THE COMPLEAT OPTION PLAYER

Revised and Updated
New 2nd Edition

By KENNETH R. TRESTER

Institute for Options Research, Inc.
P.O. Box 6586, Lake Tahoe, NV 89449
e-mail: **ior@sierra.net** *Internet:* **http://www.options-inc.com**

Cover design by Bud Willis
Illustrations by Tim Sheppard
Text design by Gale Williams, Media West Group

First Edition Hardcover, 1977 — Seven Printings
First Paperback printing, 1992
Second Paperback printing, 1993
Third Paperback printing, 1996

Published by:
Institute for Options Research, Inc.
P.O. Box 6586, Lake Tahoe, NV 89449
e-mail: **ior@sierra.net** *Internet:* **http://www.options-inc.com**

ISBN: 0-89709-200-200-7

To Merle

She helped make an impossible dream possible.

Also by Kenneth R. Trester

THE OPTION PLAYER'S ADVANCED GUIDEBOOK

SECRETS TO STOCK OPTION SUCCESS

Contents

Part III: Secrets of the Professional Option Trader

INTRODUCTION

Why options? Options are that rare investment that meets the needs of both the speculator and the conservative investor. Options can provide lottery-like returns of more than 10,000% and you can enter this game for a small price tag. Options can provide the investor with important insurance not available anywhere else, and options can provide a lot more income to your portfolio.

But, what I like best about options is that you can mathematically measure the true worth of an option—unlike stocks, bonds, gold, silver or other investment assets.

Can You Beat The Options Game?

Many analysts claim that the small investor cannot beat the options markets, but the results of my newsletter recommendations over the past eight years suggest that the options game is quite beatable, even for the small investor who risks very little. Since I first started writing *The Trester Compleat Option Report*, we have recommended almost 800 options for purchase in the newsletter. My objective over the years was to select options that had the potential to hit a homerun, and yet were low-priced, usually priced under $100 (1), and sometimes priced as low as $12.50 (1/8) to control 100 shares of stock. The options that were recommended were always undervalued according to my mathematical pricing models. The theoretical track record for these eight hundred recommendations showed consistently high and sometimes spectacular profits. In 1985, *Profit Logic*, an independent newsletter advisory rating service credited *The Trester Compleat Option Report* with a 1,500% return.

From June 1989 to December 1990, 44% of all recommendations showed a profit, a much better percentage than our record in the past, as the following chart shows:

	Time Period	Net Profit	% Profitable Positions
1)	6/89 to 12/90	$145,344	44%
2)	6/88 to 5/89	24,060	33
3)	6/87 to 5/88	124,623	21.5

Our net profit is figured using the same guidelines we set forth in every issue of the newsletter, and that we've used in every review since the newsletter was first published.

A portfolio that invested $1,000 in each position beginning in June 1989 would have returned a gross profit of $152,849, before commissions of $30 per trade (at a deep discount broker). After commissions, net profit would have been $145,344. A portfolio starting with $16,000 would have realized a theoretical 19-month return of 914%.

Using the same guidelines, the theoretical track record has been profitable each year since the *Option Report* was first published in 1983.

The record does show that a strategy of buying cheap, theoretically underpriced options according to our pricing model did generate an advantage in the market.

But the track record is strictly theoretical, and there can be a big difference between theoretical returns and actual trading profits. Yet you can beat the game and you can beat it big!

Those investors who want much more frequent payoffs should consider our second most successful strategy over the past several years in my newsletters—an *index credit spread*. There is no need to understand the strategy at this point. But the theoretical track record should attract your attention. As of July of 1991, twenty-seven index credit spreads were recommended in the *Option Report* since December 1988, and only two did lose money. Over 90% of the recommendations were winning positions. All positions were held for one month or less, some were held for only one week.

We had similar results from my other newsletter, *The Put & Call Tactician*. We recommended thirty-six such spreads. Only four of the thirty-six lost money before commissions. 89% of the positions showed a profit. As far as profits go, the annualized return after commissions was over 50%. Not bad for a strategy that paid off 90% of the time with limited risk.

These results show the potential of option trading, but you need to do your homework and gain some experience to achieve such results. This book is your starting point. Options may seem complex at times, but they are as simple as making a two-dollar bet at the horse races. So, stick with it and you should achieve some of the potential of option trading.

THE COMPLEAT OPTION PLAYER was first published in 1977. Of course, since that date, option strategies and option pricing have not changed. But many new option vehicles have been introduced, and many lessons have been learned in the listed options market. In the 1980's, index options and commodity options were introduced. Index options over the past decade have been the hottest item, drawing both institutions and small investors.

The Crash of 1987, and the Mini Crash of 1989, taught investors some important lessons, such as the importance of hedging for option writers. Since 1977, we have also seen many more discount brokers giving much deeper discounts and better service.

These changes and lessons are covered in this second edition, with many new chapters being added, and with numerous additions to the other chapters. So, sit back and enjoy.

PART I

THE OPTIONS GAME

THE ONLY GAME IN TOWN

1

THE ONLY GAME IN TOWN

A Winning Investment System: Fantasy or Fact?

Consider an investment game where you have a small risk and a high probability of reward. Consider an investment game where you win if your investments go up a little, down a little, down a lot, or don't move at all. Then consider the results of the following system:

"1. The system gained more than 25% per year for seventeen years.

2. From September, 1929, to June, 1930, the system could have doubled an investment.

3. The system showed a real five-year track record generating average returns of 25% per year.

4. The system actually doubled $100,000 in four years."[1]

Could such a game, or such a system, truly exist? To answer this question, let's turn the clock back several decades. During

[1] Edward O. Thorp, Sheen T. Kassouf, *BEAT THE MARKET,* Random House, Inc., New York, 1967.

the 1960's, two university professors, using computer technology, took on the challenge of the stock market. These two pioneers were Edward O. Thorp and Sheen T. Kassouf, and their goal was to *beat the market scientifically*. Using the computer, Thorp had already beaten the casinos of Las Vegas, forcing them to change their rules for blackjack.

Now he had taken on a far more formidable challenge: design a system to beat the stock market. After extensive experimentation, Thorp arrived at one major conclusion—the stock market is unpredictable. Stock prices move in an unforeseeable manner, and profits are as difficult to anticipate as profits at the gaming tables in Las Vegas. In other words, anyone who buys or sells stocks is taking a random walk down Wall Street.

Having made these findings, Dr. Thorp began to investigate possible stock market methods that would not require the prediction of stock price behavior. Finally, he discovered a system utilizing a special hedging strategy in convertible securities. The key element of the system was *to sell warrants short*. (Warrants are securities issued by companies giving the right to buy their common stock at a set price during a given period.) The results of this system are demonstrated in the four points above. The only problem was the limited number of investment opportunities available to the game player.

New Convertible Security Created

In 1973, a revolutionary new convertible security was born—the "listed call option." The new entity traded on the first options exchange, the Chicago Board Options Exchange (CBOE), which began operations on April 26, 1973. The new listed option, along with the recently formed CBOE, opened a whole spectrum of opportunities for the use of Thorp's stock market system; this new Exchange gave his system the spark that was needed and had been lacking in the warrant and convertible securities market.

Advances in the Thorp System Created

The new listed options are a close relative of both the warrant and the old over-the-counter (OTC) option, meaning that any systems or investment techniques which were successful with the old vehicles for investment are also directly applicable to this new medium. Being a strong advocate and user of Thorp's warrant system, I was extremely enthusiastic about the birth of the unique Options Exchange. Thus, when the Exchange opened and began operations, I altered Thorp's basic system and applied it to the new Options Exchange. The results far surpassed my greatest expectations. I documented these results in a two-year market letter, which showed an annualized return of over 40%.

Using Thorp's work as a base, I began to develop new types of strategies, such as: ratio calendar spreads; ratio vertical spreads; and unique naked option writing strategies. Sound like some kind of pornographic game? Well, believe it or not, the results of this game are far more interesting.

Professionals Take Up The Strategies

My success was not rare; other professionals began to discover these new exciting strategies. Normally, these option traders came out of the old OTC options market, where their past experience gave them a clear picture of the profit potential of the new listed option.

One of the first institutional money managers to enter this market was Jerry M. Traver, of the small Bank of Commerce in Fort Worth, Texas. Traver boasted an excellent four-year track record using the OTC options market. The strategy he employed was called "covered option writing," the most well known and also the most conservative option strategy. Using this technique, Traver raised the accounts held by his bank by approximately 4% in 1969, 15% in 1970, 18% in 1971, and 20% in 1972. Then, with the birth of the CBOE, Mr. Traver immediately moved into this new market, and from May, 1973 through April, 1974, the Bank's average option writing account rose 12.6%. In comparison, it is interesting to note that during this period, the Dow was off almost 10%, the Standard & Poor's 500 fell 15%, and the New York Stock Exchange Composite declined 15%.

Another professional who entered this new game was actually our pioneer of options strategies—Ed Thorp. Thorp and Kassouf's unique warrant system attracted many investors to Ed Thorp's door. An investment pool (using variations of his warrant system), which he began managing in 1969, has since grown to about 20 million dollars, and out-performed all but one of the more than four hundred mutual funds tracked by Standard & Poor's Mutual Fund Guide. Exact performance figures are not available. However, reliable brokerage house sources close to the funds said that they averaged better than 20% a year in net asset growth since 1969, an enviable record considering the general market decline during that period.[2]

Thorp became an active member of the options market, where a gold mine of systems opportunities is available. His performance results demonstrate the success of options strategies, and the potential of the options market.

The Listed Call Option

Given these results, the *listed call option* has proven to be an investment vehicle which:

[2] J.R. Laing, *"Computer Formulas are One Man's Secret to Success in Market"* reprinted with permission of the Wall Street Journal, Dow Jones & Co., Inc., 1974. All rights reserved.

1. Can be used to reduce risk to almost zero.
2. Can promise consistent and high profit return, without the need to predict action in the market.
3. Can be a trading medium that, if applied properly, will provide the consistent return described at the beginning of this chapter.

The Listed Put Option

Another new dimension was then added to the options market—the *"listed put option."* The advent of this new option, the counterpart to the listed call option, opened up still another new realm of investment opportunities to the individual investor. The ability to trade in listed put options adds tremendous flexibility and firing power to options strategies. The evidence presented in this chapter has demonstrated the outstanding attributes of listed call options. In later chapters, we will look more closely at the listed put option, and prove that by integrating the use of *listed put options* with *listed call options,* you can develop an investment vehicle that will far surpass the results attained in any other investment medium.

Is the Options Market For Everyone?

You may wonder then, if this options market is so great, why isn't everybody using it?

The average investor fears the complicated or the novel investment. Listed options are very complex and difficult to visualize and comprehend. Numerous amateurs have entered this game uneducated, unskilled, and unprepared for the fast and diverse action of the options market. They have been introduced to the game by inexperienced brokers who suddenly call themselves "options specialists." Consequently, these investors have been burned—receiving an expensive education. This book is dedicated to those who wish to avoid paying such a high tuition, and to those who wish to come prepared to play the game.

In conclusion, the options market is the best investment medium the author has experienced, finally giving the small investor an advantage. The small investor now has a weapon to counter the institutions. He can take his turn at being the house, rather than being a pawn to be pushed and shoved by the big boys.

However, the road to riches offered by this game is not an easy one. Don't throw caution to the wind. To succeed in this market requires you to do your homework and acquire some specialized knowledge and trading skills. You must become a COMPLEAT OPTION PLAYER—an options player well prepared for the unusual action of the options markets.

2

THE NAME OF THE GAME

Becoming a Compleat Option Player

To become a COMPLEAT OPTION PLAYER, you must gain a complete understanding of the focal point of this game—*the listed option*. You must be able to easily visualize the listed option from every angle, and then become an options psychologist, totally familiar with the behavior of these unique and unpredictable artificial beings. The option player who fails to clearly see, touch, taste and feel the listed option will never reach the winner's circle.

Now let us unravel some of the mysteries of the listed option. A look at an example will help us begin our discussion:

XEROX Jul 60

What is described above is a listed call option, listed or available on the Chicago Board Options Exchange (CBOE). You will notice that there are three parts to the option.

Part I: "XEROX"—This represents the stock name. This option is the *right* to buy 100 shares of Xerox Corporation common stock.

Part II: "JUL" — This represents the *time* when your right expires. This element is termed the "expiration date," which falls on the Saturday immediately following the third Friday of the expiration month. In this case, it is in the month of July.

Part III: "60" — This represents the *exercise price* at which the Xerox stock can be purchased. This price is also referred to as the "strike price."

Now, let's add to our example one more item:

XEROX Jul 60 (at) 3

Part IV: "(at) 3" — This refers to the *last transaction price* at which this option was bought or sold, with one qualifying point. The 3 represents $3, the price to buy the option of one share of stock. All listed options carry the right to buy or sell 100 shares of stock. Therefore, always multiply the price by 100 to get the true price of the option. In this case, the true price is $300. ($3 x 100 = $300)

A listed option then has four major segments:

I. The RIGHT — to buy or sell 100 shares of a specific stock.

II. The EXPIRATION DATE — the date that your right ends or expires.

III. The EXERCISE PRICE — the price at which you can buy or sell.

IV. The OPTION PRICE—the price you paid for the right to buy or sell 100 shares at an exercise price until an expiration date.

Let's look at a few more examples of listed call options:

EXAMPLE I: IBM Oct 100 at 2-1/2
This listed option is: the right to buy 100 shares of IBM, which expires in the month of October, on the Saturday immediately following the third Friday of the month. The price of this option is $250, and the option gives you the right to purchase 100 shares of IBM stock at a price of $100 a share, which is the exercise, or strike price.

EXAMPLE II: CITICORP Nov 15 at 3/16
This listed option gives you the right to buy 100 shares of CITICORP at a price of $15 a share, which ends in the month of November, again on the Saturday immediately following the third Friday of that month. The price of this option is 3/16, which converts to $18.75.

Now that you have a clear idea of what a listed option looks like, and which parts compose it, let's see if we can properly define this entity.

Listed Option Defined

A listed option is a stock option. An option is simply a contract, one that gives you the right to buy or sell, in this case, 100 shares of stock at a specific price, for a specific period of time. While stock options have been with us for a long time, the brilliant idea of creating a *listed option* opened up a whole new investment medium.

Further, listed options are stock options which are liquid, standardized, and are continually created at the changing price levels of the common stock. When we say a listed option is liquid, we mean that it can be bought and sold at any time in an auction market, similar to the New York Stock Exchange.

Formerly in the old over-the-counter (OTC) market, stock options could be purchased, if you could find a seller. But, in order to have taken your profits from that option, you would have had to *exercise* the option, actually buying the 100 shares of the stock that you had the right to purchase. Now, with the options exchanges, this costly process of actually buying the stock, or selling the stock, is not necessary. All you have to do is to go back to the Exchange and sell your option, just as you would sell shares of common stock. And, even better, commissions are lower, and the profits are fatter with listed options than with the old type of option.

Thus, we can see that the listed option has several clear advantages: you can buy and sell freely; there is a continuous market in each specific class of options; and, when necessary, a new class of options can be established by the Exchange.

How the Listed Option Works

To demonstrate how the listed option works, let's look at our second example of the CITICORP Nov 15 option. Let's say that you, as an investor, went into the market and purchased that option for a price of 3/16, which is $18.75. Then, one hour later, you find that the stock has moved upward, which means that your option has also moved up in price on the Exchange. Now this listed option is priced at $50, rather than $18.75, and you decide that you wish to sell it. All you have to do is to call your broker, and have him put in an order to sell your option at $50. Within one brief hour, you have bought and sold the same stock option. This never would have been possible in the old OTC options market, but with the exciting options exchanges, the game has been totally changed. In the course of one day, you can buy and sell the same option many times.

Two Categories of Listed Options Defined

At this point, you understand the listed option, and researching it more carefully, you discover that there are two types: the listed "call" option, and the listed "put" option. Since the advent of the CBOE in 1973, the only type of option that had been traded in these new markets had been the listed "call" option, which is simply *the right to buy stock.* When you purchase a call, you are betting that the underlying stock price will move *up.*

But there is another listed option which is called the listed "put" option, which is *the right to sell stock.* When you purchase a put (a put is similar to selling short without the extensive risk), you are betting that the underlying stock price will move *down.* With the addition of the put option to the market, we have another revolutionary tool with which to work in the listed options field.

A Bet To Win and A Bet To Lose

Another way to describe the difference between a "put" and a "call" is to use an analogy. Let's say that you have gone to the race track, and have placed a bet on a horse to win the race. The bet you've placed on the horse to win would be similar to a "call" option. If the horse does win the race, then the bet becomes valuable. Just as your bet becomes valuable only if the horse wins, so in the options market the call option becomes

THREE HEADED LISTED CALL OPTION

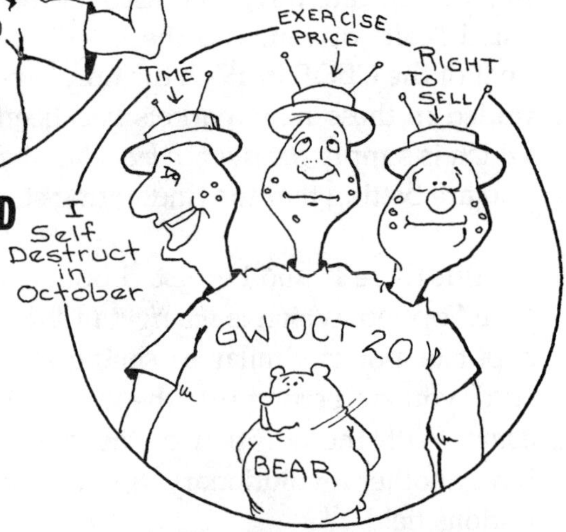

THREE HEADED LISTED PUT OPTION

valuable only if the common stock that the option represents moves *up*.

Now let's take the opposite example. Let's say that you go to the horse race, and rather than betting at the pari-mutuel windows on a horse to win, you bet on the side with a friend that the horse will come in *dead last*. This bet would be analogous to purchasing a "put" option. If the horse comes in last, the bet becomes valuable. Similarly, in the options market, the put option becomes valuable only when the common stock price that the option represents moves *down*.

Listed put options retain the same advantages that listed call options possess. They are liquid, which means that you can buy and sell them as freely as you wish on the Exchange, they are standardized, and puts are created as the stock price moves to different price levels.

Let's take a look at a sample listed put option, in order to clarify the manner in which it differs from a listed call option. For example:

XEROX Jul 60 (at) 2

Here we have a listed put option, which looks just like a listed call. But the difference is that this option is *not* the right to *buy* 100 shares of stock, it is the right to *sell* 100 shares of stock, at a price of $60 a share. The price of this option is $200.

Now let us say that after intense analysis, you have decided that the Xerox Corp.'s stock price will decline significantly in the next two weeks. Hypothetically, let's say that the Xerox stock price at the present time is $65, and you feel it will move down to $58 a share. Now, how can you place a side bet on your belief that Xerox will move *down* in this market? You can do this easily, by purchasing the put option we have just discussed—a

Xerox Jul 60—at the present price of $200 an option. So, you pull $200 out of your coffers and buy one Xerox Jul 60 put.

Watch—as you had predicted, the stock moves down the next day from $65 a share to $60 a share. This kind of a move *down* increased the value of your put option. The value of the put option now moves *up* to 4-1/2 ($450) in the market. Immediately, not being greedy, you move in and sell your put option on the Exchange for $450. You have made a nice, easy $250 profit within one day by buying a put option. What you have done is purchased a side bet, betting that the Xerox stock price would move down.

Now, if you had believed that the Xerox stock price was going to move up, then you would have wanted to buy a listed *call option*, which would be a side bet that the stock price would move up.

Thus far, you have a better feel for listed options, understand what they represent, and comprehend the difference between a listed put and a listed call. You are ready to move on to the next chapter. In it, we will discuss the arena in which these listed options are traded, and the rules by which you can buy and sell listed options.

3

THE RULES OF THE GAME

How Listed Put Options and Listed Call Options Are Traded

Having had some exposure to listed options in your early training, you're ready to talk about the ball park in which these listed put and call options are traded. This ball park is called an "Options Exchange." An options exchange, like a stock exchange, is an auction market where buyers and sellers gather to trade securities. In this case, the security is a listed option.

The first of these exchanges, the Chicago Board Options Exchange (CBOE), was established in April of 1973, and it is probably the one best structured to handle the job. Since then, several other exchanges have been established, including the American Options Exchange, the Philadelphia Options Exchange, the Pacific Options Exchange, and finally, the New York Stock Exchange. All jumped into the game after they had seen the tremendous success which came from the trading of listed options.

Each exchange operates under similar rules, and each uses the same clearing corporation, which means that they all have the same bookkeeping activities. However, the CBOE, being more

THE LISTED OPTION EXCHANGE IS AN AUCTION MARKET FOR STANDARDIZED OPTIONS

experienced than the other exchanges, has a more unique type of trading setup. As we move through this material, we will continually be referring back to the arenas of action when we discuss the Options Exchange.

Now let's take a closer look at the option transactions that occur in the options markets. There are two parties to every listed option. If you're the buyer, you may be wondering, "who is the seller?" The seller is a new man on the scene, often called an "option writer." An option writer is analogous to the casino operator who backs your bet at the gaming tables—he will pay off if you win. (This is a simplistic presentation of an option writer, but it will suffice for now.) Later on, you will discover that with the Options Exchange, you, the small investor, actually have the opportunity to become an option writer, a person who backs bets, rather than simply the person who makes bets. It's an exciting position to be in, and there is tremendous profit potential in option writing.

A listed option, as you have just learned, is similar to a side bet on the price action of a specific common stock. The stocks which are selected to have options listed on the options exchanges must meet a set of strict criteria. These criteria are available from your brokerage house. After reading through all the legal jargon, you will find that only common stocks of the highest quality can meet the tough standards for options listed on the exchanges. Even with these limitations, there are over 400 different common stocks which have options listed on the different options exchanges. This includes stocks listed on one of the exchanges and stocks trading on the over-the-counter market.

Options are also available on stock market indexes (similar to the Dow Jones Industrial Average) such as the Major Market Index, which is made up of 20 blue chip stocks, most of which are part of the Dow Jones Industrial Average, or the S&P 100

Index, which includes 100 large capitalized stocks in its average.

Stock Options Available

Each individual stock must have at least three different options listed on the Exchange, but can have many more. Each common stock has listed options that expire in the next two months, and every three months—up to nine months in the future.

For example, on September 1, IBM would have listed options which expire in September, October, January and April. On January 1, IBM would have listed options which expire in January, February, April and July. IBM is in the January cycle, where they have options that expire in January, April, July and October, with three of these months available at any time. A stock in the February cycle would have expiration dates in February, May, August and November, and the March cycle includes options that expires in March, June, September and December, all with three dates available at any one time.

In addition, in 1990, long term options were introduced on a select group of blue chip stocks. The long term options can run more than two years before they expire.

Examples Of Stock Options Available

A glance at the option prices published in most daily newspapers, in the *Wall Street Journal,* and in *Investor's Business Daily* (an example is presented in Figure 1) will quickly show some of the listed options that are available.

For the options quotations for September 27, 1991, you will find that AMR Corp (American Airlines) has options showing different strike prices, ranging from 50 to 70. You will also notice that options are available at these strike prices with three different expiration months (October, November, February). Add all these options together and you get twenty one put and call options available to the option trader in AMR Corp. But what you see on the newspaper page is only part of the story. you should also know now that AMR had options that expire in April. These options are not listed in the newspaper and, sometimes, options with different strike prices that didn't trade that day will not be listed, but such options can be bought and sold. You will need to call your broker to get quotations on these options. Look closely at the "Vol."—Volume, or the number of options traded on September 27 for each specific option. If you look at the AMR Corp (AMR) Oct 55 call option, you will find that 55 AMR Oct 55 calls were traded on September 27. This volume figure is important to the option trader and will be expanded upon later.

Why Options Vary

You are probably wondering why some stocks have more options and more strike prices than others. When options for a stock are first listed on the Exchange, options with one or two strike prices will become available. According to the rules, each will have four expiration months. Therefore, we start with four to eight listed options for a specific stock. If there is a significant change in the market price of the underlying common stock, new options with new strike prices then become available. Normally, options with new strike prices are established at 5-point intervals, unless the stock is below 25. Then strike prices are set at 2-1/2-point intervals.

A look at an example may help (refer to Figure 1).

FIGURE 1
Option Prices published in *Investor's Business Daily*

26 **Investor's Business Daily** ★ Monday, September 30, 1

Call (C) Put (P) / Exch.	Strike Price	Oct Vol.	Oct Last Price	Nov Vol.	Nov Last Price	Vol.	Last Price
A A R Corp				Stk Close 13¾			**Jan**
C X	15	no trade		6	⅜	no trade	
A M P Inc				Stk Close 51¾			**Feb**
C C	55	no trade		5	⅞	3	2⅛
P C	50	no trade		no trade		2	2¼
A M R Corp				Stk Close 57¾			**Feb**
C A	55	55	3½	7	5	no trade	
C A	60	346	1	41	2	1	4½
C A	65	11	⅛	87	⅝	109	2⅝
C A	70	no trade		no trade		105	1½
P A	50	no trade		50	5/16	25	1⅜
P A	55	38	½	30	1¼	10	2½
P A	60	335	2¾	8	3	no trade	
A S T Research				Stk Close 29⅜			**Feb**
C A	22½	no trade		8	8	no trade	
C A	25	37	4½	310	5⅝	no trade	
C A	30	334	1¼	661	2	no trade	
C A	35	no trade		10	9/16	7	1 13/16
P A	22½	no trade		10	¼	no trade	
P A	25	84	3/16	21	13/16	no trade	
P A	30	90	2	21	2⅝	no trade	
Abbott Labs				Stk Close 53¾			**Feb**
C X	45	no trade		175	9	no trade	
C X	50	no trade		4	4½	no trade	
C X	55	32	½	171	1 3/16	58	2¾
C X	60	no trade		4	3/16	13	1
P X	45	no trade		1	⅛	2	½
P X	50	26	¼	84	⅝	8	1 3/16
P X	55	no trade		2	2 3/16	5	3⅛
Acuson Corp				Stk Close 32½			**Jan**
C P	30	26	2⅝	no trade		no trade	
C P	35	5	½	8	1	no trade	
P P	30	5	¼	20	13/16	no trade	
P P	35	no trade		15	2⅞	no trade	
Adobe Systems Inc				Stk Close 50¼			**Jan**
C P	45	no trade		no trade		10	8⅝
C P	50	267	2¾	10	3⅝	no trade	
C P	55	141	¾	no trade		20	3
C P	60	75	¼	no trade		no trade	
P P	45	23	⅜	no trade		10	2⅛
P P	50	30	1⅜	23	2⅝	no trade	
P P	55	10	4⅞	2	5½	no trade	
P P	60	no trade		no trade		6	10½
Adv Micro Devices				Stk Close 9⅝			**Jan**
C P	7½	85	1⅞	no trade		30	2⅝
C P	10	138	⅜	184	¾	274	1
C P	12½	366	1/16	no trade		203	½
C P	15	no trade		no trade		77	¼
P P	7½	5	⅛	no trade		no trade	
P P	10	672	⅞	75	1	42	1¼
P P	12½	384	3⅛	15	3⅛	5	2⅞
Aetna Life&Casualty				Stk Close 33⅜			**Jan**
C A	35	no trade		no trade		25	1¼
P A	30	15	¼	no trade		no trade	
P A	35	27	1¾	no trade		2	3¼
Agency RentACar				Stk Close 12			**Jan**
C A	12½	no trade		no trade		6	1
Ahmanson HF&Co				Stk Close 17⅞			**Jan**
P A	15	10	1/16	no trade		no trade	
P A	20	no trade		no trade		4	2¾
Air Prod & Chem				Stk Close 66¼			**Dec**
C X	65	no trade		no trade		100	3¼
Airborne Freight Cp				Stk Close 26			**Feb**
P C	25	20	⅝	30	1⅜	no trade	
Alaska Air Group				Stk Close 22			**Jan**

Call (C) Put (P) / Exch.	Strike Price	Oct Vol.	Oct Last Price	Nov Vol.	Nov Last Price	Vol.	Last Price
Anheuser Busch				Stk Close 52⅜			**Dec**
C X	55	10	½	1	13/16	18	1⅜
P X	50	no trade		no trade		7	1
Anthem Electronics				Stk Close 29¼			**Jan**
C X	30	4	1⅛	no trade		no trade	
C N	30	no trade		no trade		4	2¾
Apache Corp				Stk Close 18½			**Jan**
C N	17½	no trade		no trade		5	2⅛
C N	20	20	⅛	no trade		77	¾
P N	20	no trade		140	1⅞	no trade	
Apple Computer				Stk Close 49			**Jan**
C A	40	28	10⅜	no trade		1	10¾
C A	45	24	4⅞	no trade		no trade	
C A	50	394	1 13/16	81	2 11/16	244	4
C A	55	388	7/16	347	1 1/16	120	2⅜
C A	60	4	⅛	no trade		15	1⅜
P A	40	18	⅛	no trade		11	13/16
P A	45	439	9/16	25	1 1/16	6	2⅛
P A	50	129	2⅝	215	3¼	6	4½
P A	55	11	6¼	no trade		no trade	
Applied Magnetics				Stk Close 7⅝			**Dec**
C C	10	no trade		no trade		5	1/16
Applied Materials				Stk Close 27⅞			**Jan**
C P	30	no trade		no trade		50	2
C P	35	no trade		no trade		50	¾
P P	30	no trade		10	2⅝	30	3¼
Arch o				Stk Close 25¼			**Dec**
C X	25	no trade		no trade		21	1 5/16
Arkla Inc				Stk Close 16⅛			**Feb**
C A	15	no trade		no trade		6	1⅜
C A	17½	no trade		no trade		25	⅜
C A	20	no trade		15	⅛	no trade	
Armco Inc				Stk Close 5⅛			**Feb**
C X	5	no trade		153	⅜	35	¾
P X	5	no trade		8	⅜	40	½
Armstrong World				Stk Close 33¼			**Dec**
P X	30	no trade		no trade		15	½
P X	35	no trade		1	2⅜	no trade	
Asarco Inc				Stk Close 27⅞			**Dec**
C A	25	no trade		no trade		10	3
P A	25	no trade		no trade		20	⅝
Ashland Oil Inc				Stk Close 29¾			**Jan**
C X	25	15	4⅞	no trade		no trade	
C X	30	2	1	no trade		no trade	
Ashton Tate				Stk Close 15			**Jan**
C P	15	460	1 1/16	no trade		no trade	
C P	17½	100	3/16	no trade		4	1
P P	10	20	⅛	no trade		no trade	
P P	12½	1400	7/16	no trade		no trade	
P P	15	674	1⅛	15	1½	no trade	
Atlantic Richfield				Stk Close 116⅞			**Jan**
C C	110	5	6¾	no trade		no trade	
C C	115	no trade		no trade		3	5½
C C	120	1	¾	20	1¾	1	3¼
C C	130	28	1/16	no trade		no trade	
P C	110	5	5/16	no trade		no trade	
P C	115	11	1 5/16	no trade		1	3⅞
P C	120	30	4½	no trade		no trade	
Autodesk Inc				Stk Close 50¼			**Jan**
C P	45	5	5½	no trade		no trade	
C P	50	20	2⅜	12	3⅜	20	4¾
C P	60	no trade		no trade		10	1½
P P	50	19	1⅞	no trade		no trade	
Automatic Data Prc				Stk Close 33⅞			**Feb**
C X	25	7	9	no trade		no trade	

Call (C) Put (P) / Exch.	Strike Price	Oct Vol.	Oct Last Price	Nov Vol.	Nov Last Price	Vol.	Last Price
Borden Inc				Stk Close 32⅜			**Jan**
C P	30	no trade		no trade		50	3¾
C P	35	5	7/16	26	15/16	9	1 5/16
C P	40	106	⅛	no trade		22	11/16
P P	30	no trade		no trade		32	1⅛
Bordn Chem&plstc				Stk Close 12⅜			**Feb**
C N	15	no trade		42	1/16	15	⅛
Borland Intl				Stk Close 45¾			**Jan**
C C	40	no trade		55	6	no trade	
C C	45	179	1⅜	150	3⅛	7	5⅜
C C	50	132	½	10	1⅜	no trade	
C C	55	18	⅛	no trade		no trade	
C C	60	no trade		no trade		10	¾
P C	40	140	½	no trade		no trade	
P C	45	334	1⅜	no trade		no trade	
P C	50	154	5⅛	1	6	no trade	
P C	55	4	10	no trade		2	11⅜
P C	60	no trade		no trade		2	15⅞
Bowater Inc				Stk Close 23⅜			**Dec**
C P	25	no trade		no trade		5	1
Bristol-Myers Co				Stk Close 81⅜			**Dec**
C C	70	no trade		no trade		10	12⅜
C C	75	no trade		no trade		25	7⅞
C C	80	790	2	146	3⅜	426	4¼
C C	85	1059	7/16	154	1¼	603	2
C C	90	701	1/16	346	⅜	117	¾
P C	70	no trade		no trade		97	⅜
P C	75	no trade		no trade		73	¾
P C	80	1339	1	163	1⅞	416	2¼
P C	85	74	4⅛	53	4½	148	5¼
P C	90	2	8¼	no trade		10	8½
British Petroleum				Stk Close 70⅞			**Jan**
C P	65	30	6	no trade		no trade	
C P	70	32	1⅞	no trade		no trade	
C P	75	no trade		50	11/16	2	1⅜
P P	65	20	⅛	no trade		no trade	
British Steel Plc Adr				Stk Close 23			**Jan**
C N	22½	3	1	no trade		3	1¾
Broad Inc				Stk Close 15			**Dec**
C X	15	no trade		20	1	no trade	
C X	17½	9	1/16	no trade		no trade	
P X	15	no trade		no trade		3	1⅜
Browning-Ferris				Stk Close 19¼			**Dec**
C A	20	15	½	40	⅞	20	15/16
C A	22½	no trade		no trade		1	⅜
P A	17½	no trade		no trade		1	9/16
P A	20	25	13/16	no trade		5	1⅜
Brunos Inc				Stk Close 15¼			**Feb**
C C	15	no trade		no trade		11	1 3/16
Brunswick Corp				Stk Close 12			**Dec**
C C	12½	212	¼	35	½	41	11/16
Burlingtn Resource				Stk Close 41½			**Feb**
C X	40	no trade		24	2⅝	5	4
C X	45	no trade		no trade		56	1 7/16
Burlington Northern				Stk Close 35¼			**Jan**
C C	30	12	5⅛	no trade		25	5¾
C C	35	183	15/16	no trade		2	2
P C	30	2	⅛	no trade		no trade	
C & S Sovran Corp				Stk Close 28⅛			**Feb**
C A	25	20	3¼	10	3¾	no trade	
C P	25	no trade		20	3⅝	no trade	
C A	30	10	7/16	6	¾	no trade	
P A	25	4	¼	no trade		no trade	
C B I Industries Inc				Stk Close 30⅛			**Dec**
P X	30	no trade		no trade		10	⅞

Borden Inc. (BN) call options listed:

BN	Oct	30	at	No trade
BN	Oct	35	at	7/16
BN	Oct	40	at	1/8
BN	Nov	30	at	No trade
BN	Nov	35	at	15/16
BN	Nov	40	at	No trade
BN	Jan	30	at	3-3/4
BN	Jan	35	at	1-5/16
BN	Jan	40	at	11/16

BN common stock is trading at 32-3/8. If the BN stock rises to 42-1/2, a new set of options with a strike price of 45 will be listed. If BN stock falls to 27-1/2, a new set of options with a strike price of 25 will then become available. You should also be able to identify, from your training in the previous chapter, that the last option price paid for each option is also presented in quotations.

"No trades" indicates that the specific option did not trade on September 27. But such options almost always have a bid and asked price and therefore can be bought or sold at any time during the trading day.

One more discovery that you will make as you glance over the options quotations is the fact that each specific option—such as the BN Oct 35 call—is not just one option, but a whole class of options, all with the same standardized characteristics. As a buyer and a seller settle on an option price for the BN Oct 35, another BN Oct 35 call option contract is created. Consequently, you create the volume figure presented. If you buy a BN Oct 35 call one day, you have created an option contract. If you sell that same option the next day, you theoretically dissolve that contract. As we move along through this book, many of these subtleties will become much clearer.

Now that you're aware of the rules by which listed options are established, let's go to the next chapter, in which we will take an even more specific look at the listed option.

The Incredible Shrinking Option

4

THE INCREDIBLE SHRINKING OPTION

In this chapter, we will take the listed option, put it under a microscope, and look even more closely at the option price. The price, you will discover, is the most important element of a listed option. The price of an option is set on the Options Exchange according to two different values:

1. THE INTRINSIC VALUE
2. THE TIME VALUE

Intrinsic and Time Value Defined

The "intrinsic" value is defined as the *real* value of the option. This means that if you were to exercise your call option contract (which you will normally never do in the options market), you would purchase 100 shares of the common stock at a lower price than the current market price of the common stock. Thus, the option has some *real* value. If you were to exercise a put option contract with intrinsic value, you would sell 100 shares of stock at a higher price than the current market value of the common stock—the put option would then have real value.

How does this differ from "time" value? Remember that an option is a right you have for a period of time. You must pay for that right, and the amount of money that you pay is referred to as *time value.* As time passes, the time value of an option decreases, and as a result (if we disregard the intrinsic value), the price of that option will decrease. The time value is the most important factor that we work with. In many cases, the options you buy will be options with time value only—no intrinsic value.

Examples of Intrinsic and Time Value

Let's take two examples to help clarify the two types of values which will make up the option price, first looking at a call option:

CPQ 25	JUL	OCT	JAN	Compaq Computer (CPQ) Common Stock PRICE
(Call)	2	2-3/4	3-1/4	26

Look closely at the CPQ Jul 25 call option, which, as you can see, is priced at 2 ($200), with three months remaining before July expiration. The current market value of Compaq Computer at 26 is higher than the strike price (25). This option is then called an "in-the-money" option, which means that *it does have intrinsic value.*

CURRENT MARKET PRICE OF STOCK	26
LESS STRIKE PRICE OF CALL OPTION STOCK...	- 25
= INTRINSIC VALUE	1

The intrinsic value, as you can see, is $100. Now, if you will refer to the example above, the price of the CPQ Jul 25 is 2.

OPTION PRICE	2
LESS INTRINSIC VALUE	- 1
= TIME VALUE	1

The remaining value of the option price is *time value*.

Now let's look at the same CPQ Jul 25 option price on the day in July when the option will expire, and let us assume that the stock price has not moved.

CPQ 25	JUL	OCT	JAN	Compaq Computer Common Stock
	1	2	2-3/4	26

Again the CPQ Jul 25 has 1 point of intrinsic value because the stock price is 1 point in-the-money.

But, on this date, there is no more time left in the life of the July option, and consequently, there is no time value remaining.

CPQ Jul 25 Option Price	1
Less Intrinsic Value	- 1
= Time Value	0

You will also notice that the CPQ Oct 25 and the CPQ Jan 25 have also lost some of their time value. The CPQ Oct 25 has lost $75 of value, and the CPQ Jan 25 has lost $50 of time value.

TIME VALUE IS WHAT THE MARKET THINKS THE INTRINSIC VALUE OF AN OPTION WILL BE IN THE FUTURE

CONCLUSION: The option price is made up of two values: *Intrinsic Value* and *Time Value*. Based on these facts, the following formula can be developed:

INTRINSIC VALUE + TIME VALUE = OPTION PRICE

To clarify this further, let's take another example using a put option instead of the call option we just used. Our second example has three months remaining before it expires in April:

				POLAROID (PRD) Common Stock
PRD 35	APR	JUL	OCT	PRICE
(Put)	2	3	4-1/4	37

Remembering that a *put* is the right to *sell*, not to buy, you will notice the PRD 35 options do not have any intrinsic value. Look closely at the PRD Apr 35:

Exercise Price of PRD Apr 35	35
Current Market Price of PRD (out-of-the-money)	37
Intrinsic Value	0

Intrinsic Value	+	Time Value	=	Option Price
0	+	2	=	2

Here the *full price* of the PRD Apr 35 is *time value*. You have an "out-of-the-money" option, which means that it has *no intrinsic value* (real value)—it has only time value. You are paying for time, enough time, you hope, for the Polaroid stock price to move below $35 a share.

Time passes...now let's look at the same option on that day in April when the PRD Apr 35 expires—again assuming the Polaroid stock price is unchanged at 37.

PRD 35	APR	JUL	OCT	STOCK PRICE
(Put)	1/16	2	3	37

With the Polaroid stock price unchanged, there still is no *intrinsic value* in the PRD 35 options. Look at the PRD Apr 35—the option price is down to 1/16, because there is no more time left in the option. Therefore:

Intrinsic Value	+	Time Value	=	Option Price
0	+	1/16	=	1/16

You will discover as you move through this book that the experienced player, whether he is a buyer or a writer, will spend most of his time with out-of-the-money options—options that only have *time* value.

Table 1 presents more examples of listed puts and calls breaking down their intrinsic and time values. Looking at this table will help you to remove any lingering confusion.

Tables 2 and 3 show how changes in the underlying stock price will effect the time value and the intrinsic value of a specific listed option.

Tables 4 and 5 show time value declines with a constant stock price for both a listed put and a listed call as these options approach their expiration.

Shrinking Options and the Buyer

You may be wondering why I have named this chapter, THE INCREDIBLE SHRINKING OPTION. You should have seen by now that an option is a depreciating asset which shrinks in value as time elapses; therefore, when the life of an option ends, it has "zero" value. To the option buyer and seller this is a super critical concept, which should always be a *top priority* consideration. If you purchase an option with a two-month life remaining, every day that you hold that option, its value declines, even if the underlying stock price is moving in the correct direction. To the option buyer, this price behavior is the major handicap; to the option writer, it is the major advantage.

It is of great importance that you brand this rule into your mind:

THE TIME VALUE OF AN OPTION CONTINUALLY DECLINES TO "O" AS TIME PASSES AND THE OPTION REACHES THE END OF ITS LIFE.

From my experience, the major error of the option buyer is to disregard this law when playing the game. In the options game, "time is money." Those who use this concept to their benefit will reach the winner's circle; those who ignore the law of time value will fall by the wayside.

TAKE HEED—make sure you buy plenty of time with your options. Then, don't stick your options in a closet and forget about them, for as time passes, your options also pass away.

As we move on to study other aspects of listed options,

keep in mind that the option price is determined by adding *intrinsic value* to *time value.* Intrinsic value is the *real* value of the option. The time value is the value that you place on the possibility that the option will attain some intrinsic value by having the stock price move through the strike price and into-the-money.

TABLE 1
Dissecting the Listed Option

Listed Call Options	Stock Price	Option Price	Intrinsic Value	Time Value	Out-of-the-Money	In-the-Money
Boeing May 50	48	1-1/2	0	1-1/2	X	
CBS Aug 150	152	4	2	2		X
Mobil Oil Feb 70	65	4-5/8	0	4-5/8	X	
Am Tel Apr 40	35	3	0	3	X	
Avon Jul 45	47	3-1/4	2	1-1/4		X
Bank Am Oct 40	41	2-1/2	1	1-1/2		X
Texas Instr Apr 100	80	3/4	0	3/4	X	
Pepsi Apr 80	85	6-1/8	5	1-1/8		X
IBM July 100	99	4	0	4	X	
Chips & Tech Feb 10	11	1-3/4	1	3/4		X
Rockwell June 35	34	1	0	1	X	
ASA May 45	50	5-1/2	5	1/2		X
Beverly Ent Aug 10	12	4	2	2		X
Listed Put Options						
Gen Motors May 35	30	6	5	1		X
Texas Instr Apr 80	75	8	5	3		X
Upjohn Oct 40	38	3-1/2	2	1-1/2		X
Syntex Oct 40	42	1-1/8	0	1-1/8	X	
N Semi May 25	19	7-1/4	6	1-1/4		X
Tandy Aug 20	22	1-1/2	0	1-1/2	X	
Sears Oct 40	43	2-3/4	0	2-3/4	X	
MMM July 50	44	8-1/4	6	2-1/4		X
Baxter Apr 30	29	2-1/2	1	1-1/2		X
K-Mart July 25	30	1-1/4	0	1-1/4	X	
Monsanto Oct 90	87	5-1/2	3	2-1/2		X
IBM Apr 100	100	10	0	10	X	
Coke May 80	75	9	5	4		X

TABLE 2
Listed Call Option Behavior

XEROX July 60 Call Option

Value of Option	Common Stock Price	Option Price	Time Value	Intrinsic Value
In-the-Money	70	10-7/8	7/8	10
In-the-Money	68	9	1	8
In-the-Money	66	7-1/4	1-1/4	6
In-the-Money	64	6	2	4
In-the-Money	62	5-5/8	3-5/8	2
AT-THE-MONEY	60	4-3/8	4-3/8	0
Out-of-the-Money	58	3-1/2	3-1/2	0
Out-of-the-Money	56	2-3/4	2-3/4	0
Out-of-the-Money	54	2	2	0
Out-of-the-Money	52	1-1/8	1-1/8	0
Out-of-the-Money	50	1/2	1/2	0

TABLE 3
Listed Put Option Behavior

AUTOMATIC DATA PROCESSING
February 30 Put Option

Value of Option	Common Stock Price	Option Price	Time Value	Intrinsic Value
Out-of-the-Money	40	1/4	1/4	0
Out-of-the-Money	38	1/2	1/2	0
Out-of-the-Money	36	1	1	0
Out-of-the-Money	34	1-3/8	1-3/8	0
Out-of-the-Money	32	1-7/8	1-7/8	0
AT-THE-MONEY	30	2-5/8	2-5/8	0
In-the-Money	28	4-1/8	2-1/8	2
In-the-Money	26	5-3/4	1-3/4	4
In-the-Money	24	7	1	6
In-the-Money	22	8-3/4	3/4	8
In-the-Money	20	10-1/8	1/8	10

TABLE 4
The Option Life Cycle

CBS Inc. Oct 150 Put

Time Remaining Before Expiration	4 Months	3 Months	2 Months	1 Month	2 Weeks	Expiration Day
CBS Inc. Stock Price	155	155	155	155	155	155
Option Price	5	4	3	1-1/2	1	1/16
Intrinsic Value	0	0	0	0	0	0
Time Value	5	4	3	1-1/2	1	1/16

TABLE 5
The Option Life Cycle

GTE Corp Nov 30 Call

Time Remaining Before Expiration	4 Months	3 Months	2 Months	1 Month	2 Weeks	Expiration Day
GTE Stock Price	29	29	29	29	29	29
Option Price	3-1/2	2-3/4	1-3/4	1	1/2	1/16
Intrinsic Value	0	0	0	0	0	0
Time Value	3-1/2	2-3/4	1-3/4	1	1/2	1/16

PRACTICE OPTIONS PSYCHOLOGY

5

THE PSYCHIATRIC GUIDE TO OPTIONS BEHAVIOR

Welcome to your introduction to OPTIONS PSYCHOLOGY. In this chapter you will encounter a brief training course in the study of *option price behavior*. As a prerequisite to success, the astute option player must become an expert in predicting and understanding listed option price behavior. As you study and analyze listed price behavior, you will discover that it can be erratic, especially when you work with out-of-the-money options, which have no intrinsic value. The price of that option is determined by time value, which is also referred to as PREMIUM.

Time value is a value based on opinion. How do you place value on two days in the market, or on two weeks or six months in the market? Every investor will place a different value on that period of time, injecting numerous variables to come up with those values. Place these out-of-the-money listed options in an auction market, and the results can be amazing.

Eleven Factors Influencing Option Price Behavior

To gain a complete understanding of option price behavior, let's take a close look at the eleven factors which have the greatest influence on this behavior:

1. The price and movement of the underlying common stock.

2. The time left in the life of the option.

3. The volatility of the underlying common stock.

4. Market rallies and market declines.

5. The psychology and mood in the market.

6. Supply and demand.

7. Institutions.

8. The liquidity of the option in the market.

9. The number and type of listed options available for the underlying common stock.

10. The yield of the underlying common stock.

11. Interest rates.

Chief Factors

Out of this list of influencing factors, two have a significant effect on the price of a listed option. In fact, these two factors constitute from 50% to 80% of the price of the listed option. They are the *price* of the underlying common stock, and the *time* left in the life of the option.

Since an option is the right to purchase or sell 100 shares of a specific stock at a specified price, the price of that common stock will be a great determiner of the price of the option. Because of the critical nature of time value, when you purchase an option, the time left in the option has a strong bearing on the price you pay for that option. Time value thus becomes more significant as the option nears its expiration.

Volatility

Another element that controls the price of a listed option is the price volatility of the underlying common stock, the amount that the stock price moves up and down. A common stock price which has high volatility normally moves in very wide ranges over a period of time. A volatile stock may move from 40% to 60% of its base price annually. Such wide price movements give it a much greater probability of moving through the strike price of a listed option, and as a result, that option will take on more premium (time value).

On the other hand, a stock with low volatility normally trades within a narrow range, not moving very far in any one direction. This will have a negative effect on the option price because the probability of the stock price moving through the strike price is diminished.

Understanding stock volatility in the options market can be tricky. In some cases, a common stock that has been historically quite volatile may reach periods in which it is somewhat dormant, and conversely, stocks which are normally quite low in price volatility will suddenly move dramatically in one direction or another. These shifts in price behavior will alter the influence of this factor on the listed option.

As we move through the text, we will continually refer to volatility, and will study this important component much more closely. Many option players place *far too much* importance on volatility of a specific stock, and overvalue or undervalue the options which are associated with the stock.

In summary, the three major factors which influence option behavior include: (1) the price of the underlying stock; (2) the time left in the life of the options; and (3) the volatility of the underlying stock. These three factors can constitute up to 90% of the price of the listed option.

Rallies and Declines: How To Handle Call Options & Put Options

There are other influences which, in some cases, have very marked effects on the price behavior of the listed option. Two important influences are market rallies and market declines. Option prices can make significant moves without much movement in their underlying stock prices during a market rally or a market decline. For example, optimism rises during a market rally, large amounts of money flow into listed call options, and prices become over-inflated, in some cases regardless of the price movement of the underlying stock. In addition, during a market rally, some investors have visions of grandeur, whereby the investor sees the market climbing another 100 or 200 points on the Dow. These visions may be unrealistic, but they do have a strong bearing on the prices of listed options.

Conversely, during market declines, there is extreme pessimism which overflows into the options market. Call option prices may become depressed, even though the underlying stock prices may not be moving in any direction. As the market declines, the investor has visions that disaster is near—believing that the world will fall apart, and therefore, the prices of call options will decrease while put option prices will increase in value, although close-to-the-money puts and calls tend to have similar relative premiums due to arbitrage.

The option player must use these market rallies and declines to execute strategies, buying and selling at these optimum points in time. *Market rallies are the best time to sell call options.* The price of the option is over-inflated at this time as the market makers and option traders attempt to cover their short positions. *At the depth of market declines, in some cases, it is best to buy call options,* or to cover option writing positions (short options).

The ability to use market rallies and declines to your benefit is an important skill that you, as an option player, must develop. Unfortunately, this skill counters your natural impulses because during market rallies, not only will everyone else be overflowing with optimism, but you will also be overflowing with optimism. However, you must counter this impulse, and do your selling during these optimistic periods of time. Conversely, you should do your buying at the depths of a market decline.

Note that if you are working with listed *puts,* you do exactly the opposite from what you do with calls. At the peak of market rallies, you want to buy puts, and in the later stages of market declines, you sell puts.

Market Mood & Psychology

Another factor closely related to market rallies and declines, and which has an important effect on option price behavior, is the market mood and psychology. Although you may not be in the midst of a market rally, or in a desperate decline, there is normally some kind of mood and psychology to the market, and this will have an influence on the price behavior of your options. At certain times, there is a total lack of interest in the market. Stocks move nowhere, investors are on vacation, or there is definite indecision on the part of the investors as to whether the market will be moving upward or downward. Normally at these times, option prices decline.

A stock market which has been drifting for several months will have a very damaging effect on the prices of all listed options, both puts and calls. For either a listed put or a call to have a healthy premium, that option requires that the common stock price maintain "active" price movement, or that the overall market maintain active price movement. When stock prices in the overall market move in a slow and sideways motion, this has a surprisingly negative effect on most option prices.

Supply, Demand, and the Institutional Investor

Another element which the option player must consider when attempting to predict option price behavior is the supply and demand factor. How many buyers are out there, and how many sellers? This, of course, will have an effect on the price of an option.

Add to this the influence of institutions in the options market. Institutional investors have had a major impact on the option market, especially on index options which usually have much better liquidity than stock options. Good liquidity has attracted the institutions who trade hundreds of options at a time. Many buy a lot of index put options to insure portions of their stock portfolios. Such action causes index put options to be overpriced most of the time. In the stock option arena, institutions have chiefly been option writers instead of option buyers, writing (selling) both put and call options to improve the income from their stock portfolios. But most stock options don't have good liquidity—keeping the institutions from trading large numbers of options at any one time. Small investors who deal in 5 or 10 options at a time can enter and exit their positions much more easily.

Yet the institutional investors are one of the most important factors in the market today, and they will continue to be so. Therefore, option players, BEWARE of the institutional influence.

Other supply and demand considerations come into play during market rallies and market declines. During market rallies, we normally have significant *volume* in the market, and this volume also carries over to the options market. Consequently, there is a much greater demand during market rallies for the purchase of listed call options. Normally during market declines, the volume in the stock market dries up—one of the reasons why the decline occurs—and there is a lack of buying interest in the market.

Then, this lack of buying interest in the stock market carries over to the options market, where the same lack of demand ensues. As the market declines, puts become more attractive, but because of the low volume factor, the amount of demand is not as great for puts during a decline as for calls during market advances. Therefore, as you will discover, puts may not have as high a price as calls in the market. As a result, put buying may be a more attractive ploy for the option player.

Liquidity

Another factor which has a powerful indirect influence on option price behavior is the amount of *liquidity* that exists in a specific listed option. Liquidity refers to trading volume, or the ability to move in and out of an option position easily. Liquidity requires that plenty of buyers and sellers be available to ensure such transactions. Options which do not have liquidity may trap you into a position, or prevent you from taking a large enough position to make the transaction worthwhile. Liquidity in the options market can be measured by the number of specific listed options that are traded every day.

For example, how may Xerox Jul 60 calls are traded on the average day? Calculating this average would give you an idea of Xerox Jul 60 liquidity. Note that liquidity changes throughout the life of a specific option. The Xerox Jul 60 may have no liquidity at all when the stock is at 90 because the option is so far "in-the-money" that no one is interested in that option. Or, it may not have any liquidity at all if the stock is at 30 because now the option is so far "out-of-the-money" that it hardly has any value at all.

Also, if there are eight months left in that Xerox Jul 60 call, its price may be so high that it will lack the necessary liquidity to be an effective trading vehicle. In fact, options which usually have lives of seven, eight, or nine months normally do not have the liquidity that an option of two or three months would maintain. This again is an important consideration when you design strategies, and decide when and where to take certain positions.

Classes of Options Available and Stock Yield

Still another factor that the astute option player looks at when predicting option price behavior is the number of classes of options that are presently available for a common stock. If only a few standardized options are available, all the demand for the options of that stock is channeled into these few options. This becomes an important consideration when a stock that has been dormant for an extended period of time begins to attract some price action. Suddenly there is a demand to purchase the common stock's listed options. Of course, there are only a few options to chose from, and the result is inflated option prices.

A key factor to consider would be the yield of the stock. High yielding stocks become attractive covered option writing vehicles, and we will discuss this later in the text. *Covered writing* indicates that people will purchase the stock, and write or sell an option against it. When institutions and individuals carry out these writing activities extensively, the option premiums will decrease. Therefore, stocks with high yields normally will have options with low premiums (prices), as compared to the average listed option.

Stocks with high yields are usually less volatile for they pay out most of their earnings to generate a large dividend (i.e., electric utilities). Therefore, such stocks would have small option premiums. Such stocks will also increase in value as they approach the ex-dividend day (the date after the dividend is issued), and then the stock price will lose the value of the dividend on the ex-dividend date. This price action will influence the option price.

Interest Rates

Due to the fact that an option is a surrogate for its underlying stock, you are able to control one hundred shares of stock for a small price tag. Because you can control a stock for a few hundred dollars, rather than a few thousand dollars, high interest rates cause the option to increase in value, for these thousands of dollars can be in interest-bearing instruments instead of tying the money up in the underlying stock. So, as interest rates increase, option premiums increase.

The Life and Times of the Listed Option

Now that you have a more extensive knowledge for determining what effect various factors will have on option price behavior, we are ready to look at the life cycle of a listed option, and see what changes occur in that option as it moves from its birth, when it has nine months of life remaining, to its death at the date of expiration.

Options will take on many changes in their price behavior as they move through the nine-month period. They will move from an inactive price period to a very active period. Surprisingly, the most active period in the life of an option normally begins when it has three months left. From this point in time, it becomes more and more active until it approaches its expiration. In many cases, when the underlying stock price is still very close to the exercise price as the option approaches expiration, the option becomes feverishly active. Every movement in the underlying stock, whether it is a quarter or a half a point, causes significant movement in the option price.

Table 6 draws out the complete life of a Xerox Jul 60 call option, showing what the theoretical values of the option would be at each point in its life, and at each possible stock price. You can also look at the Appendix in the back of the book where we determine the fair value of each option, at each point in its life, and at each underlying stock price.

By looking at these examples, you will note that during the first three months of life, the value of a listed option depreciates at a very slow rate. In the second three months, the price depreciates at a more accelerated rate, but it has not yet reached its peak rate of depreciation. In the fourth month of the life of an option, it normally has the highest time value it will have per the amount of time left before expiration. If you were buying an option at that time, you would generally pay the highest percentage rate possible on that option. (We are holding all other variables constant, so that we can see what occurs to the price, and the price alone, as time passes through the option's life.)

As the option passes into its last three months of life, its depreciation begins to accelerate. But when the option approaches the last month of its life, the depreciation speeds up, ending with no time value at all. The last month of an option's life causes the greatest damage to the option price and all option

Table 6
The Life and Times of a Listed Call Option

Xerox July 60

Months Left in Option Life	Xerox Price	52	54	56	58	60	62	64	68
9 Months	Option Price	3-1/2	4-3/8	5-1/8	5-1/8	6-3/4	7-3/4	8-3/8	11
	Time Value	3-1/2	4-3/4	5-1/8	5-7/8	6-3/4	5-3/4	4-3/8	3
	Intrinsic Value	0	0	0	0	0	2	4	8
6 Months	Option Price	2-3/4	3-1/2	4-1/4	5	5-1/8	6-3/4	7-1/2	10-3/4
	Time Value	2-3/4	3-1/2	4-1/4	5	5-7/8	4-3/4	3-1/2	2-3/4
	Intrinsic Value	0	0	0	0	0	2	4	8
4 Months	Option price	1-1/2	2-1/4	3	3-3/4	4-3/4	5-1/2	6-1/4	9-3/4
	Time Value	1-1/2	2-1/4	3	3-3/4	4-3/4	3-1/2	2-1/4	1-3/4
	Intrinsic Value	0	0	0	0	0	2	4	8
3 Months	Option Price	3/4	1-3/8	2-1/4	3	4	4-7/8	5-1/2	9-1/4
	Time Value	3/4	1-3/8	2-1/4	3	4	2-5/8	1-3/8	1-1/4
	Intrinsic Value	0	0	0	0	0	2	4	8
2 Months	Option Price	1/4	7/8	1-3/4	2-3/8	3-1/4	4	5	8-3/4
	Time Value	1/4	7/8	1-3/4	2-3/8	3-1/4	2	1	3/4
	Intrinsic Value	0	0	0	0	0	2	4	8
1 Month	Option Price	1/16	1/4	5/8	1-3/8	2-1/4	2-7/8	4-1/2	8-1/4
	Time Value	1/16	1/4	5/8	1-3/8	2-1/4	7/8	1/2	1/4
	Intrinsic Value	0	0	0	0	0	2	4	8
2 Weeks	Option Price	1/16	1/16	1/16	3/4	1-5/8	2-1/2	4-1/4	8-1/8
	Time Value	1/16	1/16	1/16	3/4	1-5/8	1/2	1/4	1/8
	Intrinsic Value	0	0	0	0	0	2	4	8
The Expiration Date	Option Price	0	0	0	0	0	2	4	8
	Time Value	0	0	0	0	0	0	0	0
	Intrinsic Value	0	0	0	0	0	2	4	8

traders should consider this fact carefully.

Option Prices and Common Stock Prices

How does the declining option price described above relate to the price of the underlying common stock? Holding all other variables constant, when the stock price is right at the exercise price of the listed option, the listed option will have its maximum possible time value.

For example, if we are looking at the Xerox Jul 60 option, and Xerox is priced exactly at 60, the Xerox Jul 60 will hold its maximum time value in this option (will have its highest premium), taking into consideration the amount of time left in that option. This is an important point to the option trader. Buying options when the stock is at strike price, whether you are covering a position or taking a new position, normally results in your paying the highest possible time value for that option.

When the stock price moves away from the exercise price (out-of-the-money), the amount of option premium will decrease at a constant rate. Thus, as it moves from 20% to 30% out-of-the-money, the option will lose most of its time value. If the stock price moves across the exercise price (in-the-money) again, the premium (time value) that is built into the price of that option will decrease, and will continue to decrease as the stock moves farther and farther into-the-money.

As an example, let's look at the Xerox Jul 60 call, with three months left in the option. The Xerox stock is priced at 60; the option is priced at 4, as you can see from Table 6. All four points are time value.

Let's say that the stock moves from 60 to 64. Presently the option is worth 5-1/2, but the time value of that option has decreased from 4 to 1-1/2.

Now let's say that the Xerox stock moves from 64 to 68; looking at the Xerox Jul 60 price, it is currently 9-1/4. Our time value has now decreased to 1-1/4.

Next, let's move in the other direction. Let's say that the Xerox stock has moved from 60 to 56. At 56, the Xerox Jul 60 is priced at 2-1/4, so the option has moved from a time value of 4 to a premium of 2-1/4. At 52, the Xerox Jul 60 is worth 3/4; so now the time value has moved from 4 to less than 1. There is almost the same type of decrease in time value whether the stock moves up or the stock moves down.

Unfortunately, option players often forget the principle that you just observed. Yet this is an important principle for you to consider when you design strategies, and when you attempt to alter or change your strategies. It is also an important principle for the option player who is attempting to pay a bargain basement price. As you can see, there are times in the life cycle when you should be buying the option, and times when you should not, all depending on the location of the stock price, and the number of months left in that option.

Effects of Stock Prices on Options

During the many phases in the life cycle of a listed option, probably one of the greatest combined effects on the option price will be the trend of the stock price in one direction or the other, and the speed of that trend. Suppose we are working with a listed call option. If the stock price trend is upward, and if the speed of that trend is accelerated, then the option premium accelerates in value quickly, and shows far more time value than would normally be expected. On the other hand, if the trend is upward, but the movement of that trend is slow, the effect on the option price would be small but positive. Finally, the opposite result would occur if we had a downtrend in the stock price and the movement was either accelerated or slow.

Note that when we are working with listed put options, the exact opposite of the effects described above would be true. A fast moving downtrend in the stock price would greatly increase the price of the listed put option, and vice versa.

To summarize, in this chapter we have introduced a large number of factors which effect the price behavior of listed options. We have briefly looked at the life cycle of the listed option, and have demonstrated the effect of both stock prices and time on the listed call and put options.

Should "Options Psychology" continue to bewilder you, I suggest that you reread this chapter, study the tables closely, look over your newspaper each morning, and attempt to secure a feel for the pricing behavior of an option.

One technique for practicing options psychology is to collect a series of listed options, then follow them closely and attempt to estimate their value at the closing each day before you look at their actual quotations. In the beginning, you will probably be a little frustrated, but eventually you will develop the skill which will allow you to measure what the value of an option should be at any one point in time.

These last few chapters have provided you with many of the basics. You probably are a little perplexed in certain areas, and this is to be expected. In succeeding chapters, we are going to move into some of the applications of all this theory, and as we work through different examples, and cover new material, the basics already covered will become more familiar. You will be well on your way to acquiring the knowledge and skills of the COMPLEAT OPTION PLAYER.

OPTIONS GAME
Play for as little as $6.25--
Control thousands of dollars
for pennies--
You can win a fortune
with little risk!
ENTER
EXIT
WINNER
WINNER

6

HOW TO GET STARTED ON SMALL CAPITAL

How Much Capital Do You Need To Start a Successful Venture Into The Options Market?

That is a question that can be answered in a thousand different ways, but for the speculator, the exact amount isn't great, provided you have all the other prerequisites that you need to beat the game. This chapter is aimed at the speculator who wishes to enter this exciting game with a minimal amount of capital, or who only has a small amount of pure risk capital. If an investor is going to move into this market with small capital, the risks will be great, but the possible rewards may be even greater.

One rule that you, as a speculator, must follow is to be sure that you are financially able to handle the possible loss of the capital that you are investing. It should not be borrowed or distressed money, or money taken out of the necessary living expenses that should be provided for your family. When you work with such capital, it places too much pressure on your mind; you become too emotional, and you lose the key factor of success in the options market, which is *rationality*. You must be able to make quick, rational decisions without having outside factors influence you. As soon as the money becomes more important than playing chips on a table, your factor of success decreases tremendously.

As a speculator entering this game with a limited amount of risk capital, there is only one road that you can follow, and that is to *buy options.* (The opposite of *buying* options is *writing* options, which will be covered further on in this text. In the case of the latter, the more capital you have, the more effectively you should be able to operate.)

Later you will discover that there are many more profitable strategies available in this new market than buying options, but they require minimum investments of at least $2,000. However, beginning with a small investment can be a definite asset rather than a detriment, as the successful purchase and sale of options requires effective bargain hunting, effective use of specialized knowledge, and extreme patience. A small amount of capital will force you into some of these successful behavioral patterns.

One special feature of the options market is the outstanding leverage that you can obtain by buying options. For the modest amount of $6.25, you can control over $25,000 worth of stock. Under the proper conditions, and with the appropriate moves in that stock, your investment may multiply a hundredfold. This is the pot of gold of the options game, and it is available to the small speculator.

Many of the prodigious number of books available on the options game have stated that this low capital buyer's game is a loser's game, or a sucker's game. This kind of statement shows the amount of ignorance prevalent among the "self proclaimed" authorities on the subject. For the arguments which will be presented in this text will show that buying options can be as profitable as many other strategies available to the player.

Capital Needed To Start Playing

The exact dollar figure is hard to pin down, but normally $200 would be a minimum starting figure for the novice. Setting a $200 or $300 limit on your losses will force you to take, at the maximum, only two or three positions. One important consideration is that commission costs will constitute a large portion of your purchase price at this level, and should be incorporated into your risk-reward analysis. Of course, you incur these costs in any game that you enter, be it a visit to Las Vegas, or a visit to one of your local racetracks. In these situations, you have transportation costs, entrance fees, program costs, and the other additional expenses that are incurred when traveling to and from your local gaming activity. The stock market has these same costs. Your options trading skill must pay for these costs and add a profit onto your investment. Remember, starting with small capital forces you to take on relatively high commission costs.

The Smallest Amount of Capital You Should Invest in The Options Market

As mentioned before, an option can be purchased for as little as $6.25, giving you the right to profit from the price move of 100 shares of a specific common stock, for a specific period of time. Add to that your commission costs, which may run from $15 to $40, and you have a pretty accurate figure of what a minimum investment can be. But that gives you only one very long shot in this game, and the commission costs will eat up some of your potential profit.

Therefore, a rule for the investor with small capital to follow would state:

Bring enough capital to be able to take at least two or three positions, with each position containing at least five options.

Following such a rule will force you to diversify by not putting all your eggs in one basket, and will reduce commission costs per option, giving you a chance to stay and profit in this game.

7

THE ART OF BUYING OPTIONS

Playing the Game

Are you tired of the basics? Then, let's begin playing the game. The easiest way to play this game is to buy options. If you are betting that the market is going up, then you buy call options; if you are betting that the market is going down, then you buy listed put options. If you believe the market is going to fluctuate violently, then you can buy straddles, strips, straps, or both puts and calls. Although buying options may seem to be a strategy specifically designed for the small investor, it is a viable investment tool for all investment managers, even those who manage millions of dollars of institutional funds.

Advantages of Buying Options

Buying options has three distinct advantages. These include:

1. LEVERAGE
2. LIMITED RISK
3. SMALL CAPITAL REQUIREMENT

In the previous chapter, we have already discussed the advantages of entering this buying game with small capital. *Leverage* gives the option buyer the ability to control thousands of dollars worth of price action for pennies. You discovered that for $6.25 you could control and participate in the price action of up to $25,000 or more of stock. Normally, by paying from $50 to $200, you can control the price action on a $5,000 or a $10,000 round lot of common stock. If the stock price goes up 10, 15, or 20 points, you can cash in your $100 or $200 option, and collect up to $2,000. That could be the exact amount that you would have gained if you had owned the actual stock itself. In other words, an option gives you a chance for the action and excitement of owning 100 shares of stock without having to put down all the money and taking all the risk incurred in owning that stock. The only risk is the $200, or whatever price you pay for that option. If the price action of the stock is not positive, then you may lose a portion of that risk capital, but you will not lose $5,000 or $10,000, which would be possible if you owned the stock.

So, when you buy options, you gain tremendous leverage in the market by controlling a large amount of money for a very small investment, and here is where the *limited risk* factor comes into play.

The Options Exchange helps you to reduce the risk of buying options because of its liquidity, which provides tremendous flexibility for the option buyer. If you purchase an option, and the next day, decide that that was an incorrect move, you can immediately go back into the market and sell that option. As the option buyer, you can also take advantage of small movements in that 100 shares of stock that you are controlling by moving in and out of your option positions as the stock moves up and down. In some cases, the stock price may not have to move at all for you to make a slight profit on your options. The market itself, in many cases, will generate premiums in options even when the stock price of a specific option is not moving.

For example, let's look at the flexibility of the options market in the following case. Let us assume that you have been closely following the Ford Motor Co. stock, and have decided that at its present price of 52, it will move down to 45 in the next three weeks. To take advantage of this price action, you decide to purchase one Ford Jan 50 put option at a price of 2 ($200). You purchase this one put, and sit back to watch the price action of the stock. After one week's time, the stock price rises from 52 to 55. Your prediction of the stock price movement is incorrect. Therefore, you immediately move into the market, and sell your Ford Jan 50 put, now priced on the Exchange at 1-1/8. You receive proceeds of $112.50, having reduced your loss on that option to $87.50, plus the commissions of moving in and out of that position.

So, even if your predictions are incorrect regarding the price actions of a stock, you can salvage much of the value of that option if you act quickly and move out of that option position immediately.

Option Buying and the Investment Manager

Though this chapter is aimed at the speculator, buying options can also be a sophisticated investment tool for the investment manager. There are numerous ways in which an investment manager can buy options—for insurance, for hedging, or to take advantage of other stock and option positions. For example, the astute investment manager who handles $100,000 in cash for a client (who must be protected and cannot be exposed to any risk), will invest the cash in 91-day Treasury bills at $100,000 face value. Such a purchase will cost approximately $98,500 (depending on prevailing interest rates), leaving $1,500 cash for further investment.

Instead of leaving this cash sitting in the account, he will purchase "bargain priced" listed puts and calls. Now the client can participate in big moves in the stock market without risking any of his *principal*.

Some Disadvantages of Option Buying

Now let's take a look at the disadvantages of buying options. Our whole discussion in talking about the "cons" of buying options focuses around one thing—*time*. The purchaser of 100 shares of stock may not have the leverage or the limited risk that the option buyer has, but he can hang on to that stock for five, ten or twenty years, and wait for it to reach his price objective. Normally, the option buyer will only have from one or two days up to nine months in which to attain his price objectives. Also, common stocks generally will not depreciate in value as you hold them, but options will. Therefore, as you hold onto options, waiting for the underlying stock price to increase, the option price is continually depreciating. This factor of time and depreciation is the major obstacle that has been the downfall of the majority of option buyers.

To beat the option buying game, you have to beat the clock, a sometimes difficult task. In the next section of this chapter, we will spell out a set of guidelines that will give you a chance to beat the game, and we hope that you will follow them. To become a successful option buyer, you must become shrewd, patient and be a quick decision maker. With these tactics, excellent profits will flow your way.

To begin your further training in the art of option buying, I have developed the following "Ten Commandments of Option Buying." Read these commandments, memorize them, and follow them.

The Ten Commandments of Option Buying

I.	***Be Patient***
II.	***Play Only Volatile Stocks***
III.	***Buy "Out-Of-The-Money" Options***
IV.	***Plan Before You Play***
V.	***Play Only Undervalued Options***
VI.	***Diversify***
VII.	***Maximize Your Leverage***
VIII.	***Minimize Your Risk***
IX.	***Don't Be Greedy***
X.	***Be Patient***

The first and last commandments are: *Be Patient* because it is the most important commandment of option buying. You must wait for option opportunities and you must wait until your playable options become extremely underpriced. If you require action every day, this chapter is not for you; possibly this book is not for you. Without patience, you might as well disregard the rest of these commandments because they will not help you. The only way to beat the options game from the buyer's position is to be selective in picking your spots, wait until you can get your price, wait for the big payoffs, and be able to handle a lot of losses along the way.

Play Only Volatile Stocks — Remember, you only have a limited amount of time to work with when you own an option. You are betting on price action; therefore, play stocks that are big on price action, that move around very frequently, and move within wide ranges of their base value.

Buy Out-of-the-Money Options — Options which are "in-the-money" are far too fat for the option buyer, and although they may have intrinsic value, they also have far more risk. Out-of-the-money options normally will have much lower prices, and as a result, will have less risk and far more leverage.

Plan Before You Play — This commandment is critical to your success. Even though you are buying options, you must have a game plan which maps out exactly what you will do at every point while you own an option. You must set a parameter for the length of time that you will hold the option, and decide when you will take your profits. If you do not have a plan of action through each stage of your purchase of each option, you are doomed.

Play Only Undervalued Options — The successful option buyer is a meticulous bargain hunter. When making decisions, wait for your price, pay no more than the price you demand, and make sure that price is far below the true value of that option. The Appendix at the end of this book displays the fair value of all options on stocks with average volatility, under most price and time conditions. Use these tables as a guide to determine which options are underpriced, and which are overpriced.

Diversify — In order to improve the probability of profit in the game, do not put all of your eggs in one basket. Take at least two or three option positions, and try to maintain at least five options in each position to reduce your commission costs. Try to spread your purchases over a long period of time and own both puts and calls. Then you will be in the market during volatile times, times when home runs are hit in the options market.

THE SUCCESSFUL OPTION BUYER IS A DEDICATED BARGAIN HUNTER

Maximize Your Leverage — Attempt to select an option which will increase in value at least 200% if there is a 10% move in the stock price. Attempt to derive at least a 3:1 risk-reward ratio for any option that you purchase. If you do this, the long term odds should be in your favor.

Minimize Your Risk — The best way to minimize your risk is to pay as little as possible for each of your options. A rule I like to follow is that I rarely pay more than $100 for an option. I will attempt to find positive risk-reward plays where I only have to invest from $12.50 to $100 per option. By doing this, I normally attain outstanding leverage, and of course, have a very limited risk. All I can lose is the small amount that I paid for that option.

Don't Be Greedy — The downfall of 90% of all investors, especially in the options market, is greed. They wait for that next move in the stock, wait for another week to get another point or two out of that option. To avoid this natural tendency toward greed, make sure that you follow your game plan to a "T." Place your limit orders when you take the position, and leave those limit orders in, regardless of what factors develop. But always let part of your option position ride so that you have a chance at a home run. As soon as you rely on your emotions, rather than on your game plan, your portfolio will become a disaster area.

Be Patient — Again, we see the most important commandment, and the one that you will have the roughest time following. Wait for your spots, wait for your plays, wait for your price, and pay no more than the price you demand. Finally, wait for the home runs. Most option investors do not have this patience. But to succeed, you must!

In the next chapters, we will demonstrate how these Ten Commandments can be applied in the selection of options, and we will cover some of the finer points to be followed in successful option buying.

The 4 S's: To Be Used by the Experienced Buyer Only

But, before we move on to the finer points of option buying, you should be aware of some of the other option merchandise available to the option purchaser. We mentioned that the option buyer can buy a listed put or a listed call. Now he can also purchase:

— A *Straddle* — which is actually a set of options, both a put and a call, both at the same exercise price, with the same underlying stock.

— A *Strap* — which is the purchase of two calls, and a put, again at the same exercise price.

— A *Strip* — which is the purchase of two puts and one call, both with the same exercise price.

— A *Spread* — which is the purchase of a put and a call with different exercise prices.

You need to be careful with these, for sometimes this wide array of merchandise simply confuses option buyers, and may lead you astray in making your critical buy decisions. Another problem with these fancy buy strategies involves *commission costs.* They can run very high with these types of strategies and will cut deeply into your potential profits.

The time to use these types of buy strategies occurs when you are working with an extremely volatile stock, which has a high probability of making some voluminous fluctuations.

In entering such strategies, make sure that you get the right price for both legs of the strategy, a sometimes impossible task.

Because of the difficulties involved, I suggest that you stay away from such strategies unless you have extensive experience and sophistication in the art of option buying. These strategies may have a look of glamour, but they are very expensive and can inhibit the *necessary* bargain hunting behavior of the successful option buyer.

8

THE PLAYABLE STOCK

Having looked at the "art of buying options," and at the guidelines that will put you on the road to success in this challenging game, it is time for you to put these guidelines into action. In the process of making the key decision regarding which options you should purchase, and determining the all important *time* when you should purchase them, you will discover that there is a tremendous amount of homework that must be completed in preparation for this difficult task. If you pass over this homework, and do not prepare yourself for playing this game, you are doomed to failure.

Selecting the Right Stocks — Time & Trends

The first step that the successful option buyer must take before he makes his key purchase decisions is to decide which common stocks are playable in this option buying market. A common stock must meet some special prerequisites before it can be classified as a playable stock by the sophisticated option buyer. The first requirement, and the most crucial, is the *trend* of the stock price. If you are planning on buying *call* options, or developing bullish buy strategies, the underlying stock should usually be in an *uptrend*. When buying call options, avoid buying options on a stock that is in a downtrend, or moving in a neutral pattern.

The exact opposite would be true when purchasing listed put options. Avoid the purchase of a put option unless its underlying stock is moving in a downward direction and maintains a declining trend channel.

Time is a factor so valuable in the option buying game that you cannot afford to wait for a stock to change its trend of price action. Nor can you wait for a stock to move out of a neutral trading range. There is no time to hope or pray that a stock will reverse trend, or that it will move from a dormant position to an active upward or downward position. But if you find a super bargain priced option, it is probably worthwhile to buck the trend, for stocks can be unpredictable at times.

The "Fundamental Approach" Outdated

In the evaluation of the trend and the future behavior of a stock price, the "fundamental approach" to stock analysis is a waste of time. This approach to stock evaluation measures the true value of a stock, assuming that eventually the stock will adjust to this true value. Since we don't have time to wait for that adjustment in the options market, the option buyer is not concerned with the long term value of a stock. He is concerned with the price action of that stock *today,* not in six months, or in five years. We must have that price action *now.* Therefore, the fundamental approach, and any other approach that requires a lag time of any type, should not be considered in evaluating the stock price action.

Analyzing Market Trends and Industry Trends

Another trend that you should be concerned about as you go about selecting the playable stock is the *trend of the market* and the trend of the industry that your stock is in. These two trends should be congruent—moving along with the trend in your stock. If the market is going in an adverse direction to your stock's trend, it will definitely have an adverse effect on the value of the options you have purchased. Any delay in the price movement of your stock will begin to destroy the value of the options you hold.

Another suggestion when measuring the trend of a stock price is to avoid looking at all the statistics and advice that stock brokers and brokerage houses throw your way. Look at only one thing: *the stock price.* Look at the past action of that stock price. Chart the price action of that stock. Then, to determine the strength of an upward or downward move in the stock, look at the volume it attracts as it moves. This will indicate the strength of a price move, and will determine how authentic the uptrend or the downtrend really is.

For example, if a stock price is moving in an upward direction, and is receiving above average volume as it carries out this price move, that would be a bullish sign. If the stock move is in an upward direction, and there is a below average dose of volume moving into the stock, this would be a sign that you should proceed with caution. Possibly this price move is artificial, and a decline is pending.

If a stock price is moving in a downward declining trend channel, and the stock is receiving significant volume, this would be a bearish sign. On the other hand, if this declining stock was receiving below average volume, again there is a possible sign of caution, although low volume on declining moves in stock prices can be a very deceptive signal for either a bullish or a bearish move.

Need for Volatile Price Action

The playable stock should also meet another important prerequisite—it should have *volatile price action,* or have a history of such action. We mentioned before that measuring the volatility of stock can be difficult. Volatility in some cases is unpredictable, but you must make the best attempt that you can at measuring past and future volatility.

To aid you in this process, we are presenting here a formula which helps measure past volatility:[4]

$$\text{VOLATILITY} = \frac{\text{12-MONTH STOCK PRICE RANGE}}{\text{Average 12-Month Stock Price}}$$

or, in algebraic terms:

$$\text{VOLATILITY} = \frac{\text{STOCK HIGH - STOCK LOW}}{(\text{Stock High} + \text{Stock Low}) \div 2}$$

Stock High = The Stock's 12-Month High
Stock Low = The Stock's 12-Month Low

Example: Xerox high and low for 1975 was 86 and 46.

$$\text{VOLATILITY} = \frac{86 - 46}{(86 + 46) \div 2}$$

$$\text{VOLATILITY} = \frac{40}{66}$$

Xerox Volatility = 60.6%

[4] Reprinted from *Strategies and Rational Decisions in the Securities Options Market* by Burton G. Malkiel and Richard E. Quandt, by permission of The MIT Press, 1969, Cambridge, Massachusetts.

This volatility formula measures the percentage move that a stock is likely to have above or below its average price for a one year period of time. In this case, Xerox, trading at an average price of 50, is likely to move as high as 80, or as low as 20. This formula of volatility can also be used to measure volatility in a stock price for shorter periods of time.

This information may be more helpful for the option player who is concerned with volatility for one or two months, rather than a full year. By plotting the volatility for each quarter during the past thirty months, you may get a better picture of the price range of the stock for the next three months. One guideline that I suggest that you follow when using this volatility formula is to select only stocks which have at least a 20% volatility record over a twelve-month period of time. The higher the volatility for a common stock, the more playable that common stock becomes with regard to a stock option purchase. In this age of computers, a far more accurate method of calculating volatility can be done by taking a standard deviation of changes in the stock price. Based on my research, the best volatility can be derived from weekly changes in stock prices from 10 to 20 weeks. Option software such as Option Master®[5] will calculate such volatility.

Need For Action

Another more subjective method of evaluating a common stock price's volatility is to look at its daily, weekly, and monthly price ranges, and to study the cyclical action of the stock over the past few months. The wider the trading range of the stock, the more attractive it becomes. The perfect playable stock is one that moves in deep and rapid wave formations; the more violent the fluctuations, the better. Stocks which have wide trading ranges, receive good volume, and are moving in an upward

[5] Option Master® computer software is available from Institute for Options Research, Inc., P.O. Box 6586, Lake Tahoe, NV 89449.

trend are excellent candidates for the purchase of call options. Stocks which have wide trading ranges, good cyclical patterns, and are moving in a declining channel are excellent candidates for the purchase of put options.

Monitoring Your Stocks

Once you have identified a series of stocks that meet the volatility requirements we have discussed, and have the necessary action, you are ready to closely monitor these stocks, and begin to identify playable options associated with them. Normally, it is wise to monitor from one to ten different common stocks. By spending your time in a select group of stocks, you will get a better feel for the price action of these stocks, become far more familiar with them, and of course, you will have much greater success in predicting their future price action. If you attempt to follow too many stocks, you lose the price sensitivity which is important to the option buyer.

In the process of monitoring these stocks, attempt to chart the price action—the influx of volume into these stocks. Once you have a total familiarity with the stocks you are monitoring, then you are ready to begin monitoring their *playable options*, and can wait for the proper price and time to make your first purchase of playable options.

9

THE PLAYABLE OPTIONS

Price and Timing

Having carefully selected and monitored your stocks, you are ready to select the playable options. In the process of selecting the playable options, there are two factors that should have priority over all others, and the first is: *the option price*. Regardless of whether or not the options you are considering buying meet all other requirements, they must be properly priced before you can take any action on that option. They must meet the price that you demand that they meet. If you cannot purchase an option at your price—a bargain price—then either forget it, or continue to monitor that option until it reaches your price.

The second important factor to consider as you hunt, compare and attempt to identify the playable option is *timing*—the timing of your purchase of the winning option. Remember, you are continually working against the clock. Every minute that passes chips a piece of the value out of the options that you own.

Other Factors

When comparing the attributes of candidates as possible playable options, the following characteristics also must be a part of the makeup of such options:

1. The strike price of the options that you plan to purchase should be as close as possible to the stock price. Normally, as a rule of thumb, you should avoid buying options that have exercise prices that are further than 15% to 20% away from the stock price.

2. Attempt to select options which have as long a life as possible. Remember the rule we discussed before: "as the option approaches expiration, it depreciates at a faster rate."

3. Select options which are extremely undervalued. Option value can be measured by using the Appendix of this text, which displays the true value of puts and calls at most possible strike prices, for all possible stages in the option's life cycle.

One important plus you will have when owning an undervalued option is the possibility that the time value of the option will return to a more normal evaluation during the time that you hold the option. This will provide an additional source of profit for your portfolio.

Risk — Reward Analysis

To repeat, the playable option must have the right price, a price that minimizes your risk and maximizes your leverage and reward. The exact price that you pay for an option should be determined by your risk-reward analysis. Normally, as a rule of thumb, attempt to avoid paying more than $200 for any one option, unless there is a definite risk-reward advantage in taking this step. If you only pay $50 or $100 for an option, you can lose no more than that amount. For the beginner, this can be a big advantage.

We have discussed risk-reward analysis, and you may be confused by this investment concept. Actually, risk-reward analysis is just a way of comparing the *potential return on your investment* to the *risk of your investment.*

Using the Playable Option Comparison Chart Prediction & Projections

In order to aid you in comparing and selecting the playable option, and determining the return on investment, we have developed the PLAYABLE OPTION COMPARISON CHART. This chart will greatly aid you in the selection of ideal option purchases. The Comparison Chart forces the option buyer to put down in black and white all the key factors to be considered in making the selection decision. This type of an approach to option selection will remove much of the emotionality that interferes with your decision making process.

You will notice as you go over this invaluable chart that it also requests that you, the option buyer, *predict* where you believe the *stock* price will move, *predict* where you believe the *option* price will move, and *predict how long* it will take the stock price and the option price to move to the target areas. Your ability to predict the price action of the common stock in the future will be an important determinant of your success as an option buyer.

Predicting the future option price is a far easier task than predicting the stock price. First, determine the target date of your option price move, the date that your stock price will reach

Playable Option Comparison Chart

Option (Call or Put)	1 Stock Price	2 % Distance Stock Price From Exercise Price	3 Stock Target Price	4 Time Stock Price Will Take To Reach Target	5 % Stock Price Move To Reach Target	6 Option Price	7 Normal Value of Option	8 Option Target Price
Apple Computer Aug 50 Call	43	16%	50	9 Weeks	16%	1-1/4	7/8	2-1/2
Xerox Oct 70 Call	55	27%	65	10 Weeks	18%	1/2	1/2	3
Texas Inst Oct 100 Call	83	20%	95	8 Weeks	14%	1	2-3/8	5-1/2
ASA Nov 20 Put	25	20%	20	9 Weeks	20%	1/4	0	1
Eastman Kodak Oct 70 Put	80	12.5%	72	4 Weeks	10%	1-1/2	2-3/8	4-1/2
Digital Equip July 45 Put	50	10%	46	3 Weeks	8%	1/4	7/8	1-3/4

Playable Option Comparison Chart (continued)

Option (Call or Put)	9 Stock Trend	10 Market Trend	11 Time Left in Option Life	12 Stock Volatility	13 Risk-Reward Ratio	14 Return on Investment
Apple Computer Aug 50 Call	UP	UP	17 Weeks	45%	1 – 1	100%
Xerox Oct 70 Call	UP	UP	26 Weeks	35%	5 – 1	500%
Texas Inst Oct 100 Call	UP	UP	26 Weeks	30%	4.5 – 1	450%
ASA Nov 20 Put	DOWN	DOWN	21 Weeks	25%	3 – 1	300%
Eastman Kodak Oct 70 Put	DOWN	DOWN	26 Weeks	23%	1.7 – 1	170%
Digital Equip July 45 Put	DOWN	DOWN	13 Weeks	40%	6 – 1	600%

its goal. Then go back to your option tables in the Appendix at the back of this book and you can easily determine what the normal value of that listed option will be at that point in time. With this projected option price, you can determine your expected return on investment. This will give you an important guide in the option selection process.

Our goal in using the Comparison Chart is to determine the probable return on investment if your stock price predictions are correct. Next, to measure risk, you must write off the amount you invest in your option purchase, even though you may salvage some of the value of the option when your predictions go astray.

Don't worry if you find prediction tricky. The best stock traders in the business are only "right" 55% of the time, for stock price prediction is a very difficult game. Some authorities believe the stock market is a random world, and it is impossible to accurately predict stock price action. Even the astute technical analysts will admit that it is very difficult to predict when and where a stock price will move. Many say they can tell you where a stock will move, but to indicate the timing of this move is a totally different matter. In order to profit in the option buying game, you *must* determine where a stock will move and the maximum amount of time it will take to make this move. If you have done your homework, you will probably be successful at this feat 35% of the time, depending on your experience; 65% of the time your predictions will be off target. Therefore, your projected return on investment for any option buying strategy should be at least 200% to generate a profit in the long run.

To determine the return on investment figures, complete the Comparison Chart for each playable option you are considering.

Now let's look closely at some of the variables on the chart:

(2) To identify the percentage distance that the stock price must move to reach the exercise price, look at the Apple Computer example. Apple Computer is 43, 7 points from the exercise price. Dividing 7 by 43 will give us .16, or 16%.

(3) Identifying the stock target price is one of the most difficult tasks of the option buyer. The stock target price is your projection of the future price of the underlying stock.

(4) Once you have identified the stock target price, you must project how long it will take to reach your price objective, another difficult endeavor—usually a guessing game.

(5) Then by looking at our target price objective for our common stock, we can determine the distance it must move to reach the target. In our Xerox example, our target price is 65 and the present price is 55, a 10-point move. We can find the percentage move by dividing 10 by 55, and multiplying by 100.

$$55 \div 10 = .181 \times 100 = 18.1\%$$

(7) The present fair value of the option candidates is readily available in the Appendix. Use these guidelines to identify bargain options.

(8) The option target price can be easily identified by going to the Appendix and by using the information from (3) and (4). We can then identify the fair value of the option if your projections are correct.

(12)Stock volatility can be determined for a year or for a shorter, more revealing time frame.

(13)The risk-reward ratio is determined by comparing the potential reward to the potential risk. In the ASA Nov put example, if all target prices were reached, the profit, or reward, would be $75 per option. ($100 less $25, the initial price of the option). The potential risk is the maximum you can lose, which is $25, the initial price of the ASA Nov 20 put. Therefore, the risk-reward ratio is $75 to $25, or 3-to-1.

(14)Once we know our risk-reward ratio, we can then determine our potential return on investment in the case of the ASA Nov put. A 3-to-1 risk-reward ratio is the same as a 300% return on investment.

The examples we have used should provide some insight into how to complete the Comparison Chart and to use the variables as a means of comparison in the selection process.

Puts Are Cheaper

One comment should be made as you carry out the option selection process. Listed puts are usually far better priced than calls. Normally, puts will be priced from 10% to 50% lower than calls. Consequently, playing with puts may be much wiser than playing with calls. The typical investor has a difficult time betting that the market will go down. THE COMPLEAT OPTION PLAYER has no difficulty at all.

Other Hints

A few additional guidelines to help you to eliminate stiff (loser) options should also be mentioned here:

— Never require more than a 15% move from the common

stock in order for it to reach its target price.

— Never select an option which generates a potential profit of less than 100% return on an investment.

— Avoid buying options whose strike price is more than 20% away from the stock price.

— Avoid buying options that have less than one month before they expire.

— Never buy options on stocks with a volatility of less than 20% annually.

— Never buy index options—stock indexes don't give you enough volatility.

Finally, as we conclude our discussion of the playable option, remember the "Golden Rule" of the successful option buyer—"WAIT FOR A PRICE THAT WILL GIVE YOU A HIGH RETURN ON INVESTMENT...A HIGH RISK-REWARD RATIO." To do this requires a lot of patience, and a lot of maturity in the options player. The greatest problem the option player encounters is enthusiasm for a possible common stock. After extensive study, we will see a stock preparing for a big move, and jump into the options market, playing an option with a relatively poor risk-reward ratio.

The unsuccessful option player will not wait for an acceptable price, or will he be willing to skip the stock's action if he can't get a good price. In fact, most option players will have a difficult time walking away from a very attractive opportunity on which they have spent a lot of time, even though they cannot get the "right" price. Using every emotional defense mechanism in the book, they will talk themselves into taking an undesirable option price. Remember—before you buy any option, *all* systems must be go; *all* factors must be right before the purchase can be made. THE COMPLEAT OPTION PLAYER will have this discipline. The unsuccessful option player will not.

10

THE GAME PLAN

At last you have made your decision. You have selected an option with an excellent potential return, an option which meets the guidelines that we have established; your homework has disclosed a potential rally in the market and in your common stock. ALL SYSTEMS ARE GO. You move into the option market and get "your" price. You are now the proud owner of a listed call option. Now you can relax. WRONG!

This is exactly the point at which most option buyers go wrong. Remember—as every minute passes, your option is slowly depreciating away. Like a hawk, you should be watching your option, the underlying stock, and the market. In fact, before you buy any option, you must have a "game plan."

Variables in Your Game Plan

Table 7 presents the format I suggest for this game plan. Variables from your Playable Option Comparison Chart are used in this table to map out the action points you have established in your preliminary plans. This game plan should display the underlying common stock's target price that you have established,

Table 7 – The Game Plan

Date 4-30-

Option	Stock Price	Stock Target Price	Option Target Price	Time to Reach Target Price	Maximum Time to Liquidate or Hold Option	Anticipated Return on Investment	Time Before Option Expires
Texas Inst. Oct 100 Call at 1	83	95	5-1/2	2 months	2-1/2 months on June 16	450%	6 months
Digital Equip July 45 Put at 1/4	50	46	1-3/4	1 month	5 weeks on June 4	600%	3 months

the target price for your option, and the time you have predicted it will take these prices to reach their objectives.

Another important variable that you have added to this game plan is the maximum time that you will hold your option. You must set this time parameter and follow it. The most frequent mistake that an option buyer will make is to hold onto an option too long, either because of greed or desperation. To avoid this emotional impulse, set a *point of no return* and sell out your option positions when the maximum amount of time you allot the option has passed. In determining the maximum hold period, avoid retaining options in the last two weeks of their life, unless they are very cheap. At this point in time, the option depreciates at its fastest rate and only the most sophisticated day trader can handle such action.

A side comment is appropriate here—buying and selling options during the last month of their life is an exciting and action-filled game, but it is full of dangers and only the most experienced and skilled option player can handle these dangers.

Monitoring Your Option Game Plan

Now that you have a game plan, it is important that you closely monitor the price action of your option, the underlying stock, and the market, to identify any changes in trend or trading activity. If the underlying stock price doesn't move according to your game plan, you should immediately abort your mission and sell out your option positions. To paraphrase the old saying, "He who retreats today can return to fight another day." Take heed and follow these famous words.

Too many option players are in the class of the hopers and the prayers; they have lost control of their destiny. The common stock buyer can afford to wait for his stock price to come back,

Don't! The stock will go up soon.
Quick, decisive action is required when one owns options.
HOPE
GREED
REASON
Sell the XYZ July 40 option.
XYZ
Projected Price
50
40
30
20
10
APRIL
MAY
JUNE
JULY
TIME IS MONEY

the option player cannot. As soon as the COMPLEAT OPTION PLAYER feels "uncomfortable" with his option positions, he sells them. As soon as his stock price predictions go astray, he salvages what he can from his option position and moves on to new opportunities.

When you are planning to buy options, PATIENCE is the key to success. But now that you *own* options, QUICK, DECISIVE ACTION is also a key to success.

Go For The Home Run

There is an old adage on Wall Street that states, "Cut your losses and let your profits run." Try to apply this adage when buying options. To be a successful option buyer, you need to hit some home runs—options that generate a 1,000% to 10,000% return. The only way to accomplish this is to let a portion of your option positions ride. However, once you have big gains, you can't afford to let those profits slip away. So, as the stock price moves into-the-money and your options increase in value, use a *trailing stop-loss price* on the underlying stock. As the stock prices move in your direction, keep changing the stop-loss price, following the price of the underlying stock. But, if the stock price starts to move against you, and hits the stop-loss price, take profits and exit the whole option position.

11

THE INDEX CRAZE

One of the hottest games on Wall Street today is the Index Option Game, a game where you can bet on a whole stock market average, using either index futures options or options on the actual stock indexes.

This whole new game began in February of 1982, when the Kansas City Board of Trade introduced the first index futures contract, which was a futures contract on the Value Line Index, an unweighted market average of 1,700 stocks. In April of that year, the Chicago Mercantile Exchange introduced contracts on the Standard & Poor's 500 Composite Stock Index, and in May, the New York Futures Exchange introduced futures contracts on the NYSE Composite Index of 1,530 stocks.

These new and different futures contracts were a big hit and were followed closely by options on these index futures contracts. Then, in 1983, the Chicago Board Options Exchange (CBOE) and the American Stock Exchange (AMEX) got into the act by introducing their own type of options that were not on the futures contracts, but rather on custom designed indexes. For example, the CBOE developed index options on a weighted index of 100 CBOE underlying stocks (the CBOE 100), and the AMEX developed an unweighted index on only 20 blue chip stocks, which it refers to as a Major Market Index. The CBOE then became more aggressive by introducing options on the actual Standard & Poor's 500 Composite Index and changed the name of their CBOE 100 Index to the Standard & Poor's 100.

Let us first take a close look at the index futures contracts, and by understanding these contracts, we can further understand the full scope and meaning of index options.

What is an Index Futures Contract?

To determine the difference between an index futures contract and other futures—such as a gold futures contract—let's look at an example.

The Standard & Poor's 500 Index futures contract enables you to buy or sell a contract representing a hypothetical 500 shares of an average of all of the 500 stocks in the Standard & Poor's 500 Index. Contracts are available with delivery dates of up to one year in the future. Actually, delivery date is a misnomer, since physical delivery is never made. It would be extremely difficult to deliver even a percentage of all the 500 stocks in the Index. Rather, contracts have a cash settlement price. Cash settlement versus delivery also has the advantage of eliminating the danger of someone cornering the market.

As each contract is for a hypothetical 500 shares of the Index, the contracts are valued at 500 times the Index price. If the Standard & Poor's 500 Index is priced at 370, the Index is worth $37,000. But the futures contract is probably worth over $185,000 (500 x $370 = $185,000). If the Index increases one point, the futures buyer profits by $500, while the seller loses $500. A four-point move in the Index will result in either a profit or a loss of $2,000. If you want to buy an index contract, you must presently put up a margin of about 15% of the value of the contracts.

Why Index Futures?

Index futures contracts have advantages both for the speculator and the hedger. For the speculator, they provide good leverage and diversification, but at a high and almost unlimited risk. The big advantage of these futures contracts (and index options) goes to the hedgers, institutional money managers, and investors who have portfolios to protect. If an investor holding a diversified portfolio of stock (it might even include options and mutual funds) feels that the market is in danger of falling, he might be reluctant to sell because of tax consequences, high transaction costs, and other restrictions on the sale of the shares, or because his shares constitute so large a block that their sale would cause the price to drop. By selling enough index contracts, the investor may be able to offset losses in his own portfolio with the profits from the contracts should the market fall. But this technique failed during the crash of 1987.

A Bigger Bang For Your Buck — Index Options

If you are an investor who does not hold a sizeable stock portfolio or does not want to take high risks, how can you take only a small risk and profit from the index craze? Well, as you have just learned, in addition to index futures contracts, there are also options on the actual cash indexes and options on those index futures contracts.

These index options have all the same advantages that listed options on equities have today, including leverage, limited risk, liquidity, and flexibility. In addition, for as little as a few hundred dollars, you can obtain outstanding diversification and profit from broad changes in market prices. Index options offer you a solution to a frequent dilemma that is all too common—to be right on the market, and wrong on the stocks you pick.

Index Futures Options versus Index Options

As you have just discovered, there are two types of index options that are available: there are options on futures contracts and options on the actual indexes. Futures options include: options on the Standard & Poor's 500 Index futures contracts and the NYSE Composite Index futures contracts.

Options now available for the actual cash indexes include the Standard & Poor's 500 Index options, the Standard & Poor's 100 Index options, the Major Market Index options, and options on a variety of other indexes (see a sample of option quotes for indexes that presently have options in Figure 2).

There are two major differences between options on index futures contracts and options on the actual indexes. First, options on the futures contracts are just that—options on the futures index contract, NOT on the index itself, and you will find that there is usually a discrepancy between the contract price and the actual index value. The second major difference is that an index futures contract constitutes 500 shares, or a 500 multiplier of the index for delivery in the future, while the options on the actual indexes are normally options that constitute 100 shares, or a multiplier of 100 of the actual index.

Viewing the differences between these two types of options, the index futures contract options have one big disadvantage to options investors, and that is that the futures contracts are much larger than are the actual indexes in dollar figures. For example, when the Standard & Poor's 500 Composite futures contract is valued at approximately $185,000, the Standard & Poor's 500 actual index is valued at only $37,000.

Consequently, the option investor will have to pay a much higher price for options on the futures contracts than he would for options on the actual indexes. For a few hundred dollars, for

FIGURE 2
Index Option Prices published in *Investor's Business Daily*

Index Options

Call (C) / Put (P) · Exch (X) · Strike Price · Vol. · Last Price

AMEX Institutional — Index Close 432.95

Option	Feb Vol.	Feb Last Price	Mar Vol.	Mar Last Price	Apr Vol.	Apr Last Price
C A 420	3	15½				
C A 430	81	8½	245	13		
C A 435	3	5¾	150	9⅝		
C A 440	20	4				
C A 445	103	1 15/16				
C A 450	10	1 3/16	2	3¼		
C A 455	1510	¾				
C A 460	114	7/16	5	1½		
C A 465	30	⅜	1500	15/16		
C A 470			10	⅜		
C A 475	270	3/16				
P A 325					20	5/16
P A 355			20	7/16		
P A 400	6	⅞	50	2 3/16		
P A 405	50	1				
P A 410	25	1⅜	400	3¼		
P A 415	50	2				
P A 420	35	2½				
P A 425	175	4	50	6⅝		
P A 430	235	5⅜	425	7⅞	55	11
P A 435	2	8	350	10⅜		
P A 440	164	9¼	100	13⅛		

AMEX Major Market — Index Close 346.77

Option	Feb Vol.	Feb Last Price	Mar Vol.	Mar Last Price	Apr Vol.	Apr Last Price
C A 290			3	56⅝		
C A 300	2	48¼				
C A 335	25	14⅝				
C A 340	1080	9⅝				
C A 345	135	6⅜				
C A 350	587	3⅝				
C A 355	136	2				
C A 360	97	1 1/16				
C A 365	65	½	215	1⅝	34	3⅛
C A 370	5	5/16			15	2⅛
P A 270	130	1/16				
P A 280	40	1/16				
P A 290	100	⅛				
P A 300	80	3/16				
P A 305					7	1⅝
P A 315	45	½				
P A 320	19	⅝				
P A 325	14	1	300	2½		
P A 330	62	1 5/16			1	4¾
P A 335	277	2				
P A 340	321	3⅛				
P A 345	301	4⅝	304	7⅞	7	9½
P A 350	200	7	11	9¼		
P A 355	38	9½				
P A 360	5	14¼				

AMEX Oil — Index Close 232.56

Option	Feb Vol.	Feb Last Price	Mar Vol.	Mar Last Price	Apr Vol.	Apr Last Price
C A 235	40	2¾	2	5⅝		
C A 240	5	2	20	3¼		
C A 245	10	15/16				
P A 225	2	2				

Financial News Composite — Index Close 283.26

Option	Feb Vol.	Feb Last Price	Mar Vol.	Mar Last Price	Jun Vol.	Jun Last Price
C P 270	2	14⅛				
C P 285	30	3⅜				
P P 275			80	3⅞		
P P 280			10	5½		

Japan Index — Index Close 211.97

Option	Feb Vol.	Feb Last Price	Mar Vol.	Mar Last Price	Apr Vol.	Apr Last Price
C A 205	25	13⅝				
C A 210	22	10¼				
C A 215	12	7⅝			1	13⅜
C A 220	33	5½	150	8¼		
C A 225	6	3⅞			2	8¼
C A 230			166	4½		
C A 240	4	⅞				
C A 245	5	⅜				
C A 250					10	1⅞
P A 90	63	2			10	4⅞
P A 95	40	3	54	5⅛	3	6
P A 200	30	3⅝	75	6⅛		
P A 205	51	5⅛				
P A 210	222	7	20	9½		
P A 215	59	9	20	11¾	20	13
P A 220	10	12				
P A 225			10	16⅝		
P A 230			15	21¼		

NYSE Composite — Index Close 229.17

Option	Feb Vol.	Feb Last Price	Mar Vol.	Mar Last Price	Apr Vol.	Apr Last Price
C N 40	6	½				
C N 230	10	3¼				
P N 210	10	5/16				
P N 220	11	1				
P N 225	15	1 11/16	3	3⅝		
P N 230	20	4⅝	15	5⅞		
P N 235	50	6 9/16	5	9		

Philadelphia Gold/Silver — Index Close 81.50

Option	Feb Vol.	Feb Last Price	Mar Vol.	Mar Last Price	Apr Vol.	Apr Last Price
C X 70	20	12⅜				
C X 75	16	6⅞				
C X 80					10	5⅝
C X 85	29	1⅞	32	3		
C X 90	10	½	30	1½		
C X 105					10	5/16
P X 75	16	⅛				
P X 80	20	2 3/16	50	2⅞	10	3⅜
P X 85			3	5⅞		

Philadelphia OTC 100 — Index Close 499.86

Option	Feb Vol.	Feb Last Price	Mar Vol.	Mar Last Price	Apr Vol.	Apr Last Price
C X 510	5	7⅝				
P X 450			10	2 15/16		

Philadelphia Utility — Index Close 255.70

Option	Feb Vol.	Feb Last Price	Mar Vol.	Mar Last Price	Apr Vol.	Apr Last Price
C X 250			10	6⅜		
C X 255	43	2¾	20	3⅝		
C X 265	10	½				
P X 255			10	5¾		
P X 265	20	11				

S&P 100 — Index Close 386.73

Option	Feb Vol.	Feb Last Price	Mar Vol.	Mar Last Price	Apr Vol.	Apr Last Price
C C 350	94	37½	3	38		
C C 355	75	32¾	3	34⅛		
C C 360	350	28	12	28½	4	31
C C 365	127	22⅜				
C C 370	816	18¾	12	22½		
C C 375	177	14½	15	17½		
C C 380	2637	10	110	13¾	12	17
C C 385	13820	6¾	499	10⅛	14	13
C C 390	14503	4	588	7¼	56	9¾
C C 395	10100	2 5/16	554	5⅛	14	8
C C 400	4828	1¼	776	4	178	5½
C C 405	1875	⅝	396	2⅞	3	4¼
C C 410	2876	⅜	312	1⅜	75	3
P C 330	448	3/16	10	11/16		
P C 335	18	¼	71	⅞		
P C 340	103	¼	126	1 1/16	8	1 15/16
P C 345	445	⅜	452	1¼	1	2 3/16
P C 350	648	½	384	1 9/16	50	2 9/16
P C 355	684	⅝	640	1 15/16	44	3⅛
P C 360	2101	13/16	534	2 7/16	499	4
P C 365	2162	1⅛	917	3¼	20	4⅞
P C 370	5832	1¾	467	4	54	5⅝
P C 375	6019	2 9/16	446	5⅛	32	6¾
P C 380	11420	3¾	824	6¾	238	8¼
P C 385	17196	5⅝	718	8⅝	63	10⅝
P C 390	13135	8⅛	598	10¾	60	12¾
P C 395	718	11¼	3	14¼		
P C 400	42	14	10	16		
P C 410	1	24				

S&P 500 — Index Close 415.48

Option	Feb Vol.	Feb Last Price	Mar Vol.	Mar Last Price	Apr Vol.	Apr Last Price
C C 250			167	165		
C C 370			74	48¾		
C C 385			45	33⅜		
C C 390			5	29¾		
C C 400	120	18	167	21⅛		
C C 405	217	13¾	13	17¼		
C C 410	40	11				
C C 415	740	6⅞	106	10⅜		
C C 420	188	4¼	4	7¼		
C C 425	111	2⅜	547	6⅜		
C C 430	190	1 9/16				
C C 435	20	⅞				
C C 440			55	1⅝		
C C 450			3	9/16		
P C 250			167	⅛		
P C 275						
P C 300						
P C 310	35	1/16				
P C 360			65	1 1/16		
P C 370			38	1⅜		
P C 375	200	5/16	601	1½		
P C 380	5	11/16	42	2		
P C 385	80	⅞	1335	2½		
P C 390	24	1 1/16	23	2 15/16		
P C 395	87	1 9/16	600	3½		
P C 400	632	2 3/16	364	4½	19	6⅝
P C 405	230	3	1238	5⅝	10	8⅛
P C 410	186	4⅜				
P C 415	644	6¼	709	9¼		
P C 420	226	8½	2	11⅜	2	13
P C 425	2	12				
P C 435			5	21⅜		
P C 440			3	24⅜		

Value Line Arithmetic — Index Close 352.76

Option	Feb Vol.	Feb Last Price	Mar Vol.	Mar Last Price	Apr Vol.	Apr Last Price
C X 345	2	11⅞	130	14⅜		
C X 350	10	7				
C X 355	13	5				
C X 360	13	3	305	5⅞		
C X 365	20	1⅝			5	5⅛
P X 315			1	1		
P X 335	15	1½				
P X 345			100	5⅜		
P X 350	11	4⅜				
P X 360	10	8½				

example, you can buy an option on an actual index, while it takes thousands of dollars to do the same on the futures contract. Therefore, options on the actual indexes provide much more flexibility. In addition, in order to be able to trade stock index *futures* options, you must have a net worth of $50,000-$100,000 or more, exclusive of your home. But to buy options on the actual stock indexes, there are usually no such guidelines.

Pricing Index Options and Index Futures

An index futures contract is a commitment to buy at a future date, while an index option does not require a buyer to take delivery. If the price of the underlying asset falls, only the futures contract continues to lose, because with an index futures contract, the investor has almost unlimited risk unless hedged. The loss to the index option holder, on the other hand, is limited to the premium he paid for the option. The price of an index option is determined by interest rates, the index price, its volatility, the expiration date, and its strike price.

An index option's real worth is measured by its chances of being greater than its strike price at expiration. An index futures contract price reflects the current market value of the stock index and the carrying charges of holding the index portfolio (less dividends collected on the portfolio) during the contract period.

The 1987 Crash

The S & P 500 Index futures contract played a major role in causing the stock market crash of 1987. Institutional money managers adopted the S & P 500 Index contract as insurance to protect their large stock portfolios. Money managers who handled billions of dollars mirrored their portfolios after the S & P 500 and then had computer programs monitored by clerks pinpointing when the market had dropped to a degree where these clerks would then sell enough index futures contracts to offset all the downside risks to the portfolio.

In theory, the index futures contract provided perfect portfolio insurance. In practice, on the day of the crash, so many money managers started *selling* the futures contract that its price went to almost a 30% discount, meaning that if you sold the futures contract, you automatically took a 30% loss on your portfolio. Unable to sell the futures contract to offset the downside risk, as the market was declining, the institutions panicked and sold most of their stocks. An avalanche of selling ensued, resulting in the worst market crash in our history.

Program Traders

Blame for the crash was wrongly placed on the shoulders of the program traders. But program traders are an important part of the futures markets. They keep the markets efficient by keeping the futures contract price in line with the cash index. Similar arbitrators keep such balance in most other futures markets, including the commodity markets. But on the day of the crash, the program traders were not there. They had run out of stock to sell, and therefore could not keep the futures contracts in line with the actual index.

Program traders continue to receive the blame when the stock market moves up or down. But they are strictly the effect, not the cause of those movements. The *cause* are the speculators and institutions who buy and sell the futures contracts for only 15% of its value (before the Crash—10%).

With such leverage, the speculators move the market, not the program traders. The program traders strictly put the futures contracts back in balance with the actual index by buying or selling the stocks in the index.

Puts — A Better Insurance

After the crash, institutional money managers moved to buying put options on the indexes instead of selling futures contracts as a method of providing portfolio insurance. Buying index put options to reduce portfolio risk is such a rage now that index puts are presently quite expensive, and have been since the crash of 1987, telling you to avoid buying such puts.

A Look at the Indexes

Standard & Poor's 100 — An Example

This Index was designed to reflect the market as a whole and is, therefore, broadly based and highly representative of the whole stock market. It has many of the highly capitalized blue chip stocks, and more important than that, it is a weighted index, which means that capitalization (number of shares outstanding) determines the influence of each stock in the index. Consequently, a stock such as IBM has much more influence on movements of the Index than do other stocks with fewer numbers of shares outstanding.

The S & P 100 Index has a strong correlation with both the Standard & Poor's 500 Composite Index and the Dow Jones Industrial Average. An analysis of the daily returns from January 1976 through December 1982 shows a correlation coefficient of .97 with the S & P 500 and .95 with the Dow Jones Industrial Average (DJIA). Such figures demonstrate that even though you may not have the opportunity to buy listed options on the Dow, the S & P 100 would move step for step, percentage-wise at least, with the Dow and give you the same kind of action you would be looking for with the more popular indexes.

The Major Market Index

The Major Market Index over the past year has had the same close correlation with the Dow Jones Industrial Average. However, unlike the S & P 100, the Major Market Index is unweighted, meaning that changes in the Index correspond to percentage changes in the sum of the prices of the 20 stocks in the Index. Due to the fact there are far fewer stocks in this index than the S & P 100, this index is more volatile than the S & P 100 Index.

Index Options versus Stock Options

The Similarities

To understand how to trade stock index options, it is important to remember that they are almost identical in treatment to stock options. Index options have the same contract size as stock options. The index price can be viewed as the price of one share of an underlying stock. (But here the underlying asset, the index, and the strike price are more symbolic than real.) An index option, like a stock option, covers 100 shares. Therefore, a S & P 100 Index call option priced at 2-1/4 represents $225. Strike prices for index options are usually set five points apart.

The One Major Difference

There is one major difference between stock and index options, and the best way to describe that difference is to look again at the definition of options. I always like to refer to options as side bets. In the case of stock options, they are side bets on common stocks, but in reality, they are not, because you can, for example, always exercise your call options and acquire the underlying common stock.

However, in the case of listed index options, the definition of an option as a side bet is perfect. Index options are in reality side bets on the stock market index prices (usually multiplied by 100). Index call options are bets that the market will rise, and index puts are bets that the market will fall.

The major difference arises in that you *cannot* exercise the index option and acquire all the stocks in the index. Exercising the index option only results in a cash settlement, and the words *cash settlement* are the key difference between listed index options and stock options.

Cash settlement means that when exercise occurs, settlement of the transaction is settled in cash and not by exchange of stock.

Stock or Index Options — Your Best Choice

Since the advent of index options, many small investors have jumped on the index band wagon. Buying index options is more popular than buying stock options. Every speculator loves to bet on what the Dow will do tomorrow. Buying index options is the perfect betting vehicle.

In addition, the S & P 100 Index (OEX) options have excellent liquidity, for far more OEX options trade than any class of stock options. Therefore, it is easy to move in and out of your option position. But index options are not your best choice for option buying. When you buy options, you are betting on *volatility*, big movements in the underlying stock, index or futures contracts. When you buy index options, you are buying options on a composite of stocks. The more stocks in the index, the less volatile it becomes, and the chances of a big move are reduced. For example, the NYSE Index is an index of about 1,700 stocks, and therefore this index moves slowly. Of course, there are times when an index will make a big move as we saw in 1987 when the Dow dropped 500 points in one day, or during the mini crash of 1989 when the Dow dropped 180 points in one day. But when the indexes make big moves, so do the common stocks, and some stocks make bigger moves. Yet each individual stock may also make a violent move due to an earnings report, a buy or sell recommendation by a major broker, news events or a variety of other reasons, even when the index is totally quiet.

The Importance of Volatility

When you buy index options, you lose that extra level of volatility. This point demonstrates that not only should you buy stock options instead of index options, but also you should search out options on stocks that have a better chance for surprise violent moves, such as takeover targets, or stocks with high price-earnings ratios, high flyers, or stocks such as Biotech in industries where surprise news events are likely. Also, select stocks that have smaller capitalization (shares outstanding) and those traded over-the-counter on the NASDAQ. Avoid the Big Blue Chips such as IBM or General Electric where it takes huge amounts of buying or selling to move the stock prices. Remember, the name of the game is volatility, so bet on the rabbit rather than the tortoise.

12

PUT OPTIONS: THE ULTIMATE INSURANCE POLICY

Options are usually considered a highly speculative investment. But there is a conservative side to options. Options can be used as an excellent INSURANCE POLICY for your investment portfolio.

Insurance For Your Nest Egg

We live in an insurance-oriented society—always trying to reduce risk, usually financial risk. The average American buys insurance against a whole variety of risks. We buy life, medical, dental, automobile and home insurance.

The purpose of all this insurance is to avoid a major financial catastrophe, such as having your home burn down, or having to pay heavy medical expenses. But few, if any, investors ever consider buying insurance for their *investment portfolio* or for their *savings*. And yet, these investments are assets that most people have worked a lifetime to build. You may have far more money at risk in the investment markets than in your home, or in the other potential catastrophes you normally insure against.

Even Lloyd's of London probably won't insure your stock portfolio. But with options, you now have the opportunity to create an insurance policy on your investment portfolio. If you do it right, the cost of this insurance can be quite low. In some cases, you can create this investment insurance and increase your overall profit picture, too.

Be Your Own Insurance Broker

With listed options, you can design an insurance policy for almost any asset in your investment portfolio. Options are now available on listed stocks, over-the-counter (OTC) stocks, a variety of stock market averages (i.e., S & P 100 Index), long- and short-term bonds and Treasury Notes, gold and silver, and a host of other commodities, including soybeans, cattle, and wheat.

There are even listed options available on the price of foreign currencies such as the British Pound, or the Japanese Yen. These currency options make it possible to protect a business investment (such as import-export) that is affected by changes in foreign currency values.

With listed options available on all of these investments, you can create a comprehensive insurance policy that removes much of the "downside" (loss) risk in your investment portfolio, or at least the risk of a catastrophic loss.

Listed options can also be used to hedge the business risks that you take. For example, when you start up or invest in a small business, listed options can insulate you from interest rates, recessions and other risks encountered in that business.

Hedging With Put Options

The art of using options to reduce the risks in your investment portfolio is referred to as HEDGING. The goal of hedging is to reduce risk as much as possible and yet maximize your return or profit. There are a variety of ways to do this.

The easiest way for the small investor to create an insurance policy for his investment portfolio is to buy PUT OPTIONS. Put options are a good bet whether you are using them as a method of hedging, or strictly for speculation. Why? Because put options are usually 20% to 30% lower in price than call options.

There are two major reasons why put options are lower priced.

The first major reason is that when you buy a put option, the stock can theoretically only fall to a price of "0." Therefore, there is limited profit on the DOWNSIDE. When you buy a call option, however, you theoretically have unlimited UPSIDE profit potential.

The second, psychological, reason for the lower price of a put option is that investors don't like to bet that the market will fall or that the value of their investment will drop. Investors are far more prone to bet that the market or the value of their investment will RISE. So they usually buy CALL options. This general tendency among investors creates a higher demand for call options, and that demand increases call option prices.

In addition, stocks tend to rise slower and fall faster in price, as was demonstrated by the crash of 1987, and the minor crash of 1989. Therefore, put options are the better bet.

Options As Insurance For Your Stocks Or Mutual Funds

One easy way to buy insurance for your stock or mutual fund portfolio is to buy PUT options on STOCK INDEXES such as the S & P 100 Index (OEX), the Major Market Index (XMI), and other stock indexes. If you hold a stock portfolio or a series of mutual funds that contain mostly "blue chip" stocks, you would buy options on the S & P 100 Index or the Major Market Index. Both of these indexes usually mirror the moves of these "blue chip" stocks.

In other words, try to buy put options on an index that moves with the type of stocks that you hold in your mutual fund or portfolio.

The problem with index options is the fact that they don't give you enough bang for your buck as was indicated in the previous chapter. In addition, the institutions use such puts for portfolio insurance, therefore, over the past several years, such puts have been somewhat overpriced.

So rather than buy index options, follow sound option buying procedures and buy options on stocks that are similar to the stocks in your portfolio. Or better yet, on the stocks that you own.

Here's an example: Let's say in November you own 100 shares of Pfizer which sells for 68 ($6,800 investment). You could buy one June 60 put option priced at 1 ($100). The put allows you to sell 100 shares of Pfizer at 60, anytime before the option expires on the third Friday in June. If Pfizer falls below 60 during that time, your losses on the stock will be partly offset by the appreciation of the put. For example, if Pfizer falls to 50, the put would be worth $1,000 (60 - 50 X $100), offsetting part of the $1,800 decline in the stock. If it falls to 40, the put would be worth $2,000, versus a $2,800 stock decline. If the stock rises, or just stays above 60, the put option would expire worthless.

One hundred dollars buys you insurance for seven months, but in this case, the "deductible" is high—you must absorb the first $800 of the decline.

The Kennecott Caper

In the early 1980's, I wanted to buy shares in *Kennecott Copper*, priced at $27 a share. Based on my research, I felt that the stock was somewhat undervalued. But the stock did have some downside risk, so I bought 100 shares of Kennecott and a nine-month put on Kennecott, with a strike price of 30, and paid 4 ($400) for the put. How much did I pay for this insurance? Well, the stock was three points in-the-money, so the put had only one point of time value. Therefore, I only paid $100 for this insurance.

For example, if Kennecott dropped to 0, I would have lost $2,700 on the stock, but the put would be worth $3,000 (30 points in-the-money). Hence, I would only lose $100 if I paid $2,700 for the stock plus $400 for the put, and got back $3,000.

Kennecott was bought out by Standard of Ohio three weeks later for $62 a share, so I made $3,500 on the stock (62 - 27 = 35). I lost the $400 for the put, generating a profit of $3,100.

Here is a way to buy a put to remove almost all of the risk of owning the stock.

Catastrophic Insurance

Americans have a tendency to buy too much insurance, so go for a big deductible and treat such put buying as catastrophic insurance, designed to pay off big in a major decline in the market. Select cheap puts—puts purchased for under $100, and, better yet, under $50 (1/2 or lower).

For example, in August before the crash of 1987, I recommended in the *Trester Compleat Option Report* a November ITT put for 1/8 ($12.50), to be purchased for the purpose of portfolio insurance. When the market crashed, the put rose from 1/8 ($12.50) to 16 ($1,600), over a 10,000% gain. A few of those puts would have provided a lot of profit to cover your stock losses.

A good put buying program will not only provide your portfolio with a deductible insurance policy, but also could be a profit center—even if the market doesn't suffer a major decline. In other words, when you buy underpriced puts on a stock that has a chance for some surprise moves, you could see some big gains from your puts, even during normal market conditions.

But even if your puts expire worthless, they are no different than any of your insurance policies. You don't hope your house burns down just so you can collect on fire insurance, do you? It's the same with portfolio insurance.

When To Buy

When should you own puts for insurance? In a bull market? In a bear market? The answer is: *in any market*. Before the crash of 1987, a well known money manager bought index puts for portfolio insurance, but only when he felt the market was ready to decline. During the crash, he did not own any puts, and his portfolio took a devastating loss. You don't know when or if your house will burn down, so you always own fire insurance. The same logic applies to stock market insurance.

Guidelines

Here are some guidelines that summarize how you should buy portfolio insurance.

1. Buy underpriced puts.

2. Buy longer term, low cost puts, preferably for less than $100—less than $50 is even better.

3. Stay away from index puts.

4. Diversify over time. Buy puts every few months—when they expire, buy some more.

5. Follow sound option buying procedures as covered in the previous chapters.

6. Try to buy options on stocks similar to ones that you own (i.e., in the same industry). But stay with puts on stocks that are vulnerable to a big surprise move. If you own mutual funds, buy puts on stocks similar to those in the mutual fund.

If you follow these guidelines, especially the first one, puts will provide insurance and should generate profits over the long haul, even if the market does not crash. Only with put options is it possible to turn an expense into income. You can't do that with auto insurance.

PART II

WINNING THROUGH OPTION WRITING STRATEGIES

THE OPTION WRITER IS ANALOGOUS TO A CASINO OPERATOR

13

TAKING THE BETS, RATHER THAN MAKING THE BETS

Option Writers Defined

In our early discussion of the option buying game, we've indicated that option buying is analogous to a side bet on the price action of a specific stock. The backer of that side bet is referred to as the *option writer*. He takes the bets of the option buyer, and, in a sense, he pays off when the option buyer is a winner, and pockets the option proceeds when the option buyer is a loser. Option buying has been with us for many decades.

However, option writing, as it is today, is a creation of the options exchanges. Option writing, for those who are market players, is similar to selling short a stock, or in this case, selling short an option. Actually, what you are doing is *selling* an option, rather than buying an option. The option seller, or the option writer, has a huge advantage over the option buyer. While time works *against* the option buyer, time works *for* the option seller. As time passes, the value of an option depreciates, and this depreciation, this value, slips into the pocket of the option writer.

Let's take an example. Let's say that you purchase a call option—a Compaq Computer October 25 call. Let's say that there are three months left in the life of that option, and you pay a price of $300, plus commissions. At the same time that you are buying that option, someone unknown to you, on the other side of the Options Exchange, is selling (writing) that option, and is receiving your $300. This money will go into his account; so, in a sense, you have just put $300 into the pocket of the option writer. Now, he has certain obligations. If you request 100 shares of Compaq Computer by exercising your option, he must deliver to you 100 shares of Compaq Computer stock at a price of 25.

Let's assume that the Compaq Computer (CPQ) price is now at 23, which means we are working with an "out-of-the-money" option. One month passes, and the stock has moved from 23 to 24. The CPQ Oct 25 has depreciated in value from $300 to $200, even though the stock has moved upward. The option writer now has a paper profit of $100, less commissions. If he wishes, he can go back into the Options Exchange, and buy that option back for $200, and take his profits, and in a sense, close the casino door. Or, if he feels that CPQ is going to stay where it is, or not move any further than 26 or 27 on the upside, he can hang onto that option and wait for it to continue to depreciate to zero. If you, the option buyer, hold onto the option, you will continue to see it depreciate in value, unless the stock moves up suddenly in a strong and positive direction.

So, the option writer has a huge advantage. While he is backing your bet, or option, it is depreciating; while the option buyer is holding that bet, he is losing money.

Let's look at this example in a different context. The call option writer will be a winner if the stock moves up a little, does not move at all, moves down a little, or moves down a lot. The option buyer will be the winner, will profit from an option purchase, *only* if the stock moves up a great deal. Another way of putting it is to say that the option seller (writer) has, in a sense, an 80% chance of winning, while the option buyer has only a 20% chance of winning. Here is the advantage of option writing. Of course, if the option buyer pays a very small amount for that option, his risk-reward ratio can be significant, and he can afford to take that 20% chance of winning.

The option writer then has the odds in his favor. As time passes, that option depreciates, and the depreciation slips right into his pocket. This is the reason why the options game has become so popular, why the institutions are jumping onto this band wagon, attempting to take advantage of the lucrative profits that are made by the option writer.

The Types of Option Writers

There are two types of option writers: there are the option writers that go *covered,* and there are the option writers that go *uncovered,* or "naked." The covered option writer is in a very conservative position; the uncovered option writer is in a very speculative position.

Covered option writing refers to a situation in which the option writer protects himself in case of a possible exercise of his option (assignment), or an increase in the value of that option. At the same time that he writes (sells) an option, he buys (or owns) 100 shares of the stock on which he wrote the option. In this way, he receives *premium* (time value) from the option; yet if the stock moves upward, he still profits from the move in the stock, offsetting any possible losses from the option that he has just written (sold). This kind of strategy is the most popular today; it is the one that most institutions are moving into. It is simple to understand; it generates a reasonable return on investment; and it has low risk. This strategy will be covered extensively in a later chapter.

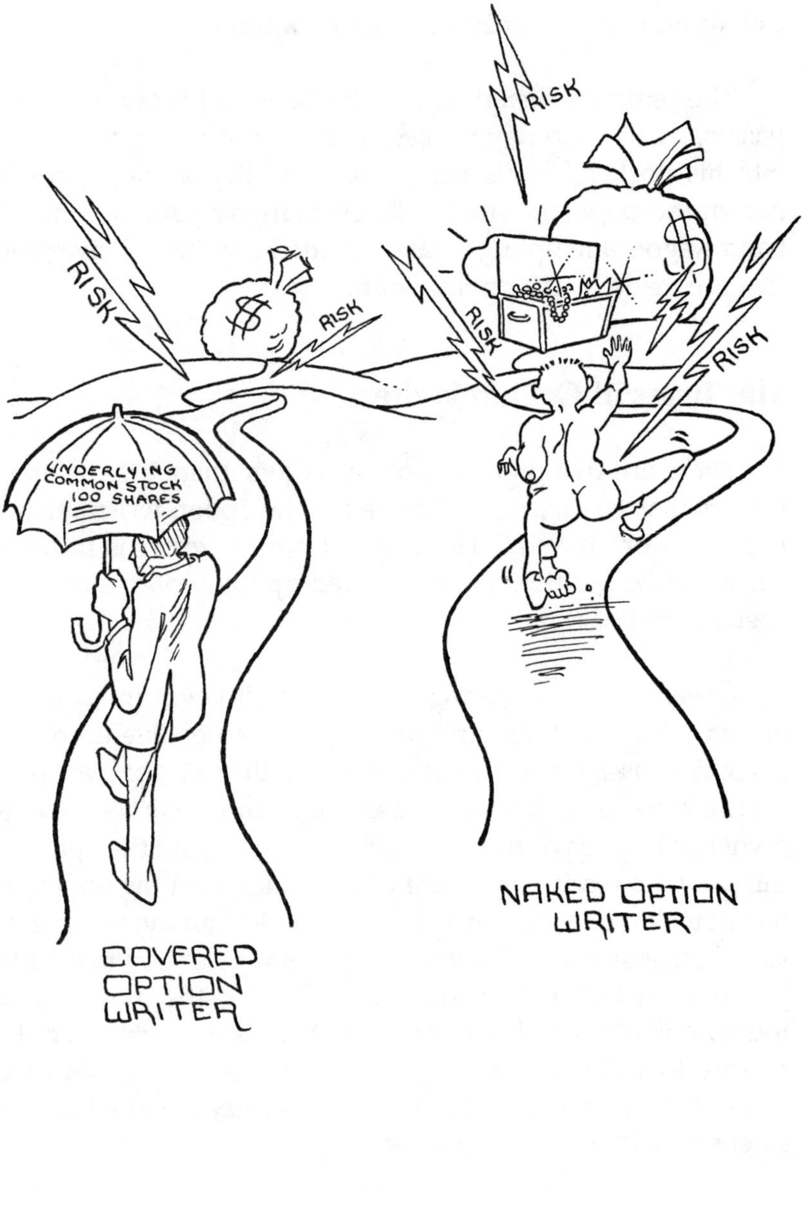
RISK
RISK
RISK
RISK
RISK
UNDERLYING
COMMON STOCK
100 SHARES
COVERED
OPTION
WRITER
NAKED OPTION
WRITER

On the other hand, the uncovered writer, rather than buying 100 shares of stock to protect the option that he has written, decides to take the gamble, and write the option without any type of hedge, or protection. He is referred to as a *naked writer*. Now this type of a position does have some risk. There is unlimited risk to the naked call writer and extensive risk to the naked put writer. But, you must remember that this is only a theoretical risk; it is not an actual risk in many cases, for the sophisticated option writer knows when the risk is great, and when it is minimal.

To guarantee to both the options buyer, and to the Options Exchange, that the naked writer will make good on the option that he writes, he must put up cash and/or collateral to back up his naked option writing position.

Naked option writing is probably the most revolutionary investment medium which has come out of this exciting options market. Naked option writing is an unusual investment tool which can provide flexibility and protection to almost any stock or bond portfolio. The numerous strategies which can be designed from naked option writing positions would take many volumes of text to describe, but I will present what I feel are the most profitable means of using naked option writing, and will identify strategies which have proven to be successful in the past.

The Mechanics of Option Writing

Many an investor who is still fuzzy about what option writing is all about will discover that it is as easy to do as buying stock, or buying options, as long as you put up the necessary cash or collateral in your account—therefore, the ease of writing options is the greatest danger to the novice investor. The investor can so easily write many options, abusing this investment medium and creating a dangerous portfolio position.

The only difference between buying and writing options lies in the order in which you carry out the process. The option writer sells an option to *open* a position, and buys an option to *close* that position. This process releases him from the responsibilities which are part of his option obligations.

Conversely, the option buyer buys an option to *open* a position, and sells an option to *close* the position, an act which relinquishes the rights which he purchased with that option.

The option writer, like the option buyer in the options market, has the advantage of liquidity. At one moment, he can write an option, and at the next moment, he can close out that position on the Exchange by buying back the option. In this way, the shrewd option writer can avoid being assigned (exercised) by the option buyer, or exposing himself to the potential dangers of option writing.

The Risks of Option Writing

A discussion of the option writer's risks is appropriate at this time. The writer of a call option, like the individual who sells short 100 shares of stock, has unlimited risk on the upside. If you write an option, and the stock goes up 50 points while you hold the position, you would lose up to $5,000—one hundred dollars for each point that the stock rose above the exercise price. This is the possible risk, the unlimited risk, a rise in the stock price can create. This factor alone scares many an option player.

The writer of a put option, on the other hand, has limited risk. For example, if you were to write a CPQ Jan 25 put option, when the stock price was right at 25, your risk can be easily determined. When you write a put, you are backing the side bet of the option buyer, a side bet that the stock will fall below the strike price of the option, which in this case is 25.

How far can that stock fall? Theoretically, it can fall to zero. For each point that it falls, the option buyer *makes* $100, and you, the option writer, *lose* $100. Consequently, with the CPQ Jan 25 put, your maximum risk, less the premium you received from the option buyer, is $2,500. Therefore, theoretically, the writing of puts has less risk than the writing of calls. But practically speaking, the risk for writing both puts and calls is actually about the same, and we will be covering this point again later when we discuss option writing strategies involving both put and call options.

The second risk to the option writer is the risk of assignment, or exercise, and the real danger does not lie in being exercised—it lies in the *cost* of exercise. The cost of the exercise is a roundtrip commission on 100 shares of stock that you will have to buy and then deliver to the option buyer.

In the next chapter, we will be discussing the problems of assignment at length, and the secrets of avoiding the exercise of options you have written. In Chapter 14, we will dispel some of the old wives' tales which have filtered through the market regarding the mystical dangers of assignment.

THE ART OF EXERCISE

14

THE SECRETS OF EXERCISE

The first major secret of exercise is: TO AVOID EXERCISE.

The second major secret of exercise is: IT IS EASY TO AVOID EXERCISE.

Exercise Defined

What is this game of exercise all about? When you buy an option, whether it is a put or a call, you are buying a right to exercise. When we say "exercise" with regard to a call option, we mean to "call" from the writer (backer) of the option the 100 shares of stock as specified in the option, at the specified option exercise price. The writer is required to deliver that 100 shares of stock at the specified exercise price to the buyer, if the option is exercised by the buyer.

With regard to a put option, we mean to "put" (sell) to the writer of the option the 100 shares of stock as specified in the option, at the specified option exercise price. The writer is required to buy that 100 shares of stock at the specified exercise price from the option buyer, if the option is exercised by the buyer.

The writer who is exercised is being *assigned* the obligation to deliver or buy the stock randomly by the Options Clearing Corporation. Therefore, the process of exercise is called *assignment*.

In practical terms, the options market has been designed to avoid the use of exercise. It is constituted so that rather than exercising if you are a buyer, under most circumstances, you can sell your option position on the Options Exchange, and avoid this more costly process. To the seller, it means that rather than being assigned, you can go back into the options market and just buy back your option, paying the prevailing option market price to discontinue your obligation to the option buyer.

Exercise and Market Specialists

Sometimes the problem of exercise does occur, although probably less than 10% of all options are ever exercised. Many of these are exercised by specialists and market makers on the floor of the options exchanges. These market makers and specialists are taking advantage of what is referred to as a "discount" in the price of the option. In this situation, there is normally no time value at all, or there is actually a negative time value; the price of the option is less than the intrinsic value of that option. But the average investor cannot take advantage of this negative price because the cost of exercise is too high. On the other hand, the specialist or market maker on the floor, because he is able to avoid paying commissions, can take advantage of these negative premiums, and usually does this by exercising the options that he purchases.

Dangers in Exercise

The real danger to the option buyer who is forced to exercise, or to the option writer whose option is assigned, lies in the cost of exercise—the commission. That cost is the only real concern that the option buyer should have with exercise. To the option writer, the assignment of an option may put him in jeopardy if it removes an element in his option strategy. All the other mechanics of the process will be taken care of neatly by the internal mechanisms of the options market, and your brokerage firm.

Why Options are Exercised

Although options are rarely exercised, the reasons why they would be should be well known to the option player:

1. The first, and most important reason for exercise relates to the time value of the option. Options which have little or no time value are ripe for exercise. Options included in this class would be options which are "deep-in-the-money," referring to the fact that the stock has moved far beyond the strike price of the option.

   For example, by looking at Table 8, three options are displayed which have no time value, and therefore, would be open to exercise.

2. Options with a negative premium, or what is referred to as a discount on their price, would also be extremely ripe for exercise. Normally, this situation would only exist when there is little time left in the option.

   Table 8 provides three examples of options which have a negative premium, or no time value.

There are other incidental reasons why options could possibly be exercised, but normally they all relate back to the fact that there is little or no more time value in that option. An option

Table 8
Options Ripe for Exercise

Option	Option Price	Stock Price	Time Value	Intrinsic Value
Disney Jan 135 Call	3	138	0	3
Loews Jan 100 Put	1	99	0	1
Charmin Dec 25 Put	4-7/8	20-1/8	0	4-7/8
Xerox Jan 50 Call	7-3/4	58	-1/4 Negative	8
Alcoa Jan 60 Put	5-7/8	54	-1/8 Negative	6
ITT Jan 30 Call	6-5/8	37	-3/8 Negative	7

exercised with time value would create a loss for the option buyer. He would, in a sense, be throwing away the time value of the option which is still built into the option price. Consequently, this type of an option would rarely be exercised, and if it were, it would provide a cushion of profit to protect the option writer from the commission costs incurred by the assignment.

How to Avoid Exercise

Now that we know the root cause of your option being exercised, we will see that it is quite easy to take steps to avoid this costly experience.

Whenever an option writer holds an option which has a price approaching zero time value, or zero premium, he should immediately buy back that option, and write another option which still maintains some time value. This action will have two benefits:

1. It will avoid possible exercise.

2. It will place you into an option which has time value, which works to the benefit of the option writer, because time value depreciates as time passes.

As you enter the option writing game, you will discover that in some cases, you forget about your options. They are not monitored closely enough, and an option writing position will be sitting in your hands without time value to protect you from possible exercise. In this case, your only real danger is the exercise cost, and that will probably run no more than $150 per 100 shares.

To summarize, exercise is the greatest concern of most

beginners in this options game, but exercise is a minor concern of most professionals.

Index Options and Exercise

Due to cash settlement, index options can cause some additional problems for options writers. By the fact that index options do not involve the transfer of assets, such as common stocks, or the assignment of such assets, they make for an easier transaction. On the other hand, under cash settlement conditions, the ability to arbitrage or hedge those positions is made much more difficult. Let us look more closely at cash settlement and make sure that you understand the concept.

The Ins and Outs of Cash Settlement

The exercise of an index call or index put gives the index option holder the right to the cash difference between the strike price and the index price at the close on the day of the exercise. Confusing? Let's take an example.

You own a S & P 100 call option with an exercise price of 370, and the index price today closes at 372. If you exercise your call today, you will receive $200 less commissions. Why? Because the index option is 2 points in-the-money at the close of trading on the day that you exercise that option. The index stocks are not delivered to you, but the cash difference between the strike price and the price of the index at the close of trading on the day that you exercise the option is delivered in cash.

Now, what happens if during the trading day the stock index rises to 374 and you decide to exercise your call options at that point in time. Will you get the difference between 370 and 374, for a total of $400? No. Again, remember that the rule states you will receive the cash amount difference between the strike price and the index value at the *close* of trading on the day that you exercise your option. If the index closes at 372 on that day, you only get $200, not $400 (372 - 370 = 2 x $100 = $200).

Risks to the Hedger

If you plan to write index options as part of spreads, or to do some covered writing of index options against mutual funds that either mirror these indexes or have some similarities to these indexes, or if you have a portfolio that moves in conjunction with an index (and most properly diversified portfolios do), there are some risks that you should be aware of with regard to cash settlement.

As an index option writer, if you are assigned, which means the options you have written are exercised, you are not allowed to deliver a mutual fund that mirrors the index or a conglomeration of stocks that mirror the index. You must come up with cash for settlement. Therefore, there is no such thing as a covered writer in the index options game. You can, of course, attempt to "write covered" by writing an index call option, for example, against a mutual fund that mirrors the index. (At the present time, a mutual fund exists that mirrors the S & P 500 Index.) But, if you are assigned, you cannot deliver that mutual fund to the buyer. This creates a problem because of the delay that may occur in receiving that assignment.

AN EXAMPLE

For example, if the S & P 100 Index today is at 372, you have written a 370 call option against that index, and you are assigned, you must pay the option buyer $200, the difference between the strike price and the index value at the close of trading today. However, you may not receive notice of exercise until tomorrow (the next business day) during trading hours, and at that point in time, the index may have dropped below 372. If the mutual fund that mirrors that index dropped to 369, in order to get out of the position, you must first provide $200 in cash settlement for the assignment of the index option. Then to remove the long (purchased) leg of your covered writing position, you must sell the mutual fund. But if you sell it at 369, you have taken an unexpected $300 loss (372 - 369 = 3 x 100 = $300).

In the case of equity options, if you were writing IBM calls against IBM and you were assigned, all you would have to do would be to deliver the IBM stock. No additional risk would be incurred. With index options, however, there is nothing to be delivered, and to get out of the total strategy, you must settle with cash. You have then opened yourself up to more risk than would normally be anticipated.

Risks to the Spreaders

Not only is this true for the covered writer, but it is also true for spreaders. Spreaders usually are guaranteed specific, limited risk by the amount that they spread a long (purchased option) and a short (written option) position. But if your short position is exercised, you will not discover that until the next trading day. At that time, the option you own (opposite side of spread) may have moved in the wrong direction. In the equity market, you could have limited the risk by just exercising the long position (the option you hold).

Unfortunately, with index options, if you exercise the long position the next morning, you are only guaranteed the index value at the end of that second day—a one-day difference between the price that you were assigned and the price at which you exercised the purchased option. By the close monitoring of your positions to avoid being exercised, the risks that cash settlement exposes the spreader and the hedger to can be reduced or eliminated.

When the time value disappears in your short positions, you should immediately take action by rolling into new options or liquidating the whole spread position, or you will risk being assigned. Specific instructions should be given to your broker to sell out the remaining portion of your position immediately if you are assigned and cannot be reached.

If this discussion is confusing, just remember that if you are writing an index option as part of a spread, and the index moves in-the-money, exit immediately when the time value starts to disappear.

European Exercise versus American Exercise

You can avoid this whole problem by sticking with index options that have European Exercise instead of American Exercise. American Exercise means that you can exercise your options at any time—all stock options have American Exercise as do some index options such as the S & P 100 Index options. Other index options have European Exercise, meaning that you can only exercise the options on the last day of trading before expiration. The S & P 500 Index (SPX) option and the Major Market Index (XMI) options both have European Exercise.

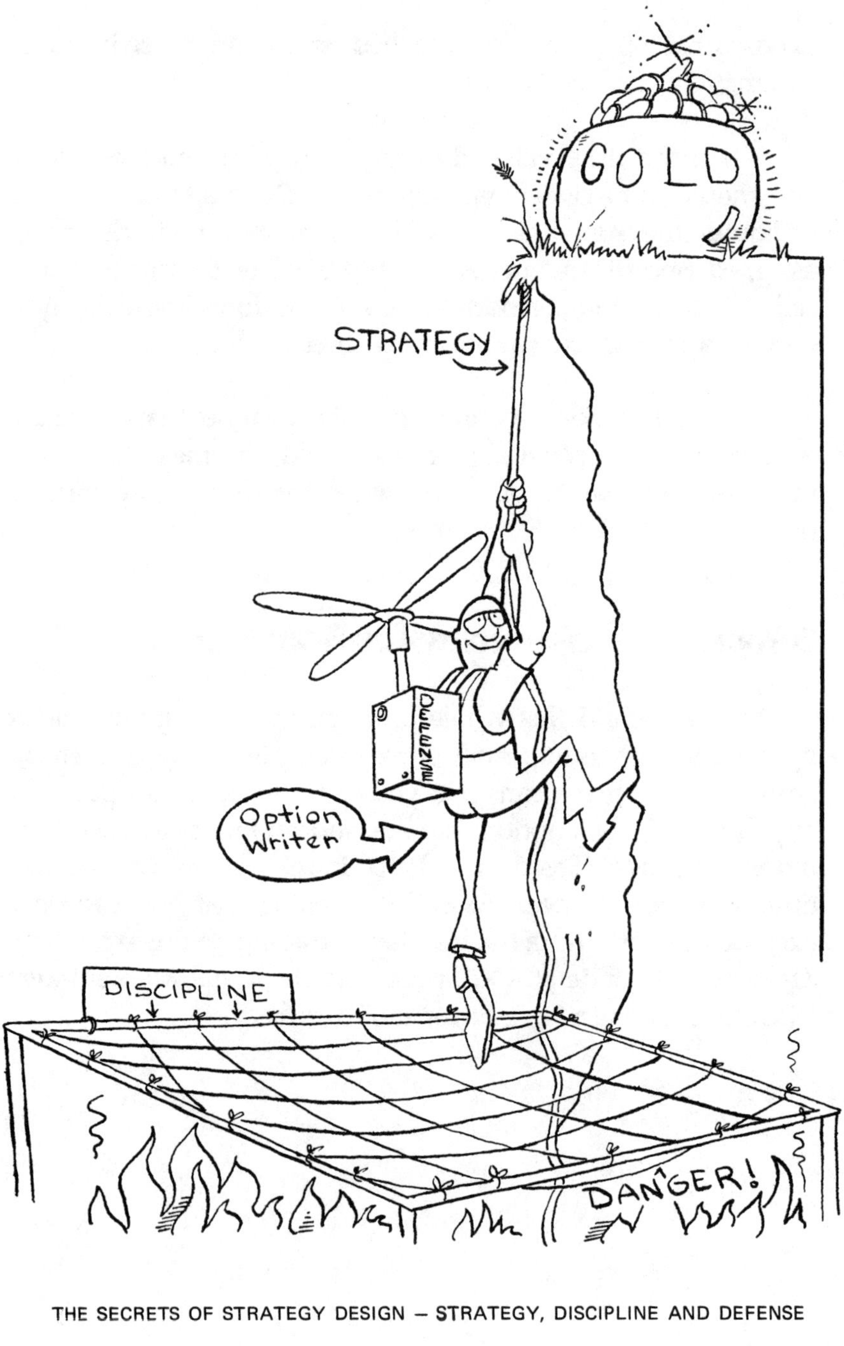

THE SECRETS OF STRATEGY DESIGN – STRATEGY, DISCIPLINE AND DEFENSE

15

THE SECRETS OF STRATEGY DESIGN

Three Magic Words

Three words will expose the secrets of strategy design. These three magic words are: STRATEGY, DISCIPLINE, and DEFENSE.

1. Strategy

The first hidden secret of strategy design is a simple prescription—make sure that you always have a well defined *strategy*, a well defined plan of attack. The options market has generated a high powered method of making money, but with this high powered potential, we also have some high powered risk. The game player requires a carefully planned out strategy to control that risk. With such a strategy, the limitless risks which are continually present to the option writer can be controlled to a degree. The game player who enjoys the glamour and glory in flying by the seat of his pants will surely crash land when he enters the options game.

2. Discipline

The second key word of strategy design is *discipline*. Discipline relates to your ability to *follow* your game plan. You may consider this secret to be elementary, but usually it is totally ignored by the option player. The greatest enemy of any option player is his emotions. As you begin to play with your own personal money, the most powerful elements of your emotions come into play, attempting to coax you off of your plan of action. Once you have lost your rationality in the options game, you have lost the options game.

You must have the discipline to follow your well defined strategy to the letter, not breaking one rule or parameter that you have set. True, this may result in some inflexibility, but in the long run, discipline will provide for a far more consistent return, and a far safer, more successful venture into the extremely volatile options market. Remember, the options market attracts the most brilliant game players in the world; the COMPLEAT OPTION PLAYER must be cool, calculating, and totally disciplined, able to disregard past losses with ease, without disturbing his present strategies and tactics.

3. Defense

If you have ever watched a college football team, you have seen many teams that will let it all hang out. Hook or crook, they will put all their offense on the line, trying to win big, throwing numerous passes, trying out exotic plays, taking every risk in the book in order to win the game. Many of these teams falter in the dust because of the numerous errors that occur from such a wide open offensive stance.

Then we look at the professional football team which plays a much duller game. They have good offense, but their defense is where all the action lies; a defense that creates openings for the team, prevents any damage from occurring, and that generates a far more consistent win record than teams with a wide open offense.

In the options market, *defense* is the name of the game. As we grow older and wiser, we discover that it is far more practical and there is a far better return if we conserve and protect our capital, and aim for a consistent return rather than laying everything on the line and going for that one super victory, using all of our resources in one burst of energy.

The options market has been beautifully designed to aid the investor in building a powerful defense. The wise option player uses these investment tools to create strategies which provide a high degree of safety and a high and consistent return, not strategies which will live or die on the price action of the stock market. The wise option player paces himself, follows his strategies carefully to avoid any type of costly error, and shows tremendous maturity in using his offense. He continually conserves his resources, using his offense only when the time is ripe, patiently waiting for the best opportunities to develop, and then striking hard leaving enough in reserve to be able to return another day.

Option strategies have tremendous potential if you remember the three key words to success: STRATEGY, DISCIPLINE, and DEFENSE. If you do not heed these words, there are numerous risks and tremendous disappointments that will face you.

16

THE BUSINESS OF OPTION WRITING

The number of different option writing strategies available to the option player is almost limitless. To provide proper treatment for each type of strategy would require several volumes of text. Therefore, I will present a select few of the most powerful and successful option strategies. We will be looking at strategies which have a sound theoretical and academic foundation, proven track records, and the potential to generate surprisingly high returns on investments over a long period of time.

This chapter presents you with the most elementary and conservative of all option writing strategies, the one that contains a good dose of safety and consistency. If you have any knowledge of the options market, you have already guessed what this strategy is. Of course, it is COVERED WRITING, probably the most popular option writing strategy today. This is the most understandable strategy available to the public. Therefore, many brokers and money managers have jumped on the band wagon, and are touting this system.

The Business of Covered Option Writing

The best way to introduce you to covered option writing is to look at this approach to the options market as a *business*, not a strategy, or a game, or an investment. Covered option writing is a business, just like running a book store or a supermarket. When you enter the business of option writing, the merchandise or inventory that will be on your shelves will be common stocks which have options listed on the Options Exchange.

The objective of your business will be the same as any other business—to generate a cash flow, and to generate a flow of income. You will generate income, cash flow, and capital gains from your merchandise—your common stock—by writing options against it.

In the past, the investor purchased a common stock with the *hope* that it would appreciate in value through an increase in price in the marketplace. However, the new Options Exchange has greatly changed that picture, and with covered option writing, we are not involved in such a "hoping" and "praying" game. The business manager who is running a covered option writing program is not concerned with significant stock price increases. But he is concerned with generating a high flow of cash, and capital gains, not from movements in the common stock price, but from the continual writing of options against that common stock, against that merchandise he has on the shelves.

Covered option writing is a rational and rewarding approach to the market. If you own common stock, you should be involved in the business of option writing, generating a cash flow and income from that stock. If you are not, you are letting that common stock go to waste. You are allowing your inventory to sit on the shelves, not opening the store for business. When you own rental property, you rent it, or when you run a book store, you sell books; you don't lock the doors and hope the books

COVERED OPTION WRITING IS SIMILAR TO OPERATING A BUSINESS

will increase in value over the years. The same analogy applies to the stock market.

The Pros and Cons of Covered Option Writing

The major advantage to the investor is that the business of covered option writing is far safer than the straightforward ownership of common stock and most other securities. For example:

An investor owns 100 shares of Skyline, presently priced at 19-3/4. His risk in holding these shares is $1,975, the total value of the 100 shares of stock. Now if he were to write a Skyline Nov 20 call option at 2 in July, he would receive a cash refund, or discount of $200 on that stock. For that $200, he has traded the right to deliver the stock to the buyer of the option at a price of 20 any time before the expiration date in November. If the 100 shares of Skyline are exercised (called) by the option buyer, the option writer would have a locked-in profit of $225, less commissions. However, if the stock moves down in price, the stock will never be exercised (remember we are working with an "out-of-the-money" option—it has no real value).

The investor, by writing the option, has bought an insurance policy with $200 worth of downside protection. If the stock price has not changed by the end of November, the investor has generated a cash return of 10% for a four-month period of time (30% return per annum). In each case, the investor comes out a winner, unless the stock price drops more than 2 points during that period of time.

On the other side of the coin, if Skyline went from 19-3/4 to 26, the investor would not be able to participate in the total price move of the stock. All he would receive would be the $225 worth of locked in profit.

The above example brings up two of the disadvantages of covered option writing:

1. The downside risk in ownership of the stock is not eliminated, only reduced.

2. The limited profit or opportunity is lost if the stock price makes a significant upward move.

Thus, the covered option writer only partially reduces his risk of stock ownership and cannot take total advantage of good moves in the stock price.

On the other hand, counter arguments can be presented to offset these disadvantages. If a stock price falls, we can buy back the option that we have written for a lower price, then write another option against our stock with a lower exercise price and different expiration date.

Referring back to our last example:

Suppose that Skyline now falls from 19-3/4 to 16. The Skyline Nov 20 call option is now priced at 3/8. We buy back the Skyline Nov 20 at 3/8, making a profit of $162.50, less commissions. Now there is also a Skyline Feb 15 option available on the Exchange priced at 3-1/2. If we write this option, we will receive $350 in additional cash to protect our position and add to our gross profits of $162.50. As Skyline continues to fall, we can buy back options and continue writing options in order to provide additional insurance and cash flow to our portfolio. In this way, we can reduce the downside risk of our stock position.

Though this situation may look like a super deal for the covered option writer, sometimes the stock price will drop at too rapid a rate to enable the writer to roll over into a new option, or the call option premiums for new options may be too low to make them a worthwhile ploy.

The covered option writer now becomes a wise investor. He has taken a guaranteed 10% return on investment for a four-month period. After a year has passed, he has probably received option premiums equal to 30% of the value of his stock, a comfortable return on investment.

Conversely, the typical investor does not write covered options; he holds onto his stock and hopes to reap high profits if the stock rises significantly during the same period of time. When the stock price does rise significantly, rarely does the investor take the cream off the top or profit from the move. Over a year's period of time, the stock investor might get lucky and get a 20% rise in the value of his stock. On the other hand, the stock may have fallen in price, or may be right where it was when he started a year ago. He has not received any insurance whatsoever, or any return on his investment.

Principles of Covered Option Writing

Now that we have looked at the pros and cons of covered option writing, let's start looking at the process of option writing itself—how do you run this business? The examples we have presented demonstrate that covered option writing involves the purchase of stock, and the writing of one option against each 100 shares of stock. In this way, the option writer is totally covered. He has no upside risk. If the stock goes up in value, the profits he gains from the stock will cover the losses he incurs from writing the option against the stock. If the stock goes down in price, the premiums (cash) that he receives from the sale of the options will cover some of the loss and decline of the stock price. Therefore the investor who buys and writes one option against each 100 shares of stock is referred to as a "covered option writer."

It may be helpful to look at an actual example which the author recommended on Dec. 21, 1973, using International Harvester (HR) common stock.

Buy 100 shares of HR at 25	$2,500
Sell 1 HR Apr 25 call option at 3	less 300 (proceeds received)
Total Investment	$2,200

If International Harvester is purchased on margin, the required investment would be $1,325.

The profit-loss table is presented below:

HR Price at the end of April	Gross Profit	Loss
20		(200)
21		(100)
22	0	0
23	$100	
24	$200	
25 or higher	$300	

Using this covered option writing strategy, if International Harvester is 25 or greater at the end of April, a gross profit return of 22% for the four-month period will be generated, which also works out to a 66% gross return on an annualized basis. This is true when International Harvester is purchased on margin. Commissions and interest costs plus dividends received are not included in this example.

The result of this covered option writing strategy actually showed a gross profit of $300 before commissions when the HR Apr 25 expired at the end of April. International Harvester was then priced at 25-1/8 at the close on April 27, 1973.

Objectives in the Option Writing Business

Option writing is not as easy as it sounds. There are many decisions that the investor must make before he jumps into this business. Just like any other business, it requires some training in order to give you a better chance of succeeding.

To open up shop, and begin our option writing business, we should have some specific objectives to guide us, and the two which I feel are the most important to the covered option writer are the following:

1. To maximize the flow of income per month.

2. To minimize the risk to the portfolio.

In order to maximize the flow of income from this covered option writing business, the covered option writer should attempt to extract at least a 20% annual return on the value of each 100 shares of stock that he holds in his portfolio.

The second objective is to continually gather enough option premium to reduce the downside risk of holding common stock, and to sell off stock positions which become unattractive because of changes in their inherent price trend.

With these objectives in mind, we must make some important decisions in choosing which stocks we will purchase for the purpose of option writing. Many investors are in the position of already owning a portfolio of common stock which they definitely plan to keep for tax reasons or other considerations. These stock positions will greatly influence their flexibility and profits when writing options. Others will have the freedom to select stocks that are more conducive to option writing.

Guidelines for Stock Selection

In the search for the correct stocks for covered option writing, consider the following guidelines closely to aid you in attaining the objectives that we have set:

1. **Select stocks with a high volatility.**

There are conflicting arguments over this point. Many option players believe that stocks with a low volatility are far easier to handle, are assigned less often, and require less surveillance. But stocks that maintain a low volatility normally have poor premiums, and it would be difficult to use these types of stocks in your portfolio and attain the goals we have set for operating our business.

On the other hand, you will find as you get into this new business, that stocks with a high volatility have much higher premiums in their listed options. These stocks normally have better liquidity, as do their listed options. Normally, stocks with high volatility also act in a much healthier and predictable manner. Further, volatile stocks will create a good income flow—one that can generate up to a 30% to a 40% return per year.

2. **Select stocks which are in an uptrend—sell any stocks which show a reversal of trend.**

In covered option writing, we buy stock and sell call options against each 100 shares of stock. Therefore, it is important for the reduction of risk to insure that the stocks that you do purchase and place in your inventory are in an uptrend.

In a bear market, you cannot write options fast enough to protect your behind; if the stock is moving down at a rapid pace, you are going to take a loss. Volatile stocks provide good premiums, and normally you can write fast enough to protect some of that downside risk, although it is very difficult to protect all of it. Therefore, you should only stock your shelves with common stocks that are in a bullish trend, and when a stock price changes its trend, you should divest yourself of that position.

Investors locked into a situation where they cannot afford to divest themselves of stock positions must, of course, take their losses during the periods when their stock is moving down significantly. But it is far better to be writing options during this period than to be sitting on your stocks praying for the next bull market.

3. **Diversify your inventory of common stocks—hold at least four different common stocks, in different industries.**

The wise covered option writer will always have a good range of common stocks in his portfolio. This diversity greatly diminishes risk. If you have only one position, and the stock dives downward in price, your performance will suffer, as you would not be able to write options fast enough to protect the total downside risk. To smooth out the peaks and troughs of the stock values which are being held in your portfolio, attempt to hold at least four positions; this number has been academically proven to provide good diversity.

4. **Favor low-priced stocks over high-priced ones.**

Low-priced stocks, such as $10, $15, or $20 a share, have a tendency to have higher premiums per the value of that stock as compared to stocks that are running at $100 or $200 a share.

Commissions are another area in which the writer of low-priced stocks has an advantage. If you use your funds to purchase 1,000 shares of Skyline at 20, rather than 100 shares of Eastman Kodak at 100, you can reduce the commission costs of writing options because you now can work with ten options, rather than one option.

Later, when we talk about the tools and tactics of trading, you will find that commissions are a real obstacle in this game. The covered option writer who carefully watches and measures his commission costs, and takes every opportunity he can to reduce these costs, will show a far better annual return than the covered writer who ignores this important consideration.

5. **Purchase stocks on margin—fill your stores as full as possible with merchandise.**

When you begin your option writing business, set aside a lump sum which you will use to purchase your merchandise, the common stock that you will be writing options against. If you are aggressive, you should attempt to get the maximum leverage from your investment. If you have $20,000 to invest in covered option writing, you should be purchasing as much stock as you possibly can with that money, even if you have to buy stock on margin (borrow money from the brokerage firm to buy stock). The going interest rate for borrowing money to buy stock normally runs from 8-1/2% to 10%. But by following the guidelines we have provided, you will generate better than a 10% return from writing options, making marginal stock profitable. Thus, the option writer will buy as much stock, or merchandise, as he can on margin.

Another great advantage of covered option writing is that when you write options, you receive the premium from that option back immediately in the form of cash, which goes directly into your account, and can help to finance the purchase of more stock. Then as you continue to generate more and more premium from your option writing business, this premium should be used to re-invest and obtain more and more stock, and at the same time, make more margin available to purchase additional merchandise. By holding a philosophy of expansion, you will obtain an attractive return on your investments and see your portfolio grow rapidly.

6. **Select stocks which have the highest yield.**

A final consideration in the selection of which playable stocks should fill the shelves of your portfolio is the yield of that stock. Again, remember, our objective—to maximize the flow of income per month. Dividends, of course, would be part of that income flow. Therefore, the option writer should not only look at what kind of a premium he is going to obtain from writing options against 100 shares of stock, but also at the dividend of that stock, adding the dividend to the return which he will receive from his other option writing premiums.

Guidelines for Options Selection

Now that you have the key steps to follow in selecting the merchandise (stocks) to put on the shelves of your portfolio, you have come to another important decision in the operation of your covered option writing business—which option should you write for each 100 shares of stock that you own? The Options Exchange is like a supermarket—each stock has several options with different strike prices, and different expiration dates available to the option writer and the option buyer. As the option writer, you must select the option that will do the best job for you.

Remembering our objectives of high return and low risk, let's look at the following as we move to select the best options:

1. **Select options which show the maximum income flow per month.**

This guideline is critical. In measuring the income generated by an option, the only thing that we can consider is the time value, or the premium value of that option. The intrinsic value of the option should not be considered in this analysis. You should only consider the intrinsic value of an option when you are attempting to provide some downside protection, but are not looking for actual income generation from that portion of the option.

Table 9 shows how to break down the option price to determine the income flow per month. Let's go back to our example of the Skyline Nov 20 call. We received $200 for a four-month period of time. The whole value of the call is time value, as indicated in the table. Thus on a per month basis, we receive $50 of time value for each month. Now let's compare that to the Nov 15 Skyline at 6. In this case we receive $600 of cash flow. We obtain $600 from the option, but only 1-1/4 points of that option price is true time value. The other part of that option price is intrinsic value; in other words, the option is in-the-money. In this case, the true return is the time value, which is 1-1/4 points. This is broken down over a four-month period to approximately $31 per month. The formula for determining the per month flow is presented as follows:

Income Per Month =
Time Value ÷ Number of Months to Expiration

As you can see from Table 9, the Skyline Feb 20 option generates a monthly income of $41, as compared to the $50 you would receive on a monthly basis from the Skyline Nov 20. Therefore, we find the Skyline Nov 20 option to be the most attractive.

Having determined which option produces the most income per month, you need to look at another factor—how important

Table 9
Covered Option Comparison Table

(Skyline at 19-3/4 on July 15)

Option	Price	Intrinsic Value	Time Value	No. of Months to Expiration	Income per Month
Skyline Nov 20	2	0	2	4	$50
Skyline Nov 15	6	4-3/4	1-1/4	4	$31
Skyline Feb 20	2-7/8	0	2-7/8	7	$41

is it to reduce your downside risk? If you believe that the stock is ready for a short downtrend, then possibly you should be more concerned about the total price of the option because that provides the total cash flow, and you should be writing in-the-money options such as the Nov 15 at 6. Remember, if the trend of the stock turns bearish, you should sell that stock, should not continue to write options against it. But, if you are unable to do this, or if you feel the downtrend is only a short-term move, then writing an option which is in-the-money might be a wiser move at this time, rather than strictly considering the amount of income which the option produces.

2. **Generally avoid deep-in-the-money options which show little time value.**

The example we have just examined would be the one exception to this rule. When you are hunting for reduction of downside risk, then in-the-money options can be attractive because they do provide more of a cash flow to protect a downside move of the stock.

But note that such options as we viewed in the preceding example, and other deep-in-the-money options, normally provide little income because there is little time value in them; consequently, they are always in danger of assignment. Therefore, *avoid* getting involved with deep-in-the-money options, unless you are forced to protect a downside risk.

3. **Maintain a policy of continuous option writing, roll over into new options when old options lose their time value.**

There are two ways in which the covered option writer can run his business. The first is to write options against his stock positions, and either wait for the options to expire, or for the options to be exercised. This method requires less surveillance by the option writer, but it also generates less premium.

In contrast, another more sophisticated technique, one that takes far more time and surveillance, is called CONTINUOUS OPTION WRITING. Of particular advantage with this approach is that it actually will reduce downside risk if a stock falls at a fast rate.

The procedure involved in "continuous option writing" is to "roll over" into new options when old ones lose their time value. What does this mean? It means that when an option loses almost all its premium, even though there may be a lot more time left in the life of that option, the option businessman goes in and buys the option back and writes a new option which is fat in time value. This may occur when the stock drops, or when it declines away from the exercise price, or it may occur when the stock moves deep-in-the-money, far over the exercise price. Under these circumstances, the option writer will buy back the option, and roll over into another option with a different strike price or a different expiration date. In this way, he can generate a much greater amount of premium over a period of time, thereby providing far more protection from downside risk.

Such a procedure will also avoid assignment, and will create a much more active portfolio—a much more active business. Continuous option writing, then, takes more time and more surveillance, but it generates more premium and provides much more protection for your portfolio of common stock.

4. Beware of the danger of commissions.

As mentioned before, commissions are your greatest obstacle in the option writing game. Not only will you have to pay the commissions from purchasing common stock, but you also will have to pay commissions created by buying and selling options on a periodic basis. If you "roll over" into new options every month or two, the commissions can mount up drastically. So, as you decide on which options to write, always consider the question of commissions.

In many cases, it is far wiser to write an option which has a more distant expiration date, even though the income per month may be lower, because such a transaction only requires *one* commission. If you write an option with a much shorter life, you may have to write another option, which requires a duplication of commissions. In other words, when determining which option to write, always consider the *total* commission costs that will be involved over the same period of time. If you are comparing writing a three-month option to writing a six-month option, the six-month option may have a better per month flow of income, after you subtract the additional commission costs of writing two three-month options, as opposed to the cost of writing only one six-month option.

5. Do not write undervalued options.

At the back of this text, there is a set of tables which you can use to determine when an option is overvalued, and when it is undervalued. Always use these tables in measuring the options premiums that are available for writing, or better yet, use a computer program that measures the fair value of an option. The options which are overvalued are the ones which should be the prime targets for option writing; the undervalued ones should be avoided. In the end, writing undervalued options will definitely affect your return on investment.

If you follow these guidelines closely, your probability of generating a 20% to a 30% return annually will greatly increase. The business of covered option writing, like any business, requires some experience, so your first year or two in this activity may be a little rocky. But do your homework, follow your guidelines, and direct all your attention towards attaining your objectives.

Your rewards will be handsome.

The Track Record

Although covered option writing was a lucrative business during the first years of the Option Exchange, over the past 15 years the performance of mutual funds that do covered call writing has been disappointing. In other words, successful covered call writing is more difficult than it looks. The first major obstacles that you face include finding over-priced options to write that give you enough income to make the practice worthwhile. The second obstacle is to be properly diversified—usually a portfolio valued at $50,000 to $100,000 is needed for such diversification. Although some investors have had great success with smaller portfolios, that only includes low-priced stocks.

Buy It, and Bury It

Another approach to covered writing is one that should be followed by the long-term investor. I have discovered over the past 20 years that the most successful stock investors are those who hold stock positions for long periods of time. These investors seek out fundamentally undervalued stocks. They try to buy such stocks in the midst of a major decline, when there is blood in the streets, or when there is a panic sell-off. They then buy the stocks, like real estate, rarely looking at the current price of their assets, confidently knowing that the stock will return to its true value, and continue to grow and reap dividends year after year.

This approach has two major advantages. First, there is a major tax savings. If you never sell a stock, you never incur a tax obligation. Or if you hold a stock for several years before taking profits, you gain the use of those lost tax dollars for several years, which is much more powerful than most think.

The second advantage is that you are not mislead by random short-term moves in the market. Stock market action approaches randomness in the short-term, and few can consistently outguess the market. As one stock investor stated, "When I do sell stock, whether to take a profit or get out of the market during a decline, it may work out in the short run, but I would have been better off holding the position in the long run."

The "buy it and bury it" approach has its merits, but can you do covered option writing with such a portfolio? Absolutely! Follow the same guidelines as indicated earlier in the chapter, but with a few alterations:

1. Only write out-of-the-money options where the stock is several points from the strike price—avoid in-the-money calls.

2. To avoid losing your stock, set a stop-loss on the underlying stock that is slightly in-the-money. If the stop-loss is hit, buy back the call and close the position. For example, if Pfizer is priced at 56 and you write the 60 call at 3, set your stop-loss at 63. If Pfizer reaches 63 before expiration, close out the option position by buying back the 60 call. With such a stop-loss, your losses should be small.

3. Avoid writing calls when the underlying stock is in a strong uptrend.

4. If you use a computer program such as *Option Master®*, only write calls if your probability of profit is 80% or greater.

5. Buy back a call if it loses all of its time value.

If you only write overpriced calls, this approach to covered option writing should generate an attractive profit, year after year, separate from your stock portfolio. Rarely will you lose the underlying stock, nor will you limit the profits from your stocks—a major disadvantage of traditional covered writing. The key is that you treat your option writing as a totally separate portfolio. Of course, at times, some losses will be incurred here as well.

17

HOW TO BUY STOCK AT A DISCOUNT PRICE

Believe it or not, naked put writing, usually an aggressive option strategy, can be a conservative investment strategy to be considered by all stock investors. In fact, such a practice is quite similar to covered call writing.

A "put" is the right to *put* the stock to the option writer. In other words, the writer has the obligation to buy the stock from a put holder who exercises the option at the strike price.

Remembering this concept, let's say you wish to buy 100 shares of Home Depot (HD), priced at 54, if it drops to 50. You could put in a good-till-cancelled limit order to buy the stock at 50. Or better yet, you could write a Home Depot put naked. If the HD Jan 50 put is priced at 4, you could sell (write) that put. Now if the Home Depot stock price is below 50 at expiration in January, or if you are assigned before that time, you will be required to buy (or be put) the stock at a price of 50—exactly what you wanted in the first place. In addition, you will have $400 in your account for initially writing the put at 4.

Your real cost will be only $46 per share (50 - 4 = 46). If Home Depot does not fall below 50 at expiration, you will not get the stock, but you will receive a **consolation prize**. You receive $400 cash for writing the put at 4.

How To Get What You Want

Naked put writing is a unique way of buying the underlying stock, and getting paid for waiting to get your price for the stock. Under these conditions, naked put writing is more conservative than buying the stock. With lower priced stocks, some attractive plays can develop. For example, one of my recommendations was to write the Bolar Pharmaceutical July 5 put priced at 1-1/2 in March, when the stock was priced at 7. This was a great play if you wanted to buy the stock, because instead of paying 7, you would wait to buy the stock at 5.

If Bolar Pharmaceutical did fall below 5 and you were assigned the stock at 5, you would receive an additional 30% discount. You have $150 in your account from writing the put, reducing the cost of the stock to 3-1/2 (5 - 1-1/2 = 3-1/2). By writing the put to buy the stock, you would save 50%. You would pay 3-1/2, instead of 7, and if you didn't buy the stock, you would receive a $150 consolation prize. What a deal!

Naked put writing is a safe, prudent investment technique as long as you plan to buy the stock and have the capital to do so. Naked put writing becomes dangerous when you write too many puts, don't intend to buy the stock, or are unable to do so. Then naked put writing is a high risk game for gladiators only.

When you begin conservative put writing, follow the same guidelines that were presented in the previous chapter on covered call writing.

There is a familiar adage on Wall Street that states, "Buy low, sell high." Naked put writing forces you to *buy* stocks when they decline, and covered call writing can force you to *sell* stocks when they are higher.

18

PLAY IT NAKED

You have received your first application of option writing with a conservative, defensive strategy—covered option writing. Now let's pull out some of the stops and play a far more exciting game. Let's PLAY IT NAKED.

Up to this point, we have been discussing the position of the covered option writer, who *covers* his option writing risk by owning the underlying common stock. He gains only part of the benefit of option writing by playing it safe and maintaining a conservative defense; he cannot reap all the various profits available to the option writer.

In contrast, "playing it naked" is a method which reaps *all* of the benefits and potential profit of the sport of option writing. The naked option writer writes options *without the common stock covering his position*.

Although there are some substantial risks in this game, which we will explore later, let us first look at some of the important benefits to be gained.

Advantages of Naked Option Writing

1. The Potential Rewards Are Outstanding.

To the professional option player, naked option writing is the Cadillac division of the options market. The profit potentials here are greater than in any other segment of the options market. The skilled and disciplined naked option writer can generate from a 50% to a 100% return annually on his investment, and normally can do this consistently over a long period of time. The naked writer can become a "man for all seasons," confronting numerous opportunities in bull, bear, and nomad market conditions.

2. The Odds of Winning Are Strongly in The Writer's Favor.

You will discover, if you decide to participate in this Grand Prix of the options market, that when you run a naked option writing portfolio, a high percentage of your positions will be winners. By following the rules that we will set out in Chapter 19, 80% of your positions are likely to come out profitable, and only 20% will be losers. In other words, the odds are stacked heavily in your favor. Naked option writing is probably the only game in town where the investor truly has a strong advantage over the rest of the market. Consider this analogy:

The casino operator who offers roulette, craps, and blackjack to patrons who visit his casino is similar to the option writer. The casino operator backs the bets of the gaming customers. He pays off when the customers are big winners; he takes in the profits when they are losers. The casino operator has a slight advantage in each game. In the game of roulette, for instance, he has approximately a 5% advantage over the gaming customer. The option writer is in a similar position, but his advantage is better than 5%. The academic studies and research that have been done so far have indicated that the option writer (seller) actually has approximately a 10% to 20% advantage over the option buyer (if he writes over-valued options). The option writer, like the casino owner, provides the option buyer with a market in which to speculate, in which to gamble. For this service, the option writer receives better odds.

The major advantage that gives him this percentage edge is TIME. The option buyer bets that the stock will go up significantly when he buys a call. But the option writer wins under all other stock price conditions. The call option writer is a winner even if the stock moves up too slowly because as time passes, the premium that the option writer receives from the option buyer for backing his bet depreciates, moving into the pocket of the option writer.

The option writer has two important factors in his favor:

1. He does not require that the underlying stock price moves to make a profit.

2. He is continually making a profit as the option shrinks in value with passing time.

The option writer who writes strictly naked options with no hedges, no stock, and no long options to cover his naked positions is attempting to maximize these two advantages. For example:

An option buyer purchases an Upjohn Jan 40 call option at 3, with three months to run. The stock price is at 37—there is actually no real value in that option at the time the option buyer purchases the option. The only value the option holds is time value. The $300 option price goes to the option writer.

In order for that option to take on any real value at all, the stock price must move above 40. For the option buyer to break even at the end of that three-month period, the stock price must be at 43. If the Upjohn stock price is below 40 at the end of the three-month period, the option will expire worthless. The writer will have made $300 less commissions, and the buyer will have lost $300.

Therefore, the profit parameters for the option writer would read—by the end of January, if the stock price is *below* 43, he wins. Conversely, if the stock price is *above* 43, the option buyer wins. However, the option writer starts with the advantage because when the option was purchased, the stock was 6 points below the breakeven point for the buyer. Actually, the option writer starts with a profit—he has $300 and 6 points to work with before the time period begins.

3. **Success Does Not Depend on Predicting Stock Price Behavior.**

The option writer, unlike the option buyer, is not required to predict the exact extent of a stock price move. By the fact that the option writer begins the game with the odds stacked in his favor, he can afford a wide margin of error in measuring and predicting what a stock price will do in the future.

In fact, there are many theorists who believe that it is impossible to predict the price action of a stock in the future. They consider the stock market a random walk down Wall Street. As you operate your naked option writing portfolio, although you should not ignore the trend of the market, or the trend of a stock, you can partially adopt a random walk theory. Even if you write an option, and the stock moves in the wrong direction, if that move is slow enough, or is short enough, you can still come out ahead.

Remember that in our scenario regarding the price action of a specific stock, a stock can move up significantly, can move up a little, can stay where it is, can move down a little, or can move down a lot. Thus when you are writing calls, the only time that you will lose is if the stock moves up significantly during the period that you back that contract. If you are writing puts, the only time that you will lose is if the stock moves down significantly.

4. **The Theoretical and Academic Arguments Supporting Naked Option Writing Are Excellent.**

Before the existence of the options exchanges, naked option writing was practiced by a select few in the old over-the-counter (OTC) market, and was a far more dangerous game than writing listed options today. The OTC option writer faced numerous obstacles which made it unfeasible for most investors to enter that game. Yet, even with these dangerous pitfalls, studies of the old OTC market show encouraging results which support the more advantageous position of the option writer today. The opinions of the experts indicate that almost 65% of all options in the OTC market were never exercised (expired without value).

In the old OTC market, when an option was written, or sold, the stock price was right at the strike price. This is not true today; now you can write options where the stock price is a great distance from the strike price. We refer to these as *out-of-the-money* options. In the old OTC market, normally the only type of option that was written was an *at-the-money* option, an option in which the strike price and the stock price were identical.

Even in the OTC options market, and even when options were at-the-money, the writer had a slight advantage in the fact that only 35% of all options were exercised. These performance claims are backed by a considerable body of research. In the book, *Strategies and Rational Decisions in the Securities Options Market*, the authors, Burton G. Malkiel and Richard E. Quandt, reported that their research conducted from 1960-1964 proved that writing OTC options on a random basis, without any judgments or safeguards, was indeed a profitable game in all cases.[6]

In contrast, those who *bought* during that period, regardless of what strategy was used, always ended up with a negative result. Therefore, they discovered that the writing of *naked* call options was one of the optimum strategies available in the options market, generating over a 10% annual return. With such encouraging results on a random basis, imagine what the returns would be if a little skill, a little knowledge and the proper timing were added to this investment mode!

Another study which indicated the feasibility of option writing came from the book, *Beat The Market*, by Sheen Kassouf and Ed Thorp. The results of their strategy, based on the shorting of warrants on the Stock Exchange (which is almost the same process as writing call options on the Options Exchange), were presented at the beginning of this text in Chapter 1. These results are impressive, and will be discussed further in a later chapter. Kassouf and Thorp proved, through the use of track records and through some sound theoretical and academic studies, that the short selling of warrants can provide a high and consistent profit when the investor also uses a hedging strategy. Though they did not discuss writing warrants without any type of hedge, the maximum flow of profit came from this technique.

Finally, documentation verifies that in the first year-and-a-half of operation of the CBOE, only 10% of all options in the new options markets had any real value when their lives expired.

Disadvantages of Naked Option Writing

When we look at the disadvantages of naked option writing, one stands out clearly above all others—RISK. There is *unlimited*

6 Reprinted from *Strategies and Rational Decisions in the Securities Options Market* by Burton G. Malkiel and Richard E. Quandt, by permission of The MIT Press, 1969, Cambridge, Massachusetts.

risk when writing naked call options, and extensive risk when writing naked puts—the risk that the underlying stock price will move through and far above or below the option strike price. This highly publicized risk scares many investors away from the naked option writing game, and many who have played in this unusual game have been wiped out by the volatility and action of naked options.

Regulatory agencies, brokers, and many option players cringe when you talk about naked options; there is probably more fear floating around about naked options than about any other investment vehicle available today. But although a definite risk does exist in the naked option writing market, this risk is usually greatly exaggerated.

To show why this is true, let us examine these possible risks of naked option writing in detail, and decide which actions to take to guard against them.

1. The Risk of Not Being Covered by Common Stock

We have already mentioned the unlimited risk that the option writer has when he is not covered by the common stock. For example:

If you were to write five call options on Upjohn with a strike price of 40, and Upjohn were to move through the 40 strike price in an upward direction, you would be responsible for delivering 500 shares of Upjohn to the buyer, if he at any time chose to exercise his options. Your risk for each point that Upjohn moves above 40 will be $100 per option position that you hold. In the case of the five Upjohn calls, you would have $500 of risk for each point that Upjohn moved above the strike price of 40. If Upjohn were to move from a price of 40 to 45, your actual loss would be $500 per option for the 5 points that the stock moved, which comes out to $2,500.

2. Negative Risk-Reward Ratio

A second related risk that scares many a player away is the possibility of a negative risk-reward ratio. In our first example of Upjohn, we mentioned the fact that the maximum amount that the option writer could gain by writing an Upjohn Jan 40 at 3 was $300 in profit.

On the other hand, his counterpart, the option buyer, has unlimited profit potential from that option position. If the Upjohn price were to move from 37 to 60 within a short period of time, the option buyer would generate a profit of $1,700, less commissions, on his $300 investment. The option writer, who only had $300 to gain, would lose $1,700 on that naked option writing position. Consequently, the risk-reward ratio in this example does not look very attractive to the naked option writer.

However, there are two counter-arguments in favor of the naked option writer regarding this risk.

1. The probability that Upjohn or any stock would make such a large move within a short period of time is small. The likelihood that the buyer will be a winner in his option positions is normally minimal. It is important for you to consider the probabilities with any stock in order to reduce the negative risk-reward scenario which can occur to the naked option writer.

2. The shrewd naked option writer rarely owns an option which has become so fat as to provide a big reward for the option buyer. He will usually never allow such a negative risk-reward scenario to develop. The professional naked option writer will have left that option position long before this occurs. One of the beauties of the options markets is the ability to close out a transaction at any time. Here the all-important quality of DISCIPLINE comes

into play. When the stock moves in the wrong direction, moves through your parameters (which you must *always* set before entering a position), you as a naked option writer *must* immediately extricate yourself from that position by buying back the option.

If you use these tools (to be discussed further in a future chapter) the naked option writing game can lead you to a large pot of gold rather than a dangerous pit of fire.

War Stories

Before you become too enthusiastic about naked option writing, be warned that this game is for high risk players ONLY. Sometimes those theoretical unlimited risks do become a reality. In the 1980's, leveraged buyouts of one company by another were the rage. Such events caused dramatic overnight changes in a stock price. Kennecott Copper common stock price rose almost 30 points overnight when Standard of Ohio bought them out. If you were a Kennecott naked call writer, there was no way to exit your position before the damage was done. You would have taken a 30-point ($3,000) loss on each call that you had written.

The takeover rage has died down, for junk bond financing has gone out of favor, and banks have become far more conservative. But takeovers will occur in the future, and they are the naked stock option call writer's greatest danger. On the other side of the coin, naked put writing has dangers of its own. Stocks may drop sharply when a news event or negative earnings report is published and institutions rush out of the stock. If the stock gaps down in price, the naked put writer cannot limit his loses, and will take a bad hit. Here is a case where you cannot close the casino door to minimize your losses.

How can you protect yourself from such losses? DIVERSIFY! Maintain extremely small positions in each stock. Then, if you do take a big hit, you will limit your loss to just a few options. In addition, avoid stocks that are takeover targets, or those vulnerable to a surprise move, such as some over-the-counter stocks.

One war story that demonstrates the risk of naked writing involves index options. Index options seem to be an ideal candidate for option writing. Index options tend to be overpriced, indexes move slowly and are not vulnerable to takeovers or surprise earnings reports. Before the crash of 1987, naked index option writing was a lucrative game. Rumor has it that one investor started with $15,000 two years before the crash, and made it grow (writing naked index options) to $750,000 before the crash occurred. But on the day of the crash, he lost the $750,000, and $2 million more that he did not have!

Before the crash, the Major Market Index (XMI) was priced at 520 (520 x 100 = $52,000), and one XMI 480 put was priced at 1 ($100). If you would have sold the 480 put, you would have received $100, and the XMI would have to drop 40 points, or 200 points on the Dow, to get you in trouble. On the day of the crash, the XMI dropped to 380. How much have you lost? First, the XMI was 100 points in-the-money (480 - 380 = 100), so the intrinsic value of the put was 100 ($10,000). But due to fear, (during the crash) to buy back that put on the exchange, you would have had to pay 200 ($20,000). If you had sold five options, your losses would have been close to $100,000.

Many small investors who were writing naked index options were caught in this disaster and saw the value of their accounts disappear. In addition, many investors owed their brokerage firms huge amounts of money from their writing losses. The brokerage firms ate most of these losses, and hence lost millions. Such events turned the brokerage firms dead against naked writers. So now many firms will not allow naked writing, even if it is conservative put writing to buy the underlying stock.

In addition, the exchanges now can stop the trading of index options when the market drops or rises extensively during the same day. Such action makes it quite dangerous to write naked index options, for you may be prevented from closing your position if the market moves against you. Stock options don't have this problem. And, of course, you can always buy or sell the underlying stock to cover your position if you are unable to deal in the option.

Margin Requirements for Naked Option Writing

The naked option writer, unlike the covered option writer, must put up a certain amount of cash or other form of collateral for each option position that he establishes. This cash or collateral (referred to as a margin requirement) guarantees to the Exchange and the brokerage house that the writer will make good on his contract if the underlying stock suddenly moves in the wrong direction.

There are many firms who continue to live in ignorance, and thus set up ridiculous margin requirements for naked option writers, requiring an initial deposit running from $25,000 to $100,000. There are, however, brokerage houses that are far more reasonable, which provide minimal margin requirements and initial deposits to enter this exciting game. These are the types of firms you should seek out if you wish to take on the supreme challenge of the options market.

During the first two years of the existence of the Options Exchange, the margin requirements were minimal in many CBOE member firms, giving the naked option writer significant leverage, and, therefore, significant return on investment during that bear market period. Portfolios multiplied within weeks; gains of 1,000% to 2,000% were not unusual. Pressure from the SEC, the New York Stock Exchange and its member firms has forced margin rules upward to a point where now, in order to write a naked option, you must put up, in the form of cash or collateral, 20% of the value of the underlying common stock. For example:

If you were to write an option on Xerox when Xerox was selling for $60 a share, you would have to put up a deposit of 20% of the value of the 100 shares of Xerox stock, which comes out to $1,200. This $1,200 margin requirement would be increased or decreased, depending on how far the stock price was from the strike price of the option you have written.

A major obstacle that the professional option writer faces is his ability to get a high enough return on investment for each position he enters. The margin requirements will be the greatest hurdle that he encounters in meeting this challenge, so he must continually attempt to identify naked options which require a minimum amount of margin.

Using Naked Options as a Defense

Naked options, combined with common stock, fixed securities, convertible bonds, or long option purchases provide protection and consistent returns. Some money managers are beginning to discover this fact, and use naked option writing to cushion their portfolios from the uncertainty of the stock market. For example:

A money manager with a portfolio consisting of common stock, or fixed securities, might consider taking 10% of his portfolio, and just write naked options with that portion. Writing naked puts and calls will provide a cushion against risk in both bull and bear markets and provide excellent results in nomad markets. Overall, this approach to the market is defensive, providing some protection to such a portfolio.

The next chapter will move into the keys to success in operating a portfolio in which you *only* write naked options.

In conclusion, when you write naked options, if you are careful, and if you follow the guidelines and the safeguards I have developed, your rewards could be more handsome than in any other strategy presented in this text, or available in today's investment markets.

19

THE SECRETS OF NAKED OPTION WRITING

As we disclose more of the secrets of the mysterious art of naked option writing, you will learn that they are based on simple and concrete principles. In Chapter 15, we discussed the secrets of strategy design, and found that a solid strategy, a good defense, and the discipline to follow them are critical to the success of the option player. The secrets that we will disclose regarding naked option writing follow that scenario closely.

The naked option writer must develop and adhere to a solid strategy which has several lines of defense built in to protect and control the numerous risks that surround him as he plays the game of naked option writing. You must have the discipline to follow the controls that you set up, you must follow your strategy, you must follow your defense. Most important of all, you must be able to "pull the trigger" and take a loss gracefully.

Only by using the following guidelines will you protect yourself from the numerous risks that scare many brokers, brokerage houses, and many option players away from this game. But if you do follow these guidelines, you will reap the rewards that this game offers.

Let's begin by looking closely at THE ELEVEN SECRETS OF NAKED OPTION WRITING:

1. Set a Bail-Out Point and Use It.

A bail-out point is the price, or the point in your strategy, at which you wish to buy back your naked positions in order to limit your losses. This stock price, or option price, at which you wish to bail out of your position is the most important segment of your naked option writing strategy. With naked options, you *must* have a set of safeguards as a defense to limit your losses and control the tremendous risks. You must have a point at which you will bite the bullet if your naked options go astray.

As you remember, the outstanding feature of the options markets is the right that you have, as an option writer, to go into the market at any time and buy back your naked options, thereby limiting all possible future losses. Setting a bail-out point is a way of insuring that you will use this right when the price hits the parameters that you have set.

How do you bail out of a position?

There are actually two approaches that you can take to limit your losses in a naked option position:

The first requires an option player of strong mind and body, an option player with nerves of steel, and with outstanding discipline. This type of an option player can afford to have the prerogative of voluntarily moving into the market when the underlying stock price touches his bail-out parameter, and buying back his options at his own discretion.

One point which should always be kept uppermost in the option player's mind when he carries out this process is that if he does not bail out at this point, there is a chance that he will lose everything. When you are running a naked option writing portfolio, your overall goal should be to stay in the game, and the only way you will ever stay in the game to participate in the eventual profits is by bailing out whenever your loss parameters are touched.

Stop-Loss Order

A second approach to bailing out of an option position has been designed for the option player who is not as experienced, or feels that he doesn't want to rely totally on his own discipline. This method requires the use of a "stop-loss order." Just think of jumping out of an airplane as analogous to taking a loss in a naked option position. If you feel that you can easily parachute out of that airplane every time, without getting a push, then you may have the discipline necessary to voluntarily move out of your option positions. On the other hand, if it might be easier for you to receive a little push when you jump out of that plane, then the use of a stop-loss order to bail you out of your option positions would probably be the wiser alternative.

Remember, it might be easy now to say, "Yes, I'll voluntarily cover my naked shorts, and buy my options back when the underlying stock hits my loss parameters." But when you actually get into the midst of the battle, investors have a hard time making decisions which involve taking losses. They will not bite the bullet; they would rather wait and hope that the stock will change direction. Their emotions take over; they have illusions which are totally unrealistic; they start to build stories around why their stock will not move any further. All these factors can come into play, and the investor must win over these emotions, or else in most cases he will lose. Therefore, the stop-loss order might be a much wiser alternative than attempting to jump out of that plane voluntarily.

USE STOP-LOSS ORDERS TO GIVE YOU A LITTLE PUSH WHEN YOUR STRATEGIES TOUCH THEIR BAIL-OUT POINTS

What is a "stop-loss order"? A stop-loss order is a special order placed on the Options Exchange whereby your naked option position will be covered (bought back) under one of two conditions:

1. If the underlying stock price reaches a certain price, which you have set as your bail-out price.

2. If the option price reaches a predetermined price.

I strongly suggest that you use the first of these. Attempt to set the point at which you have decided to limit your loss by using the stock price's action, rather than by using the option price. Option prices move in erratic patterns, and in many cases, they may become extremely inflated, even though the stock price has not moved accordingly. Your major concern as a naked option writer is where the stock price is going to end up. Consequently, you should select a stop-loss order which is contingent upon the stock price if possible. For example:

Let's say that you wrote a Xerox Jan 60 call option when the stock was at 50, and you set your bail-out point at 58. This order would indicate that if the Xerox price reached 58, your option would immediately be bought back, and your position would be closed out. The order to buy back your option would be a market order.

The market order feature of a stop-loss order is the only real disadvantage to using stop-loss orders in the options market. Market orders in the stock market usually work out well, but on the Options Exchange, a market order can be dangerous. Some options trade in thin markets. In other words, they have low liquidity, and market orders in thin markets can be costly experiences. On the floor of the exchange, market makers love to take advantage of market orders when there are few buyers and sellers around. But there are limits on the spread between the bid and asked price, so market orders work out better now.

Note: Several options exchanges and brokerage houses do not accept option stop-loss orders.

2. **Write Naked Call Options in Bear Markets;**

   Write Naked Put Options in Bull Markets.

This secret of naked option writing is self-explanatory. To improve your probability of winning this game, it is far wiser to write calls when the stock prices in general are moving down, and to write puts when stock prices are moving up. This strategy puts the odds in your favor. However, naked call options during bull markets can be profitable, and naked put writing during bear markets can be profitable because of the inherent advantage the naked option writer holds. By following these rules, you will improve your probability of winning the game, and reduce some of the risk.

3. **Write Naked Calls on Underlying Stocks that are in a Major Downtrend;**

   Write Naked Puts on Underlying Stocks that are in a Major Uptrend.

Your profits will be much greater in the naked option writing game if you write calls when the underlying stock is moving downward, and if you write puts when the underlying stock is moving upward. The best way to project this type of price behavior is to look at the underlying trend of each of the optionable stocks.

Never buck a strong uptrending stock, or in Wall Street parlance, "Don't Fight the Tape."

4. Select Stock Candidates with a Low Price Volatility.

While the option buyer always hunts and pecks for options on stocks which are extremely volatile, the option writer loves stocks that don't move anywhere. He wants stocks that move slowly, and ones that move in a narrow range, because the option writer always has time working in his favor. The slower a stock price moves, the more money he makes. Options with slow moving underlying stocks will depreciate to zero before the stock ever reaches a bail-out point. Unfortunately, the stocks with the highest volatility maintain the highest and fattest premiums for option writing, and so the option writer must attempt to find options with low volatility, and correspondingly high premiums (time values) when possible.

5. Diversify — Maintain at Least Four Different Option Positions with Different Underlying Stock.

You've heard this before in previous chapters. Naked option writing, with its extreme risks, requires diversity. Remember, one of your overall goals is to stay in the game, and the best way to do that is to avoid betting all your money on one horse. Although the odds are heavily in your favor, losers can put you out of the game if everything you have is bet on that one position. Finally, maintain very small positions in each stock so that a takeover does not nail you with a devastating loss.

6. Write Puts and Calls Which Are at Least 15% Out-of-the-Money.

I feel that when you are carrying out a naked option writing program, the only options you should ever consider as writing candidates are those that have no real (intrinsic) value, that are not in-the-money. Use only those options that are out-of-the-money, which have only *time* value. Select options which are *significantly* out-of-the-money, so that it will take a strong move in the stock (a move that normally would not occur in a two or three-month time period) to hit your bail-out parameters. These *out-of-the-money* options, which require a major move in the stock to take on any value at all, have a low probability of ever being exercised, or of ever having any real value, and this low probability is a strong advantage to the naked writer. In other words, in selecting your option positions, select those options which have the highest probability of expiring before the stock price ever gets close to the strike price. It is your ability to carry out this patient selection process, and to wait for those opportunities to develop, that will determine the degree of your success. If you have a computer program such as *Option Master®*, only write options if you have an 80% or better chance of profit.

7. **Write Naked Options with No More than Three Months Left in Their Life.**

Remember that as an option approaches expiration, its rate of depreciation normally increases, especially in the last month. Consequently, these are the times to write naked options. You will receive a higher rate of premium in the last three months of the option than at any other time in its life. The shorter the time before expiration, the better.

8. **Write Options Which Are at Least 25% Overpriced According to Their Fair Value.**

One of the most important secrets to successful naked option writing is to write only options which have been *overpriced* by the market, options for which the buyer is paying too much. This will add insurance to your profit potential, and is an important key to successful option writing. The Appendix again provides the fair values of all options. Make sure that the options you plan to write are at least 25% over the fair value presented in these tables.

9. Write Options Against Treasury Bills.

I've mentioned before that when writing options, you must put up a margin requirement. That margin requirement can be in the form of cash, or it can be in the form of securities. It can also be in the form of *Treasury Bills*. If it is in the form of securities, you can only use the loan value of the securities.

However, Treasury Bills are treated just like cash, and this is one major advantage of using them. Treasury Bills will generate from 2% to 10% annually, depending on the money market, and this will be an added dividend to your option writing portfolio. Not only will you generate the profit from option writing, but also you will generate the return each year from your Treasury Bills. Most brokerage houses place your credit balances in the money market, so you will still earn interest if you don't have Treasury Bills.

10. Maintain a Strict Stock/Option Surveillance Program.

Watch your stock and option prices like a hawk. Monitor every move that the stock and option prices make during the periods of time that you are holding these naked option positions. The professional naked option writer will keep a close eye on the price action of the underlying stock, and will cover a position, bail out of a position, or buy back a position if there is a change in the trend of the underlying stock.

He will also take profits early, when the option shrinks in value quickly, because of an advantageous stock price move, or he may take action when the options become extremely undervalued, according to the value of the stock price. The closer you carry out a surveillance program, the better your profits will be, and the smaller your losses will be.

This surveillance program should also contain a continuous

writing feature which is best described as a method of re-investing funds into new naked option writing positions as profits are taken. This process is similar to compounding interest in your bank account, although in a naked option writing account, the profits that are being compounded are much greater. By continually re-investing in new positions, and by actively taking profits when they develop, your portfolio will grow at a far faster rate than is possible if you maintain a static program of waiting until options expire.

There is a tremendous difference between an active naked option writing program, and a static one where no action occurs until the expiration date arrives. The compounding of profits in a naked option writing portfolio can be a significant factor in providing outstanding returns.

11. Set a Bail-Out Point and Use It.

Yes, you've heard this one before, and you will hear it again many times. This is the most important safeguard of your naked option writing program. Make sure that you use it. Make sure that you *set a bail-out point,* a price at which you will always, regardless of any other circumstances, buy back your position, and bail out. The best way to insure this action is to use a stop-loss order. I cannot over-emphasize the importance of this secret of naked option writing. Fortunes can be made or lost by the manner in which you pull the trigger to take your losses. As the saying has it, "He who hesitates is lost."

Now, let's take all of these important rules of naked option writing and map out a game plan. Table 10 displays the many pieces of information needed by the professional naked writer in order to select, and then later monitor, his naked option positions. This strategy format will be indispensable to the naked writer in planning and building his naked option writing portfolio.

Table 10
Naked Option Writing Strategy Chart

Date 7-20

Option Candidate	Option Price	Underlying Stock Price	% Distance Stock Price from Exercise Price	Bail-Out Stock Price	Normal Value of Option	% Option Price over Normal Value	Initial Margin Requirement	Time Left in Option	Anticipated Return on Investment (Annual)	Trend of Stock	Anticipated Commission Costs (In and Out)
Home Depot HD Oct 60 Call	4	52	15.3%	64	1-1/4	260%	$520*	18 Weeks	240%	Down	$50
Eastman Kodak EK Jan 50 Put	2	60	16.6%	48	1-1/4	60%	$600*	30 Weeks	58%	Up	$50
Pfizer PFE Oct 70 Call	3-1/2	60	16.6%	73-1/2	1-1/4	200%	$600*	18 Weeks	224%	Down	$50
Data General Corp DGN Nov 15 Put	1/2	20	25%	14-1/2	1/16	700%	$200*	22 Weeks	47%	Up	$40

*The initial *minimum* margin requirement is 10% of the value of the stock or index plus the option premium received from the sale of the option. The margin requirement shown above excludes the option premium.

A WARNING is appropriate here: make sure that you always have your naked option positions mapped out in the manner demonstrated in Table 10 before you enter them. Attempting to design and implement strategies which are not displayed on paper, in black and white, is a dangerous game, especially with naked options.

20

THE ROAD TO ADVENTURE — THE NAKED STRANGLE

You have seen the advantages and disadvantages of naked option writing, and have been exposed to a totally naked option writing portfolio. Now let us look at a new variation of the naked option writing strategy, one which will reduce your margin requirement by 50%, will improve your leverage, and will reduce some of the highly publicized risk of naked option writing. This is a strategy with an extremely solid theoretical foundation that will double your return on investment.

The "naked strangle" involves using only naked options as its base; we don't work with common stock, or with purchased options. In the past, the naked strangle has been called a "naked combination," or a "naked spread."

The major difference between this strategy and the one that we presented in the previous chapter relates to the *selection* of naked options; they are not selected strictly on market timing, or on the bear or bull of the market. Naked options for this strategy are chosen based on the criterion of margin requirements, in order to minimize the use of margin. By doing this, we are able to increase the return on investment by up to 100% over straight naked option writing. This new strategy also factors out some of the risk by the manner in which the naked options are selected. The track record of such strategies has been successful even in the old over-the-counter (OTC) market.

Naked Strangle Defined

To get into the thick of things, let's first define a naked strangle. A *naked strangle* combines the writing of a naked call and a naked put, both with the same underlying common stock, and the same expiration date, but with *different* strike prices.

For example:

Write 1 Intel Apr 50 call option
Write 1 Intel Apr 40 put option

Writing both of these options at the same time would create a naked strangle.

Of course, within the definition of a naked strangle, we can have in-the-money spreads, partially-in-the-money spreads, and out-of-the-money spreads. As an experienced option player, you have discovered that the skilled option writer always writes out-of-the-money naked options. Therefore, when designing a portfolio full of naked spreads, both the put and the call should be out-of-the-money.

For example:

Write 1 McDonald's Jul 40 call option
Write 1 McDonald's Jul 35 put option

McDonald's common stock price is 37. Therefore, both the naked put and the naked call are out-of-the-money.

In Table 11, I have mapped out the profit picture for a naked strangle in order to demonstrate the advantages of this sophisticated strategy. The naked strangle in Table 11 entails the writing of:

1. One Xerox Jul 70 call at 4

2. One Xerox Jul 60 put at 3

By writing these two options, we generate premiums of $700, which goes into our account. At the time that we carry out this position in May, the price of the Xerox stock is 65.

Now let us look at this picture in July when the options expire: if Xerox is anywhere between 70 and 60, we will make a full profit of $700 on this strategy. If the stock is anywhere between 53 and 77, we will definitely have some profit. In other words, we have placed a tent, or a canvas of profit, over the movement of the Xerox stock.

Of course, if during the life of the option, the price hits the parameter of 77, or the parameter of 53 (our bail-out points), we should immediately buy back both options, and close out the strategy. Be sure to move out of both options; do not hang on to your opposing option when an outside parameter is hit.

If this event occurs late in the option period, we will come close to breaking even before commission costs, because our bail-out points are so far in-the-money for each of the options we have written that there will be little time value left in the options.

For example, if the Xerox stock price hits 53 a few weeks before the options expire in July, the following picture would hold true:

Table 11
The Naked Strangle

Sell	1	Xerox	Jul	70	Call	at	4
Sell	1	Xerox	Jul	60	Put	at	3

The Xerox common stock price is 65 at the time of entry on May 1 for this theoretical strategy.

The Initial Margin Requirement would be $800.

The Profit-Loss Table is presented below.

XEROX Price at the End of July			Gross Profit	Loss
80				($300)
79				(200)
78				(100)
77	Bail-out Point		0	
76			100	
75		^	200	
74			300	
73			400	
72			500	
71			600	
70			700	
69			700	
68			700	
67			700	
66			700	
65	Present Price	Profit Zone	700	
64			700	
63			700	
62			700	
61			700	
60			700	
59			600	
58			500	
57			400	
56			300	
55			200	
54		v	100	
53	Bail-Out Point..........................		0	
52			(100)	
51			(200)	
50			(300)	

With this strategy, if the Xerox price is between 53 and 77 at the end of July when the options expire, a gross profit will be realized. If the Xerox stock price moves to 77 or 53 before, we should bail out of both naked options to minimize potential losses. Commission costs are not included in this profit-loss scenario.

Table 11A

In order to demonstrate how we come up with the profit-loss scenario presented in Table 11, we have generated another table below, mapping out the same strategy in a different manner, again looking at the profit-loss picture at expiration in July.

XRX Stock Price at End of July	Value of Put	Value of Call	Profit or (Loss) from Call	Profit or (Loss) from Put	Gross Profit or Loss
80	0	$1,000	($600)	$300	($300)
79	0	900	(500)	300	(200)
78	0	800	(400)	300	(100)
77	0	700	(300)	300	0
76	0	600	(200)	300	100
75	0	500	(100)	300	200
74	0	400	0	300	300
73	0	300	100	300	400
72	0	200	200	300	500
71	0	100	300	300	600
70	0	0	400	300	700
69	0	0	400	300	700
68	0	0	400	300	700
67	0	0	400	300	700
66	0	0	400	300	700
65	0	0	400	300	700
64	0	0	400	300	700
63	0	0	400	300	700
62	0	0	400	300	700
61	0	0	400	300	700
60	0	0	400	300	700
59	$100	0	400	200	600
58	200	0	400	100	500
57	300	0	400	0	400
56	400	0	400	(100)	300
55	500	0	400	(200)	200
54	600	0	400	(300)	100
53	700	0	400	(400)	0
52	800	0	400	(500)	(100)
51	900	0	400	(600)	(200)
50	1,000	0	400	(700)	(300)

Price of the XRX Jul 70 = 1/16
Price of the XRX Jul 60 = 7-1/8

We would have already received $700 in cash when we initiated the strategy. That will cover all but 1/8 of the cost to buy back the Xerox Jul 60. The cost to close out the XRX Jul 70 is only 1/16. Total cost less commissions to exit the strategy is only 3/16 ($18.75). The same picture would develop in reverse if Xerox hit 77 rather than 53.

When designing such a strategy, the potential of your naked strangle will all depend on the prices you receive for writing your put and your call, and the volatility of the stock with which you are working.

Selecting Stocks with Limited Volatility

Unlike other types of strategies which depend on market timing and market moves for their success, the naked strangle does not require this kind of prognostication. In fact, a stock market that is moving nowhere is excellent for the naked strangle writer. The naked strangle is ideal for those who believe that the stock market is a random walk scenario, where it is impossible to predict stock price behavior.

Through a study of stock volatility tables, you will discover that even the more volatile stocks do not move very dramatically. The lack of volatility in the movement of a stock is important to the naked strangle writer. You are betting that a stock will not move outside of a wide trading range when you write a naked strangle, and if it stays within that range, you are a winner. If it hits the outside parameters, you will usually take a small loss.

The name of the game is to build naked strangles which have a wide enough trading range so that the stock price has a low probability of touching your parameters. In Table 11A, a 40% trading range was developed for the Xerox naked strangle. Normally, a high percentage of all stocks will rarely move more than 20% in any direction, especially within a three month period. As a result, such a naked strangle has a high probability of coming out a winner.

To conclude, the most important principle in naked strangle writing is to map out the naked strangle, ensuring that the range of profit that you develop for that naked strangle is wider than the price movements of the underlying stock price during the life of the strategy. Tables 12 and 13 demonstrate another naked strangle and map out the manner in which profits and outside parameters are developed. You should study these tables closely and follow this format in designing and mapping out your own naked strangle strategies.

The Selection and Design of Naked Strangles

Selecting naked strangles, unlike selecting other option strategies, is more of an art than a science. Going back to our Xerox example, if Xerox rarely moves more than 20% in either direction during a three-month period, that would be an excellent strategy, because there is little likelihood of your profit parameters being violated. When there is a low probability of this occurring, you have a high quality naked strangle strategy.

In order to come up with ideal naked strangles, the following guidelines should be followed:

1. **Know Your Stocks.**

In order to determine whether or not a naked strangle will be successful, you must have a thorough understanding of the price movement of the underlying stock, and that understanding

Table 12
Another Naked Strangle

August 21, 19____

Sell	1	Digital Equip	Oct	45	Call	at	1-1/2
Sell	1	Digital Equip	Oct	35	Put	at	1

Digital Equipment common stock price is 40. The position is theoretically taken on August 21.

The Initial Margin Requirement would be $300.

The Profit-Loss picture is presented below.

Table 13 shows how we generate this profit picture using our custom worksheet.

Digital Equip. Price at Expiration Date in Oct.		Gross Profit	Loss
49			($150)
48			(50)
47	Breakeven Point	50	
46		150	
45	<---- Profit Zone ---->	250	
44		250	
43		250	
42		250	
41		250	
40	Present Price	250	
39		250	
38		250	
37		250	
36		250	
35		250	
34		150	
33	Breakeven Point	50	
32			(50)
31			(150)
30			(250)

TABLE 13
THE NAKED SPREAD
WORKSHEET

Date June 21, 19

WRITE (SELL) 1 Digital Equip. Oct. 45 CALL at 1 1/2 PROCEEDS = $ 150

WRITE (SELL) 1 Digital Equip. Oct. 35 PUT at 1 PROCEEDS = $ 100

Digital Equip. STOCK PRICE 40

INITIAL MARGIN REQUIREMENT $ 450

TOTAL PROCEEDS RECEIVED $ 250

MAXIMUM MARGIN REQUIREMENT $1360

PROJECTED COMMISSION COSTS $ 75

Digital Eq. PRICE EXPIRATION DATE IN October	(1) PROCEEDS FROM CALL	–	(2) VALUE OF CALL	=	(3) PROFIT OR (LOSS) FROM CALL	(4) PROCEEDS FROM PUT	–	(5) VALUE OF PUT	=	(6) PROFIT OR (LOSS) FROM PUT	(7) GROSS PROFIT OR (LOSS) (3) + (6) = (7)
49	$150		$400		($250)	$100		0		$100	($150)
48	150		300		(150)	100		0		100	(50)
47 Bail-out Point	150		200		(50)	100		0		100	50
46	150		100		50	100		0		100	150
45	150		0		150	100		0		100	250
44	150		0		150	100		0		100	250
43	150		0		150	100		0		100	250
42	150		0		150	100		0		100	250
41	150		0		150	100		0		100	250
40	150		0		150	100		0		100	250
39	150		0		150	100		0		100	250
38	150		0		150	100		0		100	250
37	150		0		150	100		0		100	250
36	150		0		150	100		0		100	250
35	150		0		150	100		0		100	250
34	150		0		150	100		100		0	150
33 Bail-out Point	150		0		150	100		200		(100)	50
32	150		0		150	100		300		(200)	(50)
31	150		0		150	100		400		(300)	(150)
30	150		0		150	100		500		(400)	(250)

should lie basically in the area of its volatility. Plot out what the three-month volatility has been for the past three to five years. Doing this will give you a good feeling for projecting the maximum possible move in that stock. With this knowledge, you can then begin to seek out and compare naked strangle strategies.

2. Select Option Candidates Which Are Over-Priced.

You should always attempt to write options which are over-valued by the market, as this will give you much more premium to work with and will also provide an additional bonus for your strategy. With naked strangles, your goal is to get as much cash (premium) as possible from each option that you write, to provide a wider profit range within which the common stock price can fluctuate.

3. Carefully Map Out Each Potential Strategy.

This is the only way to compare the profitability of different spread strategies. You must determine what the profit range is for each naked spread that you are considering, and what percentage move in the stock would be required to violate that range. By following this procedure, you can determine what the probability is that each strategy will be profitable.

4. Beware of Commissions.

Commissions are always a critical consideration. They have not been included in our tables and examples in this chapter, because we do not want to confuse the issue at this time. However, they are of critical importance, and we will spend a full chapter discussing the use of commissions and how to select strategies which will reduce your commission costs.

The Naked Straddle

The "naked straddle" is another sophisticated strategy, similar to the naked strangle, with many of the same benefits. I will not cover this area extensively, because the naked straddle contains many of the same elements as the naked strangle. However, the naked straddle is more market sensitive than the naked strangle, the volatility of the underlying stock is more critical, and the chances of being forced out of your strategy are greater.

A "naked straddle" is a situation where you write a put and a call, with the same underlying common stock, the same expiration date, and in this case, the *same strike price.*

Tables 14 and 15 map out a naked straddle and show the profit parameters and breakeven points for the straddle. Using the Xerox Jul 70 put and call, the profit parameters for the Xerox naked straddle run from 60 to 80. The profit range is smaller for this strategy, as are the profits at each level compared to the naked strangle. Consequently, there is a better possibility of being forced out of a strategy.

In their book, *Strategies and Rational Decisions in the Securities Options Market*, authors Malkiel and Quandt studied the options market between 1960 and 1964, and compared the naked straddle to all of the other option buying and writing strategies. The results were outstanding. They found that the return on investment was much higher than the favorable return for writing naked call options. In their research, the writing of naked straddles showed a 28-1/2% annual return. This return was based on a random approach to the selection of straddles, with no judgment, timing, or other rational considerations involved.[7]

You have an excellent arsenal of investment weapons to choose from if you plan to become a naked option writer. You can write naked puts or calls, or you can combine these two

[7] B.G. Malkiel and R.E. Quandt, *Strategies and Rational Decisions in the Securities Options Market,* MIT Press, Cambridge, Mass. 1969.

Table 14

Table 14
A Naked Straddle

Theoretical Date
May 1, 19____

Write (Sell)	1	Xerox	Jul	70	Call	at	5
Write	1	Xerox	Jul	70	Put	at	4-1/2

The Xerox common stock is 70 at the time of entry into this theoretical strategy.

The profit-loss table is presented below. With this strategy, if the Xerox price is between 79 and 61 at the expiration date in July, a gross profit will be realized. If Xerox moves to 79 or 61 before that time, you must bail out of both sides of this strategy.

Table 15 presents a worksheet which demonstrates how the profit-loss table is developed.

Xerox Price at Expiration Date in July		Gross Profit	Loss
81			(150)
80			(50)
79	Bail-out Point	50	
78	^	150	
77	Profit Zone	250	
76		350	
75		450	
74		550	
73		650	
72		750	
71		850	
70		950	
69		850	
68		750	
67		650	
66		550	
65		450	
64		350	
63		250	
62	v	150	
61	Bail-out Point	50	
60			(50)
59			(150)
58			(250)

TABLE 15
THE NAKED STRADDLE
WORKSHEET

Date May 1, 19

WRITE (SELL) XRX Jul 70 — CALL at 5 — PROCEEDS = $ 500

WRITE (SELL) XRX Jul 70 — PUT at 4 1/2 — PROCEEDS = $ 450

XRX STOCK PRICE 70

INITIAL MARGIN REQUIREMENT $ 1150

MAXIMUM MARGIN REQUIREMENT $ 2320

TOTAL PROCEEDS RECEIVED $ 950

PROJECTED COMMISSION COST $ 75

Xerox PRICE EXPIRATION DATE IN July	(1) PROCEEDS FROM CALL –	(2) VALUE OF CALL In July =	(3) PROFIT OR (LOSS) FROM CALL	(4) PROCEEDS FROM PUT –	(5) VALUE OF PUT In July =	(6) PROFIT OR (LOSS) FROM PUT	(7) GROSS PROFIT OR (LOSS) (3) + (6) = (7)
81	$500	$1100	($600)	$450	0	$450	($150)
80	500	1000	(500)	450	0	450	(50)
79 Bail-out Point	500	900	(400)	450	0	450	50
78	500	800	(300)	450	0	450	150
77	500	700	(200)	450	0	450	250
76	500	600	(100)	450	0	450	350
75	500	500	0	450	0	450	450
74	500	400	100	450	0	450	550
73	500	300	200	450	0	450	650
72	500	200	300	450	0	450	750
71	500	100	400	450	0	450	850
70	500	0	500	450	0	450	950
69	500	0	500	450	100	350	850
68	500	0	500	450	200	250	750
67	500	0	500	450	300	150	650
66	500	0	500	450	400	50	550
65	500	0	500	450	500	(50)	450
64	500	0	500	450	600	(150)	350
63	500	0	500	450	700	(250)	250
62	500	0	500	450	800	(350)	150
61 Bail-out Point	500	0	500	450	900	(450)	50
60	500	0	500	450	1000	(550)	(50)
59	500	0	500	450	1100	(650)	(150)
58	500	0	500	450	1200	(750)	(250)

types of options, and write naked strangles, or naked straddles. Naked strangles and naked straddles improve your return on investment because they greatly reduce your margin requirement, and actually reduce your risk.

But BE WARNED, naked strangles and straddles do involve naked option writing, and therefore do have high, unlimited risk. Hence, you must take very small positions in each stock to neutralize some of the risk. There is always a chance a stock will gap up or down, not allowing you to get out at your bailout point. Also, when writing naked strangles, stick with stock options. Don't use index options.

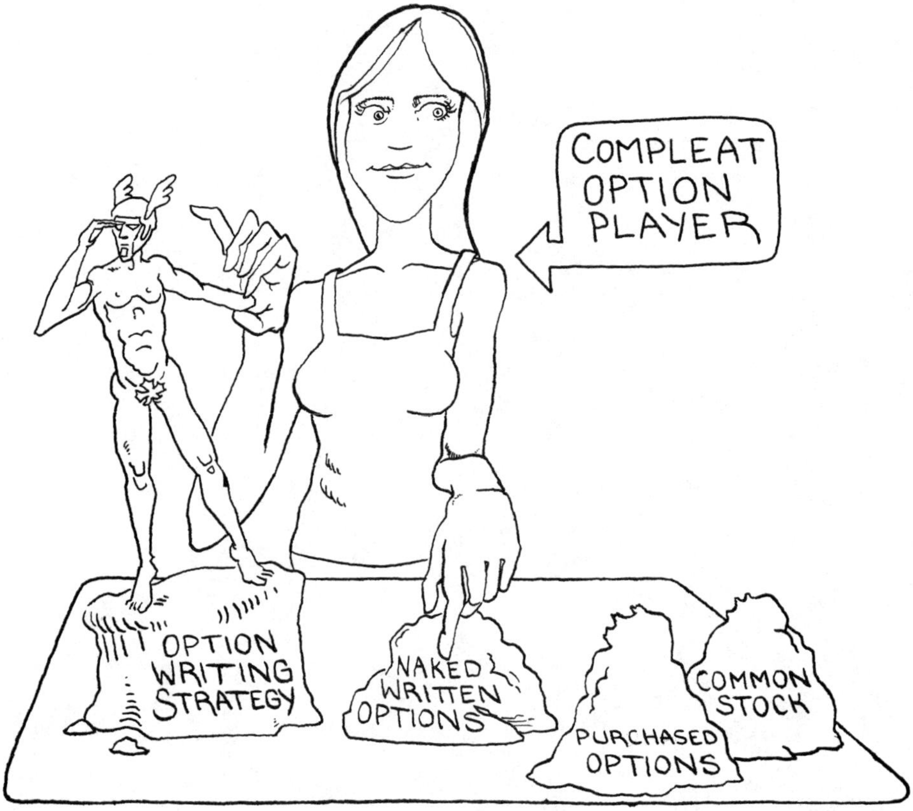

MOLDING INNOVATIVE STRATEGIES

21

MOLDING INNOVATIVE STRATEGIES

By now, you have discovered the rewards of naked option writing. We have demonstrated how naked option writing can be used as a strategy in and of itself, how to alter it to reduce the inherent risk, and how to improve profits.

Up to this point, we have discussed naked option writing strategies which involve the writing of naked options exclusively. Now we are going to look at some new approaches which utilize not only naked options, but also other investment vehicles as well. As we did in Chapter 20, we are going to mold strategies which have a small possibility of incurring loss. If a loss is incurred, it will probably be slight.

The Ratio Hedge

The major strategy we will study is referred to as the "ratio hedge," or the "variable hedge." The foundation of a ratio hedge strategy is 100 shares of common stock, similar to that of a covered option writing strategy. In the case of a ratio hedge, we take several naked call options, and wrap them around the 100 shares of underlying stock. We take the benefits of naked option writing, the high probability of reward, and use it to protect a common stock position. At the same time that we are protecting the 100 shares of stock, the 100 shares of stock is shielding the naked option writing positions from a severe loss. As the stock price moves up, the common stock will appreciate in value, countering potential losses from the naked options, which will also expand in value. If the stock moves down, you will take a loss in the stock, but you will profit from the depreciation in the price of the naked options.

The ratio hedge was practiced long before the Options Exchange was established. In fact, the ratio hedge is the heart of the Thorp and Kassouf system, which they present in their book, *Beat The Market*. The authors provide a tremendous amount of documentation to support their findings, and the results are impressive. I presented these findings at the beginning of this text, and will present them again so that we may look at them more closely. Their research shows:

"1. The system, using a ratio hedge as its base, showed a gain of more than 25% per year for 17 years.
2. From Sept., 1929 to June, 1930, the system could have doubled an investment.
3. The system showed a real five-year track record, generating average annual returns of 25%.
4. The system actually doubled $100,000 in four years."[8]

These results should prove the viability of ratio hedge strategies. The work of Thorp and Kassouf in this area used warrants rather than naked options, which were not readily available at that time. They shorted warrants, and used these vehicles as a means of providing a canvas of protection over the common stock. The short sale of a warrant is a very close relative to the writing of a listed call option. Therefore, the material in this chapter can be seen as an out-growth of the work that Thorp and Kassouf completed in their book.

[8] Edward O. Thorp, Sheen T. Kassouf, *Beat The Market*, Random House, Inc., New York, 1967.

The major objective of the ratio hedge is to create a strategy which is not market dependent, which does not require the proper prediction of where stock prices will move in the future, or the proper timing to take advantage of market moves. This strategy is designed assuming that the market moves in a random fashion. Your goal is to move into positions and wait until the options expire and then move out; or to wait until the stock price breaks one of your outside parameters.

In this strategy, you will want to design a profit pattern in which the underlying common stock price fluctuates *within* the parameters of the strategy. This strategy is designed so that the stock price can move in a wide range, and if it stays within that range, it will generate a profit when either the options expire, or shrink in value.

Let us take a close look at a ratio hedge strategy. Tables 16 and 17 map out a ratio hedge strategy using 100 shares of National Semiconductor (NSM) as the base. We have used as our molding material, three NSM Nov 45 call options, which we will write to protect the common stock position. You will notice the wide profit range that has been created. If NSM stays within that range (which runs from 30 to 53) until the end of November, and does not break through our parameters before that time, a profit will be generated. If the NSM stock hits one of the outside parameters, the strategy requires that you remove yourself from the total position, including selling the stock and buying back all the options. When you bail out, there is a good probability that there will be a small time value left in your naked options, and therefore, you may break even (before commission costs are incurred).

Table 16
A Ratio Hedge

July 19, 19____

Buy	100	NSM	Common Stock at 43-3/4	Cost = $4,375
Write	3	NSM	Nov 45 Calls at 4-3/4	Proceeds = $1,425

The profit-loss table is presented below.

NSM Price at the end of November		Gross Profit	Loss
55			(450)
54			(250)
53	Bail-out Parameter		(50)
52		$150	
51	<--- Profit Zone --->	350	
50		550	
49		750	
48		950	
47		1,150	
46		1,350	
45		1,550	
44		1,450	
43		1,350	
42		1,250	
41		1,150	
40		1,050	
39		950	
38		850	
37		750	
36		650	
35		550	
34		450	
33		350	
32		250	
31		150	
30	Bail-out Parameter	50	
29			(50)
28			(150)

TABLE 17
THE RATIO HEDGE
WORKSHEET

Date July 19, 19

BUY 100 NSM Common at 43 3/4 COST = $ 4375

WRITE (Sell) 3 NSM Nov 45 Calls at 4 3/4 PROCEEDS = $ 1425

INITIAL MARGIN REQUIREMENT $ 5800

MAXIMUM MARGIN REQUIREMENT $ 7620 at 52

PROJECTED COMMISSION COSTS $ 210

NSM PRICE EXPIRATION DATE IN November	(1) VALUE OF STOCK	–	(2) COST OF STOCK	=	(3) PROFIT or (LOSS) from STOCK	(4) PROCEEDS FROM WRITTEN OPTIONS	–	(5) VALUE OF WRITTEN OPTIONS	=	(6) PROFIT OR (LOSS) FROM WRITTEN OPTIONS	(7) TOTAL GROSS PROFIT OR (LOSS) (3) + (6) = (7)
54	$ 5400		$ 4375		$ 1025	$ 1425		$ 2700		($1275)	($250)
53	5300		4375		925	1425		2400		(975)	(50)
52 Bail-out Point	5200		4375		825	1425		2100		(675)	150
51	5100		4375		725	1425		1800		(375)	350
50	5000		4375		625	1425		1500		(75)	550
49	4900		4375		525	1425		1200		225	750
48	4800		4375		425	1425		900		525	950
47	4700		4375		325	1425		600		825	1150
46	4600		4375		225	1425		300		1125	1350
45	4500		4375		125	1425		0		1425	1550
44	4400		4375		25	1425		0		1425	1450
43	4300		4375		(75)	1425		0		1425	1350
42	4200		4375		(175)	1425		0		1425	1250
41	4100		4375		(275)	1425		0		1425	1150
40	4000		4375		(375)	1425		0		1425	1050
39	3900		4375		(475)	1425		0		1425	950
38	3800		4375		(575)	1425		0		1425	850
37	3700		4375		(675)	1425		0		1425	750
36	3600		4375		(775)	1425		0		1425	650
35	3500		4375		(875)	1425		0		1425	550
34	3400		4375		(975)	1425		0		1425	450
33	3300		4375		(1075)	1425		0		1425	350
32	3200		4375		(1175)	1425		0		1425	250
31	3100		4375		(1275)	1425		0		1425	150
30 Bail-out Point	3000		4375		(1375)	1425		0		1425	50
29	2900		4375		(1475)	1425		0		1425	(50)
28	2800		4375		(1575)	1425		0		1425	(150)
27	2700		4375		(1675)	1425		0		1425	(250)

The Art of Ratio Hedge Design

The designing of ratio hedges is as much an art as a science; yet through practice, you will gain more and more skill in mapping out these potential strategies. Table 18 presents a form that I highly recommend you use to develop these strategies, and to map out the potential returns at each price level of the stock. This formula also identifies the breakout points at which the total strategy begins to lose money on the upside and on the downside.

The ratio hedge is an ideal strategy for an investor who does not have the time to watch his positions every minute of the day, or the time to develop a technical or a fundamental analysis of the market.

In order to design ratio hedge strategies properly, the following guidelines should be followed:

1. Three is a Lucky Number.

The work of Thorp and Kassouf indicates that three options is the ideal number to write against each 100 shares of stock in a ratio hedge strategy. If you wish to input market direction into your strategy, then you could change this mix. But now you move away from a random walk approach to the market, and your market predictability will determine some of your profitability. For example:

If you were bullish, and felt that the Sears stock price had a higher probability of moving up than moving down, you might wish to write only two calls against each 100 shares of stock. On the other hand, if you are bearish regarding the price action of Sears, you might want to write four calls against your 100 share stock position.

TABLE 18

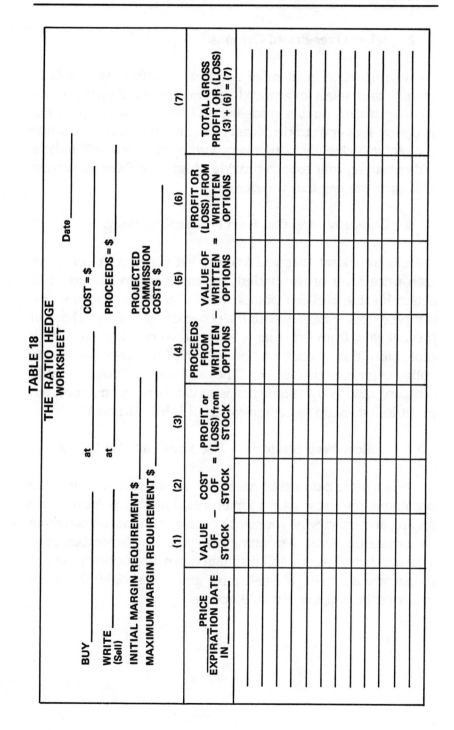

THE RATIO HEDGE
WORKSHEET

Date ____________

BUY ____________ at ____________ COST = $ ____________

WRITE (Sell) ____________ at ____________ PROCEEDS = $ ____________

INITIAL MARGIN REQUIREMENT $ ____________

MAXIMUM MARGIN REQUIREMENT $ ____________

PROJECTED COMMISSION COSTS $ ____________

______ PRICE EXPIRATION DATE IN ______	(1) VALUE OF STOCK	−	(2) COST OF STOCK	=	(3) PROFIT or (LOSS) from STOCK	(4) PROCEEDS FROM WRITTEN OPTIONS	−	(5) VALUE OF WRITTEN OPTIONS	=	(6) PROFIT OR (LOSS) FROM WRITTEN OPTIONS	(7) TOTAL GROSS PROFIT OR (LOSS) (3) + (6) = (7)

2. Select Over-Priced Options.

An important element of any option writing system is to identify and select overpriced options. In the Appendix, we provide this invaluable guideline and indicate whether or not an option is over or underpriced by comparing its normal value to its actual value. By using overpriced options, you will build a wide enough profit zone to provide a high probability of success with each strategy that you design.

3. Carefully Map Out Each Potential Strategy.

It is important that you know what your profit will be at each price level of the underlying common stock. You must determine the bail-out points for the stock so that you can compare stock volatility with the potential profit zone. This will prevent you from entering a strategy where there is a high probability that a stock will break out of that zone before the option expiration date arrives. The only way that you can really compare ratio hedge strategies is to compare the mapped out profit-loss scenario as demonstrated in Tables 16 and 17.

4. Follow Your Strategy — Use Your Bail Out Points.

When these parameters are hit by the stock, move out of the positions. You may take a small loss, but that is better than hoping and praying as your stock continues to move strongly in the wrong direction, generating heavy losses. Remember, even with a ratio hedge, you still maintain two naked option positions (when you are using a 3-to-1 mix), and you should always be aware of the dangers of naked options.

5. Write Out-of-the-Money Options, On-the-Money Options, or Options that are Only Slightly In-the-Money.

Normally, the ideal options for a ratio hedge strategy are those that are close to-the-money. They will usually provide the most premium, the most protection, and the maximum possible profit zones.

With these guidelines, you should now be able to design and compare ratio hedge strategies with considerable success. The best way to approach this unique type of strategy is to practice designing numerous strategies; try them out on paper before jumping into the market. Map them out and watch what occurs. Try to limit your strategies to a three or four-month period. Although ratio hedge strategies can run for four, five, six, or even nine months, the longer the life of the strategy, the better the chance that the underlying stock price will move through its outside parameters, ejecting you from the strategy. Consider contingency stop-loss orders to help build the necessary discipline into your strategies.

Also make sure commissions are included in your strategy design considerations. Each strategy has two separate transactions, and as a result, commissions can build up suddenly. I have not included a discussion of commissions in this chapter to avoid confusing you and to provide for more simplification, but as I have mentioned many times, they are a critically important consideration.

Although the strategies presented in this chapter are not as high powered as a straight naked option writing portfolio, they have less risk, and show a solid track record.

In the next chapter, we will discuss variations of the ratio hedge, some of which are far more attractive, others which are less appealing, and many which have market timing and market direction built into their systems. We will be discussing hedges which, rather than using common stock, employ the purchase of stock options as a means of building a foundation for the system.

22

THE SPREAD GAME

The spreading game is becoming one of the hottest games on Wall Street. Brokers who think they know a lot about options talk in terms of spreading, rather than covered writing, or other more conservative terms.

Advantages and Disadvantages of Spreads

The basic element of the highly popular spread is the *purchase of an option*. We combine this purchase of an option with the sale (or the writing) of another option, both with the same underlying common stock.

The basic advantage of the spread is the minimum amount of cash outlay that is required for any one position. Actually a spread costs a lot less than buying an option by itself.

Following are the major advantages of spreads:

1. Stock ownership is not required.

2. Spreads require a small amount of cash outlay.

3. There is limited risk.

4. The risk is clearly identified.

5. There is good leverage.

6. Your maximum profit is clearly spelled out.

I feel that if given a choice, spreading is normally a better game than buying options. When spreading, you are able to reduce your risk.

To the average investor, spreading can have some drawbacks, such as commissions, which can get out of hand quickly in this fast moving game. Trading skills are also needed to reap the rewards of spreading. For those without these skills, the spreading game can be a painful experience.

Following are the major disadvantages of spreads:

1. Spreads generate a lot of commissions.

2. Spreads are more difficult to move into and out of.

3. Spreads contain some risk.

4. Spreads are normally market sensitive.

Furthermore, spreading is usually more market sensitive than other writing strategies. Therefore, timing and the study and knowledge of future market conditions are critical to success in the spreading game. Yet there are spreads which have advantageous profit-loss scenarios, and can be successful in an uncertain market. Spreads can be designed for all types of market conditions, and can be altered to meet the moods and changes in the market. Thus, they can be an excellent hedge, or the ideal offensive weapon for a portfolio.

In order to enter spreads, a $2,000 initial margin requirement is necessary for most brokerage houses, for that is the amount needed to set up a margin account. And, a margin account is needed to do spreading. If you have $2,000, a spreading vehicle is an excellent trading medium.

With a wide variety of options available for each underlying stock, there is an extremely wide range of spreads from which to choose. There are what we call backspreads, vertical spreads, butterfly spreads—the list goes on and on. All these spreads do not have any naked options attached to them. They are similar to a covered option writing position, which was discussed in Chapter 16. Each long option position is covered by a short option position. Consequently, the investor does not have to handle the highly risky naked option. A spread that does not have any naked options is referred to as a "one-on-one" spread.

Now let's look at a few spreads. Table 19 presents examples of several different one-on-one spreads. In the next chapter, I will cover my favorite one-on-one spreads in greater depth .

The Variable Spread

Using the one-on-one spread as a base, we can now develop a far more sophisticated spread, one which adds naked options to its makeup.

We already know the value of writing naked options. Therefore, in order to build more firing power into our strategies, we may consider writing naked options in molding spread strategies. Again when you use naked options, you must be aware of the dangers and unlimited risks.

Table 19
The World of Spreads

Given 6 listed options of ASA, here are just a few of the possible spreads that can be created:

ASA	May	45	call				
ASA	May	40	call	ASA	Aug	40	call
ASA	May	45	put				
ASA	May	40	put	ASA	Aug	40	put

The Bull Spread I (a Vertical Call Spread)
Buy 1 ASA May 40 call
Sell 1 ASA May 45 call

The Bull Spread II (a Vertical Put Spread)
Buy 1 ASA May 45 put
Sell 1 ASA May 40 put

The Bear Spread I (a Vertical Call Spread)
Buy 1 ASA May 45 call
Sell 1 ASA May 45 call

The Bear Spread II (a Vertical Put Spread)
Buy 1 ASA May 40 put
Sell 1 ASA May 40 put

The Calendar Call Spread
Buy 1 ASA Aug 40 call
Sell 1 ASA May 40 call

The Calendar Put Spread
Buy 1 ASA Aug 40 put
Sell 1 ASA May 40 put

The *variable spread* is similar to the ratio hedge which we discussed in Chapter 21, with the exception that we do not purchase 100 shares of stock. The foundation of the variable spread is a one-on-one spread. Around this spread, we again mold a strategy writing naked options.

We found in Chapter 21 that the ideal number of options to write against each long position was *three*. The beauty of using an option instead of the common stock is that a stock has a tremendous amount of value that must be protected; an option does not.

Sub-Classification of Variable Spreads

In Tables 20 and 21, we map out two different variable spreads. The first is a "variable call spread," and the second is a "variable put spread." You will notice that both sides of the spread have the same expiration date, with different strike prices. This would be defined as a "vertical spread."

It is also possible to develop what are referred to as "calendar spreads." In Table 22, we show a variable calendar call spread, which is mapped out to demonstrate the profit parameters of such a strategy.

In all the strategies in the examples, you will notice that we write out-of-the-money options at all times, again following our rules regarding naked option writing.

One of the major advantages of using variable spreads is greatly increased flexibility. As demonstrated, you can use calendar spreads, which are spreads with different expiration dates, rather than different strike prices. In addition, you can use vertical spreads, whereby you have the same expiration date, with different strike prices, or you can use either puts or

Table 20
A Variable Call Spread

(An actual strategy I recommended on Oct. 22, 1973)

Buy	1	Polaroid	Jan	110	Call	at	11-3/4
Sell	3	Polaroid	Jan	130	Calls	at	4-3/4

Polaroid Price is 105-5/8

With this strategy, if the Polaroid stock is below 141 at the expiration date in January, a gross profit will be realized. If Polaroid moves above 141, you must bail out of the strategy.

The profit-loss table is presented below.

Table 20A shows how to map out the profit-loss picture using our suggested worksheet.

Polaroid Price at the end of January	Gross Profit	Loss
$145		($750)
142		(150)
141 Bail-out Point	$50	
140	250	
137	850	
135	1,250	
132	1,850	
130	2,250	
127	1,950	
125	1,750	
122	1,450	
120	1,250	
118	1,050	
116	850	
114	650	
112	450	
110 or Lower	250	

TABLE 20A
THE RATIO SPREAD
WORKSHEET

Date Oct. 22, 1973

BUY 1 PRD Jan 110 Call at 11 3/4 COST = $ 1175

WRITE (Sell) 3 PRD Jan 130 Calls at 4 3/4 PROCEEDS = $ 1425

INITIAL MARGIN REQUIREMENT $ 1113

MAXIMUM MARGIN REQUIREMENT $ 5143 at 41

PROJECTED COMMISSION COSTS $ 120

Polaroid PRICE EXPIRATION DATE IN January	(1) VALUE OF PURCHASED OPTION(S) In January	− (2) COST OF OPTION(S)	= (3) PROFIT OR (LOSS) FROM OPTIONS	(4) PROCEEDS FROM WRITTEN OPTIONS In January	− (5) VALUE OF WRITTEN OPTIONS	= (6) PROFIT OR (LOSS) FROM WRITTEN OPTIONS	(7) TOTAL GROSS PROFIT OR (LOSS) (3) + (6) = (7)
145	$ 3500	$1175	$ 2325	$ 1425	$4500	($3075)	($750)
142	3200	1175	2025	1425	3600	(2175)	(150)
141 Bail-out Point	3100	1175	1925	1425	3300	(1875)	50
140	3000	1175	1825	1425	3000	(1575)	250
137	2700	1175	1525	1425	2100	(675)	850
135	2500	1175	1325	1425	1500	(75)	1250
132	2200	1175	1025	1425	600	825	1850
130	2000	1175	825	1425	0	1425	2250
127	1700	1175	525	1425	0	1425	1950
125	1500	1175	325	1425	0	1425	1750
122	1200	1175	25	1425	0	1425	1450
120	1000	1175	(175)	1425	0	1425	1250
118	800	1175	(375)	1425	0	1425	1050
116	600	1175	(575)	1425	0	1425	850
114	400	1175	(775)	1425	0	1425	650
112	200	1175	(975)	1425	0	1425	450
110 or Lower	0	1175	(1175)	1425	0	1425	250

Table 21
A Vertical Ratio Put Spread Strategy

Theoretical Date
July 15, 19____

Buy	1	DuPont	Jan	130	Put	at	8
Sell	2	DuPont	Jan	120	Puts	at	4

DuPont's theoretical price at the time of the strategy is 125.

In this strategy, we use a 2-to-1 ratio rather than 3-to-1. When the proceeds from 2 of the out-of-the-money options equals or exceeds your option positions (as in this case), you normally have a good strategy.

The beauty of the ratio spread comes in the fact that there usually is only one bail-out point. In this case, that bail-out point is on the downside at 110. On the upside, there is no risk except the commission costs.

The profit picture is presented below.

Table 21A shows how we determine these figures using our custom worksheet.

DuPont Price at the expiration date in January	Gross Profit	Loss
130 or higher	0	
129	$100	
128	200	
127	300	
126	400	
125	500	
124	600	
123	700	
122	800	
121	900	
120	1,000	
119	900	
118	800	
117	700	
116	600	
115	500	
114	400	
113	300	
112	200	
110 Breakeven Point	0	
109		(100)
108		(200)

TABLE 21A
THE RATIO SPREAD
WORKSHEET

Date July 15, 19____

BUY 1 Dupont Jan 130 Put at 8 COST = $ 800

WRITE (Sell) 2 Dupont Jan 120 Puts at 4 PROCEEDS = $800

INITIAL MARGIN REQUIREMENT $ 2750

MAXIMUM MARGIN REQUIREMENT $ 3800 at 110

PROJECTED COMMISSION COSTS $ 100

Dupont PRICE EXPIRATION DATE IN January	(1) VALUE OF PURCHASED OPTION(S) In January	− (2) COST OF OPTION(S)	= (3) PROFIT OR (LOSS) FROM OPTIONS	(4) PROCEEDS FROM WRITTEN OPTIONS	− (5) VALUE OF WRITTEN OPTIONS In January	= (6) PROFIT OR (LOSS) FROM WRITTEN OPTIONS	(7) TOTAL GROSS PROFIT OR (LOSS) (3) + (6) = (7)
130 or Higher	$ 0	$ 800	($800)	$ 800	$ 0	$ 800	$ 0
129	100	800	(700)	800	0	800	100
128	200	800	(600)	800	0	800	200
127	300	800	(500)	800	0	800	300
126	400	800	(400)	800	0	800	400
125 Present Price	500	800	(300)	800	0	800	500
124	600	800	(200)	800	0	800	600
123	700	800	(100)	800	0	800	700
122	800	800	0	800	0	800	800
121	900	800	100	800	0	800	900
120	1000	800	200	800	0	800	1000
119	1100	800	300	800	200	600	900
118	1200	800	400	800	400	400	800
117	1300	800	500	800	600	200	700
116	1400	800	600	800	800	0	600
115	1500	800	700	800	1000	(200)	500
114	1600	800	800	800	1200	(400)	400
113	1700	800	900	800	1400	(600)	300
112	1800	800	1000	800	1600	(800)	200
111	1900	800	1100	800	1800	(1000)	100
110 Bail-out Point	2000	800	1200	800	2000	(1200)	0
109	2100	800	1300	800	2200	(1400)	(100)
108	2200	800	1400	800	2400	(1600)	(200)

Table 22
A Ratio Calendar Call Spread

Theoretical Date
August 1, 19____

Buy	1	EK	Jan	70	call	at	2
Sell	2	EK	Oct	70	calls	at	1

Eastman Kodak's theoretical price at the time of the strategy is 60.

With a ratio calendar spread, a 2-to-1 ratio is normally recommended. With this option writing strategy, the only risk would be incurred on the upside. With a ratio calendar spread, the bail-out point is located near the exercise price of both options, a key disadvantage, if you remember options psychology. The most premium will be incurred at the exercise price; therefore, it may be more expensive than normal to bail-out of the strategy.

The estimated profit-loss picture is presented below. The strategy terminates when the October options expire. Then the profit picture will be dependent on the value of the January option in October.

Table 22A shows how we generate this picture using our custom worksheet.

EK Stock Price at the Expiration Date in October	Gross Profit	Loss
73		($25)
72 Bail-out Point	$125	
71	287.50	
70	450	
69	412.50	
68	375	
67	325	
66	287.50	
65	250	
64	212.50	
63	175	
62	125	
61	87.50	
60	62.50	
59	12.50	
58	0	
57	0	
56	0	
55	0	
54 or Lower	0	

TABLE 22A
THE RATIO SPREAD
WORKSHEET

Date August 1, 19

BUY 1 EK Jan 70 Call at 2 COST = $ 200 (2)

WRITE (Sell) 2 EK Oct 70 Calls at 1 PROCEEDS = $200 (4)

INITIAL MARGIN REQUIREMENT $ 1900

MAXIMUM MARGIN REQUIREMENT $ 3200

PROJECTED COMMISSION COSTS $ 77.00

EK PRICE EXPIRATION DATE IN October	(1) VALUE OF PURCHASED OPTION(S) – EK Jan 70	(2) COST OF OPTION(S) =	(3) PROFIT OR (LOSS) FROM OPTIONS	(4) PROCEEDS FROM WRITTEN OPTIONS – 2 EK Oct 70s	(5) VALUE OF WRITTEN OPTIONS = In October	(6) PROFIT OR (LOSS) FROM WRITTEN OPTIONS	(7) TOTAL GROSS PROFIT OR (LOSS) (3) + (6) = (7)
73 Bail-out Point	$575.00	$200	$375.00	$200	$600	($400)	($25.00)
72	525.00	200	325.00	200	400	(200)	125.00
71	487.50	200	287.50	200	200	0	287.50
70	450.00	200	250.00	200	0	200	450.00
69	412.50	200	212.50	200	0	200	412.50
68	375.00	200	175.00	200	0	200	375.00
67	325.00	200	125.00	200	0	200	325.00
66	287.50	200	87.50	200	0	200	287.50
65	250.00	200	50.00	200	0	200	250.00
64	212.50	200	12.50	200	0	200	212.50
63	175.00	200	(25.00)	200	0	200	175.00
62	125.00	200	(75.00)	200	0	200	125.00
61	87.50	200	(112.50)	200	0	200	87.50
60 Present Price	62.50	200	(137.50)	200	0	200	62.50
59	12.50	200	(187.50)	200	0	200	12.50
58	0	200	(200.00)	200	0	200	0
57	0	200	(200.00)	200	0	200	0
56	0	200	(200.00)	200	0	200	0
55	0	200	(200.00)	200	0	200	0
54	0	200	(200.00)	200	0	200	0

(Obtained from normal value tables)

calls in designing your variable spreads. The spread which you do select will depend on your feel for the market.

With the ratio hedge, your only alternative was to buy stock, and to write a number of call options against that stock. Now we have greatly expanded our horizon of opportunities, because we can move into a variable vertical put spread, a variable vertical call spread, and many others. We are again using the premise of designing and molding naked options around a long option position (purchased option), and designing and developing a defensive, powerful strategy, which has a win or breakeven profit-loss scenario.

The types of variations of ratio spreads and one-on-one spreads are almost unlimited. One-on-one spreads are usually far more market sensitive. Like option buying strategies, their success depends on your success in calling the market. Ratio spreads have the ability to generate a win or breakeven profit-loss picture, where your probability of incurring a loss is usually small.

The spreading game is an unbelievable game, with an almost infinite number of opportunities for the creative player. When you write naked options in developing these strategies, you add a tremendous amount of firing power to them, and develop profit scenarios which make the game worthwhile.

Spreading is a complex art. To the novice, it can be a dangerous game. But to the professional, it is an outstanding investment tool.

23

CREDIT AND DEBIT SPREADS

Variable spreads involve naked option writing, and therefore are for higher risk players only. But one-on-one spreads usually have limited risk.

Two specific one-on-one spreads which have an attractive theoretical profit picture and an impressive track record are a special type of index credit spread and a vertical stock debit spread.

Spreads are classified as either debit or credit spreads, depending on whether they initially put money into your account, which is a *credit* to your account, or take money out of your account, or *debit* your account.

Credit spreads are usually writing strategies—they are a way to write a naked option with limited risk. On the other hand, debit spreads are usually buying strategies where you, in a sense, buy options at discount prices, also with limited risk.

An Index Credit Spread

As mentioned in Chapter 18, writing naked index options theoretically seems like a powerful strategy. But that strategy backfired for many during the crash, when they discovered what unlimited risk really means. There is a way to neutralize most of that risk and prevent the devastating losses that occurred in 1987. The answer is an index credit spread. You write (sell) one index option, and to reduce the risk of a naked writer, you buy a cheaper, further out-of-the-money option with the same expiration date.

For example, if you write the S & P 100 Index (OEX) July 380 call for 1-1/2, you may then buy the 385 call for 1/2. Therefore, you would receive in your account a credit of $100, less commissions (1-1/2 – 1/2 = 1 [$100]).

You have an option writing position, so if the S & P 100 Index does not move above 380 before expiration, both the 380 and 385 calls will expire and you will pocket the $100. But if the S & P 100 Index moves against you, the most you can lose is $400. Why? You have added a new, more important line of defense. By purchasing the 385 call, you stop losing money if the OEX moves above 385, because the 385 call will increase in value at the same rate as the 380 call you have written. Therefore, the most that you can lose is the difference between the strike price of the call you are writing, and the call you are buying (385 – 380 = 5), or $500 less your credit of $100, giving you a maximum loss of $400.[9] This is naked writing with limited risk.

With credit spreading, you have limited risk, but your risk can be high if the difference between the option that you write and buy is large, or if you write a lot of options. For example, a 15-point spread involves a possible loss of $1,500. If you do ten of the spreads, your possible loss is $15,000.

[9] There is a small probability of a larger loss if the option that is written is assigned, due to a possible delay in notification of assignment, but only if the option is deep in-the-money and the purchased position moves against you before you close the position.

A 90% Winner

I have been recommending index credit spreads in my newsletters for several years. The theoretical track record for these spreads has been impressive. These credit spreads have some unique features that will be elaborated upon later.

The Track Record

Between December, 1988 and June, 1991, I recommended twenty-seven index credit spreads in my newsletter, *The Trester Compleat Option Report*. The theoretical results of these spreads showed that two were losers, and twenty-five were profitable. In other words, over 90% were profitable. If you had entered ten contracts on each credit spread, your net profit would have been $10,518, after subtracting deep discount commissions of $1,920. The average margin requirement per position would have been $9,365, and the profit per position would be $389.

Between June of 1988 and June of 1991, thirty-six similar index credit spreads were recommended in my other newsletter, *The Put and Call Tactician*. The theoretical portfolio shows that thirty-two, or 89%, were profitable. The recommended position size ranged from five to ten contracts. The average margin required for each position was $7,875. The net profit for all positions was $16,186, less commissions of $2,460, giving a net profit of $13,726. Almost all positions were held for less than one month, and twelve out of thirty-six were held for less than one or two weeks. Therefore, the annualized return would have been over 70%.

In addition to the track record results, many of the students who have taken my investment seminars and college classes have had great success with this strategy over all other option plays.

Here are the guidelines for developing an index credit spread as described in the track record above.

1. Only write overpriced index options on broad-based indexes, such as the S & P 100 Index, or Major Market Index.

2. Only write options that are far out-of-the-money. The key to success in designing such a spread is to write an index option where the index price is far from the strike price. Then the chance is small that you will ever take a loss. This action is another line of defense against risk.

3. Set a stop-loss that is out-of-the-money on the underlying index. Never let the index price move into-the-money. Make sure to close out the whole spread before the index price can cause a lot of damage to your spread. With such a stop-loss, rarely if ever will you incur the maximum loss.

4. Never enter a credit spread where the credit is less than 7/16. A credit of 1/4 or 3/8 is too small a reward for a potential risk of 5, 10 or 15 points, especially after commissions.

5. Try to stay with 5 or 10-point spreads (the difference between the option you are writing and buying). Don't go beyond a 15-point spread.

6. Only write index spreads that have one month or less before expiration. Maximum depreciation occurs in the last month, and with less time you have a higher probability of profit.

7. Only use spread orders to enter and exit such spreads (check Chapter 25).

8. Only use deep discount brokers and do at least five

options at a time to reduce the commission cost per option. Such spreads require two, and sometimes four commissions—don't let them eat up all your profits.

9. Avoid bucking the market trend. If the market is in a strong uptrend, only enter put credit spreads. If the market is in a major decline, only enter call credit spreads. When the market moves against you, cover your position—even if the stop-loss has not been touched. This is another line of defense.

The rewards from such credit spreading may seem small. But due to the fact that you win almost all of the time, the annualized return is quite high. How can you tell if you have designed a good credit spread? *Option Master®*, a computer program, tells you your probability of profit. If it is 85% or higher and if you followed the guidelines just presented, you have a theoretically profitable credit spread. Table 23A and 23B show two examples of successful credit spreads I recommended.

In each example, the spread price is the difference between the price of the option you are selling and the price of the option you are buying. In Table 23A, the one-month call credit spread will be profitable if the Major Market Index does not rise to the stop-loss price of 593.11 by expiration in September, about a 265-point move in the Dow Industrials. This is a long way to move in one month as demonstrated by the probability of profit of 96% calculated by *Option Master®*.[10] If the stop-loss is not hit, you pocket the $68.75, less commissions. In Table 23B, you see another index credit spread using puts, showing the prices of the July 455 and 450 puts to demonstrate how the spread price is derived.

[10] *Option Master®* is available from Institute for Options Research, Inc., P.O. Box 6586, Lake Tahoe, NV 89449.

Table 23A
Index Call Credit Spread

Recommendation Date 8/17/90

Index	Index Price	Spread
Major Market Index (XMI)	540.87	Sell XMI Sept 595 Call Buy XMI Sept 600 Call
Minimum Spread Price	**Theoretical Probability of Profit**	**Index Stop-Loss Price**
11/16	96%	593.11

Maximum Loss: ($431.25)
Maximum Profit: $68.75

Table 23B
Index Put Credit Spread

Recommendation Date 6/16/89

Index	Index Price	Spread
Major Market Index (XMI)	486.89	Sell XMI July 455 Put at 1-3/16 Buy XMI July 450 Put at 3/4
Minimum Spread Price	**Theoretical Probability of Profit**	**Index Stop-Loss Price**
7/16	93%	455

Maximum Loss: ($456.25)
Maximum Profit: $43.75

Before you begin trading credit spreads, play them on paper for awhile, and when you enter the market, just do a few at a time initially until you learn the art of credit spreading.

Margin Requirements

One of the big advantages of credit spreading over naked index option writing is a much smaller margin requirement. With a 5-point credit spread, your minimum margin requirement is your maximum risk, or $500 less your credit. But if you write an OEX 380 call *naked*, when the OEX is priced at 380, your margin requirement would be 15% of the underlying index, or $5,700—what a difference!

How To Buy Options at Discount Prices

On the other side of the coin from credit spreading is debit spreading. A debit spread can be a way to buy an option at a discount price. Here we use option writing income to offset the cost of buying an option. I have had best results with debit spreads where you buy an at-the-money or slightly in-the-money option with at least one month before expiration, and write a farther out-of-the-money option that is either five or ten points out-of-the-money.

One disadvantage to such spreads is that you limit your profits. You can hit singles and doubles, but usually no home runs. Your maximum profit is determined by the spread. With a 5-point spread, your maximum profit is $500, less the cost of the spread. Never enter a spread if the option you are writing is less than 1/2. It is not worth the effort. Finally, only enter a spread if your maximum possible return is 200% or higher. With a 5-point spread, the biggest debit you want to pay is 1-5/8.

For example, Table 23C demonstrates how to design a debit spread. Here you buy the close-to-the-money Nike May 70 call for 3-1/8. To offset the cost of that option, you sell the Nike May 75 call for 2. Therefore, your spread price and your cost is only 1-1/8 (3-1/8 – 2 = 1-1/8). That is the most you can lose. Instead of paying 3-1/8 for the May 70 call, you only pay 1-1/8. What a deal! But you do limit your profits. If Nike stock price moves from 68 to 75, you stop making money at 75, for you wrote (sold) the 75 call. Hence, the most you can make is a 5-point profit (75 – 70 = 5), less the cost of the spread 1-1/8. Your maximum profit is 3-7/8 (5 – 1-1/8 = 3-7/8), or $387.50. That is a 344% return on investment. To receive the same return on investment by just buying the Nike May 70 call at 3-1/8, Nike's stock price would have to rise to 83-7/8, instead of 75, a much less likely occurrence.

This debit spread gives you a much better profit picture than just buying an option. If Nike does keep moving above 75, you lock in a 344% maximum return, no matter how high the stock rises. Table 23D demonstrates a put debit spread using the guidelines previously described.

To summarize, this type of debit spread is a great way to buy an option, but it does have its drawbacks:

1. You put a cap on your profits—there are no home runs.

2. Maximum profits usually cannot be captured until expiration, unless the underlying stock moves deep in-the-money.

3. Transaction costs are higher than buying options. You have two commissions to enter a position, and two commissions to exit. In addition, executions are more difficult.

Margin Requirements

Due to the fact you are writing an option when you enter a debit spread, there is a margin requirement. But that requirement is just the debit, or what you paid for the spread. So if you bought the Nike spread for 1-1/8. Your margin would be 1-1/8, plus commissions, the maximum risk of this debit spread.

Table 23C – Call Debit Spread

Recommendation Date 4-12-90

Stock	Stock Price	Spread
Nike, Inc. (NIKE)	68	Buy NIKE May 70 Call at 3-1/8 Sell NIKE May 75 Call at 2 **Spread Price:** 1-1/8

Theoretical Probability of Profit: 35%

Maximum Loss: ($112.50)
Maximum Profit: $387.50
Maximum Return: 344%

Table 23D – Put Debit Spread

Recommendation Date 1-12-90

Stock	Stock Price	Spread
Digital Equipment (DEC)	84-5/8	Buy Feb 85 Put at 2-15/16 Sell Feb 80 Put at 1-3/8 **Spread Price:** 1-9/16

Theoretical Probability of Profit: 43%

Maximum Loss: ($156)
Maximum Profit: $344
Maximum Return: 220%

PART III

SECRETS OF THE PROFESSIONAL OPTION TRADER

24

THE COMPLEAT OPTION TRADER

You have been introduced to the basics and the rules of the options game and have the resources necessary to become a skilled option strategist. We have covered a lot of information up to this point, and now we must break some important new ground. It is time to graduate from college, and to move into the real world. You have seen some outstanding strategies, and have been exposed to new and exciting ways of making money in the options market.

You are ready to reap the rewards that are available, but this is not an easy task. Implementing the strategies we have presented, monitoring these strategies, making the right decisions at the right times, pulling the trigger when it needs to be pulled—these are all critical skills that the COMPLEAT OPTION PLAYER must have. Therefore, in the next few chapters, we will provide you with the secrets necessary to develop and to use these critical skills.

Once you have mapped out your strategies and are prepared to play the game, you come to the important area of strategy implementation and surveillance—in other words, getting these strategies off the ground and keeping them up in the air.

Many novice players who have entered the options market fully knowledgeable in the use and design of option strategies have been severely injured because of their inability to carry out these two important steps:

1. **To implement strategies properly**

2. **To carry out a proper surveillance program**

Implementation of Strategies

In the stock market, when you purchase stock, implementation of the order normally is quite an easy task. You simply make a call to your stock broker, and tell him that you want 100 shares of XYZ stock. You may tell him what price you would like, or you may just say, "go get it in the market." Either way, you will easily obtain 100 shares of stock.

The average investor then hangs onto that stock, in many cases for years, before he ever decides to sell it. Such an investment system, used by the majority of investors, requires a small amount of time for implementation and surveillance.

But options are a different breed of cat. Unlike stock, they "self-destruct" after a short period of time. *Time* is the name of the game, and an option has a microscopic life, compared to the life of a stock. Options are extremely volatile instruments—they can self-destruct, or explode in value, or they can expire very quietly. One option may have many violent moves in price over its short life.

Options, because of their volatile nature, because of their tendency toward self-destruction, and because of their short lives, require a larger amount of attention. The option player will move in and out of positions on a rapid basis, if he closely follows the strategies he has mapped out. Therefore, the matter of executions and implementation is critical, and the skilled option player is a skilled option TRADER who knows how to get a good execution, and how to face the complexities of the options trading arena.

The option player must face many obstacles in handling, implementing and monitoring his options portfolio. These obstacles include: the need for simultaneous transactions to implement different types of strategies; the many complicated types of orders that can be utilized; the complexities of the trading floor; and the questionable liquidity of each separate class of options.

Another obstacle that the option player faces as he attempts to implement his strategies is the question of margins. Even the most experienced options specialist may have questions regarding what margin is required for each type of option strategy.

Add to this the problem of commissions. Commissions in the options market are far more important than they are in the stock market, because of the large amount of trading activity that you are forced to be involved in as you implement, monitor, and maintain your option strategies. You must keep a close watch on commissions which are tacked onto the numerous trades that you will make. As in any business, the option player must be extremely cost conscious.

In summary, the COMPLEAT OPTION PLAYER must also be a Compleat Option *Trader*. You must be an expert in the use of option trading tactics, have a complete understanding of margin rules, and know how to use them properly. You must be extremely cost conscious, and must be able to properly monitor and guide your options portfolio, in order to reap the profits that are possible in the options market.

It will take time for you to acquire the proper trading tactics. In order to help you with this process, I will present to you the many secrets I have discovered in the options market, and dispel the false assumptions regarding options trading.

Remember, being an options strategist able to map out outstanding strategies is only half of the game—the other half is getting those strategies off the ground; and hence become a Compleat Option Trader.

Seek a Professional

"I don't have the time to spend monitoring and altering my options positions every moment of every trading day."

This is a familiar comment made by many potential options enthusiasts. However, the option player entering this investment game can greatly reduce the time involved in trading activities. He can do this through the use of special trading tactics (which will be introduced later), and through the selection of a *competent options specialist*.

To the beginner, the most important decision will be the selection of an options specialist, who will help him implement and maintain your options portfolio. The options specialist is an indispensable member of the option player's winning team. He will take much of the weight off your shoulders and save you a great deal of time and money. Therefore, I have dedicated a full chapter to the selection of your options specialist.

25

PROFESSIONAL TRADING TACTICS

To be a winner in the options game, the option player must be a nimble trader. To handle the large volume of transactions that will occur in your options portfolio, you must be a compleat trader, becoming competent in the area of trading options.

When we talk about trading tactics, we are talking about *executions*. Good executions mean: getting into your options positions at the right price, being able to move out of options positions and options strategies with ease and with honor, and protecting the profits that you have built into your strategies.

The Trading Arena

In order to learn these important trading tactics, you must first completely understand the arena in which options are traded. Several markets trade listed options today, and some of these Exchanges trade in a different manner. For our purposes, we will concentrate on the activity and the manner in which options are traded on the floor of the Chicago Board Options Exchange (CBOE). The CBOE was the first Exchange to enter and initiate this game, and it is the one that uses the most sophisticated trading methods for listed options.

When you deal with the CBOE, you will want to be acquainted with three types of people. These are:

1. The Floor Broker
2. The Market Maker
3. The Board Broker

Let us take an example of an option order, and see how each of these individuals participates in the execution of that order.

Suppose that we wish to buy one Xerox (XRX) Jul 60 call option, and we want to put a limit order in at 2-1/2 (we wish to pay no more than $250 for that option). We call our broker, and he takes our order. He then either places it on the wire, or (if he has a direct line to the floor), calls it directly onto the floor of the Exchange.

When the order reaches the floor of the CBOE, the order is given to the *floor broker,* who works for our brokerage firm. Floor brokers are sometimes called $2 brokers, because in the past, they received $2 for each order that they executed on the Exchange. The floor broker takes our order to the Xerox pit, which is the trading area for the XRX Jul 60.

In that area, there are numerous *market makers* who are trading for their own account, and maintaining a market in the XRX Jul 60, very much like a specialist on the New York Stock Exchange (NYSE) does. The market maker's job is to maintain the market in that option, and of course, to profit from trading for their own account. On the NYSE, there is just *one* market maker (specialist) who makes a market in a common stock; but on the CBOE, many market makers compete against each other, which provides for a more honest and competitive option price.

The floor broker, holding our order to buy one XRX Jul 60

THE LISTED OPTIONS TRADING ARENA

call option, calls out the order to the market makers, attempting to find an interested seller of an XRX Jul 60 at 2-1/2. If the market makers are not able to sell that option at that price, the floor broker then goes to the *board broker*.

Unlike the market maker, the board broker does not trade for his own account. He is an employee of the Exchange. His job is to list in his book for XRX Jul 60's, our order to buy one XRX Jul 60 at the limit order price of 2-1/2. What does this mean? It means that when that order goes into the book, it has *priority* over any other order, except for orders that were entered earlier. When the asked price of the XRX Jul 60 moves to 2-1/2, our order will be executed immediately.

You should be aware that if the floor broker is required to put an order in the book, giving that order to the board broker, he usually does not receive any individual compensation for that order. Consequently, it is to his advantage to execute the order immediately, before it goes into the book. By doing this, he is able to attain $2, or whatever compensation he receives for executing that order.

These three individuals are important as we begin to look at the different types of orders that you can enter, and the different problems that are encountered in getting that execution.

Getting That Execution

The ability to "enter" and to "exit" different option positions effectively (i.e., to buy and sell options) is truly an art, and only through experience will you be able to carry out this trading activity with finesse. Let's look closely at the different types of orders that can be used to ENTER an option position, whether you are going to buy an option initially, or to write an option.

1. Market Orders

The first and the simplest order that can be utilized is called a *market order*, and it acts just like a market order for the purchase or sale of stock. The market order is the best way of making sure that you get an execution, whether you are buying or selling an option. The major problem with this type of order is that you are going into the market blind—you do not know what price you will get for the purchase or the sale of your option. The price will be whatever the market will bear.

This tactic can be dangerous in the options market when you attempt to buy or sell an option which has poor liquidity. (Poor liquidity means that there are not many options being traded in that market.) Because of the large number of different options available in the various option markets, poor liquidity can occur quite frequently, especially in deep-in-the-money options, or far-out-of-the-money options. There is a chance if you are buying an option that you will pay far more than you would have expected, or if you are selling an option, that you will sell your options for far less than you expected. In a sense, you will be paying for a night out on the town for the market maker, who takes advantage of the lack of liquidity in this market.

Of course, you have quotes available from your option broker to indicate current prices in the market. But those quotes can be misleading. Price action in options can move so fast that a quote that you receive from your broker is probably five or ten minutes behind the real action in that market. At the time that you place your market order, the situation may have changed from the bid or the asked price that you were quoted. The bid or the asked may have disappeared, and only a market maker is available to support that market.

So, when you enter a market order, make sure that a large number of options are continually trading in that option class.

In this way, at least you will be moving into a market that has liquidity. Then a market maker cannot sneak in and rake you over by giving you a poor price on your option.

Market orders are also dangerous when you attempt to buy or sell too many options at one time. For example, let's say that you wish to buy 100 XRX Jul 60 call options. Well, the market may not be able to handle that number of options, but some market maker surely would move in there and charge you an outrageous price for the remaining options you requested. For all of these reasons, be careful when you play with market orders.

2. The Limit Order

Another type of order that you can use to get an execution is called a *limit order*. This is a far safer order, but does not guarantee that you will get your execution. You are setting a limit on what price you will pay to buy an option, and also setting a minimum on what price you will receive for selling an option. In our example of the XRX Jul 60, we had set a limit order of 2-1/2, which means we would pay *no* more than 2-1/2, although we could pay less than 2-1/2.

When you wish to buy options, or to write options, it is best to use a limit order if you have the time to wait for your price, rather than going blindly into the market, and impatiently using the market order.

However, when you are in the opposite position, and must *exit* a strategy because a stock price has hit one of your bailout parameters, the limit order can be dangerous, because it does not guarantee that you will execute your trade. Again, I warn you not to rely too much on the quotes that you receive from your broker before you enter an order. Those quotes are behind the action, and can be almost worthless in a fast moving market.

The Hidden Cost

There is an important hidden cost to trading both stocks and options, but especially options. That cost is the difference between the bid and asked prices. The bid and asked prices are established by the market makers and specialists on the floors of the exchanges. The *asked* price is the price at which you can buy an option at that moment, and the *bid* price is the price at which you can sell an option. The difference between the two prices is that hidden cost, and is the profit that goes to the market makers and specialists.

For example, if you wanted to buy a S & P 100 Index (OEX) July 360 call, you would call your broker and ask for a quote. Your broker may give you the *last price* traded for that option—this is the price that is published in a newspaper. But that price could have been established through a trade that occurred several minutes or hours ago. What you really need is the bid and asked price. If the real quote is 1-1/2 at 1-3/4, the 1-1/2 is the bid price—that is the price at which you can sell the OEX 360 call. The 1-3/4 is the asked price—the price at which you can buy the OEX 360 call at that moment. The 1/4 difference (1-3/4 – 1-1/2 = 1/4) is an extra cost of the trade in addition to the commission you pay. With low priced options, that cost can be a sizeable percentage of the price of the option.

For over a decade, there was no limit on the size of the spread between the bid and asked price. So with illiquid options, the distance between the bid and asked price could be large. But today, the options exchanges have established limits on the spread between the bid and asked price, and market makers and specialists must allow you to buy at least 10 options at the asked price and sell at least 10 options at the bid price. (Such beneficial rules are not presently available in the commodity options market.)

For example, on the AMEX Options Exchange, the maximum allowed difference between the bid and asked price for options priced under 2 is 1/4; for options priced between 2 and 5, the spread is 3/8; for options priced between 5 and 10, the spread is 1/2; and for options priced between 10 and 20, the spread is 3/4. Similar guidelines are present on the other equity options exchanges. Such rules are a great advantage for the option investor, preventing a market maker or specialist from taking advantage of the investor. But this transaction cost can have a real impact on your profit picture. For example, an option with a bid and asked price of 1/4 at 1/2 is permissible under exchange rules, but the asked price is 100% of the bid price. In other words, you must pay 100% more to buy the option than to sell it.

Trading Tactics

When entering and exiting options positions, one of your goals should be to reduce the transaction cost—the difference between the bid and asked price. If you trade in liquid options such as S & P 100 Index (OEX) options, the difference will be quite small. For example, with active OEX options priced under 2, the difference is usually only 1/16. But there will be many occasions when you will deal with more illiquid options. In these circumstances, you must become an aggressive bargain hunter. For example, if you want to buy the Xerox Oct 60 call, and the quote is 1-1/2 at 1-3/4, normally you would have to pay 1-3/4 to buy the option. But before you pay that price, test the waters for a better price.

One way is to put in a limit order at a lower price, such as 1 or 1-1/4, and wait for the market to move to that price. Here you can put in a "day order"—or a "Good Till Cancelled order"—and wait for a day or two in hopes of getting a real bargain. This is a good tactic with lower priced options, where intra-day fluctuations in a stock price could give you a very good price, but don't leave these limit orders in too long, or you will get the option at your limit price—after the underlying stock has moved significantly against you.

Another tactic when you want an immediate execution is to test the waters with a limit order, but here make an offer just above the bid price to give the market maker a little profit. In our Xerox Oct 60 example quoted 1-1/2 at 1-3/4, use a limit order of 1-9/16. Many market makers will fill your order at that price, even with only a 1/16 profit, especially if there is little action in the option. To help persuade the market maker or specialist to fill your order, use a *fill* or *kill* order. This order states that if your order is not filled immediately when the floor broker calls out the order at the option post, the order is *cancelled!* So here the market maker is more likely to fill the order, knowing you will leave if he doesn't fill it. In addition, you are immediately notified if the order is not filled, so you can enter another order at a different limit price.

Another method that gives you a better chance of an execution is a "limit order with discretion." In our Xerox example, you would enter a limit order at 1-9/16 with 3/16 discretion. Here the floor broker tries to get you a price of 1-9/16. If he can't, he moves the price up to 1-5/8, then 1-11/16, and finally 1-3/4. This technique gives you the best price at that moment.

But test this technique first. If you find that you always pay the asked price, the floor broker is probably tipping off the market makers. Then either switch brokers, or do not use this type of order.

When You're Naked

When you are a naked option writer, and you hit a point where you must get out, there is no time to bargain—you must use a *market order* to cover the position.

Executing Strategies

Because of the outstanding profits that can be made in the area of strategy design, taking positions is not always simple for many option players. Many options strategies involve not just one option purchase or sale, but a simultaneous transaction in which you write some options and buy some other options, or write some options and buy stock, or a combination of the two. The need for simultaneous transactions makes trading in the options market a difficult task. Let us examine some of these simultaneous transactions.

1. The Spread Order

One of your needs might be to buy and sell options at the same time, either to enter or to leave a position. The *spread order* has been especially designed for this type of transaction. Use the spread order when you wish to buy one class of options, and sell another class of options at the same time. For example:

Say you wish to buy one XRX Jul 70 put and sell one XRX Jul 60 put, a good example of a vertical spread. You could enter that order as a spread order, requesting that your broker sell a 60, and buy the 70, either at market, which would be easily executed, or with a specific spread limit. In other words, if you wish to sell the 60 and buy the 70 with a maximum of two points difference between the two option prices, you can enter it in that manner, with a spread of 2. Try to always use limit spread orders to enter either debit or credit spreads.

Before a spread order can be executed, the conditions regarding the bid or asked on both sides of the spread must be perfect, although some floor brokers have indicated that sometimes executing spread orders is easier than single transactions.

Whether or not you are able to execute spread orders will depend on the skill of your floor brokers (attached to your brokerage house), the amount of discretion you give the broker (the size of the spread between the two option prices), and the amount of time you are willing to wait for a potential spread execution.

Spread orders are an important trading tactic, but sometimes professionals depend on other orders to insure faster and sometimes better executions, although at far more risk. The best advise here is to always use a spread order when entering or exiting a spread.

2. The Contingency Order

Another order used to implement simultaneous transactions between options and stock, or between options and options, is called a *contingency order*. With a contingency order, you place a limit order for one of your transactions, *and* either a market or a limit order for your other transaction. This second order will be put into play after the first transaction is completed. For example:

Let's say that you wish to buy 100 shares of General Motors (GM) and wish to write 3 GM Jan 25 calls against that position. Let's say hypothetically that the GM Jan 25's are trading in the range of 2 to 2-1/2. The best way to approach this simultaneous transaction is to enter a contingency order with the purchase of the stock contingent upon the sale of the 3 GM Jan 25's.

Because the premium received from the options is the most

LIMIT ORDER
SPREAD ORDER
MARKET ORDER
CONTINGENCY ORDER
OPTIONS MONITOR
COMPLEAT OPTION TRADER
OPTION STRATEGY
ROAR!

important element of your strategy, you should set a limit order to implement the execution of a sale of the 3 GM Jan 25's. Let's say that we wish to sell the three options for 2-1/2, so we will place a limit order in at 2-1/2. Contingent upon the execution of these three options, we instruct the broker to buy 100 shares of GM at the market. Now we sit back and let the contingency order work for us. As soon as we get our price for the sale of the GM Jan 25 options, the stock will be purchased for us in the market.

Remember, we have used a market order to purchase our stock. It is important when we enter a market order to ensure that the market which we are entering is liquid, in order to provide for a fair price. Market orders used in the purchase of stock are far safer than market orders which are used to buy or sell options, because of the big question of liquidity in the options market.

Another type of contingency order is one that uses *two* limit orders—one to enter the first position, and one to enter the second, once the first position has been executed. In our example of General Motors, we would place a limit order to sell three GM Jan 25's at 2-1/2, contingent upon that order being executed to buy 100 shares of GM at 25. When the three options were sold, the limit order would then be placed automatically to purchase 100 shares of GM at 25.

The danger with this type of contingency order is that you may not get the second leg of the order off; you may not purchase the 100 shares of GM at 25, because the price might be above your limit.

Consequently, if you wish to ensure a simultaneous transaction, half of your order must be a market order. Contingency orders are also used to exit an option strategy and this feature will be discussed in the following section.

3. Legging into a Position

The third type of trading technique for executing simultaneous transactions is one that the novice option player should not touch. Only those who are extremely skilled in option trading should consider this tactic. This method of execution is referred to in the business as *legging into a position*. This method has far more risk than either the contingency order, or the spread order. On the other hand, it has the advantage of being able to generate better executions and profits than the more conservative trading tactics. *Legging-in* refers to the taking of one side of your strategy first, and then moving into the second phase of your strategy.

With our General Motors example, you would first put a limit order in to sell your three GM options. When that order has been executed, you would then move in and attempt to get the price to execute your 100 shares of GM. In some cases, it might take the whole trading day to complete this simultaneous transaction.

The problem with this tactic is that when you enter one leg of your strategy, you become exposed to some risks. The option player who attempts to leg-in, in many cases, will fail to accomplish his total strategy because he becomes too greedy as he moves into the second leg. Or, equally disastrously, he will move into the wrong leg first, and then find that the market has moved in the wrong direction, before he has put on the second leg. The last pitfall is that the option player is far too dependent on the mood and whims of the market with this tactic.

I, therefore, feel that the legging into and the legging out of option strategies should be left to the professional or to the options specialist. What should you do? Generally, it is far better to rely on a contingency or a spread order, where you are GUARANTEED both sides of a transaction.

Pulling the Trigger

Up to this time, we have only discussed how to get executions to *enter* both option positions and option strategies which require simultaneous transactions. Now let's talk about methods to obtain executions to EXIT option strategies. I refer to this section as "Pulling the Trigger" because in many cases, the orders that you use to exit positions will force you to take a loss or to shave important profit from your option strategy.

Moving out of option positions is probably the most difficult task that the option player must face. To guard against the inherent risks in the naked options used in many of the strategies we are discussing, you must extricate yourself from option strategies when the underlying common stock price touches your bail-out parameters. Often the option player must "pull the trigger" in the midst of a strategy in order to take a profit that has developed. The ability to exit a position with honor, in many cases, is dependent on the type of execution orders that you use.

For the novice option player, the best way to approach this problem is to use *stop-loss orders*. By using stop-loss orders, the novice has removed the position from his own hands and put it in the hands of his brokerage house. These stop-loss orders normally should be put on as soon as you enter a strategy. In this way, you will greatly reduce the amount of time spent in monitoring and guiding your options portfolio. A stop-loss order is a market order, and as you already know the dangers of market orders, you have to be prepared to take some of the disadvantages that go with them.

Let's say that you purchased one Teledyne (TDY) Oct 30 put at 4, and you place a stop-loss order on the option at 2. If the option price goes down to 2 at any time during the life of that option, then you wish to move out of the position immediately, and your stop-loss order would automatically be activated. This means that the board broker would immediately sell your one option at whatever the market would bear. Remember that a stop-loss order is a market order, and you are not guaranteed a full price of 2, but at least you are assured of an execution. Further, you do not have to be there to activate that order, and this is the major advantage of a stop-loss order. At this writing, stop-loss orders on options are only accepted on the American Options Exchange.

The Contingency Order

Because of the complicated nature of option strategies, you should consider a more sophisticated way of handling stop-loss orders. The more sophisticated approach is to integrate a stop-loss order with a contingency order. However, many brokerage houses will not handle these complicated contingency orders, and few if any will guarantee executions.

The contingency order that we are going to look at is one that is contingent upon the price level of the stock. Most of your option strategies will be strongly influenced by the price action in the common stock underlying your options. Therefore, it makes sense for you to understand and be able to use a contingency order which deals with the common stock price.

With a ratio hedge, a ratio spread, or with a naked option writing position, you have breakeven or bail-out parameters, and you must move out of the position if the stock price reaches a specific point, whether on the upside or the downside.

For example, if we moved into a ratio hedge centered around General Motors common stock, and our upward breakeven point was $30 a share, then we would want to move out of our total position, and sell our stock at $30. We could ensure that this would be accomplished through a contingency (stop-loss) order, which would automatically detonate at 30, selling out our stock position, and covering our option positions immediately.

For the novice option player then, the contingency (stop-loss) order should be considered for all option strategies which involve naked options, or credit spreads. This contingency order would probably also be appropriate for the closing of single option positions. The major problem you face is finding a brokerage house that will handle the order.

26

THE TEN COMMANDMENTS OF OPTION TRADING

By now, you have discovered that option trading tactics are an important part of the option player's "bag of tricks." Through my experience, I have developed ten major principles that you should follow if you wish to be a successful option trader. We have discussed some of these concepts before and they summarize many key points.

These Ten Commandments relate to your ability to *implement* the strategies you have designed, and to *monitor* those strategies. These rules also should help you decide when and where to take profits, or how to exit the strategies, should your options or stock touch a red alert zone.

Now let us look briefly at these Ten Commandments, and then cover them in detail:

The Ten Commandments of Option Trading

I DON'T BE GREEDY

II LOOK BEFORE YOU LEAP

III FOLLOW YOUR STRATEGY

IV PULL THE TRIGGER

V USE CONTINGENCY ORDERS

VI BEWARE OF COMMISSIONS

VII AVOID EXERCISE

VIII BE PATIENT

IX USE AN OPTIONS SPECIALIST

X MANAGE YOUR MARGIN

I. Don't be greedy.

The first commandment of option trading is a simple one, but it is probably the most important one. Don't be greedy. You may laugh, but this is probably the root cause of many an option player's failure to succeed in the options game. When we say, "Don't be greedy," we just mean, "Do not be unrealistic when you take a position, or take profits, or move out of a position."

An old option trader with plenty of experience frequently states the following seasoned principle: **"You can buy the world for an eighth."** What he is referring to is simply an eighth of a point. Option players incur significant losses and lose significant opportunities because they do not give their broker enough room to execute new trades, or to execute and take profits properly. They spend their time looking for that extra eighth of a point profit whenever they conduct an option transaction, and unfortunately this prevents them either from taking advantage of many profitable opportunities, or from exiting a position when the danger zone has been reached. When you get too greedy in the options market, your portfolio will suffer the consequences; you may pay a high price for an eighth of a point.

II. Look before you leap.

In the options game, as in any other game, it is critical that you have some kind of a plan, and that you carefully map out a detailed picture of what will occur in the future to your strategy. Because of the nature of options, strategies can be formulated in great detail. Right in front of you, you have the exact amount of time left in the life of each option. This can help you clearly map out what will happen at every point in the life of your strategy. By doing this, you will have no surprises and you can build a defense against any unexpected contingencies. Without a strategy, you are playing with dynamite, especially when you write naked options.

III. Follow your strategy.

You have now spent many hours mapping out several alternative strategies and you have selected the strategies you feel have the highest profit potential and the lowest possible risk. Now follow them. This may be easy to say, but in the heat of battle, your emotions may attempt to take command of your actions. Many an option player will fall by the roadside because he has been swayed by his emotions, rather than following the detailed strategies he mapped out before he entered this action filled market.

IV. Pull the trigger.

This recommendation may be the hardest one to follow. We have discussed this concept many times throughout the text. I have repeated it numerous times because it is so important. You have been trained to build defense mechanisms into your strategies: danger points, breakeven points, parameters where you bail-out of your positions to avoid a potential loss. Because of the inherent dangers in the writing of naked options, it is critical that you take action when these points are reached, that you pull the trigger and immediately move out of all these positions. We've talked about ways of building this ejection system into your strategies through the use of contingency orders and stop-losses. Whether you use a stop-loss, or whether you rely on your own discretion to pull the trigger, it must be pulled. The only way you will open yourself up to financial disaster in the options market is to hesitate one time and not pull the trigger.

When we talk about pulling the trigger, we also refer to your ability to take profits *when they develop* in your strategies. The best comment I can make here is never, never be afraid to take a profit. Then don't have any regrets because the strategy would later have become more profitable. Once you are out of a strategy, do not consider what happens to it in the future.

V. Use contingency orders.

We've talked about the many types of trading tactics that can be used in the options market. For the extremely experienced option player, legging-in and legging-out techniques might be considered—they provide the most profit and take advantage of market moods. But to the player who does not have the time or the inclination to monitor his positions closely on an hour-by-hour basis, or to spend large amounts of time moving into and out of strategies, or for the player who does not have that good intuitive feel for the market, the contingency order is the best type to use.

VI. Beware of commissions.

I have not, in my examples, clearly displayed the commission costs involved in different types of options transactions. In the next chapter, I will identify the different possible commission costs involved in each type of option strategy, and discuss which ones can best minimize commission costs over an extended period of time. Being aware of commission costs is one of the Ten Commandments because commissions are so important in your options portfolio. Options are traded far more extensively than are stocks, and therefore, commission costs per dollar of investment are much greater. These commission costs should be offset by the many advantages of the options market, but they are there, and they must be watched closely and controlled carefully.

The use of options as a trading vehicle, where you move in and out of option positions on a daily basis, can be extremely dangerous unless you carefully watch the buildup of commission costs. Options have been highly touted as an excellent trading vehicle, but if you look closely at the amount of commission costs involved in such transactions, this method could become far less attractive. Only those who have commission advantages, where they receive heavy discounts, or where they have a seat on the Exchange, can be viable *daily* option traders.

VII. Avoid exercise.

We spent one full chapter talking about exercise, and dispelling some myths that are passed on about the dangers, uncertainties and the fears of exercise. Exercise is nothing to fear, but when you are exercised, there are additional costs.

There is a simple prescription to guard against exercise. *To avoid exercise, never hold a short position (a writing position) in an option where the option has no time value, or a negligible time value.* This is an easy principle to follow, and it will save you a lot of money if you follow this commandment.

VIII. Be patient.

We have talked about being patient when you plan to buy options because you are starting with a slight disadvantage, and, therefore, you must get an excellent price. Only through a good price can your overall results be profitable. Consequently you may have to wait extensive periods of time until the market and the option price are ideal.

In strategy development, the same rules apply. Do not be overly impatient in attempting to find an interesting option strategy. Wait for the ideal strategies to develop, those which have high profit potential and low risk considerations. As you bide your time and continue to compare different strategy alternatives, you can always have your money invested in Treasury Bills. They are acceptable collateral when you are writing options, and the time that you wait will be productive.

Because of the high commission costs of different strategies, and the importance of executions, it is vital that you select the most powerful strategies that are available, but these strategies may not be present every day of the week; you may have to wait for them. The question of getting the right prices for that strategy is another story, and if you cannot, you must pass and move onto other strategies. There are over 400 stocks that have options on the options exchanges, and there are over 1,500 different options available. So, there are plenty of strategies to pick from. Take your time and pick the best of the crop. Make sure you get the prices you need and the strategy that satisfies you before you make a move.

IX. Use an options specialist.

Even though this is the ninth Commandment, it is probably one of the most important ones. Because of the intricacies of the options market, and the numerous strategies available, because of the complicated and complex problems involved in options trading, because of the need for effective option implementation and execution, and because of the need for day to day surveillance of all strategies, your broker is an important member of your team.

A competent options specialist (not a stock broker) who spends all of his time in the options market and has years of experience in that market can be an indispensable asset to your portfolio and to your performance. He will get you out of a lot of tough spots, get you into some good strategies, and obtain good executions for you.

He will solve many problems and guide you through many of the commandments that we have talked about. Equally important, he will provide you with the on-the-job experience and education that I cannot cover in this text. So, when you select your broker, choose an options specialist to guide you. It will be one of the best moves you make toward winning the options game.

X. Manage your margin.

Another subject the option player must be concerned with is margin, the good faith deposit you will put up in order to initiate and maintain your naked option writing strategies and spreads.

The amount of margin required for an option position or strategy will have a significant impact on your return on investment. Maintenance margin calls may force you out of potentially profitable strategies and cause havoc to your portfolio. Therefore, managing margin requirements is an important activity to the option trader. Your ability to select low margin strategies and to avoid margin calls will be a strong determinant in the profit picture of your portfolio.

GOLD
COMMISSION COST $97.60
COST $89
COMMISSION COST $156.00
COST $39.50
DANGER!! BEWARE OF COMMISSIONS
OPTION PLAYER

27

DANGER: BEWARE OF COMMISSIONS

One of our Ten Commandments of option trading states: beware of option commissions. As in any other sport, there are admission fees and expenses that must be paid to play the game. In the options game, these expenses are high. A moderately active options portfolio will generate from 10% to 30% of the value of that portfolio in the form of commissions per annum. In other words, if you have a $10,000 options portfolio, at the end of your first year of trading, you may incur commission costs running from $1,000 to $3,000. So, if you do not *earn* more than $1,000 in that account, you will lose.

The options game, then, has a high cost of doing business. The option player should be wary of commissions, which should be carefully watched, mapped out, and avoided whenever possible. Of course, the stock market does have commission costs, too. But by their very nature (because of their short life), options tend to be traded frequently. In fact, the major criticism of playing in the options game is that the investor must pay excessive commissions, because of the excessive trading options create.

However, there are ways to avoid and reduce high commission costs, and means of instituting defenses to protect yourself against them.

Although commissions are high in the options game, they are high in many games that you play, and in many business activities. What you are looking for is the bottom line, the net profit margin at the end of the year. With good option writing strategies, that bottom line is fat, even with the higher commissions.

Strategy Selection

To control your commission costs, you should attempt to select strategies which incur the smallest commission costs per dollar invested. The ideal strategies are the *simplest*.

1. **Buying Options, Writing Naked Options.**

The buying of options, and the *writing of naked options* create the smallest amount of commission costs. Why? Because when you enter an option buying position, you are only required to pay one commission, and if you exit that position, there is only one commission charge, which nets out to two total commissions.

If you are absolutely wrong about the purchase, and the market goes in the opposite direction, you may never have to close out the position. It will be worthless before you can take any kind of constructive action. Therefore, the commission costs in buying options are low, especially when you are working with the simplest strategy, which is buying very cheap options, and hoping that they will appreciate.

In many cases, when you are writing naked options, especially if they are way out-of-the-money, you may not have to close out the position at all. The option simply expires, and when it does, there are no commissions involved in the closing of the transaction.

When you write such out-of-the-money options, the chance that you will have to close out that option position may occur only 20% to 30% of the time; the other 70% of the time, the options that you write will expire with no exit commission costs. So, the writing of naked options is probably another ideal strategy if you wish to reduce commission costs.

2. The Out-Of-The-Money Spreads

The second most attractive strategy is the out-of-the-money spread. For example, far-out-of-the-money index credit spreads will expire 80% to 90% of the time, therefore, there will usually be only two commissions incurred to enter, but none to exit the position. Out-of-the-money debit spreads will also tend to expire 65% or more of the time, and therefore, usually you will only incur two commissions, instead of four (two commissions to enter and two to exit).

3. Naked Strangles

The third most attractive strategy with regard to commissions is the writing of a naked strangle, where both the naked call and the naked put are out-of-the-money. Here again, your only commission costs are your costs of moving into both positions. The odds are in your favor that one or both options will expire, and you will not be forced to close out your positions by buying back the options, thereby avoiding additional commissions.

4. Covered Option Writing

The fourth ranking strategy with regard to commission costs per dollar invested is the conservative covered option writing program. We mentioned before that this approach is similar to operating a business, and this strategy normally will generate small commission costs. This is true if you hang onto your pivotal common stocks, and are not active in buying and selling common stocks to use as the merchandise in your covered option writing program. By avoiding excessive trading of both options and common stock under a covered option writing program, you will greatly reduce the commission costs per dollar of investment.

5. The Ratio Hedge

Moving down the list, our commission costs rise at a much faster rate as we move into the more sophisticated, more complicated types of strategies. For instance, the ratio hedge accrues far more commission costs because you must make two simultaneous transactions to move into the position, and two simultaneous transactions to move out of the position, unless the options that you write against each 100 shares of stock expire. (The self-destructive nature of naked options is the one advantage you have going for you with a ratio hedge over some of the spreads that we have discussed.) You may, if forced out of your position, incur four different commission costs. Yet with the ratio hedge, because you are doing a lot of naked writing, you do have the odds in your favor, and this should offset some of the additional commission costs that are incurred with this fancier strategy.

6. The Ratio Spread

The next type of strategy, the ratio spread, again incurs two commissions when you move into the strategy, and two when you move out of it, unless some of your naked options, or long options expire. Thus normally, you must pay for four commissions—two roundtrips.

7. The In-The-Money Spread

Spreads where the underlying stock is in-the-money of one of the options in the spread have an increased likelihood of generating four commissions because the spread will probably not expire worthless. Four commissions on every strategy can take quite a toll on your expense ledger. For not only do you have the commission costs, but you also have the other transaction costs—the difference between the bid and asked price on each of your trades.

In addition, when you are in an in-the-money credit spread, you increase your chance of being assigned, and incurring more commission costs. Hence, avoid in-the-money spreads unless they are slightly in-the-money debit spreads. The transaction costs are just too high for the average investor.

8. Butterfly Spreads

Probably the most expensive of all option strategies is the "butterfly spread." This is a strategy that is often touted by stock brokers because they want to improve their own income. It sounds fancy, and the profits look pretty good, but CAUTION: the butterfly spread has not *four* commissions, but *six* commissions. This spread requires three different option positions to establish and maintain the strategy, and that adds up to six different commissions incurred during the life of that strategy. At the bottom line, there is not enough profit to cover these commission costs and the difference between the bid and asked price. So, beware of the butterfly spread.

Only if you are a market maker on the floor of the Options Exchange can you afford to play with butterfly spreads! If you are just a typical option player who works through a brokerage house and pays his bill of fare, you cannot afford to play with such fancy strategies.

In conclusion, the fancier the strategy gets, the more expensive it gets, and although it may show reduced risk, the commissions will take such a toll that the strategy probably will not have been worth attempting.

The Day Trader

One approach to the options market which we have not yet covered in this text is *daily* option trading. Options, because of their extreme leverage, limited risk, and their tremendous volatility, are ideal for the day to day trader, who can take a one hour move in a stock or index and play it in the options market. In many cases, the day trader will use spreads—bear spreads, bull spreads, butterfly spreads, every spread under the sun. He will employ naked writing, the buying of options or any technique which best plays on the moves of the most active common stocks or indexes. By doing this, he can profit from a one or two-point move in a stock, or a several point move in an index.

This sounds like great fun; there is a lot of action involved, and there are some who are able to make a good living at this sport. However, I do not recommend this course of action for the average investor, because of the tremendous commission costs you will incur. Many novice players have attempted to be a day option trader and have found that within two or three weeks, their account has disappeared into the night. It has been dissipated, not by trading losses, but by commission costs. I have seen it happen many times—the more active you are, the more excessive your trading activity, the sooner your account will disappear, just through the cost of doing business.

True, there are some who have made spectacular profits, even when they have had to pay commissions, but it was only their outstanding ability to call the market, and to manipulate options on a day to day basis that allowed them to survive. Most of the traders who are able to make a living at trading options on a day to day basis generally are on the floor of the Options Exchange because they do not incur the high commission costs. Day trading is a costly art, and we have not covered it in depth because I feel the discussion would be academic for the average investor, due to the commission costs incurred.

What about the Discount Commission Brokers?

You have heard of them—the discount broker—one who gives you a discount on your commission costs, in some cases, as much as 80% off. This sounds attractive, and to many it is an excellent alternative. But the major problem for the beginning option player is the fact that the discount broker does not provide services; he only provides a trading facility.

In the options market, unlike the case in the stock market, the beginning option player may need some backup from his brokerage house in the form of a competent options specialist, a competent trading staff, and sophisticated option trading facilities. This support includes lines to the floor of the Exchanges, publications, and anything else that will aid you in making investment decisions. Remember, option trading requires far more activity than stock trading, far more surveillance, far more planning, and far more expertise. You may think you are an expert, but you should use all the help you can get, and with a discount broker, you usually receive relatively little, because you are not paying for that assistance.

So as a beginner, a full service option broker may be your best choice. But as you gain experience, or if you are a skilled trader and feel comfortable with option strategies, or if you trade the more complicated commission generating strategies, a discount broker is A MUST!

Yet you can have the best of both worlds. There are many full service option brokers who will now give discounts to option traders. The advent of deep discount brokers has forced many option brokers to be more competitive. So if you like your option broker, don't be afraid to ask him for a discount on your commissions, and ask for a big discount. You will probably be surprised at what you can negotiate. Some of the big brokerage houses will negotiate their options commissions even with a small investor, especially if you threaten to move your account to another firm.

When you trade the more complicated strategies, or strategies that have thin profit margins (index credit spreads), you must eventually use a *deep* discount broker. Try to get your commission costs down to below $5 per option. Some deep discounters charge as little as $3 per option on orders of ten options or more.

Another important consideration when you select a discount broker is to make sure they charge a *low minimum charge* on any trade. Some discounters charge over a $35 minimum on an option trade. That is too high! You will be surprised how many times you will do a small trade where the minimum will be invoked, and cause your cost per option to be much too high.

For example, if you buy back two options at 1/8 to cover a writing position, at a minimum commission of $40, your cost per option is $20. Or if you want to buy just one option, the commission for that option would be $40—too much.

One big advantage with discount brokers is that you're dealing with impersonal clerks. Therefore, you will feel more comfortable about calling for option quotes, and your broker won't put any personal pressure on you as you trade. When your personal option specialist is monitoring your positions, your ego is at stake if a strategy goes bad, and you may hesitate to take a loss because you believe you would look inferior in the eyes of your broker. Such hesitation could be disastrous.

Now that you know what the best strategies to use in your cost reduction program are, it is time to look at a few steps which you can follow to reduce commission costs. They are simple, and should not alter your overall strategies to any great degree. They may not provide as much action as you would like, but then, remember, the more action, the more your commission costs will rise and the smaller your profits will be.

Steps to Reduce Commission Costs

1. Avoid excessive trading in your account.

Remember, option portfolios have a high propensity for trading activity. Even the most conservative options account has a high degree of trading activity. As you get into this game, you may become over-zealous and do far more trading in your account than you should, and this will be costly. The more trading you do, the more your costs will increase. So, attempt at all times to avoid excessive trading activity if you can. Avoid strategies which require a lot of activity. When you finish one strategy, attempt to use some of the same positions in the old strategy to create a new one. This will reduce some of the activity that is required.

It is hard to describe in theory how to avoid excessive trading activity. You will learn this art through experience.

2. Plan for commissions.

Before you enter a strategy, build your commission costs into the profit and loss picture of that strategy. Do not assume that they will be a certain percentage of your profit. If you have two roundtrip commissions that could be incurred in a strategy, build them in before you ever enter it. Map out your costs, know what those costs will be before they are incurred. This will greatly aid you in your selection process, and it will direct you towards strategies which have much higher profits because of much lower commission costs.

In this text, I have factored out the commission costs in displaying examples, as we mentioned before, to simplify the explanation, and to avoid the confusion of introducing yet another variable. But, because we have not dealt with commission costs does not mean that they should not be figured into your strategy design activities. They must be incorporated into your strategies before you consider which one you will select. The special forms used here have room set aside for these commission costs. Use them. Make them a part of your investment decision.

3. Beware of the over-zealous broker.

Brokers have a tendency to ignore, or factor out, commission costs, especially when they are recommending strategies to the customers. Your broker may not be aware of commission costs, but you had better be aware of them. Even the most competent options specialist around must be controlled by this kind of thinking. So, when your options specialist makes a recommendation to move into a strategy, check on the commission costs first. Then you should make the decision, incorporating those commission costs into your profit-loss scenario.

4. Get a quantity discount.

Just as in any other business, the more options you buy or sell, the lower the price that you will pay for each option. Using this principle, attempt to move into strategies where you are buying and selling a quantity of options. In this way, you will reduce the commission costs per option, significantly in many cases. The option player who comes into this game with a small amount of capital, and only buys one option, or sells one option, is taking on huge commissions. In order to reduce that cost, buy and sell in quantity, and pay a low minimum.

I strongly suggest that you always work with at least five options when you move in and out of positions. By doing this, you will reduce your commission costs down to one-fifth or less per option, and that can be a significant reduction in your overall profit-loss scenario.

The more options you buy, the more you sell, the lower your costs per option. The ideal number, of course, is *ten;* if you can get to a working level of ten options for each strategy, then you will have attained a nominal commission cost level. However, you might note that using more than ten options, although it may reduce your commission costs a slight bit more, may also create some trading problems. Many classes of options don't have the liquidity to take on large positions. And it is far more difficult to get the right price with a large position than with a smaller one.

5. Select a brokerage house carefully.

We are in an era of competitive commission rates; every brokerage house charges different commissions, and you may want to look at the full range of brokerage houses to find those that will charge the lowest commissions for the number of services that you receive. A warning here: do not forsake a competent options specialist for a 5% or 10% difference in commissions. In the long run, you may pay for that difference, many times over.

6. Select the cheapest strategies.

I have mentioned the priorities of the strategies based on commission costs per dollar of investment. Use that priority list.

7. Avoid exercise (assignment).

This is one of our Ten Commandments of option trading, and it is important because exercise costs money. It costs commissions, and when you have an assignment, you may be shocked at the commission costs involved. By avoiding assignment, you avoid commission costs.

8. Let options expire.

When you are an option writer, the name of the game is to write an option, and let it die. Let it pass on, thereby incurring only one commission, the commission to move into that position. One caution here: in many cases, an option will become almost worthless long before it will expire. In these situations, it is best to cover your positions and use your money wisely in other areas. Whenever you write naked options, there are margin requirements (collateral requirements) that must be put up, and if you are letting that money sit there because you are holding a naked option which is worthless, you are wasting the use of that money. In addition, when you are writing an option, there is theoretical risk and you don't want to continue to hold that risk for just 1/16 or 1/8. So, although it is wise to let your options expire, should they become almost worthless before their life comes to an end, go ahead and take your profits, cover those positions, and put your money to use in some other option strategy.

WATCH YOUR COMMISSION COSTS LIKE A PARANOID ACCOUNTANT

Again, one of the key points of this chapter is to stress the importance of commission costs to the survival of the option player. When we get into the heat of the battle, when we are involved in playing the game, we have a tendency to rationalize commission costs; to flip them under a stone, to hide them from our sight. That practice can be dangerous.

On the other hand, don't let commissions interfere with your tactical and strategic actions once strategies are put into play. When there are profits to be made, take them. When you are required to get out of a strategy, *get out*. Do not consider commissions *at these points* in time, although you can consider tactics to reduce the commissions in taking these actions. Once in the game, do not let commissions interfere with the critical, tactical maneuvers that you must make during the life of your strategies.

To conclude, remember, commission costs will probably eat up 10% to 30% of your portfolio every year. Plan for them; take defensive positions to reduce them; be cost conscious—put on your "accountant's hat" and control those costs. Following these simple steps should reduce your commission costs.

28

WINNING THE MARGIN GAME

To be a COMPLEAT OPTION PLAYER, you must know how to play the margin game, and in the options market this is probably the most confusing and complex subject that you will ever encounter. Even the experts, the back office people who handle the measuring of margin requirements and maintenance requirements, have trouble determining what the margin requirement is for each type of strategy. Even the best options specialists at times have questions; so, if you become confused and lost in the maze of requirements, you are not alone.

What is Margin: What are Margin Requirements?

Many players in the options market never really have a clear understanding of what it's all about. They let their options specialist handle that problem, and they are amazed both at the figures he comes up with, and by the margin calls that they receive throughout the lives of their strategies.

Margin in the options market is *not* the same as in the stock market, where margin relates to the borrowing of money to take and maintain a stock position. In the options market, margin is *not* the borrowing of money from a brokerage house. Margin in options is a totally different concept, and because it is different, it has caused many problems.

So, clean the slates regarding your knowledge of margin requirements and margin calls, and let's talk about a new breed of cat—the margin requirements in the options market.

A margin requirement is a deposit—of cash, or collateral—that you, the investor, put up *to guarantee that you will deliver on options that you have written.*

Therefore, the only option players who should be concerned with margins are those who are *writing* options. If you are writing covered options, you have already put up your margin requirements, this requirement being the 100 shares of stock underlying that option (covering the short position that you have written). So, when you are writing covered options, we do not have too heady a problem in calculating your margin requirement.

Instead, the problem arises when we are writing naked options, or are involved in spreads, ratio hedges, or ratio spreads. In this case we are required to put up cash, or collateral, to guarantee that we will deliver if the options we have written are ever exercised; that is, you guarantee that you will make good on the option contracts you have written. This good faith deposit, if you would like to call it that, differs depending on which strategy we enter.

This deposit is required, and it is an important consideration in your strategy selection process, because it will determine your return on investment. Therefore, you want to select profitable strategies that require *little margin.*

In determining the margin requirement for each strategy, a little knowledge and a few basic rules will do the job. If figures confuse you, you might want to leave this problem for your broker.

Both cash and Treasury Bills can be used for this deposit. Treasury Bills, as we have stated before, are an excellent way for the investor to put up collateral. You can also use stocks and bonds as collateral, but only a portion of their value can be used as margin (i.e., 50% of the value of the stock).

Margin requirements are a major obstacle in the options game; make sure that you always know what your margin will be, and if you can't calculate your margin requirements, make sure somebody on your team calculates them for you before you enter a strategy. Too many option players are confused by this issue—they attempt to factor it out, just as they attempt to ignore commissions, and this habit is dangerous. You can't afford to ignore margins. They will get you one way or the other if you do.

Types of Margin Requirements

Now, let's discuss the different kinds of margin requirements. There are two basic types of margin requirements, and you must understand the difference thoroughly. They are:

1. The INITIAL margin requirement

2. The MAINTENANCE margin requirement

The *initial* margin requirement is the amount of deposit that you must put down when you *first* enter your strategy. But the second type of margin, the *maintenance* margin requirement, will probably cause you more headaches than anything else. You need to pay maintenance margin in the following situation: you have taken a position, and suddenly the underlying stock price moves against your naked option positions; now you must pay additional good faith deposits, or maintenance margin.

You must pay because the potential value of the option has increased and now you must guarantee the good faith of that position. To do that, you must deposit additional margin (cash, or Treasury Bills). You can easily calculate what the margin will be by yourself. But if you don't, your brokerage house will, and they will notify you when additional margin is required. At that time, you must immediately put up more margin to maintain that position.

Margin Requirements

Minimum margin requirements as set by the Option Exchange have changed several times since the advent of the Options Exchange in 1973. And the margin requirements will vary dramatically from one brokerage house to another. Some will hold to the minimums set up by the Option Exchange, and others have ridiculously high requirements. When selecting a broker, try to select one that sticks close to the minimum requirements that are set by the exchanges.

At this point, let's go back to discuss the initial margin requirement. Then we will look at maintenance margin requirements and discuss how to handle them.

Initial Margin Requirements

We can best analyze the initial margin requirements by looking at some of the strategies that require these good faith deposits.

1. Covered Writing

As we mentioned at the beginning of this chapter, covered writing strategies have *no* special margin requirement, because you are writing options against your underlying stock. In addition, there is an advantage to this transaction—the option proceeds (the price of the option you have written) is directly credited to your account, and you can withdraw that money as soon as you write that option, even if you have purchased the stock on margin.

For example:

XRX = Xerox

Buy 100 XRX Common Stock at 50 with 50% margin ($5,000 x 50% = $2,500) — Cost.....$2,500

Sell 1 XRX Oct 50 at 3 — Less Proceeds $300

Total Cost.....$2,200

Example 1: an On-The-Money Naked Option

Sell 1 XRX Jul 60 Put at 3
XRX Stock Price at 60
100 Shares x 60 = $6,000

$6,000 x 20% = ...$1,200
Initial Margin Requirement $1,200

Example 2: an In-The-Money Naked Option

Sell 1 XRX Jul 60 Put at 3
XRX Stock Price at 57
$5,700 x 20% = $1,140

Margin Before Adjustment		$1,140
Strike Price	60	
XRX Stock Price	– 57	
Plus	3	+ $300
Initial Margin Requirement		$1,440

Example 3: an Out-of-The-Money Naked Option

Sell 1 XRX Jul 60 Call at 3
XRX Stock Price at 57
$5,700 x 20% = $1,140

Margin Before Adjustment		$1,140
Strike Price	60	
XRX Stock Price	– 57	
Less	3	($300)
Initial Margin Requirement		$840

Example 4:
an Out-of-The-Money Index Naked Option

Sell S & P 100 Index July 370 call at 3
S & P 100 Index Price at 365
\$36,500 x 15% = \$5,475

Margin Before Adjustment		\$5,475
Strike Price	370	
S & P 100 Index Price	−365	
Less	5	(\$500)
Initial Margin Requirement		\$4,957

2. Naked Writing

The minimum initial margin requirement should be viewed in the light that many brokerage firms require that you have from \$50,000 to over \$100,000 in your account before you start naked writing. Others are more lenient, requiring smaller initial deposits before you start writing naked options, but do require that your liquid net worth be at least \$50,000. Some don't allow any naked writing at all. So, if you are an option writer, you again need to shop around for the best margin deal.

The minimum margin requirement for writing one naked stock put or naked call is 20% of the value of the 100 shares of the underlying stock. This means that you must put up enough cash or Treasury Bills to constitute a value equal to 20% of the underlying stock, in order to establish that naked position—plus the option proceeds. In addition, another segment to this margin rule exists. If the option strike price is different from the stock price, an adjustment must be made to the initial margin requirement. If the option is in-the-money (has intrinsic value), your margin requirement will increase above that 20% level. Thus each point that your option is out-of-the-money will reduce your margin requirement by $100, and each point that it is in-the-money will increase it by $100. Broad-based index options, such as the S & P 100 Index or the Major Market Index, require 15% of the value of the index, rather than 20% that applies to stocks.

For examples of these cases, please refer to Examples 2 – 4.

3. Debit Spreads

Debit spreads, where both options expire in the same month or the purchased option expires in a longer term month, have an initial margin requirement. But that requirement is only the price, or debit, that you paid for the spread. Why? Because that is the most you can lose with that spread.

For example, if you buy the IBM Oct 100 call at 3 and sell (write) the IBM Oct 105 call at 2, your cost, or debit, for this spread is 1, or $100 (3 – 2 = 1). That $100 is the most you could ever lose with this spread, plus commissions. Therefore, that should be your maximum margin requirement. But to carry out spreading activities, you must have a margin account, and to establish a margin account, you must start with an account of $2,000.

4. Credit Spreads

The margin requirement for a credit spread (with both options expiring in the same month) is the difference between the strike price of the option you buy and the option you sell, less the credit you receive. This difference is the maximum risk possible to the credit spread position. (Index options with an American exercise may have more risk due to a possible delay in assignment notification.)

For example, if you sell the OEX July 360 call for 2, and buy the OEX 365 call for 1, your credit here is 1 (2 – 1 = 1). Your margin would be 4, or $400 (365 – 360 = 5 – 1 (credit) = 4). Why? Because the most you can lose here is 4 ($400), no matter what the OEX (S & P 100 Index) does.

5. Other Strategies

The initial margin requirement for more complicated strategies, such as a ratio spread or ratio hedge, is a combination of the margin rules we have just discussed. For example, a ratio spread, where you buy one option and sell three options against that position, involves two naked options and a debit spread. So the margin would include margins for two naked options, plus the margin for one debit spread.

When you write a naked strangle, or a naked straddle, you write a put and a call on the same stock. Here, rather than having to come up with the margin for two naked options, you are only required to put up half of that margin—an advantage to these two strategies.

Maintenance Margin Requirements

Now that we have covered the initial margin requirements for each type of strategy, it is time to look at the second type of good faith deposit that is required, and that is the *maintenance* requirement. You will have maintenance requirements only if you write naked options. If your writing strategies move in the right direction, you will never be bothered with a maintenance requirement. However, as soon as one of your strategies goes astray, and even though you may not be taking any realized losses (in fact, your strategy may still be in great shape based on your profit parameters), you may receive margin maintenance calls. This means you must put up additional deposits. Why? Because the stock or index price is approaching the strike prices of your naked options.

For naked stock options, the maintenance requirement is the current premium on the option, plus 20% of the underlying stock. For naked broad-based index options (i.e., OEX), the maintenance requirement is the market price of the option, plus 10% of the underlying index value.

Keys to Winning the Margin Game

Now that we have discovered the rules of the margin game, let's look at the keys to winning this game. Margins are important to the option player because they will dictate his return on investment and may dictate the actions he will take in the midst of an option strategy.

Your maintenance margin requirement is an important determination of the freedom you will have to operate your options portfolio. You must always consider not only the initial margin requirement, but also the maximum maintenance requirement possible within the life of a strategy or an option position.

Find out the maximum amount of margin that may be required in the strategy before it reaches its bail-out points. Then you will know ahead of time exactly how much money you will have to set aside in your account to meet a potential maintenance requirement. If you don't have enough money in your account, and you cannot acquire that money, you will have to bail out before you want to, and that can be a costly process. Further, if you are forced out of strategy positions because of margin, your commission costs will really mount up. You will not be taking advantage of all the time that you spent in developing that strategy; you will be at the mercy of the moods and whims of the market, and that is one position in which the option player cannot afford to be.

You CANNOT let margin calls dictate the actions you will take in the options market. Therefore, an important rule to follow is to MAKE SURE YOU HAVE ENOUGH MARGIN TO MEET ALL MAINTENANCE REQUIREMENTS. This is the key principle to winning the margin game. If you don't follow this principle, margin calls will dictate your option life, and as soon as that occurs, you will have a short life as an options player because you will be eaten alive by commissions. You will be forced to take action long before you should, and you will be covering positions in many cases when the premiums in your naked positions are much too fat. Margin management is a skill you will need to develop to be a COMPLEAT OPTION PLAYER.

Closing Comments

If you are confused by this margin game, you are not alone. One suggestion: use your options specialist or broker to guide you in determining margins. That is what he gets paid to do. He will give you the initial margin requirement, and determine the maximum deposit that may be needed to maintain the profit parameters that you have designed into the strategy.

The Winning Option Team
RISK
GREED
MARKET MAKER
OPTION BROKERAGE
OPTION SPECIALIST
COMPUTER
COMPLEAT OPTION PLAYER
1

29

SELECTING YOUR OPTIONS TEAM

Now we come to the important task of selecting the options team which will help determine whether you win or lose the options game.

One of the most important members of your team is the options specialist who will handle your account. The selection of the options specialist is an important decision in options trading.

Why an Options Specialist?

When you start trading, an options specialist can be an indispensable member of your investment team. Unlike the case with the stock market, and with stock investment portfolios, an options portfolio demands a tremendous amount of attention, as there is more activity and surveillance involved. Consequently, your broker is a far more important member of your team than if you were merely investing in stocks or bonds. Add to this the intricacies involved in the use of listed options, the confusion over margin requirements, and the complexity and number of strategies that can be designed through the use of listed options, and you will understand why you may need a specialist. A specialist can answer many of your questions, guide you, and carry out a lot of the legwork that is needed to design and implement profitable strategies in the options market.

Even though you may be your own man or woman, a person who wishes to make his own decisions, and does not want the advice and help of a broker, the options specialist could still be an indispensable aid to your success. He can clarify margin rules for you, help monitor your portfolio, and be a "devil's advocate" for the strategies and ideas that you develop.

There is another alternative—you can have someone else manage your money, and maybe by watching what he does, you can learn something without an expensive trial and error education. There are investment managers around who do not work on commissions, they simply charge a small percentage fee based on the size of your portfolio.

However, one of the problems with using an investment manager or investment counselor is that they require large chunks of money to begin a management program, and you may not qualify. Another disadvantage is that, as a rule, investment managers specialize only in covered option writing programs, if they manage money in the options market. Although a covered option writing program should generate a decent return, you may be looking for more action, and more potential return, and therefore may wish to use some of the more inherently profitable strategies available.

Investment managers who work for fees rather than commissions cannot afford to spend a tremendous amount of time handling a portfolio, and therefore will avoid managing complicated option portfolios. If you use an investment manager, make sure he has a long track record of five to ten years.

Many investors will be tempted to try to find an options specialist to manage their options account for them. There are several major problems here. First, the options specialist earns his income by generating commissions. If you must pay full commissions for each trade, your options portfolio will not survive. Even if the options specialist gives you a discount as he manages your account, he will trade enough to make sure he gets paid well for managing your account, and the portfolio will suffer.

In addition, such brokers handle a lot of accounts, and probably will not dedicate much time to yours. Over the years in the commodity options markets, there have been many commodity brokers who advertise options managed accounts. A good guess is that 90% of those accounts have been wiped out in a short period of time. In a high risk game such as options, it is too dangerous to let someone else handle your money.

There's an old adage among poker players that says, "When you have money in the pot, play your own cards." Think of option trading the same way. Only you can give it the time, effort and commitment needed to succeed, and only you can have the responsibility. If you can't handle it, don't trade options, and never use a managed account unless you thoroughly understand options and the risk you're taking.

My advice is, "Don't use managed accounts." There's another adage that fits here: "Beware of the socialist dressed in broker's clothes; he wants to redistribute the wealth—your wealth."

Your only choice, then, is to make your own decisions and get limited aid from a commissioned options specialist who earns his bread through your commissions. As we mentioned, this is unfortunate because you and your options specialist may have conflicting interests. *You* wish to keep the commissions low, and in order for him to earn his living, *he* wishes to keep the commissions high. This is one tendency you will have to keep in line. You must control your commissions as we mentioned in Chapter 27.

We've given you a large task to complete: finding a person who can be your partner, your team member in this options game. He will take a lot of weight off of your shoulders, and should help your profit margins. He will answer all the questions that are outside the scope of this book. He will provide all the experience you do not have, and he will be a gold mine of new information, new ideas and new strategies.

Brokers To Avoid

Many an investor will say: "Well, I have a broker. I have had the same one for ten years, and he is a good broker." But this is analogous to going to your family General Practitioner for a skin ailment, instead of going to a Dermatologist.

You don't need an *all purpose* stock broker. You need a *specialist* in the options field, one who spends all his time in the options market. And, unlike calling in a medical specialist, consulting an options specialist will cost you no more than working with a general broker, as the commissions are the same—there is no additional cost for the options broker that you affiliate with.

Most stock brokers will claim that they know options pretty well. They will say that they have been dabbling for awhile. Be wary of this type of statement; it takes a tremendous amount of time and effort to become a skilled options specialist. An all purpose stock broker will not have the depth, the knowledge and the information needed to do an effective job. He has just spread himself too thin.

In the process of seeking out a true options specialist, you are going to have difficulties, because the brokerage business tends to breed *salesmen* rather than stock technicians, or options technicians. In other words, usually the salesman is far more successful in obtaining new accounts than is the truly brilliant market specialist or options specialist. The salesman has "personality," he is often able to "con" the customer into believing that he knows it all.

In many cases, the salesman sells a package presented to him by his brokerage house, especially in the larger chain brokerage firms. Therefore, you are going to have to weed out the truly competent options specialist from the salesman who merely touts the ideas put out by his brokerage house. The salesman will not do the job for you. You need the expertise of a specialist who knows what he is doing and knows his business—a good trader, a good strategist, a good technician. And you will probably have to shuffle through a few salesmen to get to that man. So what we're looking for here is not "personality plus," but "intelligence plus."

Also, avoid the broker who has jumped on the bandwagon and suddenly calls himself an OPTIONS EXPERT. Generally, he is in there to grab some of the commissions that have been highly touted in the brokerage industry, or he is a dropout from the stock market who is looking for a new method of grinding out commissions.

Learn to be leery of "active trading" options specialists. Remember, it is hard to survive in the market as a trader, and although the options specialist who does a lot of trading might be quite competent, following his habits can be dangerous.

The selection of an options specialist is as tough a job as selecting a spouse, or bringing a partner into your business, but we hope there is a lot less emotion involved in this process! You must find someone whom you feel comfortable with, and who is comfortable with you—someone with whom you can communicate. Remember, he or she is human too, and likely to make mistakes at times. You have to be willing to forgive and forget in some cases. Attempt to avoid using your options specialist as a scapegoat because this game is tough enough as it is, and we want cooperation, not hostility, in the process of getting these strategies off the ground, and building profits into your portfolio.

The options specialist is a broker who spends all his time in the options market, who has been in the options market for a long time. Therefore, he has gained every minute of experience that has been available in this options field. This kind of depth will provide you with a tremendous bank of knowledge when you need it.

How to Select an Options Specialist

One way to avoid selecting a salesman in place of an options specialist is to look at his resume. You're right! Brokers usually don't have a resume, or if they did, they would be insulted if you asked them for one. However, a few good, well directed questions, as follows, may disclose some of the important aspects of their education and background.

1. Experience

How much experience does this so-called options specialist have—not stock experience, but options experience?

How long has he been an options specialist?

What track record does he have?

The ideal specialists started when the listed options were born; they are the ones who foresaw the opportunities of this market, and were willing to stick their necks out, and commit themselves to this industry. Of course, the knowledge that you have gained through reading this text should help you to decipher the true blue, experienced specialist from the phony one, and it should not take long for you to determine whether or not he knows what he is talking about.

2. Originality and Creativity

Some big houses discourage this, but some of the smaller regional firms who still have New York Stock Exchange membership encourage this kind of attitude. Originality and creativity are two of the key attributes needed in the options market. There are so many strategies that can be designed in the options market, and so many ways of doing the same thing that the options market is a cornucopia of opportunities for the creative person. The creative and original go wild in the options market because there are so many new and imaginative strategies that can be designed—new and inventive ways of using margin and reducing commissions and improving profits. What you need on your options team is at least one creative person to trade ideas with you, to look for pitfalls in potential strategies, and to help you work out the complexities of the margin rules and the trading schemes that confront you as you play the game.

3. Mathematics Orientation

Mathematics and statistics are excellent prerequisites for entrance into the options markets. You might want to look for an options specialist who has a math orientation, if this is not your forte.

Selecting the Option Brokerage House

Once you have selected what you feel are the prime candidates to represent your options portfolio, it is then time to look at the second criterion, the selection of the brokerage house.

There are several things to consider when attempting to select your brokerage house: trading facilities, bookkeeping facilities, and an avenue to the floor of the Exchange. Normally, an extremely competent options specialist will be affiliated with a brokerage house which meets many of the needs of the option player. It will be a brokerage house that caters to options, one that has good margin requirements, and that provides a lot of options support. Your primary guide to identifying which brokerage house with which to work is your options specialist.

Before you settle that question, let's look at some of the other factors that you will want to investigate before you decide which brokerage house will service your account.

Besides commissions, the most important consideration that you should review is the brokerage house's margin requirements. To generate a sufficient profit in this game, you must have the best margin requirements available in the market. Consequently, you should try to stay with brokerage houses which maintain close to the minimum margin requirements set by the Exchange. Some firms today have moved in this direction, and are using these minimums, but there are many that do not, and these are the firms that you should avoid.

The following are aspects to investigate in choosing a firm:

1. **Trading Facilities**

   Does the firm have a direct telephone line to the floor of the Exchange?

How long does it take to get off an execution?

What types of orders will this firm accept? (In many cases, some contingency orders will not be accepted by certain firms.)

2. **Commissions**

What kind of commissions does this firm charge?

What kind of discount will you get for option trades?

What is the minimum commission for an option trade?

3. **Services**

How much research and development do they generate for you, not in the area of stocks, but in the area of optionable stock?

Will they provide you with charts, or with an accessibility to technical charts?

How well do they handle your bookkeeping problems?

4. **Computers**

What kind of computer services do they provide for the option trader?

Do they provide any kind of computer augmented information on a daily basis for their customers?

When looking at different computer systems that each brokerage house provides, determine whether or not the strategy systems that are built into the computer systems are in-house or nationwide. Many of the large brokerage houses use a nationwide computer service which generates the same strategies to all their brokerage firms throughout the country. Unfortunately, such a widespread distribution of data nullifies the information that is provided before you can ever get to the floor of the Exchange, rendering such information almost worthless. On the other hand, a small brokerage house, which has in-house computer software, generates unique strategies which are distributed only to that house, and these can be a real advantage to the option player.

Again, even though you may not find all the advantages we have mentioned in a brokerage house, if you can find a competent specialist, take him. Some of the small disadvantages you may encounter in the brokerage house will be far offset by the aid and help you will receive from your man on the street. But remember, getting big discounts on your commissions is your top priority, especially after you have gained some trading experience. You will be dead in the water if you pay too much for commissions.

To conclude, as we mentioned in the chapter on commissions, support from your brokerage house and from your options specialist is more important in this options game than it ever was in the stock market. With a competent options specialist, you will get through this complex and confusing jungle and will reap the many profits that are available in this options game.

30

TOOLS NEEDED FOR PROFESSIONAL PLAY

Now that you have a good feel for the tactics necessary for effective option trading, let's look at some of the aids that are in the toolbox of the professional option player.

1. Your Daily Newspaper

Most major daily newspapers provide the option prices for shorter term options on the Options Exchange. *Investor's Business Daily* provides the best display of prices, listed according to the alphabetical order of the underlying stock. *Investor's Business Daily* also provides the volume—the number of options traded for each standardized option class. This information is not available in any other daily newspaper. No prices will be available for options that don't trade on a specific day. But these options still have bid and asked prices, as do longer term options that are not listed in the paper. To get prices on these options, just call your broker.

How do you make use of the newspaper? It keeps you in touch with the options market, is an indispensable aid for monitoring your positions, and it is your resource document for developing a strategy. From the data in the newspaper's options listing, you will derive many of your strategies.

Try to collect the daily prices from this newspaper and keep them in a looseleaf notebook, in a file, or some place where you can have easy access to the prices for the past three months. This gives you a feel for the way the option prices have been behaving over the last few weeks and months so that you can more nearly estimate whether or not option prices for specific stocks are overpriced, underpriced, or normally priced at any point in time. This will greatly aid you in comparing strategies and anticipating what option prices will be in the next three to six months. These prices will give you a good feel for the options market, and are an important intuitive aid as you play the game.

To recapitulate—your first major tools are your daily newspaper, and a collection of option prices; these will be indispensable in helping you to design, implement and monitor option strategies.

2. Option Normal Value Tables

The second aid, one that you must also have to be competitive in this options market (if you do not have a computer), is your Option Normal Value Tables (see Appendix). These tables tell you what the price of an option should be at any one point in time, on any week in the life of that option. I have provided you with what I feel is a reasonable guide, a set of Normal Value Tables for stocks which have average volatility. These tables will be indispensable in the operation of your options portfolio, in the design of your strategies, in monitoring your strategies, and in telling you what will happen in the future if certain changes occur in the underlying stock prices of your strategies.

The market makers on the Options Exchanges receive a printout every morning which provides the fair values for all options on the Exchange. So, in order to be competitive, you

THE NORMAL VALUE OPTION TABLES FORETELL OPTION PRICES IN THE FUTURE

need to have the same information they have. You must know whether or not an option is over or underpriced in order for you to maintain a competitive edge with the market makers and professional players on the floor of the Exchange.

If you really get serious about option trading, you should have a computer and a pricing program, such as *Option Master®*.[11]

3. Stock Volatility Tables

Measuring the volatility of the underlying stocks is also critical to your success. You should know the volatility of your stocks backwards, forwards, and upside down. The formula for identifying the volatility of a stock price has been provided in Chapter 8. This formula gives you a feel for the volatility of a stock, but a much more accurate method is to use a pricing program such as *Option Master®*, where a 10-week to 20-week volatility should be measured. In addition, several publications provide a stock's volatility. One is *The Put and Call Tactician*, published by the Institute for Options Research, Inc. Once you have measured the volatility, set up a table that shows the price volatility of the stocks that you are monitoring. This will be an excellent reference guide for you in determining which option strategies you will select.

4. Stock Price Charts

Another aid to understanding the past price behavior of a stock is the stock charts—graphs that plot out the price action of stocks on a daily, weekly and monthly basis. These charts will be valuable in helping you to better understand the underlying stock that you will be working with as you design option strategies.

There are many stock chart services available; some are quite expensive, so you may wish to use the services provided by

[11] *Option Master®* is available from Institute for Options Research, Inc., P.O. Box 6586, Lake Tahoe, NV 89449.

your own brokerage house, or by your options specialist.

There are also excellent references in the library and you can easily update your charts each week using their copier to copy the reference material.

When deciding which type of charts to order, or to use, we strongly suggest that you work with daily stock price charts, not weekly or monthly ones. Remember, the life of an option is very short. We are not working with months and years; we are working with hours and days. An excellent chart book service is the *Daily Graphs Option Guide,* put out by the publishers of *Investor's Business Daily.*

5. Strategy Forms

Now that you have some of the basics for designing strategies, you need some format to map out these strategies, and we strongly suggest a uniform, formalized *strategy sheet* where you can put all your strategies down on paper—a worksheet of some type where you can map out your strategies, and easily compare the different types of strategies that you are considering.

I have used several forms in this text and include these forms in this chapter for your use. There are many types that you can design, and the design of your strategy sheet will depend on what approach you will take in this options market. A strategy sheet will force you to put your strategies down in black and white. It will also provide you with a record of which strategies were available, which ones you selected, and how they performed. It makes an excellent reference to review to find out where you made your errors, and what the actual outcomes were, as compared to the outcomes that you had projected in your preliminary worksheet.

You will also want to keep a *position record* to keep track of what positions you have at any one time.

6. Commission Charts

In Chapter 27, we talked about the importance of commissions, stressing the fact that you must be very cost conscious and watch your commissions like a paranoid accountant. To aid you in planning exactly what you are going to be paying, and when you are going to pay it, we have provided two commission charts in this chapter. One chart breaks down commissions by cost per commission, and the other rates commissions on a quantity basis. The commissions charged in the charts are typical commissions at a full service house. You should never pay such high commissions. Make sure to get a big discount off these commissions once you select a broker. Create a chart similar to the charts we present in this chapter. Then it will be easy to determine the cost of any trade or strategy quickly and you will be able to tell how many options you will need to buy or sell.

7. A Bookkeeping System

Another required piece of information that all option players and investors must have is some kind of a bookkeeping system, possibly of the type that you are now using for your stock portfolio. You need a system that will record the trades and provide a record for your own surveillance system, in effect, charting your own track record, and also—you guessed it—providing a record for the IRS to determine taxes you must pay.

You might also consider using a set of index cards and placing each active strategy on a card. When the strategy is terminated or expires, you may wish to record how much profit or loss you made on each card. In this way, you can gauge what kind of strategies are generating what kind of profits, and also, you can

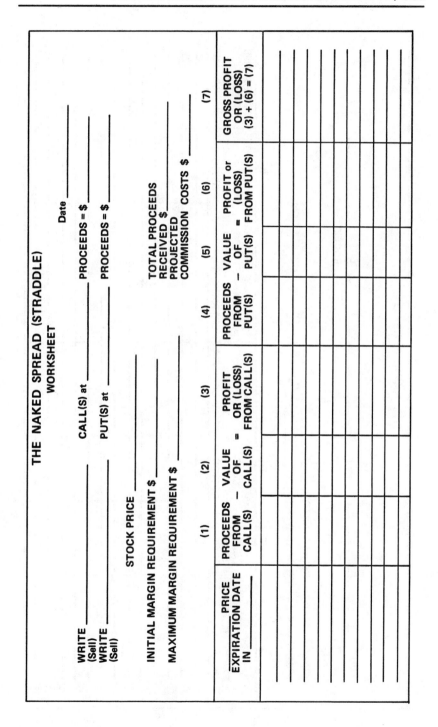

THE NAKED SPREAD (STRADDLE)
WORKSHEET

Date ____________

WRITE (Sell) ____________________ CALL(S) at ____________ PROCEEDS = $ ____________

WRITE (Sell) ____________________ PUT(S) at ____________ PROCEEDS = $ ____________

STOCK PRICE ________________

INITIAL MARGIN REQUIREMENT $ ______________

MAXIMUM MARGIN REQUIREMENT $ ______________

TOTAL PROCEEDS RECEIVED $ ______________

PROJECTED COMMISSION COSTS $ ________

________ PRICE EXPIRATION DATE IN ________	(1) PROCEEDS FROM CALL(S)	–	(2) VALUE OF CALL(S)	=	(3) PROFIT OR (LOSS) FROM CALL(S)	(4) PROCEEDS FROM PUT(S)	–	(5) VALUE OF PUT(S)	=	(6) PROFIT or (LOSS) FROM PUT(S)	(7) GROSS PROFIT OR (LOSS) (3) + (6) = (7)

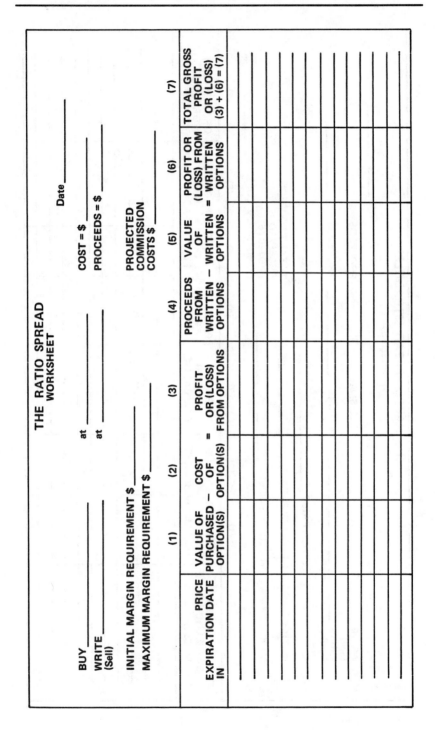

THE RATIO SPREAD
WORKSHEET

Date __________

BUY __________ at __________ COST = $ __________

WRITE (Sell) __________ at __________ PROCEEDS = $ __________

INITIAL MARGIN REQUIREMENT $ __________

MAXIMUM MARGIN REQUIREMENT $ __________

PROJECTED COMMISSION COSTS $ __________

PRICE IN EXPIRATION DATE	(1) VALUE OF PURCHASED OPTION(S)	−	(2) COST OF OPTION(S)	=	(3) PROFIT OR (LOSS) FROM OPTIONS	(4) PROCEEDS FROM WRITTEN OPTIONS	−	(5) VALUE OF WRITTEN OPTIONS	=	(6) PROFIT OR (LOSS) FROM WRITTEN OPTIONS	(7) TOTAL GROSS PROFIT OR (LOSS) (3) + (6) = (7)

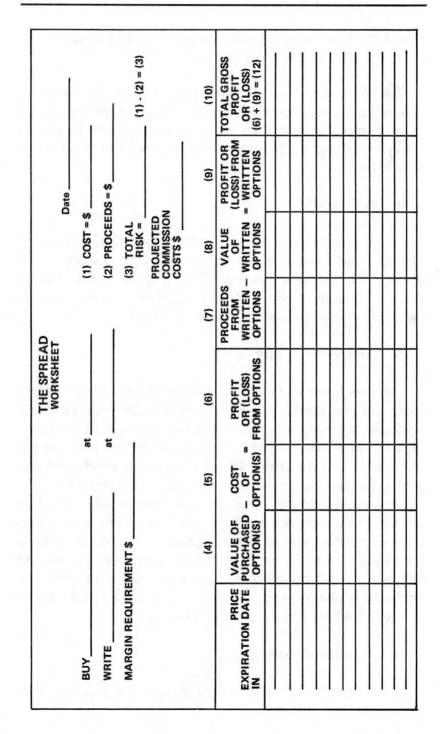

THE SPREAD
WORKSHEET

Date ______________

BUY ______________ at ______________

WRITE ______________ at ______________

MARGIN REQUIREMENT $ ______________

(1) COST = $ ______________

(2) PROCEEDS = $ ______________

(3) TOTAL RISK = ______________ (1) - (2) = (3)

PROJECTED COMMISSION COSTS $ ______________

PRICE EXPIRATION DATE IN	(4) VALUE OF PURCHASED OPTION(S)	– (5) COST OF OPTION(S)	= (6) PROFIT OR (LOSS) FROM OPTIONS	(7) PROCEEDS FROM WRITTEN OPTIONS	– (8) VALUE OF WRITTEN OPTIONS	= (9) PROFIT OR (LOSS) FROM WRITTEN OPTIONS	(10) TOTAL GROSS PROFIT OR (LOSS) (6) + (9) = (12)

keep a more meaningful record for your portfolio (and for your own edification).

So, some sort of simple bookkeeping system is necessary, both as a matter of good management, and as a matter of meeting the requirements of the IRS. Your accountant may be able to help you in designing the system if you are at a loss to determine how to set it up.

8. A Calendar

Another tool which is simple, but is something that all option players must have, is a calendar—one that spells out in red letters when options will expire. Believe it or not, investors forget that their options are sitting there wasting away; some investors even lose sight of the options' expiration date!

9. An Options Diary

Another important tool which we recommend is an options diary. All you need is a notebook, which lists your successful strategies, tells why they were successful, and records what kind of return on investment you received. Then don't forget to put down a list of your errors. Where did you go wrong, did you get too greedy, did you ask for too much, did you take off one leg and hang onto the other? In other words, when did you stray from the beaten path? Remember, the player who makes the fewest errors will have the highest profits. Normally he is the player who is not afraid to pull the trigger every time, and although he will make errors, he makes fewer than most. The only way to eliminate errors is to study your past performance to find out where you are making mistakes.

10. A Personal Computer

Even though a computer is not necessary, it will sure help.

**COMMISSION SCHEDULE
PER OPTION ORDER**

NUMBER OF OPTIONS IN ORDER

Price of Options	1	2	3	4	5	6	7	8	9	10	15	20	25	30	35	40	45	50
$1	25.00	26.60	33.90	41.20	48.50	55.80	63.10	70.40	77.70	85.00	111.50	138.00	164.50	189.00	213.50	238.00	262.50	287.00
2	25.00	29.20	37.80	46.40	55.00	63.60	72.20	80.80	89.40	98.00	129.00	158.00	182.00	216.00	245.00	274.00	303.00	332.00
3	25.00	31.80	41.70	51.60	61.50	71.40	81.30	91.20	100.30	109.00	142.50	176.00	209.50	243.00	276.50	310.00	343.50	377.00
4	25.00	34.40	45.60	56.80	68.00	79.20	89.20	98.80	108.40	118.00	156.00	194.00	232.00	270.00	308.00	346.00	394.00	422.00
5	25.00	37.00	49.50	62.00	74.50	85.00	95.50	106.00	116.50	127.00	169.50	212.00	254.50	297.00	339.50	392.00	417.00	452.00
6	25.00	39.60	52.40	67.20	79.00	90.40	101.80	113.20	124.60	136.00	183.00	230.00	277.00	324.00	368.00	406.00	444.00	482.00
7	25.00	42.20	57.30	71.20	83.50	95.80	108.10	120.40	133.70	145.00	196.50	248.00	299.50	348.00	389.00	430.00	468.00	502.00
8	25.00	44.80	61.20	74.80	88.00	101.20	114.40	127.60	140.80	154.00	210.00	266.00	322.00	366.00	410.00	450.00	486.00	522.00
9	25.00	47.40	64.30	78.40	92.50	106.60	120.70	134.80	148.90	163.00	223.50	284.00	337.00	384.00	428.00	466.00	504.00	542.00
10	25.00	50.00	67.00	82.00	97.00	112.00	127.00	142.00	157.00	172.00	237.00	302.00	352.00	402.00	442.00	482.00	522.00	562.00
11	26.30	52.60	69.70	85.60	101.00	117.40	133.30	149.20	165.10	181.00	250.50	314.00	367.00	414.00	456.00	498.00	540.00	582.00
12	27.60	55.20	72.40	89.20	106.00	122.80	139.60	156.40	173.20	190.00	264.00	326.00	382.00	426.00	470.00	514.00	558.00	602.00
13	28.90	57.40	75.10	92.80	110.50	128.20	145.90	163.60	181.30	199.00	277.50	338.00	392.00	438.00	484.00	530.00	576.00	622.00
14	30.20	59.20	77.80	96.40	115.00	133.60	152.20	170.80	189.40	208.00	288.00	350.00	402.00	450.00	498.00	546.00	594.00	642.00
15	31.50	61.00	80.50	100.00	119.50	139.00	158.50	178.60	197.50	217.00	297.00	362.00	412.00	462.00	512.00	562.00	612.00	662.00
20	38.00	70.00	94.00	118.00	142.00	166.00	190.00	214.00	238.00	262.00	342.00	402.00	462.00	522.00	582.00	642.00	702.00	762.00
25	44.50	79.00	107.50	130.00	164.50	193.00	221.50	250.00	271.00	292.00	372.00	442.00	512.00	582.00	652.00	722.00	792.00	862.00
30	49.00	88.00	121.00	154.00	187.00	220.00	250.00	274.00	298.00	322.00	402.00	482.00	562.00	642.00	722.00	802.00	882.00	962.00
35	53.50	97.00	134.50	172.00	209.50	244.00	271.00	298.00	322.00	342.00	432.00	522.00	612.00	702.00	792.00	882.00	972.00	1062.00
40	58.00	106.00	148.00	190.00	232.00	262.00	292.00	318.00	340.00	362.00	462.00	562.00	662.00	762.00	862.00	962.00	1062.00	1162.00
45	62.50	115.00	161.50	208.00	247.00	280.00	310.00	334.00	358.00	382.00	492.00	602.00	712.00	822.00	932.00	1042.00	1052.00	1262.00
50	65.00	124.00	175.00	226.00	262.00	298.00	324.00	350.00	376.00	402.00	522.00	642.00	762.00	882.00	1002.00	1122.00	1242.00	1362.00

Based on minimum CBOE commissions charged before May 1, 1975.

BASE COMMISSION COST PER OPTION

Number of Options in Order	OPTION PRICE 1	2	3	4	5	6	7	8	9	10	15	20	25	30	40	50
1	25.00	25.00	25.00	25.00	25.00	25.00	25.00	25.00	25.00	25.00	31.50	38.00	44.50	49.00	58.00	65.00
2	13.30	14.80	15.90	17.20	18.50	19.80	21.10	22.40	23.70	25.00	30.50	35.00	39.00	44.00	53.00	62.00
3	11.30	12.60	13.90	15.20	16.50	17.80	19.10	20.40	21.43	22.33	26.83	31.33	35.83	40.33	49.33	58.33
4	10.30	11.60	12.90	14.20	15.50	16.80	17.80	18.70	19.60	20.50	25.00	29.50	34.00	38.50	47.90	56.50
5	9.70	11.00	12.30	13.60	14.90	15.80	16.70	17.60	18.50	19.40	23.90	28.40	32.90	37.40	46.40	52.40
6	9.30	10.60	11.90	13.20	14.16	15.06	15.96	16.86	17.76	18.60	23.16	27.66	32.16	36.60	43.66	49.66
7	9.00	10.31	11.61	12.74	13.64	14.54	15.44	16.34	17.24	18.14	22.64	27.22	31.64	35.71	41.71	46.28
8	8.80	10.10	11.40	12.35	13.25	14.15	15.05	15.95	16.85	17.75	22.32	26.75	31.25	34.25	39.75	43.75
9	8.63	9.93	11.14	12.04	12.94	13.84	14.74	15.64	16.54	17.44	21.94	26.44	30.11	33.11	37.84	44.77
10	8.50	9.20	10.90	11.80	12.70	13.60	14.50	15.40	16.30	17.20	21.70	26.20	29.20	32.20	36.20	40.00
15	7.43	8.60	9.50	10.40	11.30	12.20	13.10	14.00	14.90	15.80	19.80	22.80	24.80	26.20	30.80	34.80
20	6.90	7.90	8.80	9.70	10.60	11.50	12.40	13.30	14.20	15.10	18.10	20.10	22.10	24.10	28.10	32.10
25	6.58	7.48	8.38	9.28	10.18	11.09	11.98	12.88	13.42	14.08	16.48	18.48	20.48	22.48	26.48	30.40
30	6.30	7.20	8.10	9.00	9.90	10.80	11.60	12.20	12.80	13.40	16.06	17.40	19.40	21.40	25.40	29.40
35	6.10	7.00	7.90	8.80	9.70	10.51	11.11	11.71	12.12	12.62	14.62	16.62	18.62	20.62	24.62	28.62
40	5.95	6.85	7.75	8.65	9.55	10.15	10.75	11.25	11.65	12.05	14.05	16.05	18.05	20.05	24.05	28.05
50	5.74	6.64	7.54	8.44	9.04	9.64	10.04	10.43	10.84	11.24	13.24	15.24	17.24	19.24	23.24	27.24

Listed options priced under $1 normally receive the following commission charges:

(a) $5 per option for options priced between 7/16 and 15/16.
(b) $2.50 per option for options priced between 1/16 and 6/16.
(c) Minimum commission charge per order will run from $20 to $25.

And now you can buy a personal computer for a few hundred dollars. So you should be able to get this investment back many times by improved performance in the option markets. The computer's most important function in the options market is to measure the fair value of an option.

In addition, a computer program such as *Option Master®* will calculate a stock's price volatility and will measure your probability of profit when you buy or sell an option or enter an option strategy.

A computer will also enable you to get option quotes throughout the day, will help you identify option strategies and will help you do your options bookkeeping.

Finally, remember most market makers use computers. To be competitive, you should have a computer, along with a good option pricing program.

Okay, you've now been given all the necessary tools that are needed for professional play. Actually, this list is not very long. Make sure that you *use* all these aids and your probability of success will be high. If you just place them in your tool kit and never use them, well, I hope you are lucky, because you'll be substituting luck for method and training.

31

OPTION PRICING: THE KEY TO SUCCESS

The Forgotten Secret

In the options game, there is one secret to success. This secret is followed religiously by the market makers and specialists on the floors of the option exchanges. Yet most investors do not follow this important action. Surprisingly, this simple secret provides an unusual advantage in the options market that is not available in other investment markets.

Unlocking the Secret

The secret to successful investing always is to identify an investment that is priced below its *true value*. But what is the true value of a share of IBM stock, or one ounce of gold, or a two-bedroom house? Finding assets that are being sold at less than their true worth is a goal of every investor, yet in most cases the tools to measure worth are difficult to find, or non-existent.

Consequently, the majority of investors and analysts selecting undervalued investments fumble with systems that are founded on superstition and wishful thinking. But the *options* market is the one place where the tools to scientifically analyze true value exist, and are available to every investor.

The unique nature of listed put and call options enables their true values to be determined by statistical and computer analysis, thus allowing you to spot genuine bargains.

Why Options?

The value of a stock option is dependent on price changes in the underlying common stock against which the option is trading. Naturally, the majority of option investors purchase options based on their assessment of the underlying common stock. For example, usually investors will buy calls on stocks that are priced below what they feel is their true value, or when they believe that the common stock price will move up in the present market environment for a variety of prevalent reasons. Although the true value of a common stock is hard to determine, investors are always trying.

Some use systems of fundamental analysis—studying corporate earnings, net worth, market shares, etc. Others use technical analysis—studying past price movements.

Evidence indicates that fundamental analysis is helpful only in determining long-term potential movements, but in the short term, a stock's price is influenced by investors' emotions, unpredictable economic conditions, unexpected news events, and other factors that tend to cause the price to move in a random pattern.

If we can assume that short-term stock price moves are truly random—and the body of statistical and scientific evidence supports this position—then we have a basis for measuring the real worth of individual options. Nevertheless, investors believe in their ability to predict short-term price movements, and are constantly wagering on their ability to do so. I believe there are some services and statistical measures that can outperform the random market in the short term, but short-term stock price actions do approach randomness.

Therefore, the intelligent way to invest in the options market is to assume that the market is random in the short term, and make your moves accordingly.

It is the random nature of stock price movements, coupled with investors' ignorance of this phenomenon, that provides the foundation for locating undervalued or overvalued options on a scientific basis.

Listed options have a very short life. This makes their values highly dependent on short-term random moves in the prices of the underlying stocks. If you are able to determine the degree of volatility of a stock (the average amount the price fluctuates up or down in a given time), and you can assume that the price fluctuations are random, you can apply statistical and computer analysis to determine what the probability is that the price will be higher or lower at some particular time in the future.

With this information, it is then relatively easy to determine the *proper price* for an option, and to determine whether its present price is too high or too low.

A Matter of Odds

Investors have a hard time understanding the pricing of options. When an investor identifies an option as being underpriced, and later sees that option expire worthless, he then assumes he was wrong, and that the option was not underpriced, for it became worthless. But to understand why an option is underpriced or overpriced, you must understand the laws of probability and odds.

When we say an option is underpriced, we mean in the *long run* if you buy an option over and over again and hold it for the same exact period of time, your overall result would show a gross profit on that position. Of course, that is only a theoretical profit, because there is no way to buy the same option under the same conditions thousands of times.

But many option players need immediate gratification. If they lose on various options, they begin to think that the price of the option means nothing, and they resort to looking only at the underlying stock's prospects, and forget the option's price—a faulty approach to the options market.

Understanding that you can lose in the short term but win in the long term is as simple as flipping a coin. For example, when you flip a coin, you have a 50% chance that the coin will turn up heads. Flip it 10 times, and you might see heads come up only two times, or it might even come up seven or eight times, rather than five times, which are the *true odds*. When you flip it 1,000 times, however, the probability is that it will turn up heads very close to 500 times. The greater the number of flips, the higher the probability that the results will be 50% heads and 50% tails.

This same phenomenon is true in all situations where random events are concerned, such as the options market. When you buy options that are underpriced, according to the laws of probability you may lose many times, but in the long run, you will win.

The Secret: Scientifically Pricing Options

The secret then to successful options trading is to buy options that are underpriced and sell options that are overpriced. Better yet, in the options market you have the rare ability to measure the true value of your investment (options) through scientific means.

But if the real worth of any option can be quickly and clearly measured, then why are all options not priced at their true worth in the options market? Like any investment market, the options market is filled with investors and speculators who think they can predict the unpredictable. They believe they can predict short-term moves in the stock market (but most of them can't). Therefore, they purchase options based only on the merits of the underlying stock, without bothering to look at the price of the option itself. In addition, the emotion and uncertainty present in the stock market is magnified in the options market. Options, being highly leveraged instruments, exaggerate the emotional optimism or pessimism of the market, causing option prices to vary widely from their true worth.

The Key to the Treasure Chest

The key to determining the true worth of a put or call revolves around identifying the volatility of the underlying stock. Most common stocks usually have a consistent volatility pattern over the years. By measuring the average price volatility for the past three to five years, an estimate of future volatility can be obtained. If you can combine your longer-term volatility estimate with a short-term measure of volatility, you can better pinpoint the future volatility of the underlying stock.

The more time spent in estimating the price volatility of the underlying stock, the more accurate you will be in determining the true worth of a put or call.

The Art of Pricing Options

If pricing options is the key to success in the options game, how can you as an investor scientifically measure whether an option is over- or underpriced? The professionals and market makers on the options exchanges use computers to determine whether options are over- or underpriced, and they usually use a pricing formula called the Black & Scholes Model, or a variation of that pricing formula. The Black & Scholes pricing formula estimates what the market price of an option should be, and it does this by determining the cost of creating a perfect hedge in the market, using options and stock.

The Black & Scholes model provides a good estimate of the true worth of an option, but because it weights interest rates, it in some cases distorts that true worth when interest rates are high.

From a practical point of view, don't be alarmed by the mathematics of measuring the proper price of an option. Many of the established methods for scientifically pricing options can be followed, and any method is better than none. The important consideration is that you make some attempt to determine whether an option is over- or underpriced. Here are some suggested ways to handle the pricing of options.

First, approach the pricing of options the way you approach the pricing of a used car. When you buy a used car, you should have a *blue book* in hand to measure what the proper price should be. In the options market, when you attempt to find some puts or calls for purchase, you of course select stocks that you feel are the best prospects for option buying.

Your next step is to identify what are the best options available for option buying. Here, to ensure that you are going to be buying the best priced options, you need a blue book, and that blue book could be the Normal Value Tables at the back of this text. These tables can be used to make an estimate of what the price of an option should be. After looking up your chosen option in the tables, you then compare it to its actual price in the market today. This is a broad-brush, simple and fast method of pricing options.

Better yet, you can compete with the professionals by using your own home computer to measure whether or not an option's price is undervalued. *Option Master*®* can be used on a Macintosh®* or IBM* computer, and does a sophisticated job of pricing options. This is how you can become far more exact in measuring the real worth of an option price.

There is another alternative, and that is to use option advisory services, such as the *The Trester Compleat Option Report**, where much of the work in identifying underpriced options has been done for you. Many man-hours are spent identifying the best underpriced options in the market. But, be wary of advisory services that recommend options, and ignore option *prices*.

Whether you use an advisory service, your computer, or this book to price those options, some attempt must be made to make sure that the options you are purchasing are, at the very least, fairly priced; better yet, that the options are underpriced if you are buying options, and overpriced if you are writing options.

Just remember, the difference between a professional and an amateur in the options market is determined by the amount of time spent pricing options. Regardless of what you think the underlying stock will do in the future, don't buy an option if it is overpriced, or write an option if it is underpriced. When you

**Option Master*® and *The Trester Compleat Option Report* are available from the Institute for Options Research, Inc., P.O. Box 6586, Lake Tahoe, NV 89449. *Option Master*® is a registered trademark of Institute for Options Research, Inc. All other trade names referenced are the proprietary registered trademark of the respective manufacturer.

buy overpriced options, you are no different from the gambler who throws his dollars into the slot machines in Las Vegas. In the end, you will lose.

32

PREPARING FOR ACTION

The Psychological Battlefield

As you prepare to enter the options game, your greatest obstacle to success probably will be the psychological battlefield that you must survive. To be a winner, most novice option traders think that all they need is a little luck—a few big winners right off the bat and they'll be on Easy Street. It's just a matter of being at the right place at the right time, or so they think. Of course, they couldn't be more wrong.

Proper money management is just as important as using the right strategy, probably more so. Most people fail to realize that. For example, if they just buy options (even if they are theoretically undervalued), they could have a long losing streak and, if they're not careful, lose their entire investment capital. Most people aren't careful. Typically, after a few losses traders become hesitant—they take profits quickly so they can't hit any home runs, and they run up their commissions by over-trading. Their goose was cooked before they began, because they were emotionally unprepared to trade options.

Your foremost opponent when you trade options is not the exchange and its members, nor the other traders. It's your emotions, and if you can't control them, you're going to be licked. Don't get down about it though, most money managers have the same problem.

The Game Plan

The best way to keep your emotions out of your investment decisions is to have a well-defined game plan. Write it down and stick to it.

1. Decide how much money you are willing to risk in options during the next twelve months, and don't blow it all in the first few months. This is really important—plan to spread your option trades over the entire year. Can you risk that much money? Is the money you could lose more important to you than the money you could make? Would a loss affect your lifestyle? If you answer "yes," you shouldn't be trading at all. You also should trade as if options are chips on a poker table—if you're afraid to lose, you will.

2. Plan to diversify, both over time and position. If you spread your purchases over one year, for example, and buy both puts and calls on several stocks, you won't be wiped out if the stock market is dull for months on end (it can happen). Also, you'll have a better chance of being around when things pick up and options pay off. Always invest the same dollar amount in each position. If you do, you'll eliminate the risk of having small investments in the winners and big investments in the losers.

You should also diversify by using different option strategies. Buying cheap options pays off about 20% to 25% of the time, so, if that's all you do, you're going to have some long losing streaks. That's why you should also use debit and credit spreads to increase your probability of profiting. Theoretically, these strategies usually have more risk than option buying. But in practice, the amount of loss is usually less because you lose so often buying options.

The best game plan will be of no use unless you have both the patience and discipline to stick to it through thick and thin, to play it on paper until you understand how options work, to wait for the home runs, to invest gradually, and to use stop-loss orders where they are called for (always when writing options).

Don't Overdose

When you start trading options, go easy. Start by trading on paper. Then gradually enter the market. Just buy a few cheap options, or a few credit or debit spreads, so you risk very little. You will make mistakes when you first start trading, so don't put much on the line. Then you will pay a small tuition for learning how to trade. Treat your first few months of trading as exhibition season, or for baseball fans, spring training.

Your greatest danger is to overdose when you trade options. After some initial successes, the novice investor then plunges into the market, taking far too much risk, and usually losing all. Or the investor gets a strong feeling about a stock or the market and plunges—usually when an investor has a very strong feeling about the market, he is wrong.

The most successful professional traders have stated that the major mistake they have made was to plunge, risking much or all of their assets. DON'T PLUNGE!

Your biggest danger in the options market is to take too big an options position and overdose on options. They can be hazardous to your financial health!

33

THE PAST, THE PRESENT, AND THE FUTURE

In the first edition of *The Compleat Option Player* (1977), I forecast an explosion of new option products, including option exchanges across the globe, the advent of commodity options, options on over-the-counter stocks, and spreads that are sold as individual options. All of these forecasts have come to pass.

Commodity Options

A comprehensive treatment of commodity options is beyond the scope of this book. But, *options are options,* whether they are stock, index or commodity options. They act the same way, are theoretically priced in a similar manner, and the same type of strategies can be designed with each type of option. Once you thoroughly understand how to use stock options, there is a tremendous amount of learning transferable to commodity and other futures options.

Presently, there are options available on commodities, such as wheat, corn, soybeans, soybean oil, cattle, hogs, pork bellies, cocoa, coffee, orange juice, sugar, lumber, cotton, gold, silver, copper, crude oil, and heating oil. In addition, there are options on financial futures contracts such as Treasury Bonds, Treasury

Bills, Eurodollars and the foreign currencies, such as the British pound, the German mark, the Japanese yen, and the Swiss franc. All of these options are traded on the floors of the commodity exchanges, such as the Chicago Board of Trade.

Futures options, like index options, are options on much larger contracts than stock options. For example, an option on soybeans is an option on a future contract of 5,000 bushels of soybeans. If soybeans are priced at $6.00 a bushel, then that contract is valued at $30,000 (5,000 x $6 = $30,000). So you may have much greater leverage with commodity options. Each type of commodity option usually expires on a different day, unlike stock options that all expire at the same time of the month, and commodity options usually expire in the month before the underlying futures contract is due for delivery (currency options are one exception).

Commodity options are more difficult to trade than stock options, for the small investor doesn't have some of the safeguards that are available to the investor on the stock option trading floor (i.e., limits on the spread between the bid and asked price). In addition, commodity options have higher commissions because rarely can you set a quantity discount as you can with stock options. Each commodity option commission is a round-trip commission, meaning you pay up front both for entering and exiting the trade. But commodity options do provide some interesting opportunities for the option player using the strategies covered in this text.

Before you begin trading commodity options, make sure to do your homework and thoroughly understand underlying futures contracts.

Capped Index Options

Capped index options are index spreads that are bought and sold as individual options. Option players love to trade index options. However, index options are usually overpriced and lack that extra level of volatility that individual stocks possess. Yet, if you write naked index options, you then take on the type of limitless risk that was strongly demonstrated during the crash of 1987.

Now there is a better way to trade index options.

The CBOE and AMEX have recently introduced *Capped Index Options*. If you are an option buyer, they are the same as debit spreads; if you're a seller or writer, they are like entering a credit spread. The difference between a capped option and a regular call or put is that your maximum gain (if you're a buyer) or loss (if you're a seller) is limited.

Here's an example:

Capped options on the Major Market Index (XMI) have a 20-point cap. If an XMI capped March 325 call sold for 6-1/2 when the Index was 315, and you bought the option for 6-1/2, your maximum profit would be 13-1/2, the cap (20) less your cost (6-1/2). If the XMI closes at or above 345, the strike price plus the 20-point cap, the call will automatically be exercised, the call owner will receive 20 ($2,000), and the person who sold the option must pay the same amount.

There are also capped options on the Institutional Index (XII), which measures 75 stocks that are the most widely held by institutions. XII capped options also have a 20-point cap.

The S & P 100 Index (OEX) has capped options as does the S & P 500 Index (SPX). Both have 30-point caps.

Since capped options duplicate debit spreads, they cost less than an outright index option purchase. Actually, the automatic exercise feature makes them even better than debit spreads, because they pay off as soon as the index closes at or above the cap. With regular index option debit spreads, you usually have to wait until the options expire to generate the maximum profit. That could be months away.

Capped options have other advantages over debit spreads. First, they cost less to trade. Debit spreads require the purchase and sale of two options; you only need to buy one capped option to have the same effect. Second, it's easier to get a good execution with capped options.

While capped options are better than debit spreads for buyers, sellers will find that they're not as good as credit spreads because of automatic exercise.

How To Use Capped Index Options

Capped options make an excellent trading vehicle, especially if you are the option writer. Capped index options remove the greatest obstacle to writing such options for they limit your risk. Therefore, if you think the market is going to decline, you could write an XMI March 325 call at 6-1/2 when the XMI is at 315. If the XMI moves down, stays where it is, or slowly moves up just a little, the March 325 call will lose value and eventually expire worthless if the XMI is below 325, and you would pocket the 6-1/2 ($650).

But, if you are wrong and the XMI races up to 345 or higher, the most you can lose is 13-1/2, and if you use the proper stop-loss, you probably will take a small loss. So, if you want to bet on the indexes, USE CAPPED INDEX OPTIONS.

In the future, we should continue to see new unique option vehicles, such as capped index options. The advent of new option games will provide a multitude of opportunities. Winning strategies will continually be developing.

The Drying of the Well

Will the explosion in outstanding option opportunities ever end? Will this well of opportunities ever run dry? Once a game becomes extremely popular and the masses enter that game, the game is usually over.

But wait a minute—the options game is not such a simple game. Because of the complex nature of the options game, because of a multitude of vehicles that can be used to participate in this game, the well may never run dry. If covered writing dries up because of heavy institutional participation, then option buying will become attractive. If credit spreading is overplayed, then maybe the debit spreading will become attractive.

In other words, because there is such a huge number of vastly different strategies, when one strategy becomes overplayed, another will pop up for the astute player. The option market is now and will probably continue to be in a state of continual adjustment. It will over-adjust to one strategy and then under-adjust to that strategy. The COMPLEAT OPTION PLAYER will take advantage of this over and under adjustment.

One thing you should remember—if the masses enter the options game, they will enter the simplest strategies, those that are easy to understand. Therefore, the COMPLEAT OPTION PLAYER will select strategies which are more complex and difficult to follow, ones which are not popular. These are the strategies where outstanding opportunities will be gained.

But, before we assume that our options well will remain full of opportunities, there are some other factors to consider. The heavy influence in the securities industry of regulation could some day destroy the options game. And, don't forget the influence of our illustrious Congress, which may some day shut down the game.

Preparing for the Future

Now that you have had a look ahead, how can you prepare for the future? I suggest that you follow these three steps:

1. Take a graduate course in options and spreading.
2. Use all the aids you can get.
3. Be flexible and patient.

1. Take a graduate course in options and spreading.

We have only touched on spreading in this text because it is a complex art and science.

Once you have gotten your feet wet in the options market, your next step will be to begin to play around with spreads. Read everything you can about spreads and play a lot of different ones on paper. Remember, spreads take a lot of trading skill, and trading skill takes a lot of time to develop, so be patient and prepare yourself before you enter the spreading game.

Once in this unique game, you will find the opportunities limitless. Spreads are complex, but because they are, they keep the masses out and the COMPLEAT OPTION PLAYER in the money.

2. Use all the aids you can get.

To maintain that competitive edge over the increased sophistication by the market makers, the institutions and the public, the COMPLEAT OPTION PLAYER will utilize all the aids available to him. He will use the best computer technology available, the best options specialist available, and the best software (publications, charts and other resource aids, see Chapter 30) that are available.

3. Be flexible and patient.

You've heard this before, but in the future it will be even more important to be flexible and patient. Don't get stuck on a special strategy; move on to new option vehicles when old ones run out of gas. Then be patient and wait for really good opportunities to develop. You, the public investor, have the advantage in the options game only if you are willing to sit and wait for your key strategies to develop.

The time has come to wish you the best of luck in this super game. You have all the resources you need to win. If you are still uncomfortable with the listed option, a re-reading or review of this book will help. Options are a complicated subject, even for the intelligent person.

If you use the tools and strategies I have given you and apply them according to the guidelines I have set, you will join the ranks of successful COMPLEAT OPTION PLAYERS.

APPENDIX

NORMAL VALUE OPTION TABLES

How To Use the Normal Value Option Tables

The Normal Value Option Tables are one of the most indispensable aids to the option player. They will tell you when to buy, when to sell, and project what a specific option price will be in the future.

Normal Value Option Tables are your crystal ball. They are critical to your success (if you don't have an option pricing computer program). They will identify bargain priced options, and options which are ripe for naked or covered writing. The Normal Value Option Tables give the true option price, based on the underlying common stock price, and the number of weeks left in the life of the option.

Options with strike prices as high as $150 are provided in the tables. Very few optionable common stocks are priced above $150, and those that do reach these heights normally are split in order to make their shares more attractive to the market. So, if you are evaluating a listed option with a strike price at 150 or lower, you should be able to easily determine the true value of that option today, or at any time in the option's life.

The normal option prices presented in these tables are to be used as GUIDELINES—not as an absolute measure of value. The prices given are based on an underlying common stock with average volatility. Volatility is a key you will have to input in evaluating these normal prices. Common stocks with a higher than average volatility should have a higher price than the prices listed in the Normal Value Option Tables. Underlying common stocks with low volatility should have a lower price than the listed option prices in the tables.

Therefore, volatility should be carefully considered when you view the normal values we have given to each option. Use the volatility formula we have presented, or look at the underlying common stock's Beta Factor (provided by most chart services).

When the volatility is much greater than 30% or the Beta Factor is much greater than 1.00, the corresponding option price should be adjusted accordingly. The same adjustment should be made for underlying common stocks which have a volatility which is significantly below 30%, or which maintain a Beta Factor well below 1.00.

Remember, the normal value prices are to be used as a guideline—a beacon to guide you in this fast moving and confusing game. You will find these tables invaluable, both in strategy design and in making tactical maneuvers. These tables will clearly tell you when option prices are out of line. So, keep these tables at your side when you play the options game.

Interpolation

Under certain conditions, you will encounter an option *exercise price* not listed in our Normal Value Option Tables, such as 55 or 22-1/2, etc. In order to measure the normal price of options with abnormal exercise prices, interpolation is required.

For example, you are evaluating an EXXON Oct 55 put with 6 weeks until expiration, with the stock price at 55. This option is not presented in the tables. Therefore, identify the two option prices with the closest exercise prices and the same number of weeks to expiration. Add these two prices together and, in this case, divide by two. This will give you the normal value of the Oct 55 option with six weeks remaining until expiration.

(a)	Normal value of the Oct 50 put is when the underlying stock is 50.	1.7
(b)	Add the normal value of the Oct 60 put when the underlying stock is 60.	+ 2.1
	NORMAL VALUE =	3.8 ÷ 2 = 1.9

Sum of (a) and (b) divided by two equals the normal value of the Oct 55 put option, which is 1.9 ($190).

You can also use interpolation to measure the normal value of an option for a specific number of days rather than a specific number of weeks before expiration. However, I feel that the normal value prices given for each week will provide quite adequate guidelines, and such interpolation is probably unnecessary.

How To Find the Normal Value of an Option

Using our Normal Value Option Tables is an easy task. For example, to find the real value of a Sears July 40 call with ten weeks remaining, with Sears priced at $40 a share—turn to the Call tables and the page with the exercise price of 40. Look down the table to the point where the common stock price is 40. Move across to the column which states that ten weeks are remaining, and you will find the normal value of the Sears July 40 call, which is 2.3 ($230).

Practice with a few more options and you will get the hang of using these tables quite rapidly. But remember, I highly recommend that you use an options pricing computer program, such as *Option Master*® when you really get serious about trading options.

THE NORMAL VALUE LISTED CALL OPTION TABLES

LISTED CALL OPTION PRICE WHEN EXERCISE PRICE IS 10

Common Stock Price	NUMBER OF WEEKS BEFORE THE OPTION EXPIRES																																					
	1	2	3	4	5	6	7	8	9	10	11	12	13	14	15	16	17	18	19	20	21	22	23	24	25	26	27	28	29	30	31	32	33	34	35	36	37	38	39
14	4.0	4.0	4.0	4.0	4.0	4.0	4.0	4.1	4.1	4.1	4.1	4.1	4.1	4.1	4.1	4.1	4.1	4.1	4.1	4.1	4.1	4.1	4.2	4.2	4.2	4.2	4.2	4.2	4.2	4.2	4.2	4.2	4.2	4.2	4.2	4.2	4.2	4.2	4.3
13.5	3.5	3.5	3.5	3.5	3.5	3.6	3.6	3.6	3.6	3.6	3.6	3.6	3.6	3.6	3.6	3.6	3.7	3.7	3.7	3.7	3.7	3.7	3.7	3.7	3.7	3.7	3.7	3.8	3.8	3.8	3.8	3.8	3.8	3.8	3.8	3.8	3.8	3.8	3.9
13	3.0	3.0	3.0	3.0	3.1	3.1	3.1	3.1	3.1	3.1	3.1	3.1	3.2	3.2	3.2	3.2	3.2	3.2	3.2	3.2	3.2	3,3	3,3	3,3	3,3	3,3	3,3	3,3	3,3	3.4	3.4	3.4	3.4	3.4	3.4	3.4	3.4	3.4	3.5
12.5	2.5	2.5	2.5	2.6	2.6	2.6	2.6	2.6	2.6	2.6	2.7	2.7	2.7	2.7	2.7	2.7	2.7	2,8	2,8	2,8	2,8	2,8	2,8	2,8	2.9	2.9	2.9	2.9	2.9	2.9	2.9	3.0	3.0	3.0	3.0	3.0	3.0	3.0	3.1
12	2.0	2.0	2.1	2.1	2.1	2.1	2.1	2.1	2.2	2.2	2.2	2.2	2.2	2.2	2.3	2.3	2.3	2.3	2.3	2.3	2.4	2.4	2.4	2.4	2.4	2.4	2.5	2.5	2.5	2.5	2.5	2.5	2.6	2.6	2.6	2.6	2.6	2.6	2.7
11.5	1.5	1.5	1.6	1.6	1.6	1.6	1.6	1.7	1.7	1.7	1.7	1.7	1.8	1.8	1.8	1.8	1.8	1.8	1.9	1.9	1.9	1.9	1.9	2.0	2.0	2.0	2.0	2.0	2.1	2.1	2.1	2.1	2.1	2.2	2.2	2.2	2.2	2.2	2.3
11	1.0	1.1	1.1	1.2	1.2	1.2	1.2	1.2	1.3	1.3	1.3	1.3	1.3	1.4	1.4	1.4	1.4	1.4	1.5	1.5	1.5	1.5	1.6	1.6	1.6	1.6	1.6	1.6	1.7	1.7	1.7	1.7	1.7	1.8	1.8	1.8	1.8	1.9	1.9
10.5	0.6	0.7	0.7	0.7	0.8	0.8	0.8	0.8	0.9	0.9	0.9	0.9	0.9	1.0	1.0	1.0	1.0	1.0	1.1	1.1	1.1	1.1	1.2	1.2	1.2	1.2	1.2	1.2	1.3	1.3	1.3	1.3	1.3	1.4	1.4	1.4	1.4	1.4	1.5
10	0.2	0.3	0.3	0.4	0.4	0.4	0.5	0.5	0.5	0.6	0.6	0.6	0.6	0.7	0.7	0.7	0.7	0.8	0.8	0.8	0.8	0.8	0.9	0.9	0.9	0.9	0.9	0.9	1.0	1.0	1.0	1.0	1.0	1.0	1.1	1.1	1.1	1.1	1.1
9.5	0.0	0.1	0.1	0.2	0.2	0.2	0.3	0.3	0.3	0.4	0.4	0.4	0.4	0.5	0.5	0.5	0.5	0.6	0.6	0.6	0.6	0.6	0.7	0.7	0.7	0.7	0.7	0.7	0.8	0.8	0.8	0.8	0.8	0.8	0.9	0.9	0.9	0.9	0.9
9	0.0	0.0	0.0	0.0	0.0	0.0	0.1	0.1	0.1	0.2	0.2	0.2	0.2	0.3	0.3	0.3	0.3	0.4	0.4	0.4	0.4	0.4	0.5	0.5	0.5	0.5	0.5	0.5	0.6	0.6	0.6	0.6	0.6	0.6	0.7	0.7	0.7	0.7	0.7
8.5	0.0	0.0	0.0	0.0	0.0	0.0	0.0	0.0	0.0	0.0	0.0	0.0	0.0	0.1	0.1	0.1	0.1	0.2	0.2	0.2	0.2	0.2	0.3	0.3	0.3	0.3	0.3	0.3	0.4	0.4	0.4	0.4	0.4	0.4	0.5	0.5	0.5	0.5	0.5
8	0.0	0.0	0.0	0.0	0.0	0.0	0.0	0.0	0.0	0.0	0.0	0.0	0.0	0.0	0.0	0.0	0.0	0.0	0.0	0.0	0.0	0.0	0.1	0.1	0.1	0.1	0.1	0.1	0.2	0.2	0.2	0.2	0.2	0.2	0.3	0.3	0.3	0.3	0.3
7.5	0.0	0.0	0.0	0.0	0.0	0.0	0.0	0.0	0.0	0.0	0.0	0.0	0.0	0.0	0.0	0.0	0.0	0.0	0.0	0.0	0.0	0.0	0.0	0.0	0.0	0.0	0.0	0.0	0.0	0.0	0.0	0.0	0.0	0.0	0.1	0.1	0.1	0.1	0.1
7	0.0	0.0	0.0	0.0	0.0	0.0	0.0	0.0	0.0	0.0	0.0	0.0	0.0	0.0	0.0	0.0	0.0	0.0	0.0	0.0	0.0	0.0	0.0	0.0	0.0	0.0	0.0	0.0	0.0	0.0	0.0	0.0	0.0	0.0	0.0	0.0	0.0	0.0	0.0
6.5	0.0	0.0	0.0	0.0	0.0	0.0	0.0	0.0	0.0	0.0	0.0	0.0	0.0	0.0	0.0	0.0	0.0	0.0	0.0	0.0	0.0	0.0	0.0	0.0	0.0	0.0	0.0	0.0	0.0	0.0	0.0	0.0	0.0	0.0	0.0	0.0	0.0	0.0	0.0
6	0.0	0.0	0.0	0.0	0.0	0.0	0.0	0.0	0.0	0.0	0.0	0.0	0.0	0.0	0.0	0.0	0.0	0.0	0.0	0.0	0.0	0.0	0.0	0.0	0.0	0.0	0.0	0.0	0.0	0.0	0.0	0.0	0.0	0.0	0.0	0.0	0.0	0.0	0.0

LISTED CALL OPTION PRICE WHEN EXERCISE PRICE IS 15

NUMBER OF WEEKS BEFORE THE OPTION EXPIRES

Common Stock Price	1	2	3	4	5	6	7	8	9	10	11	12	13	14	15	16	17	18	19	20
21	6.0	6.0	6.0	6.0	6.0	6.1	6.1	6.1	6.1	6.1	6.1	6.1	6.1	6.1	6.1	6.2	6.2	6.2	6.2	6.2
20	5.0	5.0	5.0	5.1	5.1	5.1	5.1	5.1	5.1	5.1	5.2	5.2	5.2	5.2	5.2	5.2	5.3	5.3	5.3	5.3
19	4.0	4.0	4.1	4.1	4.1	4.1	4.1	4.2	4.2	4.2	4.2	4.2	4.3	4.3	4.3	4.3	4.3	4.4	4.4	4.4
18	3.0	3.1	3.1	3.1	3.1	3.2	3.2	3.2	3.2	3.3	3.3	3.3	3.3	3.4	3.4	3.4	3.4	3.5	3.5	3.5
17	2.0	2.1	2.1	2.1	2.2	2.2	2.2	2.2	2.3	2.3	2.3	2.4	2.4	2.4	2.5	2.5	2.5	2.5	2.6	2.6
16	1.1	1.2	1.2	1.3	1.3	1.4	1.4	1.5	1.5	1.5	1.6	1.6	1.6	1.7	1.7	1.8	1.8	1.8	1.9	1.9
15	0.3	0.4	0.5	0.5	0.6	0.7	0.7	0.8	0.8	0.8	0.9	0.9	1.0	1.0	1.0	1.1	1.1	1.1	1.2	1.2
14.5	0.1	0.2	0.3	0.3	0.4	0.5	0.5	0.6	0.6	0.6	0.7	0.7	0.8	0.8	0.8	0.9	0.9	0.9	1.0	1.0
14	0.0	0.0	0.1	0.1	0.2	0.3	0.3	0.4	0.4	0.4	0.5	0.5	0.6	0.6	0.6	0.7	0.7	0.7	0.8	0.8
13.5	0.0	0.0	0.0	0.0	0.0	0.1	0.1	0.2	0.2	0.2	0.3	0.3	0.4	0.4	0.4	0.5	0.5	0.5	0.6	0.6
13	0.0	0.0	0.0	0.0	0.0	0.0	0.0	0.0	0.0	0.0	0.1	0.1	0.2	0.2	0.2	0.3	0.3	0.3	0.4	0.4
12.5	0.0	0.0	0.0	0.0	0.0	0.0	0.0	0.0	0.0	0.0	0.0	0.0	0.0	0.0	0.0	0.1	0.1	0.1	0.2	0.2
12	0.0	0.0	0.0	0.0	0.0	0.0	0.0	0.0	0.0	0.0	0.0	0.0	0.0	0.0	0.0	0.0	0.0	0.0	0.0	0.0
11.5	0.0	0.0	0.0	0.0	0.0	0.0	0.0	0.0	0.0	0.0	0.0	0.0	0.0	0.0	0.0	0.0	0.0	0.0	0.0	0.0
11	0.0	0.0	0.0	0.0	0.0	0.0	0.0	0.0	0.0	0.0	0.0	0.0	0.0	0.0	0.0	0.0	0.0	0.0	0.0	0.0
10.5	0.0	0.0	0.0	0.0	0.0	0.0	0.0	0.0	0.0	0.0	0.0	0.0	0.0	0.0	0.0	0.0	0.0	0.0	0.0	0.0
10	0.0	0.0	0.0	0.0	0.0	0.0	0.0	0.0	0.0	0.0	0.0	0.0	0.0	0.0	0.0	0.0	0.0	0.0	0.0	0.0
9.5	0.0	0.0	0.0	0.0	0.0	0.0	0.0	0.0	0.0	0.0	0.0	0.0	0.0	0.0	0.0	0.0	0.0	0.0	0.0	0.0
9	0.0	0.0	0.0	0.0	0.0	0.0	0.0	0.0	0.0	0.0	0.0	0.0	0.0	0.0	0.0	0.0	0.0	0.0	0.0	0.0

Common Stock Price	21	22	23	24	25	26	27	28	29	30	31	32	33	34	35	36	37	38	39
21	6.2	6.2	6.2	6.2	6.2	6.3	6.3	6.3	6.3	6.3	6.3	6.3	6.3	6.3	6.3	6.4	6.4	6.4	6.4
20	5.3	5.3	5.3	5.4	5.4	5.4	5.4	5.4	5.4	5.4	5.5	5.5	5.5	5.5	5.5	5.5	5.6	5.6	5.6
19	4.4	4.4	4.5	4.5	4.5	4.5	4.5	4.6	4.6	4.6	4.6	4.6	4.7	4.7	4.7	4.7	4.7	4.8	4.8
18	3.5	3.6	3.6	3.6	3.6	3.7	3.7	3.7	3.7	3.8	3.8	3.8	3.8	3.9	3.9	3.9	3.9	4.0	4.0
17	2.6	2.7	2.7	2.7	2.8	2.8	2.8	2.8	2.9	2.9	2.9	3.0	3.0	3.0	3.1	3.1	3.1	3.2	3.2
16	1.9	1.9	1.9	2.0	2.0	2.0	2.0	2.0	2.1	2.1	2.1	2.2	2.2	2.3	2.3	2.4	2.4	2.5	2.5
15	1.2	1.3	1.3	1.3	1.3	1.4	1.4	1.4	1.4	1.5	1.5	1.5	1.5	1.6	1.6	1.6	1.6	1.6	1.7
14.5	1.0	1.1	1.1	1.1	1.1	1.2	1.2	1.2	1.2	1.3	1.3	1.3	1.3	1.4	1.4	1.4	1.4	1.4	1.5
14	0.8	0.9	0.9	0.9	0.9	1.0	1.0	1.0	1.0	1.1	1.1	1.1	1.1	1.2	1.2	1.2	1.2	1.2	1.3
13.5	0.6	0.7	0.7	0.7	0.7	0.8	0.8	0.8	0.8	0.9	0.9	0.9	0.9	1.0	1.0	1.0	1.0	1.0	1.1
13	0.4	0.5	0.5	0.5	0.5	0.6	0.6	0.6	0.6	0.7	0.7	0.7	0.7	0.8	0.8	0.8	0.8	0.8	0.9
12.5	0.2	0.3	0.3	0.3	0.3	0.4	0.4	0.4	0.4	0.5	0.5	0.5	0.5	0.6	0.6	0.6	0.6	0.6	0.7
12	0.0	0.1	0.1	0.1	0.1	0.2	0.2	0.2	0.2	0.3	0.3	0.3	0.3	0.4	0.4	0.4	0.4	0.4	0.5
11.5	0.0	0.0	0.0	0.0	0.0	0.0	0.0	0.0	0.0	0.1	0.1	0.1	0.1	0.2	0.2	0.2	0.2	0.2	0.3
11	0.0	0.0	0.0	0.0	0.0	0.0	0.0	0.0	0.0	0.0	0.0	0.0	0.0	0.0	0.0	0.0	0.0	0.0	0.1
10.5	0.0	0.0	0.0	0.0	0.0	0.0	0.0	0.0	0.0	0.0	0.0	0.0	0.0	0.0	0.0	0.0	0.0	0.0	0.0
10	0.0	0.0	0.0	0.0	0.0	0.0	0.0	0.0	0.0	0.0	0.0	0.0	0.0	0.0	0.0	0.0	0.0	0.0	0.0
9.5	0.0	0.0	0.0	0.0	0.0	0.0	0.0	0.0	0.0	0.0	0.0	0.0	0.0	0.0	0.0	0.0	0.0	0.0	0.0
9	0.0	0.0	0.0	0.0	0.0	0.0	0.0	0.0	0.0	0.0	0.0	0.0	0.0	0.0	0.0	0.0	0.0	0.0	0.0

LISTED CALL OPTION PRICE WHEN EXERCISE PRICE IS 20

Common Stock Price	NUMBER OF WEEKS BEFORE THE OPTION EXPIRES 1	2	3	4	5	6	7	8	9	10	11	12	13	14	15	16	17	18	19	20	21	22	23	24	25	26	27	28	29	30	31	32	33	34	35	36	37	38	39
28	8.0	8.0	8.0	8.1	8.1	8.1	8.1	8.1	8.1	8.1	8.1	8.2	8.2	8.2	8.2	8.2	8.2	8.2	8.2	8.3	8.3	8.3	8.3	8.3	8.3	8.3	8.4	8.4	8.4	8.4	8.4	8.4	8.4	8.4	8.5	8.5	8.5	8.5	8.5
27	7.0	7.0	7.1	7.1	7.1	7.1	7.1	7.1	7.2	7.2	7.2	7.2	7.2	7.3	7.3	7.3	7.3	7.3	7.3	7.4	7.4	7.4	7.4	7.4	7.5	7.5	7.5	7.5	7.5	7.5	7.6	7.6	7.6	7.6	7.6	7.7	7.7	7.7	7.7
26	6.0	6.0	6.1	6.1	6.1	6.1	6.2	6.2	6.2	6.2	6.3	6.3	6.3	6.3	6.4	6.4	6.4	6.4	6.4	6.5	6.5	6.5	6.5	6.6	6.6	6.6	6.6	6.7	6.7	6.7	6.7	6.7	6.8	6.8	6.8	6.8	6.9	6.9	6.9
25	5.0	5.1	5.1	5.1	5.1	5.2	5.2	5.2	5.3	5.3	5.3	5.3	5.4	5.4	5.4	5.5	5.5	5.5	5.5	5.6	5.6	5.6	5.7	5.7	5.7	5.7	5.8	5.8	5.8	5.9	5.9	5.9	5.9	6.0	6.0	6.0	6.1	6.1	6.1
24	4.0	4.1	4.1	4.1	4.2	4.2	4.2	4.3	4.3	4.3	4.4	4.4	4.4	4.5	4.5	4.5	4.6	4.6	4.6	4.7	4.7	4.7	4.8	4.8	4.8	4.9	4.9	4.9	5.0	5.0	5.0	5.1	5.1	5.1	5.2	5.2	5.2	5.3	5.3
23	3.0	3.1	3.1	3.2	3.2	3.2	3.3	3.3	3.3	3.4	3.4	3.5	3.5	3.5	3.6	3.6	3.7	3.7	3.7	3.8	3.8	3.9	3.9	3.9	4.0	4.0	4.0	4.1	4.1	4.2	4.2	4.2	4.3	4.3	4.4	4.4	4.4	4.5	4.5
22	2.1	2.1	2.2	2.3	2.3	2.3	2.4	2.5	2.6	2.6	2.7	2.7	2.7	2.8	2.9	2.9	3.0	3.0	3.0	3.0	3.1	3.1	3.1	3.1	3.2	3.2	3.3	3.3	3.3	3.4	3.4	3.4	3.5	3.5	3.6	3.6	3.6	3.7	3.7
21	1.1	1.2	1.2	1.3	1.4	1.5	1.6	1.7	1.8	1.8	1.9	1.9	1.9	2.0	2.0	2.1	2.2	2.2	2.2	2.3	2.3	2.4	2.4	2.4	2.5	2.5	2.5	2.5	2.6	2.6	2.7	2.7	2.8	2.8	2.8	2.8	2.9	2.9	2.9
20	0.4	0.5	0.6	0.7	0.8	0.9	0.9	1.0	1.1	1.1	1.2	1.2	1.3	1.3	1.4	1.4	1.5	1.5	1.6	1.6	1.6	1.7	1.7	1.7	1.8	1.8	1.8	1.9	1.9	1.9	2.0	2.0	2.0	2.1	2.1	2.1	2.2	2.2	2.2
19	0.0	0.1	0.2	0.3	0.4	0.5	0.5	0.6	0.7	0.7	0.8	0.8	0.9	0.9	1.0	1.0	1.1	1.1	1.2	1.2	1.2	1.3	1.3	1.3	1.4	1.4	1.4	1.5	1.5	1.5	1.6	1.6	1.6	1.7	1.7	1.7	1.8	1.8	1.8
18	0.0	0.0	0.0	0.0	0.0	0.1	0.1	0.2	0.3	0.3	0.4	0.4	0.5	0.5	0.6	0.6	0.7	0.7	0.8	0.8	0.8	0.9	0.9	0.9	1.0	1.0	1.0	1.1	1.1	1.1	1.2	1.2	1.2	1.3	1.3	1.3	1.4	1.4	1.4
17	0.0	0.0	0.0	0.0	0.0	0.0	0.0	0.0	0.0	0.0	0.0	0.0	0.1	0.1	0.2	0.2	0.3	0.3	0.4	0.4	0.4	0.5	0.5	0.5	0.6	0.6	0.6	0.7	0.7	0.7	0.8	0.8	0.8	0.9	0.9	0.9	1.0	1.0	1.0
16	0.0	0.0	0.0	0.0	0.0	0.0	0.0	0.0	0.0	0.0	0.0	0.0	0.0	0.0	0.0	0.0	0.0	0.0	0.0	0.0	0.0	0.1	0.1	0.1	0.2	0.2	0.2	0.3	0.3	0.3	0.4	0.4	0.4	0.5	0.5	0.5	0.6	0.6	0.6
15	0.0	0.0	0.0	0.0	0.0	0.0	0.0	0.0	0.0	0.0	0.0	0.0	0.0	0.0	0.0	0.0	0.0	0.0	0.0	0.0	0.0	0.0	0.0	0.0	0.0	0.0	0.0	0.0	0.0	0.0	0.0	0.0	0.0	0.1	0.1	0.1	0.2	0.2	0.2
14.5	0.0	0.0	0.0	0.0	0.0	0.0	0.0	0.0	0.0	0.0	0.0	0.0	0.0	0.0	0.0	0.0	0.0	0.0	0.0	0.0	0.0	0.0	0.0	0.0	0.0	0.0	0.0	0.0	0.0	0.0	0.0	0.0	0.0	0.0	0.0	0.0	0.0	0.0	0.0
14	0.0	0.0	0.0	0.0	0.0	0.0	0.0	0.0	0.0	0.0	0.0	0.0	0.0	0.0	0.0	0.0	0.0	0.0	0.0	0.0	0.0	0.0	0.0	0.0	0.0	0.0	0.0	0.0	0.0	0.0	0.0	0.0	0.0	0.0	0.0	0.0	0.0	0.0	0.0
13.5	0.0	0.0	0.0	0.0	0.0	0.0	0.0	0.0	0.0	0.0	0.0	0.0	0.0	0.0	0.0	0.0	0.0	0.0	0.0	0.0	0.0	0.0	0.0	0.0	0.0	0.0	0.0	0.0	0.0	0.0	0.0	0.0	0.0	0.0	0.0	0.0	0.0	0.0	0.0
13	0.0	0.0	0.0	0.0	0.0	0.0	0.0	0.0	0.0	0.0	0.0	0.0	0.0	0.0	0.0	0.0	0.0	0.0	0.0	0.0	0.0	0.0	0.0	0.0	0.0	0.0	0.0	0.0	0.0	0.0	0.0	0.0	0.0	0.0	0.0	0.0	0.0	0.0	0.0
12.5	0.0	0.0	0.0	0.0	0.0	0.0	0.0	0.0	0.0	0.0	0.0	0.0	0.0	0.0	0.0	0.0	0.0	0.0	0.0	0.0	0.0	0.0	0.0	0.0	0.0	0.0	0.0	0.0	0.0	0.0	0.0	0.0	0.0	0.0	0.0	0.0	0.0	0.0	0.0
12	0.0	0.0	0.0	0.0	0.0	0.0	0.0	0.0	0.0	0.0	0.0	0.0	0.0	0.0	0.0	0.0	0.0	0.0	0.0	0.0	0.0	0.0	0.0	0.0	0.0	0.0	0.0	0.0	0.0	0.0	0.0	0.0	0.0	0.0	0.0	0.0	0.0	0.0	0.0

LISTED CALL OPTION PRICE WHEN EXERCISE PRICE IS 25

NUMBER OF WEEKS BEFORE THE OPTION EXPIRES

Common Stock Price	1	2	3	4	5	6	7	8	9	10	11	12	13	14	15	16	17	18	19	20
35	10.0	10.0	10.0	10.1	10.1	10.1	10.1	10.1	10.1	10.2	10.2	10.2	10.2	10.2	10.2	10.3	10.3	10.3	10.3	10.3
34	9.0	9.0	9.1	9.1	9.1	9.1	9.2	9.2	9.2	9.2	9.2	9.3	9.3	9.3	9.3	9.3	9.4	9.4	9.4	9.4
33	8.0	8.1	8.1	8.1	8.1	8.2	8.2	8.2	8.2	8.3	8.3	8.3	8.3	8.4	8.4	8.4	8.5	8.5	8.5	8.5
32	7.0	7.1	7.1	7.1	7.2	7.2	7.2	7.3	7.3	7.3	7.3	7.4	7.4	7.4	7.5	7.5	7.5	7.6	7.6	7.6
31	6.0	6.1	6.1	6.1	6.2	6.2	6.3	6.3	6.3	6.4	6.4	6.4	6.5	6.5	6.6	6.6	6.6	6.7	6.7	6.7
30	5.0	5.1	5.1	5.2	5.2	5.3	5.3	5.3	5.4	5.4	5.5	5.5	5.5	5.6	5.6	5.7	5.7	5.8	5.8	5.8
29	4.0	4.1	4.1	4.2	4.2	4.3	4.3	4.4	4.4	4.5	4.5	4.6	4.6	4.7	4.7	4.8	4.8	4.8	4.9	4.9
28	3.1	3.1	3.2	3.2	3.3	3.3	3.4	3.4	3.5	3.5	3.6	3.6	3.7	3.7	3.8	3.8	3.9	3.9	4.0	4.0
27	2.2	2.3	2.4	2.4	2.5	2.6	2.7	2.7	2.7	2.8	2.9	2.9	3.0	3.0	3.1	3.1	3.2	3.2	3.2	3.3
26	1.3	1.4	1.6	1.7	1.8	1.9	1.9	1.9	1.9	2.0	2.1	2.1	2.2	2.3	2.4	2.5	2.5	2.5	2.6	2.6
25	0.4	0.6	0.8	0.9	1.0	1.1	1.2	1.3	1.3	1.4	1.5	1.5	1.6	1.7	1.7	1.8	1.8	1.9	1.9	2.0
24	0.0	0.2	0.4	0.5	0.6	0.7	0.8	0.9	0.9	1.0	1.1	1.1	1.2	1.3	1.3	1.4	1.4	1.5	1.5	1.6
23	0.0	0.0	0.0	0.1	0.2	0.3	0.4	0.5	0.5	0.6	0.7	0.7	0.8	0.9	0.9	1.0	1.0	1.1	1.1	1.2
22	0.0	0.0	0.0	0.0	0.0	0.0	0.0	0.1	0.1	0.2	0.3	0.3	0.4	0.5	0.5	0.6	0.6	0.7	0.7	0.8
21	0.0	0.0	0.0	0.0	0.0	0.0	0.0	0.0	0.0	0.0	0.0	0.0	0.0	0.1	0.1	0.2	0.2	0.3	0.3	0.4
20	0.0	0.0	0.0	0.0	0.0	0.0	0.0	0.0	0.0	0.0	0.0	0.0	0.0	0.0	0.0	0.0	0.0	0.0	0.0	0.0
19	0.0	0.0	0.0	0.0	0.0	0.0	0.0	0.0	0.0	0.0	0.0	0.0	0.0	0.0	0.0	0.0	0.0	0.0	0.0	0.0
18	0.0	0.0	0.0	0.0	0.0	0.0	0.0	0.0	0.0	0.0	0.0	0.0	0.0	0.0	0.0	0.0	0.0	0.0	0.0	0.0
17	0.0	0.0	0.0	0.0	0.0	0.0	0.0	0.0	0.0	0.0	0.0	0.0	0.0	0.0	0.0	0.0	0.0	0.0	0.0	0.0
16	0.0	0.0	0.0	0.0	0.0	0.0	0.0	0.0	0.0	0.0	0.0	0.0	0.0	0.0	0.0	0.0	0.0	0.0	0.0	0.0
15	0.0	0.0	0.0	0.0	0.0	0.0	0.0	0.0	0.0	0.0	0.0	0.0	0.0	0.0	0.0	0.0	0.0	0.0	0.0	0.0

Common Stock Price	21	22	23	24	25	26	27	28	29	30	31	32	33	34	35	36	37	38	39
35	10.3	10.4	10.4	10.4	10.4	10.4	10.4	10.5	10.5	10.5	10.5	10.5	10.5	10.6	10.6	10.6	10.6	10.6	10.6
34	9.5	9.5	9.5	9.5	9.5	9.6	9.6	9.6	9.6	9.6	9.7	9.7	9.7	9.7	9.8	9.8	9.8	9.8	9.8
33	8.6	8.6	8.6	8.6	8.7	8.7	8.7	8.7	8.8	8.8	8.8	8.9	8.9	8.9	8.9	9.0	9.0	9.0	9.0
32	7.7	7.7	7.7	7.8	7.8	7.8	7.9	7.9	7.9	8.0	8.0	8.0	8.0	8.1	8.1	8.1	8.2	8.2	8.2
31	6.8	6.8	6.8	6.9	6.9	7.0	7.0	7.0	7.1	7.1	7.1	7.2	7.2	7.3	7.3	7.3	7.4	7.4	7.4
30	5.9	5.9	6.0	6.0	6.0	6.1	6.1	6.2	6.2	6.3	6.3	6.3	6.4	6.4	6.5	6.5	6.6	6.6	6.6
29	5.0	5.0	5.1	5.1	5.2	5.2	5.3	5.3	5.4	5.4	5.5	5.5	5.6	5.6	5.6	5.7	5.7	5.8	5.8
28	4.1	4.1	4.2	4.3	4.3	4.4	4.4	4.5	4.5	4.6	4.6	4.7	4.7	4.8	4.8	4.9	4.9	5.0	5.0
27	3.3	3.4	3.4	3.5	3.5	3.6	3.6	3.7	3.7	3.8	3.8	3.9	3.9	4.0	4.1	4.1	4.1	4.2	4.2
26	2.7	2.7	2.7	2.8	2.8	2.9	2.9	3.0	3.0	3.0	3.1	3.1	3.2	3.2	3.2	3.3	3.3	3.3	3.4
25	2.0	2.1	2.1	2.2	2.2	2.3	2.3	2.4	2.4	2.4	2.5	2.5	2.6	2.6	2.6	2.7	2.7	2.7	2.8
24	1.6	1.7	1.7	1.8	1.8	1.9	1.9	2.0	2.0	2.0	2.1	2.1	2.2	2.2	2.2	2.3	2.3	2.3	2.4
23	1.2	1.3	1.3	1.4	1.4	1.5	1.5	1.6	1.6	1.6	1.7	1.7	1.8	1.8	1.8	1.9	1.9	1.9	2.0
22	0.8	0.9	0.9	1.0	1.0	1.1	1.1	1.2	1.2	1.2	1.3	1.3	1.4	1.4	1.4	1.5	1.5	1.5	1.6
21	0.4	0.5	0.5	0.6	0.6	0.7	0.7	0.8	0.8	0.8	0.9	0.9	1.0	1.0	1.0	1.1	1.1	1.1	1.2
20	0.0	0.1	0.1	0.2	0.2	0.3	0.3	0.4	0.4	0.4	0.5	0.5	0.6	0.6	0.6	0.7	0.7	0.7	0.8
19	0.0	0.0	0.0	0.0	0.0	0.0	0.0	0.0	0.0	0.0	0.1	0.1	0.2	0.2	0.2	0.3	0.3	0.3	0.4
18	0.0	0.0	0.0	0.0	0.0	0.0	0.0	0.0	0.0	0.0	0.0	0.0	0.0	0.0	0.0	0.0	0.0	0.0	0.0
17	0.0	0.0	0.0	0.0	0.0	0.0	0.0	0.0	0.0	0.0	0.0	0.0	0.0	0.0	0.0	0.0	0.0	0.0	0.0
16	0.0	0.0	0.0	0.0	0.0	0.0	0.0	0.0	0.0	0.0	0.0	0.0	0.0	0.0	0.0	0.0	0.0	0.0	0.0
15	0.0	0.0	0.0	0.0	0.0	0.0	0.0	0.0	0.0	0.0	0.0	0.0	0.0	0.0	0.0	0.0	0.0	0.0	0.0

LISTED CALL OPTION PRICE WHEN EXERCISE PRICE IS 30

Common Stock Price	NUMBER OF WEEKS BEFORE THE OPTION EXPIRES																																					
	1	2	3	4	5	6	7	8	9	10	11	12	13	14	15	16	17	18	19	20	21	22	23	24	25	26	27	28	29	30	31	32	33	34	35	36	37	38	39
42	12.0	12.0	12.1	12.1	12.1	12.1	12.1	12.2	12.2	12.2	12.2	12.2	12.3	12.3	12.3	12.3	12.3	12.4	12.4	12.4	12.4	12.4	12.5	12.5	12.5	12.5	12.5	12.5	12.6	12.6	12.6	12.6	12.6	12.7	12.7	12.7	12.7	12.7	12.8
41	11.0	11.0	11.1	11.1	11.1	11.1	11.2	11.2	11.2	11.2	11.3	11.3	11.3	11.3	11.4	11.4	11.4	11.4	11.5	11.5	11.5	11.5	11.6	11.6	11.6	11.6	11.7	11.7	11.7	11.7	11.8	11.8	11.8	11.8	11.9	11.9	11.9	11.9	12.0
40	10.0	10.1	10.1	10.1	10.1	10.2	10.2	10.2	10.3	10.3	10.3	10.4	10.4	10.4	10.4	10.5	10.5	10.5	10.6	10.6	10.6	10.7	10.7	10.7	10.7	10.8	10.8	10.8	10.9	10.9	10.9	11.0	11.0	11.0	11.0	11.1	11.1	11.1	11.2
39	9.0	9.1	9.1	9.1	9.2	9.2	9.2	9.3	9.3	9.3	9.4	9.4	9.5	9.5	9.5	9.6	9.6	9.6	9.7	9.7	9.7	9.8	9.8	9.8	9.9	9.9	9.9	9.9	10.0	10.0	10.1	10.1	10.2	10.2	10.2	10.3	10.3	10.3	10.4
38	8.0	8.1	8.1	8.2	8.2	8.2	8.3	8.3	8.4	8.4	8.4	8.5	8.5	8.6	8.6	8.6	8.7	8.7	8.8	8.8	8.8	8.9	8.9	9.0	9.0	9.0	9.1	9.1	9.2	9.2	9.2	9.3	9.3	9.4	9.4	9.4	9.5	9.5	9.6
37	7.0	7.1	7.1	7.2	7.2	7.3	7.3	7.4	7.4	7.5	7.5	7.5	7.6	7.6	7.7	7.7	7.8	7.8	7.9	7.9	8.0	8.0	8.0	8.1	8.1	8.2	8.2	8.3	8.3	8.4	8.4	8.4	8.5	8.5	8.6	8.6	8.7	8.7	8.8
36	6.1	6.1	6.2	6.2	6.3	6.3	6.4	6.4	6.5	6.5	6.6	6.6	6.7	6.7	6.8	6.8	6.9	6.9	7.0	7.0	7.1	7.1	7.2	7.2	7.3	7.3	7.4	7.4	7.5	7.5	7.6	7.6	7.7	7.7	7.8	7.8	7.9	7.9	8.0
35	5.1	5.1	5.2	5.2	5.3	5.3	5.4	5.4	5.5	5.6	5.6	5.7	5.7	5.8	5.8	5.9	5.9	6.0	6.1	6.1	6.2	6.2	6.3	6.3	6.4	6.4	6.5	6.6	6.6	6.7	6.7	6.8	6.8	6.9	6.9	7.0	7.1	7.1	7.2
34	4.1	4.1	4.2	4.2	4.3	4.4	4.4	4.5	4.5	4.6	4.7	4.7	4.8	4.8	4.9	5.0	5.0	5.1	5.2	5.2	5.3	5.3	5.4	5.5	5.5	5.6	5.6	5.7	5.8	5.8	5.9	5.9	6.0	6.1	6.1	6.2	6.2	6.3	6.4
33	3.2	3.2	3.2	3.3	3.4	3.5	3.6	3.6	3.7	3.8	3.8	3.9	4.0	4.0	4.1	4.2	4.2	4.3	4.4	4.4	4.5	4.5	4.6	4.6	4.7	4.8	4.8	4.9	4.9	4.9	5.0	5.1	5.2	5.3	5.3	5.4	5.4	5.5	5.6
32	2.2	2.3	2.4	2.5	2.6	2.7	2.8	2.9	2.9	3.0	3.1	3.1	3.2	3.3	3.4	3.4	3.5	3.6	3.6	3.7	3.7	3.8	3.9	3.9	4.0	4.0	4.1	4.1	4.2	4.2	4.3	4.3	4.4	4.4	4.5	4.5	4.6	4.7	4.8
31	1,3	1.5	1.6	1.8	1.9	2.0	2.1	2.2	2.2	2.2	2.3	2.3	2.4	2.5	2.6	2.7	2.8	2.9	2.9	3.0	3.0	3.1	3.2	3.2	3.3	3.3	3.4	3.4	3.5	3.5	3.6	3.6	3.7	3.8	3.8	3.9	3.9	4.0	4.0
30	0.5	0.8	0.9	1.1	1.2	1.3	1.4	1.5	1.6	1.7	1.8	1.8	1.9	2.0	2.1	2.1	2.2	2.3	2.3	2.4	2.4	2.5	2.6	2.6	2.7	2.7	2.8	2.8	2.9	2.9	3.0	3.0	3.1	3.1	3.2	3.2	3.2	3.3	3.3
29	0.1	0.4	0.5	0.7	0.8	0.9	1.0	1.1	1.2	1.3	1.4	1.4	1.5	1.6	1.7	1.7	1.8	1.9	1.9	2.0	2.0	2.1	2.2	2.2	2.3	2.3	2.4	2.4	2.5	2.5	2.6	2.6	2.7	2.7	2.8	2.8	2.8	2.9	2.9
28	0.0	0.0	0.1	0.3	0.4	0.5	0.6	0.7	0.8	0.9	1.0	1.0	1.1	1.2	1.3	1.3	1.4	1.5	1.5	1.6	1.6	1.7	1.8	1.8	1.9	1.9	2.0	2.0	2.1	2.1	2.2	2.2	2.3	2.3	2.4	2.4	2.4	2.5	2.5
27	0.0	0.0	0.0	0.0	0.0	0.1	0.2	0.3	0.4	0.5	0.6	0.6	0.7	0.8	0.9	0.9	1.0	1.1	1.1	1.2	1.2	1.3	1.4	1.4	1.5	1.5	1.6	1.6	1.7	1.7	1.8	1.8	1.9	1.9	2.0	2.0	2.0	2.1	2.1
26	0.0	0.0	0.0	0.0	0.0	0.0	0.0	0.0	0.0	0.1	0.2	0.2	0.3	0.4	0.5	0.5	0.6	0.7	0.7	0.8	0.8	0.9	1.0	1.0	1.1	1.1	1.2	1.2	1.3	1.3	1.4	1.4	1.5	1.5	1.6	1.6	1.6	1.7	1.7
25	0.0	0.0	0.0	0.0	0.0	0.0	0.0	0.0	0.0	0.0	0.0	0.0	0.0	0.0	0.1	0.1	0.2	0.3	0.3	0.4	0.4	0.5	0.6	0.6	0.7	0.7	0.8	0.8	0.9	0.9	1.0	1.0	1.1	1.1	1.2	1.2	1.2	1.3	1.3
24	0.0	0.0	0.0	0.0	0.0	0.0	0.0	0.0	0.0	0.0	0.0	0.0	0.0	0.0	0.0	0.0	0.0	0.0	0.0	0.0	0.0	0.1	0.2	0.2	0.3	0.3	0.4	0.4	0.5	0.5	0.6	0.6	0.7	0.7	0.8	0.8	0.8	0.9	0.9
23	0.0	0.0	0.0	0.0	0.0	0.0	0.0	0.0	0.0	0.0	0.0	0.0	0.0	0.0	0.0	0.0	0.0	0.0	0.0	0.0	0.0	0.0	0.0	0.0	0.0	0.0	0.0	0.0	0.1	0.1	0.2	0.2	0.3	0.3	0.4	0.4	0.4	0.5	0.5
22	0.0	0.0	0.0	0.0	0.0	0.0	0.0	0.0	0.0	0.0	0.0	0.0	0.0	0.0	0.0	0.0	0.0	0.0	0.0	0.0	0.0	0.0	0.0	0.0	0.0	0.0	0.0	0.0	0.0	0.0	0.0	0.0	0.0	0.0	0.0	0.0	0.0	0.1	0.1
21	0.0	0.0	0.0	0.0	0.0	0.0	0.0	0.0	0.0	0.0	0.0	0.0	0.0	0.0	0.0	0.0	0.0	0.0	0.0	0.0	0.0	0.0	0.0	0.0	0.0	0.0	0.0	0.0	0.0	0.0	0.0	0.0	0.0	0.0	0.0	0.0	0.0	0.0	0.0
20	0.0	0.0	0.0	0.0	0.0	0.0	0.0	0.0	0.0	0.0	0.0	0.0	0.0	0.0	0.0	0.0	0.0	0.0	0.0	0.0	0.0	0.0	0.0	0.0	0.0	0.0	0.0	0.0	0.0	0.0	0.0	0.0	0.0	0.0	0.0	0.0	0.0	0.0	0.0
19	0.0	0.0	0.0	0.0	0.0	0.0	0.0	0.0	0.0	0.0	0.0	0.0	0.0	0.0	0.0	0.0	0.0	0.0	0.0	0.0	0.0	0.0	0.0	0.0	0.0	0.0	0.0	0.0	0.0	0.0	0.0	0.0	0.0	0.0	0.0	0.0	0.0	0.0	0.0
18	0.0	0.0	0.0	0.0	0.0	0.0	0.0	0.0	0.0	0.0	0.0	0.0	0.0	0.0	0.0	0.0	0.0	0.0	0.0	0.0	0.0	0.0	0.0	0.0	0.0	0.0	0.0	0.0	0.0	0.0	0.0	0.0	0.0	0.0	0.0	0.0	0.0	0.0	0.0

LISTED CALL OPTION PRICE WHEN EXERCISE PRICE IS 35

Common Stock Price — NUMBER OF WEEKS BEFORE THE OPTION EXPIRES

	1	2	3	4	5	6	7	8	9	10	11	12	13	14	15	16	17	18	19	20	21	22	23	24	25	26	27	28	29	30	31	32	33	34	35	36	37	38	39
49	14.0	14.0	14.1	14.1	14.1	14.1	14.2	14.2	14.2	14.2	14.3	14.3	14.3	14.3	14.3	14.4	14.4	14.4	14.4	14.5	14.5	14.5	14.5	14.5	14.6	14.6	14.6	14.6	14.7	14.7	14.7	14.7	14.8	14.8	14.8	14.8	14.8	14.9	14.9
48	13.0	13.1	13.1	13.1	13.1	13.2	13.2	13.2	13.3	13.3	13.3	13.3	13.4	13.4	13.4	13.4	13.5	13.5	13.5	13.6	13.6	13.6	13.6	13.7	13.7	13.7	13.8	13.8	13.8	13.8	13.9	13.9	13.9	14.0	14.0	14.0	14.0	14.1	14.1
47	12.0	12.1	12.1	12.1	12.2	12.2	12.2	12.3	12.3	12.3	12.4	12.4	12.4	12.5	12.5	12.5	12.6	12.6	12.6	12.7	12.7	12.7	12.8	12.8	12.8	12.9	12.9	12.9	13.0	13.0	13.0	13.1	13.1	13.1	13.2	13.2	13.2	13.3	13.3
46	11.0	11.1	11.1	11.2	11.2	11.2	11.3	11.3	11.3	11.4	11.4	11.5	11.5	11.5	11.6	11.6	11.7	11.7	11.7	11.8	11.8	11.8	11.9	11.9	12.0	12.0	12.0	12.1	12.1	12.1	12.2	12.2	12.3	12.3	12.3	12.4	12.4	12.5	12.5
45	10.0	10.1	10.1	10.2	10.2	10.3	10.3	10.3	10.4	10.4	10.5	10.5	10.6	10.6	10.7	10.7	10.7	10.8	10.8	10.9	10.9	11.0	11.0	11.0	11.1	11.1	11.2	11.2	11.3	11.3	11.3	11.4	11.4	11.5	11.5	11.6	11.6	11.6	11.7
44	9.0	9.1	9.1	9.2	9.2	9.3	9.3	9.4	9.4	9.5	9.5	9.6	9.6	9.7	9.7	9.8	9.8	9.9	9.9	9.9	10.0	10.1	10.1	10.2	10.2	10.3	10.3	10.4	10.4	10.5	10.5	10.6	10.6	10.6	10.7	10.7	10.8	10.8	10.9
43	8.1	8.1	8.2	8.2	8.3	8.3	8.4	8.4	8.5	8.5	8.6	8.6	8.7	8.8	8.8	8.9	8.9	9.0	9.0	9.1	9.1	9.2	9.2	9.3	9.3	9.4	9.4	9.5	9.6	9.6	9.7	9.7	9.8	9.8	9.9	9.9	9.9	10.0	10.1
42	7.1	7.1	7.2	7.2	7.3	7.4	7.4	7.5	7.5	7.6	7.6	7.7	7.8	7.8	7.9	7.9	8.0	8.1	8.1	8.2	8.2	8.3	8.4	8.4	8.5	8.5	8.6	8.6	8.7	8.8	8.8	8.9	8.9	9.0	9.1	9.1	9.2	9.2	9.3
41	6.1	6.1	6.2	6.3	6.3	6.4	6.4	6.5	6.6	6.6	6.7	6.8	6.8	6.9	7.0	7.0	7.1	7.2	7.2	7.3	7.3	7.4	7.5	7.5	7.6	7.7	7.7	7.8	7.9	7.9	8.0	8.0	8.1	8.2	8.2	8.3	8.4	8.4	8.5
40	5.1	5.1	5.2	5.3	5.3	5.4	5.5	5.6	5.6	5.7	5.8	5.8	5.9	6.0	6.0	6.1	6.2	6.3	6.3	6.4	6.4	6.5	6.6	6.7	6.7	6.8	6.9	6.9	7.0	7.1	7.1	7.2	7.3	7.3	7.4	7.5	7.6	7.6	7.7
39	4.1	4.1	4.2	4.3	4.4	4.4	4.5	4.6	4.7	4.7	4.8	4.9	5.0	5.0	5.1	5.2	5.3	5.3	5.4	5.5	5.6	5.6	5.7	5.8	5.9	5.9	6.0	6.1	6.2	6.2	6.3	6.4	6.4	6.5	6.6	6.7	6.7	6.8	6.9
38	3.2	3.2	3.3	3.4	3.5	3.6	3.6	3.8	3.8	3.9	4.0	4.0	4.1	4.2	4.3	4.4	4.5	4.5	4.6	4.7	4.8	4.8	4.9	5.0	5.0	5.1	5.2	5.3	5.4	5.4	5.5	5.6	5.6	5.7	5.8	5.9	5.9	6.0	6.1
37	2.2	2.3	2.4	2.5	2.5	2.6	2.6	2.7	2.9	3.0	3.1	3.2	3.3	3.4	3.5	3.6	3.7	3.8	3.9	4.0	4.1	4.1	4.2	4.3	4.3	4.4	4.4	4.5	4.6	4.6	4.7	4.8	4.8	4.9	5.0	5.1	5.2	5.2	5.3
36	1.4	1.6	1.8	1.9	2.0	2.1	2.2	2.4	2.5	2.6	2.7	2.8	2.8	2.9	3.0	3.1	3.2	3.2	3.3	3.4	3.5	3.5	3.6	3.7	3.7	3.8	3.8	3.9	4.0	4.0	4.1	4.1	4.2	4.2	4.3	4.4	4.5	4.5	4.6
35	0.6	0.9	1.1	1.2	1.4	1.5	1.6	1.8	1.9	2.0	2.1	2.2	2.2	2.3	2.4	2.5	2.6	2.6	2.7	2.8	2.9	2.9	3.0	3.1	3.1	3.2	3.2	3.3	3.4	3.4	3.5	3.5	3.6	3.6	3.7	3.7	3.8	3.8	3.9
34	0.2	0.5	0.7	0.8	1.0	1.1	1.2	1.4	1.5	1.6	1.7	1.8	1.8	1.9	2.0	2.1	2.2	2.2	2.3	2.4	2.5	2.5	2.6	2.7	2.7	2.8	2.8	2.9	3.0	3.0	3.1	3.1	3.2	3.2	3.3	3.3	3.4	3.4	3.5
33	0.0	0.1	0.3	0.4	0.6	0.7	0.8	1.0	1.1	1.2	1.3	1.4	1.4	1.5	1.6	1.7	1.8	1.8	1.9	2.0	2.1	2.1	2.2	2.3	2.3	2.4	2.4	2.5	2.6	2.6	2.7	2.7	2.8	2.8	2.9	2.9	3.0	3.0	3.1
32	0.0	0.0	0.0	0.0	0.2	0.3	0.4	0.6	0.7	0.8	0.9	1.0	1.0	1.1	1.2	1.3	1.4	1.4	1.5	1.6	1.7	1.7	1.8	1.9	1.9	2.0	2.0	2.1	2.2	2.2	2.3	2.3	2.4	2.4	2.5	2.5	2.6	2.6	2.7
31	0.0	0.0	0.0	0.0	0.0	0.0	0.0	0.2	0.3	0.4	0.5	0.6	0.6	0.7	0.8	0.9	1.0	1.0	1.1	1.2	1.3	1.3	1.4	1.5	1.5	1.6	1.6	1.7	1.8	1.8	1.9	1.9	2.0	2.0	2.1	2.1	2.2	2.2	2.3
30	0.0	0.0	0.0	0.0	0.0	0.0	0.0	0.0	0.0	0.0	0.1	0.2	0.2	0.3	0.4	0.5	0.6	0.6	0.7	0.8	0.9	0.9	1.0	1.1	1.1	1.2	1.2	1.3	1.4	1.4	1.5	1.5	1.6	1.6	1.7	1.7	1.8	1.8	1.9
29	0.0	0.0	0.0	0.0	0.0	0.0	0.0	0.0	0.0	0.0	0.0	0.0	0.0	0.0	0.0	0.1	0.2	0.2	0.3	0.4	0.5	0.5	0.6	0.7	0.7	0.8	0.8	0.9	1.0	1.0	1.1	1.1	1.2	1.2	1.3	1.3	1.4	1.4	1.5
28	0.0	0.0	0.0	0.0	0.0	0.0	0.0	0.0	0.0	0.0	0.0	0.0	0.0	0.0	0.0	0.0	0.0	0.0	0.0	0.0	0.1	0.1	0.2	0.3	0.3	0.4	0.4	0.5	0.6	0.6	0.7	0.7	0.8	0.8	0.9	0.9	1.0	1.0	1.1
27	0.0	0.0	0.0	0.0	0.0	0.0	0.0	0.0	0.0	0.0	0.0	0.0	0.0	0.0	0.0	0.0	0.0	0.0	0.0	0.0	0.0	0.0	0.0	0.0	0.0	0.0	0.0	0.1	0.2	0.2	0.3	0.3	0.4	0.4	0.5	0.5	0.6	0.6	0.7
26	0.0	0.0	0.0	0.0	0.0	0.0	0.0	0.0	0.0	0.0	0.0	0.0	0.0	0.0	0.0	0.0	0.0	0.0	0.0	0.0	0.0	0.0	0.0	0.0	0.0	0.0	0.0	0.0	0.0	0.0	0.0	0.0	0.0	0.0	0.1	0.1	0.2	0.2	0.3
25	0.0	0.0	0.0	0.0	0.0	0.0	0.0	0.0	0.0	0.0	0.0	0.0	0.0	0.0	0.0	0.0	0.0	0.0	0.0	0.0	0.0	0.0	0.0	0.0	0.0	0.0	0.0	0.0	0.0	0.0	0.0	0.0	0.0	0.0	0.0	0.0	0.0	0.0	0.0
24	0.0	0.0	0.0	0.0	0.0	0.0	0.0	0.0	0.0	0.0	0.0	0.0	0.0	0.0	0.0	0.0	0.0	0.0	0.0	0.0	0.0	0.0	0.0	0.0	0.0	0.0	0.0	0.0	0.0	0.0	0.0	0.0	0.0	0.0	0.0	0.0	0.0	0.0	0.0
23	0.0	0.0	0.0	0.0	0.0	0.0	0.0	0.0	0.0	0.0	0.0	0.0	0.0	0.0	0.0	0.0	0.0	0.0	0.0	0.0	0.0	0.0	0.0	0.0	0.0	0.0	0.0	0.0	0.0	0.0	0.0	0.0	0.0	0.0	0.0	0.0	0.0	0.0	0.0
22	0.0	0.0	0.0	0.0	0.0	0.0	0.0	0.0	0.0	0.0	0.0	0.0	0.0	0.0	0.0	0.0	0.0	0.0	0.0	0.0	0.0	0.0	0.0	0.0	0.0	0.0	0.0	0.0	0.0	0.0	0.0	0.0	0.0	0.0	0.0	0.0	0.0	0.0	0.0
21	0.0	0.0	0.0	0.0	0.0	0.0	0.0	0.0	0.0	0.0	0.0	0.0	0.0	0.0	0.0	0.0	0.0	0.0	0.0	0.0	0.0	0.0	0.0	0.0	0.0	0.0	0.0	0.0	0.0	0.0	0.0	0.0	0.0	0.0	0.0	0.0	0.0	0.0	0.0

LISTED CALL OPTION PRICE WHEN EXERCISE PRICE IS 40′

NUMBER OF WEEKS BEFORE THE OPTION EXPIRES

Common Stock Price	1	2	3	4	5	6	7	8	9	10	11	12	13	14	15	16	17	18	19	20	21	22	23	24	25	26	27	28	29	30	31	32	33	34	35	36	37	38	39
56	16.0	16.1	16.1	16.1	16.1	16.2	16.2	16.2	16.2	16.3	16.3	16.3	16.3	16.4	16.4	16.4	16.4	16.5	16.5	16.5	16.5	16.6	16.6	16.6	16.7	16.7	16.7	16.7	16.8	16.8	16.8	16.8	16.9	16.9	16.9	16.9	17.0	17.0	17.0
55	15.0	15.1	15.1	15.1	15.2	15.2	15.2	15.3	15.3	15.3	15.3	15.4	15.4	15.4	15.5	15.5	15.5	15.6	15.6	15.6	15.7	15.7	15.7	15.8	15.8	15.8	15.8	15.9	15.9	15.9	16.0	16.0	16.0	16.1	16.1	16.1	16.2	16.2	16.2
54	14.0	14.1	14.1	14.1	14.2	14.2	14.3	14.3	14.3	14.4	14.4	14.4	14.5	14.5	14.5	14.6	14.6	14.7	14.7	14.7	14.8	14.8	14.8	14.9	14.9	14.9	15.0	15.0	15.1	15.1	15.1	15.2	15.2	15.2	15.3	15.3	15.3	15.4	15.4
53	13.0	13.1	13.1	13.2	13.2	13.2	13.3	13.3	13.4	13.4	13.5	13.5	13.5	13.6	13.6	13.7	13.7	13.7	13.8	13.8	13.9	13.9	14.0	14.0	14.0	14.1	14.1	1.42	14.2	14.2	14.3	14.3	14.4	14.4	14.5	14.5	14.5	14.6	14.6
52	12.0	12.1	12.1	12.2	12.2	12.3	12.3	12.4	12.4	12.5	12.5	12.6	12.6	12.7	12.7	12.7	12.8	12.8	12.9	12.9	13.0	13.0	13.1	13.1	13.2	13.2	13.3	13.3	13.4	13.4	13.4	13.5	13.5	13.6	13.6	13.7	13.7	13.8	13.8
51	11.1	11.1	11.2	11.2	11.3	11.3	11.4	11.4	11.5	11.5	11.6	11.6	11.7	11.7	11.8	11.8	11.9	11.9	12.0	12.0	12.1	12.1	12.2	12.2	12.3	12.3	12.4	12.5	12.5	12.6	12.6	12.7	12.7	12.8	12.8	12.9	12.9	13.0	13.0
50	10.1	10.1	10.2	10.2	10.3	10.3	10.4	10.5	10.5	10.6	10.6	10.7	10.7	10.8	10.9	10.9	11.0	11.0	11.1	11.1	11.2	11.3	11.3	11.4	11.4	11.5	11.5	11.6	11.7	11.7	11.8	11.8	11.9	11.9	12.0	12.0	12.1	12.2	12.2
49	9.1	9.1	9.2	9.2	9.3	9.4	9.4	9.5	9.6	9.6	9.7	9.7	9.8	9.9	9.9	9.9	10.1	10.1	10.2	10.2	10.3	10.4	10.4	10.5	10.6	10.6	10.7	10.7	10.8	10.9	10.9	11.0	11.0	11.1	11.2	11.2	11.3	11.4	11.4
48	8.1	8.1	8.2	8.3	8.3	8.4	8.5	8.5	8.6	8.7	8.7	8.8	8.9	8.9	9.0	9.1	9.1	9.2	9.3	9.3	9.4	9.5	9.5	9.6	9.7	9.7	9.8	9.9	9.9	10.0	10.1	10.1	10.2	10.3	10.4	10.4	10.5	10.6	10.6
47	7.1	7.1	7.2	7.3	7.4	7.4	7.5	7.6	7.7	7.7	7.8	7.9	7.9	8.0	8.1	8.2	8.2	8.3	8.4	8.4	8.5	8.6	8.7	8.7	8.8	8.9	9.0	9.0	9.1	9.2	9.2	9.3	9.4	9.5	9.5	9.6	9.7	9.7	9.8
46	6.1	6.2	6.2	6.3	6.4	6.5	6.5	6.6	6.7	6.8	6.9	6.9	7.0	7.1	7.2	7.2	7.3	7.4	7.5	7.5	7.6	7.7	7.8	7.9	7.9	8.0	8.1	8.2	8.2	8.3	8.4	8.5	8.6	8.6	8.7	8.8	8.9	8.9	9.0
45	5.1	5.2	5.2	5.3	5.4	5.5	5.6	5.7	5.7	5.8	5.9	6.0	6.1	6.2	6.2	6.3	6.4	6.5	6.6	6.7	6.7	6.8	6.9	7.0	7.1	7.1	7.2	7.3	7.4	7.5	7.6	7.6	7.7	7.8	7.9	8.0	8.1	8.1	8.2
44	4.1	4.2	4.3	4.3	4.4	4.5	4.6	4.7	4.8	4.9	5.0	5.1	5.2	5.3	5.3	5.3	5.4	5.5	5.6	5.7	5.7	5.8	6.1	6.2	6.2	6.3	6.4	6.5	6.6	6.8	6.8	6.8	6.9	6.9	7.0	7.1	7.2	7.3	7.4
43	3.2	3.3	3.5	3.6	3.7	3.8	4.0	4.1	4.2	4.3	4.5	4.6	4.8	4.9	5.0	5.0	5.1	5.1	5.1	5.3	5.5	5.5	5.7	5.8	5.8	5.9	5.9	5.9	6.0	6.2	6.2	6.2	6.3	6.3	6.4	6.5	6.6	6.7	6.8
42	2.3	2.5	2.7	2.9	3.1	3.2	3.4	3.5	3.6	3.7	3.9	4.0	4.2	4.3	4.4	4.4	4.5	4.5	4.6	4.7	4.9	4.9	5.1	5.2	5.2	5.3	5.4	5.4	5.5	5.5	5.6	5.6	5.7	5.7	5.8	5.8	5.9	6.0	6.1
41	1.5	1.7	1.9	2.1	2.3	2.4	2.6	2.7	2.9	3.0	3.2	3.3	3.5	3.6	3.7	3.7	3.8	3.8	3.9	4.0	4.1	4.1	4.3	4.4	4.4	4.5	4.6	4.6	4.6	4.7	4.7	4.7	4.8	4.8	4.9	5.0	5.1	5.2	5.2
40	0.7	1.0	1.2	1.4	1.6	1.7	1.9	2.0	2.1	2.3	2.4	2.5	2.6	2.7	2.8	2.8	2.9	3.0	3.1	3.2	3.3	3.3	3.4	3.5	3.6	3.6	3.7	3.8	3.8	3.9	4.0	4.0	4.1	4.1	4.2	4.3	4.3	4.4	4.4
39	0.3	0.6	0.8	1.0	1.2	1.3	1.5	1.6	1.7	1.9	2.0	2.1	2.2	2.3	2.4	2.4	2.5	2.6	2.7	2.8	2.9	2.9	3.0	3.1	3.2	3.2	3.3	3.4	3.4	3.5	3.6	3.6	3.7	3.7	3.8	3.9	3.9	4.0	4.0
38	0.0	0.2	0.4	0.6	0.8	0.9	1.1	1.2	1.3	1.5	1.6	1.7	1.8	1.9	2.0	2.0	2.1	2.2	2.3	2.4	2.5	2.5	2.6	2.7	2.8	2.8	2.9	3.0	3.0	3.1	3.2	3.2	3.3	3.3	3.4	3.5	3.5	3.6	3.6
37	0.0	0.0	0.0	0.2	0.4	0.5	0.7	0.8	0.9	1.1	1.2	1.3	1.4	1.5	1.6	1.6	1.7	1.8	1.9	2.0	2.1	2.1	2.2	2.3	2.4	2.4	2.5	2.6	2.6	2.7	2.8	2.8	2.9	2.9	3.0	3.1	3.1	3.2	3.2
36	0.0	0.0	0.0	0.0	0.0	0.1	0.3	0.4	0.5	0.7	0.8	0.9	1.0	1.1	1.2	1.2	1.3	1.4	1.5	1.6	1.7	1.7	1.8	1.9	2.0	2.0	2.1	2.2	2.2	2.3	2.4	2.4	2.5	2.5	2.6	2.7	2.7	2.8	2.8
35	0.0	0.0	0.0	0.0	0.0	0.0	0.0	0.0	0.1	0.3	0.4	0.5	0.6	0.7	0.8	0.8	0.9	1.0	1.1	1.2	1.3	1.3	1.4	1.5	1.6	1.6	1.7	1.8	1.8	1.9	2.0	2.0	2.1	2.1	2.2	2.3	2.3	2.4	2.4
34	0.0	0.0	0.0	0.0	0.0	0.0	0.0	0.0	0.0	0.0	0.0	0.1	0.2	0.3	0.4	0.4	0.5	0.6	0.7	0.8	0.9	0.9	1.0	1.1	1.2	1.2	1.3	1.4	1.4	1.5	1.6	1.6	1.7	1.7	1.8	1.9	1.9	2.0	2.0
33	0.0	0.0	0.0	0.0	0.0	0.0	0.0	0.0	0.0	0.0	0.0	0.0	0.0	0.0	0.0	0.0	0.1	0.2	0.3	0.4	0.5	0.5	0.6	0.7	0.8	0.8	0.9	1.0	1.0	1.1	1.2	1.2	1.3	1.3	1.4	1.5	1.5	1.6	1.6
32	0.0	0.0	0.0	0.0	0.0	0.0	0.0	0.0	0.0	0.0	0.0	0.0	0.0	0.0	0.0	0.0	0.0	0.0	0.0	0.0	0.1	0.1	0.2	0.3	0.4	0.4	0.5	0.6	0.6	0.7	0.8	0.8	0.9	0.9	1.0	1.1	1.1	1.2	1.2
31	0.0	0.0	0.0	0.0	0.0	0.0	0.0	0.0	0.0	0.0	0.0	0.0	0.0	0.0	0.0	0.0	0.0	0.0	0.0	0.0	0.0	0.0	0.0	0.0	0.0	0.0	0.1	0.2	0.2	0.3	0.4	0.4	0.5	0.5	0.6	0.7	0.7	0.8	0.8
30	0.0	0.0	0.0	0.0	0.0	0.0	0.0	0.0	0.0	0.0	0.0	0.0	0.0	0.0	0.0	0.0	0.0	0.0	0.0	0.0	0.0	0.0	0.0	0.0	0.0	0.0	0.0	0.0	0.0	0.0	0.0	0.0	0.1	0.1	0.2	0.3	0.3	0.4	0.4
29	0.0	0.0	0.0	0.0	0.0	0.0	0.0	0.0	0.0	0.0	0.0	0.0	0.0	0.0	0.0	0.0	0.0	0.0	0.0	0.0	0.0	0.0	0.0	0.0	0.0	0.0	0.0	0.0	0.0	0.0	0.0	0.0	0.0	0.0	0.0	0.0	0.0	0.0	0.0

LISTED CALL OPTION PRICE WHEN EXERCISE PRICE IS 45

Common Stock Price	NUMBER OF WEEKS BEFORE THE OPTION EXPIRES 1	2	3	4	5	6	7	8	9	10	11	12	13	14	15	16	17	18	19	20	21	22	23	24	25	26	27	28	29	30	31	32	33	34	35	36	37	38	39
63	18.0	18.1	18.1	18.1	18.1	18.2	18.2	18.2	18.3	18.3	18.3	18.4	18.4	18.4	18.4	18.5	18.5	18.5	18.6	18.6	18.6	18.6	18.7	18.7	18.7	18.8	18.8	18.8	18.9	18.9	18.9	18.9	19.0	19.0	19.0	19.1	19.1	19.1	19.1
62	17.0	17.1	17.1	17.1	17.2	17.2	17.2	17.3	17.3	17.3	17.4	17.4	17.4	17.5	17.5	17.6	17.6	17.6	17.7	17.7	17.7	17.8	17.8	17.8	17.9	17.9	17.9	18.0	18.0	18.0	18.1	18.1	18.1	18.2	18.2	18.2	18.3	18.3	18.3
61	16.0	16.1	16.1	16.2	16.2	16.2	16.3	16.3	16.4	16.4	16.4	16.5	16.5	16.6	16.6	16.6	16.7	16.7	16.8	16.8	16.8	16.9	16.9	17.0	17.0	17.0	17.1	17.1	17.2	17.2	17.2	17.3	17.3	17.3	17.4	17.4	17.5	17.5	17.5
60	15.0	15.1	15.1	15.2	15.2	15.3	15.3	15.4	15.4	15.4	15.5	15.5	15.6	15.6	15.7	15.7	15.8	15.8	15.9	15.9	15.9	16.0	16.0	16.1	16.1	16.2	16.2	16.3	16.3	16.3	16.4	16.4	16.5	16.5	16.6	16.6	16.7	16.7	16.7
59	14.0	14.1	14.1	14.2	14.2	14.3	14.3	14.4	14.4	14.5	14.5	14.6	14.6	14.7	14.7	14.8	14.8	14.9	14.9	15.0	15.0	15.1	15.1	15.2	15.2	15.3	15.3	15.4	15.4	15.5	15.5	15.6	15.6	15.7	15.7	15.8	15.8	15.9	15.9
58	13.1	13.1	13.2	13.2	13.3	13.3	13.4	13.4	13.5	13.6	13.6	13.7	13.7	13.8	13.8	13.9	13.9	14.0	14.0	14.1	14.2	14.2	14.3	14.3	14.4	14.4	14.5	14.5	14.6	14.7	14.7	14.8	14.8	14.9	14.9	15.0	15.0	15.1	15.1
57	12.1	12.1	12.2	12.2	12.3	12.4	12.4	12.5	12.5	12.6	12.7	12.7	12.8	12.8	12.9	13.0	13.0	13.1	13.1	13.2	13.3	13.3	13.4	13.4	13.5	13.6	13.6	13.7	13.7	13.8	13.9	13.9	14.0	14.0	14.1	14.2	14.2	14.3	14.3
56	11.1	11.1	11.2	11.3	11.3	11.4	11.5	11.5	11.6	11.7	11.7	11.8	11.8	11.9	12.0	12.0	12.1	12.2	12.2	12.3	12.4	12.4	12.5	12.6	12.6	12.7	12.8	12.8	12.9	13.0	13.0	13.1	13.2	13.2	13.3	13.4	13.4	13.5	13.5
55	10.1	10.1	10.2	10.3	10.4	10.4	10.5	10.6	10.6	10.7	10.8	10.8	10.9	11.0	11.1	11.1	11.2	11.3	11.3	11.4	11.5	11.5	11.6	11.7	11.8	11.8	11.9	12.0	12.0	12.1	12.2	12.3	12.3	12.4	12.5	12.5	12.6	12.7	12.7
54	9.1	9.2	9.2	9.3	9.4	9.5	9.5	9.6	9.7	9.8	9.8	9.9	9.9	10.1	10.1	10.2	10.3	10.4	10.4	10.5	10.6	10.7	10.7	10.8	10.9	11.0	11.0	11.1	11.2	11.3	11.3	11.4	11.5	11.6	11.6	11.7	11.8	11.9	11.9
53	8.1	8.2	8.2	8.3	8.4	8.5	8.6	8.6	8.7	8.8	8.9	9.0	9.0	9.1	9.2	9.3	9.4	9.5	9.5	9.6	9.7	9.8	9.9	9.9	10.0	10.1	10.2	10.3	10.3	10.4	10.5	10.6	10.7	10.7	10.8	10.9	11.0	11.1	11.1
52	7.1	7.2	7.3	7.3	7.4	7.5	7.6	7.7	7.8	7.9	7.9	8.0	8.1	8.2	8.3	8.4	8.5	8.5	8.6	8.7	8.8	8.9	9.0	9.1	9.1	9.2	9.3	9.4	9.5	9.6	9.7	9.7	9.8	9.9	10.0	10.1	10.2	10.3	10.3
51	6.1	6.2	6.3	6.4	6.5	6.5	6.6	6.7	6.8	6.9	7.0	7.1	7.2	7.3	7.4	7.5	7.5	7.6	7.7	7.8	7.9	8.0	8.1	8.2	8.3	8.4	8.5	8.5	8.6	8.7	8.8	8.9	9.0	9.1	9.2	9.3	9.4	9.5	9.5
50	5.1	5.2	5.3	5.4	5.5	5.6	5.7	5.8	5.9	6.0	6.1	6.2	6.2	6.3	6.4	6.5	6.6	6.7	6.8	6.9	7.0	7.1	7.2	7.3	7.4	7.5	7.6	7.7	7.8	7.9	8.0	8.1	8.2	8.3	8.4	8.5	8.6	8.7	8.7
49	4.2	4.3	4.3	4.5	4.6	4.7	4.8	4.9	5.0	5.1	5.2	5.3	5.3	5.4	5.5	5.6	5.7	5.8	5.9	6.0	6.1	6.2	6.3	6.4	6.5	6.7	6.8	6.9	7.0	7.0	7.1	7.2	7.3	7.4	7.5	7.6	7.8	7.9	8.0
48	3.3	3.4	3.4	3.6	3.7	3.8	3.9	4.1	4.2	4.3	4.4	4.5	4.5	4.6	4.7	4.8	4.9	5.0	5.1	5.2	5.3	5.4	5.5	5.6	5.7	5.8	5.9	6.0	6.1	6.2	6.3	6.4	6.5	6.6	6.7	6.8	7.0	7.1	7.2
47	2.4	2.6	2.6	2.8	3.1	3.3	3.4	3.6	3.7	3.8	3.9	4.0	4.0	4.1	4.2	4.3	4.4	4.5	4.6	4.7	4.8	4.8	4.8	4.9	5.0	5.1	5.2	5.3	5.4	5.5	5.6	5.6	5.7	5.8	5.9	6.0	6.2	6.3	6.4
46	1.6	1.8	2.0	2.2	2.4	2.6	2.7	2.9	3.0	3.1	3.3	3.4	3.5	3.6	3.7	3.8	3.9	4.0	4.1	4.2	4.3	4.4	4.4	4.5	4.6	4.7	4.8	4.9	5.0	5.1	5.2	5.2	5.2	5.3	5.3	5.4	5.5	5.6	5.6
45	0.8	1.1	1.4	1.6	1.8	2.0	2.1	2.3	2.4	2.5	2.7	2.8	2.9	3.0	3.1	3.2	3.3	3.4	3.5	3.6	3.7	3.8	3.8	3.9	4.0	4.1	4.2	4.2	4.3	4.4	4.5	4.5	4.6	4.7	4.7	4.8	4.9	4.9	5.0
44	0.4	0.7	1.0	1.2	1.4	1.6	1.7	1.9	2.0	2.1	2.3	2.4	2.5	2.6	2.7	2.8	2.9	3.0	3.1	3.2	3.3	3.4	3.4	3.5	3.6	3.7	3.8	3.8	3.9	4.0	4.1	4.1	4.2	4.3	4.3	4.4	4.5	4.5	4.6
43	0.0	0.3	0.6	0.8	1.0	1.2	1.3	1.5	1.6	1.7	1.9	2.0	2.1	2.2	2.3	2.4	2.5	2.6	2.7	2.8	2.9	3.0	3.0	3.1	3.2	3.3	3.4	3.4	3.5	3.6	3.7	3.7	3.8	3.9	3.9	4.0	4.1	4.1	4.2
42	0.0	0.0	0.2	0.4	0.6	0.8	0.9	1.1	1.2	1.3	1.5	1.6	1.7	1.8	1.9	2.0	2.1	2.2	2.3	2.4	2.5	2.6	2.6	2.7	2.8	2.9	3.0	3.0	3.1	3.2	3.3	3.3	3.4	3.5	3.5	3.6	3.7	3.7	3.8
41	0.0	0.0	0.0	0.0	0.2	0.4	0.5	0.7	0.8	0.9	1.1	1.2	1.3	1.4	1.5	1.6	1.7	1.8	1.9	2.0	2.1	2.2	2.2	2.3	2.4	2.5	2.6	2.6	2.7	2.8	2.9	2.9	3.0	3.1	3.1	3.2	3.3	3.3	3.4
40	0.0	0.0	0.0	0.0	0.0	0.0	0.1	0.3	0.4	0.5	0.7	0.8	0.9	1.0	1.1	1.2	1.3	1.4	1.5	1.6	1.7	1.8	1.8	1.9	2.0	2.1	2.2	2.2	2.3	2.4	2.5	2.5	2.6	2.7	2.7	2.8	2.9	2.9	3.0
39	0.0	0.0	0.0	0.0	0.0	0.0	0.0	0.0	0.0	0.1	0.3	0.4	0.5	0.6	0.7	0.8	0.9	1.0	1.1	1.2	1.3	1.4	1.4	1.5	1.6	1.7	1.8	1.8	1.9	2.0	2.1	2.1	2.2	2.3	2.3	2.4	2.5	2.5	2.6
38	0.0	0.0	0.0	0.0	0.0	0.0	0.0	0.0	0.0	0.0	0.0	0.0	0.1	0.2	0.3	0.4	0.5	0.6	0.7	0.8	0.9	1.0	1.0	1.1	1.2	1.3	1.4	1.4	1.5	1.6	1.7	1.7	1.8	1.9	1.9	2.0	2.1	2.1	2.2
37	0.0	0.0	0.0	0.0	0.0	0.0	0.0	0.0	0.0	0.0	0.0	0.0	0.0	0.0	0.0	0.0	0.1	0.2	0.3	0.4	0.5	0.6	0.6	0.7	0.8	0.9	1.0	1.0	1.1	1.2	1.3	1.3	1.4	1.5	1.5	1.6	1.7	1.7	1.8
36	0.0	0.0	0.0	0.0	0.0	0.0	0.0	0.0	0.0	0.0	0.0	0.0	0.0	0.0	0.0	0.0	0.0	0.0	0.0	0.0	0.1	0.2	0.2	0.3	0.4	0.5	0.6	0.6	0.7	0.8	0.9	0.9	1.0	1.1	1.1	1.2	1.3	1.3	1.4
35	0.0	0.0	0.0	0.0	0.0	0.0	0.0	0.0	0.0	0.0	0.0	0.0	0.0	0.0	0.0	0.0	0.0	0.0	0.0	0.0	0.0	0.0	0.0	0.0	0.0	0.1	0.2	0.2	0.3	0.4	0.5	0.5	0.6	0.7	0.7	0.8	0.9	0.9	1.0
34	0.0	0.0	0.0	0.0	0.0	0.0	0.0	0.0	0.0	0.0	0.0	0.0	0.0	0.0	0.0	0.0	0.0	0.0	0.0	0.0	0.0	0.0	0.0	0.0	0.0	0.0	0.0	0.0	0.0	0.0	0.1	0.1	0.2	0.3	0.3	0.4	0.5	0.5	0.6
33	0.0	0.0	0.0	0.0	0.0	0.0	0.0	0.0	0.0	0.0	0.0	0.0	0.0	0.0	0.0	0.0	0.0	0.0	0.0	0.0	0.0	0.0	0.0	0.0	0.0	0.0	0.0	0.0	0.0	0.0	0.0	0.0	0.0	0.0	0.0	0.0	0.1	0.1	0.2
32	0.0	0.0	0.0	0.0	0.0	0.0	0.0	0.0	0.0	0.0	0.0	0.0	0.0	0.0	0.0	0.0	0.0	0.0	0.0	0.0	0.0	0.0	0.0	0.0	0.0	0.0	0.0	0.0	0.0	0.0	0.0	0.0	0.0	0.0	0.0	0.0	0.0	0.0	0.0
31	0.0	0.0	0.0	0.0	0.0	0.0	0.0	0.0	0.0	0.0	0.0	0.0	0.0	0.0	0.0	0.0	0.0	0.0	0.0	0.0	0.0	0.0	0.0	0.0	0.0	0.0	0.0	0.0	0.0	0.0	0.0	0.0	0.0	0.0	0.0	0.0	0.0	0.0	0.0
30	0.0	0.0	0.0	0.0	0.0	0.0	0.0	0.0	0.0	0.0	0.0	0.0	0.0	0.0	0.0	0.0	0.0	0.0	0.0	0.0	0.0	0.0	0.0	0.0	0.0	0.0	0.0	0.0	0.0	0.0	0.0	0.0	0.0	0.0	0.0	0.0	0.0	0.0	0.0
29	0.0	0.0	0.0	0.0	0.0	0.0	0.0	0.0	0.0	0.0	0.0	0.0	0.0	0.0	0.0	0.0	0.0	0.0	0.0	0.0	0.0	0.0	0.0	0.0	0.0	0.0	0.0	0.0	0.0	0.0	0.0	0.0	0.0	0.0	0.0	0.0	0.0	0.0	0.0
28	0.0	0.0	0.0	0.0	0.0	0.0	0.0	0.0	0.0	0.0	0.0	0.0	0.0	0.0	0.0	0.0	0.0	0.0	0.0	0.0	0.0	0.0	0.0	0.0	0.0	0.0	0.0	0.0	0.0	0.0	0.0	0.0	0.0	0.0	0.0	0.0	0.0	0.0	0.0
27	0.0	0.0	0.0	0.0	0.0	0.0	0.0	0.0	0.0	0.0	0.0	0.0	0.0	0.0	0.0	0.0	0.0	0.0	0.0	0.0	0.0	0.0	0.0	0.0	0.0	0.0	0.0	0.0	0.0	0.0	0.0	0.0	0.0	0.0	0.0	0.0	0.0	0.0	0.0

LISTED CALL OPTION PRICE WHEN EXERCISE PRICE IS 50

NUMBER OF WEEKS BEFORE THE OPTION EXPIRES

Common Stock Price	1	2	3	4	5	6	7	8	9	10	11	12	13	14	15	16	17	18	19	20	21	22	23	24	25	26	27	28	29	30	31	32	33	34	35	36	37	38	39
65	15.1	15.1	15.2	15.2	15.3	15.3	15.4	15.5	15.5	15.6	15.6	15.7	15.8	15.8	15.9	15.9	16.0	16.0	16.1	16.2	16.2	16.3	16.3	16.4	16.5	16.5	16.6	16.6	16.7	16.8	16.8	16.9	16.9	17.0	17.0	17.1	17.2	17.2	17.3
64	14.1	14.1	14.2	14.3	14.3	14.4	14.4	14.5	14.6	14.6	14.7	14.8	14.8	14.9	15.0	15.0	15.1	15.1	15.2	15.3	15.3	15.4	15.5	15.5	15.6	15.6	15.7	15.8	15.8	15.9	16.0	16.0	16.1	16.2	16.2	16.3	16.3	16.4	16.5
63	13.1	13.1	13.2	13.3	13.3	13.4	13.5	13.5	13.6	13.7	13.8	13.8	13.9	14.0	14.0	14.1	14.2	14.2	14.3	14.4	14.4	14.5	14.6	14.6	14.7	14.8	14.9	14.9	15.0	15.1	15.1	15.2	15.3	15.3	15.4	15.5	15.5	15.6	15.7
62	12.1	12.1	12.2	12.3	12.4	12.4	12.5	12.6	12.7	12.7	12.8	12.9	13.0	13.0	13.1	13.2	13.3	13.3	13.4	13.5	13.5	13.6	13.7	13.8	13.8	13.9	14.0	14.1	14.1	14.2	14.3	14.4	14.4	14.5	14.6	14.7	14.7	14.8	14.9
61	11.1	11.2	11.2	11.3	11.4	11.5	11.6	11.6	11.7	11.8	11.9	11.9	12.0	12.1	12.2	12.3	12.3	12.4	12.5	12.6	12.7	12.7	12.8	12.9	13.0	13.1	13.1	13.2	13.3	13.4	13.4	13.5	13.6	13.7	13.8	13.8	13.9	14.0	14.1
60	10.1	10.2	10.3	10.3	10.4	10.5	10.6	10.7	10.8	10.8	1.09	11.0	11.1	11.2	11.3	11.3	11.4	11.5	11.6	11.7	11.8	11.8	11.9	12.0	12.1	12.2	12.3	12.4	12.4	12.5	12.6	12.7	12.8	12.9	12.9	13.0	13.1	13.2	13.3
59	9.1	9.2	9.3	9.4	9.4	9.5	9.6	9.7	9.8	9.9	9.9	10.1	10.2	10.2	10.3	10.4	10.5	10.6	10.7	10.8	10.9	11.0	11.0	11.1	11.2	11.3	11.4	11.5	11.6	11.7	11.8	11.9	11.9	12.0	12.1	12.2	12.3	12.4	12.5
58	8.1	8.2	8.3	8.4	8.5	8.6	8.7	8.8	8.8	8.9	9.0	9.1	9.2	9.3	9.4	9.5	9.6	9.7	9.8	9.9	9.9	10.1	10.2	10.3	10.4	10.5	10.5	10.6	10.7	10.8	10.9	11.0	11.1	11.2	11.3	11.4	11.5	11.6	11.7
57	7.1	7.2	7.3	7.4	7.5	7.6	7.7	7.8	7.9	8.0	8.1	8.2	8.3	8.4	8.5	8.6	8.7	8.8	8.9	9.0	9.1	9.2	9.3	9.4	9.5	9.6	9.7	9.8	9.9	9.9	10.1	10.2	10.3	10.4	10.5	10.6	10.7	10.8	10.9
56	6.1	6.2	6.3	6.4	6.5	6.6	6.7	6.8	6.9	7.0	7.1	7.3	7.4	7.5	7.6	7.7	7.8	7.9	8.0	8.1	8.2	8.3	8.4	8.5	8.6	8.7	8.8	8.9	9.0	9.1	9.2	9.3	9.4	9.6	9.7	9.8	9.9	9.9	10.1
55	5.2	5.2	5.3	5.4	5.5	5.6	5.8	5.9	6.0	6.1	6.3	6.4	6.5	6.6	6.7	6.8	6.9	7.0	7.1	7.2	7.3	7.4	7.5	7.6	7.7	7.8	7.9	8.0	8.1	8.2	8.3	8.4	8.5	8.7	8.8	8.9	9.0	9.1	9.2
54	4.2	4.3	4.4	4.5	4.6	4.7	4.9	5.0	5.1	5.3	5.5	5.6	5.7	5.8	5.9	6.0	6.1	6.2	6.3	6.4	6.5	6.6	6.7	6.8	6.9	7.0	7.1	7.2	7.3	7.4	7.5	7.6	7.8	7.9	8.0	8.1	8.2	8.3	8.4
53	3.3	3.4	3.5	3.6	3.8	3.9	4.1	4.2	4.4	4.5	4.7	4.8	4.9	5.0	5.1	5.2	5.3	5.5	5.6	5.7	5.8	5.9	6.0	6.1	6.2	6.3	6.4	6.5	6.6	6.7	6.8	6.9	7.0	7.2	7.3	7.4	7.5	7.6	7.7
52	2.3	2.5	2.7	3.0	3.2	3.4	3.6	3.7	3.9	3.9	4.1	4.2	4.3	4.4	4.5	4.7	4.8	4.9	5.0	5.1	5.2	5.3	5.4	5.5	5.5	5.6	5.7	5.8	5.9	6.0	6.1	6.2	6.3	6.5	6.6	6.7	6.8	6.9	7.0
51	1.4	1.8	2.0	2.3	2.5	2.7	2.9	3.0	3.2	3.3	3.5	3.6	3.7	3.8	3.9	4.1	4.2	4.3	4.4	4.5	4.6	4.7	4.8	4.9	4.9	5.0	5.1	5.2	5.3	5.4	5.4	5.5	5.6	5.7	5.8	5.9	6.0	6.1	6.2
50	0.9	1.3	1.5	1.8	2.0	2.2	2.4	2.5	2.7	2.8	3.0	3.1	3.2	3.3	3.4	3.6	3.7	3.8	3.9	4.0	4.1	4.2	4.3	4.4	4.4	4.5	4.6	4.7	4.8	4.9	5.0	5.0	5.1	5.2	5.3	5.3	5.4	5.5	5.6
49	0.5	0.9	1.1	1.4	1.6	1.8	2.0	2.1	2.3	2.4	2.6	2.7	2.8	2.9	3.0	3.2	3.3	3.4	3.5	3.6	3.7	3.8	3.9	4.0	4.0	4.1	4.2	4.3	4.4	4.5	4.6	4.6	4.7	4.8	4.9	4.9	5.0	5.1	5.2
48	0.1	0.5	0.7	1.0	1.2	1.4	1.6	1.7	1.9	2.0	2.2	2.3	2.4	2.5	2.6	2.8	2.9	3.0	3.1	3.2	3.2	3.4	3.5	3.6	3.6	3.7	3.8	3.9	4.0	4.1	4.2	4.2	4.3	4.4	4.5	4.5	4.6	4.7	4.8
47	0.0	0.1	0.3	0.6	0.8	1.0	1.2	1.3	1.5	1.6	1.8	1.9	2.0	2.1	2.2	2.4	2.5	2.6	2.7	2.8	2.9	3.0	3.1	3.2	3.2	3.3	3.4	3.5	3.6	3.7	3.8	3.8	3.9	4.0	4.1	4.1	4.2	4.3	4.4
46	0.0	0.0	0.0	0.2	0.4	0.6	0.8	0.9	1.1	1.2	1.4	1.5	1.6	1.7	1.8	2.0	2.1	2.2	2.3	2.4	2.5	2.6	2.7	2.8	2.8	2.9	3.0	3.1	3.2	3.3	3.4	3.4	3.5	3.6	3.7	3.7	3.8	3.9	4.0
45	0.0	0.0	0.0	0.0	0.0	0.2	0.4	0.5	0.7	0.8	1.0	1.1	1.2	1.3	1.4	1.6	1.7	1.8	1.9	2.0	2.1	2.2	2.3	2.4	2.4	2.5	2.6	2.7	2.8	2.9	3.0	3.0	3.1	3.2	3.3	3.3	3.4	3.5	3.6
44	0.0	0.0	0.0	0.0	0.0	0.0	0.0	0.1	0.3	0.4	0.6	0.7	0.8	0.9	1.0	1.2	1.3	1.4	1.5	1.6	1.7	1.8	1.9	2.0	2.0	2.1	2.2	2.3	2.4	2.5	2.6	2.6	2.7	2.8	2.9	2.9	3.0	3.1	3.2
43	0.0	0.0	0.0	0.0	0.0	0.0	0.0	0.0	0.0	0.0	0.2	0.3	0.4	0.5	0.6	0.8	0.9	1.0	1.1	1.2	1.3	1.4	1.5	1.6	1.6	1.7	1.8	1.9	2.0	2.1	2.2	2.2	2.3	2.4	2.5	2.5	2.6	2.7	2.8
42	0.0	0.0	0.0	0.0	0.0	0.0	0.0	0.0	0.0	0.0	0.0	0.0	0.0	0.1	0.2	0.4	0.5	0.6	0.7	0.8	0.9	1.0	1.1	1.2	1.2	1.3	1.4	1.5	1.6	1.7	1.8	1.8	1.9	2.0	2.1	2.1	2.2	2.3	2.4
41	0.0	0.0	0.0	0.0	0.0	0.0	0.0	0.0	0.0	0.0	0.0	0.0	0.0	0.0	0.0	0.0	0.1	0.2	0.3	0.4	0.5	0.6	0.7	0.8	0.8	0.9	1.0	1.1	1.2	1.3	1.4	1.4	1.5	1.6	1.7	1.7	1.8	1.9	2.0
40	0.0	0.0	0.0	0.0	0.0	0.0	0.0	0.0	0.0	0.0	0.0	0.0	0.0	0.0	0.0	0.0	0.0	0.0	0.0	0.0	0.1	0.2	0.3	0.4	0.4	0.5	0.6	0.7	0.8	0.9	1.0	1.0	1.1	1.2	1.3	1.3	1.4	1.5	1.6
39	0.0	0.0	0.0	0.0	0.0	0.0	0.0	0.0	0.0	0.0	0.0	0.0	0.0	0.0	0.0	0.0	0.0	0.0	0.0	0.0	0.0	0.0	0.0	0.0	0.0	0.1	0.2	0.3	0.4	0.5	0.6	0.6	0.7	0.8	0.9	0.9	1.0	1.1	1.2
38	0.0	0.0	0.0	0.0	0.0	0.0	0.0	0.0	0.0	0.0	0.0	0.0	0.0	0.0	0.0	0.0	0.0	0.0	0.0	0.0	0.0	0.0	0.0	0.0	0.0	0.0	0.0	0.0	0.0	0.1	0.2	0.2	0.3	0.4	0.5	0.5	0.6	0.7	0.8
37	0.0	0.0	0.0	0.0	0.0	0.0	0.0	0.0	0.0	0.0	0.0	0.0	0.0	0.0	0.0	0.0	0.0	0.0	0.0	0.0	0.0	0.0	0.0	0.0	0.0	0.0	0.0	0.0	0.0	0.0	0.0	0.0	0.0	0.0	0.1	0.1	0.2	0.3	0.4
36	0.0	0.0	0.0	0.0	0.0	0.0	0.0	0.0	0.0	0.0	0.0	0.0	0.0	0.0	0.0	0.0	0.0	0.0	0.0	0.0	0.0	0.0	0.0	0.0	0.0	0.0	0.0	0.0	0.0	0.0	0.0	0.0	0.0	0.0	0.0	0.0	0.0	0.0	0.0
35	0.0	0.0	0.0	0.0	0.0	0.0	0.0	0.0	0.0	0.0	0.0	0.0	0.0	0.0	0.0	0.0	0.0	0.0	0.0	0.0	0.0	0.0	0.0	0.0	0.0	0.0	0.0	0.0	0.0	0.0	0.0	0.0	0.0	0.0	0.0	0.0	0.0	0.0	0.0

LISTED CALL OPTION PRICE WHEN EXERCISE PRICE IS 60

NUMBER OF WEEKS BEFORE THE OPTION EXPIRES

Common Stock Price	1	2	3	4	5	6	7	8	9	10	11	12	13	14	15	16	17	18	19	20	21	22	23	24	25	26	27	28	29	30	31	32	33	34	35	36	37	38	39
78	18.1	18.1	18.2	18.3	18.3	18.4	18.5	18.6	18.6	18.7	18.8	18.8	18.9	19.0	19.1	19.1	19.2	19.3	19.3	19.4	19.5	19.5	19.6	19.7	19.8	19.8	19.9	19.9	20.0	20.1	20.2	20.2	20.3	20.4	20.4	20.5	20.6	20.7	20.7
77	17.1	17.2	17.2	17.3	17.4	17.5	17.5	17.6	17.7	17.8	17.8	17.9	18.0	18.1	18.1	18.2	18.3	18.4	18.4	18.5	18.6	18.7	18.7	18.8	18.9	19.0	19.0	19.1	19.2	19.3	19.3	19.4	19.5	19.6	19.6	19.7	19.8	19.9	19.9
76	16.1	16.2	16.2	16.3	16.4	16.5	16.6	16.6	16.7	16.8	16.9	17.0	17.0	17.1	17.2	17.3	17.4	17.4	17.5	17.6	17.7	17.8	17.8	17.9	18.0	18.1	18.2	18.2	18.3	18.4	18.5	18.6	18.6	18.7	18.8	18.9	19.0	19.0	19.1
75	15.1	15.2	15.3	15.3	15.4	15.5	15.6	15.7	15.8	15.9	15.9	16.0	16.1	16.2	16.3	16.4	16.5	16.5	16.6	16.7	16.8	16.9	17.0	17.0	17.1	17.2	17.3	17.4	17.5	17.6	17.6	17.7	17.8	17.9	18.0	18.1	18.2	18.2	18.3
74	14.1	14.2	14.3	14.4	14.5	14.5	14.6	14.7	14.8	14.9	15.0	15.1	15.2	15.3	15.4	15.4	15.5	15.6	15.7	15.8	15.9	16.0	16.1	16.2	16.3	16.4	16.4	16.5	16.6	16.7	16.8	16.9	17.0	17.1	17.2	17.3	17.3	17.4	17.5
73	13.1	13.2	13.3	13.4	13.5	13.6	13.7	13.8	13.9	14.0	14.1	14.1	14.2	14.3	14.4	14.5	14.6	14.7	14.8	14.9	15.0	15.1	15.2	15.3	15.4	15.5	15.6	15.7	15.8	15.9	16.0	16.1	16.2	16.3	16.3	16.4	16.5	16.6	16.7
72	12.1	12.2	12.3	12.4	12.5	12.6	12.7	12.8	12.9	13.0	13.1	13.2	13.3	13.4	13.5	13.6	13.7	13.8	13.9	14.0	14.1	14.2	14.3	14.4	14.5	14.6	14.7	14.8	14.9	15.0	15.1	15.2	15.3	15.4	15.5	15.6	15.7	15.8	15.9
71	11.1	11.2	11.3	11.4	11.5	11.6	11.7	11.8	12.0	12.1	12.2	12.3	12.4	12.5	12.6	12.7	12.8	12.9	13.0	13.1	13.2	13.3	13.4	13.5	13.6	13.8	13.9	14.0	14.1	14.2	14.3	14.4	14.5	14.6	14.7	14.8	14.9	15.0	15.1
70	10.1	10.2	10.3	10.4	10.6	10.7	10.8	10.9	11.0	11.1	11.2	11.3	11.4	11.6	11.7	11.8	11.9	12.0	12.1	12.2	12.3	12.4	12.6	12.7	12.8	12.9	13.0	13.1	13.2	13.3	13.4	13.6	13.7	13.8	13.9	14.0	14.1	14.2	14.3
69	9.1	9.2	9.3	9.5	9.6	9.7	9.8	9.9	10.0	10.2	10.3	10.4	10.5	10.6	10.7	10.9	11.0	11.1	11.2	11.3	11.4	11.6	11.7	11.8	11.9	12.0	12.1	12.3	12.4	12.5	12.6	12.7	12.8	12.9	13.1	13.2	13.3	13.4	13.5
68	8.1	8.2	8.4	8.5	8.6	8.7	8.8	9.0	9.1	9.2	9.3	9.5	9.6	9.7	9.8	9.9	10.1	10.2	10.3	10.4	10.5	10.7	10.8	10.9	11.0	11.2	11.3	11.4	11.5	11.6	11.8	11.9	12.0	12.1	12.2	12.4	12.5	12.6	12.7
67	7.1	7.3	7.4	7.5	7.6	7.8	7.9	8.0	8.1	8.3	8.4	8.5	8.6	8.8	8.9	9.0	9.1	9.3	9.4	9.5	9.7	9.8	9.9	10.0	10.2	10.3	10.4	10.5	10.7	10.8	10.9	11.0	11.2	11.3	11.4	11.6	11.7	11.8	11.9
66	6.2	6.3	6.4	6.6	6.7	6.9	7.0	7.1	7.2	7.4	7.5	7.6	7.7	7.9	8.0	8.1	8.2	8.4	8.5	8.6	8.8	8.9	9.0	9.1	9.3	9.4	9.5	9.6	9.8	9.9	10.0	10.1	10.3	10.4	10.5	10.7	10.8	10.9	11.0
65	5.2	5.3	5.4	5.8	5.8	6.0	6.1	6.2	6.3	6.5	6.6	6.7	6.8	7.0	7.1	7.3	7.4	7.5	7.7	7.8	7.9	8.0	8.2	8.3	8.4	8.5	8.7	8.8	8.9	9.1	9.2	9.3	9.5	9.6	9.7	9.8	9.9	10.0	10.1
64	4.2	4.4	4.5	4.9	5.0	5.1	5.2	5.4	5.6	5.7	5.8	5.9	6.0	6.2	6.3	6.5	6.6	6.7	6.9	7.0	7.1	7.2	7.4	7.5	7.6	7.7	7.9	8.0	8.1	8.3	8.4	8.5	8.7	8.8	8.9	9.0	9.1	9.2	9.3
63	3.3	3.4	3.7	3.8	4.1	4.3	4.4	4.6	4.8	5.0	5.1	5.2	5.3	5.5	5.6	5.7	5.8	5.9	6.1	6.2	6.3	6.4	6.7	6.8	6.9	7.0	7.1	7.2	7.3	7.5	7.6	7.7	7.9	8.0	8.1	8.2	8.3	8.4	8.5
62	2.3	2.5	2.8	3.1	3.4	3.6	3.8	4.0	4.2	4.4	4.5	4.6	4.7	4.9	5.0	5.2	5.3	5.4	5.6	5.7	5.8	5.9	6.0	6.1	6.2	6.3	6.4	6.5	6.6	6.8	6.9	7.0	7.2	7.3	7.4	7.5	7.6	7.7	7.8
61	1.5	1.9	2.2	2.5	2.8	3.0	3.2	3.4	3.6	3.8	3.9	4.1	4.2	4.4	4.5	4.7	4.8	4.9	5.1	5.2	5.3	5.4	5.5	5.6	5.7	5.8	5.9	6.0	6.1	6.2	6.3	6.4	6.5	6.6	6.7	6.8	6.9	7.0	7.1
60	1.1	1.5	1.8	2.1	2.4	2.6	2.8	3.0	3.2	3.4	3.5	3.7	3.8	4.0	4.1	4.3	4.4	4.5	4.7	4.8	4.9	5.0	5.1	5.2	5.3	5.4	5.5	5.6	5.7	5.8	5.9	6.0	6.1	6.2	6.3	6.4	6.5	6.6	6.7
59	0.7	1.1	1.4	1.7	2.0	2.2	2.4	2.6	2.8	3.0	3.1	3.3	3.4	3.6	3.7	3.9	4.0	4.1	4.3	4.4	4.5	4.6	4.7	4.8	4.9	5.0	5.1	5.2	5.3	5.4	5.5	5.6	5.7	5.8	5.9	6.0	6.1	6.2	6.3
58	0.3	0.7	1.0	1.3	1.6	1.8	2.0	2.2	2.4	2.6	2.7	2.9	3.0	3.2	3.3	3.5	3.6	3.7	3.9	4.0	4.1	4.2	4.3	4.4	4.5	4.6	4.7	4.8	4.9	5.0	5.1	5.2	5.3	5.4	5.5	5.6	5.7	5.8	5.9
57	0.0	0.3	0.6	0.9	1.2	1.4	1.6	1.8	2.0	2.2	2.3	2.5	2.6	2.8	2.9	3.1	3.2	3.3	3.5	3.6	3.7	3.8	3.9	4.0	4.1	4.2	4.3	4.4	4.5	4.6	4.7	4.8	4.9	5.0	5.1	5.2	5.3	5.4	5.5
56	0.0	0.0	0.2	0.5	0.8	1.0	1.2	1.4	1.6	1.8	1.9	2.1	2.2	2.4	2.5	2.7	2.8	2.9	3.1	3.2	3.3	3.4	3.5	3.6	3.7	3.8	3.9	4.0	4.1	4.2	4.3	4.4	4.5	4.6	4.7	4.8	4.9	5.0	5.1
55	0.0	0.0	0.0	0.1	0.4	0.6	0.8	1.0	1.2	1.4	1.5	1.7	1.8	2.0	2.1	2.3	2.4	2.5	2.7	2.8	2.9	3.0	3.1	3.2	3.3	3.4	3.5	3.6	3.7	3.8	3.9	4.0	4.1	4.2	4.3	4.4	4.5	4.6	4.7
54	0.0	0.0	0.0	0.0	0.0	0.2	0.4	0.6	0.8	1.0	1.1	1.3	1.4	1.6	1.7	1.9	2.0	2.1	2.3	2.4	2.5	2.6	2.7	2.8	2.9	3.0	3.1	3.2	3.3	3.4	3.5	3.6	3.7	3.8	3.9	4.0	4.1	4.2	4.3
53	0.0	0.0	0.0	0.0	0.0	0.0	0.0	0.2	0.4	0.6	0.7	0.9	1.0	1.2	1.3	1.5	1.6	1.7	1.9	2.0	2.1	2.2	2.3	2.4	2.5	2.6	2.7	2.8	2.9	3.0	3.1	3.2	3.3	3.4	3.5	3.6	3.7	3.8	3.9
52	0.0	0.0	0.0	0.0	0.0	0.0	0.0	0.0	0.0	0.2	0.3	0.5	0.6	0.8	0.9	1.1	1.2	1.3	1.5	1.6	1.7	1.8	1.9	2.0	2.1	2.2	2.3	2.4	2.5	2.6	2.7	2.8	2.9	3.0	3.1	3.2	3.3	3.4	3.5
51	0.0	0.0	0.0	0.0	0.0	0.0	0.0	0.0	0.0	0.0	0.0	0.1	0.2	0.4	0.5	0.7	0.8	0.9	1.1	1.2	1.3	1.4	1.5	1.6	1.7	1.8	1.9	2.0	2.1	2.2	2.3	2.4	2.5	2.6	2.7	2.8	2.9	3.0	3.1
50	0.0	0.0	0.0	0.0	0.0	0.0	0.0	0.0	0.0	0.0	0.0	0.0	0.0	0.0	0.1	0.3	0.4	0.5	0.7	0.8	0.9	1.0	1.1	1.2	1.3	1.4	1.5	1.6	1.7	1.8	1.9	2.0	2.1	2.2	2.3	2.4	2.5	2.6	2.7
49	0.0	0.0	0.0	0.0	0.0	0.0	0.0	0.0	0.0	0.0	0.0	0.0	0.0	0.0	0.0	0.0	0.0	0.1	0.3	0.4	0.5	0.6	0.7	0.8	0.9	1.0	1.1	1.2	1.3	1.4	1.5	1.6	1.7	1.8	1.9	2.0	2.1	2.2	2.3
48	0.0	0.0	0.0	0.0	0.0	0.0	0.0	0.0	0.0	0.0	0.0	0.0	0.0	0.0	0.0	0.0	0.0	0.0	0.0	0.0	0.1	0.2	0.3	0.4	0.5	0.6	0.7	0.8	0.9	1.0	1.1	1.2	1.3	1.4	1.5	1.6	1.7	1.8	1.9
47	0.0	0.0	0.0	0.0	0.0	0.0	0.0	0.0	0.0	0.0	0.0	0.0	0.0	0.0	0.0	0.0	0.0	0.0	0.0	0.0	0.0	0.0	0.0	0.0	0.1	0.2	0.3	0.4	0.5	0.6	0.7	0.8	0.9	1.0	1.1	1.2	1.3	1.4	1.5
46	0.0	0.0	0.0	0.0	0.0	0.0	0.0	0.0	0.0	0.0	0.0	0.0	0.0	0.0	0.0	0.0	0.0	0.0	0.0	0.0	0.0	0.0	0.0	0.0	0.0	0.0	0.0	0.0	0.1	0.2	0.3	0.4	0.5	0.6	0.7	0.8	0.9	1.0	1.1
45	0.0	0.0	0.0	0.0	0.0	0.0	0.0	0.0	0.0	0.0	0.0	0.0	0.0	0.0	0.0	0.0	0.0	0.0	0.0	0.0	0.0	0.0	0.0	0.0	0.0	0.0	0.0	0.0	0.0	0.0	0.0	0.0	0.1	0.2	0.3	0.4	0.5	0.6	0.7
44	0.0	0.0	0.0	0.0	0.0	0.0	0.0	0.0	0.0	0.0	0.0	0.0	0.0	0.0	0.0	0.0	0.0	0.0	0.0	0.0	0.0	0.0	0.0	0.0	0.0	0.0	0.0	0.0	0.0	0.0	0.0	0.0	0.0	0.0	0.0	0.0	0.1	0.2	0.3
43	0.0	0.0	0.0	0.0	0.0	0.0	0.0	0.0	0.0	0.0	0.0	0.0	0.0	0.0	0.0	0.0	0.0	0.0	0.0	0.0	0.0	0.0	0.0	0.0	0.0	0.0	0.0	0.0	0.0	0.0	0.0	0.0	0.0	0.0	0.0	0.0	0.0	0.0	0.0
42	0.0	0.0	0.0	0.0	0.0	0.0	0.0	0.0	0.0	0.0	0.0	0.0	0.0	0.0	0.0	0.0	0.0	0.0	0.0	0.0	0.0	0.0	0.0	0.0	0.0	0.0	0.0	0.0	0.0	0.0	0.0	0.0	0.0	0.0	0.0	0.0	0.0	0.0	0.0

LISTED CALL OPTION PRICE WHEN EXERCISE PRICE IS 70

Common Stock Price	NUMBER OF WEEKS BEFORE THE OPTION EXPIRES 1	2	3	4	5	6	7	8	9	10	11	12	13	14	15	16	17	18	19	20	21	22	23	24	25	26	27	28	29	30	31	32	33	34	35	36	37	38	39
91	21.1	21.2	21.2	21.3	21.4	21.5	21.6	21.7	21.7	21.8	21.9	22.0	22.1	22.1	22.2	22.3	22.4	22.5	22.6	22.6	22.7	22.8	22.9	23.0	23.0	23.1	23.2	23.3	23.4	23.4	23.5	23.6	23.7	23.8	23.9	23.9	24.0	24.1	24.2
90	20.1	20.2	20.3	20.3	20.4	20.5	20.6	20.7	20.8	20.9	21.0	21.0	21.1	21.2	21.3	21.4	21.5	21.6	21.6	21.7	21.8	21.9	22.0	22.1	22.2	22.3	22.3	22.4	22.5	22.6	22.7	22.8	22.9	23.0	23.0	23.1	23.2	23.3	23.4
89	19.1	19.2	19.3	19.4	19.5	19.6	19.6	19.7	19.8	19.9	20.0	20.1	20.2	20.3	20.4	20.5	20.6	20.7	20.7	20.8	20.9	21.0	21.1	21.2	21.3	21.4	21.5	21.6	21.7	21.8	21.8	21.9	22.0	22.1	22.2	22.3	22.4	22.5	22.6
88	18.1	18.2	18.3	18.4	18.5	18.6	18.7	18.8	18.9	19.0	19.1	19.2	19.3	19.4	19.5	19.6	19.6	19.7	19.8	19.9	20.0	20.1	20.2	20.3	20.4	20.5	20.6	20.7	20.8	20.9	21.0	21.1	21.2	21.3	21.4	21.5	21.6	21.7	21.8
87	17.1	17.2	17.3	17.4	17.5	17.6	17.7	17.8	17.9	18.0	18.1	18.2	18.3	18.4	18.5	18.6	18.7	18.8	18.9	19.0	19.1	19.2	19.4	19.5	19.6	19.7	19.8	19.9	19.9	20.1	20.2	20.3	20.4	20.5	20.6	20.7	20.8	20.9	21.0
86	16.1	16.2	16.3	16.4	16.5	16.6	16.8	16.9	17.0	17.1	17.2	17.3	17.4	17.5	17.6	17.7	17.8	17.9	18.0	18.1	18.3	18.4	18.5	18.6	18.7	18.8	18.9	19.0	19.1	19.2	19.3	19.4	19.5	19.6	19.8	19.9	19.9	20.1	20.2
85	15.1	15.2	15.3	15.4	15.6	15.7	15.8	15.9	16.0	16.1	16.2	16.3	16.5	16.6	16.7	16.8	16.9	17.0	17.1	17.2	17.4	17.5	17.6	17.7	17.8	17.9	18.0	18.1	18.3	18.4	18.5	18.6	18.7	18.8	18.9	19.0	19.2	19.3	19.4
84	14.1	14.2	14.4	14.5	14.6	14.7	14.8	14.9	15.1	15.2	15.3	15.4	15.5	15.6	15.8	15.9	16.0	16.1	16.2	16.4	16.5	16.6	16.7	16.8	16.9	17.1	17.2	17.3	17.4	17.5	17.6	17.8	17.9	18.0	18.1	18.2	18.3	18.5	18.6
83	13.1	13.2	13.4	13.5	13.6	13.7	13.9	14.0	14.1	14.2	14.3	14.5	14.6	14.7	14.8	15.0	15.1	15.2	15.3	15.5	15.6	15.7	15.8	15.9	16.1	16.2	16.3	16.4	16.6	16.7	16.8	16.9	17.0	17.2	17.3	17.4	17.5	17.7	17.8
82	12.1	12.3	12.4	12.5	12.6	12.8	12.9	13.0	13.2	13.3	13.4	13.5	13.7	13.8	13.9	14.0	14.2	14.3	14.4	14.6	14.7	14.8	14.9	15.1	15.2	15.3	15.5	15.6	15.7	15.8	16.0	16.1	16.2	16.3	16.5	16.6	16.7	16.9	17.0
81	11.1	11.3	11.4	11.5	11.7	11.8	11.9	12.1	12.2	12.3	12.5	12.6	12.7	12.9	13.0	13.1	13.3	13.4	13.5	13.7	13.8	13.9	14.1	14.2	14.3	14.5	14.6	14.7	14.9	15.0	15.1	15.3	15.4	15.5	15.7	15.8	15.9	16.1	16.2
80	10.1	10.3	10.4	10.6	10.7	10.8	11.0	11.1	11.2	11.4	11.5	11.7	11.8	11.9	12.1	12.2	12.3	12.5	12.6	12.8	12.9	13.0	13.2	13.3	13.5	13.6	13.7	13.9	14.0	14.1	14.3	14.4	14.6	14.7	14.8	15.0	15.1	15.2	15.4
79	9.1	9.3	9.4	9.6	9.7	9.9	10.0	10.1	10.3	10.4	10.6	10.7	10.9	11.0	11.1	11.3	11.4	11.6	11.7	11.9	12.0	12.2	12.3	12.4	12.6	12.7	12.9	13.0	13.2	13.3	13.4	13.6	13.7	13.9	14.0	14.2	14.3	14.4	14.6
78	8.1	8.3	8.4	8.6	8.7	8.9	9.0	9.2	9.3	9.5	9.6	9.8	9.9	10.1	10.2	10.4	10.5	10.7	10.8	11.0	11.1	11.3	11.4	11.6	11.7	11.9	12.0	12.2	12.3	12.4	12.6	12.7	12.9	13.0	13.2	13.3	13.5	13.6	13.8
77	7.1	7.3	7.5	7.6	7.8	7.9	8.1	8.3	8.4	8.6	8.7	8.9	9.0	9.2	9.3	9.5	9.6	9.8	9.9	10.1	10.2	10.4	10.5	10.7	10.8	11.0	11.1	11.3	11.4	11.5	11.7	11.8	11.9	12.1	12.2	12.3	12.5	12.6	12.8
76	6.2	6.4	6.5	6.7	6.9	7.0	7.2	7.4	7.5	7.7	7.8	8.0	8.1	8.3	8.4	8.6	8.7	8.9	9.0	9.2	9.3	9.5	9.6	9.8	9.9	10.1	10.2	10.4	10.5	10.6	10.8	10.9	11.0	11.2	11.3	11.4	11.6	11.7	11.8
75	5.2	5.4	5.5	5.8	6.0	6.1	6.3	6.5	6.6	6.8	6.9	7.1	7.2	7.4	7.5	7.7	7.8	8.0	8.1	8.3	8.4	8.6	8.7	8.9	9.0	9.2	9.3	9.5	9.6	9.7	9.9	10.0	10.1	10.3	10.4	10.5	10.6	10.7	10.8
74	4.3	4.4	4.6	4.9	5.1	5.2	5.5	5.7	5.8	6.0	6.1	6.3	6.4	6.6	6.7	6.9	7.0	7.2	7.3	7.5	7.6	7.8	7.9	8.1	8.2	8.3	8.5	8.6	8.7	8.8	9.0	9.1	9.2	9.4	9.5	9.6	9.7	9.8	9.9
73	3.3	3.4	3.6	4.0	4.3	4.5	4.7	4.9	5.1	5.1	5.3	5.5	5.7	5.9	6.0	6.2	6.3	6.5	6.6	6.8	6.9	7.0	7.2	7.3	7.4	7.5	7.7	7.8	7.9	8.0	8.1	8.2	8.4	8.5	8.6	8.7	8.8	8.9	9.0
72	2.4	2.6	3.0	3.3	3.6	3.9	4.1	4.3	4.5	4.7	4.9	5.1	5.3	5.5	5.6	5.8	5.9	6.1	6.2	6.4	6.5	6.6	6.8	6.9	7.0	7.1	7.3	7.4	7.5	7.6	7.7	7.8	8.0	8.1	8.2	8.3	8.4	8.5	8.6
71	1.6	2.2	2.6	2.9	3.2	3.5	3.7	3.9	4.1	4.3	4.5	4.7	4.9	5.1	5.2	5.4	5.5	5.7	5.8	6.0	6.1	6.2	6.4	6.5	6.6	6.7	6.9	7.0	7.1	7.2	7.3	7.4	7.6	7.7	7.8	7.9	8.0	8.1	8.2
70	1.2	1.8	2.2	2.5	2.8	3.1	3.3	3.5	3.7	3.9	4.1	4.3	4.5	4.7	4.8	5.0	5.1	5.3	5.4	5.6	5.7	5.8	6.0	6.1	6.2	6.3	6.5	6.6	6.7	6.8	6.9	7.0	7.2	7.3	7.4	7.5	7.6	7.7	7.8
69	0.8	1.4	1.8	2.1	2.4	2.7	2.9	3.1	3.3	3.5	3.7	3.9	4.1	4.3	4.4	4.6	4.7	4.9	5.0	5.2	5.3	5.4	5.6	5.7	5.8	5.9	6.1	6.2	6.3	6.4	6.5	6.6	6.8	6.9	7.0	7.1	7.2	7.3	7.4
68	0.4	1.0	1.4	1.7	2.0	2.3	2.5	2.7	2.9	3.1	3.3	3.5	3.7	3.9	4.0	4.2	4.3	4.5	4.6	4.8	4.9	5.0	5.2	5.3	5.4	5.5	5.7	5.8	5.9	6.0	6.1	6.2	6.4	6.5	6.6	6.7	6.8	6.9	7.0
67	0.0	0.6	1.0	1.3	1.6	1.9	2.1	2.3	2.5	2.7	2.9	3.1	3.3	3.5	3.6	3.8	3.9	4.1	4.2	4.4	4.5	4.6	4.8	4.9	5.0	5.1	5.3	5.4	5.5	5.6	5.7	5.8	6.0	6.1	6.2	6.3	6.4	6.5	6.6
66	0.0	0.2	0.6	0.9	1.2	1.5	1.7	1.9	2.1	2.3	2.5	2.7	2.9	3.1	3.2	3.4	3.5	3.7	3.8	4.0	4.1	4.2	4.4	4.5	4.6	4.7	4.9	5.0	5.1	5.2	5.3	5.4	5.6	5.7	5.8	5.9	6.0	6.1	6.2
65	0.0	0.0	0.2	0.5	0.8	1.1	1.3	1.5	1.7	1.9	2.1	2.3	2.5	2.7	2.8	3.0	3.1	3.3	3.4	3.6	3.7	3.8	4.0	4.1	4.2	4.3	4.5	4.6	4.7	4.8	4.9	5.0	5.2	5.3	5.4	5.5	5.6	5.7	5.8
64	0.0	0.0	0.0	0.1	0.4	0.7	0.9	1.1	1.3	1.5	1.7	1.9	2.1	2.3	2.4	2.6	2.7	2.9	3.0	3.2	3.3	3.4	3.6	3.7	3.8	3.9	4.1	4.2	4.3	4.4	4.5	4.6	4.8	4.9	5.0	5.1	5.2	5.3	5.4
63	0.0	0.0	0.0	0.0	0.0	0.3	0.5	0.7	0.9	1.1	1.3	1.5	1.7	1.9	2.0	2.2	2.3	2.5	2.6	2.8	2.9	3.0	3.2	3.3	3.4	3.5	3.7	3.8	3.9	4.0	4.1	4.2	4.4	4.5	4.6	4.7	4.8	4.9	5.0
62	0.0	0.0	0.0	0.0	0.0	0.0	0.1	0.3	0.5	0.7	0.9	1.1	1.3	1.5	1.6	1.8	1.9	2.1	2.2	2.4	2.5	2.6	2.8	2.9	3.0	3.1	3.3	3.4	3.5	3.6	3.7	3.8	4.0	4.1	4.2	4.3	4.4	4.5	4.6
61	0.0	0.0	0.0	0.0	0.0	0.0	0.0	0.0	0.1	0.3	0.5	0.7	0.9	1.1	1.2	1.4	1.5	1.7	1.8	2.0	2.1	2.2	2.4	2.5	2.6	2.7	2.9	3.0	3.1	3.2	3.3	3.4	3.6	3.7	3.8	3.9	4.0	4.1	4.2
60	0.0	0.0	0.0	0.0	0.0	0.0	0.0	0.0	0.0	0.0	0.1	0.3	0.5	0.7	0.8	1.0	1.1	1.3	1.4	1.6	1.7	1.8	2.0	2.1	2.2	2.3	2.5	2.6	2.7	2.8	2.9	3.0	3.2	3.3	3.4	3.5	3.6	3.7	3.8
59	0.0	0.0	0.0	0.0	0.0	0.0	0.0	0.0	0.0	0.0	0.0	0.0	0.1	0.3	0.4	0.6	0.7	0.9	1.0	1.2	1.3	1.4	1.6	1.7	1.8	1.9	2.1	2.2	2.3	2.4	2.5	2.6	2.8	2.9	3.0	3.1	3.2	3.3	3.4
58	0.0	0.0	0.0	0.0	0.0	0.0	0.0	0.0	0.0	0.0	0.0	0.0	0.0	0.0	0.0	0.2	0.3	0.5	0.6	0.8	0.9	1.0	1.2	1.3	1.4	1.5	1.7	1.8	1.9	2.0	2.1	2.2	2.4	2.5	2.6	2.7	2.8	2.9	3.0
57	0.0	0.0	0.0	0.0	0.0	0.0	0.0	0.0	0.0	0.0	0.0	0.0	0.0	0.0	0.0	0.0	0.0	0.1	0.2	0.4	0.5	0.6	0.8	0.9	1.0	1.1	1.3	1.4	1.5	1.6	1.7	1.8	2.0	2.1	2.2	2.3	2.4	2.5	2.6
56	0.0	0.0	0.0	0.0	0.0	0.0	0.0	0.0	0.0	0.0	0.0	0.0	0.0	0.0	0.0	0.0	0.0	0.0	0.0	0.0	0.1	0.2	0.4	0.5	0.6	0.7	0.9	1.0	1.1	1.2	1.3	1.4	1.6	1.7	1.8	1.9	2.0	2.1	2.2
55	0.0	0.0	0.0	0.0	0.0	0.0	0.0	0.0	0.0	0.0	0.0	0.0	0.0	0.0	0.0	0.0	0.0	0.0	0.0	0.0	0.0	0.0	0.0	0.1	0.2	0.3	0.5	0.6	0.7	0.8	0.9	1.0	1.2	1.3	1.4	1.5	1.6	1.7	1.8
54	0.0	0.0	0.0	0.0	0.0	0.0	0.0	0.0	0.0	0.0	0.0	0.0	0.0	0.0	0.0	0.0	0.0	0.0	0.0	0.0	0.0	0.0	0.0	0.0	0.0	0.0	0.1	0.2	0.3	0.4	0.5	0.6	0.8	0.9	1.0	1.1	1.2	1.3	1.4
53	0.0	0.0	0.0	0.0	0.0	0.0	0.0	0.0	0.0	0.0	0.0	0.0	0.0	0.0	0.0	0.0	0.0	0.0	0.0	0.0	0.0	0.0	0.0	0.0	0.0	0.0	0.0	0.0	0.0	0.0	0.1	0.2	0.4	0.5	0.6	0.7	0.8	0.9	1.0
52	0.0	0.0	0.0	0.0	0.0	0.0	0.0	0.0	0.0	0.0	0.0	0.0	0.0	0.0	0.0	0.0	0.0	0.0	0.0	0.0	0.0	0.0	0.0	0.0	0.0	0.0	0.0	0.0	0.0	0.0	0.0	0.0	0.0	0.1	0.2	0.3	0.4	0.5	0.6
51	0.0	0.0	0.0	0.0	0.0	0.0	0.0	0.0	0.0	0.0	0.0	0.0	0.0	0.0	0.0	0.0	0.0	0.0	0.0	0.0	0.0	0.0	0.0	0.0	0.0	0.0	0.0	0.0	0.0	0.0	0.0	0.0	0.0	0.0	0.0	0.0	0.0	0.1	0.2
50	0.0	0.0	0.0	0.0	0.0	0.0	0.0	0.0	0.0	0.0	0.0	0.0	0.0	0.0	0.0	0.0	0.0	0.0	0.0	0.0	0.0	0.0	0.0	0.0	0.0	0.0	0.0	0.0	0.0	0.0	0.0	0.0	0.0	0.0	0.0	0.0	0.0	0.0	0.0
49	0.0	0.0	0.0	0.0	0.0	0.0	0.0	0.0	0.0	0.0	0.0	0.0	0.0	0.0	0.0	0.0	0.0	0.0	0.0	0.0	0.0	0.0	0.0	0.0	0.0	0.0	0.0	0.0	0.0	0.0	0.0	0.0	0.0	0.0	0.0	0.0	0.0	0.0	0.0

LISTED CALL OPTION PRICE WHEN EXERCISE PRICE IS 80

Common Stock Price	NUMBER OF WEEKS BEFORE THE OPTION EXPIRES																																					
	1	2	3	4	5	6	7	8	9	10	11	12	13	14	15	16	17	18	19	20	21	22	23	24	25	26	27	28	29	30	31	32	33	34	35	36	37	38	39
104	24.1	24.2	24.3	24.4	24.5	24.6	24.7	24.7	24.8	24.9	25.0	25.1	25.2	25.3	25.4	25.5	25.6	25.7	25.8	25.9	26.0	26.1	26.1	26.2	26.3	26.4	26.5	26.6	26.7	26.8	26.9	27.0	27.1	27.2	27.3	27.4	27.5	27.5	27.6
102	22.1	22.2	22.3	22.4	22.5	22.6	22.7	22.8	22.9	23.0	23.1	23.2	23.3	23.5	23.6	23.7	23.8	23.9	24.0	24.1	24.2	24.3	24.4	24.5	24.6	24.7	24.8	24.9	25.0	25.1	25.2	25.3	25.4	25.5	25.6	25.7	25.8	25.9	26.0
100	20.1	20.2	20.3	20.5	20.6	20.7	20.8	20.9	21.0	21.1	21.3	21.4	21.5	21.6	21.7	21.8	21.9	22.0	22.2	22.3	22.4	22.5	22.6	22.7	22.8	23.0	23.1	23.2	23.3	23.4	23.5	23.6	23.8	23.9	24.0	24.1	24.2	24.3	24.4
99	19.1	19.2	19.4	19.5	19.6	19.7	19.8	19.9	20.1	20.2	20.3	20.4	20.5	20.7	20.8	20.9	21.0	21.1	21.3	21.4	21.5	21.6	21.7	21.9	22.0	22.1	22.2	22.3	22.5	22.6	22.7	22.8	22.9	23.0	23.2	23.3	23.4	23.5	23.6
98	18.1	18.2	18.4	18.5	18.6	18.7	18.9	19.0	19.1	19.2	19.4	19.5	19.6	19.7	19.9	19.9	20.1	20.2	20.4	20.5	20.6	20.7	20.9	21.0	21.1	21.2	21.4	21.5	21.6	21.7	21.8	22.0	22.1	22.2	22.3	22.5	22.6	22.7	22.8
97	17.1	17.3	17.4	17.5	17.6	17.8	17.9	18.0	18.2	18.3	18.4	18.6	18.7	18.8	18.9	19.1	19.2	19.3	19.5	19.6	19.7	19.8	19.9	20.1	20.2	20.4	20.5	20.6	20.7	20.9	21.0	21.1	21.3	21.4	21.5	21.7	21.8	21.9	22.0
96	16.1	16.3	16.4	16.5	16.7	16.8	16.9	17.1	17.2	17.3	17.5	17.6	17.7	17.9	18.0	18.1	18.3	18.4	18.6	18.7	18.8	19.0	19.1	19.2	19.4	19.5	19.6	19.8	19.9	20.0	20.2	20.3	20.4	20.6	20.7	20.8	21.0	21.1	21.2
95	15.1	15.3	15.4	15.6	15.7	15.8	16.0	16.1	16.3	16.4	16.5	16.7	16.8	17.0	17.1	17.2	17.4	17.5	17.7	17.8	17.9	18.1	18.2	18.3	18.5	18.6	18.8	18.9	19.0	19.2	19.3	19.5	19.6	19.7	19.9	20.0	20.2	20.3	20.4
94	14.1	14.3	14.4	14.6	14.7	14.9	15.0	15.2	15.3	15.4	15.6	15.7	15.9	16.0	16.2	16.3	16.5	16.6	16.7	16.9	17.0	17.2	17.3	17.5	17.6	17.8	17.9	18.0	18.2	18.3	18.5	18.6	18.8	18.9	19.1	19.2	19.4	19.5	19.6
93	13.1	13.3	13.4	13.6	13.7	13.9	14.0	14.2	14.3	14.5	14.6	14.8	14.9	15.1	15.2	15.4	15.5	15.7	15.8	16.0	16.1	16.3	16.4	16.6	16.7	16.9	17.0	17.2	17.3	17.5	17.6	17.8	17.9	18.1	18.2	18.4	18.5	18.7	18.8
92	12.2	12.3	12.5	12.6	12.8	12.9	13.1	13.2	13.4	13.5	13.7	13.9	14.0	14.2	14.3	14.5	14.6	14.8	14.9	15.1	15.3	15.4	15.6	15.7	15.9	16.0	16.2	16.3	16.5	16.6	16.8	17.0	17.1	17.3	17.4	17.6	17.7	17.9	18.0
91	11.2	11.3	11.5	11.6	11.8	12.0	12.1	12.3	12.4	12.6	12.8	12.9	13.1	13.2	13.4	13.6	13.7	13.9	14.0	14.2	14.4	14.5	14.7	14.8	15.0	15.2	15.3	15.5	15.6	15.8	16.0	16.1	16.3	16.4	16.6	16.8	16.9	17.1	17.2
90	10.2	10.3	10.5	10.7	10.8	11.0	11.2	11.3	11.5	11.7	11.8	12.0	12.1	12.3	12.5	12.6	12.8	13.0	13.1	13.3	13.5	13.6	13.8	14.0	14.1	14.3	14.5	14.6	14.8	15.0	15.1	15.3	15.4	15.6	15.8	15.9	16.1	16.3	16.4
89	9.2	9.3	9.5	9.7	9.9	10.0	10.2	10.4	10.5	10.7	10.9	11.0	11.2	11.4	11.6	11.7	11.9	12.1	12.2	12.4	12.6	12.7	12.9	13.1	13.3	13.4	13.6	13.8	13.9	14.1	14.3	14.4	14.6	14.8	15.0	15.1	15.3	15.5	15.6
88	8.2	8.3	8.5	8.7	8.9	9.1	9.3	9.5	9.6	9.8	9.9	10.1	10.2	10.4	10.6	10.7	11.0	11.2	11.3	11.4	11.6	11.7	11.9	12.1	12.3	12.4	12.6	12.8	13.0	13.2	13.4	13.5	13.7	13.9	14.1	14.2	14.4	14.6	14.7
87	7.2	7.4	7.5	7.8	7.9	8.2	8.4	8.6	8.6	8.8	9.0	9.1	9.3	9.5	9.7	9.8	10.1	10.3	10.4	10.5	10.7	10.8	11.0	11.2	11.4	11.5	11.7	11.9	12.1	12.3	12.5	12.6	12.8	13.0	13.2	13.4	13.5	13.7	13.8
86	6.2	6.4	6.6	6.8	7.0	7.3	7.5	7.7	7.7	7.9	8.0	8.2	8.4	8.6	8.8	8.9	9.2	9.4	9.5	9.6	9.8	9.9	10.1	10.3	10.5	10.6	10.8	11.0	11.2	11.4	11.7	11.7	11.9	12.1	12.3	12.5	12.6	12.8	12.9
85	5.3	5.4	5.6	5.9	6.1	6.4	6.6	6.8	6.8	6.9	7.1	7.3	7.5	7.7	7.9	8.0	8.3	8.5	8.6	8.7	8.9	9.0	9.2	9.4	9.6	9.7	9.9	10.1	10.3	10.5	10.9	10.9	11.1	11.2	11.4	11.6	11.7	11.9	12.0
84	4.3	4.4	4.6	4.9	5.2	5.5	5.7	5.9	6.1	6.2	6.3	6.5	6.7	6.9	7.1	7.3	7.5	7.6	7.8	8.0	8.1	8.3	8.4	8.6	8.7	8.9	9.0	9.3	9.4	9.6	10.0	10.1	10.2	10.3	10.5	10.7	10.8	11.0	11.1
83	2.4	3.4	3.7	4.1	4.4	4.7	5.0	5.2	5.5	5.7	5.9	6.1	6.3	6.5	6.7	6.9	7.1	7.2	7.4	7.6	7.7	7.9	8.0	8.2	8.3	8.5	8.6	8.7	8.9	9.0	9.1	9.3	9.4	9.5	9.6	9.9	10.0	10.2	10.2
82	2.4	2.8	3.3	3.6	4.0	4.3	4.6	4.8	5.1	5.3	5.5	5.7	5.9	6.1	6.3	6.5	6.7	6.8	7.0	7.2	7.3	7.5	7.6	7.8	7.9	8.1	8.2	8.3	8.5	8.6	8.7	8.9	9.0	9.1	9.2	9.3	9.5	9.6	9.7
81	1.8	2.4	2.9	3.2	3.6	3.9	4.2	4.4	4.7	4.9	5.1	5.3	5.5	5.7	5.9	6.1	6.3	6.4	6.6	6.8	6.9	7.1	7.2	7.4	7.5	7.7	7.8	7.9	8.1	8.2	8.3	8.5	8.6	8.7	8.8	8.9	9.1	9.2	9.3
80	1.4	2.0	2.5	2.8	3.2	3.5	3.8	4.0	4.3	4.5	4.7	4.9	5.1	5.3	5.5	5.7	5.9	6.0	6.2	6.4	6.5	6.7	6.8	7.0	7.1	7.3	7.4	7.5	7.7	7.8	7.9	8.1	8.2	8.3	8.4	8.5	8.7	8.8	8.9
79	1.0	1.6	2.1	2.4	2.8	3.1	3.4	3.6	3.9	4.1	4.3	4.5	4.7	4.9	5.1	5.3	5.5	5.6	5.8	6.0	6.1	6.3	6.4	6.6	6.7	6.9	7.0	7.1	7.3	7.4	7.5	7.7	7.8	7.9	8.0	8.1	8.3	8.4	8.5
78	0.6	1.2	1.7	2.0	2.4	2.7	3.0	3.2	3.5	3.7	3.9	4.1	4.3	4.5	4.7	4.9	5.1	5.2	5.4	5.6	5.7	5.9	6.0	6.2	6.3	6.5	6.6	6.7	6.9	7.0	7.1	7.3	7.4	7.5	7.6	7.7	7.9	8.0	8.1
77	0.2	0.8	1.3	1.6	2.0	2.3	2.6	2.8	3.1	3.3	3.5	3.7	3.9	4.1	4.3	4.5	4.7	4.8	5.0	5.2	5.3	5.5	5.6	5.8	5.9	6.1	6.2	6.3	6.5	6.6	6.7	6.9	7.0	7.1	7.2	7.3	7.5	7.6	7.7
76	0.0	0.4	0.9	1.2	1.6	1.9	2.2	2.4	2.7	2.9	3.1	3.3	3.5	3.7	3.9	4.1	4.3	4.4	4.6	4.8	4.9	5.1	5.2	5.4	5.5	5.7	5.8	5.9	6.1	6.2	6.3	6.5	6.6	6.7	6.8	6.9	7.1	7.2	7.3
75	0.0	0.0	0.5	0.8	1.2	1.5	1.8	2.0	2.3	2.5	2.7	2.9	3.1	3.3	3.5	3.7	3.9	4.0	4.2	4.4	4.5	4.7	4.8	5.0	5.1	5.3	5.4	5.5	5.7	5.8	5.9	6.1	6.2	6.3	6.4	6.5	6.7	6.8	6.9
74	0.0	0.0	0.1	0.4	0.8	1.1	1.4	1.6	1.9	2.1	2.3	2.5	2.7	2.9	3.1	3.3	3.5	3.6	3.8	4.0	4.1	4.3	4.4	4.6	4.7	4.9	5.0	5.1	5.3	5.4	5.5	5.7	5.8	5.9	6.0	6.1	6.3	6.4	6.5
73	0.0	0.0	0.0	0.0	0.4	0.7	1.0	1.2	1.5	1.7	1.9	2.1	2.3	2.5	2.7	2.9	3.1	3.2	3.4	3.6	3.7	3.9	4.0	4.2	4.3	4.5	4.6	4.7	4.9	5.0	5.1	5.3	5.4	5.5	5.6	5.7	5.9	6.0	6.1
72	0.0	0.0	0.0	0.0	0.0	0.3	0.6	0.8	1.1	1.3	1.5	1.7	1.9	2.1	2.3	2.5	2.7	2.8	3.0	3.2	3.3	3.5	3.6	3.8	3.9	4.1	4.2	4.3	4.5	4.6	4.7	4.9	5.0	5.1	5.2	5.3	5.5	5.6	5.7
71	0.0	0.0	0.0	0.0	0.0	0.0	0.2	0.4	0.7	0.9	1.1	1.3	1.5	1.7	1.9	2.1	2.3	2.4	2.6	2.8	2.9	3.1	3.2	3.4	3.5	3.7	3.8	3.9	4.1	4.2	4.3	4.5	4.6	4.7	4.8	4.9	5.1	5.2	5.3
70	0.0	0.0	0.0	0.0	0.0	0.0	0.0	0.0	0.3	0.5	0.7	0.9	1.1	1.3	1.5	1.7	1.9	2.0	2.2	2.4	2.5	2.7	2.8	3.0	3.1	3.3	3.4	3.5	3.7	3.8	3.9	4.1	4.2	4.3	4.4	4.5	4.7	4.8	4.9
69	0.0	0.0	0.0	0.0	0.0	0.0	0.0	0.0	0.0	0.1	0.3	0.5	0.7	0.9	1.1	1.3	1.5	1.6	1.8	2.0	2.1	2.3	2.4	2.6	2.7	2.9	3.0	3.1	3.3	3.4	3.5	3.7	3.8	3.9	4.0	4.1	4.3	4.4	4.5
68	0.0	0.0	0.0	0.0	0.0	0.0	0.0	0.0	0.0	0.0	0.0	0.1	0.3	0.5	0.7	0.9	1.1	1.2	1.4	1.6	1.7	1.9	2.0	2.2	2.3	2.5	2.6	2.7	2.9	3.0	3.1	3.3	3.4	3.5	3.6	3.7	3.9	4.0	4.1
67	0.0	0.0	0.0	0.0	0.0	0.0	0.0	0.0	0.0	0.0	0.0	0.0	0.0	0.1	0.3	0.5	0.7	0.8	1.0	1.2	1.3	1.5	1.6	1.8	1.9	2.1	2.2	2.3	2.5	2.6	2.7	2.9	3.0	3.1	3.2	3.3	3.5	3.6	3.7
66	0.0	0.0	0.0	0.0	0.0	0.0	0.0	0.0	0.0	0.0	0.0	0.0	0.0	0.0	0.0	0.1	0.3	0.4	0.6	0.8	0.9	1.1	1.2	1.4	1.5	1.7	1.8	1.9	2.1	2.2	2.3	2.5	2.6	2.7	2.8	2.9	3.1	3.2	3.3
65	0.0	0.0	0.0	0.0	0.0	0.0	0.0	0.0	0.0	0.0	0.0	0.0	0.0	0.0	0.0	0.0	0.0	0.0	0.2	0.4	0.5	0.7	0.8	1.0	1.1	1.3	1.4	1.5	1.7	1.8	1.9	2.1	2.2	2.3	2.4	2.5	2.7	2.8	2.9
64	0.0	0.0	0.0	0.0	0.0	0.0	0.0	0.0	0.0	0.0	0.0	0.0	0.0	0.0	0.0	0.0	0.0	0.0	0.0	0.0	0.1	0.3	0.4	0.6	0.7	0.9	1.0	1.1	1.3	1.4	1.5	1.7	1.8	1.9	2.0	2.1	2.3	2.4	2.5
63	0.0	0.0	0.0	0.0	0.0	0.0	0.0	0.0	0.0	0.0	0.0	0.0	0.0	0.0	0.0	0.0	0.0	0.0	0.0	0.0	0.0	0.0	0.0	0.2	0.3	0.5	0.6	0.7	0.9	1.0	1.1	1.3	1.4	1.5	1.7	1.8	1.9	2.0	2.1
62	0.0	0.0	0.0	0.0	0.0	0.0	0.0	0.0	0.0	0.0	0.0	0.0	0.0	0.0	0.0	0.0	0.0	0.0	0.0	0.0	0.0	0.0	0.0	0.0	0.0	0.1	0.2	0.3	0.5	0.6	0.7	0.9	1.0	1.1	1.2	1.3	1.5	1.6	1.7
61	0.0	0.0	0.0	0.0	0.0	0.0	0.0	0.0	0.0	0.0	0.0	0.0	0.0	0.0	0.0	0.0	0.0	0.0	0.0	0.0	0.0	0.0	0.0	0.0	0.0	0.0	0.0	0.0	0.1	0.2	0.3	0.5	0.6	0.7	0.8	0.9	1.1	1.2	1.3
60	0.0	0.0	0.0	0.0	0.0	0.0	0.0	0.0	0.0	0.0	0.0	0.0	0.0	0.0	0.0	0.0	0.0	0.0	0.0	0.0	0.0	0.0	0.0	0.0	0.0	0.0	0.0	0.0	0.0	0.0	0.0	0.1	0.2	0.3	0.4	0.5	0.7	0.8	0.9
59	0.0	0.0	0.0	0.0	0.0	0.0	0.0	0.0	0.0	0.0	0.0	0.0	0.0	0.0	0.0	0.0	0.0	0.0	0.0	0.0	0.0	0.0	0.0	0.0	0.0	0.0	0.0	0.0	0.0	0.0	0.0	0.0	0.0	0.0	0.0	0.1	0.3	0.4	0.5
58	0.0	0.0	0.0	0.0	0.0	0.0	0.0	0.0	0.0	0.0	0.0	0.0	0.0	0.0	0.0	0.0	0.0	0.0	0.0	0.0	0.0	0.0	0.0	0.0	0.0	0.0	0.0	0.0	0.0	0.0	0.0	0.0	0.0	0.0	0.0	0.0	0.0	0.0	0.1
57	0.0	0.0	0.0	0.0	0.0	0.0	0.0	0.0	0.0	0.0	0.0	0.0	0.0	0.0	0.0	0.0	0.0	0.0	0.0	0.0	0.0	0.0	0.0	0.0	0.0	0.0	0.0	0.0	0.0	0.0	0.0	0.0	0.0	0.0	0.0	0.0	0.0	0.0	0.0

LISTED CALL OPTION PRICE WHEN EXERCISE PRICE IS 90

NUMBER OF WEEKS BEFORE THE OPTION EXPIRES

Common Stock Price	1	2	3	4	5	6	7	8	9	10	11	12	13	14	15	16	17	18	19	20	21	22	23	24	25	26	27	28	29	30	31	32	33	34	35	36	37	38	39
118	28.1	28.2	28.3	28.4	28.5	28.6	28.7	28.8	28.9	29.0	29.1	29.2	29.3	29.4	29.5	29.6	29.7	29.8	29.9	29.9	30.1	30.2	30.3	30.4	30.5	30.6	30.7	30.8	30.9	31.0	31.1	31.2	31.3	31.4	31.5	31.6	31.7	31.8	31.9
116	26.1	26.2	26.3	26.4	26.6	26.7	26.8	26.9	27.0	27.1	27.2	27.3	27.4	27.5	27.7	27.8	27.9	28.0	28.1	28.2	28.3	28.4	28.5	28.6	28.8	28.9	29.0	29.1	29.2	29.3	29.4	29.5	29.6	29.7	29.8	29.9	30.1	30.2	30.3
114	24.1	24.2	24.4	24.5	24.6	24.7	24.8	25.0	25.1	25.2	25.3	25.4	25.6	25.7	25.8	25.9	26.0	26.2	26.3	26.4	26.5	26.6	26.8	26.9	27.0	27.1	27.3	27.4	27.5	27.6	27.7	27.9	28.0	28.1	28.2	28.3	28.5	28.6	28.7
112	22.1	22.3	22.4	22.5	22.7	22.8	22.9	23.0	23.2	23.3	23.4	23.6	23.7	23.8	24.0	24.1	24.2	24.4	24.5	24.6	24.7	24.9	25.0	25.1	25.3	25.4	25.5	25.7	25.8	25.9	26.0	26.2	26.3	26.4	26.6	26.7	26.8	27.0	27.1
110	20.1	20.3	20.4	20.6	20.7	20.8	21.0	21.1	21.3	21.4	21.5	21.7	21.8	22.0	22.1	22.3	22.4	22.5	22.7	22.8	23.0	23.1	23.2	23.4	23.5	23.7	23.8	23.9	24.1	24.2	24.4	24.5	24.6	24.8	24.9	25.1	25.2	25.4	25.5
108	18.2	18.3	18.5	18.6	18.8	18.9	19.1	19.2	19.4	19.5	19.7	19.8	19.9	20.1	20.3	20.4	20.6	20.7	20.9	21.0	21.2	21.3	21.5	21.6	21.8	21.9	22.1	22.2	22.4	22.5	22.7	22.8	23.0	23.1	23.3	23.4	23.6	23.7	23.9
106	16.2	16.3	16.5	16.6	16.8	17.0	17.1	17.3	17.5	17.6	17.8	17.9	18.1	18.3	18.4	18.6	18.7	18.9	19.1	19.2	19.4	19.6	19.7	19.9	20.0	20.2	20.4	20.5	20.7	20.8	21.0	21.2	21.3	21.5	21.6	21.8	22.0	22.1	22.3
104	14.2	14.3	14.5	14.7	14.9	15.0	15.2	15.4	15.5	15.7	15.9	16.1	16.2	16.4	16.6	16.7	16.9	17.1	17.3	17.4	17.6	17.8	17.9	18.1	18.3	18.5	18.6	18.8	19.0	19.1	19.3	19.5	19.7	19.8	20.0	20.2	20.4	20.5	20.7
102	12.2	12.4	12.5	12.7	12.9	13.1	13.3	13.5	13.6	13.8	14.0	14.2	14.4	14.5	14.7	14.9	15.1	15.3	15.5	15.6	15.8	16.0	16.2	16.4	16.5	16.7	16.9	17.1	17.3	17.5	17.6	17.8	18.0	18.2	18.4	18.5	18.7	18.9	19.1
100	10.2	10.4	10.6	10.8	11.0	11.2	11.3	11.5	11.7	11.9	12.1	12.3	12.5	12.7	12.9	13.1	13.3	13.5	13.7	13.8	14.0	14.2	14.4	14.6	14.8	15.0	15.2	15.4	15.6	15.8	16.0	16.1	16.3	16.5	16.7	16.9	17.1	17.3	17.5
99	9.2	9.4	9.6	9.8	10.0	10.2	10.4	10.6	10.7	10.9	11.1	11.4	11.6	11.8	12.0	12.2	12.4	12.6	12.8	12.9	13.1	13.3	13.5	13.7	13.9	14.1	14.3	14.5	14.7	14.9	15.1	15.2	15.4	15.6	15.8	16.0	16.2	16.4	16.6
98	8.2	8.4	8.6	8.8	9.1	9.3	9.4	9.6	9.8	10.0	10.2	10.5	10.7	10.9	11.1	11.3	11.5	11.7	11.9	12.0	12.2	12.4	12.6	12.8	13.0	13.2	13.4	13.6	13.8	14.0	14.2	14.3	14.5	14.7	14.9	15.1	15.3	15.4	15.7
97	7.2	7.4	7.6	7.9	8.1	8.3	8.5	8.7	8.8	9.0	9.3	9.6	9.8	10.0	10.2	10.4	10.6	10.8	11.0	11.1	11.3	11.5	11.7	11.9	12.1	12.3	12.5	12.7	12.9	13.1	13.3	13.4	13.6	13.8	14.0	14.2	14.4	14.6	14.8
96	6.3	6.5	6.7	6.9	7.2	7.4	7.5	7.7	7.9	8.1	8.4	8.7	8.9	9.1	9.3	9.5	9.7	9.9	10.1	10.2	10.4	10.6	10.8	11.0	11.2	11.4	11.6	11.8	12.0	12.2	12.4	12.5	12.7	12.9	13.1	13.3	13.5	13.7	13.9
95	5.3	5.5	5.7	6.0	6.3	6.5	6.6	6.8	7.0	7.2	7.5	7.8	8.0	8.2	8.4	8.6	8.8	9.0	9.2	9.3	9.5	9.7	9.9	10.1	10.3	10.5	10.7	10.9	11.1	11.3	11.5	11.6	11.8	12.0	12.2	12.4	12.6	12.8	13.0
94	4.4	4.5	4.8	5.1	5.4	5.6	5.8	6.1	6.4	6.7	6.9	7.1	7.4	7.6	7.8	8.0	8.2	8.4	8.6	8.8	8.9	9.1	9.3	9.4	9.6	9.8	9.9	10.1	10.2	10.4	10.6	10.7	10.9	11.1	11.3	11.5	11.7	11.9	12.1
93	3.4	3.5	4.0	4.4	4.8	5.1	5.4	5.7	6.0	6.3	6.5	6.7	7.0	7.2	7.4	7.6	7.8	8.0	8.2	8.4	8.5	8.7	8.9	9.0	9.2	9.4	9.5	9.7	9.8	9.9	10.1	10.3	10.4	10.5	10.7	10.8	10.9	11.1	11.2
92	2.5	3.1	3.6	4.0	4.4	4.7	5.0	5.3	5.6	5.9	6.1	6.3	6.6	6.8	7.0	7.2	7.4	7.6	7.8	8.0	8.1	8.3	8.5	8.6	8.8	9.0	9.1	9.3	9.4	9.6	9.7	9.9	9.9	10.1	10.3	10.4	10.5	10.7	10.8
91	2.0	2.7	3.2	3.6	4.0	4.3	4.6	4.9	5.2	5.5	5.7	5.9	6.2	6.4	6.6	6.8	7.0	7.2	7.4	7.6	7.7	7.9	8.1	8.2	8.4	8.6	8.7	8.9	9.0	9.2	9.3	9.5	9.6	9.7	9.9	10.0	10.1	10.3	10.4
90	1.6	2.3	2.8	3.2	3.6	3.9	4.2	4.5	4.8	5.1	5.3	5.5	5.8	6.0	6.2	6.4	6.6	6.8	7.0	7.2	7.3	7.5	7.7	7.8	8.0	8.2	8.3	8.5	8.6	8.8	8.9	9.1	9.2	9.3	9.5	9.6	9.7	9.9	10.0
89	1.2	1.9	2.4	2.8	3.2	3.5	3.8	4.1	4.4	4.7	4.9	5.1	5.4	5.6	5.8	6.0	6.2	6.4	6.6	6.8	6.9	7.1	7.3	7.4	7.6	7.8	7.9	8.1	8.2	8.4	8.5	8.7	8.8	8.9	9.1	9.2	9.3	9.5	9.6
88	0.8	1.5	2.0	2.4	2.8	3.1	3.4	3.7	4.0	4.3	4.5	4.7	5.0	5.2	5.4	5.6	5.8	6.0	6.2	6.4	6.5	6.7	6.9	7.0	7.2	7.4	7.5	7.7	7.8	8.0	8.1	8.3	8.4	8.5	8.7	8.8	8.9	9.1	9.2
87	0.4	1.1	1.6	2.0	2.4	2.7	3.0	3.3	3.6	3.9	4.1	4.3	4.6	4.8	5.0	5.2	5.4	5.6	5.8	6.0	6.1	6.3	6.5	6.6	6.8	7.0	7.1	7.3	7.4	7.6	7.7	7.9	8.0	8.1	8.3	8.4	8.5	8.7	8.8
86	0.0	0.7	1.2	1.6	2.0	2.3	2.6	2.9	3.2	3.5	3.7	3.9	4.2	4.4	4.6	4.8	5.0	5.2	5.4	5.6	5.7	5.9	6.1	6.2	6.4	6.6	6.7	6.9	7.0	7.2	7.3	7.5	7.6	7.7	7.9	8.0	8.1	8.3	8.4
85	0.0	0.3	0.8	1.2	1.6	1.9	2.2	2.5	2.8	3.1	3.3	3.5	3.8	4.0	4.2	4.4	4.6	4.8	5.0	5.2	5.3	5.5	5.7	5.8	6.0	6.2	6.3	6.5	6.6	6.8	6.9	7.1	7.2	7.3	7.5	7.6	7.7	7.9	8.0
84	0.0	0.0	0.4	0.8	1.2	1.5	1.8	2.1	2.4	2.7	2.9	3.1	3.4	3.6	3.8	4.0	4.2	4.4	4.6	4.8	4.9	5.1	5.3	5.4	5.6	5.8	5.9	6.1	6.2	6.4	6.5	6.7	6.8	6.9	7.1	7.2	7.3	7.5	7.6
83	0.0	0.0	0.0	0.4	0.8	1.1	1.4	1.7	2.0	2.3	2.5	2.7	3.0	3.2	3.4	3.6	3.8	4.0	4.2	4.4	4.5	4.7	4.9	5.0	5.2	5.4	5.5	5.7	5.8	6.0	6.1	6.3	6.4	6.5	6.7	6.8	6.9	7.1	7.2
82	0.0	0.0	0.0	0.0	0.4	0.7	1.0	1.3	1.6	1.9	2.1	2.3	2.6	2.8	3.0	3.2	3.4	3.6	3.8	4.0	4.1	4.3	4.5	4.6	4.8	5.0	5.1	5.3	5.4	5.6	5.7	5.9	6.0	6.1	6.3	6.4	6.5	6.7	6.8
81	0.0	0.0	0.0	0.0	0.0	0.3	0.6	0.9	1.2	1.5	1.7	1.9	2.2	2.4	2.6	2.8	3.0	3.2	3.4	3.6	3.7	3.9	4.1	4.2	4.4	4.6	4.7	4.9	5.0	5.2	5.3	5.5	5.6	5.7	5.9	6.0	6.1	6.3	6.4
80	0.0	0.0	0.0	0.0	0.0	0.0	0.2	0.5	0.8	1.1	1.3	1.5	1.8	2.0	2.2	2.4	2.6	2.8	3.0	3.2	3.3	3.5	3.7	3.8	4.0	4.2	4.3	4.5	4.6	4.8	4.9	5.1	5.2	5.3	5.5	5.6	5.7	5.9	6.0
79	0.0	0.0	0.0	0.0	0.0	0.0	0.0	0.1	0.4	0.7	0.9	1.1	1.4	1.6	1.8	2.0	2.2	2.4	2.6	2.8	2.9	3.1	3.3	3.4	3.6	3.8	3.9	4.1	4.2	4.4	4.5	4.7	4.8	4.9	5.1	5.2	5.3	5.5	5.6
78	0.0	0.0	0.0	0.0	0.0	0.0	0.0	0.0	0.0	0.3	0.5	0.7	1.0	1.2	1.4	1.6	1.8	2.0	2.2	2.4	2.5	2.7	2.9	3.0	3.2	3.4	3.5	3.7	3.8	4.0	4.1	4.3	4.4	4.5	4.7	4.8	4.9	5.1	5.2
77	0.0	0.0	0.0	0.0	0.0	0.0	0.0	0.0	0.0	0.0	0.1	0.3	0.6	0.8	1.0	1.2	1.4	1.6	1.8	2.0	2.1	2.3	2.5	2.6	2.8	3.0	3.1	3.3	3.4	3.6	3.7	3.8	4.0	4.1	4.3	4.4	4.5	4.7	4.8
76	0.0	0.0	0.0	0.0	0.0	0.0	0.0	0.0	0.0	0.0	0.0	0.0	0.2	0.4	0.6	0.8	1.0	1.2	1.4	1.6	1.7	1.9	2.1	2.2	2.4	2.6	2.7	2.9	3.0	3.2	3.3	3.5	3.6	3.7	3.9	4.0	4.1	4.3	4.4
75	0.0	0.0	0.0	0.0	0.0	0.0	0.0	0.0	0.0	0.0	0.0	0.0	0.0	0.0	0.2	0.4	0.6	0.8	1.0	1.2	1.3	1.5	1.7	1.8	2.0	2.2	2.3	2.5	2.6	2.8	2.9	3.1	3.2	3.3	3.5	3.6	3.7	3.9	4.0
74	0.0	0.0	0.0	0.0	0.0	0.0	0.0	0.0	0.0	0.0	0.0	0.0	0.0	0.0	0.0	0.0	0.2	0.4	0.6	0.8	0.9	1.1	1.3	1.4	1.6	1.8	1.9	2.1	2.2	2.4	2.5	2.7	2.8	2.9	3.1	3.2	3.3	3.5	3.6
73	0.0	0.0	0.0	0.0	0.0	0.0	0.0	0.0	0.0	0.0	0.0	0.0	0.0	0.0	0.0	0.0	0.0	0.0	0.2	0.4	0.5	0.7	0.9	1.0	1.2	1.4	1.5	1.7	1.8	2.0	2.1	2.3	2.4	2.5	2.7	2.8	2.9	3.1	3.2
72	0.0	0.0	0.0	0.0	0.0	0.0	0.0	0.0	0.0	0.0	0.0	0.0	0.0	0.0	0.0	0.0	0.0	0.0	0.0	0.0	0.1	0.3	0.5	0.6	0.8	1.0	1.1	1.3	1.4	1.6	1.7	1.9	2.0	2.1	2.3	2.4	2.5	2.7	2.8
71	0.0	0.0	0.0	0.0	0.0	0.0	0.0	0.0	0.0	0.0	0.0	0.0	0.0	0.0	0.0	0.0	0.0	0.0	0.0	0.0	0.0	0.0	0.1	0.2	0.4	0.6	0.7	0.9	1.0	1.2	1.3	1.5	1.6	1.7	1.9	2.0	2.1	2.3	2.4
70	0.0	0.0	0.0	0.0	0.0	0.0	0.0	0.0	0.0	0.0	0.0	0.0	0.0	0.0	0.0	0.0	0.0	0.0	0.0	0.0	0.0	0.0	0.0	0.0	0.0	0.2	0.3	0.5	0.6	0.8	0.9	1.1	1.2	1.3	1.5	1.6	1.7	1.9	2.0
69	0.0	0.0	0.0	0.0	0.0	0.0	0.0	0.0	0.0	0.0	0.0	0.0	0.0	0.0	0.0	0.0	0.0	0.0	0.0	0.0	0.0	0.0	0.0	0.0	0.0	0.0	0.0	0.1	0.2	0.4	0.5	0.7	0.8	0.9	1.1	1.2	1.3	1.5	1.6
68	0.0	0.0	0.0	0.0	0.0	0.0	0.0	0.0	0.0	0.0	0.0	0.0	0.0	0.0	0.0	0.0	0.0	0.0	0.0	0.0	0.0	0.0	0.0	0.0	0.0	0.0	0.0	0.0	0.0	0.0	0.1	0.3	0.4	0.5	0.7	0.8	0.9	1.1	1.2
67	0.0	0.0	0.0	0.0	0.0	0.0	0.0	0.0	0.0	0.0	0.0	0.0	0.0	0.0	0.0	0.0	0.0	0.0	0.0	0.0	0.0	0.0	0.0	0.0	0.0	0.0	0.0	0.0	0.0	0.0	0.0	0.0	0.0	0.1	0.3	0.4	0.5	0.7	0.8
66	0.0	0.0	0.0	0.0	0.0	0.0	0.0	0.0	0.0	0.0	0.0	0.0	0.0	0.0	0.0	0.0	0.0	0.0	0.0	0.0	0.0	0.0	0.0	0.0	0.0	0.0	0.0	0.0	0.0	0.0	0.0	0.0	0.0	0.0	0.0	0.0	0.1	0.3	0.4
65	0.0	0.0	0.0	0.0	0.0	0.0	0.0	0.0	0.0	0.0	0.0	0.0	0.0	0.0	0.0	0.0	0.0	0.0	0.0	0.0	0.0	0.0	0.0	0.0	0.0	0.0	0.0	0.0	0.0	0.0	0.0	0.0	0.0	0.0	0.0	0.0	0.0	0.0	0.0
64	0.0	0.0	0.0	0.0	0.0	0.0	0.0	0.0	0.0	0.0	0.0	0.0	0.0	0.0	0.0	0.0	0.0	0.0	0.0	0.0	0.0	0.0	0.0	0.0	0.0	0.0	0.0	0.0	0.0	0.0	0.0	0.0	0.0	0.0	0.0	0.0	0.0	0.0	0.0

LISTED CALL OPTION PRICE WHEN EXERCISE PRICE IS 100

NUMBER OF WEEKS BEFORE THE OPTION EXPIRES

Common Stock Price	1	2	3	4	5	6	7	8	9	10	11	12	13	14	15	16	17	18	19	20	21	22	23	24	25	26	27	28	29	30	31	32	33	34	35	36	37	38	39
130	30.1	30.2	30.3	30.5	30.6	30.7	30.8	30.9	31.0	31.2	31.3	31.4	31.5	31.6	31.8	31.9	32.0	32.1	32.2	32.3	32.4	32.6	32.7	32.8	32.9	33.0	33.2	33.3	33.4	33.5	33.6	33.7	33.8	34.0	34.1	34.2	34.3	34.4	34.6
128	28.1	28.3	28.4	28.5	28.6	28.8	28.9	29.0	29.1	29.3	29.4	29.5	29.7	29.8	29.9	30.0	30.2	30.3	30.4	30.5	30.7	30.8	30.9	31.0	31.2	31.3	31.4	41.6	31.7	31.8	31.9	32.1	32.2	32.3	32.4	32.6	32.7	32.8	33.0
126	26.1	26.3	26.4	26.5	26.7	26.8	27.0	27.1	27.2	27.4	27.5	27.6	27.8	27.9	28.1	28.2	28.3	28.5	28.6	28.7	28.9	29.0	29.2	29.3	29.4	29.6	29.7	29.8	29.9	30.1	30.3	30.4	30.5	30.7	30.8	30.9	31.1	31.2	31.3
124	24.1	24.3	24.4	24.6	24.7	24.9	25.0	25.2	25.3	25.5	25.6	25.8	25.9	26.1	26.2	26.4	26.5	26.7	26.8	26.9	27.1	27.2	27.4	27.5	27.7	27.8	28.0	28.1	28.3	28.4	28.6	28.7	28.9	29.0	29.2	29.3	29.5	29.6	29.8
122	22.2	22.3	22.5	22.6	22.8	22.9	23.1	23.3	23.4	23.6	23.7	23.9	24.1	24.2	24.4	24.5	24.7	24.8	25.0	25.2	25.3	25.5	25.6	25.8	25.9	26.1	26.3	26.4	26.6	26.7	26.9	27.0	27.2	27.4	27.5	27.7	27.8	28.0	28.2
120	20.2	20.3	20.5	20.7	20.8	21.0	21.2	21.3	21.5	21.7	21.8	22.0	22.2	22.4	22.5	22.7	22.9	23.0	23.2	23.4	23.5	23.7	23.9	24.0	24.2	24.4	24.5	24.7	24.9	25.0	25.2	25.4	25.5	25.7	25.9	26.0	26.2	26.4	26.6
118	18.2	18.4	18.5	18.7	18.9	19.1	19.2	19.4	19.6	19.8	19.9	20.1	20.3	20.5	20.7	20.9	21.0	21.2	21.4	21.6	21.7	21.9	22.1	22.3	22.5	22.6	22.8	23.0	23.2	23.3	23.5	23.7	23.9	24.1	24.2	24.4	24.6	24.8	25.0
116	16.2	16.4	16.6	16.8	16.9	17.1	17.3	17.5	17.7	17.9	18.1	18.3	18.5	18.6	18.8	19.0	19.2	19.4	19.6	19.8	19.9	20.1	20.3	20.5	20.7	20.9	21.1	21.3	21.5	21.7	21.8	22.0	22.2	22.4	22.6	22.8	23.0	23.2	23.4
114	14.2	14.4	14.6	14.8	15.0	15.2	15.4	15.6	15.8	16.0	16.2	16.4	16.6	16.8	17.0	17.2	17.4	17.6	17.8	18.0	18.2	18.4	18.6	18.8	19.0	19.2	19.4	19.6	19.8	19.9	20.2	20.4	20.6	20.8	21.0	21.2	21.4	21.6	21.8
112	12.2	12.4	12.6	12.8	13.0	13.3	13.5	13.7	13.9	14.1	14.3	14.5	14.7	14.9	15.1	15.3	15.6	15.8	16.0	16.2	16.4	16.6	16.8	17.0	17.2	17.4	17.6	17.9	18.1	18.3	18.5	18.7	18.9	19.1	19.3	19.5	19.7	19.9	20.1
110	10.2	10.4	10.6	10.8	11.0	11.3	11.5	11.7	12.0	12.2	12.4	12.6	12.8	13.0	13.4	13.6	13.9	14.1	14.2	14.4	14.6	14.9	15.1	15.3	15.5	15.7	15.9	16.2	16.4	16.6	16.7	16.9	17.1	17.3	17.4	17.6	17.8	18.0	18.2
108	8.2	8.4	8.7	8.9	9.2	9.4	9.6	9.8	10.1	10.3	10.6	10.8	11.0	11.2	11.7	11.9	12.2	12.4	12.6	12.8	13.0	13.2	13.4	13.6	13.8	14.0	14.2	14.5	14.7	14.9	15.0	15.2	15.4	15.6	15.7	15.7	15.9	16.1	16.3
106	6.3	6.5	6.8	7.0	7.3	7.5	7.7	7.9	8.2	8.6	8.8	9.0	9.3	9.6	10.0	10.2	10.5	10.7	10.9	11.1	11.3	11.5	11.7	11.9	12.1	12.3	12.5	12.8	13.0	13.2	13.3	13.5	13.7	13.9	14.0	14.0	14.1	14.3	14.5
104	4.4	4.6	4.8	5.2	5.6	6.0	6.3	6.6	6.9	7.2	7.5	7.8	8.0	8.3	8.5	8.7	8.9	9.1	9.4	9.6	9.8	9.9	10.1	10.3	10.5	10.7	10.8	11.0	11.2	11.3	11.5	11.7	11.8	12.0	12.1	12.3	12.4	12.6	12.7
102	2.6	3.3	4.0	4.4	4.8	5.2	5.5	5.8	6.1	6.4	6.7	7.0	7.2	7.5	7.7	7.9	8.1	8.3	8.6	8.8	9.0	9.1	9.3	9.5	9.7	9.9	10.0	10.2	10.4	10.5	10.7	10.9	11.0	11.2	11.3	11.5	11.6	11.8	11.9
100	1.8	2.5	3.1	3.6	4.0	4.4	4.7	5.0	5.3	5.6	5.9	6.2	6.4	6.7	6.9	7.1	7.3	7.5	7.8	8.0	8.2	8.3	8.5	8.7	8.9	9.1	9.2	9.4	9.6	9.7	9.9	10.1	10.2	10.4	10.5	10.7	10.8	11.0	11.1
99	1.4	2.1	2.7	3.2	3.6	4.0	4.3	4.6	4.9	5.2	5.5	5.8	6.0	6.3	6.5	6.7	6.9	7.1	7.4	7.6	7.8	7.9	8.1	8.3	8.5	8.7	8.8	9.0	9.2	9.3	9.5	9.7	9.8	9.9	10.1	10.3	10.4	10.6	10.7
98	1.0	1.7	2.3	2.8	3.2	3.6	3.9	4.2	4.5	4.8	5.1	5.4	5.6	5.9	6.1	6.3	6.5	6.7	7.0	7.2	7.4	7.5	7.7	7.9	8.1	8.3	8.4	8.6	8.8	8.9	9.1	9.3	9.4	9.6	9.7	9.9	10.0	10.2	10.3
97	0.6	1.3	1.9	2.4	2.8	3.2	3.5	3.8	4.1	4.4	4.7	5.0	5.2	5.5	5.7	5.9	6.1	6.3	6.6	6.8	7.0	7.1	7.3	7.5	7.7	7.9	8.0	8.2	8.4	8.5	8.7	8.9	9.0	9.2	9.3	9.5	9.6	9.8	9.9
96	0.2	0.9	1.5	2.0	2.4	2.8	3.1	3.4	3.7	4.0	4.3	4.6	4.8	5.1	5.3	5.5	5.7	5.9	6.2	6.4	6.6	6.7	6.9	7.1	7.3	7.5	7.6	7.8	8.0	8.1	8.3	8.5	8.6	8.8	8.9	9.1	9.2	9.4	9.5
95	0.0	0.5	1.1	1.6	2.0	2.4	2.7	3.0	3.3	3.6	3.9	4.2	4.4	4.7	4.9	5.1	5.3	5.5	5.8	6.0	6.2	6.3	6.5	6.7	6.9	7.1	7.2	7.4	7.6	7.7	7.9	8.1	8.2	8.4	8.5	8.7	8.8	9.0	9.1
94	0.0	0.1	0.7	1.2	1.6	2.0	2.3	2.6	2.9	3.2	3.5	3.8	4.0	4.3	4.5	4.7	4.9	5.1	5.4	5.6	5.8	5.9	6.1	6.3	6.5	6.7	6.8	7.0	7.2	7.3	7.5	7.7	7.8	8.0	8.1	8.3	8.4	8.6	8.7
93	0.0	0.0	0.3	0.8	1.2	1.6	1.9	2.2	2.5	2.8	3.1	3.4	3.6	3.9	4.1	4.3	4.5	4.7	5.0	5.2	5.4	5.5	5.7	5.9	6.1	6.3	6.4	6.6	6.8	6.9	7.1	7.3	7.4	7.6	7.7	7.9	8.0	8.2	8.3
92	0.0	0.0	0.0	0.4	0.8	1.2	1.5	1.8	2.1	2.4	2.7	3.0	3.2	3.5	3.7	3.9	4.1	4.3	4.6	4.8	5.0	5.1	5.3	5.5	5.7	5.9	6.0	6.2	6.4	6.5	6.7	6.9	7.0	7.2	7.3	7.5	7.6	7.8	7.9
91	0.0	0.0	0.0	0.0	0.4	0.8	1.1	1.4	1.7	2.0	2.3	2.6	2.8	3.1	3.3	3.5	3.7	3.9	4.2	4.4	4.6	4.7	4.9	5.1	5.3	5.5	5.6	5.8	6.0	6.1	6.3	6.5	6.6	6.8	6.9	7.1	7.2	7.4	7.5
90	0.0	0.0	0.0	0.0	0.0	0.4	0.7	1.0	1.3	1.6	1.9	2.2	2.4	2.7	2.9	3.1	3.3	3.5	3.8	4.0	4.2	4.3	4.5	4.7	4.9	5.1	5.2	5.4	5.6	5.7	5.9	6.1	6.2	6.4	6.5	6.7	6.8	7.0	7.1
89	0.0	0.0	0.0	0.0	0.0	0.0	0.3	0.6	0.9	1.2	1.5	1.8	2.0	2.3	2.5	2.7	2.9	3.1	3.4	3.6	3.8	3.9	4.1	4.3	4.5	4.7	4.8	5.0	5.2	5.3	5.5	5.7	5.8	6.0	6.1	6.3	6.4	6.6	6.7
88	0.0	0.0	0.0	0.0	0.0	0.0	0.0	0.2	0.5	0.8	1.1	1.4	1.6	1.9	2.1	2.3	2.5	2.7	3.0	3.2	3.4	3.5	3.7	3.9	4.1	4.3	4.4	4.6	4.8	4.9	5.1	5.3	5.4	5.6	5.7	5.9	6.0	6.2	6.3
87	0.0	0.0	0.0	0.0	0.0	0.0	0.0	0.0	0.1	0.4	0.7	1.0	1.2	1.5	1.7	1.9	2.1	2.3	2.6	2.8	3.0	3.1	3.3	3.5	3.7	3.9	4.0	4.2	4.4	4.5	4.7	4.9	5.0	5.2	5.3	5.5	5.6	5.8	5.9
86	0.0	0.0	0.0	0.0	0.0	0.0	0.0	0.0	0.0	0.0	0.3	0.6	0.8	1.1	1.3	1.5	1.7	1.9	2.2	2.4	2.6	2.7	2.9	3.1	3.3	3.5	3.6	3.8	4.0	4.1	4.3	4.5	4.6	4.8	4.9	5.1	5.2	5.4	5.5
85	0.0	0.0	0.0	0.0	0.0	0.0	0.0	0.0	0.0	0.0	0.0	0.2	0.4	0.7	0.9	1.1	1.3	1.5	1.8	2.0	2.2	2.3	2.5	2.7	2.9	3.1	3.2	3.4	3.6	3.7	3.9	4.1	4.2	4.4	4.5	4.7	4.8	5.0	5.1
84	0.0	0.0	0.0	0.0	0.0	0.0	0.0	0.0	0.0	0.0	0.0	0.0	0.0	0.3	0.5	0.7	0.9	1.1	1.4	1.6	1.8	1.9	2.1	2.3	2.5	2.7	2.8	3.0	3.2	3.3	3.5	3.7	3.8	4.0	4.1	4.3	4.4	4.6	4.7
83	0.0	0.0	0.0	0.0	0.0	0.0	0.0	0.0	0.0	0.0	0.0	0.0	0.0	0.0	0.1	0.3	0.5	0.7	1.0	1.2	1.4	1.5	1.7	1.9	2.1	2.3	2.4	2.6	2.8	2.9	3.1	3.3	3.4	3.6	3.7	3.9	4.0	4.2	4.3
82	0.0	0.0	0.0	0.0	0.0	0.0	0.0	0.0	0.0	0.0	0.0	0.0	0.0	0.0	0.0	0.0	0.1	0.3	0.6	0.8	1.0	1.1	1.3	1.5	1.7	1.9	2.0	2.2	2.4	2.5	2.7	2.9	3.0	3.2	3.3	3.5	3.6	3.8	3.9
81	0.0	0.0	0.0	0.0	0.0	0.0	0.0	0.0	0.0	0.0	0.0	0.0	0.0	0.0	0.0	0.0	0.0	0.0	0.2	0.4	0.6	0.7	0.9	1.1	1.3	1.5	1.6	1.8	2.0	2.1	2.3	2.5	2.6	2.8	2.9	3.1	3.2	3.4	3.5
80	0.0	0.0	0.0	0.0	0.0	0.0	0.0	0.0	0.0	0.0	0.0	0.0	0.0	0.0	0.0	0.0	0.0	0.0	0.0	0.0	0.2	0.3	0.5	0.7	0.9	1.1	1.2	1.4	1.6	1.7	1.9	2.1	2.2	2.4	2.5	2.7	2.8	3.0	3.1
79	0.0	0.0	0.0	0.0	0.0	0.0	0.0	0.0	0.0	0.0	0.0	0.0	0.0	0.0	0.0	0.0	0.0	0.0	0.0	0.0	0.0	0.0	0.1	0.3	0.5	0.7	0.8	1.0	1.2	1.3	1.5	1.7	1.8	2.0	2.1	2.3	2.4	2.6	2.7
78	0.0	0.0	0.0	0.0	0.0	0.0	0.0	0.0	0.0	0.0	0.0	0.0	0.0	0.0	0.0	0.0	0.0	0.0	0.0	0.0	0.0	0.0	0.0	0.0	0.1	0.3	0.4	0.6	0.8	0.9	1.1	1.3	1.4	1.6	1.7	1.9	2.0	2.2	2.3
77	0.0	0.0	0.0	0.0	0.0	0.0	0.0	0.0	0.0	0.0	0.0	0.0	0.0	0.0	0.0	0.0	0.0	0.0	0.0	0.0	0.0	0.0	0.0	0.0	0.0	0.0	0.0	0.2	0.4	0.5	0.7	0.9	1.0	1.2	1.3	1.5	1.6	1.8	1.9
76	0.0	0.0	0.0	0.0	0.0	0.0	0.0	0.0	0.0	0.0	0.0	0.0	0.0	0.0	0.0	0.0	0.0	0.0	0.0	0.0	0.0	0.0	0.0	0.0	0.0	0.0	0.0	0.0	0.0	0.1	0.3	0.5	0.6	0.8	0.9	1.1	1.2	1.4	1.5
75	0.0	0.0	0.0	0.0	0.0	0.0	0.0	0.0	0.0	0.0	0.0	0.0	0.0	0.0	0.0	0.0	0.0	0.0	0.0	0.0	0.0	0.0	0.0	0.0	0.0	0.0	0.0	0.0	0.0	0.0	0.0	0.1	0.2	0.4	0.5	0.7	0.8	1.0	1.1
74	0.0	0.0	0.0	0.0	0.0	0.0	0.0	0.0	0.0	0.0	0.0	0.0	0.0	0.0	0.0	0.0	0.0	0.0	0.0	0.0	0.0	0.0	0.0	0.0	0.0	0.0	0.0	0.0	0.0	0.0	0.0	0.0	0.0	0.0	0.1	0.3	0.4	0.6	0.7
73	0.0	0.0	0.0	0.0	0.0	0.0	0.0	0.0	0.0	0.0	0.0	0.0	0.0	0.0	0.0	0.0	0.0	0.0	0.0	0.0	0.0	0.0	0.0	0.0	0.0	0.0	0.0	0.0	0.0	0.0	0.0	0.0	0.0	0.0	0.0	0.0	0.0	0.2	0.3
72	0.0	0.0	0.0	0.0	0.0	0.0	0.0	0.0	0.0	0.0	0.0	0.0	0.0	0.0	0.0	0.0	0.0	0.0	0.0	0.0	0.0	0.0	0.0	0.0	0.0	0.0	0.0	0.0	0.0	0.0	0.0	0.0	0.0	0.0	0.0	0.0	0.0	0.0	0.0
71	0.0	0.0	0.0	0.0	0.0	0.0	0.0	0.0	0.0	0.0	0.0	0.0	0.0	0.0	0.0	0.0	0.0	0.0	0.0	0.0	0.0	0.0	0.0	0.0	0.0	0.0	0.0	0.0	0.0	0.0	0.0	0.0	0.0	0.0	0.0	0.0	0.0	0.0	0.0
70	0.0	0.0	0.0	0.0	0.0	0.0	0.0	0.0	0.0	0.0	0.0	0.0	0.0	0.0	0.0	0.0	0.0	0.0	0.0	0.0	0.0	0.0	0.0	0.0	0.0	0.0	0.0	0.0	0.0	0.0	0.0	0.0	0.0	0.0	0.0	0.0	0.0	0.0	0.0

LISTED CALL OPTION PRICE WHEN EXERCISE PRICE IS 110

Common Stock Price	NUMBER OF WEEKS BEFORE THE OPTION EXPIRES																																					
	1	2	3	4	5	6	7	8	9	10	11	12	13	14	15	16	17	18	19	20	21	22	23	24	25	26	27	28	29	30	31	32	33	34	35	36	37	38	39
144	34.1	34.2	34.4	34.5	34.6	34.7	34.9	35.0	35.1	35.2	35.4	35.5	35.6	35.7	35.8	36.0	36.1	36.2	36.3	36.5	36.6	36.7	36.8	37.0	37.1	37.2	37.3	37.4	37.6	37.7	37.8	37.9	38.1	38.2	38.3	38.4	38.6	38.7	38.8
142	32.1	32.3	32.4	32.5	32.7	32.8	32.9	33.1	33.2	33.3	33.5	33.6	33.7	33.9	34.0	34.1	34.3	34.4	34.5	34.7	34.8	34.9	35.1	35.2	35.3	35.5	35.6	35.7	35.9	36.0	36.1	36.3	36.4	36.5	36.7	36.8	36.9	37.1	37.2
140	30.1	30.3	30.4	30.6	30.7	30.9	31.0	31.1	31.3	31.4	31.6	31.7	31.9	32.0	32.2	32.3	32.4	32.6	32.7	32.9	33.0	33.2	33.3	33.4	33.6	33.7	33.9	34.0	34.2	34.3	34.5	34.6	34.7	34.9	35.0	35.2	35.3	35.5	35.6
138	28.2	28.3	28.5	28.6	28.8	28.9	29.1	29.2	29.4	29.5	29.7	29.8	30.0	30.2	30.3	30.5	30.6	30.8	30.9	31.1	31.2	31.4	31.5	31.7	31.8	32.0	32.2	32.3	32.5	32.6	32.8	32.9	33.1	33.2	33.4	33.5	33.7	33.9	34.0
136	26.2	26.3	26.4	26.7	26.8	27.0	27.1	27.3	27.5	27.6	27.8	28.0	28.1	28.3	28.5	28.6	28.8	29.0	29.1	29.3	29.4	29.6	29.8	29.9	30.1	30.3	30.4	30.6	30.8	30.9	31.1	31.3	31.4	31.6	31.7	31.9	32.1	32.2	32.4
134	24.2	24.3	24.5	24.7	24.9	25.0	25.2	25.4	25.6	25.7	25.9	26.1	26.3	26.4	26.6	26.8	27.0	27.1	27.3	27.5	27.7	27.8	28.0	28.2	28.4	28.5	28.7	28.9	29.1	29.2	29.4	29.6	29.8	29.9	30.1	30.3	30.5	30.6	30.8
132	22.2	22.4	22.6	22.7	22.9	23.1	23.3	23.5	23.7	23.8	24.0	24.2	24.4	24.6	24.8	25.0	25.1	25.3	25.5	25.7	25.9	26.1	26.2	26.4	26.6	26.8	27.0	27.2	27.4	27.5	27.7	27.9	28.1	28.3	28.5	28.7	28.8	29.0	29.2
130	20.2	20.4	20.6	20.8	21.0	21.2	21.4	21.6	21.8	22.0	22.1	22.3	22.5	22.7	22.9	23.1	23.3	23.5	23.7	23.9	24.1	24.3	24.5	24.7	24.9	25.1	25.3	25.5	25.7	25.9	26.0	26.2	26.4	26.6	26.8	27.0	27.2	27.4	27.6
128	18.2	18.4	18.6	18.8	19.0	19.2	19.4	19.6	19.8	20.1	20.3	20.5	20.7	20.9	21.1	21.3	21.5	21.7	21.9	22.1	22.3	22.5	22.7	22.9	23.1	23.3	23.5	23.7	24.0	24.2	24.4	24.6	24.8	25.0	25.2	25.4	25.6	25.8	26.0
126	16.2	16.4	16.6	16.9	17.1	17.3	17.5	17.7	17.9	18.2	18.4	18.6	18.8	19.0	19.2	19.4	19.7	19.9	20.1	20.3	20.5	20.7	21.0	21.2	21.4	21.6	21.8	22.0	22.2	22.5	22.7	22.9	23.1	23.3	23.5	23.8	24.0	24.2	24.4
124	14.2	14.5	14.7	14.9	15.1	15.4	15.6	15.8	16.0	16.3	16.5	16.7	16.9	17.2	17.4	17.6	17.8	18.1	18.3	18.5	18.7	19.0	19.2	19.4	19.6	19.9	20.1	20.3	20.5	20.8	21.0	21.2	21.5	21.7	21.9	22.1	22.4	22.6	22.8
122	12.2	12.5	12.7	12.9	13.2	13.4	13.7	13.9	14.1	14.4	14.6	14.8	15.1	15.3	15.5	15.8	16.0	16.2	16.5	16.7	17.0	17.2	17.4	17.7	17.9	18.1	18.4	18.6	18.8	19.1	19.3	19.6	19.8	20.0	20.3	20.5	20.7	21.0	21.2
120	10.2	10.5	10.7	11.0	11.3	11.5	11.8	12.0	12.3	12.6	12.8	13.0	13.2	13.5	13.7	14.0	14.2	14.5	14.8	15.0	15.3	15.5	15.7	16.0	16.1	16.3	16.6	16.8	17.0	17.3	17.5	17.8	18.0	18.2	18.5	18.7	18.9	19.2	19.4
118	8.3	8.5	8.8	9.1	9.4	9.6	9.9	10.2	10.5	10.8	11.0	11.2	11.5	11.8	12.0	12.3	12.5	12.8	13.0	13.2	13.5	13.7	13.9	14.2	14.4	14.6	14.9	15.1	15.2	15.5	15.7	16.0	16.2	16.4	16.7	16.9	17.1	17.4	17.6
116	6.3	6.6	6.8	7.2	7.5	7.7	8.1	8.4	8.7	9.0	9.3	9.6	9.9	10.3	10.5	10.8	11.0	11.3	11.5	11.7	12.0	12.2	12.4	12.7	12.9	13.1	13.3	13.5	13.7	14.0	14.2	14.5	14.7	14.8	14.9	15.1	15.3	15.6	15.8
114	4.5	4.7	5.0	5.5	6.0	6.4	6.8	7.1	7.5	7.8	8.1	8.4	8.7	8.9	9.2	9.4	9.7	9.9	10.1	10.4	10.6	10.8	11.0	11.2	11.4	11.6	11.8	12.0	12.1	12.3	12.5	12.7	12.8	13.0	13.2	13.3	13.5	13.7	13.8
112	2.8	3.6	4.2	4.7	5.2	5.6	6.0	6.3	6.7	7.0	7.3	7.6	7.9	8.1	8.4	8.6	8.9	9.1	9.3	9.6	9.8	9.9	10.2	10.4	10.6	10.8	11.0	11.2	11.3	11.5	11.7	11.9	12.0	12.2	12.4	12.5	12.7	12.9	13.0
110	2.0	2.8	3.4	3.9	4.4	4.8	5.2	5.5	5.9	6.2	6.5	6.8	7.1	7.3	7.6	7.8	8.1	8.3	8.5	8.8	9.0	9.2	9.4	9.6	9.8	9.9	10.2	10.4	10.5	10.7	10.9	11.1	11.2	11.4	11.6	11.7	11.9	12.1	12.2
108	1.2	2.0	2.6	3.1	3.6	4.0	4.4	4.7	5.1	5.4	5.7	6.0	6.3	6.5	6.8	7.0	7.3	7.5	7.7	8.0	8.2	8.4	8.6	8.8	9.0	9.2	9.4	9.6	9.7	9.9	10.1	10.3	10.4	10.6	10.8	10.9	11.1	11.3	11.4
106	0.4	1.2	1.8	2.3	2.8	3.2	3.6	3.9	4.3	4.6	4.9	5.2	5.5	5.7	6.0	6.2	6.5	6.7	6.9	7.2	7.4	7.6	7.8	8.0	8.2	8.4	8.6	8.8	8.9	9.1	9.3	9.5	9.6	9.8	9.9	10.1	10.3	10.5	10.6
104	0.0	0.4	1.0	1.5	2.0	2.4	2.8	3.1	3.5	3.8	4.1	4.4	4.7	4.9	5.2	5.4	5.7	5.9	6.1	6.4	6.6	6.8	7.0	7.2	7.4	7.6	7.8	8.0	8.1	8.3	8.5	8.7	8.8	9.0	9.2	9.3	9.5	9.7	9.8
102	0.0	0.0	0.2	0.7	1.2	1.6	2.0	2.3	2.7	3.0	3.3	3.6	3.9	4.1	4.4	4.6	4.9	5.1	5.3	5.6	5.8	6.0	6.2	6.4	6.6	6.8	7.0	7.2	7.3	7.5	7.7	7.9	8.0	8.2	8.4	8.5	8.7	8.9	9.0
100	0.0	0.0	0.0	0.0	0.4	0.8	1.2	1.5	1.9	2.2	2.5	2.8	3.1	3.3	3.6	3.8	4.1	4.3	4.5	4.8	5.0	5.2	5.4	5.6	5.8	6.0	6.2	6.4	6.5	6.7	6.9	7.1	7.2	7.4	7.6	7.7	7.9	8.1	8.2
99	0.0	0.0	0.0	0.0	0.0	0.4	0.8	1.1	1.5	1.8	2.1	2.4	2.7	2.9	3.2	3.4	3.7	3.9	4.1	4.4	4.6	4.8	5.0	5.2	5.4	5.6	5.8	6.0	6.1	6.3	6.5	6.7	6.8	7.0	7.2	7.3	7.5	7.7	7.8
98	0.0	0.0	0.0	0.0	0.0	0.0	0.4	0.7	1.1	1.4	1.7	2.0	2.3	2.6	2.8	3.0	3.3	3.5	3.7	4.0	4.2	4.4	4.6	4.8	5.0	5.2	5.4	5.6	5.7	5.9	6.1	6.3	6.4	6.6	6.8	6.9	7.1	7.3	7.4
97	0.0	0.0	0.0	0.0	0.0	0.0	0.0	0.3	0.7	1.0	1.3	1.6	1.9	2.1	2.4	2.6	2.9	3.1	3.3	3.6	3.8	4.0	4.2	4.4	4.6	4.8	5.0	5.2	5.3	5.5	5.7	5.9	6.0	6.2	6.4	6.5	6.7	6.9	7.0
96	0.0	0.0	0.0	0.0	0.0	0.0	0.0	0.0	0.3	0.6	0.9	1.2	1.5	1.7	2.0	2.2	2.5	2.7	2.9	3.2	3.4	3.6	3.8	4.0	4.2	4.4	4.6	4.8	4.9	5.1	5.3	5.5	5.6	5.8	6.0	6.1	6.3	6.5	6.6
95	0.0	0.0	0.0	0.0	0.0	0.0	0.0	0.0	0.0	0.2	0.5	0.8	1.1	1.3	1.6	1.8	2.1	2.3	2.5	2.8	3.0	3.2	3.4	3.6	3.8	4.0	4.2	4.4	4.5	4.7	4.9	5.1	5.2	5.4	5.6	5.7	5.9	6.1	6.2
94	0.0	0.0	0.0	0.0	0.0	0.0	0.0	0.0	0.0	0.0	0.1	0.4	0.7	0.9	1.2	1.4	1.7	1.9	2.1	2.4	2.6	2.8	3.0	3.2	3.4	3.6	3.8	4.0	4.1	4.3	4.5	4.7	4.8	5.0	5.2	5.3	5.5	5.7	5.8
93	0.0	0.0	0.0	0.0	0.0	0.0	0.0	0.0	0.0	0.0	0.0	0.0	0.3	0.5	0.8	1.0	1.3	1.5	1.7	2.0	2.2	2.4	2.6	2.8	3.0	3.2	3.4	3.6	3.7	3.9	4.1	4.3	4.4	4.6	4.8	4.9	5.1	5.3	5.4
92	0.0	0.0	0.0	0.0	0.0	0.0	0.0	0.0	0.0	0.0	0.0	0.0	0.0	0.1	0.4	0.6	0.9	1.1	1.3	1.6	1.8	2.0	2.2	2.4	2.6	2.8	3.0	3.2	3.3	3.5	3.7	3.9	4.0	4.2	4.4	4.5	4.7	4.9	5.0
91	0.0	0.0	0.0	0.0	0.0	0.0	0.0	0.0	0.0	0.0	0.0	0.0	0.0	0.0	0.0	0.2	0.5	0.7	0.9	1.2	1.4	1.6	1.8	2.0	2.2	2.4	2.6	2.8	2.9	3.1	3.3	3.5	3.6	3.8	4.0	4.1	4.3	4.5	4.6
90	0.0	0.0	0.0	0.0	0.0	0.0	0.0	0.0	0.0	0.0	0.0	0.0	0.0	0.0	0.0	0.0	0.1	0.3	0.5	0.8	1.0	1.2	1.4	1.6	1.8	2.0	2.2	2.4	2.5	2.7	2.9	3.1	3.2	3.4	3.6	3.7	3.9	4.1	4.2
89	0.0	0.0	0.0	0.0	0.0	0.0	0.0	0.0	0.0	0.0	0.0	0.0	0.0	0.0	0.0	0.0	0.0	0.0	0.1	0.4	0.6	0.8	1.0	1.2	1.4	1.6	1.8	2.0	2.1	2.3	2.5	2.7	2.8	3.0	3.2	3.3	3.5	3.7	3.8
88	0.0	0.0	0.0	0.0	0.0	0.0	0.0	0.0	0.0	0.0	0.0	0.0	0.0	0.0	0.0	0.0	0.0	0.0	0.0	0.0	0.2	0.4	0.6	0.8	1.0	1.2	1.4	1.6	1.7	1.9	2.1	2.3	2.4	2.6	2.8	2.9	3.1	3.3	3.4
87	0.0	0.0	0.0	0.0	0.0	0.0	0.0	0.0	0.0	0.0	0.0	0.0	0.0	0.0	0.0	0.0	0.0	0.0	0.0	0.0	0.0	0.0	0.2	0.4	0.6	0.8	1.0	1.2	1.3	1.5	1.7	1.9	2.0	2.2	2.4	2.5	2.7	2.9	3.0
86	0.0	0.0	0.0	0.0	0.0	0.0	0.0	0.0	0.0	0.0	0.0	0.0	0.0	0.0	0.0	0.0	0.0	0.0	0.0	0.0	0.0	0.0	0.0	0.0	0.2	0.4	0.6	0.8	0.9	1.1	1.3	1.5	1.6	1.8	2.0	2.1	2.3	2.5	2.6
85	0.0	0.0	0.0	0.0	0.0	0.0	0.0	0.0	0.0	0.0	0.0	0.0	0.0	0.0	0.0	0.0	0.0	0.0	0.0	0.0	0.0	0.0	0.0	0.0	0.0	0.0	0.2	0.4	0.5	0.7	0.9	1.1	1.2	1.4	1.6	1.7	1.9	2.1	2.2
84	0.0	0.0	0.0	0.0	0.0	0.0	0.0	0.0	0.0	0.0	0.0	0.0	0.0	0.0	0.0	0.0	0.0	0.0	0.0	0.0	0.0	0.0	0.0	0.0	0.0	0.0	0.0	0.0	0.1	0.3	0.5	0.7	0.8	1.0	1.2	1.3	1.5	1.7	1.8
83	0.0	0.0	0.0	0.0	0.0	0.0	0.0	0.0	0.0	0.0	0.0	0.0	0.0	0.0	0.0	0.0	0.0	0.0	0.0	0.0	0.0	0.0	0.0	0.0	0.0	0.0	0.0	0.0	0.0	0.0	0.1	0.3	0.4	0.6	0.8	0.9	1.1	1.3	1.4
82	0.0	0.0	0.0	0.0	0.0	0.0	0.0	0.0	0.0	0.0	0.0	0.0	0.0	0.0	0.0	0.0	0.0	0.0	0.0	0.0	0.0	0.0	0.0	0.0	0.0	0.0	0.0	0.0	0.0	0.0	0.0	0.0	0.0	0.2	0.4	0.5	0.7	0.9	1.0
81	0.0	0.0	0.0	0.0	0.0	0.0	0.0	0.0	0.0	0.0	0.0	0.0	0.0	0.0	0.0	0.0	0.0	0.0	0.0	0.0	0.0	0.0	0.0	0.0	0.0	0.0	0.0	0.0	0.0	0.0	0.0	0.0	0.0	0.0	0.0	0.1	0.3	0.5	0.6
80	0.0	0.0	0.0	0.0	0.0	0.0	0.0	0.0	0.0	0.0	0.0	0.0	0.0	0.0	0.0	0.0	0.0	0.0	0.0	0.0	0.0	0.0	0.0	0.0	0.0	0.0	0.0	0.0	0.0	0.0	0.0	0.0	0.0	0.0	0.0	0.0	0.0	0.1	0.2
79	0.0	0.0	0.0	0.0	0.0	0.0	0.0	0.0	0.0	0.0	0.0	0.0	0.0	0.0	0.0	0.0	0.0	0.0	0.0	0.0	0.0	0.0	0.0	0.0	0.0	0.0	0.0	0.0	0.0	0.0	0.0	0.0	0.0	0.0	0.0	0.0	0.0	0.0	0.0
78	0.0	0.0	0.0	0.0	0.0	0.0	0.0	0.0	0.0	0.0	0.0	0.0	0.0	0.0	0.0	0.0	0.0	0.0	0.0	0.0	0.0	0.0	0.0	0.0	0.0	0.0	0.0	0.0	0.0	0.0	0.0	0.0	0.0	0.0	0.0	0.0	0.0	0.0	0.0
77	0.0	0.0	0.0	0.0	0.0	0.0	0.0	0.0	0.0	0.0	0.0	0.0	0.0	0.0	0.0	0.0	0.0	0.0	0.0	0.0	0.0	0.0	0.0	0.0	0.0	0.0	0.0	0.0	0.0	0.0	0.0	0.0	0.0	0.0	0.0	0.0	0.0	0.0	0.0

LISTED CALL OPTION PRICE WHEN EXERCISE PRICE IS 120

NUMBER OF WEEKS BEFORE THE OPTION EXPIRES

Common Stock Price	1	2	3	4	5	6	7	8	9	10	11	12	13	14	15	16	17	18	19	20	21	22	23	24	25	26	27	28	29	30	31	32	33	34	35	36	37	38	39
156	36.1	36.3	36.4	36.6	36.7	36.8	37.0	37.1	37.3	37.4	37.5	37.7	37.8	38.0	38.1	38.2	38.4	38.5	38.7	38.8	38.9	39.1	39.2	39.4	39.5	39.6	39.8	39.9	40.1	40.2	40.3	40.5	40.6	40.8	40.9	41.0	41.2	41.3	41.5
154	34.2	34.3	34.5	34.6	34.8	34.9	35.1	35.2	35.4	35.5	35.7	35.8	36.0	36.1	36.3	36.4	36.6	36.7	36.9	37.0	37.2	37.3	37.5	37.6	37.8	37.9	38.1	38.2	38.4	38.5	38.7	38.8	39.0	39.1	39.3	39.4	39.6	39.7	39.9
152	32.2	32.3	32.5	32.6	32.8	33.0	33.1	33.3	33.4	33.6	33.8	33.9	34.1	34.2	34.4	34.6	34.7	34.9	35.0	35.2	35.4	35.5	35.7	35.9	36.0	36.2	36.3	36.5	36.7	36.8	37.0	37.1	37.3	37.5	37.6	37.8	37.9	38.1	38.3
150	30.2	30.3	30.5	30.7	30.9	31.0	31.2	31.4	31.5	31.7	31.9	32.0	32.2	32.4	32.6	32.7	32.9	33.1	33.2	33.4	33.6	33.8	33.9	34.1	34.3	34.4	34.6	34.8	35.0	35.1	35.3	35.5	35.6	35.8	36.0	36.1	36.3	36.5	36.7
148	28.2	28.4	28.5	28.7	28.9	29.1	29.3	29.4	29.6	29.8	29.9	30.2	30.4	30.5	30.7	30.9	31.1	31.3	31.4	31.6	31.8	32.0	32.2	32.3	32.5	32.7	32.9	33.1	33.2	33.4	33.6	33.8	34.0	34.2	34.3	34.5	34.7	34.9	35.1
146	26.2	26.4	26.6	26.8	27.0	27.1	27.3	27.5	27.7	27.9	28.1	28.3	28.5	28.7	28.9	29.1	29.3	29.4	29.6	29.8	30.0	30.2	30.4	30.6	30.8	31.0	31.2	31.4	31.5	31.7	31.9	32.1	32.3	32.5	32.7	32.9	33.1	33.3	33.5
144	24.2	24.4	24.6	24.8	25.0	25.2	25.4	25.6	25.8	26.0	26.2	26.4	26.6	26.8	27.0	27.2	27.4	27.6	27.8	28.0	28.2	28.4	28.6	28.8	29.0	29.2	29.4	29.6	29.8	30.0	30.2	30.4	30.7	30.9	31.1	31.3	31.5	31.7	31.9
142	22.2	22.4	22.6	22.8	23.1	23.3	23.5	23.7	23.9	24.1	24.3	24.5	24.8	25.0	25.2	25.4	25.6	25.8	26.0	26.2	26.4	26.7	26.9	27.1	27.3	27.5	27.7	27.9	28.1	28.4	28.6	28.8	29.0	29.2	29.4	29.6	29.8	30.0	30.3
140	20.2	20.4	20.7	20.9	21.1	21.3	21.6	21.8	22.0	22.2	22.4	22.7	22.9	23.1	23.3	23.6	23.8	24.0	24.2	24.4	24.7	24.9	25.1	25.3	25.6	25.8	26.0	26.2	26.4	26.7	26.9	27.1	27.3	27.5	27.8	28.0	28.2	28.4	28.7
138	18.2	18.5	18.7	18.9	19.2	19.4	19.6	19.9	20.1	20.3	20.6	20.8	21.0	21.3	21.5	21.7	21.9	22.2	22.4	22.6	22.9	23.1	23.3	23.6	23.8	24.0	24.3	24.5	24.7	25.0	25.2	25.4	25.7	25.9	26.1	26.4	26.6	26.8	27.1
136	16.2	16.5	16.7	17.0	17.2	17.5	17.7	17.9	18.2	18.4	18.7	18.9	19.2	19.4	19.6	19.9	20.1	20.4	20.6	20.9	21.1	21.3	21.6	21.8	22.1	22.3	22.5	22.8	23.0	23.3	23.5	23.8	24.0	24.2	24.5	24.7	25.0	25.2	25.5
134	14.3	14.5	14.8	15.0	15.3	15.5	15.8	16.0	16.3	16.5	16.8	17.0	17.3	17.5	17.8	18.0	18.3	18.6	18.8	19.1	19.3	19.6	19.8	20.1	20.3	20.6	20.8	21.1	21.3	21.6	21.8	22.1	22.3	22.6	22.8	23.1	23.4	23.6	23.9
132	12.3	12.5	12.8	13.0	13.3	13.5	13.9	14.1	14.4	14.6	15.0	15.3	15.6	15.8	16.1	16.3	16.6	16.9	17.1	17.4	17.6	17.9	18.1	18.2	18.4	18.7	18.9	19.2	19.4	19.7	19.9	20.2	20.4	20.7	20.9	21.2	21.5	21.7	22.0
130	10.3	10.5	10.8	11.1	11.4	11.6	12.1	12.3	12.6	12.8	13.2	13.5	13.9	14.1	14.4	14.6	14.9	15.2	15.4	15.7	15.9	16.2	16.4	16.7	16.9	17.2	17.4	17.7	17.9	18.2	18.4	18.7	18.9	19.2	19.3	19.4	19.6	19.8	20.1
128	8.4	8.6	8.9	9.2	9.5	9.8	10.3	10.5	10.8	11.0	11.5	11.8	12.2	12.4	12.7	12.9	13.2	13.5	13.7	14.0	14.2	14.5	14.7	15.0	15.2	15.5	15.7	16.0	16.2	16.5	16.7	17.0	17.2	17.5	17.6	17.8	17.8	17.9	18.2
126	6.5	6.7	7.0	7.3	7.6	8.0	8.6	8.8	9.3	9.6	10.1	10.4	10.8	11.0	11.3	11.5	11.8	12.1	12.3	12.6	12.8	13.1	13.3	13.6	13.8	14.1	14.3	14.6	14.8	15.1	15.3	15.6	15.7	15.8	15.9	16.0	16.1	16.2	16.4
124	4.6	4.9	5.3	5.9	6.4	6.8	7.2	7.6	8.0	8.4	8.7	9.0	9.3	9.6	9.9	10.1	10.4	10.7	10.9	11.1	11.4	11.6	11.8	12.1	12.3	12.5	12.7	12.9	13.1	13.3	13.5	13.7	13.9	14.0	14.2	14.4	14.6	14.8	14.9
122	2.9	3.8	4.5	5.1	5.6	6.0	6.4	6.8	7.2	7.6	7.9	8.2	8.5	8.8	9.1	9.3	9.6	9.9	10.1	10.3	10.6	10.8	11.0	11.3	11.5	11.7	11.9	12.1	12.3	12.5	12.7	12.9	13.1	13.2	13.4	13.6	13.8	14.0	14.1
120	2.1	3.0	3.7	4.3	4.8	5.2	5.6	6.0	6.4	6.8	7.1	7.4	7.7	8.0	8.3	8.5	8.8	9.1	9.3	9.5	9.8	10.0	10.2	10.5	10.7	10.9	11.1	11.3	11.5	11.7	11.9	12.1	12.3	12.4	12.6	12.8	13.0	13.2	13.3
118	1.3	2.2	2.9	3.5	4.0	4.4	4.8	5.2	5.6	6.0	6.3	6.6	6.9	7.2	7.5	7.7	8.0	8.3	8.5	8.7	9.0	9.2	9.4	9.7	9.9	10.1	10.3	10.5	10.7	10.9	11.1	11.3	11.5	11.6	11.8	12.0	12.2	12.4	12.5
116	0.5	1.4	2.1	2.7	3.2	3.6	4.0	4.4	4.8	5.2	5.5	5.8	6.1	6.4	6.7	6.9	7.2	7.5	7.7	7.9	8.2	8.4	8.6	8.9	9.1	9.3	9.5	9.7	9.9	10.1	10.3	10.5	10.7	10.8	11.0	11.2	11.4	11.6	11.7
114	0.0	0.6	1.3	1.9	2.4	2.8	3.2	3.6	4.0	4.4	4.7	5.0	5.3	5.6	5.9	6.1	6.4	6.7	6.9	7.1	7.4	7.6	7.8	8.1	8.3	8.5	8.7	8.9	9.1	9.3	9.5	9.7	9.9	10.0	10.2	10.4	10.6	10.8	10.9
112	0.0	0.0	0.5	1.1	1.6	2.0	2.4	2.8	3.2	3.6	3.9	4.2	4.5	4.8	5.1	5.3	5.6	5.9	6.1	6.3	6.6	6.8	7.0	7.3	7.5	7.7	7.9	8.1	8.3	8.5	8.7	8.9	9.1	9.2	9.4	9.6	9.8	9.9	10.1
110	0.0	0.0	0.0	0.3	0.8	1.2	1.6	2.0	2.4	2.8	3.1	3.4	3.7	4.0	4.3	4.5	4.8	5.1	5.3	5.5	5.8	6.0	6.2	6.5	6.7	6.9	7.1	7.3	7.5	7.7	7.9	8.1	8.3	8.4	8.6	8.8	9.0	9.2	9.3
108	0.0	0.0	0.0	0.0	0.0	0.4	0.8	1.2	1.6	2.0	2.3	2.6	2.9	3.2	3.5	3.7	4.0	4.3	4.5	4.7	5.0	5.2	5.4	5.7	5.9	6.1	6.3	6.5	6.7	6.9	7.1	7.3	7.5	7.6	7.8	8.0	8.2	8.4	8.5
106	0.0	0.0	0.0	0.0	0.0	0.0	0.0	0.4	0.8	1.2	1.5	1.8	2.1	2.4	2.7	2.9	3.2	3.5	3.7	3.9	4.2	4.4	4.6	4.9	5.1	5.3	5.5	5.7	5.9	6.1	6.3	6.5	6.7	6.8	7.0	7.2	7.4	7.6	7.7
104	0.0	0.0	0.0	0.0	0.0	0.0	0.0	0.0	0.0	0.4	0.7	1.0	1.3	1.6	1.9	2.1	2.4	2.7	2.9	3.1	3.4	3.6	3.8	4.1	4.3	4.5	4.7	4.9	5.1	5.3	5.5	5.7	5.9	6.0	6.2	6.4	6.6	6.8	6.9
102	0.0	0.0	0.0	0.0	0.0	0.0	0.0	0.0	0.0	0.0	0.0	0.2	0.5	0.8	1.1	1.3	1.6	1.9	2.1	2.3	2.6	2.8	3.0	3.3	35.	3.7	3.9	4.1	4.3	4.5	4.7	4.9	5.1	5.2	5.4	5.6	5.8	6.0	6.1
100	0.0	0.0	0.0	0.0	0.0	0.0	0.0	0.0	0.0	0.0	0.0	0.0	0.0	0.0	0.3	0.5	0.8	1.1	1.3	1.5	1.8	2.0	2.2	2.5	2.7	2.9	3.1	3.3	3.5	3.7	3.9	4.1	4.3	4.4	4.6	4.8	5.0	5.2	5.3
99	0.0	0.0	0.0	0.0	0.0	0.0	0.0	0.0	0.0	0.0	0.0	0.0	0.0	0.0	0.0	0.1	0.4	0.7	0.9	1.1	1.4	1.6	1.8	2.1	2.3	2.5	2.7	2.9	3.1	3.3	3.5	3.7	3.9	4.0	4.2	4.4	4.6	4.8	4.9
98	0.0	0.0	0.0	0.0	0.0	0.0	0.0	0.0	0.0	0.0	0.0	0.0	0.0	0.0	0.0	0.0	0.0	0.3	0.5	0.7	1.0	1.2	1.4	1.7	1.9	2.1	2.3	2.5	2.7	2.9	3.1	3.3	3.5	3.6	3.8	4.0	4.2	4.4	4.5
97	0.0	0.0	0.0	0.0	0.0	0.0	0.0	0.0	0.0	0.0	0.0	0.0	0.0	0.0	0.0	0.0	0.0	0.0	0.1	0.3	0.6	0.8	1.0	1.3	1.5	1.7	1.9	2.1	2.3	2.5	2.7	2.9	3.1	3.2	3.4	3.6	3.8	4.0	4.1
96	0.0	0.0	0.0	0.0	0.0	0.0	0.0	0.0	0.0	0.0	0.0	0.0	0.0	0.0	0.0	0.0	0.0	0.0	0.0	0.0	0.2	0.4	0.6	0.9	1.1	1.3	1.5	1.7	1.9	2.1	2.3	2.5	2.7	2.8	3.0	3.2	3.4	3.6	3.7
95	0.0	0.0	0.0	0.0	0.0	0.0	0.0	0.0	0.0	0.0	0.0	0.0	0.0	0.0	0.0	0.0	0.0	0.0	0.0	0.0	0.0	0.0	0.2	0.5	0.7	0.9	1.1	1.3	1.5	1.7	1.9	2.1	2.3	2.4	2.6	2.8	3.0	3.2	3.3
94	0.0	0.0	0.0	0.0	0.0	0.0	0.0	0.0	0.0	0.0	0.0	0.0	0.0	0.0	0.0	0.0	0.0	0.0	0.0	0.0	0.0	0.0	0.0	0.1	0.3	0.5	0.7	0.9	1.1	1.3	1.5	1.7	1.9	2.0	2.2	2.4	2.6	2.8	2.9
93	0.0	0.0	0.0	0.0	0.0	0.0	0.0	0.0	0.0	0.0	0.0	0.0	0.0	0.0	0.0	0.0	0.0	0.0	0.0	0.0	0.0	0.0	0.0	0.0	0.0	0.1	0.3	0.5	0.7	0.9	1.1	1.3	1.5	1.6	1.8	2.0	2.2	2.4	2.5
92	0.0	0.0	0.0	0.0	0.0	0.0	0.0	0.0	0.0	0.0	0.0	0.0	0.0	0.0	0.0	0.0	0.0	0.0	0.0	0.0	0.0	0.0	0.0	0.0	0.0	0.0	0.0	0.1	0.3	0.5	0.7	0.9	1.1	1.2	1.4	1.6	1.8	2.0	2.1
91	0.0	0.0	0.0	0.0	0.0	0.0	0.0	0.0	0.0	0.0	0.0	0.0	0.0	0.0	0.0	0.0	0.0	0.0	0.0	0.0	0.0	0.0	0.0	0.0	0.0	0.0	0.0	0.0	0.0	0.1	0.3	0.5	0.7	0.8	1.0	1.2	1.4	1.6	1.7
90	0.0	0.0	0.0	0.0	0.0	0.0	0.0	0.0	0.0	0.0	0.0	0.0	0.0	0.0	0.0	0.0	0.0	0.0	0.0	0.0	0.0	0.0	0.0	0.0	0.0	0.0	0.0	0.0	0.0	0.0	0.0	0.1	0.3	0.4	0.6	0.8	1.0	1.2	1.3
89	0.0	0.0	0.0	0.0	0.0	0.0	0.0	0.0	0.0	0.0	0.0	0.0	0.0	0.0	0.0	0.0	0.0	0.0	0.0	0.0	0.0	0.0	0.0	0.0	0.0	0.0	0.0	0.0	0.0	0.0	0.0	0.0	0.0	0.0	0.2	0.4	0.6	0.8	0.9
88	0.0	0.0	0.0	0.0	0.0	0.0	0.0	0.0	0.0	0.0	0.0	0.0	0.0	0.0	0.0	0.0	0.0	0.0	0.0	0.0	0.0	0.0	0.0	0.0	0.0	0.0	0.0	0.0	0.0	0.0	0.0	0.0	0.0	0.0	0.0	0.0	0.2	0.4	0.5
87	0.0	0.0	0.0	0.0	0.0	0.0	0.0	0.0	0.0	0.0	0.0	0.0	0.0	0.0	0.0	0.0	0.0	0.0	0.0	0.0	0.0	0.0	0.0	0.0	0.0	0.0	0.0	0.0	0.0	0.0	0.0	0.0	0.0	0.0	0.0	0.0	0.0	0.0	0.1
86	0.0	0.0	0.0	0.0	0.0	0.0	0.0	0.0	0.0	0.0	0.0	0.0	0.0	0.0	0.0	0.0	0.0	0.0	0.0	0.0	0.0	0.0	0.0	0.0	0.0	0.0	0.0	0.0	0.0	0.0	0.0	0.0	0.0	0.0	0.0	0.0	0.0	0.0	0.0
85	0.0	0.0	0.0	0.0	0.0	0.0	0.0	0.0	0.0	0.0	0.0	0.0	0.0	0.0	0.0	0.0	0.0	0.0	0.0	0.0	0.0	0.0	0.0	0.0	0.0	0.0	0.0	0.0	0.0	0.0	0.0	0.0	0.0	0.0	0.0	0.0	0.0	0.0	0.0
84	0.0	0.0	0.0	0.0	0.0	0.0	0.0	0.0	0.0	0.0	0.0	0.0	0.0	0.0	0.0	0.0	0.0	0.0	0.0	0.0	0.0	0.0	0.0	0.0	0.0	0.0	0.0	0.0	0.0	0.0	0.0	0.0	0.0	0.0	0.0	0.0	0.0	0.0	0.0

LISTED CALL OPTION PRICE WHEN EXERCISE PRICE IS 130

NUMBER OF WEEKS BEFORE THE OPTION EXPIRES

Common Stock Price	1	2	3	4	5	6	7	8	9	10	11	12	13	14	15	16	17	18	19	20	21	22	23	24	25	26	27	28	29	30	31	32	33	34	35	36	37	38	39
170	40.1	40.3	40.4	40.6	40.7	40.9	41.0	41.2	41.3	41.5	41.6	41.8	41.9	42.1	42.2	42.3	42.5	42.6	42.8	42.9	43.1	43.2	43.4	43.5	43.7	43.8	44.0	44.1	44.2	44.4	44.5	44.7	44.8	45.0	45.1	45.3	45.4	45.6	45.7
168	38.2	38.3	38.5	38.6	38.8	38.9	39.1	39.3	39.4	39.6	39.7	39.9	40.0	40.2	40.4	40.5	40.7	40.8	41.0	41.1	41.3	41.4	41.6	41.8	41.9	42.1	42.2	42.4	42.5	42.7	42.9	43.0	43.2	43.3	43.5	43.6	43.8	44.0	44.1
166	36.2	36.3	36.5	36.7	36.8	37.0	37.2	37.3	37.5	37.7	37.8	38.0	38.2	38.3	38.5	38.7	38.8	39.0	39.2	39.3	39.5	39.7	39.8	40.0	40.2	40.3	40.5	40.7	40.8	41.0	41.2	41.3	41.5	41.7	41.8	42.0	42.2	42.3	42.5
164	34.2	34.4	34.5	34.7	34.9	35.1	35.2	35.4	35.6	35.8	36.0	36.1	36.3	36.5	36.7	36.8	37.0	37.2	37.4	37.5	37.7	37.9	38.1	38.3	38.4	38.6	38.8	39.0	39.1	39.3	39.5	39.7	39.9	40.0	40.2	40.4	40.6	40.7	40.9
162	32.2	32.4	32.6	32.8	32.9	33.1	33.3	33.5	33.7	33.9	34.1	34.3	34.4	34.6	34.8	35.0	35.2	35.4	35.6	35.8	35.9	36.1	36.3	36.5	36.7	36.9	37.1	37.3	37.4	37.6	37.8	38.0	38.2	38.4	38.6	38.8	38.9	39.1	39.3
160	30.2	30.4	38.6	30.8	31.0	31.2	31.4	31.6	31.8	32.0	32.2	32.4	32.6	32.8	33.0	33.2	33.4	33.6	33.8	34.0	34.2	34.4	34.5	34.7	34.9	35.1	35.3	35.5	35.7	35.9	36.1	36.3	36.5	36.7	36.9	37.1	37.3	37.5	37.7
158	28.2	28.4	28.6	28.8	29.0	29.2	29.5	29.7	29.9	30.1	30.3	30.5	30.7	30.9	31.1	31.3	31.5	31.7	32.0	32.2	32.4	32.6	32.8	33.0	33.2	33.4	33.6	33.8	34.0	34.2	34.5	34.7	34.9	35.1	35.3	35.5	35.7	35.9	36.1
156	26.2	26.4	26.7	26.9	27.1	27.3	27.5	27.7	28.0	28.2	28.4	28.6	28.8	29.1	29.3	29.5	29.7	29.9	30.1	30.4	30.6	30.8	31.0	31.2	31.5	31.7	31.9	32.1	32.3	32.6	32.8	33.0	33.2	33.4	33.6	33.9	34.1	34.3	34.5
154	24.2	24.5	24.7	24.9	25.1	25.4	25.6	25.8	26.1	26.3	26.5	26.7	27.0	27.2	27.4	27.7	27.9	28.1	28.3	28.6	28.8	29.0	29.3	29.5	29.7	29.9	30.2	30.4	30.6	30.9	31.1	31.3	31.5	31.8	32.0	32.2	32.5	32.7	32.9
152	22.2	22.5	22.7	23.0	23.2	23.4	23.7	23.9	24.1	24.4	24.6	24.9	25.1	25.3	25.6	25.8	26.1	26.3	26.5	26.8	27.0	27.3	27.5	27.7	28.0	28.2	28.4	28.7	28.9	29.2	29.4	29.6	29.9	30.1	30.4	30.6	30.8	31.1	31.3
150	20.2	20.5	20.7	21.0	21.2	21.5	21.7	22.0	22.2	22.5	22.7	23.0	23.2	23.5	23.7	24.0	24.2	24.5	24.7	25.0	25.2	25.5	25.7	26.0	26.2	26.5	26.7	27.0	27.2	27.5	27.7	28.0	28.2	28.5	28.7	29.0	29.2	29.5	29.7
148	18.3	18.5	18.8	19.0	19.3	19.6	19.8	20.1	20.3	20.6	20.9	21.1	21.4	21.6	21.9	22.1	22.4	22.7	22.9	23.2	23.4	23.7	24.0	24.2	24.5	24.7	25.0	25.3	25.5	25.8	26.0	26.3	26.6	26.8	27.1	27.3	27.6	27.9	28.1
146	16.3	16.5	16.8	17.1	17.3	17.6	17.9	18.2	18.4	18.7	19.0	19.2	19.5	19.8	20.0	20.3	20.6	20.9	21.1	21.4	21.7	21.9	22.2	22.5	22.7	23.0	23.3	23.5	23.8	24.1	24.4	24.6	24.9	25.2	25.4	25.7	26.0	26.2	26.5
144	14.3	14.6	14.8	15.1	15.4	15.7	16.0	16.2	16.5	16.8	17.1	17.4	17.6	17.9	18.2	18.5	18.8	19.0	19.3	19.6	19.9	20.2	20.4	20.7	21.0	21.3	21.6	21.8	22.1	22.4	22.7	23.0	23.2	23.5	23.8	24.1	24.4	24.6	24.9
142	12.3	12.6	12.8	13.1	13.4	13.8	14.1	14.3	14.6	14.9	15.3	15.6	15.8	16.1	16.4	16.7	17.0	17.2	17.5	17.8	18.2	18.5	18.7	19.0	19.3	19.6	19.9	20.1	20.4	20.7	20.9	21.2	21.4	21.6	21.9	22.2	22.5	22.7	23.0
140	10.4	10.6	10.9	11.2	11.5	12.0	12.3	12.5	12.8	13.1	13.5	13.9	14.1	14.4	14.7	15.0	15.3	15.5	15.7	16.0	16.4	16.7	16.9	17.2	17.5	17.8	18.1	18.3	18.6	18.9	19.2	19.5	19.7	19.9	20.4	20.6	21.0	21.4	21.5
138	8.5	8.7	9.0	9.3	9.7	10.1	10.4	10.7	11.1	11.5	11.8	12.2	12.4	12.7	13.0	13.3	13.6	13.8	14.1	14.5	14.9	15.2	15.4	15.7	16.0	16.3	16.6	16.9	17.2	17.5	17.8	18.1	18.4	18.7	19.0	19.3	19.6	19.8	19.9
136	6.6	6.8	7.1	7.4	8.0	8.6	9.0	9.4	9.8	10.2	10.6	10.9	11.1	11.5	11.8	12.1	12.4	12.6	12.9	13.2	13.6	13.9	14.1	14.4	14.7	15.0	15.3	15.5	15.8	16.1	16.4	16.5	16.7	16.9	17.1	17.4	17.8	17.9	17.9
134	4.7	5.0	5.6	6.2	6.8	7.3	7.7	8.1	8.5	8.9	9.3	9.6	9.9	10.3	10.6	10.9	11.1	11.4	11.7	11.9	12.2	12.4	12.7	12.9	13.2	13.4	13.6	13.8	14.1	14.3	14.5	14.7	14.9	15.1	15.3	15.5	15.7	15.9	16.0
132	3.1	4.1	4.8	5.4	6.0	6.5	6.9	7.3	7.7	8.1	8.5	8.8	9.1	9.5	9.8	10.1	10.3	10.6	10.9	11.1	11.4	11.6	11.9	12.1	12.4	12.6	12.8	13.0	13.3	13.5	13.7	13.9	14.1	14.3	14.5	14.7	14.9	15.1	15.2
130	2.3	3.3	4.0	4.6	5.2	5.7	6.1	6.5	6.9	7.3	7.7	8.0	8.3	8.7	9.0	9.3	9.5	9.8	10.1	10.3	10.6	10.8	11.1	11.3	11.6	11.8	12.0	12.2	12.5	12.7	12.9	13.1	13.3	13.5	13.7	13.9	14.1	14.3	14.4
128	1.5	2.5	3.2	3.8	4.4	4.9	5.3	5.7	6.1	6.5	6.9	7.2	7.5	7.9	8.2	8.5	8.7	9.0	9.3	9.5	9.8	10.0	10.3	10.5	10.8	11.0	11.2	11.4	11.7	11.9	12.1	12.3	12.5	12.7	12.9	13.1	13.3	13.5	13.6
126	0.7	1.7	2.4	3.0	3.6	4.1	4.5	4.9	5.3	5.7	6.1	6.4	6.7	7.1	7.4	7.7	7.9	8.2	8.5	8.7	9.0	9.2	9.5	9.7	9.9	10.2	10.4	10.6	10.9	11.1	11.3	11.5	11.7	11.9	12.1	12.3	12.5	12.7	12.8
124	0.0	0.9	1.6	2.2	2.8	3.3	3.7	4.1	4.5	4.9	5.3	5.6	5.9	6.3	6.6	6.9	7.1	7.4	7.7	7.9	8.2	8.4	8.7	8.9	9.2	9.4	9.6	9.8	10.1	10.3	10.5	10.7	10.9	11.1	11.3	11.5	11.7	11.9	12.0
122	0.0	0.1	0.8	1.4	2.0	2.5	2.9	3.3	3.7	4.1	4.5	4.8	5.1	5.5	5.8	6.1	6.3	6.6	6.9	7.1	7.4	7.6	7.9	8.1	8.4	8.6	8.8	9.0	9.3	9.5	9.7	9.9	10.1	10.3	10.5	10.7	10.9	11.1	11.2
120	0.0	0.0	0.0	0.6	1.2	1.7	2.1	2.5	2.9	3.3	3.7	4.0	4.3	4.7	5.0	5.3	5.5	5.8	6.1	6.3	6.6	6.8	7.1	7.3	7.6	7.8	8.0	8.2	8.5	8.7	8.9	9.1	9.3	9.5	9.7	9.9	10.1	10.3	10.4
118	0.0	0.0	0.0	0.0	0.4	0.9	1.3	1.7	2.1	2.5	2.9	3.2	3.5	3.9	4.2	4.5	4.7	5.0	5.3	5.5	5.8	6.0	6.3	6.5	6.8	7.0	7.2	7.4	7.7	7.9	8.1	8.3	8.5	8.7	8.9	9.1	9.3	9.5	9.6
116	0.0	0.0	0.0	0.0	0.0	0.1	0.5	0.9	1.3	1.7	2.1	2.4	2.7	3.1	3.4	3.7	3.9	4.2	4.5	4.7	5.0	5.2	5.5	5.7	6.0	6.2	6.4	6.6	6.9	7.1	7.3	7.5	7.7	7.9	8.1	8.3	8.5	8.7	8.8
114	0.0	0.0	0.0	0.0	0.0	0.0	0.0	0.1	0.5	0.9	1.3	1.6	1.9	2.3	2.6	2.9	3.1	3.4	3.7	3.9	4.2	4.4	4.7	4.9	5.2	5.4	5.6	5.8	6.1	6.3	6.5	6.7	6.9	7.1	7.3	7.5	7.7	7.9	8.0
112	0.0	0.0	0.0	0.0	0.0	0.0	0.0	0.0	0.0	0.1	0.5	0.8	1.1	1.5	1.8	2.1	2.3	2.6	2.9	3.1	3.4	3.6	3.9	4.1	4.4	4.6	4.8	5.0	5.3	5.5	5.7	5.9	6.1	6.3	6.5	6.7	6.9	7.1	7.2
110	0.0	0.0	0.0	0.0	0.0	0.0	0.0	0.0	0.0	0.0	0.0	0.0	0.3	0.7	1.0	1.3	1.5	1.8	2.1	2.3	2.6	2.8	3.1	3.3	3.6	3.8	4.0	4.2	4.5	4.7	4.9	5.1	5.3	5.5	5.7	5.9	6.1	6.3	6.4
108	0.0	0.0	0.0	0.0	0.0	0.0	0.0	0.0	0.0	0.0	0.0	0.0	0.0	0.0	0.2	0.5	0.7	1.0	1.3	1.5	1.8	2.0	2.3	2.5	2.8	3.0	3.2	3.4	3.7	3.9	4.1	4.3	4.5	4.7	4.9	5.1	5.3	5.5	5.6
106	0.0	0.0	0.0	0.0	0.0	0.0	0.0	0.0	0.0	0.0	0.0	0.0	0.0	0.0	0.0	0.0	0.0	0.2	0.5	0.7	1.0	1.2	1.5	1.7	2.0	2.2	2.4	2.6	2.9	3.1	3.3	3.5	3.7	3.9	4.1	4.3	4.5	4.7	4.8
104	0.0	0.0	0.0	0.0	0.0	0.0	0.0	0.0	0.0	0.0	0.0	0.0	0.0	0.0	0.0	0.0	0.0	0.0	0.0	0.0	0.2	0.4	0.7	0.9	1.2	1.4	1.6	1.8	2.1	2.3	2.5	2.7	2.9	3.1	3.3	3.5	3.7	3.9	4.0
102	0.0	0.0	0.0	0.0	0.0	0.0	0.0	0.0	0.0	0.0	0.0	0.0	0.0	0.0	0.0	0.0	0.0	0.0	0.0	0.0	0.0	0.0	0.0	0.1	0.4	0.6	0.8	1.0	1.3	1.5	1.7	1.9	2.1	2.3	2.5	2.7	2.9	3.1	3.2
100	0.0	0.0	0.0	0.0	0.0	0.0	0.0	0.0	0.0	0.0	0.0	0.0	0.0	0.0	0.0	0.0	0.0	0.0	0.0	0.0	0.0	0.0	0.0	0.0	0.0	0.0	0.0	0.2	0.5	0.7	0.9	1.1	1.3	1.5	1.7	1.9	2.1	2.3	2.4
99	0.0	0.0	0.0	0.0	0.0	0.0	0.0	0.0	0.0	0.0	0.0	0.0	0.0	0.0	0.0	0.0	0.0	0.0	0.0	0.0	0.0	0.0	0.0	0.0	0.0	0.0	0.0	0.0	0.1	0.3	0.5	0.7	0.9	1.1	1.3	1.5	1.7	1.9	2.0
98	0.0	0.0	0.0	0.0	0.0	0.0	0.0	0.0	0.0	0.0	0.0	0.0	0.0	0.0	0.0	0.0	0.0	0.0	0.0	0.0	0.0	0.0	0.0	0.0	0.0	0.0	0.0	0.0	0.0	0.0	0.1	0.3	0.5	0.7	0.9	1.1	1.3	1.5	1.6
97	0.0	0.0	0.0	0.0	0.0	0.0	0.0	0.0	0.0	0.0	0.0	0.0	0.0	0.0	0.0	0.0	0.0	0.0	0.0	0.0	0.0	0.0	0.0	0.0	0.0	0.0	0.0	0.0	0.0	0.0	0.0	0.0	0.1	0.3	0.5	0.7	0.9	1.1	1.2
96	0.0	0.0	0.0	0.0	0.0	0.0	0.0	0.0	0.0	0.0	0.0	0.0	0.0	0.0	0.0	0.0	0.0	0.0	0.0	0.0	0.0	0.0	0.0	0.0	0.0	0.0	0.0	0.0	0.0	0.0	0.0	0.0	0.0	0.0	0.1	0.3	0.5	0.7	0.8
95	0.0	0.0	0.0	0.0	0.0	0.0	0.0	0.0	0.0	0.0	0.0	0.0	0.0	0.0	0.0	0.0	0.0	0.0	0.0	0.0	0.0	0.0	0.0	0.0	0.0	0.0	0.0	0.0	0.0	0.0	0.0	0.0	0.0	0.0	0.0	0.0	0.1	0.3	0.4
94	0.0	0.0	0.0	0.0	0.0	0.0	0.0	0.0	0.0	0.0	0.0	0.0	0.0	0.0	0.0	0.0	0.0	0.0	0.0	0.0	0.0	0.0	0.0	0.0	0.0	0.0	0.0	0.0	0.0	0.0	0.0	0.0	0.0	0.0	0.0	0.0	0.0	0.0	0.0
93	0.0	0.0	0.0	0.0	0.0	0.0	0.0	0.0	0.0	0.0	0.0	0.0	0.0	0.0	0.0	0.0	0.0	0.0	0.0	0.0	0.0	0.0	0.0	0.0	0.0	0.0	0.0	0.0	0.0	0.0	0.0	0.0	0.0	0.0	0.0	0.0	0.0	0.0	0.0
92	0.0	0.0	0.0	0.0	0.0	0.0	0.0	0.0	0.0	0.0	0.0	0.0	0.0	0.0	0.0	0.0	0.0	0.0	0.0	0.0	0.0	0.0	0.0	0.0	0.0	0.0	0.0	0.0	0.0	0.0	0.0	0.0	0.0	0.0	0.0	0.0	0.0	0.0	0.0
91	0.0	0.0	0.0	0.0	0.0	0.0	0.0	0.0	0.0	0.0	0.0	0.0	0.0	0.0	0.0	0.0	0.0	0.0	0.0	0.0	0.0	0.0	0.0	0.0	0.0	0.0	0.0	0.0	0.0	0.0	0.0	0.0	0.0	0.0	0.0	0.0	0.0	0.0	0.0

LISTED CALL OPTION PRICE WHEN EXERCISE PRICE IS 140

Common Stock Price	NUMBER OF WEEKS BEFORE THE OPTION EXPIRES																																					
	1	2	3	4	5	6	7	8	9	10	11	12	13	14	15	16	17	18	19	20	21	22	23	24	25	26	27	28	29	30	31	32	33	34	35	36	37	38	39
182	42.2	42.3	42.5	42.7	42.8	43.0	43.1	43.3	43.5	43.6	43.8	44.0	44.1	44.3	44.4	44.6	44.8	44.9	45.1	45.3	45.4	45.6	45.8	45.9	46.1	46.2	46.4	46.6	46.7	46.9	47.1	47.2	47.4	47.6	47.7	47.9	48.0	48.2	48.4
180	40.2	40.3	40.5	40.7	40.9	41.0	41.2	41.4	41.6	41.7	41.9	42.1	42.3	42.4	42.6	42.8	43.0	43.1	43.3	43.5	43.6	43.8	44.0	44.2	44.3	44.5	44.7	44.9	45.0	45.2	45.4	45.6	45.7	45.9	46.1	46.2	46.4	46.6	46.8
178	38.2	38.4	38.6	38.7	38.9	39.1	39.3	39.5	39.7	39.8	40.0	40.2	40.4	40.6	40.8	40.9	41.1	41.3	41.5	41.7	41.9	42.0	42.2	42.4	42.6	42.8	43.0	43.1	43.3	43.5	43.7	43.9	44.1	44.3	44.4	44.6	44.8	45.0	45.2
176	36.2	36.4	36.6	36.8	37.0	37.2	37.4	37.6	37.7	37.9	38.1	38.3	38.5	38.7	38.9	39.1	39.3	39.5	39.7	39.9	40.1	40.3	40.5	40.7	40.9	41.0	41.2	41.4	41.6	41.8	42.0	42.2	42.4	42.6	42.8	43.0	43.2	43.4	43.6
174	34.2	34.4	34.6	34.8	35.0	35.2	35.4	35.6	35.8	36.0	36.2	36.5	36.7	36.9	37.1	37.3	37.5	37.7	37.9	38.1	38.3	38.5	38.7	38.9	39.1	39.3	39.5	39.7	39.9	40.1	40.3	40.5	40.7	40.9	41.2	41.4	41.6	41.8	42.0
172	32.2	32.4	32.6	32.9	33.1	33.3	33.5	33.7	33.9	34.1	34.4	34.6	34.8	35.0	35.2	35.4	35.6	35.9	36.1	36.3	36.5	36.7	36.9	37.2	37.4	37.6	37.8	38.0	38.2	38.4	38.7	38.9	39.1	39.3	39.5	39.7	39.9	40.2	40.4
170	30.2	30.4	30.7	30.9	31.1	31.3	31.6	31.8	32.0	32.2	32.5	32.7	32.9	33.1	33.4	33.6	33.8	34.0	34.3	34.5	34.7	34.9	35.2	35.4	35.6	35.8	36.1	36.3	36.5	36.7	37.0	37.2	37.4	37.6	37.9	38.1	38.3	38.5	38.8
168	28.2	28.5	28.7	28.9	29.2	29.4	29.6	29.9	30.1	30.4	30.6	30.8	31.1	31.3	31.5	31.8	32.0	32.2	32.5	32.7	32.9	33.2	33.4	33.6	33.9	34.1	34.3	34.6	34.8	35.1	35.3	35.5	35.8	36.0	36.2	36.5	36.7	36.9	37.2
166	26.2	26.5	26.7	27.0	27.2	27.5	27.7	28.0	28.2	28.5	28.7	28.9	29.2	29.4	29.7	29.9	30.2	30.4	30.7	30.9	31.2	31.4	31.6	31.9	32.1	32.4	32.6	32.9	33.1	33.4	33.6	33.9	34.1	34.3	34.6	34.8	35.1	35.3	35.6
164	24.3	24.5	24.8	25.0	25.3	25.5	25.8	26.0	26.3	26.6	26.8	27.1	27.3	27.6	27.8	28.1	28.3	28.6	28.9	29.1	29.4	29.6	29.9	30.1	30.4	30.6	30.9	31.2	31.4	31.7	31.9	32.2	32.4	32.7	32.9	33.2	33.5	33.7	34.0
162	22.3	22.5	22.8	23.1	23.3	23.6	23.9	24.1	24.4	24.7	24.9	25.2	25.5	25.7	26.0	26.3	26.5	26.8	27.1	27.3	27.6	27.8	28.1	28.4	28.6	28.9	29.2	29.4	29.7	29.9	30.2	30.5	30.8	31.0	31.3	31.6	31.8	32.1	32.4
160	20.3	20.6	20.8	21.1	21.4	21.7	21.9	22.2	22.5	22.8	23.0	23.3	23.6	23.9	24.1	24.4	24.7	25.0	25.2	25.5	25.8	26.1	26.4	26.6	26.9	27.2	27.5	27.7	28.0	28.3	28.6	28.8	29.1	29.4	29.7	29.9	30.2	30.5	30.8
158	18.3	18.6	18.9	19.1	19.4	19.7	20.0	20.3	20.6	20.9	21.2	21.4	21.7	22.0	22.3	22.6	22.9	23.2	23.4	23.7	24.0	24.3	24.6	24.9	25.2	25.4	25.7	26.0	26.3	26.6	26.9	27.2	27.5	27.7	28.0	28.3	28.6	28.9	29.2
156	16.3	16.6	16.9	17.2	17.5	17.8	18.1	18.4	18.7	19.0	19.3	19.6	19.9	20.2	20.5	20.7	21.0	21.3	21.6	21.9	22.2	22.5	22.8	23.1	23.4	23.7	24.0	24.3	24.6	24.9	25.2	25.5	25.8	26.1	26.4	26.7	27.0	27.3	27.6
154	14.3	14.6	14.9	15.2	15.6	15.9	16.2	16.5	16.8	17.1	17.4	17.7	18.0	18.3	18.6	18.8	19.1	19.4	19.7	20.0	20.3	20.6	20.9	21.2	21.5	21.8	22.1	22.4	22.7	23.0	23.3	23.6	23.9	24.2	24.5	24.8	25.1	25.4	25.6
152	12.4	12.6	12.9	13.3	13.7	14.0	14.3	14.6	14.9	15.2	15.5	15.8	16.1	16.4	16.7	16.9	17.2	17.5	17.8	18.1	18.4	18.7	19.0	19.3	19.6	19.9	20.2	20.5	20.8	21.1	21.4	21.7	22.0	22.3	22.6	22.9	23.2	23.5	23.7
150	10.5	10.7	11.0	11.4	11.8	12.1	12.4	12.7	13.1	13.4	13.7	14.0	14.3	14.6	14.9	15.1	15.4	15.7	16.0	16.3	16.6	16.9	17.2	17.5	17.8	18.1	18.4	18.7	19.0	19.3	19.6	19.9	20.2	20.5	20.8	21.1	21.3	21.6	21.8
148	8.6	8.8	9.1	9.5	9.9	10.2	10.6	10.9	11.3	11.6	11.9	12.2	12.5	12.8	13.1	13.3	13.6	13.9	14.2	14.5	14.8	15.1	15.4	15.6	15.9	16.2	16.5	16.8	17.1	17.4	17.7	18.0	18.3	18.6	18.9	19.2	19.4	19.7	19.9
146	6.7	6.9	7.3	7.7	8.0	8.5	9.0	9.4	9.9	10.3	10.7	11.0	11.4	11.7	12.0	12.4	12.7	13.0	13.3	13.5	13.8	14.1	14.3	14.6	14.9	15.1	15.3	15.6	15.8	16.0	16.3	16.5	16.7	16.9	17.1	17.3	17.5	17.8	18.0
144	4.8	5.1	5.9	6.6	7.2	7.7	8.2	8.6	9.1	9.5	9.9	10.2	10.6	10.9	11.2	11.6	11.9	12.2	12.5	12.7	13.0	13.3	13.5	13.8	14.1	14.3	14.5	14.8	15.0	15.2	15.5	15.7	15.9	16.1	16.3	16.5	16.7	17.0	17.2
142	3.3	4.3	5.1	5.8	6.4	6.9	7.4	7.8	8.3	8.7	9.1	9.4	9.8	10.1	10.4	10.8	11.1	11.4	11.7	11.9	12.2	12.5	12.7	13.0	13.3	13.5	13.7	14.0	14.2	14.4	14.7	14.9	15.1	15.3	15.5	15.7	15.9	16.2	16.4
140	2.5	3.5	4.3	5.0	5.6	6.1	6.6	7.0	7.5	7.9	8.3	8.6	9.0	9.3	9.6	9.9	10.3	10.6	10.9	11.1	11.4	11.7	11.9	12.2	12.5	12.7	12.9	13.2	13.4	13.6	13.9	14.1	14.3	14.5	14.7	14.9	15.1	15.4	15.6
138	1.7	2.7	3.5	4.2	4.8	5.3	5.8	6.2	6.7	7.1	7.5	7.8	8.2	8.5	8.8	9.2	9.5	9.8	10.1	10.3	10.6	10.9	11.1	11.4	11.7	11.9	12.1	12.4	12.6	12.8	13.1	13.3	13.5	13.7	13.9	14.1	14.3	14.6	14.8
136	0.9	1.9	2.7	3.4	4.0	4.5	5.0	5.4	5.9	6.3	6.7	7.0	7.4	7.7	8.0	8.4	8.7	9.0	9.3	9.5	9.8	10.1	10.3	10.6	10.9	11.1	11.3	11.6	11.8	12.0	12.3	12.5	12.7	12.9	13.1	13.3	13.5	13.8	14.0
134	0.1	1.1	1.9	2.6	3.2	3.7	4.2	4.6	5.1	5.5	5.9	6.2	6.6	6.9	7.2	7.6	7.9	8.2	8.5	8.7	9.0	9.3	9.5	9.8	10.1	10.3	10.5	10.8	11.0	11.2	11.5	11.7	11.9	12.1	12.3	12.5	12.7	13.0	13.2
132	0.0	0.3	1.1	1.8	2.4	2.9	3.4	3.8	4.3	4.7	5.1	5.4	5.8	6.1	6.4	6.8	7.1	7.4	7.7	7.9	8.2	8.5	8.7	9.0	9.3	9.5	9.7	9.9	1.02	10.4	10.7	10.9	11.1	11.3	11.5	11.7	11.9	12.2	12.4
130	0.0	0.0	0.3	1.0	1.6	2.1	2.6	3.0	3.5	3.9	4.3	4.6	5.0	5.3	5.6	6.0	6.3	6.6	6.9	7.1	7.4	7.7	7.9	8.2	8.5	8.7	8.9	9.2	9.4	9.6	9.9	10.1	10.3	10.5	10.7	10.9	11.1	11.4	11.6
128	0.0	0.0	0.0	0.2	0.8	1.3	1.8	2.2	2.7	3.1	3.5	3.8	4.2	4.5	4.8	5.2	5.5	5.8	6.1	6.3	6.6	6.9	7.1	7.4	7.7	7.9	8.1	8.4	8.6	8.8	9.1	9.3	9.5	9.7	9.9	10.1	10.3	10.6	10.8
126	0.0	0.0	0.0	0.0	0.0	0.5	1.0	1.4	1.9	2.3	2.7	3.0	3.4	3.7	4.0	4.4	4.7	5.0	5.3	5.5	5.8	6.1	6.3	6.6	6.9	7.1	7.3	7.6	7.8	8.0	8.3	8.5	8.7	8.9	9.1	9.3	9.5	9.8	9.9
124	0.0	0.0	0.0	0.0	0.0	0.0	0.2	0.6	1.1	1.5	1.9	2.2	2.6	2.9	3.2	3.6	3.9	4.2	4.5	4.7	5.0	5.3	5.5	5.8	6.1	6.3	6.5	6.8	7.0	7.2	7.5	7.7	7.9	8.1	8.3	8.5	8.7	9.0	9.2
122	0.0	0.0	0.0	0.0	0.0	0.0	0.0	0.0	0.3	0.7	1.1	1.4	1.8	2.1	2.4	2.8	3.1	3.4	3.7	3.9	4.2	4.5	4.7	5.0	5.3	5.5	5.7	6.0	6.2	6.4	6.7	6.9	7.1	7.3	7.5	7.7	7.9	8.2	8.4
120	0.0	0.0	0.0	0.0	0.0	0.0	0.0	0.0	0.0	0.0	0.3	0.6	1.0	1.3	1.6	2.0	2.3	2.6	2.9	3.1	3.4	3.7	3.9	4.2	4.5	4.7	4.9	5.2	5.4	5.6	5.9	6.1	6.3	6.5	6.7	6.9	7.1	7.4	7.6
118	0.0	0.0	0.0	0.0	0.0	0.0	0.0	0.0	0.0	0.0	0.0	0.0	0.2	0.5	0.8	1.2	1.5	1.8	2.1	2.3	2.6	2.9	3.1	3.4	3.7	3.9	4.1	4.4	4.6	4.8	5.1	5.3	5.5	5.7	5.9	6.1	6.3	6.6	6.8
116	0.0	0.0	0.0	0.0	0.0	0.0	0.0	0.0	0.0	0.0	0.0	0.0	0.0	0.0	0.0	0.4	0.7	1.0	1.3	1.5	1.8	2.1	2.3	2.6	2.9	3.1	3.3	3.6	3.8	4.0	4.3	4.5	4.7	4.9	5.1	5.3	5.5	5.8	6.0
114	0.0	0.0	0.0	0.0	0.0	0.0	0.0	0.0	0.0	0.0	0.0	0.0	0.0	0.0	0.0	0.0	0.0	0.2	0.5	0.7	1.0	1.3	1.5	1.8	2.1	2.3	2.5	2.8	3.0	3.2	3.5	3.7	3.9	4.1	4.3	4.5	4.7	5.0	5.2
112	0.0	0.0	0.0	0.0	0.0	0.0	0.0	0.0	0.0	0.0	0.0	0.0	0.0	0.0	0.0	0.0	0.0	0.0	0.0	0.0	0.2	0.5	0.7	1.0	1.3	1.5	1.7	2.0	2.2	2.4	2.7	2.9	3.1	3.3	3.5	3.7	3.9	4.2	4.4
110	0.0	0.0	0.0	0.0	0.0	0.0	0.0	0.0	0.0	0.0	0.0	0.0	0.0	0.0	0.0	0.0	0.0	0.0	0.0	0.0	0.0	0.0	0.0	0.2	0.5	0.7	0.9	1.2	1.4	1.6	1.9	2.1	2.3	2.5	2.7	2.9	3.1	3.4	3.6
108	0.0	0.0	0.0	0.0	0.0	0.0	0.0	0.0	0.0	0.0	0.0	0.0	0.0	0.0	0.0	0.0	0.0	0.0	0.0	0.0	0.0	0.0	0.0	0.0	0.0	0.0	0.1	0.4	0.6	0.8	1.1	1.3	1.5	1.7	1.9	2.1	2.3	2.6	2.8
106	0.0	0.0	0.0	0.0	0.0	0.0	0.0	0.0	0.0	0.0	0.0	0.0	0.0	0.0	0.0	0.0	0.0	0.0	0.0	0.0	0.0	0.0	0.0	0.0	0.0	0.0	0.0	0.0	0.0	0.0	0.3	0.5	0.7	0.9	1.1	1.3	1.5	1.8	2.0
104	0.0	0.0	0.0	0.0	0.0	0.0	0.0	0.0	0.0	0.0	0.0	0.0	0.0	0.0	0.0	0.0	0.0	0.0	0.0	0.0	0.0	0.0	0.0	0.0	0.0	0.0	0.0	0.0	0.0	0.0	0.0	0.0	0.0	0.1	0.3	0.5	0.7	1.0	1.2
102	0.0	0.0	0.0	0.0	0.0	0.0	0.0	0.0	0.0	0.0	0.0	0.0	0.0	0.0	0.0	0.0	0.0	0.0	0.0	0.0	0.0	0.0	0.0	0.0	0.0	0.0	0.0	0.0	0.0	0.0	0.0	0.0	0.0	0.0	0.0	0.0	0.0	0.2	0.4
100	0.0	0.0	0.0	0.0	0.0	0.0	0.0	0.0	0.0	0.0	0.0	0.0	0.0	0.0	0.0	0.0	0.0	0.0	0.0	0.0	0.0	0.0	0.0	0.0	0.0	0.0	0.0	0.0	0.0	0.0	0.0	0.0	0.0	0.0	0.0	0.0	0.0	0.0	0.0
99	0.0	0.0	0.0	0.0	0.0	0.0	0.0	0.0	0.0	0.0	0.0	0.0	0.0	0.0	0.0	0.0	0.0	0.0	0.0	0.0	0.0	0.0	0.0	0.0	0.0	0.0	0.0	0.0	0.0	0.0	0.0	0.0	0.0	0.0	0.0	0.0	0.0	0.0	0.0
98	0.0	0.0	0.0	0.0	0.0	0.0	0.0	0.0	0.0	0.0	0.0	0.0	0.0	0.0	0.0	0.0	0.0	0.0	0.0	0.0	0.0	0.0	0.0	0.0	0.0	0.0	0.0	0.0	0.0	0.0	0.0	0.0	0.0	0.0	0.0	0.0	0.0	0.0	0.0

LISTED CALL OPTION PRICE WHEN EXERCISE PRICE IS 150

Common Stock Price	NUMBER OF WEEKS BEFORE THE OPTION EXPIRES 1	2	3	4	5	6	7	8	9	10	11	12	13	14	15	16	17	18	19	20	21	22	23	24	25	26	27	28	29	30	31	32	33	34	35	36	37	38	39
196	46.2	46.3	46.5	46.7	46.8	47.0	47.2	47.4	47.5	47.7	47.9	48.0	48.2	48.4	48.5	48.7	48.9	49.1	49.2	49.4	49.6	49.7	49.9	50.1	50.2	50.4	50.6	50.8	50.9	51.1	51.3	51.4	51.6	51.8	51.9	52.1	52.3	52.5	52.6
194	44.2	44.4	44.5	44.7	44.9	45.1	45.3	45.4	45.6	45.8	46.0	46.2	46.3	46.5	46.7	46.9	47.1	47.2	47.4	47.6	47.8	48.0	48.1	48.3	48.5	48.7	48.9	49.0	49.2	49.4	49.6	49.8	49.9	50.1	50.3	50.5	50.7	50.8	51.0
192	42.2	42.4	42.6	42.8	43.0	43.1	43.3	43.5	43.7	43.9	44.1	44.3	44.5	44.7	44.9	45.0	45.2	45.4	45.6	45.8	46.0	46.2	46.4	46.6	46.8	46.9	47.1	47.3	47.5	47.7	47.9	48.1	48.3	48.5	48.7	48.9	49.0	49.2	49.4
190	40.2	40.4	40.6	40.8	41.0	41.2	41.4	41.6	41.8	42.0	42.2	42.4	42.6	42.8	43.0	43.2	43.4	43.6	43.8	44.0	44.2	44.4	44.6	44.8	45.0	45.2	45.4	45.6	45.8	46.0	46.2	46.4	46.6	46.8	47.0	47.2	47.4	47.6	47.8
188	38.2	38.4	38.6	38.8	39.1	39.3	39.5	39.7	39.9	40.1	40.3	40.5	40.7	41.0	41.2	41.4	41.6	41.8	42.0	42.2	42.4	42.6	42.9	43.1	43.3	43.5	43.7	43.9	44.1	44.3	44.5	44.7	45.0	45.2	45.4	45.6	45.8	46.0	46.2
186	36.2	36.4	36.7	36.9	37.1	37.3	37.5	37.8	38.0	38.2	38.4	38.7	38.9	39.1	39.3	39.5	39.8	39.9	40.2	40.4	40.6	40.9	41.1	41.3	41.5	41.8	42.0	42.2	42.4	42.6	42.9	43.1	43.3	43.5	43.7	44.0	44.2	44.4	44.6
184	34.2	34.5	34.7	34.9	35.2	35.4	35.6	35.9	36.1	36.3	36.5	36.8	37.0	37.2	37.5	37.7	37.9	38.2	38.4	38.6	38.9	39.1	39.3	39.6	39.8	40.0	40.2	40.5	40.7	40.9	41.2	41.4	41.6	41.9	42.1	42.3	42.6	42.8	43.0
182	32.2	32.5	32.7	33.0	33.2	33.5	33.7	33.9	34.2	34.4	34.7	34.9	35.1	35.4	35.6	35.9	36.1	36.4	36.6	36.8	37.1	37.3	37.6	37.8	38.0	38.3	38.5	38.8	39.0	39.3	39.5	39.7	39.9	40.2	40.5	40.7	40.9	41.2	41.4
180	30.3	30.5	30.8	31.0	31.3	31.5	31.8	32.0	32.3	32.5	32.8	33.0	33.3	33.5	33.8	34.0	34.3	34.5	34.8	35.0	35.3	35.5	35.8	36.0	36.3	36.6	36.8	37.1	37.3	37.6	37.8	38.1	38.3	38.6	38.8	39.1	39.3	39.6	39.8
178	28.3	28.5	28.8	29.0	29.3	29.6	29.8	30.1	30.4	30.6	30.9	31.1	31.4	31.7	31.9	32.2	32.5	32.7	33.0	33.2	33.5	33.8	34.0	34.3	34.6	34.8	35.1	35.3	35.6	35.9	36.1	36.4	36.7	36.9	37.2	37.4	37.7	38.0	38.2
176	26.3	26.5	26.8	27.1	27.4	27.6	27.9	28.2	28.5	28.7	29.0	29.3	29.5	29.8	30.1	30.4	30.6	30.9	31.2	31.4	31.7	32.0	32.3	32.5	32.8	33.1	33.4	33.6	33.9	34.2	34.4	34.7	35.0	35.3	35.5	35.8	36.1	36.4	36.6
174	24.3	24.6	24.8	25.1	25.4	25.7	26.0	26.3	26.5	26.8	27.1	27.4	27.7	28.0	28.2	28.5	28.8	29.1	29.4	29.7	29.9	30.2	30.5	30.8	31.1	31.4	31.6	31.9	32.2	32.5	32.8	33.0	33.3	33.6	33.9	34.2	34.5	34.7	35.0
172	22.3	22.6	22.9	23.2	23.5	23.8	24.1	24.3	24.6	24.9	25.2	25.5	25.8	26.1	26.4	26.7	27.0	27.3	27.6	27.9	28.2	28.4	28.7	29.0	29.3	29.6	29.9	30.2	30.5	30.8	31.1	31.4	31.7	32.0	32.3	32.5	32.8	33.1	33.4
170	20.3	20.6	20.9	21.2	21.5	21.8	22.1	22.4	22.7	23.0	23.3	23.6	23.9	24.2	24.5	24.9	25.2	25.5	25.8	26.1	26.4	26.7	27.0	27.3	27.6	27.9	28.2	28.5	28.8	29.1	29.4	29.7	30.0	30.3	30.6	30.9	31.2	31.5	31.8
168	18.3	18.6	18.9	19.3	19.6	19.9	20.2	20.5	20.8	21.1	21.4	21.8	22.1	22.4	22.7	23.0	23.3	23.6	24.0	24.3	24.6	24.9	25.2	25.5	25.8	26.1	26.5	26.8	27.1	27.4	27.7	28.0	28.3	28.7	29.0	29.3	29.6	29.9	30.2
166	16.3	16.6	17.0	17.3	17.6	17.9	18.3	18.6	18.9	19.2	19.6	19.9	20.2	20.5	20.9	21.2	21.5	21.8	22.2	22.5	22.8	23.1	23.4	23.8	24.1	24.4	24.7	25.1	25.4	25.7	26.0	26.4	26.7	27.0	27.3	27.7	28.0	28.3	28.6
164	14.3	14.6	15.0	15.4	15.7	16.0	16.3	16.6	16.9	17.2	17.6	18.0	18.3	18.6	19.0	19.3	19.6	19.9	20.3	20.6	20.9	21.2	21.5	21.9	22.2	22.5	22.8	23.2	23.5	23.8	24.1	24.5	24.8	25.1	25.4	25.8	26.1	26.4	26.7
162	12.4	12.7	13.1	13.4	13.8	14.1	14.4	14.7	15.0	15.3	15.7	16.1	16.4	16.7	17.1	17.4	17.7	18.0	18.4	18.7	19.0	19.3	19.6	20.0	20.3	20.6	20.9	21.2	21.6	21.9	22.2	22.6	22.9	23.2	23.5	23.9	24.2	24.5	24.8
160	10.5	10.8	11.2	11.5	11.9	12.2	12.5	12.8	13.1	13.4	13.8	14.2	14.5	14.8	15.2	15.5	15.8	16.1	16.5	16.8	17.1	17.4	17.7	18.1	18.2	18.7	19.0	19.4	19.7	20.0	20.3	20.7	21.0	21.3	21.6	22.0	22.3	22.6	22.9
158	8.7	8.9	9.3	9.6	10.0	10.4	10.6	10.9	11.2	11.6	12.1	12.4	12.8	13.2	13.5	13.9	14.2	14.5	14.8	15.1	15.4	15.7	16.0	16.3	16.5	16.8	17.1	17.5	17.8	18.1	18.4	18.8	19.1	19.4	19.7	20.1	20.4	20.7	21.0
156	6.8	7.0	7.5	7.9	8.4	8.9	9.5	9.9	10.4	10.8	11.3	11.6	12.0	12.4	12.7	13.1	13.4	13.7	14.0	14.3	14.6	14.9	15.2	15.5	15.7	16.0	16.3	16.5	16.8	17.0	17.3	17.5	17.7	18.0	18.2	18.4	18.6	18.8	19.1
154	4.9	5.4	6.2	6.9	7.6	8.1	8.7	9.1	9.6	10.0	10.5	10.8	11.2	11.6	11.9	12.3	12.6	12.9	13.2	13.5	13.8	14.1	14.4	14.7	14.9	15.2	15.5	15.7	16.0	16.2	16.5	16.7	16.9	17.2	17.4	17.6	17.8	18.0	18.3
152	3.5	4.6	5.4	6.1	6.8	7.3	7.9	8.3	8.8	9.2	9.7	10.0	10.4	10.8	11.1	11.5	11.8	12.1	12.4	12.7	13.0	13.3	13.6	13.9	14.1	14.4	14.7	14.9	15.2	15.4	15.7	15.9	16.1	16.4	16.6	16.8	17.0	17.2	17.5
150	2.7	3.8	4.6	5.3	6.0	6.5	7.1	7.5	8.0	8.4	8.9	9.2	9.6	9.9	10.3	10.7	11.0	11.3	11.6	11.9	12.2	12.5	12.8	13.1	13.3	13.6	13.9	14.1	14.4	14.6	14.9	15.1	15.3	15.6	15.8	16.0	16.2	16.4	16.7
148	1.9	3.0	3.8	4.5	5.2	5.7	6.3	6.7	7.2	7.6	8.1	8.4	8.8	9.2	9.5	9.9	10.2	10.5	10.8	11.1	11.4	11.7	12.0	12.3	12.5	12.8	13.1	13.3	13.6	13.8	14.1	14.3	14.5	14.8	15.0	15.2	15.4	15.6	15.9
146	1.1	2.2	3.0	3.7	4.4	4.9	5.5	5.9	6.4	6.8	7.3	7.6	8.0	8.4	8.7	9.1	9.4	9.7	10.0	10.3	10.6	10.9	11.2	11.5	11.7	12.0	12.3	12.5	12.8	13.0	13.3	13.5	13.7	14.0	14.2	14.4	14.6	14.8	15.1
144	0.3	1.4	2.2	2.9	3.6	4.1	4.7	5.1	5.6	6.0	6.5	6.8	7.2	7.6	7.9	8.3	8.6	8.9	9.2	9.5	9.8	10.1	10.4	10.7	10.9	11.2	11.5	11.7	12.0	12.2	12.5	12.7	12.9	13.2	13.4	13.6	13.8	14.0	14.3
142	0.0	0.6	1.4	2.1	2.8	3.3	3.9	4.3	4.8	5.2	5.7	6.0	6.4	6.8	7.1	7.5	7.8	8.1	8.4	8.7	9.0	9.3	9.6	9.9	10.1	10.4	10.7	10.9	11.2	11.4	11.7	11.9	12.1	12.4	12.6	12.8	13.0	13.2	13.5
140	0.0	0.0	0.6	1.3	2.0	2.5	3.1	3.5	4.0	4.4	4.9	5.2	5.6	6.0	6.3	6.7	7.0	7.3	7.6	7.9	8.2	8.5	8.8	9.1	9.3	9.6	9.9	10.1	10.4	10.6	10.9	11.1	11.3	11.6	11.8	12.0	12.2	12.4	12.7
138	0.0	0.0	0.0	0.5	1.2	1.7	2.3	2.7	3.2	3.6	4.1	4.4	4.8	5.2	5.5	5.9	6.2	6.5	6.8	7.1	7.4	7.7	8.0	8.3	8.5	8.8	9.1	9.3	9.6	9.8	10.1	10.3	10.5	10.8	11.0	11.2	11.4	11.6	11.9
136	0.0	0.0	0.0	0.0	0.4	0.9	1.5	1.9	2.4	2.8	3.3	3.6	4.0	4.4	4.7	5.1	5.4	5.7	6.0	6.3	6.6	6.9	7.2	7.5	7.7	8.0	8.3	8.5	8.8	9.0	9.3	9.5	9.7	9.9	10.2	10.4	10.6	10.8	11.1
134	0.0	0.0	0.0	0.0	0.0	0.1	0.7	1.1	1.6	2.0	2.5	2.8	3.2	3.6	3.9	4.3	4.6	4.9	5.2	5.5	5.8	6.1	6.4	6.7	6.9	7.2	7.5	7.7	8.0	8.2	8.5	8.7	8.9	9.2	9.4	9.6	9.8	10.0	10.3
132	0.0	0.0	0.0	0.0	0.0	0.0	0.0	0.3	0.8	1.2	1.7	2.0	2.4	2.8	3.1	3.5	3.8	4.1	4.4	4.7	5.0	5.3	5.6	5.9	6.1	6.4	6.7	6.9	7.2	7.4	7.7	7.9	8.1	8.4	8.6	8.8	9.0	9.2	9.5
130	0.0	0.0	0.0	0.0	0.0	0.0	0.0	0.0	0.0	0.4	0.9	1.2	1.6	2.0	2.3	2.7	3.0	3.3	3.6	3.9	4.2	4.5	4.8	5.1	5.3	5.6	5.9	6.1	6.4	6.6	6.9	7.1	7.3	7.6	7.8	8.0	8.2	8.4	8.7
128	0.0	0.0	0.0	0.0	0.0	0.0	0.0	0.0	0.0	0.0	0.1	0.4	0.8	1.2	1.5	1.9	2.2	2.5	2.8	3.1	3.4	3.7	4.0	4.3	4.5	4.8	5.1	5.3	5.6	5.8	6.1	6.3	6.5	6.8	7.0	7.2	7.4	7.6	7.9
126	0.0	0.0	0.0	0.0	0.0	0.0	0.0	0.0	0.0	0.0	0.0	0.0	0.0	0.4	0.7	1.1	1.4	1.7	2.0	2.3	2.6	2.9	3.2	3.5	3.7	4.0	4.3	4.5	4.8	5.0	5.3	5.5	5.7	6.0	6.2	6.4	6.6	6.8	7.1
124	0.0	0.0	0.0	0.0	0.0	0.0	0.0	0.0	0.0	0.0	0.0	0.0	0.0	0.0	0.0	0.3	0.6	0.9	1.2	1.5	1.8	2.1	2.4	2.7	2.9	3.2	3.5	3.7	4.0	4.2	4.5	4.7	4.9	5.2	5.4	5.6	5.8	6.0	6.3
122	0.0	0.0	0.0	0.0	0.0	0.0	0.0	0.0	0.0	0.0	0.0	0.0	0.0	0.0	0.0	0.0	0.0	0.1	0.4	0.7	1.0	1.3	1.6	1.9	2.1	2.4	2.7	2.9	3.2	3.4	3.7	3.9	4.1	4.4	4.6	4.8	5.0	5.2	5.5
120	0.0	0.0	0.0	0.0	0.0	0.0	0.0	0.0	0.0	0.0	0.0	0.0	0.0	0.0	0.0	0.0	0.0	0.0	0.0	0.0	0.2	0.5	0.8	1.1	1.3	1.6	1.9	2.1	2.4	2.6	2.9	3.1	3.3	3.6	3.8	4.0	4.2	4.4	4.7
118	0.0	0.0	0.0	0.0	0.0	0.0	0.0	0.0	0.0	0.0	0.0	0.0	0.0	0.0	0.0	0.0	0.0	0.0	0.0	0.0	0.0	0.0	0.0	0.3	0.5	0.8	1.1	1.3	1.6	1.8	2.1	2.3	2.5	2.8	3.0	3.2	3.4	3.6	3.9
116	0.0	0.0	0.0	0.0	0.0	0.0	0.0	0.0	0.0	0.0	0.0	0.0	0.0	0.0	0.0	0.0	0.0	0.0	0.0	0.0	0.0	0.0	0.0	0.0	0.0	0.0	0.3	0.5	0.8	1.0	1.3	1.5	1.7	2.0	2.2	2.4	2.6	2.8	3.1
114	0.0	0.0	0.0	0.0	0.0	0.0	0.0	0.0	0.0	0.0	0.0	0.0	0.0	0.0	0.0	0.0	0.0	0.0	0.0	0.0	0.0	0.0	0.0	0.0	0.0	0.0	0.0	0.0	0.0	0.2	0.5	0.7	0.9	1.2	1.4	1.6	1.8	2.0	2.3
112	0.0	0.0	0.0	0.0	0.0	0.0	0.0	0.0	0.0	0.0	0.0	0.0	0.0	0.0	0.0	0.0	0.0	0.0	0.0	0.0	0.0	0.0	0.0	0.0	0.0	0.0	0.0	0.0	0.0	0.0	0.0	0.0	0.1	0.4	0.6	0.8	1.0	1.2	1.5
110	0.0	0.0	0.0	0.0	0.0	0.0	0.0	0.0	0.0	0.0	0.0	0.0	0.0	0.0	0.0	0.0	0.0	0.0	0.0	0.0	0.0	0.0	0.0	0.0	0.0	0.0	0.0	0.0	0.0	0.0	0.0	0.0	0.0	0.0	0.0	0.0	0.2	0.4	0.7
108	0.0	0.0	0.0	0.0	0.0	0.0	0.0	0.0	0.0	0.0	0.0	0.0	0.0	0.0	0.0	0.0	0.0	0.0	0.0	0.0	0.0	0.0	0.0	0.0	0.0	0.0	0.0	0.0	0.0	0.0	0.0	0.0	0.0	0.0	0.0	0.0	0.0	0.0	0.0
106	0.0	0.0	0.0	0.0	0.0	0.0	0.0	0.0	0.0	0.0	0.0	0.0	0.0	0.0	0.0	0.0	0.0	0.0	0.0	0.0	0.0	0.0	0.0	0.0	0.0	0.0	0.0	0.0	0.0	0.0	0.0	0.0	0.0	0.0	0.0	0.0	0.0	0.0	0.0

THE NORMAL VALUE

LISTED PUT OPTION

TABLES

LISTED PUT OPTION PRICE WHEN EXERCISE PRICE IS 10

Common Stock Price	NUMBER OF WEEKS BEFORE THE OPTION EXPIRES																																					
	1	2	3	4	5	6	7	8	9	10	11	12	13	14	15	16	17	18	19	20	21	22	23	24	25	26	27	28	29	30	31	32	33	34	35	36	37	38	39
14	0.0	0.0	0.0	0.0	0.0	0.0	0.0	0.0	0.0	0.0	0.0	0.0	0.0	0.0	0.0	0.0	0.0	0.0	0.0	0.0	0.0	0.0	0.0	0.0	0.0	0.0	0.0	0.0	0.0	0.0	0.0	0.0	0.0	0.0	0.0	0.0	0.0	0.0	0.0
13.5	0.0	0.0	0.0	0.0	0.0	0.0	0.0	0.0	0.0	0.0	0.0	0.0	0.0	0.0	0.0	0.0	0.0	0.0	0.0	0.0	0.0	0.0	0.0	0.0	0.0	0.0	0.0	0.0	0.0	0.0	0.0	0.0	0.0	0.0	0.0	0.0	0.0	0.0	0.1
13	0.0	0.0	0.0	0.0	0.0	0.0	0.0	0.0	0.0	0.0	0.0	0.0	0.0	0.0	0.0	0.0	0.0	0.0	0.0	0.0	0.0	0.0	0.0	0.0	0.0	0.0	0.0	0.0	0.0	0.0	0.1	0.1	0.1	0.1	0.1	0.1	0.1	0.1	0.2
12.5	0.0	0.0	0.0	0.0	0.0	0.0	0.0	0.0	0.0	0.0	0.0	0.0	0.0	0.0	0.0	0.0	0.0	0.0	0.0	0.0	0.0	0.0	0.0	0.1	0.1	0.1	0.1	0.1	0.1	0.1	0.2	0.2	0.2	0.2	0.2	0.2	0.2	0.2	0.2
12	0.0	0.0	0.0	0.0	0.0	0.0	0.0	0.0	0.0	0.0	0.0	0.0	0.0	0.0	0.0	0.0	0.1	0.1	0.1	0.1	0.1	0.1	0.1	0.2	0.2	0.2	0.2	0.2	0.2	0.2	0.3	0.3	0.3	0.3	0.3	0.3	0.3	0.3	0.4
11.5	0.0	0.0	0.0	0.0	0.0	0.0	0.0	0.0	0.0	0.0	0.1	0.1	0.1	0.1	0.1	0.2	0.2	0.2	0.2	0.2	0.2	0.3	0.3	0.3	0.3	0.3	0.3	0.3	0.3	0.4	0.4	0.4	0.4	0.4	0.4	0.4	0.4	0.5	0.5
11	0.0	0.0	0.0	0.0	0.0	0.1	0.1	0.1	0.1	0.2	0.2	0.2	0.2	0.2	0.3	0.3	0.3	0.3	0.3	0.3	0.4	0.4	0.4	0.4	0.4	0.4	0.4	0.5	0.5	0.5	0.5	0.5	0.5	0.5	0.6	0.6	0.6	0.6	0.6
10.5	0.0	0.0	0.1	0.1	0.2	0.2	0.2	0.3	0.3	0.3	0.3	0.3	0.4	0.4	0.4	0.4	0.4	0.5	0.5	0.5	0.5	0.5	0.5	0.5	0.6	0.6	0.6	0.6	0.6	0.6	0.6	0.7	0.7	0.7	0.7	0.7	0.7	0.7	0.7
10	0.1	0.2	0.2	0.3	0.3	0.3	0.4	0.4	0.4	0.5	0.5	0.5	0.5	0.5	0.6	0.6	0.6	0.6	0.6	0.6	0.7	0.7	0.7	0.7	0.7	0.7	0.7	0.8	0.8	0.8	0.8	0.8	0.8	0.8	0.8	0.9	0.9	0.9	0.9
9.5	0.5	0.5	0.6	0.6	0.6	0.6	0.7	0.7	0.7	0.7	0.8	0.8	0.8	0.8	0.8	0.9	0.9	0.9	0.9	1.0	1.0	1.0	1.0	1.1	1.1	1.1	1.1	1.1	1.2	1.2	1.2	1.2	1.3	1.3	1.3	1.3	1.4	1.4	1.4
9	1.0	1.0	1.1	1.1	1.1	1.1	1.1	1.2	1.2	1.2	1.2	1.2	1.2	1.3	1.3	1.3	1.3	1.3	1.4	1.4	1.4	1.4	1.4	1.5	1.5	1.5	1.5	1.5	1.6	1.6	1.6	1.6	1.6	1.7	1.7	1.7	1.7	1.7	1.7
8.5	1.5	1.5	1.5	1.6	1.6	1.6	1.6	1.6	1.6	1.7	1.7	1.7	1.7	1.7	1.7	1.7	1.8	1.8	1.8	1.8	1.8	1.8	1.9	1.9	1.9	1.9	1.9	1.9	1.9	2.0	2.0	2.0	2.0	2.0	2.0	2.1	2.1	2.1	2.1
8	2.0	2.0	2.0	2.0	2.1	2.1	2.1	2.1	2.1	2.1	2.1	2.1	2.1	2.2	2.2	2.2	2.2	2.2	2.2	2.2	2.2	2.3	2.3	2.3	2.3	2.3	2.3	2.3	2.3	2.3	2.4	2.4	2.4	2.4	2.4	2.4	2.4	2.4	2.4
7.5	2.5	2.5	2.5	2.5	2.5	2.5	2.6	2.6	2.6	2.6	2.6	2.6	2.6	2.6	2.6	2.6	2.6	2.6	2.6	2.6	2.7	2.7	2.7	2.7	2.7	2.7	2.7	2.7	2.7	2.7	2.7	2.7	2.7	2.8	2.8	2.8	2.8	2.8	2.8
7	3.0	3.0	3.0	3.0	3.0	3.0	3.0	3.0	3.0	3.0	3.0	3.0	3.0	3.0	3.1	3.1	3.1	3.1	3.1	3.1	3.1	3.1	3.1	3.1	3.1	3.1	3.1	3.1	3.1	3.1	3.1	3.1	3.1	3.1	3.1	3.1	3.1	3.1	3.1
6.5	3.5	3.5	3.5	3.5	3.5	3.5	3.5	3.5	3.5	3.5	3.5	3.5	3.5	3.5	3.5	3.5	3.5	3.5	3.5	3.5	3.5	3.5	3.5	3.5	3.5	3.5	3.5	3.5	3.5	3.5	3.5	3.5	3.5	3.5	3.5	3.5	3.5	3.5	3.5
6	4.0	4.0	4.0	4.0	4.0	4.0	4.0	4.0	4.0	4.0	4.0	4.0	4.0	4.0	4.0	4.0	4.0	4.0	4.0	4.0	4.0	4.0	4.0	4.0	4.0	4.0	4.0	4.0	4.0	4.0	4.0	4.0	4.0	4.0	4.0	4.0	4.0	4.0	4.0

LISTED PUT OPTION PRICE WHEN EXERCISE PRICE IS 15

NUMBER OF WEEKS BEFORE THE OPTION EXPIRES

Common Stock Price	1	2	3	4	5	6	7	8	9	10	11	12	13	14	15	16	17	18	19	20
21	0.0	0.0	0.0	0.0	0.0	0.0	0.0	0.0	0.0	0.0	0.0	0.0	0.0	0.0	0.0	0.0	0.0	0.0	0.0	0.0
20	0.0	0.0	0.0	0.0	0.0	0.0	0.0	0.0	0.0	0.0	0.0	0.0	0.0	0.0	0.0	0.0	0.0	0.0	0.0	0.0
19	0.0	0.0	0.0	0.0	0.0	0.0	0.0	0.0	0.0	0.0	0.0	0.0	0.0	0.0	0.0	0.0	0.0	0.0	0.0	0.0
18	0.0	0.0	0.0	0.0	0.0	0.0	0.0	0.0	0.0	0.0	0.0	0.0	0.0	0.0	0.0	0.1	0.1	0.1	0.1	0.2
17	0.0	0.0	0.0	0.0	0.0	0.0	0.0	0.0	0.1	0.1	0.1	0.2	0.2	0.2	0.3	0.3	0.3	0.3	0.4	0.4
16	0.0	0.0	0.1	0.1	0.2	0.2	0.3	0.3	0.3	0.4	0.4	0.4	0.5	0.5	0.5	0.6	0.6	0.6	0.6	0.7
15	0.2	0.3	0.4	0.4	0.5	0.5	0.6	0.6	0.6	0.7	0.7	0.7	0.8	0.8	0.8	0.9	0.9	0.9	0.9	1.0
14.5	0.5	0.6	0.6	0.6	0.7	0.7	0.8	0.8	0.8	0.9	0.9	0.9	1.0	1.0	1.0	1.1	1.1	1.2	1.2	1.2
14	1.0	1.1	1.1	1.1	1.2	1.2	1.2	1.3	1.3	1.3	1.4	1.4	1.4	1.5	1.5	1.5	1.6	1.6	1.6	1.7
13.5	1.5	1.6	1.6	1.6	1.6	1.7	1.7	1.7	1.8	1.8	1.8	1.8	1.9	1.9	1.9	2.0	2.0	2.0	2.0	2.1
13	2.0	2.0	2.1	2.1	2.1	2.1	2.2	2.2	2.2	2.2	2.3	2.3	2.3	2.3	2.4	2.4	2.4	2.4	2.5	2.5
12.5	2.5	2.5	2.6	2.6	2.6	2.6	2.6	2.7	2.7	2.7	2.7	2.8	2.8	2.8	2.8	2.8	2.9	2.9	2.9	2.9
12	3.0	3.0	3.1	3.1	3.1	3.1	3.1	3.1	3.2	3.2	3.2	3.2	3.2	3.2	3.3	3.3	3.3	3.3	3.3	3.3
11.5	3.5	3.5	3.5	3.6	3.6	3.6	3.6	3.6	3.6	3.6	3.6	3.7	3.7	3.7	3.7	3.7	3.7	3.7	3.8	3.8
11	4.0	4.0	4.0	4.0	4.0	4.1	4.1	4.1	4.1	4.1	4.1	4.1	4.1	4.1	4.1	4.1	4.2	4.2	4.2	4.2
10.5	4.5	4.5	4.5	4.5	4.5	4.5	4.5	4.5	4.5	4.6	4.6	4.6	4.6	4.6	4.6	4.6	4.6	4.6	4.6	4.6
10	5.0	5.0	5.0	5.0	5.0	5.0	5.0	5.0	5.0	5.0	5.0	5.0	5.0	5.0	5.0	5.0	5.0	5.0	5.0	5.0
9.5	5.5	5.5	5.5	5.5	5.5	5.5	5.5	5.5	5.5	5.5	5.5	5.5	5.5	5.5	5.5	5.5	5.5	5.5	5.5	5.5
9	6.0	6.0	6.0	6.0	6.0	6.0	6.0	6.0	6.0	6.0	6.0	6.0	6.0	6.0	6.0	6.0	6.0	6.0	6.0	6.0

Common Stock Price	21	22	23	24	25	26	27	28	29	30	31	32	33	34	35	36	37	38	39
21	0.0	0.0	0.0	0.0	0.0	0.0	0.0	0.0	0.0	0.0	0.0	0.0	0.0	0.0	0.0	0.0	0.0	0.0	0.0
20	0.0	0.0	0.0	0.0	0.0	0.0	0.0	0.0	0.0	0.0	0.0	0.0	0.0	0.0	0.1	0.1	0.1	0.1	0.1
19	0.0	0.0	0.0	0.0	0.1	0.1	0.1	0.1	0.1	0.2	0.2	0.2	0.2	0.2	0.3	0.3	0.3	0.3	0.3
18	0.2	0.2	0.2	0.2	0.3	0.3	0.3	0.3	0.3	0.4	0.4	0.4	0.4	0.4	0.5	0.5	0.5	0.5	0.5
17	0.4	0.4	0.5	0.5	0.5	0.5	0.5	0.6	0.6	0.6	0.6	0.6	0.7	0.7	0.7	0.7	0.7	0.8	0.8
16	0.7	0.7	0.7	0.7	0.8	0.8	0.8	0.8	0.8	0.9	0.9	0.9	0.9	0.9	1.0	1.0	1.0	1.0	1.0
15	1.0	1.0	1.0	1.0	1.1	1.1	1.1	1.1	1.1	1.2	1.2	1.2	1.2	1.2	1.3	1.3	1.3	1.3	1.3
14.5	1.3	1.3	1.3	1.4	1.4	1.5	1.5	1.5	1.6	1.6	1.6	1.7	1.7	1.7	1.8	1.8	1.9	1.9	1.9
14	1.7	1.7	1.8	1.8	1.8	1.9	1.9	1.9	1.9	2.0	2.0	2.0	2.1	2.1	2.1	2.2	2.2	2.2	2.3
13.5	2.1	2.1	2.2	2.2	2.2	2.2	2.3	2.3	2.3	2.4	2.4	2.4	2.5	2.5	2.5	2.5	2.6	2.6	2.6
13	2.5	2.5	2.6	2.6	2.6	2.6	2.7	2.7	2.7	2.7	2.8	2.8	2.8	2.8	2.9	2.9	2.9	2.9	3.0
12.5	2.9	3.0	3.0	3.0	3.0	3.0	3.1	3.1	3.1	3.1	3.2	3.2	3.2	3.2	3.2	3.3	3.3	3.3	3.3
12	3.4	3.4	3.4	3.4	3.4	3.4	3.5	3.5	3.5	3.5	3.5	3.5	3.6	3.6	3.6	3.6	3.6	3.6	3.7
11.5	3.8	3.8	3.8	3.8	3.8	3.8	3.9	3.9	3.9	3.9	3.9	3.9	3.9	3.9	4.0	4.0	4.0	4.0	4.0
11	4.2	4.2	4.2	4.2	4.2	4.2	4.2	4.3	4.3	4.3	4.3	4.3	4.3	4.3	4.3	4.3	4.3	4.4	4.4
10.5	4.6	4.6	4.6	4.6	4.6	4.6	4.6	4.6	4.7	4.7	4.7	4.7	4.7	4.7	4.7	4.7	4.7	4.7	4.7
10	5.0	5.0	5.0	5.0	5.0	5.0	5.0	5.0	5.0	5.0	5.0	5.0	5.0	5.0	5.0	5.1	5.1	5.1	5.1
9.5	5.5	5.5	5.5	5.5	5.5	5.5	5.5	5.5	5.5	5.5	5.5	5.5	5.5	5.5	5.5	5.5	5.5	5.5	5.5
9	6.0	6.0	6.0	6.0	6.0	6.0	6.0	6.0	6.0	6.0	6.0	6.0	6.0	6.0	6.0	6.0	6.0	6.0	6.0

LISTED PUT OPTION PRICE WHEN EXERCISE PRICE IS 20

NUMBER OF WEEKS BEFORE THE OPTION EXPIRES (weeks 1–20)

Common Stock Price	1	2	3	4	5	6	7	8	9	10	11	12	13	14	15	16	17	18	19	20
28	0.0	0.0	0.0	0.0	0.0	0.0	0.0	0.0	0.0	0.0	0.0	0.0	0.0	0.0	0.0	0.0	0.0	0.0	0.0	0.0
27	0.0	0.0	0.0	0.0	0.0	0.0	0.0	0.0	0.0	0.0	0.0	0.0	0.0	0.0	0.0	0.0	0.0	0.0	0.0	0.0
26	0.0	0.0	0.0	0.0	0.0	0.0	0.0	0.0	0.0	0.0	0.0	0.0	0.0	0.0	0.0	0.0	0.0	0.0	0.0	0.0
25	0.0	0.0	0.0	0.0	0.0	0.0	0.0	0.0	0.0	0.0	0.0	0.0	0.0	0.0	0.0	0.0	0.0	0.0	0.0	0.0
24	0.0	0.0	0.0	0.0	0.0	0.0	0.0	0.0	0.0	0.0	0.0	0.0	0.0	0.0	0.0	0.1	0.1	0.1	0.2	0.2
23	0.0	0.0	0.0	0.0	0.0	0.0	0.0	0.0	0.0	0.1	0.1	0.2	0.2	0.2	0.3	0.3	0.3	0.4	0.4	0.4
22	0.0	0.0	0.0	0.0	0.1	0.1	0.2	0.2	0.3	0.3	0.4	0.4	0.4	0.5	0.5	0.6	0.6	0.6	0.7	0.7
21	0.0	0.1	0.2	0.3	0.3	0.4	0.4	0.5	0.5	0.6	0.6	0.7	0.7	0.8	0.8	0.8	0.9	0.9	0.9	1.0
20	0.3	0.4	0.5	0.6	0.6	0.7	0.8	0.8	0.9	0.9	0.9	1.0	1.0	1.1	1.1	1.1	1.2	1.2	1.2	1.3
19	1.0	1.1	1.1	1.2	1.2	1.3	1.3	1.4	1.4	1.5	1.5	1.6	1.6	1.6	1.7	1.7	1.8	1.8	1.9	1.9
18	2.0	2.1	2.1	2.2	2.2	2.2	2.3	2.3	2.3	2.4	2.4	2.5	2.5	2.5	2.6	2.6	2.7	2.7	2.7	2.8
17	3.0	3.1	3.1	3.1	3.2	3.2	3.2	3.2	3.3	3.3	3.3	3.4	3.4	3.4	3.5	3.5	3.5	3.6	3.6	3.6
16	4.0	4.0	4.1	4.1	4.1	4.1	4.2	4.2	4.2	4.2	4.3	4.3	4.3	4.3	4.3	4.4	4.4	4.4	4.4	4.5
15	5.0	5.0	5.0	5.1	5.1	5.1	5.1	5.1	5.1	5.1	5.2	5.2	5.2	5.2	5.2	5.2	5.3	5.3	5.3	5.3
14.5	5.5	5.5	5.5	5.5	5.6	5.6	5.6	5.6	5.6	5.6	5.6	5.6	5.6	5.7	5.7	5.7	5.7	5.7	5.7	5.7
14	6.0	6.0	6.0	6.0	6.0	6.0	6.0	6.1	6.1	6.1	6.1	6.1	6.1	6.1	6.1	6.1	6.1	6.1	6.1	6.1
13.5	6.5	6.5	6.5	6.5	6.5	6.5	6.5	6.5	6.5	6.5	6.5	6.5	6.5	6.5	6.5	6.6	6.6	6.6	6.6	6.6
13	7;0	7.0	7.0	7.0	7.0	7.0	7.0	7.0	7.0	7.0	7.0	7.0	7.0	7.0	7.0	7.0	7.0	7.0	7.0	7.0
12.5	7.5	7.5	7.5	7.5	7.5	7.5	7.5	7.5	7.5	7.5	7.5	7.5	7.5	7.5	7.5	7.5	7.5	7.5	7.5	7.5
12	8.0	8.0	8.0	8.0	8.0	8.0	8.0	8.0	8.0	8.0	8.0	8.0	8.0	8.0	8.0	8.0	8.0	8.0	8.0	8.0

NUMBER OF WEEKS BEFORE THE OPTION EXPIRES (weeks 21–39)

Common Stock Price	21	22	23	24	25	26	27	28	29	30	31	32	33	34	35	36	37	38	39
28	0.0	0.0	0.0	0.0	0.0	0.0	0.0	0.0	0.0	0.0	0.0	0.0	0.0	0.0	0.0	0.0	0.0	0.0	0.0
27	0.0	0.0	0.0	0.0	0.0	0.0	0.0	0.0	0.0	0.0	0.0	0.0	0.0	0.0	0.0	0.0	0.1	0.1	0.1
26	0.0	0.0	0.0	0.0	0.0	0.0	0.0	0.0	0.1	0.1	0.1	0.1	0.2	0.2	0.2	0.2	0.3	0.3	0.3
25	0.0	0.1	0.1	0.1	0.1	0.2	0.2	0.2	0.3	0.3	0.3	0.3	0.4	0.4	0.4	0.4	0.5	0.5	0.5
24	0.2	0.3	0.3	0.3	0.4	0.4	0.4	0.4	0.5	0.5	0.5	0.5	0.6	0.6	0.6	0.6	0.7	0.7	0.7
23	0.5	0.5	0.5	0.6	0.6	0.6	0.6	0.7	0.7	0.7	0.8	0.8	0.8	0.8	0.8	0.9	0.9	0.9	0.9
22	0.7	0.8	0.8	0.8	0.8	0.9	0.9	0.9	1.0	1.0	1.0	1.0	1.1	1.1	1.1	1.1	1.1	1.2	1.2
21	1.0	1.0	1.1	1.1	1.1	1.1	1.2	1.2	1.2	1.3	1.3	1.3	1.3	1.4	1.4	1.4	1.4	1.4	1.5
20	1.3	1.3	1.4	1.4	1.4	1.5	1.5	1.5	1.5	1.6	1.6	1.6	1.6	1.7	1.7	1.7	1.7	1.8	1.8
19	2.0	2.0	2.1	2.1	2.2	2.2	2.2	2.3	2.3	2.4	2.4	2.5	2.5	2.6	2.6	2.7	2.7	2.8	2.8
18	2.8	2.8	2.9	2.9	3.0	3.0	3.0	3.1	3.1	3.2	3.2	3.2	3.3	3.3	3.3	3.4	3.4	3.5	3.5
17	3.6	3.7	3.7	3.7	3.8	3.8	3.8	3.9	3.9	3.9	3.9	4.0	4.0	4.0	4.1	4.1	4.1	4.2	4.2
16	4.5	4.5	4.5	4.5	4.6	4.6	4.6	4.6	4.7	4.7	4.7	4.7	4.8	4.8	4.8	4.8	4.8	4.9	4.9
15	5.3	5.3	5.3	5.4	5.4	5.4	5.4	5.4	5.4	5.4	5.5	5.5	5.5	5.5	5.5	5.5	5.6	5.6	5.6
14.5	5.7	5.7	5.8	5.8	5.8	5.8	5.8	5.8	5.8	5.8	5.8	5.9	5.9	5.9	5.9	5.9	5.9	5.9	5.9
14	6.1	6.2	6.2	6.2	6.2	6.2	6.2	6.2	6.2	6.2	6.2	6.2	6.2	6.2	6.2	6.3	6.3	6.3	6.3
13.5	6.6	6.6	6.6	6.6	6.6	6.6	6.6	6.6	6.6	6.6	6.6	6.6	6.6	6.6	6.6	6.6	6.6	6.6	6.6
13	7.0	7.0	7.0	7.0	7.0	7.0	7.0	7.0	7.0	7.0	7.0	7.0	7.0	7.0	7.0	7.0	7.0	7.0	7.0
12.5	7.5	7.5	7.5	7.5	7.5	7.5	7.5	7.5	7.5	7.5	7.5	7.5	7.5	7.5	7.5	7.5	7.5	7.5	7.5
12	8.0	8.0	8.0	8.0	8.0	8.0	8.0	8.0	8.0	8.0	8.0	8.0	8.0	8.0	8.0	8.0	8.0	8.0	8.0

LISTED PUT OPTION PRICE WHEN EXERCISE PRICE IS 25

Common Stock Price	NUMBER OF WEEKS BEFORE THE OPTION EXPIRES 1	2	3	4	5	6	7	8	9	10	11	12	13	14	15	16	17	18	19	20	21	22	23	24	25	26	27	28	29	30	31	32	33	34	35	36	37	38	39
35	0.0	0.0	0.0	0.0	0.0	0.0	0.0	0.0	0.0	0.0	0.0	0.0	0.0	0.0	0.0	0.0	0.0	0.0	0.0	0.0	0.0	0.0	0.0	0.0	0.0	0.0	0.0	0.0	0.0	0.0	0.0	0.0	0.0	0.0	0.0	0.0	0.0	0.0	0.0
34	0.0	0.0	0.0	0.0	0.0	0.0	0.0	0.0	0.0	0.0	0.0	0.0	0.0	0.0	0.0	0.0	0.0	0.0	0.0	0.0	0.0	0.0	0.0	0.0	0.0	0.0	0.0	0.0	0.0	0.0	0.0	0.0	0.0	0.0	0.0	0.0	0.0	0.1	0.1
33	0.0	0.0	0.0	0.0	0.0	0.0	0.0	0.0	0.0	0.0	0.0	0.0	0.0	0.0	0.0	0.0	0.0	0.0	0.0	0.0	0.0	0.0	0.0	0.0	0.0	0.0	0.0	0.0	0.0	0.0	0.0	0.1	0.1	0.1	0.2	0.2	0.2	0.3	0.3
32	0.0	0.0	0.0	0.0	0.0	0.0	0.0	0.0	0.0	0.0	0.0	0.0	0.0	0.0	0.0	0.0	0.0	0.0	0.0	0.0	0.0	0.0	0.0	0.0	0.0	0.1	0.1	0.1	0.2	0.2	0.2	0.3	0.3	0.3	0.4	0.4	0.4	0.4	0.5
31	0.0	0.0	0.0	0.0	0.0	0.0	0.0	0.0	0.0	0.0	0.0	0.0	0.0	0.0	0.0	0.0	0.0	0.0	0.0	0.0	0.1	0.1	0.2	0.2	0.2	0.3	0.3	0.3	0.4	0.4	0.4	0.5	0.5	0.5	0.6	0.6	0.6	0.6	0.7
30	0.0	0.0	0.0	0.0	0.0	0.0	0.0	0.0	0.0	0.0	0.0	0.0	0.0	0.0	0.0	0.1	0.1	0.2	0.2	0.3	0.3	0.3	0.4	0.4	0.4	0.5	0.5	0.5	0.6	0.6	0.6	0.7	0.7	0.7	0.8	0.8	0.8	0.9	0.9
29	0.0	0.0	0.0	0.0	0.0	0.0	0.0	0.0	0.0	0.0	0.1	0.1	0.2	0.2	0.3	0.3	0.4	0.4	0.4	0.5	0.5	0.6	0.6	0.6	0.7	0.7	0.7	0.8	0.8	0.8	0.9	0.9	0.9	1.0	1.0	1.0	1.1	1.1	1.1
28	0.0	0.0	0.0	0.0	0.0	0.0	0.1	0.1	0.2	0.3	0.3	0.4	0.4	0.5	0.5	0.6	0.6	0.7	0.7	0.7	0.8	0.8	0.8	0.9	0.9	1.0	1.0	1.0	1.1	1.1	1.1	1.2	1.2	1.2	1.2	1.3	1.3	1.3	1.4
27	0.0	0.0	0.0	0.1	0.2	0.3	0.3	0.4	0.5	0.5	0.6	0.6	0.7	0.7	0.8	0.8	0.9	0.9	1.0	1.0	1.0	1.1	1.1	1.2	1.2	1.2	1.3	1.3	1.3	1.4	1.4	1.4	1.5	1.5	1.5	1.5	1.6	1.6	1.6
26	0.0	0.2	0.3	0.4	0.5	0.6	0.6	0.7	0.8	0.8	0.9	0.9	1.0	1.0	1.1	1.1	1.2	1.2	1.2	1.3	1.3	1.4	1.4	1.4	1.5	1.5	1.5	1.6	1.6	1.6	1.7	1.7	1.7	1.8	1.8	1.8	1.9	1.9	1.9
25	0.4	0.5	0.6	0.7	0.8	0.9	0.9	1.0	1.1	1.1	1.2	1.2	1.3	1.3	1.4	1.4	1.5	1.5	1.6	1.6	1.6	1.7	1.7	1.7	1.8	1.8	1.8	1.9	1.9	1.9	2.0	2.0	2.0	2.1	2.1	2.1	2.2	2.2	2.2
24	1.1	1.1	1.2	1.2	1.3	1.4	1.4	1.5	1.5	1.6	1.7	1.7	1.8	1.8	1.9	2.0	2.0	2.1	2.1	2.2	2.3	2.3	2.4	2.4	2.5	2.6	2.6	2.7	2.7	2.8	2.9	2.9	2.9	3.0	3.2	3.2	3.3	3.4	3.4
23	2.1	2.1	2.2	2.2	2.3	2.3	2.4	2.4	2.5	2.5	2.6	2.6	2.7	2.7	2.8	2.8	2.9	2.9	3.0	3.0	3.1	3.1	3.2	3.2	3.3	3.4	3.4	3.5	3.5	3.6	3.6	3.7	3.7	3.8	3.8	3.9	3.9	4.0	4.0
22	3.0	3.1	3.1	3.2	3.2	3.3	3.3	3.4	3.4	3.4	3.5	3.5	3.6	3.6	3.7	3.7	3.8	3.8	3.8	3.9	3.9	4.0	4.0	4.1	4.1	4.1	4.2	4.2	4.3	4.3	4.4	4.4	4.5	4.5	4.5	4.6	4.6	4.7	4.7
21	4.0	4.1	4.1	4.1	4.2	4.2	4.3	4.3	4.3	4.4	4.4	4.4	4.5	4.5	4.5	4.6	4.6	4.7	4.7	4.7	4.8	4.8	4.8	4.9	4.9	4.9	5.0	5.0	5.1	5.1	5.1	5.2	5.2	5.2	5.3	5.3	5.3	5.4	5.4
20	5.0	5.1	5.1	5.1	5.1	5.2	5.2	5.2	5.3	5.3	5.3	5.3	5.4	5.4	5.4	5.5	5.5	5.5	5.5	5.6	5.6	5.6	5.7	5.7	5.7	5.7	5.8	5.8	5.8	5.9	5.9	5.9	5.9	6.0	6.0	6.0	6.1	6.1	6.1
19	6.0	6.0	6.1	6.1	6.1	6.1	6.1	6.2	6.2	6.2	6.2	6.2	6.3	6.3	6.3	6.3	6.4	6.4	6.4	6.4	6.4	6.5	6.5	6.5	6.5	6.5	6.6	6.6	6.6	6.6	6.6	6.7	6.7	6.7	6.7	6.7	6.8	6.8	6.8
18	7.0	7.0	7.0	7.1	7.1	7.1	7.1	7.1	7.1	7.1	7.1	7.2	7.2	7.2	7.2	7.2	7.2	7.2	7.2	7.3	7.3	7.3	7.3	7.3	7.3	7.3	7.3	7.4	7.4	7.4	7.4	7.4	7.4	7.4	7.4	7.5	7.5	7.5	7.5
17	8.0	8.0	8.0	8.0	8.0	8.0	8.0	8.0	8.0	8.0	8.1	8.1	8.1	8.1	8.1	8.1	8.1	8.1	8.1	8.1	8.1	8.1	8.1	8.1	8.1	8.1	8.1	8.1	8.1	8.1	8.2	8.2	8.2	8.2	8.2	8.2	8.2	8.2	8.2
16	9.0	9.0	9.0	9.0	9.0	9.0	9.0	9.0	9.0	9.0	9.0	9.0	9.0	9.0	9.0	9.0	9.0	9.0	9.0	9.0	9.0	9.0	9.0	9.0	9.0	9.0	9.0	9.0	9.0	9.0	9.0	9.0	9.0	9.0	9.0	9.0	9.0	9.0	9.0
15	10.0	10.0	10.0	10.0	10.0	10.0	10.0	10.0	10.0	10.0	10.0	10.0	10.0	10.0	10.0	10.0	10.0	10.0	10.0	10.0	10.0	10.0	10.0	10.0	10.0	10.0	10.0	10.0	10.0	10.0	10.0	10.0	10.0	10.0	10.0	10.0	10.0	10.0	10.0

LISTED PUT OPTION PRICE WHEN EXERCISE PRICE IS 30

Common Stock Price	NUMBER OF WEEKS BEFORE THE OPTION EXPIRES																																					
	1	2	3	4	5	6	7	8	9	10	11	12	13	14	15	16	17	18	19	20	21	22	23	24	25	26	27	28	29	30	31	32	33	34	35	36	37	38	39
42	0.0	0.0	0.0	0.0	0.0	0.0	0.0	0.0	0.0	0.0	0.0	0.0	0.0	0.0	0.0	0.0	0.0	0.0	0.0	0.0	0.0	0.0	0.0	0.0	0.0	0.0	0.0	0.0	0.0	0.0	0.0	0.0	0.0	0.0	0.0	0.0	0.0	0.0	0.0
41	0.0	0.0	0.0	0.0	0.0	0.0	0.0	0.0	0.0	0.0	0.0	0.0	0.0	0.0	0.0	0.0	0.0	0.0	0.0	0.0	0.0	0.0	0.0	0.0	0.0	0.0	0.0	0.0	0.0	0.0	0.0	0.0	0.0	0.0	0.0	0.0	0.0	0.1	0.1
40	0.0	0.0	0.0	0.0	0.0	0.0	0.0	0.0	0.0	0.0	0.0	0.0	0.0	0.0	0.0	0.0	0.0	0.0	0.0	0.0	0.0	0.0	0.0	0.0	0.0	0.0	0.0	0.0	0.0	0.0	0.0	0.0	0.1	0.1	0.1	0.2	0.2	0.2	0.3
39	0.0	0.0	0.0	0.0	0.0	0.0	0.0	0.0	0.0	0.0	0.0	0.0	0.0	0.0	0.0	0.0	0.0	0.0	0.0	0.0	0.0	0.0	0.0	0.0	0.0	0.0	0.0	0.0	0.1	0.1	0.2	0.2	0.2	0.3	0.3	0.3	0.4	0.4	0.5
38	0.0	0.0	0.0	0.0	0.0	0.0	0.0	0.0	0.0	0.0	0.0	0.0	0.0	0.0	0.0	0.0	0.0	0.0	0.0	0.0	0.0	0.0	0.0	0.1	0.1	0.2	0.2	0.2	0.3	0.3	0.4	0.4	0.4	0.5	0.5	0.5	0.6	0.6	0.6
37	0.0	0.0	0.0	0.0	0.0	0.0	0.0	0.0	0.0	0.0	0.0	0.0	0.0	0.0	0.0	0.0	0.0	0.0	0.0	0.1	0.1	0.2	0.2	0.3	0.3	0.4	0.4	0.4	0.5	0.5	0.6	0.6	0.6	0.7	0.7	0.7	0.8	0.8	0.9
36	0.0	0.0	0.0	0.0	0.0	0.0	0.0	0.0	0.0	0.0	0.0	0.0	0.0	0.0	0.1	0.1	0.2	0.2	0.3	0.3	0.4	0.4	0.4	0.5	0.5	0.6	0.6	0.7	0.7	0.7	0.8	0.8	0.9	0.9	0.9	1.0	1.0	1.0	1.1
35	0.0	0.0	0.0	0.0	0.0	0.0	0.0	0.0	0.0	0.0	0.0	0.1	0.2	0.2	0.3	0.3	0.4	0.4	0.5	0.5	0.6	0.6	0.7	0.7	0.8	0.8	0.8	0.9	0.9	1.0	1.0	1.0	1.1	1.1	1.2	1.2	1.2	1.3	1.3
34	0.0	0.0	0.0	0.0	0.0	0.0	0.0	0.1	0.2	0.2	0.3	0.3	0.4	0.5	0.5	0.6	0.6	0.7	0.7	0.8	0.8	0.9	0.9	1.0	1.0	1.0	1.1	1.1	1.2	1.2	1.2	1.3	1.3	1.4	1.4	1.4	1.5	1.5	1.5
33	0.0	0.0	0.0	0.0	0.1	0.2	0.3	0.3	0.4	0.5	0.5	0.6	0.7	0.7	0.8	0.8	0.9	0.9	1.0	1.0	1.1	1.1	1.2	1.2	1.3	1.3	1.3	1.4	1.4	1.5	1.5	1.5	1.6	1.6	1.7	1.7	1.7	1.8	1.8
32	0.0	0.0	0.1	0.3	0.4	0.4	0.5	0.6	0.7	0.8	0.8	0.9	0.9	1.0	1.1	1.1	1.2	1.2	1.3	1.3	1.4	1.4	1.4	1.5	1.5	1.6	1.6	1.7	1.7	1.7	1.8	1.8	1.9	1.9	1.9	2.0	2.0	2.0	2.1
31	0.1	0.3	0.4	0.5	0.6	0.7	0.8	0.9	1.0	1.0	1.1	1.2	1.2	1.3	1.3	1.4	1.5	1.5	1.6	1.6	1.6	1.7	1.7	1.8	1.8	1.9	1.9	1.9	2.0	2.0	2.1	2.1	2.1	2.2	2.2	2.3	2.3	2.3	2.4
30	0.4	0.6	0.7	0.9	1.0	1.0	1.1	1.2	1.3	1.4	1.4	1.5	1.5	1.6	1.7	1.7	1.8	1.8	1.9	1.9	2.0	2.0	2.0	2.1	2.1	2.2	2.2	2.3	2.3	2.3	2.4	2.4	2.5	2.5	2.5	2.6	2.6	2.6	2.7
29	1.1	1.1	1.2	1.3	1.4	1.4	1.5	1.6	1.7	1.7	1.8	1.9	2.0	2.0	2.1	2.2	2.2	2.3	2.4	2.5	2.5	2.6	2.7	2.8	2.8	2.9	3.0	3.1	3.1	3.2	3.3	3.3	3.4	3.4	3.4	3.5	3.5	3.5	3.6
28	2.1	2.1	2.2	2.3	2.3	2.4	2.5	2.5	2.6	2.7	2.7	2.8	2.9	2.9	3.0	3.0	3.1	3.2	3.2	3.3	3.4	3.4	3.5	3.6	3.6	3.7	3.8	3.8	3.9	4.0	4.0	4.1	4.2	4.2	4.2	4.3	4.4	4.4	4.5
27	3.1	3.1	3.2	3.2	3.3	3.3	3.4	3.5	3.5	3.6	3.6	3.7	3.7	3.8	3.9	3.9	4.0	4.0	4.1	4.2	4.2	4.3	4.3	4.4	4.4	4.5	4.6	4.6	4.7	4.7	4.8	4.8	4.9	5.0	5.0	5.1	5.1	5.2	5.2
26	4.0	4.1	4.1	4.2	4.2	4.3	4.3	4.4	4.4	4.5	4.5	4.6	4.6	4.7	4.7	4.8	4.8	4.9	4.9	5.0	5.0	5.1	5.1	5.2	5.2	5.3	5.3	5.4	5.4	5.5	5.5	5.6	5.6	5.7	5.7	5.8	5.8	5.9	5.9
25	5.0	5.1	5.1	5.2	5.2	5.3	5.3	5.3	5.4	5.4	5.5	5.5	5.5	5.6	5.6	5.7	5.7	5.8	5.8	5.8	5.9	5.9	6.0	6.0	6.0	6.1	6.1	6.2	6.2	6.3	6.3	6.3	6.4	6.4	6.5	6.5	6.6	6.6	6.6
24	6.0	6.1	6.1	6.1	6.2	6.2	6.2	6.3	6.3	6.3	6.4	6.4	6.4	6.5	6.5	6.5	6.6	6.6	6.6	6.7	6.7	6.8	6.8	6.8	6.9	6.9	6.9	7.0	7.0	7.0	7.1	7.1	7.1	7.2	7.2	7.2	7.3	7.3	7.3
23	7.0	7.1	7.1	7.1	7.1	7.2	7.2	7.2	7.2	7.3	7.3	7.3	7.3	7.4	7.4	7.4	7.4	7.5	7.5	7.5	7.6	7.6	7.6	7.6	7.7	7.7	7.7	7.7	7.8	7.8	7.8	7.8	7.9	7.9	7.9	7.9	8.0	8.0	8.0
22	8.0	8.0	8.1	8.1	8.1	8.1	8.1	8.1	8.2	8.2	8.2	8.2	8.2	8.3	8.3	8.3	8.3	8.3	8.4	8.4	8.4	8.4	8.4	8.4	8.5	8.5	8.5	8.5	8.5	8.6	8.6	8.6	8.6	8.6	8.6	8.7	8.7	8.7	8.7
21	9.0	9.0	9.0	9.0	9.1	9.1	9.1	9.1	9.1	9.1	9.1	9.1	9.1	9.1	9.2	9.2	9.2	9.2	9.2	9.2	9.2	9.2	9.2	9.3	9.3	9.3	9.3	9.3	9.3	9.3	9.3	9.3	9.4	9.4	9.4	9.4	9.4	9.4	9.4
20	10.0	10.0	10.0	10.0	10.0	10.0	10.0	10.0	10.0	10.0	10.0	10.0	10.0	10.0	10.0	10.0	10.0	10.1	10.1	10.1	10.1	10.1	10.1	10.1	10.1	10.1	10.1	10.1	10.1	10.1	10.1	10.1	10.1	10.1	10.1	10.1	10.1	10.1	10.1
19	11.0	11.0	11.0	11.0	11.0	11.0	11.0	11.0	11.0	11.0	11.0	11.0	11.0	11.0	11.0	11.0	11.0	11.0	11.0	11.0	11.0	11.0	11.0	11.0	11.0	11.0	11.0	11.0	11.0	11.0	11.0	11.0	11.0	11.0	11.0	11.0	11.0	11.0	11.0
18	12.0	12.0	12.0	12.0	12.0	12.0	12.0	12.0	12.0	12.0	1.20	12.0	12.0	12.0	12.0	12.0	12.0	12.0	12.0	12.0	12.0	12.0	12.0	12.0	12.0	12.0	12.0	12.0	12.0	12.0	12.0	12.0	12.0	12.0	12.0	12.0	12.0	12.0	12.0

LISTED PUT OPTION PRICE WHEN EXERCISE PRICE IS 35

NUMBER OF WEEKS BEFORE THE OPTION EXPIRES (weeks 1–20)

Common Stock Price	1	2	3	4	5	6	7	8	9	10	11	12	13	14	15	16	17	18	19	20
49	0.0	0.0	0.0	0.0	0.0	0.0	0.0	0.0	0.0	0.0	0.0	0.0	0.0	0.0	0.0	0.0	0.0	0.0	0.0	0.0
48	0.0	0.0	0.0	0.0	0.0	0.0	0.0	0.0	0.0	0.0	0.0	0.0	0.0	0.0	0.0	0.0	0.0	0.0	0.0	0.0
47	0.0	0.0	0.0	0.0	0.0	0.0	0.0	0.0	0.0	0.0	0.0	0.0	0.0	0.0	0.0	0.0	0.0	0.0	0.0	0.0
46	0.0	0.0	0.0	0.0	0.0	0.0	0.0	0.0	0.0	0.0	0.0	0.0	0.0	0.0	0.0	0.0	0.0	0.0	0.0	0.0
45	0.0	0.0	0.0	0.0	0.0	0.0	0.0	0.0	0.0	0.0	0.0	0.0	0.0	0.0	0.0	0.0	0.0	0.0	0.0	0.0
44	0.0	0.0	0.0	0.0	0.0	0.0	0.0	0.0	0.0	0.0	0.0	0.0	0.0	0.0	0.0	0.0	0.0	0.0	0.0	0.0
43	0.0	0.0	0.0	0.0	0.0	0.0	0.0	0.0	0.0	0.0	0.0	0.0	0.0	0.0	0.0	0.0	0.0	0.0	0.1	0.1
42	0.0	0.0	0.0	0.0	0.0	0.0	0.0	0.0	0.0	0.0	0.0	0.0	0.0	0.0	0.1	0.1	0.2	0.2	0.3	0.4
41	0.0	0.0	0.0	0.0	0.0	0.0	0.0	0.0	0.0	0.0	0.0	0.1	0.2	0.2	0.3	0.4	0.4	0.5	0.5	0.6
40	0.0	0.0	0.0	0.0	0.0	0.0	0.0	0.0	0.1	0.2	0.3	0.3	0.4	0.5	0.5	0.6	0.7	0.7	0.8	0.8
39	0.0	0.0	0.0	0.0	0.0	0.1	0.2	0.3	0.3	0.4	0.5	0.6	0.6	0.7	0.8	0.8	0.9	1.0	1.0	1.1
38	0.0	0.0	0.0	0.1	0.2	0.3	0.4	0.5	0.6	0.7	0.8	0.8	0.9	1.0	1.0	1.1	1.2	1.2	1.3	1.3
37	0.0	0.1	0.3	0.4	0.5	0.6	0.7	0.8	0.9	1.0	1.0	1.1	1.2	1.3	1.3	1.4	1.4	1.5	1.6	1.6
36	0.2	0.4	0.6	0.7	0.8	0.9	1.0	1.1	1.2	1.3	1.3	1.4	1.5	1.6	1.6	1.7	1.7	1.8	1.9	1.9
35	0.5	0.7	0.9	1.0	1.1	1.2	1.3	1.4	1.5	1.6	1.7	1.7	1.8	1.9	1.9	2.0	2.1	2.1	2.2	2.2
34	1.1	1.2	1.3	1.3	1.4	1.5	1.6	1.7	1.8	1.9	2.0	2.0	2.1	2.2	2.3	2.4	2.5	2.6	2.7	2.7
33	2.1	2.2	2.2	2.3	2.4	2.5	2.6	2.6	2.7	2.8	2.9	2.9	3.0	3.1	3.2	3.3	3.3	3.4	3.5	3.6
32	3.1	3.1	3.2	3.3	3.4	3.4	3.5	3.6	3.6	3.7	3.8	3.9	3.9	4.0	4.1	4.1	4.2	4.3	4.4	4.4
31	4.1	4.1	4.2	4.3	4.3	4.4	4.4	4.5	4.6	4.6	4.7	4.8	4.8	4.9	5.0	5.0	5.1	5.1	5.2	5.3
30	5.1	5.1	5.2	5.2	5.3	5.3	5.4	5.4	5.5	5.6	5.6	5.7	5.7	5.8	5.8	5.9	5.9	6.0	6.1	6.1
29	6.0	6.1	6.1	6.2	6.2	6.3	6.3	6.4	6.4	6.5	6.5	6.6	6.6	6.7	6.7	6.8	6.8	6.9	6.9	7.0
28	7.0	7.1	7.1	7.2	7.2	7.2	7.3	7.3	7.4	7.4	7.4	7.5	7.5	7.6	7.6	7.6	7.7	7.7	7.8	7.8
27	8.0	8.1	8.1	8.1	8.2	8.2	8.2	8.3	8.3	8.3	8.4	8.4	8.4	8.4	8.5	8.5	8.5	8.6	8.6	8.6
26	9.0	9.0	9.1	9.1	9.1	9.1	9.2	9.2	9.2	9.2	9.3	9.3	9.3	9.3	9.4	9.4	9.4	9.4	9.5	9.5
25	10.0	10.0	10.0	10.1	10.1	10.1	10.1	10.1	10.1	10.2	10.2	10.2	10.2	10.2	10.2	10.3	10.3	10.3	10.3	10.3
24	11.0	11.0	11.0	11.0	11.0	11.1	11.1	11.1	11.1	11.1	11.1	11.1	11.1	11.1	11.1	11.1	11.1	11.1	11.2	11.2

NUMBER OF WEEKS BEFORE THE OPTION EXPIRES (weeks 21–39)

Common Stock Price	21	22	23	24	25	26	27	28	29	30	31	32	33	34	35	36	37	38	39
49	0.0	0.0	0.0	0.0	0.0	0.0	0.0	0.0	0.0	0.0	0.0	0.0	0.0	0.0	0.0	0.0	0.0	0.0	0.0
48	0.0	0.0	0.0	0.0	0.0	0.0	0.0	0.0	0.0	0.0	0.0	0.0	0.0	0.0	0.0	0.0	0.0	0.0	0.1
47	0.0	0.0	0.0	0.0	0.0	0.0	0.0	0.0	0.0	0.0	0.0	0.0	0.0	0.0	0.1	0.1	0.2	0.2	0.3
46	0.0	0.0	0.0	0.0	0.0	0.0	0.0	0.0	0.0	0.1	0.1	0.1	0.2	0.2	0.3	0.3	0.4	0.4	0.4
45	0.0	0.0	0.0	0.0	0.0	0.1	0.1	0.1	0.2	0.2	0.3	0.3	0.4	0.4	0.5	0.5	0.5	0.6	0.6
44	0.0	0.0	0.1	0.1	0.2	0.2	0.3	0.3	0.4	0.4	0.5	0.5	0.6	0.6	0.7	0.7	0.7	0.8	0.8
43	0.2	0.3	0.3	0.4	0.4	0.5	0.5	0.6	0.6	0.6	0.7	0.7	0.8	0.8	0.9	0.9	0.9	1.0	1.0
42	0.4	0.5	0.5	0.6	0.6	0.7	0.7	0.8	0.8	0.9	0.9	1.0	1.0	1.0	1.1	1.1	1.2	1.2	1.2
41	0.6	0.7	0.7	0.8	0.9	0.9	0.9	1.0	1.0	1.1	1.1	1.2	1.2	1.3	1.3	1.3	1.4	1.4	1.5
40	0.9	0.9	1.0	1.0	1.1	1.1	1.2	1.2	1.3	1.3	1.4	1.4	1.5	1.5	1.5	1.6	1.6	1.7	1.7
39	1.1	1.2	1.2	1.3	1.3	1.4	1.4	1.5	1.5	1.6	1.6	1.7	1.7	1.8	1.8	1.8	1.9	1.9	2.0
38	1.4	1.5	1.5	1.6	1.6	1.7	1.7	1.8	1.8	1.8	1.9	1.9	2.0	2.0	2.1	2.1	2.1	2.2	2.2
37	1.7	1.7	1.8	1.8	1.9	1.9	2.0	2.0	2.1	2.1	2.2	2.2	2.3	2.3	2.3	2.4	2.4	2.5	2.5
36	2.0	2.0	2.1	2.1	2.2	2.2	2.3	2.3	2.4	2.4	2.5	2.5	2.6	2.6	2.6	2.7	2.7	2.8	2.8
35	2.3	2.3	2.4	2.4	2.5	2.5	2.6	2.6	2.7	2.7	2.8	2.8	2.9	2.9	2.9	3.0	3.0	3.1	3.1
34	2.8	2.9	3.0	3.1	3.2	3.3	3.3	3.4	3.5	3.6	3.7	3.7	3.7	3.8	3.8	3.9	3.9	3.9	4.0
33	3.7	3.7	3.8	3.9	4.0	4.1	4.1	4.2	4.3	4.4	4.4	4.5	4.6	4.7	4.8	4.8	4.8	4.9	4.9
32	4.5	4.6	4.6	4.7	4.8	4.9	4.9	5.0	5.1	5.1	5.2	5.3	5.3	5.4	5.5	5.6	5.6	5.7	5.8
31	5.3	5.4	5.5	5.5	5.6	5.6	5.7	5.8	5.8	5.9	6.0	6.0	6.1	6.2	6.2	6.3	6.3	6.4	6.5
30	6.2	6.2	6.3	6.3	6.4	6.4	6.5	6.6	6.6	6.7	6.7	6.8	6.8	6.9	6.9	7.0	7.1	7.1	7.2
29	7.0	7.0	7.1	7.1	7.2	7.2	7.3	7.3	7.4	7.4	7.5	7.5	7.6	7.6	7.7	7.7	7.8	7.8	7.9
28	7.8	7.9	7.9	8.0	8.0	8.0	8.1	8.1	8.2	8.2	8.2	8.3	8.3	8.4	8.4	8.4	8.5	8.5	8.6
27	8.7	8.7	8.7	8.8	8.8	8.8	8.9	8.9	8.9	9.0	9.0	9.0	9.1	9.1	9.1	9.2	9.2	9.2	9.2
26	9.5	9.5	9.6	9.6	9.6	9.6	9.7	9.7	9.7	9.7	9.7	9.8	9.8	9.8	9.8	9.9	9.9	9.9	9.9
25	10.3	10.4	10.4	10.4	10.4	10.4	10.4	10.5	10.5	10.5	10.5	10.5	10.5	10.6	10.6	10.6	10.6	10.6	10.6
24	11.2	11.2	11.2	11.2	11.2	11.2	11.2	11.2	11.2	11.3	11.3	11.3	11.3	11.3	11.3	11.3	11.3	11.3	11.3

LISTED PUT OPTION PRICE WHEN EXERCISE PRICE IS 40

Common Stock Price	NUMBER OF WEEKS BEFORE THE OPTION EXPIRES																																					
	1	2	3	4	5	6	7	8	9	10	11	12	13	14	15	16	17	18	19	20	21	22	23	24	25	26	27	28	29	30	31	32	33	34	35	36	37	38	39
56	0.0	0.0	0.0	0.0	0.0	0.0	0.0	0.0	0.0	0.0	0.0	0.0	0.0	0.0	0.0	0.0	0.0	0.0	0.0	0.0	0.0	0.0	0.0	0.0	0.0	0.0	0.0	0.0	0.0	0.0	0.0	0.0	0.0	0.0	0.0	0.0	0.0	0.0	0.0
55	0.0	0.0	0.0	0.0	0.0	0.0	0.0	0.0	0.0	0.0	0.0	0.0	0.0	0.0	0.0	0.0	0.0	0.0	0.0	0.0	0.0	0.0	0.0	0.0	0.0	0.0	0.0	0.0	0.0	0.0	0.0	0.0	0.0	0.0	0.0	0.0	0.0	0.0	0.1
54	0.0	0.0	0.0	0.0	0.0	0.0	0.0	0.0	0.0	0.0	0.0	0.0	0.0	0.0	0.0	0.0	0.0	0.0	0.0	0.0	0.0	0.0	0.0	0.0	0.0	0.0	0.0	0.0	0.0	0.0	0.0	0.0	0.0	0.0	0.0	0.1	0.1	0.2	0.2
53	0.0	0.0	0.0	0.0	0.0	0.0	0.0	0.0	0.0	0.0	0.0	0.0	0.0	0.0	0.0	0.0	0.0	0.0	0.0	0.0	0.0	0.0	0.0	0.0	0.0	0.0	0.0	0.0	0.0	0.0	0.0	0.1	0.1	0.2	0.2	0.3	0.3	0.4	0.4
52	0.0	0.0	0.0	0.0	0.0	0.0	0.0	0.0	0.0	0.0	0.0	0.0	0.0	0.0	0.0	0.0	0.0	0.0	0.0	0.0	0.0	0.0	0.0	0.0	0.0	0.0	0.0	0.1	0.1	0.2	0.2	0.3	0.3	0.4	0.4	0.5	0.5	0.6	0.6
51	0.0	0.0	0.0	0.0	0.0	0.0	0.0	0.0	0.0	0.0	0.0	0.0	0.0	0.0	0.0	0.0	0.0	0.0	0.0	0.0	0.0	0.0	0.0	0.0	0.1	0.1	0.2	0.3	0.3	0.4	0.4	0.5	0.5	0.6	0.6	0.7	0.7	0.7	0.8
50	0.0	0.0	0.0	0.0	0.0	0.0	0.0	0.0	0.0	0.0	0.0	0.0	0.0	0.0	0.0	0.0	0.0	0.0	0.0	0.0	0.0	0.1	0.2	0.2	0.3	0.3	0.4	0.5	0.5	0.6	0.6	0.7	0.7	0.8	0.8	0.9	0.9	0.9	1.0
49	0.0	0.0	0.0	0.0	0.0	0.0	0.0	0.0	0.0	0.0	0.0	0.0	0.0	0.0	0.0	0.0	0.0	0.1	0.1	0.2	0.3	0.3	0.4	0.4	0.5	0.6	0.6	0.7	0.7	0.8	0.8	0.9	0.9	1.0	1.0	1.1	1.1	1.2	1.2
48	0.0	0.0	0.0	0.0	0.0	0.0	0.0	0.0	0.0	0.0	0.0	0.0	0.0	0.0	0.1	0.1	0.2	0.3	0.3	0.4	0.5	0.5	0.6	0.7	0.7	0.8	0.8	0.9	0.9	1.0	1.0	1.1	1.1	1.2	1.2	1.3	1.3	1.4	1.4
47	0.0	0.0	0.0	0.0	0.0	0.0	0.0	0.0	0.0	0.0	0.0	0.1	0.1	0.2	0.3	0.4	0.4	0.5	0.6	0.6	0.7	0.8	0.8	0.9	0.9	1.0	1.1	1.1	1.2	1.2	1.3	1.3	1.4	1.4	1.5	1.5	1.6	1.6	1.6
46	0.0	0.0	0.0	0.0	0.0	0.0	0.0	0.0	0.0	0.1	0.2	0.3	0.4	0.5	0.5	0.6	0.7	0.7	0.8	0.9	0.9	1.0	1.1	1.1	1.2	1.2	1.3	1.3	1.4	1.4	1.5	1.6	1.6	1.6	1.7	1.7	1.8	1.8	1.9
45	0.0	0.0	0.0	0.0	0.0	0.0	0.1	0.2	0.3	0.4	0.5	0.5	0.6	0.7	0.8	0.9	0.9	1.0	1.1	1.1	1.2	1.2	1.3	1.4	1.4	1.5	1.5	1.6	1.6	1.7	1.7	1.8	1.8	1.9	1.9	2.0	2.0	2.1	2.1
44	0.0	0.0	0.0	0.0	0.1	0.2	0.3	0.4	0.5	0.6	0.7	0.8	0.9	1.0	1.0	1.1	1.2	1.3	1.3	1.4	1.4	1.5	1.6	1.6	1.7	1.7	1.8	1.8	1.9	2.0	2.0	2.1	2.1	2.2	2.2	2.3	2.3	2.3	2.4
43	0.0	0.0	0.1	0.2	0.4	0.5	0.6	0.7	0.8	0.9	1.0	1.1	1.2	1.2	1.3	1.4	1.5	1.5	1.6	1.7	1.7	1.8	1.8	1.9	2.0	2.0	2.1	2.1	2.2	2.2	2.3	2.3	2.4	2.4	2.5	2.5	2.6	2.6	2.7
42	0.0	0.2	0.4	0.5	0.7	0.8	0.9	1.0	1.1	1.2	1.3	1.4	1.4	1.5	1.6	1.7	1.7	1.8	1.9	1.9	2.0	2.1	2.1	2.2	2.2	2.3	2.3	2.4	2.5	2.5	2.6	2.6	2.7	2.7	2.8	2.8	2.9	2.9	2.9
41	0.3	0.5	0.7	0.8	1.0	1.1	1.2	1.3	1.4	1.5	1.6	1.7	1.7	1.8	1.9	2.0	2.0	2.1	2.2	2.2	2.3	2.4	2.4	2.5	2.5	2.6	2.6	2.7	2.8	2.8	2.9	2.9	3.0	3.0	3.1	3.1	3.2	3.2	3.2
40	0.6	0.8	1.0	1.1	1.3	1.4	1.5	1.6	1.7	1.8	1.9	2.0	2.1	2.1	2.2	2.3	2.3	2.4	2.5	2.5	2.6	2.7	2.7	2.8	2.8	2.9	3.0	3.0	3.1	3.1	3.2	3.2	3.3	3.3	3.4	3.4	3.5	3.5	3.6
39	1.1	1.2	1.3	1.4	1.5	1.6	1.7	1.8	1.9	2.0	2.1	2.2	2.3	2.4	2.5	2.6	2.7	2.8	2.9	3.0	3.1	3.2	3.3	3.4	3.5	3.6	3.7	3.8	3.9	4.0	4.1	4.1	4.2	4.2	4.2	4.2	4.3	4.4	4.5
38	2.1	2.2	2.3	2.4	2.5	2.6	2.6	2.7	2.8	2.9	3.0	3.1	3.2	3.3	3.4	3.5	3.6	3.7	3.8	3.9	3.9	4.0	4.1	4.2	4.3	4.4	4.5	4.6	4.7	4.8	4.9	5.0	5.1	5.1	5.1	5.1	5.2	5.3	5.4
37	3.1	3.2	3.3	3.3	3.4	3.5	3.6	3.7	3.8	3.8	3.9	4.0	4.1	4.2	4.3	4.4	4.4	4.5	4.6	4.7	4.8	4.9	4.9	5.0	5.1	5.2	5.3	5.4	5.5	5.5	5.6	5.7	5.8	5.9	6.0	6.0	6.1	6.2	6.3
36	4.1	4.2	4.2	4.3	4.4	4.5	4.5	4.6	4.7	4.8	4.8	4.9	5.0	5.1	5.2	5.2	5.3	5.4	5.5	5.5	5.6	5.7	5.8	5.8	5.9	6.0	6.1	6.2	6.2	6.3	6.4	6.5	6.5	6.6	6.7	6.8	6.8	6.9	7.0
35	5.1	5.1	5.2	5.3	5.3	5.4	5.5	5.6	5.6	5.7	5.8	5.8	5.9	6.0	6.0	6.1	6.2	6.2	6.3	6.4	6.4	6.5	6.6	6.7	6.7	6.8	6.9	6.9	7.0	7.1	7.1	7.2	7.3	7.3	7.4	7.5	7.6	7.6	7.7
34	6.1	6.1	6.2	6.2	6.3	6.4	6.4	6.5	6.6	6.6	6.7	6.7	6.8	6.9	6.9	7.0	7.0	7.1	7.2	7.2	7.3	7.3	7.4	7.5	7.5	7.6	7.7	7.7	7.8	7.8	7.9	8.0	8.0	8.1	8.1	8.2	8.3	8.3	8.4
33	7.1	7.1	7.2	7.2	7.3	7.3	7.4	7.4	7.5	7.5	7.6	7.6	7.7	7.7	7.8	7.9	7.9	8.0	8.0	8.1	8.1	8.2	8.2	8.3	8.3	8.4	8.4	8.5	8.5	8.6	8.7	8.7	8.8	8.8	8.9	8.9	9.0	9.0	9.1
32	8.0	8.1	8.1	8.2	8.2	8.3	8.3	8.4	8.4	8.5	8.5	8.5	8.6	8.6	8.7	8.7	8.8	8.8	8.9	8.9	9.0	9.0	9.0	9.1	9.1	9.2	9.2	9.3	9.3	9.4	9.4	9.5	9.5	9.5	9.6	9.6	9.7	9.7	9.8
31	9.0	9.1	9.1	9.2	9.2	9.2	9.3	9.3	9.3	9.4	9.4	9.5	9.5	9.5	9.6	9.6	9.6	9.7	9.7	9.8	9.8	9.8	9.9	9.9	9.9	9.9	10.0	10.1	10.1	10.1	10.2	10.2	10.2	10.3	10.3	10.4	10.4	10.4	10.5
30	10.0	10.1	10.1	10.1	10.1	10.2	10.2	10.2	10.3	10.3	10.3	10.4	10.4	10.4	10.4	10.5	10.5	10.5	10.6	10.6	10.6	10.7	10.7	10.7	10.7	10.8	10.8	10.8	10.9	10.9	10.9	11.0	11.0	11.0	11.0	11.1	11.1	11.1	11.2
29	11.0	11.0	11.1	11.1	11.1	11.1	11.2	11.2	11.2	11.2	11.2	11.3	11.3	11.3	11.3	11.4	11.4	11.4	11.4	11.4	11.5	11.5	11.5	11.5	11.6	11.6	11.6	11.6	11.6	11.7	11.7	11.7	11.7	11.7	11.8	11.8	11.8	11.8	11.9
28	12.0	12.0	12.0	12.1	12.1	12.1	12.1	12.1	12.1	12.1	12.2	12.2	12.2	12.2	12.2	12.2	12.2	12.3	12.3	12.3	12.3	12.3	12.3	12.3	12.4	12.4	12.4	12.4	12.4	12.4	12.4	12.5	12.5	12.5	12.5	12.5	12.5	12.5	12.6
27	13.0	13.0	13.0	13.0	13.0	13.0	13.0	13.1	13.1	13.1	13.1	13.1	13.1	13.1	13.1	13.1	13.1	13.1	13.1	13.1	13.1	13.1	13.1	13.2	13.2	13.2	13.2	13.2	13.2	13.2	13.2	13.2	13.2	13.2	13.2	13.2	13.2	13.2	13.2

LISTED PUT OPTION PRICE WHEN EXERCISE PRICE IS 45

Common Stock Price	NUMBER OF WEEKS BEFORE THE OPTION EXPIRES 1	2	3	4	5	6	7	8	9	10	11	12	13	14	15	16	17	18	19	20	21	22	23	24	25	26	27	28	29	30	31	32	33	34	35	36	37	38	39
63	0.0	0.0	0.0	0.0	0.0	0.0	0.0	0.0	0.0	0.0	0.0	0.0	0.0	0.0	0.0	0.0	0.0	0.0	0.0	0.0	0.0	0.0	0.0	0.0	0.0	0.0	0.0	0.0	0.0	0.0	0.0	0.0	0.0	0.0	0.0	0.0	0.0	0.0	0.0
62	0.0	0.0	0.0	0.0	0.0	0.0	0.0	0.0	0.0	0.0	0.0	0.0	0.0	0.0	0.0	0.0	0.0	0.0	0.0	0.0	0.0	0.0	0.0	0.0	0.0	0.0	0.0	0.0	0.0	0.0	0.0	0.0	0.0	0.0	0.0	0.0	0.0	0.0	0.1
61	0.0	0.0	0.0	0.0	0.0	0.0	0.0	0.0	0.0	0.0	0.0	0.0	0.0	0.0	0.0	0.0	0.0	0.0	0.0	0.0	0.0	0.0	0.0	0.0	0.0	0.0	0.0	0.0	0.0	0.0	0.0	0.0	0.0	0.0	0.0	0.1	0.1	0.2	0.2
60	0.0	0.0	0.0	0.0	0.0	0.0	0.0	0.0	0.0	0.0	0.0	0.0	0.0	0.0	0.0	0.0	0.0	0.0	0.0	0.0	0.0	0.0	0.0	0.0	0.0	0.0	0.0	0.0	0.0	0.0	0.0	0.0	0.1	0.1	0.2	0.2	0.3	0.3	0.4
59	0.0	0.0	0.0	0.0	0.0	0.0	0.0	0.0	0.0	0.0	0.0	0.0	0.0	0.0	0.0	0.0	0.0	0.0	0.0	0.0	0.0	0.0	0.0	0.0	0.0	0.0	0.0	0.0	0.0	0.1	0.1	0.2	0.3	0.3	0.4	0.4	0.5	0.5	0.6
58	0.0	0.0	0.0	0.0	0.0	0.0	0.0	0.0	0.0	0.0	0.0	0.0	0.0	0.0	0.0	0.0	0.0	0.0	0.0	0.0	0.0	0.0	0.0	0.0	0.0	0.0	0.1	0.2	0.2	0.3	0.3	0.4	0.5	0.5	0.6	0.6	0.7	0.7	0.8
57	0.0	0.0	0.0	0.0	0.0	0.0	0.0	0.0	0.0	0.0	0.0	0.0	0.0	0.0	0.0	0.0	0.0	0.0	0.0	0.0	0.0	0.0	0.0	0.1	0.2	0.2	0.3	0.4	0.4	0.5	0.5	0.6	0.6	0.7	0.8	0.8	0.9	0.9	1.0
56	0.0	0.0	0.0	0.0	0.0	0.0	0.0	0.0	0.0	0.0	0.0	0.0	0.0	0.0	0.0	0.0	0.0	0.0	0.0	0.0	0.1	0.2	0.2	0.3	0.4	0.4	0.5	0.6	0.6	0.7	0.7	0.8	0.9	0.9	1.0	1.0	1.1	1.1	1.2
55	0.0	0.0	0.0	0.0	0.0	0.0	0.0	0.0	0.0	0.0	0.0	0.0	0.0	0.0	0.0	0.0	0.0	0.1	0.2	0.2	0.3	0.4	0.5	0.5	0.6	0.6	0.7	0.8	0.8	0.9	0.9	1.0	1.1	1.1	1.2	1.2	1.3	1.3	1.4
54	0.0	0.0	0.0	0.0	0.0	0.0	0.0	0.0	0.0	0.0	0.0	0.0	0.0	0.0	0.1	0.2	0.2	0.3	0.4	0.5	0.5	0.6	0.7	0.7	0.8	0.9	0.9	1.0	1.0	1.1	1.2	1.2	1.3	1.3	1.4	1.4	1.5	1.5	1.6
53	0.0	0.0	0.0	0.0	0.0	0.0	0.0	0.0	0.0	0.0	0.0	0.0	0.1	0.2	0.3	0.4	0.5	0.5	0.6	0.7	0.8	0.8	0.9	1.0	1.0	1.1	1.2	1.2	1.3	1.3	1.4	1.4	1.5	1.6	1.6	1.7	1.7	1.8	1.8
52	0.0	0.0	0.0	0.0	0.0	0.0	0.0	0.0	0.0	0.1	0.2	0.3	0.4	0.5	0.5	0.6	0.7	0.8	0.9	0.9	1.0	1.1	1.1	1.2	1.3	1.3	1.4	1.5	1.5	1.6	1.6	1.7	1.7	1.8	1.9	1.9	2.0	2.0	2.1
51	0.0	0.0	0.0	0.0	0.0	0.0	0.0	0.1	0.2	0.3	0.4	0.5	0.6	0.7	0.8	0.9	0.9	1.0	1.1	1.2	1.2	1.3	1.4	1.4	1.5	1.6	1.6	1.7	1.8	1.8	1.9	1.9	2.0	2.0	2.1	2.1	2.2	2.3	2.3
50	0.0	0.0	0.0	0.0	0.0	0.1	0.3	0.4	0.5	0.6	0.7	0.8	0.9	1.0	1.0	1.1	1.2	1.3	1.4	1.4	1.5	1.6	1.6	1.7	1.8	1.8	1.9	1.9	2.0	2.1	2.1	2.2	2.2	2.3	2.3	2.4	2.5	2.5	2.6
49	0.0	0.0	0.0	0.1	0.3	0.4	0.5	0.6	0.7	0.8	0.9	1.0	1.1	1.2	1.3	1.4	1.5	1.5	1.6	1.7	1.8	1.8	1.9	2.0	2.0	2.1	2.2	2.2	2.3	2.3	2.4	2.4	2.5	2.6	2.6	2.7	2.7	2.8	2.8
48	0.0	0.0	0.2	0.4	0.5	0.7	0.8	0.9	1.0	1.1	1.2	1.3	1.4	1.5	1.6	1.7	1.7	1.8	1.9	2.0	2.0	2.1	2.2	2.2	2.3	2.4	2.4	2.5	2.5	2.6	2.7	2.7	2.8	2.8	2.9	2.9	3.0	3.0	3.1
47	0.0	0.3	0.5	0.7	0.8	1.0	1.1	1.2	1.3	1.4	1.5	1.6	1.7	1.8	1.9	1.9	2.0	2.1	2.2	2.3	2.3	2.4	2.5	2.5	2.6	2.7	2.7	2.8	2.8	2.9	3.0	3.0	3.1	3.1	3.2	3.2	3.3	3.3	3.4
46	0.3	0.6	0.8	1.0	1.1	1.3	1.4	1.5	1.6	1.7	1.8	1.9	2.0	2.1	2.2	2.2	2.3	2.4	2.5	2.6	2.6	2.7	2.8	2.8	2.9	3.0	3.0	3.1	3.1	3.2	3.3	3.3	3.4	3.4	3.5	3.5	3.6	3.6	3.7
45	0.6	0.9	1.1	1.3	1.4	1.6	1.7	1.8	1.9	2.0	2.1	2.2	2.3	2.4	2.5	2.6	2.6	2.7	2.8	2.9	2.9	3.0	3.1	3.1	3.2	3.3	3.3	3.4	3.4	3.5	3.6	3.6	3.7	3.7	3.8	3.8	3.9	3.9	4.0
44	1.1	1.2	1.3	1.5	1.7	1.8	1.9	2.0	2.2	2.3	2.4	2.5	2.6	2.7	2.8	2.9	3.0	3.1	3.2	3.3	3.4	3.5	3.6	3.7	3.8	4.0	4.1	4.2	4.3	4.4	4.5	4.5	4.6	4.6	4.7	4.7	4.8	4.8	4.9
43	2.1	2.2	2.3	2.4	2.5	2.6	2.7	2.8	3.0	3.1	3.2	3.3	3.4	3.5	3.6	3.7	3.8	3.9	4.0	4.1	4.2	4.3	4.4	4.5	4.7	4.8	4.9	5.0	5.1	5.2	5.3	5.4	5.4	5.4	5.5	5.6	5.7	5.7	5.8
42	3.1	3.2	3.3	3.4	3.5	3.6	3.7	3.8	3.9	4.0	4.1	4.2	4.3	4.4	4.5	4.6	4.7	4.8	4.9	5.0	5.1	5.2	5.3	5.4	5.5	5.6	5.7	5.8	5.8	5.9	6.0	6.1	6.2	6.3	6.4	6.5	6.5	6.6	6.7
41	4.1	4.2	4.3	4.4	4.5	4.5	4.6	4.7	4.8	4.9	5.0	5.1	5.2	5.3	5.4	5.4	5.5	5.6	5.7	5.8	5.9	6.0	6.1	6.2	6.3	6.4	6.4	6.5	6.6	6.7	6.8	6.9	7.0	7.1	7.2	7.3	7.3	7.4	7.5
40	5.1	5.2	5.2	5.3	5.4	5.5	5.6	5.7	5.7	5.8	5.9	6.0	6.1	6.2	6.2	6.3	6.4	6.5	6.6	6.7	6.7	6.8	6.9	7.0	7.1	7.1	7.2	7.3	7.4	7.5	7.6	7.6	7.7	7.8	7.9	8.0	8.1	8.1	8.2
39	6.1	6.1	6.2	6.3	6.4	6.4	6.5	6.6	6.7	6.7	6.8	6.9	7.0	7.0	7.1	7.2	7.3	7.3	7.4	7.5	7.6	7.6	7.7	7.8	7.9	7.9	8.0	8.1	8.2	8.2	8.3	8.4	8.5	8.5	8.6	8.7	8.8	8.8	8.9
38	7.1	7.1	7.2	7.3	7.3	7.4	7.5	7.5	7.6	7.7	7.7	7.8	7.9	7.9	8.0	8.1	8.1	8.2	8.3	8.3	8.4	8.5	8.5	8.6	8.7	8.7	8.8	8.9	8.9	9.0	9.1	9.1	9.2	9.3	9.3	9.4	9.5	9.5	9.6
37	8.1	8.1	8.2	8.2	8.3	8.4	8.4	8.5	8.5	8.6	8.6	8.7	8.8	8.8	8.9	8.9	9.0	9.1	9.1	9.2	9.2	9.3	9.4	9.4	9.5	9.5	9.6	9.7	9.7	9.8	9.8	9.9	9.9	10.0	10.1	10.1	10.2	10.2	10.3
36	9.1	9.1	9.2	9.2	9.3	9.3	9.4	9.4	9.5	9.5	9.6	9.6	9.7	9.7	9.8	9.8	9.9	9.9	9.9	10.0	10.1	10.1	10.2	10.2	10.3	10.3	10.4	10.4	10.5	10.5	10.6	10.6	10.7	10.7	10.8	10.8	10.9	10.9	11.0
35	10.0	10.1	10.1	10.2	10.2	10.3	10.3	10.3	10.4	10.4	10.5	10.5	10.6	10.6	10.7	10.7	10.7	10.8	10.8	10.9	10.9	11.0	11.0	11.0	11.1	11.1	11.2	11.2	11.3	11.3	11.3	11.4	11.4	11.5	11.5	11.6	11.6	11.6	11.7
34	11.0	11.1	11.1	11.1	11.2	11.2	11.2	11.3	11.3	11.4	11.4	11.4	11.5	11.5	11.5	11.6	11.6	11.6	11.7	11.7	11.7	11.8	11.8	11.9	11.9	11.9	12.0	12.0	12.0	12.1	12.1	12.1	12.2	12.2	12.2	12.3	12.3	12.4	12.4
33	12.0	12.1	12.1	12.1	12.1	12.2	12.2	12.2	12.2	12.3	12.3	12.3	12.4	12.4	12.4	12.4	12.5	12.5	12.5	12.6	12.6	12.6	12.6	12.7	12.7	12.7	12.7	12.8	12.8	12.8	12.9	12.9	12.9	12.9	13.0	13.0	13.0	13.1	13.1
32	13.0	13.0	13.1	13.1	13.1	13.1	13.1	13.2	13.2	13.2	13.2	13.2	13.3	13.3	13.3	13.3	13.3	13.4	13.4	13.4	13.4	13.4	13.5	13.5	13.5	13.5	13.5	13.6	13.6	13.6	13.6	13.6	13.7	13.7	13.7	13.7	13.7	13.8	13.8
31	14.0	14.0	14.0	14.0	14.1	14.1	14.1	14.1	14.1	14.1	14.1	14.1	14.2	14.2	14.2	14.2	14.2	14.2	14.2	14.2	14.3	14.3	14.3	14.3	14.3	14.3	14.3	14.3	14.3	14.4	14.4	14.4	14.4	14.4	14.4	14.4	14.4	14.5	14.5
30	15.0	15.0	15.0	15.0	15.0	15.0	15.0	15.0	15.0	15.0	15.0	15.1	15.1	15.1	15.1	15.1	15.1	15.1	15.1	15.1	15.1	15.1	15.1	15.1	15.1	15.1	15.1	15.1	15.1	15.1	15.1	15.1	15.1	15.1	15.1	15.2	15.2	15.2	15.2

LISTED PUT OPTION PRICE WHEN EXERCISE PRICE IS 50

NUMBER OF WEEKS BEFORE THE OPTION EXPIRES

Common Stock Price	1	2	3	4	5	6	7	8	9	10	11	12	13	14	15	16	17	18	19	20
65	0.0	0.0	0.0	0.0	0.0	0.0	0.0	0.0	0.0	0.0	0.0	0.0	0.0	0.0	0.0	0.0	0.0	0.0	0.0	0.0
64	0.0	0.0	0.0	0.0	0.0	0.0	0.0	0.0	0.0	0.0	0.0	0.0	0.0	0.0	0.0	0.0	0.0	0.0	0.0	0.0
63	0.0	0.0	0.0	0.0	0.0	0.0	0.0	0.0	0.0	0.0	0.0	0.0	0.0	0.0	0.0	0.0	0.0	0.0	0.0	0.0
62	0.0	0.0	0.0	0.0	0.0	0.0	0.0	0.0	0.0	0.0	0.0	0.0	0.0	0.0	0.0	0.0	0.0	0.0	0.0	0.1
61	0.0	0.0	0.0	0.0	0.0	0.0	0.0	0.0	0.0	0.0	0.0	0.0	0.0	0.0	0.0	0.0	0.0	0.1	0.2	0.3
60	0.0	0.0	0.0	0.0	0.0	0.0	0.0	0.0	0.0	0.0	0.0	0.0	0.0	0.0	0.1	0.2	0.3	0.4	0.4	0.5
59	0.0	0.0	0.0	0.0	0.0	0.0	0.0	0.0	0.0	0.0	0.0	0.0	0.1	0.2	0.3	0.4	0.5	0.6	0.7	0.7
58	0.0	0.0	0.0	0.0	0.0	0.0	0.0	0.0	0.0	0.0	0.2	0.3	0.4	0.5	0.5	0.6	0.7	0.8	0.9	1.0
57	0.0	0.0	0.0	0.0	0.0	0.0	0.0	0.0	0.2	0.3	0.4	0.5	0.6	0.7	0.8	0.9	1.0	1.1	1.1	1.2
56	0.0	0.0	0.0	0.0	0.0	0.0	0.2	0.3	0.4	0.5	0.6	0.8	0.9	0.9	1.0	1.1	1.2	1.3	1.4	1.5
55	0.0	0.0	0.0	0.0	0.1	0.3	0.4	0.6	0.7	0.8	0.9	1.0	1.1	1.2	1.3	1.4	1.5	1.6	1.6	1.7
54	0.0	0.0	0.0	0.2	0.4	0.6	0.7	0.8	0.9	1.1	1.2	1.3	1.4	1.5	1.6	1.7	1.7	1.8	1.9	2.0
53	0.0	0.1	0.3	0.5	0.7	0.8	1.0	1.1	1.2	1.3	1.5	1.6	1.7	1.8	1.9	1.9	2.0	2.1	2.2	2.3
52	0.1	0.4	0.6	0.8	1.0	1.1	1.3	1.4	1.5	1.6	1.7	1.8	2.0	2.0	2.1	2.2	2.3	2.4	2.5	2.6
51	0.4	0.7	0.9	1.1	1.3	1.4	1.6	1.7	1.8	1.9	2.0	2.2	2.3	2.3	2.4	2.5	2.6	2.7	2.8	2.9
50	0.7	1.0	1.2	1.4	1.6	1.7	1.9	2.0	2.1	2.3	2.4	2.5	2.6	2.7	2.8	2.8	2.9	3.0	3.1	3.2
49	1.1	1.3	1.4	1.6	1.8	1.9	2.1	2.2	2.3	2.4	2.6	2.7	2.8	2.9	3.0	3.0	3.2	3.3	3.4	3.5
48	2.1	2.2	2.4	2.5	2.6	2.7	2.8	3.0	3.1	3.2	3.3	3.4	3.6	3.7	3.8	3.9	4.0	4.2	4.3	4.4
47	3.1	3.2	3.3	3.4	3.6	3.7	3.8	3.9	4.0	4.1	4.2	4.3	4.5	4.6	4.7	4.8	4.9	5.0	5.1	5.2
46	4.1	4.2	4.3	4.4	4.5	4.6	4.7	4.8	4.9	5.0	5.1	5.2	5.4	5.5	5.6	5.7	5.8	5.9	6.0	6.1
45	5.1	5.2	5.3	5.4	5.5	5.6	5.7	5.8	5.9	6.0	6.1	6.2	6.2	6.3	6.4	6.5	6.6	6.7	6.8	6.9
44	6.1	6.2	6.3	6.4	6.4	6.5	6.6	6.7	6.8	6.9	7.0	7.1	7.1	7.2	7.3	7.4	7.5	7.6	7.7	7.8
43	7.1	7.2	7.2	7.3	7.4	7.5	7.6	7.6	7 7	7.8	7.9	8.0	8.0	8.1	8.2	8.3	8.4	8.4	8.5	8.6
42	8.1	8.1	8.2	8.3	8.4	8.4	8.5	8.6	8.7	8.7	8.8	8.9	8.9	9.0	9.1	9.2	9.2	9.3	9.4	9.5
41	9.1	9.1	9.2	9.3	9.3	9.4	9.5	9.5	9.6	9.6	9.7	9.8	9.8	9.9	9.9	10.0	10.1	10.2	10.2	10.3
40	10.1	10.1	10.2	10.2	10.3	10.3	10.4	10.5	10.5	10.6	10.6	10.7	10.7	10.8	10.9	10.9	11.0	11.0	11.1	11.1
39	11.0	11.1	11.1	11.2	11.2	11.3	11.3	11.4	11.4	11.5	11.5	11.6	11.6	11.7	11.7	11.8	11.8	11.9	11.9	12.0
38	12.0	12.1	12.1	12.2	12.2	12.2	12.3	12.3	12.4	12.4	12.5	12.5	12.5	12.6	12.6	12.7	12.7	12.7	12.8	12.8
37	13.0	13.1	13.1	13.1	13.2	13.2	13.2	13.3	13.3	13.3	13.4	13.4	13.4	13.5	13.5	13.5	13.6	13.6	13.6	13.7
36	14.0	14.1	14.1	14.1	14.1	14.2	14.2	14.2	14.2	14.3	14.3	14.3	14.3	14.4	14.4	14.4	14.4	14.5	14.5	14.5
35	15.0	15.0	15.1	15.1	15.1	15.1	15.1	15.1	15.2	15.2	15.2	15.2	15.2	15.2	15.3	15.3	15.3	15.3	15.3	15.3

Common Stock Price	21	22	23	24	25	26	27	28	29	30	31	32	33	34	35	36	37	38	39
65	0.0	0.0	0.0	0.0	0.0	0.0	0.0	0.1	0.1	0.2	0.3	0.3	0.4	0.5	0.5	0.6	0.6	0.7	0.8
64	0.0	0.0	0.0	0.0	0.1	0.1	0.2	0.3	0.3	0.4	0.5	0.5	0.6	0.6	0.7	0.8	0.8	0.9	0.9
63	0.0	0.0	0.1	0.2	0.3	0.3	0.4	0.5	0.5	0.6	0.7	0.7	0.8	0.8	0.9	1.0	1.0	1.1	1.1
62	0.2	0.2	0.3	0.4	0.5	0.5	0.6	0.7	0.7	0.8	0.9	0.9	1.0	1.1	1.1	1.2	1.2	1.3	1.3
61	0.4	0.5	0.5	0.6	0.7	0.7	0.8	0.9	0.9	1.0	1.1	1.1	1.2	1.3	1.3	1.4	1.4	1.5	1.6
60	0.6	0.7	0.7	0.8	0.9	1.0	1.0	1.1	1.2	1.2	1.3	1.4	1.4	1.5	1.5	1.6	1.7	1.7	1.8
59	0.8	0.9	1.0	1.0	1.1	1.2	1.3	1.3	1.4	1.5	1.5	1.6	1.6	1.7	1.8	1.8	1.9	1.9	2.0
58	1.1	1.1	1.2	1.3	1.4	1.4	1.5	1.6	1.6	1.7	1.8	1.8	1.9	1.9	2.0	2.1	2.1	2.2	2.2
57	1.3	1.4	1.4	1.5	1.6	1.7	1.7	1.8	1.9	1.9	2.0	2.1	2.1	2.2	2.2	2.3	2.4	2.4	2.5
56	1.5	1.6	1.7	1.8	1.8	1.9	2.0	2.1	2.1	2.2	2.2	2.3	2.4	2.4	2.5	2.6	2.6	2.7	2.7
55	1.8	1.9	2.0	2.0	2.1	2.2	2.2	2.3	2.4	2.4	2.5	2.6	2.6	2.7	2.8	2.8	2.9	2.9	3.0
54	2.1	2.2	2.2	2.3	2.4	2.4	2.5	2.6	2.6	2.7	2.8	2.8	2.9	3.0	3.0	3.1	3.1	3.2	3.3
53	2.4	2.4	2.5	2.6	2.7	2.7	2.8	2.9	2.9	3.0	3.1	3.1	3.2	3.2	3.3	3.4	3.4	3.5	3.5
52	2.6	2.7	2.8	2.9	2.9	3.0	3.1	3.2	3.2	3.3	3.3	3.4	3.5	3.5	3.6	3.7	3.7	3.8	3.8
51	2.9	3.0	3.1	3.2	3.2	3.3	3.4	3.5	3.5	3.6	3.6	3.7	3.8	3.8	3.9	4.0	4.0	4.1	4.1
50	3.3	3.3	3.4	3.5	3.6	3.6	3.7	3.8	3.8	3.9	4.0	4.0	4.1	4.1	4.2	4.3	4.3	4.4	4.4
49	3.7	3.8	3.9	4.1	4.2	4.3	4.4	4.6	4.7	4.8	4.8	4.8	5.0	5.0	5.1	5.2	5.2	5.3	5.3
48	4.5	4.6	4.8	4.9	5.0	5.1	5.2	5.3	5.5	5.6	5.7	5.7	5.8	5.8	6.0	6.1	6.1	6.2	6.2
47	5.3	5.5	5.6	5.7	5.8	5.9	6.0	6.1	6.2	6.4	6.5	6.5	6.6	6.6	6.8	7.0	7.0	7.1	7.1
46	6.2	6.3	6.4	6.5	6.6	6.7	6.8	6.9	7.0	7.1	7.2	7.3	7.4	7.5	7.6	7.7	7.8	7.9	8.0
45	7.0	7.1	7.2	7.3	7.4	7.5	7.6	7.7	7.8	7.9	8.0	8.1	8.2	8.3	8.4	8.5	8.6	8.7	8.7
44	7.9	7.9	8.0	8.1	8.2	8.3	8.4	8.5	8.6	8.6	8.7	8.8	8.9	9.0	9.1	9.2	9.3	9.4	9.4
43	8.7	8.8	8.8	8.9	9.0	9.1	9.2	9.3	9.3	9.4	9.5	9.6	9.7	9.7	9.8	9.9	9.9	10.1	10.1
42	9.5	9.6	9.7	9.7	9.8	9.9	9.9	10.0	10.1	10.2	10.3	10.3	10.4	10.5	10.5	10.6	10.7	10.8	10.8
41	10.4	10.4	10.5	10.6	10.6	10.7	10.7	10.8	10.9	10.9	11.0	11.1	11.1	11.2	11.3	11.3	11.4	11.5	11.5
40	11.2	11.3	11.3	11.4	11.4	11.5	11.5	11.6	11.7	11.7	11.8	11.8	11.9	11.9	12.0	12.0	12.1	12.2	12.2
39	12.0	12.1	12.1	12.2	12.2	12.3	12.3	12.4	12.4	12.5	12.5	12.6	12.6	12.7	12.7	12.8	12.8	12.9	12.9
38	12.9	12.9	12.9	13.0	13.0	13.1	13.1	13.2	13.2	13.2	13.3	13.3	13.4	13.4	13.4	13.5	13.5	13.6	13.6
37	13.7	13.7	13.8	13.8	13.8	13.9	13.9	13.9	14.0	14.0	14.0	14.1	14.1	14.1	14.2	14.2	14.2	14.3	14.3
36	14.5	14.6	14.6	14.6	14.6	14.7	14.7	14.7	14.7	14.8	14.8	14.8	14.8	14.9	14.9	14.9	14.9	15.0	15.0
35	15.4	15.4	15.4	15.4	15.4	15.5	15.5	15.5	15.5	15.5	15.5	15.6	15.6	15.6	15.6	15.6	15.7	15.7	15.7

LISTED PUT OPTION PRICE WHEN EXERCISE PRICE IS 60

Common Stock Price	NUMBER OF WEEKS BEFORE THE OPTION EXPIRES																																					
	1	2	3	4	5	6	7	8	9	10	11	12	13	14	15	16	17	18	19	20	21	22	23	24	25	26	27	28	29	30	31	32	33	34	35	36	37	38	39
78	0.0	0.0	0.0	0.0	0.0	0.0	0.0	0.0	0.0	0.0	0.0	0.0	0.0	0.0	0.0	0.0	0.0	0.0	0.0	0.0	0.0	0.0	0.0	0.0	0.0	0.0	0.0	0.1	0.2	0.2	0.3	0.4	0.5	0.5	0.6	0.7	0.8	0.8	0.9
77	0.0	0.0	0.0	0.0	0.0	0.0	0.0	0.0	0.0	0.0	0.0	0.0	0.0	0.0	0.0	0.0	0.0	0.0	0.0	0.0	0.0	0.0	0.0	0.0	0.0	0.1	0.2	0.3	0.4	0.4	0.5	0.6	0.7	0.7	0.8	0.9	1.0	1.0	1.1
76	0.0	0.0	0.0	0.0	0.0	0.0	0.0	0.0	0.0	0.0	0.0	0.0	0.0	0.0	0.0	0.0	0.0	0.0	0.0	0.0	0.0	0.0	0.1	0.1	0.2	0.3	0.4	0.5	0.6	0.6	0.7	0.8	0.9	0.9	1.0	1.1	1.2	1.2	1.3
75	0.0	0.0	0.0	0.0	0.0	0.0	0.0	0.0	0.0	0.0	0.0	0.0	0.0	0.0	0.0	0.0	0.0	0.0	0.0	0.0	0.1	0.2	0.3	0.3	0.4	0.5	0.6	0.7	0.8	0.8	0.9	1.0	1.1	1.1	1.2	1.3	1.4	1.4	1.5
74	0.0	0.0	0.0	0.0	0.0	0.0	0.0	0.0	0.0	0.0	0.0	0.0	0.0	0.0	0.0	0.0	0.0	0.0	0.1	0.2	0.3	0.4	0.5	0.6	0.6	0.7	0.8	0.9	1.0	1.0	1.1	1.2	1.3	1.3	1.4	1.5	1.6	1.6	1.7
73	0.0	0.0	0.0	0.0	0.0	0.0	0.0	0.0	0.0	0.0	0.0	0.0	0.0	0.0	0.0	0.0	0.1	0.2	0.3	0.4	0.5	0.6	0.7	0.8	0.9	0.9	1.0	1.1	1.2	1.3	1.3	1.4	1.5	1.6	1.6	1.7	1.8	1.8	1.9
72	0.0	0.0	0.0	0.0	0.0	0.0	0.0	0.0	0.0	0.0	0.0	0.0	0.0	0.0	0.1	0.2	0.3	0.4	0.5	0.6	0.7	0.8	0.9	1.0	1.1	1.2	1.2	1.3	1.4	1.5	1.6	1.6	1.7	1.8	1.9	1.9	2.0	2.1	2.1
71	0.0	0.0	0.0	0.0	0.0	0.0	0.0	0.0	0.0	0.0	0.0	0.0	0.1	0.2	0.3	0.4	0.5	0.6	0.7	0.8	0.9	1.0	1.1	1.2	1.3	1.4	1.5	1.5	1.6	1.7	1.8	1.9	1.9	2.0	2.1	2.1	2.2	2.3	2.4
70	0.0	0.0	0.0	0.0	0.0	0.0	0.0	0.0	0.0	0.0	0.1	0.2	0.3	0.5	0.6	0.7	0.8	0.9	1.0	1.1	1.2	1.3	1.4	1.4	1.5	1.6	1.7	1.8	1.9	1.9	2.0	2.1	2.2	2.2	2.3	2.4	2.5	2.5	2.6
69	0.0	0.0	0.0	0.0	0.0	0.0	0.0	0.0	0.1	0.2	0.3	0.5	0.6	0.7	0.8	0.9	1.0	1.1	1.2	1.3	1.4	1.5	1.6	1.7	1.8	1.8	1.9	2.0	2.1	2.2	2.3	2.3	2.4	2.5	2.5	2.6	2.7	2.8	2.8
68	0.0	0.0	0.0	0.0	0.0	0.0	0.0	0.2	0.3	0.4	0.6	0.7	0.8	0.9	1.0	1.2	1.3	1.4	1.5	1.6	1.7	1.7	1.8	1.9	2.0	2.1	2.2	2.3	2.3	2.4	2.5	2.6	2.6	2.7	2.8	2.9	2.9	3.0	3.1
67	0.0	0.0	0.0	0.0	0.0	0.1	0.3	0.4	0.6	0.7	0.8	1.0	1.1	1.2	1.3	1.4	1.5	1.6	1.7	1.8	1.9	2.0	2.1	2.2	2.3	2.3	2.4	2.5	2.6	2.7	2.7	2.8	2.9	3.0	3.0	3.1	3.2	3.3	3.3
66	0.0	0.0	0.0	0.0	0.2	0.3	0.5	0.7	0.8	1.0	1.1	1.2	1.3	1.4	1.6	1.7	1.8	1.9	2.0	2.1	2.2	2.3	2.3	2.4	2.5	2.6	2.7	2.8	2.9	2.9	3.0	3.1	3.2	3.2	3.3	3.4	3.4	3.5	3.6
65	0.0	0.0	0.0	0.2	0.4	0.6	0.8	0.9	1.1	1.2	1.4	1.5	1.6	1.7	1.8	1.9	2.0	2.1	2.2	2.3	2.4	2.5	2.6	2.7	2.8	2.9	3.0	3.0	3.1	3.2	3.3	3.4	3.4	3.5	3.6	3.6	3.7	3.8	3.9
64	0.0	0.0	0.3	0.5	0.7	0.9	1.1	1.2	1.4	1.5	1.6	1.8	1.9	2.0	2.1	2.2	2.3	2.4	2.5	2.6	2.7	2.8	2.9	3.0	3.1	3.2	3.2	3.3	3.4	3.5	3.6	3.6	3.7	3.8	3.9	3.9	4.0	4.1	4.1
63	0.0	0.3	0.6	0.8	1.0	1.2	1.3	1.5	1.6	1.8	1.9	2.0	2.2	2.3	2.4	2.5	2.6	2.7	2.8	2.9	3.0	3.1	3.2	3.3	3.4	3.4	3.5	3.6	3.7	3.8	3.8	3.9	4.0	4.1	4.1	4.2	4.3	4.3	4.4
62	0.2	0.6	0.9	1.1	1.3	1.5	1.6	1.8	1.9	2.1	2.2	2.3	2.5	2.6	2.7	2.8	2.9	3.0	3.1	3.2	3.3	3.4	3.5	3.6	3.7	3.7	3.8	3.9	4.0	4.1	4.1	4.2	4.3	4.4	4.4	4.5	4.6	4.6	4.7
61	0.5	0.9	1.2	1.4	1.6	1.8	1.9	2.1	2.2	2.4	2.5	2.6	2.8	2.9	3.0	3.1	3.2	3.3	3.4	3.5	3.6	3.7	3.8	3.9	4.0	4.0	4.1	4.2	4.3	4.4	4.4	4.5	4.6	4.7	4.7	4.8	4.9	4.9	5.0
60	0.9	1.2	1.5	1.7	1.9	2.1	2.3	2.4	2.6	2.7	2.8	3.0	3.1	3.2	3.3	3.4	3.5	3.6	3.7	3.8	3.9	4.0	4.1	4.2	4.3	4.4	4.4	4.5	4.6	4.7	4.8	4.8	4.9	5.0	5.1	5.1	5.2	5.3	5.3
59	1.2	1.3	1.6	1.8	2.1	2.3	2.5	2.6	2.8	2.9	3.0	3.2	3.3	3.4	3.5	3.6	3.7	3.8	3.9	4.1	4.2	4.4	4.6	4.7	4.9	5.0	5.2	5.3	5.5	5.6	5.6	5.7	5.8	5.9	6.0	6.0	6.1	6.2	6.2
58	2.1	2.3	2.4	2.6	2.7	2.9	3.0	3.2	3.3	3.5	3.6	3.8	3.9	4.1	4.2	4.3	4.5	4.6	4.8	4.9	5.1	5.2	5.4	5.5	5.7	5.8	6.0	6.1	6.3	6.4	6.5	6.6	6.7	6.8	6.9	6.9	7.0	7.1	7.1
57	3.1	3.3	3.4	3.6	3.7	3.8	4.0	4.1	4.2	4.4	4.5	4.7	4.8	4.9	5.1	5.2	5.4	5.5	5.6	5.8	5.9	6.1	6.2	6.3	6.5	6.6	6.7	6.9	7.0	7.2	7.3	7.4	7.6	7.7	7.7	7.8	7.9	8.0	8.0
56	4.1	4.3	4.4	4.5	4.7	4.8	4.9	5.0	5.2	5.3	5.4	5.6	5.7	5.8	6.0	6.1	6.2	6.4	6.5	6.6	6.8	6.9	7.0	7.1	7.3	7.4	7.5	7.7	7.8	7.9	8.1	8.2	8.3	8.5	8.6	8.7	8.8	8.9	8.9
55	5.1	5.2	5.4	5.5	5.6	5.7	5.9	6.0	6.1	6.2	6.4	6.5	6.6	6.7	6.8	7.0	7.1	7.2	7.3	7.5	7.6	7.7	7.8	8.0	8.1	8.2	8.3	84	8.6	8.7	8.8	8.9	9.1	9.2	9.3	9.4	9.6	9.7	9.8
54	6.1	6.2	6.3	6.5	6.6	6.7	6.8	6.9	7.0	7.2	7.3	7.4	7.5	7.6	7.7	7.8	8.0	8.1	8.2	8.3	8.4	8.5	8.7	8.8	8.9	9.0	9.1	9.2	9.3	9.5	9.6	9.7	9.8	9.9	10.0	10.2	10.3	10.4	10.5
53	7.1	7.2	7.3	7.4	7.5	7.6	7.8	7.9	8.0	8.1	8.2	8.3	8.4	8.5	8.6	8.7	8.8	8.9	9.0	9.1	9.3	9.4	9.5	9.6	9.7	9.8	9.9	10.0	10.1	10.2	10.3	10.4	10.5	10.7	10.8	10.9	11.0	11.1	11.2
52	8.1	8.2	8.3	8.4	8.5	8.6	8.7	8.8	8.9	9.0	9.1	9.2	9.3	9.4	9.5	9.6	9.7	9.8	9.9	9.9	10.1	10.2	10.3	10.4	10.5	10.6	10.7	10.8	10.9	11.0	11.1	11.2	11.3	11.4	11.5	11.6	11.7	11.8	11.9
51	9.1	9.2	9.3	9.4	9.5	9.6	9.6	9.7	9.8	9.9	10.0	10.1	10.2	10.3	10.4	10.5	10.6	10.7	10.7	10.8	10.9	11.0	11.1	11.2	11.3	11.4	11.5	11.6	11.7	11.8	11.8	11.9	12.0	12.1	12.2	12.3	12.4	12.5	12.6
50	10.1	10.2	10.3	10.3	10.4	10.5	10.6	10.7	10.8	10.8	10.9	11.0	11.1	11.2	11.3	11.3	11.4	11.5	11.6	11.7	11.8	11.8	11.9	12.0	12.1	12.2	12.3	12.4	12.4	12.5	12.6	12.7	12.8	12.9	12.9	13.0	13.1	13.2	13.3
49	11.1	11.2	11.2	11.3	11.4	11.5	11.5	11.6	11.7	11.8	11.8	11.9	12.0	12.1	12.1	12.2	12.3	12.4	12.4	12.5	12.6	12.7	12.8	12.8	12.9	13.0	13.1	13.1	13.2	13.3	13.4	13.4	13.5	13.6	13.7	13.7	13.8	13.9	14.0
48	12.1	12.1	12.2	12.3	12.3	12.4	12.5	12.5	12.6	12.7	12.8	12.8	12.9	13.0	13.0	13.1	13.2	13.2	13.3	13.4	13.4	13.5	13.6	13.6	13.7	13.8	13.8	13.9	14.0	14.0	14.1	14.2	14.3	14.3	14.4	14.5	14.5	14.6	14.7
47	13.1	13.1	13.2	13.2	13.3	13.4	13.4	13.5	13.5	13.6	13.7	13.7	13.8	13.8	13.9	14.0	14.0	14.1	14.1	14.2	14.3	14.3	14.4	14.5	14.5	14.6	14.6	14.7	14.8	14.8	14.9	14.9	15.0	15.1	15.1	15.2	15.2	15.3	15.4
46	14.1	14.1	14.2	14.2	14.3	14.3	14.4	14.4	14.5	14.5	14.6	14.6	14.7	14.7	14.8	14.8	14.9	14.9	15.0	15.1	15.1	15.2	15.2	15.3	15.3	15.4	15.4	15.5	15.5	15.6	15.6	15.7	15.7	15.8	15.8	15.9	15.9	16.0	16.1
45	15.0	15.1	15.1	15.2	15.2	15.3	15.3	15.4	15.4	15.4	15.5	15.5	15.6	15.6	15.7	15.7	15.8	15.8	15.9	15.9	15.9	16.0	16.0	16.1	16.1	16.2	16.2	16.3	16.3	16.3	16.4	16.4	16.5	16.5	16.6	16.6	16.7	16.7	16.7
44	16.0	16.1	16.1	16.1	16.2	16.2	16.3	16.3	16.3	16.4	16.4	16.4	16.5	16.5	16.6	16.6	16.6	16.7	16.7	16.7	16.8	16.8	16.9	16.9	16.9	17.0	17.0	17.0	17.1	17.1	17.1	17.2	17.2	17.3	17.3	17.3	17.4	17.4	17.4
43	17.0	17.1	17.1	17.1	17.1	17.2	17.2	17.2	17.3	17.3	17.3	17.3	17.4	17.4	17.4	17.5	17.5	17.5	17.6	17.6	17.6	17.6	17.7	17.7	17.7	17.8	17.8	17.8	17.8	17.9	17.9	17.9	18.0	18.0	18.0	18.0	18.1	18.1	18.1
42	18.0	18.0	18.1	18.1	18.1	18.1	18.1	18.2	18.2	18.2	18.2	18.3	18.3	18.3	18.3	18.3	18.4	18.4	18.4	18.4	18.4	18.5	18.5	18.5	18.5	18.6	18.6	18.6	18.6	18.6	18.7	18.7	18.7	18.7	18.7	18.8	18.8	18.8	18.8

LISTED PUT OPTION PRICE WHEN EXERCISE PRICE IS 70

NUMBER OF WEEKS BEFORE THE OPTION EXPIRES

Common Stock Price	1	2	3	4	5	6	7	8	9	10	11	12	13	14	15	16	17	18	19	20	21	22	23	24	25	26	27	28	29	30	31	32	33	34	35	36	37	38	39
91	0.0	0.0	0.0	0.0	0.0	0.0	0.0	0.0	0.0	0.0	0.0	0.0	0.0	0.0	0.0	0.0	0.0	0.0	0.0	0.0	0.0	0.0	0.0	0.0	0.0	0.0	0.0	0.1	0.2	0.3	0.4	0.5	0.6	0.6	0.7	0.8	0.9	1.0	1.1
90	0.0	0.0	0.0	0.0	0.0	0.0	0.0	0.0	0.0	0.0	0.0	0.0	0.0	0.0	0.0	0.0	0.0	0.0	0.0	0.0	0.0	0.0	0.0	0.0	0.0	0.1	0.2	0.3	0.4	0.5	0.6	0.7	0.7	0.8	0.9	1.0	1.1	1.2	1.2
89	0.0	0.0	0.0	0.0	0.0	0.0	0.0	0.0	0.0	0.0	0.0	0.0	0.0	0.0	0.0	0.0	0.0	0.0	0.0	0.0	0.0	0.0	0.0	0.1	0.2	0.3	0.4	0.5	0.6	0.7	0.8	0.9	0.9	1.0	1.1	1.2	1.3	1.4	1.4
88	0.0	0.0	0.0	0.0	0.0	0.0	0.0	0.0	0.0	0.0	0.0	0.0	0.0	0.0	0.0	0.0	0.0	0.0	0.0	0.0	0.0	0.1	0.2	0.3	0.4	0.5	0.6	0.7	0.8	0.9	1.0	1.1	1.1	1.2	1.3	1.4	1.5	1.6	1.6
87	0.0	0.0	0.0	0.0	0.0	0.0	0.0	0.0	0.0	0.0	0.0	0.0	0.0	0.0	0.0	0.0	0.0	0.0	0.0	0.1	0.2	0.3	0.4	0.5	0.6	0.7	0.8	0.9	1.0	1.1	1.2	1.3	1.3	1.4	1.5	1.6	1.7	1.8	1.8
86	0.0	0.0	0.0	0.0	0.0	0.0	0.0	0.0	0.0	0.0	0.0	0.0	0.0	0.0	0.0	0.0	0.0	0.1	0.2	0.3	0.4	0.5	0.6	0.7	0.8	0.9	1.0	1.1	1.2	1.3	1.4	1.5	1.6	1.6	1.7	1.8	1.9	2.0	2.1
85	0.0	0.0	0.0	0.0	0.0	0.0	0.0	0.0	0.0	0.0	0.0	0.0	0.0	0.0	0.0	0.0	0.2	0.3	0.4	0.5	0.6	0.7	0.8	0.9	1.0	1.1	1.2	1.3	1.4	1.5	1.6	1.7	1.8	1.9	1.9	2.0	2.1	2.2	2.3
84	0.0	0.0	0.0	0.0	0.0	0.0	0.0	0.0	0.0	0.0	0.0	0.0	0.0	0.0	0.1	0.3	0.4	0.5	0.6	0.7	0.8	0.9	1.0	1.1	1.2	1.3	1.4	1.5	1.6	1.7	1.8	1.9	2.0	2.1	2.2	2.2	2.3	2.4	2.5
83	0.0	0.0	0.0	0.0	0.0	0.0	0.0	0.0	0.0	0.0	0.0	0.0	0.1	0.2	0.4	0.5	0.6	0.7	0.8	0.9	1.1	1.2	1.3	1.4	1.5	1.6	1.7	1.8	1.9	1.9	2.0	2.1	2.2	2.3	2.4	2.5	2.6	2.6	2.7
82	0.0	0.0	0.0	0.0	0.0	0.0	0.0	0.0	0.0	0.0	0.0	0.2	0.3	0.4	0.6	0.7	0.8	0.9	1.1	1.2	1.3	1.4	1.5	1.6	1.7	1.8	1.9	2.0	2.1	2.2	2.3	2.4	2.4	2.5	2.6	2.7	2.8	2.9	2.9
81	0.0	0.0	0.0	0.0	0.0	0.0	0.0	0.0	0.0	0.1	0.3	0.4	0.6	0.7	0.8	0.9	1.1	1.2	1.3	1.4	1.5	1.6	1.7	1.8	1.9	2.0	2.1	2.2	2.3	2.4	2.5	2.6	2.7	2.8	2.9	2.9	3.0	3.1	3.2
80	0.0	0.0	0.0	0.0	0.0	0.0	0.0	0.0	0.2	0.4	0.5	0.7	0.8	0.9	1.1	1.2	1.3	1.4	1.5	1.7	1.8	1.9	2.0	2.1	2.2	2.3	2.4	2.5	2.6	2.7	2.7	2.8	2.9	3.0	3.1	3.2	3.3	3.3	3.4
79	0.0	0.0	0.0	0.0	0.0	0.0	0.1	0.3	0.4	0.6	0.8	0.9	1.0	1.2	1.3	1.4	1.6	1.7	1.8	1.9	2.0	2.1	2.2	2.3	2.4	2.5	2.6	2.7	2.8	2.9	3.0	3.1	3.2	3.3	3.3	3.4	3.5	3.6	3.7
78	0.0	0.0	0.0	0.0	0.0	0.1	0.3	0.5	0.7	0.9	1.0	1.2	1.3	1.4	1.6	1.7	1.8	1.9	2.0	2.2	2.3	2.4	2.5	2.6	2.7	2.8	2.9	3.0	3.1	3.2	3.2	3.3	3.4	3.5	3.6	3.7	3.8	3.8	3.9
77	0.0	0.0	0.0	0.0	0.2	0.4	0.6	0.8	1.0	1.1	1.3	1.4	1.6	1.7	1.8	1.9	2.1	2.2	2.3	2.4	2.5	2.6	2.7	2.8	2.9	3.0	3.1	3.2	3.3	3.4	3.5	3.6	3.7	3.8	3.9	3.9	4.0	4.1	4.2
76	0.0	0.0	0.0	0.2	0.5	0.7	0.9	1.0	1.2	1.4	1.5	1.7	1.8	2.0	2.1	2.2	2.3	2.5	2.6	2.7	2.8	2.9	3.0	3.1	3.2	3.3	3.4	3.5	3.6	3.7	3.8	3.9	4.0	4.0	4.1	4.2	4.3	4.4	4.5
75	0.0	0.0	0.2	0.5	0.7	0.9	1.1	1.3	1.5	1.7	1.8	2.0	2.1	2.2	2.4	2.5	2.6	2.7	2.8	3.0	3.1	3.2	3.3	3.4	3.5	3.6	3.7	3.8	3.9	4.0	4.1	4.1	4.2	4.3	4.4	4.5	4.6	4.6	4.7
74	0.0	0.2	0.5	0.8	1.0	1.2	1.4	1.6	1.8	1.9	2.1	2.2	2.4	2.5	2.6	2.8	2.9	3.0	3.1	3.2	3.4	3.5	3.6	3.7	3.8	3.9	4.0	4.1	4.2	4.2	4.3	4.4	4.5	4.6	4.7	4.8	4.8	4.9	5.0
73	0.1	0.5	0.8	1.1	1.3	1.5	1.7	1.9	2.1	2.2	2.4	2.5	2.7	2.8	2.9	3.1	3.2	3.3	3.4	3.5	3.6	3.8	3.9	4.0	4.1	4.2	4.3	4.4	4.4	4.5	4.6	4.7	4.8	4.9	5.0	5.1	5.1	5.2	5.3
72	0.4	0.8	1.1	1.4	1.6	1.8	2.0	2.2	2.4	2.5	2.7	2.8	3.0	3.1	3.2	3.4	3.5	3.6	3.7	3.8	3.9	4.1	4.2	4.3	4.4	4.5	4.6	4.6	4.7	4.8	4.9	5.0	5.1	5.2	5.3	5.4	5.4	5.5	5.6
71	0.7	1.1	1.4	1.7	1.9	2.1	2.3	2.5	2.7	2.8	3.0	3.1	3.3	3.4	3.5	3.7	3.8	3.9	4.0	4.1	4.2	4.4	4.5	4.6	4.7	4.8	4.9	5.0	5.0	5.1	5.2	5.3	5.4	5.5	5.6	5.7	5.7	5.8	5.9
70	1.0	1.4	1.7	2.0	2.2	2.4	2.6	2.8	3.0	3.2	3.3	3.5	3.6	3.7	3.9	4.0	4.1	4.2	4.3	4.5	4.6	4.7	4.8	4.9	5.0	5.1	5.2	5.3	5.4	5.5	5.5	5.6	5.7	5.8	5.9	6.0	6.1	6.1	6.2
69	1.2	1.5	1.8	2.1	2.3	2.6	2.8	3.0	3.2	3.4	3.6	3.7	3.8	3.9	4.1	4.2	4.3	4.4	4.6	4.8	4.9	5.0	5.2	5.4	5.5	5.7	5.9	6.1	6.3	6.4	6.4	6.5	6.6	6.7	6.8	6.9	7.0	7.0	7.1
68	2.2	2.3	2.5	2.7	2.9	3.0	3.2	3.4	3.6	3.7	3.9	4.1	4.3	4.4	4.6	4.8	5.0	5.1	5.3	5.5	5.6	5.8	6.0	6.2	6.3	6.5	6.7	6.9	7.0	7.2	7.4	7.4	7.5	7.6	7.7	7.8	7.9	7.9	8.0
67	3.2	3.3	3.5	3.7	3.8	4.0	4.2	4.3	4.5	4.7	4.8	5.0	5.2	5.3	5.5	5.7	5.8	6.0	6.2	6.3	6.5	6.6	6.8	7.0	7.1	7.3	7.5	7.6	7.8	8.0	8.1	8.3	8.4	8.5	8.6	8.7	8.8	8.8	8.9
66	4.2	4.3	4.5	4.6	4.8	4.9	5.1	5.3	5.4	5.6	5.7	5.9	6.1	6.2	6.4	6.5	6.7	6.8	7.0	7.2	7.3	7.5	7.6	7.8	8.0	8.1	8.3	8.4	8.6	8.7	8.9	9.1	9.2	9.4	9.4	9.5	9.7	9.7	9.8
65	5.2	5.3	5.5	5.6	5.8	5.9	6.1	6.2	6.4	6.5	6.7	6.8	7.0	7.1	7.3	7.4	7.6	7.7	7.9	8.0	8.2	8.3	8.5	8.6	8.8	8.9	9.1	9.2	9.4	9.5	9.7	9.8	9.9	10.1	10.3	10.4	10.6	10.6	10.7
64	6.1	6.3	6.4	6.6	6.7	6.9	7.0	7.1	7.3	7.4	7.6	7.7	7.9	8.0	8.1	8.3	8.4	8.6	8.7	8.8	9.0	9.1	9.3	9.4	9.6	9.7	9.8	9.9	10.1	10.3	10.4	10.6	10.7	10.8	11.0	11.1	11.3	11.4	11.6
63	7.1	7.3	7.4	7.5	7.7	7.8	7.9	8.1	8.2	8.3	8.5	8.6	8.7	8.9	9.0	9.2	9.3	9.4	9.6	9.7	9.8	9.9	10.1	10.2	10.4	10.5	10.6	10.8	10.9	11.0	11.2	11.3	11.4	11.6	11.7	11.8	12.0	12.1	12.2
62	8.1	8.3	8.4	8.5	8.6	8.8	8.9	9.0	9.1	9.3	9.4	9.5	9.6	9.8	9.9	10.0	10.2	10.3	10.4	10.5	10.7	10.8	10.9	11.0	11.2	11.3	11.4	11.5	11.7	11.8	11.9	12.1	12.2	12.3	12.4	12.6	12.7	12.8	12.9
61	9.1	9.2	9.4	9.5	9.6	9.7	9.8	9.9	10.1	10.2	10.3	10.4	10.5	10.7	10.8	10.9	11.0	11.1	11.3	11.4	11.5	11.6	11.7	11.9	12.0	12.1	12.2	12.3	12.4	12.6	12.7	12.8	12.9	13.0	13.2	13.3	13.4	13.5	13.6
60	10.1	10.2	10.3	10.4	10.6	10.7	10.8	10.9	11.0	11.1	11.2	11.3	11.4	11.6	11.7	11.8	11.9	12.0	12.1	12.2	12.3	12.4	12.6	12.7	12.8	12.9	13.0	13.1	13.2	13.3	13.4	13.6	13.7	13.8	13.9	14.0	14.1	14.2	14.3
59	11.1	11.2	11.3	11.4	11.5	11.6	11.7	11.8	11.9	12.0	12.1	12.2	12.3	12.4	12.5	12.7	12.8	12.9	13.0	13.1	13.2	13.3	13.4	13.5	13.6	13.7	13.8	13.9	14.0	14.1	14.2	14.3	14.4	14.5	14.6	14.7	14.8	14.9	15.0
58	12.1	12.2	12.3	12.4	12.5	12.6	12.7	12.8	12.9	13.0	13.0	13.1	13.2	13.3	13.4	13.5	13.6	13.7	13.8	13.9	14.0	14.1	14.2	14.3	14.4	14.5	14.6	14.7	14.8	14.9	15.0	15.1	15.1	15.2	15.3	15.4	15.5	15.6	15.7
57	13.1	13.2	13.3	13.4	13.4	13.5	13.6	13.7	13.8	13.9	14.0	14.1	14.1	14.2	14.3	14.4	14.5	14.6	14.7	14.8	14.8	14.9	15.0	15.1	15.2	15.3	15.4	15.5	15.5	15.6	15.7	15.8	15.9	16.0	16.1	16.2	16.2	16.3	16.4
56	14.1	14.2	14.2	14.3	14.4	14.5	14.6	14.6	14.7	14.8	14.9	15.0	15.0	15.1	15.2	15.3	15.4	15.4	15.5	15.6	15.7	15.8	15.8	15.9	16.0	16.1	16.2	16.2	16.3	16.4	16.5	16.6	16.6	16.7	16.8	16.9	16.9	17.0	17.1
55	15.1	15.1	15.2	15.3	15.4	15.4	15.5	15.6	15.6	15.7	15.8	15.9	15.9	16.0	16.1	16.1	16.2	16.3	16.4	16.4	16.5	16.6	16.7	16.7	16.8	16.9	16.9	17.0	17.1	17.2	17.2	17.3	17.4	17.4	17.5	17.6	17.7	17.7	17.8
54	16.1	16.1	16.2	16.3	16.3	16.4	16.4	16.5	16.6	16.6	16.7	16.8	16.8	16.9	17.0	17.0	17.1	17.2	17.2	17.3	17.3	17.4	17.5	17.5	17.6	17.7	17.7	17.8	17.9	17.9	18.0	18.0	18.1	18.2	18.2	18.3	18.4	18.4	18.5
53	17.1	17.1	17.2	17.2	17.3	17.3	17.4	17.4	17.5	17.6	17.6	17.7	17.7	17.8	17.8	17.9	18.0	18.0	18.1	18.1	18.2	18.2	18.3	18.3	18.4	18.5	18.5	18.6	18.6	18.7	18.7	18.8	18.9	18.9	19.0	19.0	19.1	19.1	19.2
52	18.0	18.1	18.1	18.2	18.2	18.3	18.3	18.4	18.4	18.5	18.5	18.6	18.6	18.7	18.7	18.8	18.8	18.9	18.9	19.0	19.0	19.1	19.1	19.2	19.2	19.3	19.3	19.4	19.4	19.5	19.5	19.5	19.6	19.6	19.7	19.7	19.8	19.8	19.9
51	19.0	19.1	19.1	19.2	19.2	19.2	19.3	19.3	19.4	19.4	19.4	19.5	19.5	19.6	19.6	19.6	19.7	19.7	19.8	19.8	19.9	19.9	19.9	19.9	20.0	20.1	20.1	20.1	20.2	20.2	20.3	20.3	20.3	20.4	20.4	20.5	20.5	20.5	20.6
50	20.0	20.1	20.1	20.1	20.2	20.2	20.2	20.3	20.3	20.3	20.4	20.4	20.4	20.5	20.5	20.5	20.6	20.6	20.6	20.7	20.7	20.7	20.8	20.8	20.8	20.9	20.9	20.9	20.9	21.0	21.0	21.0	21.1	21.1	21.1	21.2	21.2	21.2	21.3
49	21.0	21.0	21.1	21.1	21.1	21.1	21.2	21.2	21.2	21.2	21.3	21.3	21.3	21.3	21.4	21.4	21.4	21.4	21.5	21.5	21.5	21.5	21.6	21.6	21.6	21.6	21.7	21.7	21.7	21.7	21.8	21.8	21.8	21.8	21.9	21.9	21.9	21.9	22.0

LISTED PUT OPTION PRICE WHEN EXERCISE PRICE IS 80

Common Stock Price	NUMBER OF WEEKS BEFORE THE OPTION EXPIRES 1	2	3	4	5	6	7	8	9	10	11	12	13	14	15	16	17	18	19	20	21	22	23	24	25	26	27	28	29	30	31	32	33	34	35	36	37	38	39
104	0.0	0.0	0.0	0.0	0.0	0.0	0.0	0.0	0.0	0.0	0.0	0.0	0.0	0.0	0.0	0.0	0.0	0.0	0.0	0.0	0.0	0.0	0.0	0.0	0.0	0.0	0.0	0.1	0.2	0.3	0.4	0.5	0.6	0.7	0.8	0.9	1.0	1.1	1.2
102	0.0	0.0	0.0	0.0	0.0	0.0	0.0	0.0	0.0	0.0	0.0	0.0	0.0	0.0	0.0	0.0	0.0	0.0	0.0	0.0	0.0	0.0	0.0	0.1	0.2	0.3	0.4	0.5	0.6	0.7	0.8	0.9	1.0	1.1	1.2	1.3	1.4	1.5	1.6
100	0.0	0.0	0.0	0.0	0.0	0.0	0.0	0.0	0.0	0.0	0.0	0.0	0.0	0.0	0.0	0.0	0.0	0.0	0.0	0.0	0.1	0.2	0.3	0.5	0.6	0.7	0.8	0.9	1.0	1.1	1.2	1.3	1.4	1.5	1.6	1.7	1.8	1.9	2.0
99	0.0	0.0	0.0	0.0	0.0	0.0	0.0	0.0	0.0	0.0	0.0	0.0	0.0	0.0	0.0	0.0	0.0	0.0	0.0	0.2	0.3	0.4	0.5	0.7	0.8	0.9	1.0	1.1	1.2	1.3	1.4	1.5	1.6	1.7	1.8	1.9	2.0	2.1	2.2
98	0.0	0.0	0.0	0.0	0.0	0.0	0.0	0.0	0.0	0.0	0.0	0.0	0.0	0.0	0.0	0.0	0.0	0.1	0.3	0.4	0.5	0.6	0.8	0.9	1.0	1.1	1.2	1.3	1.4	1.5	1.6	1.7	1.8	1.9	2.0	2.1	2.2	2.3	2.4
97	0.0	0.0	0.0	0.0	0.0	0.0	0.0	0.0	0.0	0.0	0.0	0.0	0.0	0.0	0.0	0.1	0.2	0.3	0.5	0.6	0.7	0.9	1.0	1.1	1.2	1.3	1.4	1.5	1.6	1.7	1.9	2.0	2.1	2.2	2.2	2.3	2.4	2.5	2.6
96	0.0	0.0	0.0	0.0	0.0	0.0	0.0	0.0	0.0	0.0	0.0	0.0	0.0	0.0	0.1	0.3	0.4	0.6	0.7	0.8	1.0	1.1	1.2	1.3	1.4	1.5	1.6	1.8	1.9	2.0	2.1	2.2	2.3	2.4	2.5	2.6	2.7	2.8	2.8
95	0.0	0.0	0.0	0.0	0.0	0.0	0.0	0.0	0.0	0.0	0.0	0.0	0.1	0.2	0.4	0.5	0.7	0.8	0.9	1.0	1.2	1.3	1.4	1.5	1.7	1.8	1.9	2.0	2.1	2.2	2.3	2.4	2.5	2.6	2.7	2.8	2.9	3.0	3.1
94	0.0	0.0	0.0	0.0	0.0	0.0	0.0	0.0	0.0	0.0	0.0	0.1	0.3	0.4	0.6	0.7	0.9	1.0	1.2	1.3	1.4	1.5	1.6	1.8	1.9	2.0	2.1	2.2	2.3	2.4	2.5	2.6	2.7	2.8	2.9	3.0	3.1	3.2	3.3
93	0.0	0.0	0.0	0.0	0.0	0.0	0.0	0.0	0.0	0.0	0.2	0.4	0.5	0.7	0.8	1.0	1.1	1.3	1.4	1.5	1.6	1.8	1.9	2.0	2.1	2.2	2.3	2.4	2.6	2.7	2.8	2.9	3.0	3.1	3.2	3.3	3.3	3.4	3.5
92	0.0	0.0	0.0	0.0	0.0	0.0	0.0	0.0	0.1	0.3	0.4	0.6	0.8	0.9	1.1	1.2	1.4	1.5	1.6	1.8	1.9	2.0	2.1	2.2	2.4	2.5	2.6	2.7	2.8	2.9	3.0	3.1	3.2	3.3	3.4	3.5	3.6	3.7	3.8
91	0.0	0.0	0.0	0.0	0.0	0.0	0.0	0.1	0.3	0.5	0.7	0.8	1.0	1.2	1.3	1.5	1.6	1.7	1.9	2.0	2.1	2.2	2.4	2.5	2.6	2.7	2.8	2.9	3.0	3.1	3.2	3.3	3.4	3.5	3.6	3.7	3.8	3.9	4.0
90	0.0	0.0	0.0	0.0	0.0	0.0	0.2	0.4	0.6	0.8	0.9	1.1	1.3	1.4	1.6	1.7	1.9	2.0	2.1	2.2	2.4	2.5	2.6	2.7	2.8	3.0	3.1	3.2	3.3	3.4	3.5	3.6	3.7	3.8	3.9	4.0	4.1	4.2	4.3
89	0.0	0.0	0.0	0.0	0.0	0.2	0.4	0.6	0.8	1.0	1.2	1.4	1.5	1.7	1.8	2.0	2.1	2.2	2.4	2.5	2.6	2.8	2.9	3.0	3.1	3.2	3.3	3.4	3.5	3.6	3.8	3.9	4.0	4.1	4.1	4.2	4.3	4.4	4.5
88	0.0	0.0	0.0	0.0	0.2	0.5	0.7	0.9	1.1	1.3	1.4	1.6	1.8	1.9	2.1	2.2	2.4	2.5	2.6	2.8	2.9	3.0	3.1	3.3	3.4	3.5	3.6	3.7	3.8	3.9	4.0	4.1	4.2	4.3	4.4	4.5	4.6	4.7	4.8
87	0.0	0.0	0.0	0.2	0.5	0.7	1.0	1.2	1.4	1.5	1.7	1.9	2.0	2.2	2.3	2.5	2.6	2.8	2.9	3.0	3.2	3.3	3.4	3.5	3.6	3.7	3.9	4.0	4.1	4.2	4.3	4.4	4.5	4.6	4.7	4.8	4.9	5.0	5.1
86	0.0	0.0	0.2	0.5	0.8	1.0	1.2	1.4	1.6	1.8	2.0	2.2	2.3	2.5	2.6	2.8	2.9	3.0	3.2	3.3	3.4	3.6	3.7	3.8	3.9	4.0	4.1	4.2	4.3	4.5	4.6	4.7	4.8	4.9	4.9	5.0	5.1	5.2	5.3
85	0.0	0.1	0.5	0.8	1.0	1.3	1.5	1.7	1.9	2.1	2.3	2.4	2.6	2.8	2.9	3.0	3.2	3.3	3.5	3.6	3.7	3.8	4.0	4.1	4.2	4.3	4.4	4.5	4.6	4.7	4.8	4.9	5.0	5.1	5.2	5.3	5.4	5.5	5.6
84	0.0	0.4	0.8	1.1	1.3	1.6	1.8	2.0	2.2	2.4	2.6	2.7	2.9	3.0	3.2	3.3	3.5	3.6	3.7	3.9	4.0	4.1	4.2	4.4	4.5	4.6	4.7	4.8	4.9	5.0	5.1	5.2	5.3	5.4	5.5	5.6	5.7	5.8	5.9
83	0.2	0.7	1.0	1.4	1.6	1.9	2.1	2.3	2.5	2.7	2.9	3.0	3.2	3.3	3.5	3.6	3.8	3.9	4.0	4.2	4.3	4.4	4.5	4.7	4.8	4.9	5.0	5.1	5.2	5.3	5.4	5.5	5.6	5.7	5.8	5.9	6.0	6.1	6.2
82	0.5	1.0	1.3	1.7	1.9	2.2	2.4	2.6	2.8	3.0	3.2	3.3	3.5	3.6	3.8	3.9	4.1	4.2	4.3	4.5	4.6	4.7	4.8	5.0	5.1	5.2	5.3	5.4	5.5	5.6	5.7	5.8	5.9	6.0	6.1	6.2	6.3	6.4	6.5
81	0.8	1.3	1.7	2.0	2.2	2.5	2.7	2.9	3.1	3.3	3.5	3.6	3.8	3.9	4.1	4.2	4.4	4.5	4.6	4.8	4.9	5.0	5.1	5.3	5.4	5.5	5.6	5.7	5.8	5.9	6.0	6.1	6.2	6.3	6.4	6.5	6.6	6.7	6.8
80	1.1	1.6	2.0	2.3	2.5	2.8	3.0	3.2	3.4	3.6	3.8	3.9	4.1	4.3	4.4	4.6	4.7	4.8	5.0	5.1	5.2	5.3	5.5	5.6	5.7	5.8	5.9	6.0	6.1	6.2	6.3	6.4	6.5	6.6	6.7	6.8	6.9	7.0	7.1
79	1.2	1.7	2.1	2.5	2.7	3.0	3.2	3.4	3.6	3.8	4.0	4.1	4.3	4.5	4.7	4.9	5.0	5.1	5.3	5.4	5.6	5.7	5.8	6.0	6.2	6.4	6.6	6.8	7.0	7.1	7.2	7.3	7.4	7.5	7.6	7.7	7.8	7.9	8.0
78	2.2	2.4	2.6	2.8	3.0	3.2	3.4	3.6	3.8	4.0	4.2	4.4	4.6	4.8	5.0	5.2	5.4	5.6	5.8	6.0	6.2	6.4	6.6	6.8	7.0	7.2	7.4	7.6	7.8	8.0	8.1	8.2	8.3	8.4	8.5	8.6	8.7	8.8	8.9
77	3.2	3.4	3.6	3.8	4.0	4.2	4.4	4.5	4.7	4.9	5.1	5.3	5.5	5.7	5.9	6.1	6.3	6.5	6.7	6.9	7.1	7.2	7.4	7.6	7.8	8.0	8.2	8.4	8.6	8.8	9.0	9.1	9.2	9.3	9.4	9.5	9.6	9.7	9.8
76	4.2	4.4	4.6	4.7	4.9	5.1	5.3	5.5	5.7	5.9	6.0	6.2	6.4	6.6	6.8	7.0	7.1	7.3	7.5	7.7	7.9	8.1	8.3	8.4	8.6	8.8	9.0	9.2	9.4	9.6	9.7	9.9	10.1	10.2	10.3	10.4	10.5	10.6	10.7
75	5.2	5.4	5.5	5.7	5.9	6.1	6.2	6.4	6.6	6.8	6.9	7.1	7.3	7.5	7.7	7.8	8.0	8.2	8.4	8.5	8.7	8.9	9.1	9.3	9.4	9.6	9.8	9.9	10.1	10.3	10.5	10.7	10.8	11.0	11.2	11.3	11.4	11.5	11.6
74	6.2	6.3	6.5	6.7	6.8	7.0	7.2	7.4	7.5	7.7	7.9	8.0	8.2	8.4	8.5	8.7	8.9	9.0	9.2	9.4	9.6	9.7	9.9	10.1	10.2	10.4	10.6	10.7	10.9	11.1	11.3	11.4	11.6	11.8	11.9	12.1	12.3	12.4	12.5
73	7.2	7.3	7.5	7.6	7.8	8.0	8.1	8.3	8.5	8.6	8.8	8.9	9.1	9.3	9.4	9.6	9.7	9.9	10.1	10.2	10.4	10.6	10.7	10.9	11.0	11.2	11.4	11.5	11.7	11.8	12.0	12.2	12.3	12.5	12.7	12.8	13.0	13.1	13.3
72	8.2	8.3	8.5	8.6	8.8	8.9	9.1	9.2	9.4	9.5	9.7	9.8	9.9	10.2	10.3	10.5	10.6	10.8	10.9	11.1	11.2	11.4	11.5	11.7	11.8	12.0	12.2	12.3	12.5	12.6	12.8	12.9	13.1	13.2	13.4	13.5	13.7	13.8	14.0
71	9.1	9.3	9.4	9.6	9.7	9.9	10.0	10.2	10.3	10.5	10.6	10.8	10.9	11.0	11.2	11.3	11.5	11.6	11.8	11.9	12.1	12.2	12.4	12.5	12.6	12.8	12.9	13.1	13.2	13.4	13.5	13.7	13.8	14.0	14.1	14.3	14.4	14.5	14.7
70	10.1	10.3	10.4	10.6	10.7	10.8	11.0	11.1	11.2	11.4	11.5	11.7	11.8	11.9	12.1	12.2	12.3	12.5	12.6	12.8	12.9	13.0	13.2	13.3	13.5	13.6	13.7	13.9	14.0	14.1	14.3	14.4	14.6	14.7	14.8	15.0	15.1	15.2	15.4
69	11.1	11.3	11.4	11.5	11.7	11.8	11.9	12.0	12.2	12.3	12.4	12.6	12.7	12.8	13.0	13.1	13.2	13.3	13.5	13.6	13.7	13.9	14.0	14.1	14.3	14.4	14.5	14.6	14.8	14.9	15.0	15.2	15.3	15.4	15.6	15.7	15.8	15.9	16.1
68	12.1	12.2	12.4	12.5	12.6	12.7	12.9	13.0	13.1	13.2	13.3	13.5	13.6	13.7	13.8	14.0	14.1	14.2	14.3	14.4	14.6	14.7	14.8	14.9	15.1	15.2	15.3	15.4	15.5	15.7	15.8	15.9	16.0	16.2	16.3	16.4	16.5	16.7	16.8
67	13.1	13.2	13.3	13.5	13.6	13.7	13.8	13.9	14.0	14.1	14.3	14.4	14.5	14.6	14.7	14.8	14.9	15.1	15.2	15.3	15.4	15.5	15.6	15.7	15.9	16.0	16.1	16.2	16.3	16.4	16.6	16.7	16.8	16.9	17.0	17.1	17.2	17.4	17.5
66	14.1	14.2	14.3	14.4	14.5	14.6	14.7	14.9	15.0	15.1	15.2	15.3	15.4	15.5	15.6	15.7	15.8	15.9	16.0	16.1	16.2	16.3	16.5	16.6	16.7	16.8	16.9	17.0	17.1	17.2	17.3	17.4	17.5	17.6	17.7	17.8	17.9	18.1	18.2
65	15.1	15.2	15.3	15.4	15.5	15.6	15.7	15.8	15.9	16.0	16.1	16.2	16.3	16.4	16.5	16.6	16.7	16.8	16.9	17.0	17.1	17.2	17.3	17.4	17.5	17.6	17.7	17.8	17.9	18.0	18.1	18.2	18.3	18.4	18.5	18.6	18.7	18.8	18.9
64	16.1	16.2	16.3	16.4	16.5	16.5	16.6	16.7	16.8	16.9	17.0	17.1	17.2	17.3	17.4	17.5	17.5	17.6	17.7	17.8	17.9	18.0	18.1	18.2	18.3	18.4	18.5	18.6	18.6	18.7	18.8	18.9	19.0	19.1	19.2	19.3	19.4	19.5	19.6
63	17.1	17.2	17.2	17.3	17.4	17.5	17.6	17.7	17.7	17.8	17.9	18.0	18.1	18.2	18.2	18.3	18.4	18.5	18.6	18.7	18.7	18.8	18.9	19.0	19.1	19.2	19.2	19.3	19.4	19.5	19.6	19.7	19.7	19.8	19.9	19.9	20.1	20.2	20.2
62	18.1	18.2	18.2	18.3	18.4	18.5	18.5	18.6	18.7	18.8	18.8	18.9	19.0	19.1	19.1	19.2	19.3	19.4	19.4	19.5	19.6	19.7	19.7	19.8	19.9	19.9	20.0	20.1	20.2	20.3	20.3	20.4	20.5	20.6	20.6	20.7	20.8	20.9	20.9
61	19.1	19.1	19.2	19.3	19.3	19.4	19.5	19.5	19.6	19.7	19.7	19.8	19.9	19.9	20.0	20.1	20.1	20.2	20.3	20.4	20.4	20.5	20.6	20.6	20.7	20.8	20.8	20.9	21.0	21.0	21.1	21.2	21.2	21.3	21.4	21.4	21.5	21.6	21.6
60	20.1	20.1	20.2	20.2	20.3	20.4	20.4	20.5	20.5	20.6	20.7	20.7	20.8	20.8	20.9	21.0	21.0	21.1	21.1	21.2	21.3	21.3	21.4	21.4	21.5	21.6	21.6	21.7	21.7	21.8	21.9	21.9	22.0	22.0	22.1	22.2	22.2	22.3	22.3
59	21.1	21.1	21.2	21.2	21.3	21.3	21.4	21.4	21.5	21.5	21.6	21.6	21.7	21.7	21.8	21.8	21.9	21.9	22.0	22.0	22.1	22.1	22.2	22.2	22.3	22.3	22.4	22.5	22.5	22.6	22.6	22.7	22.7	22.8	22.8	22.9	22.9	23.0	23.0
58	22.0	22.1	22.1	22.2	22.2	22.3	22.3	22.4	22.4	22.4	22.5	22.5	22.6	22.6	22.7	22.7	22.7	22.8	22.8	22.9	22.9	23.0	23.0	23.1	23.1	23.1	23.2	23.2	23.3	23.3	23.4	23.4	23.5	23.5	23.5	23.6	23.6	23.7	23.7
57	23.0	23.1	23.1	23.1	23.2	23.2	23.3	23.3	23.3	23.4	23.4	23.4	23.5	23.5	23.5	23.6	23.6	23.7	23.7	23.7	23.8	23.8	23.8	23.9	23.9	23.9	24.0	24.0	24.1	24.1	24.1	24.2	24.2	24.2	24.3	24.3	24.3	24.4	24.4

LISTED PUT OPTION PRICE WHEN EXERCISE PRICE IS 90

Common Stock Price	NUMBER OF WEEKS BEFORE THE OPTION EXPIRES																																					
	1	2	3	4	5	6	7	8	9	10	11	12	13	14	15	16	17	18	19	20	21	22	23	24	25	26	27	28	29	30	31	32	33	34	35	36	37	38	39
118	0.0	0.0	0.0	0.0	0.0	0.0	0.0	0.0	0.0	0.0	0.0	0.0	0.0	0.0	0.0	0.0	0.0	0.0	0.0	0.0	0.0	0.0	0.0	0.0	0.0	0.0	0.0	0.0	0.1	0.2	0.3	0.4	0.5	0.6	0.7	0.9	1.0	1.1	1.2
116	0.0	0.0	0.0	0.0	0.0	0.0	0.0	0.0	0.0	0.0	0.0	0.0	0.0	0.0	0.0	0.0	0.0	0.0	0.0	0.0	0.0	0.0	0.0	0.0	0.0	0.1	0.2	0.3	0.4	0.6	0.7	0.8	0.9	1.0	1.1	1.2	1.3	1.4	1.5
114	0.0	0.0	0.0	0.0	0.0	0.0	0.0	0.0	0.0	0.0	0.0	0.0	0.0	0.0	0.0	0.0	0.0	0.0	0.0	0.0	0.0	0.0	0.1	0.2	0.3	0.5	0.6	0.7	0.8	1.0	1.1	1.2	1.3	1.4	1.5	1.6	1.7	1.8	1.9
112	0.0	0.0	0.0	0.0	0.0	0.0	0.0	0.0	0.0	0.0	0.0	0.0	0.0	0.0	0.0	0.0	0.0	0.0	0.0	0.1	0.2	0.4	0.5	0.6	0.7	0.9	1.0	1.1	1.2	1.4	1.5	1.6	1.7	1.8	1.9	2.0	2.1	2.2	2.3
110	0.0	0.0	0.0	0.0	0.0	0.0	0.0	0.0	0.0	0.0	0.0	0.0	0.0	0.0	0.0	0.0	0.0	0.2	0.3	0.5	0.6	0.8	0.9	1.0	1.2	1.3	1.4	1.5	1.7	1.8	1.9	2.0	2.1	2.2	2.3	2.4	2.6	2.7	2.8
108	0.0	0.0	0.0	0.0	0.0	0.0	0.0	0.0	0.0	0.0	0.0	0.0	0.0	0.0	0.2	0.3	0.5	0.6	0.8	0.9	1.1	1.2	1.3	1.5	1.6	1.7	1.9	2.0	2.1	2.2	2.3	2.4	2.6	2.7	2.8	2.9	3.0	3.1	3.2
106	0.0	0.0	0.0	0.0	0.0	0.0	0.0	0.0	0.0	0.0	0.0	0.1	0.3	0.4	0.6	0.8	0.9	1.1	1.2	1.4	1.5	1.7	1.8	1.9	2.1	2.2	2.3	2.4	2.6	2.7	2.8	2.9	3.0	3.1	3.2	3.3	3.4	3.5	3.7
104	0.0	0.0	0.0	0.0	0.0	0.0	0.0	0.0	0.0	0.2	0.4	0.6	0.7	0.9	1.1	1.2	1.4	1.6	1.7	1.9	2.0	2.1	2.3	2.4	2.5	2.7	2.8	2.9	3.0	3.1	3.3	3.4	3.5	3.6	3.7	3.8	3.9	4.0	4.1
102	0.0	0.0	0.0	0.0	0.0	0.0	0.0	0.2	0.5	0.7	0.9	1.0	1.2	1.4	1.6	1.7	1.9	2.0	2.2	2.3	2.5	2.6	2.8	2.9	3.0	3.1	3.3	3.4	3.5	3.6	3.7	3.9	4.0	4.1	4.2	4.3	4.4	4.5	4.6
100	0.0	0.0	0.0	0.0	0.0	0.3	0.5	0.7	1.0	1.2	1.4	1.6	1.7	1.9	2.1	2.2	2.4	2.6	2.7	2.8	3.0	3.1	3.3	3.4	3.5	3.7	3.8	3.9	4.0	4.1	4.3	4.4	4.5	4.6	4.7	4.8	4.9	5.0	5.1
99	0.0	0.0	0.0	0.0	0.2	0.5	0.8	1.0	1.2	1.4	1.6	1.8	2.0	2.2	2.3	2.5	2.7	2.8	3.0	3.1	3.3	3.4	3.5	3.7	3.8	3.9	4.0	4.2	4.3	4.4	4.5	4.6	4.7	4.9	5.0	5.1	5.2	5.3	5.4
98	0.0	0.0	0.0	0.2	0.5	0.8	1.0	1.3	1.5	1.7	1.9	2.1	2.3	2.4	2.6	2.8	2.9	3.1	3.2	3.4	3.5	3.7	3.8	3.9	4.1	4.2	4.3	4.4	4.5	4.7	4.8	4.9	5.0	5.1	5.2	5.3	5.4	5.5	5.6
97	0.0	0.0	0.1	0.5	0.8	1.1	1.3	1.5	1.8	2.0	2.2	2.4	2.5	2.7	2.9	3.0	3.2	3.4	3.5	3.6	3.8	3.9	4.1	4.2	4.3	4.5	4.6	4.7	4.8	4.9	5.1	5.2	5.3	5.4	5.5	5.6	5.7	5.8	5.9
96	0.0	0.0	0.4	0.8	1.1	1.3	1.6	1.8	2.0	2.3	2.4	2.6	2.8	3.0	3.2	3.3	3.5	3.6	3.8	3.9	4.1	4.2	4.3	4.5	4.6	4.7	4.9	5.0	5.1	5.2	5.3	5.4	5.6	5.7	5.8	5.9	6.0	6.1	6.2
95	0.0	0.3	0.7	1.0	1.3	1.6	1.9	2.1	2.3	2.5	2.7	2.9	3.1	3.3	3.4	3.6	3.8	3.9	4.1	4.2	4.4	4.5	4.6	4.8	4.9	5.0	5.1	5.3	5.4	5.5	5.6	5.7	5.8	6.0	6.1	6.2	6.3	6.4	6.5
94	0.1	0.6	1.0	1.3	1.6	1.9	2.2	2.4	2.6	2.8	3.0	3.2	3.4	3.6	3.7	3.9	4.1	4.2	4.4	4.5	4.6	4.8	4.9	5.0	5.2	5.3	5.4	5.6	5.7	5.8	5.9	6.0	6.1	6.2	6.4	6.5	6.6	6.7	6.8
93	0.4	0.9	1.3	1.6	1.9	2.2	2.5	2.7	2.9	3.1	3.3	3.5	3.7	3.9	4.0	4.2	4.4	4.5	4.7	4.8	4.9	5.1	5.2	5.3	5.5	5.6	5.7	5.8	6.0	6.1	6.2	6.3	6.4	6.5	6.6	6.8	6.9	7.0	7.1
92	0.7	1.2	1.6	1.9	2.2	2.5	2.8	3.0	3.2	3.4	3.6	3.8	4.0	4.2	4.3	4.5	4.7	4.8	5.0	5.1	5.2	5.4	5.5	5.6	5.8	5.9	6.0	6.2	6.3	6.4	6.5	6.6	6.7	6.8	7.0	7.1	7.2	7.3	7.4
91	1.0	1.5	1.9	2.2	2.5	2.8	3.1	3.3	3.5	3.7	3.9	4.1	4.3	4.5	4.6	4.8	5.0	5.1	5.3	5.4	5.6	5.7	5.8	6.0	6.1	6.2	6.3	6.5	6.6	6.7	6.8	6.9	7.0	7.2	7.3	7.4	7.5	7.6	7.7
90	1.3	1.8	2.2	2.6	2.9	3.1	3.4	3.6	3.8	4.1	4.2	4.4	4.6	4.8	5.0	5.1	5.3	5.4	5.6	5.7	5.9	6.0	6.1	6.3	6.4	6.5	6.7	6.8	6.9	7.0	7.1	7.2	7.4	7.5	7.6	7.7	7.8	7.9	8.0
89	1.5	1.6	2.0	2.4	2.7	3.2	3.5	3.7	4.0	4.2	4.4	4.6	4.8	5.0	5.2	5.3	5.6	5.7	5.9	6.1	6.3	6.4	6.5	6.7	6.9	7.1	7.4	7.6	7.8	7.9	8.0	8.1	8.3	8.4	8.5	8.6	8.7	8.8	8.9
88	2.2	2.5	2.7	2.9	3.1	3.4	3.6	3.8	4.1	4.3	4.5	4.7	5.0	5.2	5.4	5.6	5.9	6.1	6.3	6.6	6.8	7.0	7.2	7.5	7.7	7.9	8.2	8.4	8.6	8.8	8.9	9.0	9.2	9.3	9.4	9.5	9.6	9.7	9.8
87	3.2	3.4	3.7	3.9	4.1	4.3	4.5	4.8	5.0	5.2	5.4	5.6	5.9	6.1	6.3	6.5	6.7	7.0	7.2	7.4	7.6	7.8	8.1	8.3	8.5	8.7	8.9	9.2	9.4	9.6	9.8	9.9	10.1	10.2	10.3	10.4	10.5	10.6	10.7
86	4.2	4.4	4.6	4.8	5.1	5.3	5.5	5.7	5.9	6.1	6.3	6.5	6.8	7.0	7.2	7.4	7.6	7.8	8.0	8.2	8.5	8.7	8.9	9.1	9.3	9.5	9.7	9.9	10.2	10.4	10.6	10.8	11.0	11.1	11.2	11.3	11.4	11.5	11.6
85	5.2	5.4	5.6	5.8	6.0	6.2	6.4	6.6	6.8	7.0	7.2	7.5	7.7	7.9	8.1	8.3	8.5	8.7	8.9	9.1	9.3	9.5	9.7	9.9	10.1	10.3	10.5	10.7	10.9	11.1	11.3	11.5	11.7	11.9	12.1	10.2	12.3	12.4	12.5
84	6.2	6.4	6.6	6.8	7.0	7.2	7.4	7.6	7.8	8.0	8.2	8.4	8.6	8.8	8.9	9.1	9.3	9.5	9.7	9.9	10.1	10.3	10.5	10.7	10.9	11.1	11.3	11.5	11.7	11.9	12.1	12.3	12.5	12.7	12.9	13.1	13.2	13.3	13.4
83	7.2	7.4	7.6	7.8	7.9	8.1	8.3	8.5	8.7	8.9	9.1	9.3	9.5	9.6	9.8	10.0	10.2	10.4	10.6	10.8	11.0	11.1	11.3	11.5	11.7	11.9	12.1	12.3	12.5	12.7	12.8	13.0	13.2	13.4	13.6	13.8	14.0	14.2	14.3
82	8.2	8.4	8.5	8.7	8.9	9.1	9.3	9.4	9.6	9.8	9.9	10.2	10.4	10.5	10.7	10.9	11.1	11.3	11.4	11.6	11.8	12.0	12.2	12.3	12.5	12.7	12.9	13.1	13.2	13.4	13.6	13.8	14.0	14.1	14.3	14.5	14.7	14.9	15.1
81	9.2	9.3	9.5	9.7	9.9	10.0	10.2	10.4	10.6	10.7	10.9	11.1	11.2	11.4	11.6	11.8	11.9	12.1	12.3	12.5	12.6	12.8	13.0	13.2	13.3	13.5	13.7	13.8	14.0	14.2	14.4	14.5	14.7	14.9	15.1	15.2	15.4	15.6	15.7
80	10.2	10.3	10.5	10.7	10.8	11.0	11.2	11.3	11.5	11.7	11.8	12.0	12.1	12.3	12.5	12.6	12.8	13.0	13.1	13.3	13.5	13.6	13.8	14.0	14.1	14.3	14.5	14.6	14.8	15.0	15.1	15.3	15.4	15.6	15.8	15.9	16.1	16.3	16.4
79	11.2	11.3	11.5	11.6	11.8	11.9	12.1	12.3	12.4	12.6	12.7	12.9	13.0	13.2	13.4	13.5	13.7	13.8	14.0	14.1	14.3	14.5	14.6	14.8	14.9	15.1	15.2	15.4	15.6	15.7	15.9	16.0	16.2	16.3	16.5	16.7	16.8	17.0	17.1
78	12.1	12.3	12.4	12.6	12.7	12.9	13.0	13.2	13.3	13.5	13.6	13.8	13.9	14.1	14.2	14.4	14.5	14.7	14.8	15.0	15.1	15.3	15.4	15.6	15.7	15.9	16.0	16.2	16.3	16.5	16.6	16.8	16.9	17.1	17.2	17.4	17.5	17.7	17.8
77	13.1	13.3	13.4	13.6	13.7	13.8	14.0	14.1	14.3	14.4	14.6	14.7	14.8	15.0	15.1	15.3	15.4	15.5	15.7	15.8	16.0	16.1	16.3	16.4	16.5	16.7	16.8	17.0	17.1	17.2	17.4	17.5	17.7	17.8	18.0	18.1	18.2	18.4	18.5
76	14.1	14.3	14.4	14.5	14.7	14.8	14.9	15.1	15.2	15.3	15.5	15.6	15.7	15.9	16.0	16.1	16.3	16.4	16.5	16.7	16.8	16.9	17.1	17.2	17.3	17.5	17.6	17.7	17.9	18.0	18.1	18.3	18.4	18.5	18.7	18.8	19.0	19.1	19.2
75	15.1	15.3	15.4	15.5	15.6	15.8	15.9	16.0	16.1	16.3	16.4	16.5	16.6	16.8	16.9	17.0	17.1	17.3	17.4	17.5	17.6	17.8	17.9	18.0	18.1	18.3	18.4	18.5	18.7	18.8	18.9	19.0	19.2	19.3	19.4	19.5	19.7	19.8	19.9
74	16.1	16.2	16.4	16.5	16.6	16.7	16.8	16.9	17.1	17.2	17.3	17.4	17.5	17.7	17.8	17.9	18.0	18.1	18.2	18.4	18.5	18.6	18.7	18.8	19.0	19.1	19.2	19.3	19.4	19.5	19.7	19.8	19.9	20.0	20.1	20.3	20.4	20.5	20.6
73	17.1	17.2	17.3	17.4	17.6	17.7	17.8	17.9	18.0	18.1	18.2	18.3	18.4	18.5	18.7	18.8	18.9	19.0	19.1	19.2	19.3	19.4	19.5	19.6	19.8	19.9	19.9	20.1	20.2	20.3	20.4	20.5	20.6	20.8	20.9	21.0	21.1	21.2	21.3
72	18.1	18.2	18.3	18.4	18.5	18.6	18.7	18.8	18.9	19.0	19.1	19.2	19.3	19.4	19.5	19.6	19.7	19.8	19.9	20.0	20.2	20.3	20.4	20.5	20.6	20.7	20.8	20.9	21.0	21.1	21.2	21.3	21.4	21.5	21.6	21.7	21.8	21.9	22.0
71	19.1	19.2	19.3	19.4	19.5	19.6	19.7	19.8	19.9	19.9	20.0	20.1	20.2	20.3	20.4	20.5	20.6	20.7	20.8	20.9	21.0	21.1	21.2	21.3	21.4	21.5	21.6	21.6	21.7	21.8	21.9	22.0	22.1	22.2	22.3	22.4	22.5	22.6	22.7
70	20.1	20.2	20.3	20.3	20.4	20.5	20.6	20.7	20.8	20.9	21.0	21.0	21.1	21.2	21.3	21.4	21.5	21.6	21.6	21.7	21.8	21.9	22.0	22.1	22.2	22.3	22.3	22.4	22.5	22.6	22.7	22.8	22.9	23.0	23.0	23.1	23.2	23.3	23.4
69	21.1	21.2	21.2	21.3	21.4	21.5	21.6	21.6	21.7	21.8	21.9	21.9	22.0	22.1	22.2	22.3	22.3	22.4	22.5	22.6	22.7	22.7	22.8	22.9	23.0	23.1	23.1	23.2	23.3	23.4	23.4	23.5	23.6	23.7	23.8	23.8	23.9	24.0	24.1
68	22.1	22.1	22.2	22.3	22.4	22.4	22.5	22.6	22.6	22.7	22.8	22.9	22.9	23.0	23.1	23.1	23.2	23.3	23.4	23.4	23.5	23.6	23.6	23.7	23.8	23.8	23.9	24.0	24.1	24.1	24.2	24.3	24.3	24.4	24.5	24.6	24.6	24.7	24.8
67	23.1	23.1	23.2	23.3	23.3	23.4	23.4	23.5	23.6	23.6	23.7	23.8	23.8	23.9	23.9	24.0	24.1	24.1	24.2	24.3	24.3	24.4	24.5	24.5	24.6	24.6	24.7	24.8	24.8	24.9	25.0	25.0	25.1	25.2	25.2	25.3	25.3	25.4	25.5
66	24.1	24.1	24.2	24.2	24.3	24.3	24.4	24.4	24.5	24.6	24.6	24.7	24.7	24.8	24.8	24.9	24.9	25.0	25.1	25.1	25.2	25.2	25.3	25.3	25.4	25.4	25.5	25.6	25.6	25.7	25.7	25.8	25.8	25.9	25.9	26.0	26.1	26.1	26.2
65	25.0	25.1	25.1	25.2	25.2	25.3	25.3	25.4	25.4	25.5	25.5	25.6	25.6	25.7	25.7	25.8	25.8	25.9	25.9	26.0	26.0	26.0	26.1	26.1	26.2	26.2	26.3	26.3	26.4	26.4	26.5	26.5	26.6	26.6	26.7	26.7	26.8	26.8	26.9
64	26.0	26.1	26.1	26.2	26.2	26.2	26.3	26.3	26.4	26.4	26.4	26.5	26.5	26.6	26.6	26.6	26.7	26.7	26.8	26.8	26.8	26.9	26.9	27.0	27.0	27.0	27.1	27.1	27.2	27.2	27.2	27.3	27.3	27.4	27.4	27.4	27.5	27.5	27.6

LISTED PUT OPTION PRICE WHEN EXERCISE PRICE IS 100

NUMBER OF WEEKS BEFORE THE OPTION EXPIRES

Common Stock Price	1	2	3	4	5	6	7	8	9	10	11	12	13	14	15	16	17	18	19	20	21	22	23	24	25	26	27	28	29	30	31	32	33	34	35	36	37	38	39
130	0.0	0.0	0.0	0.0	0.0	0.0	0.0	0.0	0.0	0.0	0.0	0.0	0.0	0.0	0.0	0.0	0.0	0.0	0.0	0.0	0.0	0.0	0.0	0.0	0.0	0.0	0.0	0.1	0.3	0.4	0.5	0.7	0.8	0.9	1.0	1.2	1.3	1.4	1.5
128	0.0	0.0	0.0	0.0	0.0	0.0	0.0	0.0	0.0	0.0	0.0	0.0	0.0	0.0	0.0	0.0	0.0	0.0	0.0	0.0	0.0	0.0	0.0	0.0	0.1	0.3	0.4	0.5	0.7	0.8	0.9	1.1	1.2	1.3	1.4	1.5	1.7	1.8	1.9
126	0.0	0.0	0.0	0.0	0.0	0.0	0.0	0.0	0.0	0.0	0.0	0.0	0.0	0.0	0.0	0.0	0.0	0.0	0.0	0.0	0.0	0.1	0.2	0.4	0.5	0.7	0.8	0.9	1.1	1.2	1.3	1.4	1.6	1.7	1.8	1.9	2.1	2.2	2.3
124	0.0	0.0	0.0	0.0	0.0	0.0	0.0	0.0	0.0	0.0	0.0	0.0	0.0	0.0	0.0	0.0	0.0	0.0	0.0	0.2	0.3	0.5	0.6	0.8	0.9	1.1	1.2	1.3	1.5	1.6	1.7	1.9	2.0	2.1	2.2	2.3	2.5	2.6	2.7
122	0.0	0.0	0.0	0.0	0.0	0.0	0.0	0.0	0.0	0.0	0.0	0.0	0.0	0.0	0.0	0.0	0.1	0.3	0.4	0.6	0.8	0.9	1.1	1.2	1.3	1.5	1.6	1.8	1.9	2.0	2.2	2.3	2.4	2.5	2.6	2.8	2.9	3.0	3.1
120	0.0	0.0	0.0	0.0	0.0	0.0	0.0	0.0	0.0	0.0	0.0	0.0	0.0	0.0	0.2	0.4	0.5	0.7	0.9	1.0	1.2	1.3	1.5	1.6	1.8	1.9	2.1	2.2	2.3	2.5	2.6	2.7	2.8	3.0	3.1	3.2	3.3	3.4	3.6
118	0.0	0.0	0.0	0.0	0.0	0.0	0.0	0.0	0.0	0.0	0.0	0.0	0.3	0.4	0.6	0.8	1.0	1.2	1.3	1.5	1.6	1.8	1.9	2.1	2.2	2.4	2.5	2.6	2.8	2.9	3.0	3.2	3.3	3.4	3.5	3.7	3.8	3.9	4.0
116	0.0	0.0	0.0	0.0	0.0	0.0	0.0	0.0	0.0	0.1	0.3	0.5	0.7	0.9	1.1	1.3	1.5	1.6	1.8	2.0	2.1	2.3	2.4	2.6	2.7	2.8	3.0	3.1	3.3	3.4	3.5	3.6	3.8	3.9	4.0	4.1	4.2	4.4	4.5
114	0.0	0.0	0.0	0.0	0.0	0.0	0.0	0.1	0.3	0.6	0.8	1.0	1.2	1.4	1.6	1.8	1.9	2.1	2.3	2.4	2.6	2.7	2.9	3.0	3.2	3.3	3.5	3.6	3.7	3.9	4.0	4.1	4.2	4.4	4.5	4.6	4.7	4.8	5.0
112	0.0	0.0	0.0	0.0	0.0	0.1	0.3	0.6	0.8	1.1	1.3	1.5	1.7	1.9	2.1	2.3	2.4	2.6	2.8	2.9	3.1	3.2	3.4	3.5	3.7	3.8	4.0	4.1	4.2	4.4	4.5	4.6	4.7	4.9	5.0	5.1	5.2	5.3	5.5
110	0.0	0.0	0.0	0.0	0.3	0.6	0.9	1.1	1.4	1.6	1.8	2.0	2.2	2.4	2.6	2.8	3.0	3.1	3.3	3.5	3.6	3.8	3.9	4.1	4.2	4.3	4.5	4.6	4.8	4.9	5.0	5.1	5.3	5.4	5.5	5.6	5.7	5.9	6.0
108	0.0	0.0	0.1	0.5	0.8	1.1	1.4	1.7	1.9	2.1	2.3	2.6	2.8	3.0	3.1	3.3	3.5	3.7	3.8	4.0	4.2	4.3	4.5	4.6	4.7	4.9	5.0	5.2	5.3	5.4	5.6	5.7	5.8	5.9	6.0	6.2	6.3	6.4	6.5
106	0.0	0.2	0.7	1.0	1.4	1.7	2.0	2.2	2.5	2.7	2.9	3.1	3.3	3.5	3.7	3.9	4.1	4.2	4.4	4.6	4.7	4.9	5.0	5.2	5.3	5.4	5.6	5.7	5.9	6.0	6.1	6.2	6.4	6.5	6.6	6.7	6.8	7.0	7.1
104	0.2	0.8	1.2	1.6	2.0	2.3	2.5	2.8	3.0	3.3	3.5	3.7	3.9	4.1	4.3	4.5	4.6	4.8	5.0	5.1	5.3	5.4	5.6	5.7	5.9	6.0	6.2	6.3	6.4	6.6	6.7	6.8	6.9	7.1	7.2	7.3	7.4	7.5	7.7
102	0.8	1.4	1.8	2.2	2.6	2.9	3.1	3.4	3.6	3.9	4.1	4.3	4.5	4.7	4.9	5.1	5.2	5.4	5.6	5.7	5.9	6.0	6.2	6.3	6.5	6.6	6.8	6.9	7.0	7.2	7.3	7.4	7.5	7.7	7.8	7.9	8.0	8.1	8.3
100	1.4	2.0	2.5	2.8	3.2	3.5	3.8	4.0	4.3	4.5	4.7	4.9	5.1	5.3	5.5	5.7	5.9	6.0	6.2	6.4	6.5	6.7	6.8	7.0	7.1	7.3	7.4	7.5	7.7	7.8	7.9	8.1	8.2	8.3	8.4	8.5	8.7	8.8	8.9
99	1.6	2.2	2.7	2.9	3.3	3.6	4.0	4.2	4.5	4.8	5.0	5.1	5.4	5.6	5.8	6.0	6.2	6.4	6.6	6.8	6.9	7.1	7.2	7.3	7.6	7.8	8.1	8.4	8.6	8.7	8.8	9.0	9.1	9.2	9.3	9.4	9.6	9.7	9.8
98	2.3	2.5	2.8	3.0	3.4	3.8	4.2	4.4	4.7	5.1	5.3	5.5	5.8	6.0	6.2	6.4	6.6	6.8	7.0	7.1	7.4	7.6	7.9	8.1	8.4	8.6	8.9	9.1	9.4	9.6	9.7	9.9	10.0	10.1	10.2	10.3	10.5	10.6	10.7
97	3.2	3.5	3.7	4.0	4.2	4.5	4.7	5.0	5.2	5.5	5.7	6.0	6.2	6.5	6.7	7.0	7.2	7.4	7.7	7.9	8.2	8.4	8.7	8.9	9.2	9.4	9.7	9.9	10.2	10.4	10.6	10.8	10.9	11.0	11.1	11.2	11.4	11.5	11.6
96	4.2	4.5	4.7	5.0	5.2	5.4	5.7	5.9	6.2	6.4	6.6	6.9	7.1	7.3	7.6	7.8	8.1	8.3	8.5	8.8	9.0	9.3	9.5	9.7	9.9	10.2	10.5	10.7	10.9	11.2	11.4	11.7	11.8	11.9	12.0	12.1	12.3	12.4	12.5
95	5.2	5.5	5.7	5.9	6.2	6.4	6.6	6.9	7.1	7.3	7.5	7.8	8,0	8.2	8.5	8.7	8.9	9.2	9.4	9.6	9.9	10.1	10.3	10.6	10.8	11.0	11.2	11.5	11.7	11.9	12.2	12.4	12.6	12.8	12.9	13.0	13.2	13.3	13.4
94	6.2	6.4	6.7	6.9	7.1	7.3	7.6	7.8	8.0	8.2	8.5	8.7	8.9	9.1	9.4	9.6	9.8	10.0	10.2	10.5	10.7	10.9	11.1	11.4	11.6	11.8	12.0	12.3	12.5	12.7	12.9	13.2	13.4	13.6	13.8	14.1	14.1	14.2	14.3
93	7.2	7.4	7.6	7.9	8.1	8.3	8.5	8.7	8.9	9.2	9.4	9.6	9.8	10.0	10.2	10.5	10.7	10.9	11.1	11.3	11.5	11.7	12.0	12.2	12.4	12.6	12.8	13.0	13.3	13.5	13.7	13.9	14.1	14.3	14.5	14.8	15.0	15.1	15.2
92	8.2	8.4	8.6	8.8	9.0	9.2	9.5	9.7	9.9	10.1	10.3	10.5	10.7	10.9	11.1	11.3	11.5	11.7	11.9	12.2	12.4	12.6	12.8	13.0	13.2	13.4	13.6	13.8	14.0	14.2	14.4	14.7	14.9	15.1	15.3	15.5	15.7	15.9	16.1
91	9.2	9.4	9.6	9.8	10.0	10.2	10.4	10.6	10.8	11.0	11.2	11.4	11.6	11.8	12.0	12.2	12.4	12.6	12.8	13.0	13.2	13.4	13.6	13.8	14.0	14.2	14.4	14.6	14.8	15.0	15.2	15.4	15.6	15.8	16.0	16.2	16.4	16.6	16.8
90	10.2	10.4	10.6	10.8	11.0	11.2	11.3	11.5	11.7	11.9	12.1	12.3	12.5	12.7	12.9	13.1	13.3	13.5	13.7	13.8	14.0	14.2	14.4	14.6	14.8	15.0	15.2	15.4	15.6	15.8	16.0	16.1	16.3	16.5	16.7	16.9	17.1	17.3	17.5
89	11.2	11.4	11.6	11.7	11.9	12.1	12.3	12.5	12.7	12.8	13.0	13.2	13.4	13.6	13.8	13.9	14.1	14.3	14.5	14.7	14.9	15.1	15.2	15.4	15.6	15.8	16.0	16.2	16.3	16.5	16.7	16.9	17.1	17.3	17.5	17.6	17.8	18.0	18.2
88	12.2	12.4	12.5	12.7	12.9	13.1	13.2	13.4	13.6	13.8	13.9	14.1	14.3	14.5	14.6	14.8	15.0	15.2	15.4	15.5	15.7	15.9	16.1	16.2	16.4	16.6	16.8	16.9	17.1	17.3	17.5	17.6	17.8	18.0	18.2	18.4	18.5	18.7	18.9
87	13.2	13.3	13.5	13.7	13.8	14.0	14.2	14.3	14.5	14.7	14.9	15.0	15.2	15.4	15.5	15.7	15.9	16.0	16.2	16.4	16.5	16.7	16.9	17.0	17.2	17.4	17.6	17.7	17.9	18.1	18.2	18.4	18.6	18.7	18.9	19.1	19.2	19.4	19.6
86	14.2	14.3	14.5	14.6	14.8	15.0	15.1	15.3	15.4	15.6	15.8	15.9	16.1	16.3	16.4	16.6	16.7	16.9	17.1	17.2	17.4	17.5	17.7	17.9	18.0	18.2	18.3	18.5	19.7	18.8	19.0	19.1	19.3	19.5	19.6	19.8	19.9	20.1	20.3
85	15.2	15.3	15.5	15.6	15.8	15.9	16.1	16.2	16.4	16.5	16.7	16.8	17.0	17.1	17.3	17.4	17.6	17.8	17.9	18.1	18.2	18.4	18.5	18.7	18.8	19.0	19.1	19.3	19.4	19.6	19.7	19.9	20.0	20.2	20.4	20.5	20.7	20.8	21.0
84	16.1	16.3	16.4	16.6	16.7	16.9	17.0	17.2	71.3	17.5	17.6	17.7	17.9	18.0	18.2	18.3	18.5	18.6	18.8	18.9	19.0	19.2	19.3	19.5	19.6	19.8	19.9	20.1	20.2	20.4	20.5	20.6	20.8	20.9	21.1	21.2	21.4	21.5	21.7
83	17.1	17.3	17.4	17.5	17.7	17.8	18.0	18.1	18.2	18.4	18.5	18.6	18.8	18.9	19.1	19.2	19.3	19.5	19.6	19.7	19.9	20.0	20.2	20.3	20.4	20.6	20.7	20.8	21.0	21.1	21.3	21.4	21.5	21.7	21.8	21.9	22.1	22.2	22.4
82	18.1	18.3	18.4	18.5	18.6	18.8	18.9	19.0	19.2	19.3	19.4	19.6	19.7	19.8	19.9	20.1	20.2	20.3	20.5	20.6	20.7	20.8	21.0	21.1	21.2	21.4	21.5	21.6	21.8	21.9	22.0	22.1	22.3	22.4	22.5	22.7	22.8	22.9	23.1
81	19.1	19.2	19.4	19.5	19.6	19.7	19.9	19.9	20.1	20.2	20.3	20.5	20.6	20.7	20.8	20.9	21.1	21.2	21.3	21.4	21.6	21.7	21.8	21.9	22.0	22.2	22.3	22.4	22.5	22.7	22.8	22.9	23.0	23.1	23.3	23.4	23.5	23.6	23.7
80	20.1	20.2	20.3	20.5	20.6	20.7	20.8	20.9	21.0	21.1	21.3	21.4	21.5	21.6	21.7	21.8	21.9	22.0	22.2	22.3	22.4	22.5	22.6	22.7	22.8	23.0	23.1	23.2	23.3	23.4	23.5	23.6	23.8	23.9	24.0	24.1	24.2	24.3	24.4
79	21.1	21.2	21.3	21.4	21.5	21.6	21.7	21.8	22.0	22.1	22.2	22.3	22.4	22.5	22.6	22.7	22.8	22.9	23.0	23.1	23.2	23.3	23.4	23.5	23.7	23.8	23.9	24.0	24.1	24.2	24.3	24.4	24.5	24.6	24.7	24.8	24.9	25.0	25.1
78	22.1	22.2	22.3	22.4	22.5	22.6	22.7	22.8	22.9	23.0	23.1	23.2	23.3	23.4	23.5	23.6	23.7	23.8	23.9	24.0	24.1	24.2	24.3	24.4	24.5	24.6	24.7	24.7	24.8	24.9	25.0	25.2	25.2	25.3	25.4	25.5	25.6	25.7	25.8
77	23.1	23.2	23.3	23.4	23.5	23.5	23.6	23.7	23.8	23.9	24.0	24.1	24.2	24.3	24.4	24.4	24.5	24.6	24.7	24.8	24.9	25.0	25.1	25.2	25.3	25.3	25.4	25.5	25.6	25.7	25.8	25.9	26.0	26.1	26.2	26.3	26.3	26.4	26.5
76	24.1	24.2	24.2	24.3	24.4	24.5	24.6	24.7	24.7	24.8	24.9	25.0	25.1	25.2	25.2	25.3	25.4	25.5	25.6	25.7	25.7	25.8	25.9	26.0	26.1	26.1	26.2	26.3	26.4	26.5	26.6	26.6	26.7	26.8	26.9	27.0	27.1	27.1	27.2
75	25.1	25.1	25.2	25.3	25.4	25.4	25.5	25.6	25.7	25.7	25.8	25.9	26.0	26.0	26.1	26.2	26.3	26.3	26.4	26.5	26.6	26.6	26.7	26.8	26.9	26.9	27.0	27.1	27.2	27.2	27.3	27.4	27.5	27.5	27.6	27.7	27.8	27.8	27.9
74	26.1	26.1	26.2	26.3	26.3	26.4	26.5	26.5	26.6	26.7	26.7	26.8	26.9	26.9	27.0	27.1	27.1	27.2	27.3	27.3	27.6	27.5	27.5	27.6	27.7	27.7	27.8	27.9	27.9	28.0	28.1	28.1	28.2	28.3	28.3	28.4	28.5	28.5	28.6
73	27.1	27.1	27.2	27.2	27.3	27.4	27.4	27.5	27.5	27.6	27.6	27.7	27.8	27.8	27.9	27.9	28.0	28.1	28.1	28.2	28.2	28.3	28.4	28.4	28.5	28.5	28.6	28.7	28.7	28.8	28.8	28.9	28.9	29.0	29.1	29.1	29.2	29.2	29.3
72	28.1	28.1	28.2	28.2	28.3	28.3	28.4	28.4	28.5	28.5	28.6	28.6	28.7	28.7	28.8	28.8	28.9	28.9	29.0	29.0	29.1	29.1	29.2	29.2	29.3	29.3	29.4	29.4	29.5	29.5	29.6	29.6	29.7	29.7	29.8	29.8	29.9	29.9	29.9
71	29.0	29.1	29.1	29.2	29.2	29.3	29.3	29.3	29.4	29.4	29.5	29.5	29.6	29.6	29.7	29.7	29.7	29.8	29.8	29.9	29.9	29.9	29.9	30.0	30.1	30.1	30.2	30.2	30.3	30.3	30.3	30.4	30.4	30.5	30.5	30.6	30.6	30.6	30.7
70	30.0	30.1	30.1	30.1	30.2	30.2	30.2	30.3	30.3	30.4	30.4	30.4	30.5	30.5	30.5	30.6	30.6	30.6	30.7	30.7	30.7	30.8	30.8	30.9	30.9	30.9	31.0	31.0	31.0	31.1	31.1	31.1	31.2	31.2	31.2	31.3	31.3	31.3	31.4

LISTED PUT OPTION PRICE WHEN EXERCISE PRICE IS 110

Common Stock Price	NUMBER OF WEEKS BEFORE THE OPTION EXPIRES																																					
	1	2	3	4	5	6	7	8	9	10	11	12	13	14	15	16	17	18	19	20	21	22	23	24	25	26	27	28	29	30	31	32	33	34	35	36	37	38	39
144	0.0	0.0	0.0	0.0	0.0	0.0	0.0	0.0	0.0	0.0	0.0	0.0	0.0	0.0	0.0	0.0	0.0	0.0	0.0	0.0	0.0	0.0	0.0	0.0	0.0	0.0	0.0	0.0	0.1	0.3	0.4	0.5	0.7	0.8	1.0	1.1	1.2	1.3	1.5
142	0.0	0.0	0.0	0.0	0.0	0.0	0.0	0.0	0.0	0.0	0.0	0.0	0.0	0.0	0.0	0.0	0.0	0.0	0.0	0.0	0.0	0.0	0.0	0.0	0.0	0.1	0.2	0.4	0.5	0.6	0.8	0.9	1.1	1.2	1.3	1.5	1.6	1.7	1.8
140	0.0	0.0	0.0	0.0	0.0	0.0	0.0	0.0	0.0	0.0	0.0	0.0	0.0	0.0	0.0	0.0	0.0	0.0	0.0	0.0	0.0	0.0	0.0	0.1	0.3	0.4	0.6	0.7	0.9	1.0	1.2	1.3	1.5	1.6	1.7	1.9	2.0	2.1	2.2
138	0.0	0.0	0.0	0.0	0.0	0.0	0.0	0.0	0.0	0.0	0.0	0.0	0.0	0.0	0.0	0.0	0.0	0.0	0.0	0.0	0.0	0.2	0.4	0.5	0.7	0.8	1.0	1.1	1.3	1.4	1.6	1.7	1.9	2.0	2.1	2.3	2.4	2.5	2.6
136	0.0	0.0	0.0	0.0	0.0	0.0	0.0	0.0	0.0	0.0	0.0	0.0	0.0	0.0	0.0	0.0	0.0	0.0	0.1	0.3	0.4	0.6	0.8	0.9	1.1	1.3	1.4	1.6	1.7	1.8	2.0	2.1	2.3	2.4	2.5	2.7	2.8	2.9	3.0
134	0.0	0.0	0.0	0.0	0.0	0.0	0.0	0.0	0.0	0.0	0.0	0.0	0.0	0.0	0.0	0.0	0.2	0.3	0.5	0.7	0.9	1.0	1.2	1.4	1.5	1.7	1.8	2.0	2.1	2.3	2.4	2.6	2.7	2.8	3.0	3.1	3.2	3.3	3.5
132	0.0	0.0	0.0	0.0	0.0	0.0	0.0	0.0	0.0	0.0	0.0	0.0	0.0	0.0	0.2	0.4	0.6	0.8	1.0	1.1	1.3	1.5	1.6	1.8	2.0	2.1	2.3	2.4	2.6	2.7	2.8	3.0	3.1	3.3	3.4	3.5	3.7	3.8	3.9
130	0.0	0.0	0.0	0.0	0.0	0.0	0.0	0.0	0.0	0.0	0.0	0.0	0.2	0.4	0.6	0.8	1.0	1.2	1.4	1.6	1.8	1.9	2.1	2.3	2.4	2.6	2.7	2.9	3.0	3.2	3.3	3.4	3.6	3.7	3.8	4.0	4.1	4.2	4.4
128	0.0	0.0	0.0	0.0	0.0	0.0	0.0	0.0	0.0	0.0	0.2	0.5	0.7	0.9	1.1	1.3	1.5	1.7	1.9	2.1	2.2	2.4	2.6	2.7	2.9	3.0	3.2	3.3	3.5	3.6	3.8	3.9	4.0	4.2	4.3	4.4	4.6	4.7	4.8
126	0.0	0.0	0.0	0.0	0.0	0.0	0.0	0.0	0.2	0.5	0.7	1.0	1.2	1.4	1.6	1.8	2.0	2.2	2.4	2.5	2.7	2.9	3.0	3.2	3.4	3.5	3.7	3.8	4.0	4.1	4.2	4.4	4.5	4.7	4.8	4.9	5.1	5.2	5.3
124	0.0	0.0	0.0	0.0	0.0	0.0	0.2	0.5	0.7	1.0	1.2	1.4	1.7	1.9	2.1	2.3	2.5	2.7	2.8	3.0	3.2	3.4	3.5	3.7	3.9	4.0	4.2	4.3	4.5	4.6	4.7	4.9	5.0	5.2	5.3	5.4	5.5	5.7	5.8
122	0.0	0.0	0.0	0.0	0.0	0.4	0.7	1.0	1.2	1.5	1.7	2.0	2.2	2.4	2.6	2.8	3.0	3.2	3.4	3.5	3.7	3.9	4.0	4.2	4.4	4.5	4.7	4.8	5.0	5.1	5.3	5.4	5.5	5.7	5.8	5.9	6.1	6.2	6.3
120	0.0	0.0	0.0	0.2	0.6	0.9	1.2	1.5	1.8	2.0	2.3	2.5	2.7	2.9	3.1	3.3	3.5	3.7	3.9	4.1	4.2	4.4	4.6	4.7	4.9	5.0	5.2	5.4	5.5	5.6	5.8	5.9	6.1	6.2	6.3	6.5	6.6	6.7	6.8
118	0.0	0.0	0.3	0.7	1.1	1.4	1.8	2.0	2.3	2.6	2.8	3.0	3.3	3.5	3.7	3.9	4.1	4.3	4.4	4.6	4.8	5.0	5.1	5.3	5.4	5.6	5.7	5.9	6.0	6.2	6.3	6.5	6.6	6.7	6.9	7.0	7.1	7.3	7.4
116	0.0	0.4	0.9	1.3	1.7	2.0	2.3	2.6	2.9	3.1	3.4	3.6	3.8	4.0	4.2	4.4	4.6	4.8	5.0	5.2	5.4	5.5	5.7	5.8	6.0	6.2	6.3	6.5	6.6	6.8	6.9	7.0	7.2	7.3	7.4	7.6	7.7	7.8	8.0
114	0.3	1.0	1.5	1.9	2.3	2.6	2.9	3.2	3.5	3.7	4.0	4.2	4.4	4.6	4.8	5.0	5.2	5.4	5.6	5.8	5.9	6.1	6.3	6.4	6.6	6.7	6.9	7.0	7.2	7.3	7.5	7.6	7.8	7.9	8.0	8.2	8.3	8.4	8.5
112	0.9	1.6	2.1	2.5	2.9	3.2	3.5	3.8	4.1	4.3	4.6	4.8	5.0	5.2	5.4	5.6	5.8	6.0	6.2	6.4	6.5	6.7	6.9	7.0	7.2	7.4	7.5	7.7	7.8	7.9	8.1	8.2	8.4	8.5	8.6	8.8	8.9	9.0	9.1
110	1.6	2.2	2.7	3.1	3.5	3.8	4.1	4.4	4.7	5.0	5.2	5.4	5.6	5.9	6.1	6.3	6.5	6.6	6.8	7.0	7.2	7.3	7.5	7.7	7.8	8.0	8.1	8.3	8.4	8.6	8.7	8.9	9.0	9.1	9.3	9.4	9.5	9.7	9.8
108	2.3	2.6	3.0	3.3	3.7	4.0	4.3	4.6	4.9	5.2	5.5	5.7	6.0	6.4	6.6	6.8	7.0	7.2	7.4	7.6	7.9	8.2	8.5	8.8	9.0	9.3	9.6	9.9	10.2	10.4	10.5	10.7	10.8	10.9	11.1	11.2	11.3	11.5	11.6
106	4.3	4.5	4.8	5.1	5.3	5.6	5.9	6.1	6.4	6.7	6.9	7.2	7.5	7.7	8.0	8.3	8.5	8.8	9.1	9.3	9.6	9.9	10.1	10.4	10.7	10.9	11.2	11.5	11.7	12.0	12.3	12.5	12.6	12.7	12.8	12.9	13.1	13.3	13.4
104	6.3	6.5	6.8	7.0	7.3	7.5	7.8	8.0	8.3	8.5	8.8	9.0	9.3	9.5	9.8	10.0	10.3	10.5	10.8	11.0	11.3	11.5	11.8	12.0	12.3	12.5	12.8	13.0	13.3	13.5	13.8	14.0	14.3	14.5	14.6	14.7	14.9	15.1	15.2
102	8.2	8.5	8.7	8.9	9.2	9.4	9.6	9.9	10.1	10.3	10.6	10.8	11.1	11.3	11.5	11.8	12.0	12.2	12.5	12.7	12.9	13.2	13.4	13.6	13.9	14.1	14.3	14.6	14.8	15.0	15.3	15.5	15.8	16.0	16.2	16.5	16.7	16.9	17.0
100	10.2	10.4	10.7	10.9	11.1	11.3	11.5	11.8	12.0	12.2	12.4	12.6	12.8	13.1	13.3	13.5	13.7	13.9	14.2	14.4	14.6	14.8	15.0	15.3	15.5	15.7	15.9	16.1	16.4	16.6	16.8	17.0	17.2	17.5	17.7	17.9	18.1	18.3	18.5
99	11.2	11.4	11.6	11.8	12.1	12.3	12.5	12.7	12.9	13.1	13.3	13.5	13.7	14.0	14.2	14.4	14.6	14.8	15.0	15.2	15.4	15.7	15.9	16.1	16.3	16.5	16.7	16.9	17.1	17.3	17.6	17.8	18.0	18.2	18.4	18.6	18.8	19.0	19.2
98	12.2	12.4	12.6	12.8	13.0	13.2	13.4	13.6	13.8	14.0	14.2	14.4	14.6	14.8	15.1	15.3	15.5	15.7	15.9	16.1	16.3	16.5	16.7	16.9	17.1	17.3	17.5	17.7	17.9	18.1	18.3	18.5	18.7	18.9	19.1	19.3	19.5	19.7	19.9
97	13.2	13.4	13.6	13.8	14.0	14.2	14.4	14.6	14.8	15.0	15.2	15.3	15.5	15.7	15.9	16.1	16.3	16.5	16.7	16.9	17.1	17.3	17.5	17.7	17.9	18.1	18.3	18.5	18.7	18.9	19.1	19.3	19.5	19.7	19.9	20.0	20.2	20.4	20.6
96	14.2	14.4	14.6	14.8	14.9	15.1	15.3	15.5	15.7	15.9	16.1	16.3	16.4	16.6	16.8	17.0	17.2	17.4	17.6	17.8	17.9	18.1	18.3	18.5	18.7	18.9	19.1	19.3	19.4	19.6	19.8	20.0	20.2	20.4	20.6	20.8	21.0	21.1	21.3
95	15.2	15.4	15.5	15.7	15.9	16.1	16.3	16.4	16.6	16.8	17.0	17.2	17.3	17.5	17.7	17.9	18.1	18.2	18.4	18.6	18.8	19.0	19.1	19.3	19.5	19.7	19.9	20.0	20.2	20.4	20.6	20.8	20.9	21.1	21.3	21.5	21.7	21.8	22.0
94	16.2	16.3	16.5	16.7	16.9	17.0	17.2	17.4	17.6	17.7	17.9	18.1	18.2	18.4	18.6	18.8	18.9	19.1	19.3	19.4	19.6	19.8	19.9	20.1	20.3	20.5	20.7	20.8	21.0	21.2	21.3	21.5	21.7	21.9	22.0	22.2	22.4	22.5	22.7
93	17.2	17.3	17.5	17.7	17.8	18.0	18.2	18.3	18.5	18.6	18.8	19.0	19.1	19.3	19.5	19.6	19.8	19.9	20.1	20.3	20.5	20.6	20.8	20.9	21.1	21.3	21.4	21.6	21.8	21.9	22.1	22.3	22.6	22.6	22.8	22.9	23.1	23.2	23.4
92	18.2	18.3	18.5	18.6	18.8	18.9	19.1	19.3	19.4	19.6	19.7	19.9	20.0	20.2	20.3	20.5	20.7	20.8	21.0	21.1	21.3	21.4	21.6	21.8	21.9	22.1	22.2	22.4	22.5	22.7	22.9	23.0	23.2	23.3	23.5	23.6	23.8	23.9	24.1
91	19.1	19.3	19.4	19.6	19.7	19.9	20.0	20.2	20.3	20.5	20.6	20.8	20.9	21.1	21.2	21.4	21.5	21.7	21.8	22.0	22.1	22.3	22.4	22.6	22.7	22.9	23.0	23.2	23.3	23.5	23.6	23.8	23.9	24.1	24.0	24.4	24.5	24.7	24.8
90	20.1	20.3	20.4	20.6	20.7	20.8	21.0	21.1	21.3	21.4	21.5	21.7	21.8	22.0	22.1	22.3	22.4	22.5	22.7	22.8	23.0	23.1	23.2	23.4	23.5	23.7	23.8	23.9	24.1	24.2	24.4	24.5	24.6	24.8	24.9	25.1	25.2	25.4	25.5
89	21.1	21.3	21.4	21.5	21.7	21.8	21.9	22.1	22.2	22.3	22.5	22.6	22.7	22.9	23.0	23.1	23.3	23.4	23.5	23.7	23.8	23.9	24.1	24.2	24.3	24.5	24.6	24.7	24.9	25.0	25.1	25.3	25.4	25.5	25.7	25.8	25.9	26.1	26.2
88	22.1	22.3	22.4	22.5	22.6	22.8	22.9	23.0	23.1	23.3	23.4	23.5	23.6	23.8	23.9	24.0	24.1	24.3	24.4	24.5	24.6	24.8	24.9	25.0	25.1	25.3	25.4	25.5	25.6	25.8	25.9	26.0	26.1	26.3	26.4	26.5	26.6	26.8	26.9
87	23.1	23.2	23.4	23.5	23.6	23.7	23.8	23.9	24.1	24.2	24.3	24.4	24.5	24.6	24.8	24.9	25.0	25.1	25.2	25.3	25.5	25.6	25.7	25.8	25.9	26.1	26.2	26.3	26.4	26.5	26.6	26.8	26.9	27.0	27.1	27.2	27.3	27.5	27.6
86	24.1	24.2	24.3	24.4	24.5	24.7	24.8	24.9	25.0	25.1	25.2	25.3	25.4	25.5	25.6	25.8	25.9	26.0	26.1	26.2	26.3	26.4	26.5	26.6	26.7	26.8	27.0	27.1	27.2	27.3	27.4	27.5	27.6	27.7	27.8	27.9	28.1	28.2	28.3
85	25.1	25.2	25.3	25.4	25.5	25.6	25.7	25.8	25.9	26.0	26.1	26.2	26.3	26.4	26.5	26.6	26.7	26.8	26.9	27.0	27.1	27.2	27.3	27.4	27.5	27.6	27.7	27.8	28.0	28.1	28.2	28.3	28.4	28.5	28.6	28.7	28.8	28.9	29.0
84	26.1	26.2	26.3	26.4	26.5	26.6	26.7	26.8	26.8	26.9	27.0	27.1	27.2	27.3	27.4	27.5	27.6	27.7	27.8	27.9	28.0	28.1	28.2	28.3	28.3	28.4	28.5	28.6	28.7	28.8	28.9	29.0	29.1	29.2	29.3	29.4	29.5	29.6	29.7
83	27.1	27.2	27.3	27.3	27.4	27.5	27.6	27.7	27.8	27.9	27.9	28.0	28.1	28.2	28.3	28.4	28.5	28.5	28.6	28.7	28.8	28.9	29.0	29.1	29.2	29.2	29.3	29.4	29.5	29.6	29.7	29.8	29.8	29.9	30.0	30.1	30.2	30.3	30.4
82	28.1	28.2	28.2	28.3	28.4	28.5	28.5	28.6	28.7	28.8	28.9	28.9	29.0	29.1	29.2	29.3	29.3	29.4	29.5	29.6	29.6	29.7	29.8	29.9	29.9	30.0	30.1	30.2	30.3	30.3	30.4	30.5	30.6	30.7	30.8	30.9	30.9	31.0	31.1
81	29.1	29.1	29.2	29.3	29.4	29.4	29.5	29.6	29.6	29.7	29.8	29.8	29.9	29.9	30.1	30.1	30.2	30.3	30.3	30.4	30.5	30.5	30.6	30.7	30.8	30.8	30.9	31.0	31.0	31.1	31.2	31.3	31.3	31.4	31.5	31.5	31.6	31.7	31.7
80	30.1	30.1	30.2	30.3	30.3	30.4	30.4	30.5	30.6	30.6	30.7	30.8	30.8	30.9	30.9	31.0	31.1	31.1	31.0	31.3	31.3	31.4	31.4	31.5	31.6	31.6	31.7	31.8	31.8	31.9	31.9	32.0	32.1	32.1	32.2	32.3	32.3	32.4	32.4
79	31.1	31.1	31.2	31.2	31.3	31.3	31.4	31.4	31.5	31.5	31.6	31.7	31.7	31.8	31.8	31.9	31.9	32.0	32.0	32.1	32.1	32.2	32.3	32.3	32.4	32.4	32.5	32.5	32.6	32.6	32.7	32.8	32.8	32.9	32.9	33.0	33.0	33.1	33.1
78	32.0	32.1	32.1	32.2	32.2	32.3	32.3	32.4	32.4	32.5	32.5	32.6	32.6	32.7	32.7	32.8	32.8	32.8	32.9	32.9	33.0	33.0	33.1	33.1	33.2	33.2	33.3	33.3	33.4	33.4	33.5	33.5	33.5	33.6	33.6	33.7	33.7	33.8	33.8
77	33.0	33.1	33.1	33.2	33.2	33.2	33.3	33.3	33.4	33.4	33.4	33.5	33.5	33.5	33.6	33.6	33.7	33.7	33.7	33.8	33.8	33.9	33.9	33.9	34.0	34.0	34.1	34.1	34.1	34.2	34.2	34.3	34.3	34.3	34.4	34.4	34.4	34.5	34.5

LISTED PUT OPTION PRICE WHEN EXERCISE PRICE IS 120

NUMBER OF WEEKS BEFORE THE OPTION EXPIRES

Common Stock Price	1	2	3	4	5	6	7	8	9	10	11	12	13	14	15	16	17	18	19	20	21	22	23	24	25	26	27	28	29	30	31	32	33	34	35	36	37	38	39
156	0.0	0.0	0.0	0.0	0.0	0.0	0.0	0.0	0.0	0.0	0.0	0.0	0.0	0.0	0.0	0.0	0.0	0.0	0.0	0.0	0.0	0.0	0.0	0.0	0.0	0.0	0.0	0.2	0.3	0.5	0.6	0.8	0.9	1.1	1.2	1.4	1.5	1.7	1.8
154	0.0	0.0	0.0	0.0	0.0	0.0	0.0	0.0	0.0	0.0	0.0	0.0	0.0	0.0	0.0	0.0	0.0	0.0	0.0	0.0	0.0	0.0	0.0	0.0	0.1	0.2	0.4	0.6	0.7	0.9	1.0	1.2	1.3	1.5	1.6	1.8	1.9	2.1	2.2
152	0.0	0.0	0.0	0.0	0.0	0.0	0.0	0.0	0.0	0.0	0.0	0.0	0.0	0.0	0.0	0.0	0.0	0.0	0.0	0.0	0.0	0.0	0.1	0.3	0.5	0.6	0.8	1.0	1.1	1.3	1.4	1.6	1.7	1.9	2.0	2.2	2.3	2.4	2.6
150	0.0	0.0	0.0	0.0	0.0	0.0	0.0	0.0	0.0	0.0	0.0	0.0	0.0	0.0	0.0	0.0	0.0	0.0	0.0	0.0	0.1	0.3	0.5	0.7	0.9	1.0	1.2	1.4	1.5	1.7	1.8	2.0	2.1	2.3	2.4	2.6	2.7	2.8	3.0
148	0.0	0.0	0.0	0.0	0.0	0.0	0.0	0.0	0.0	0.0	0.0	0.0	0.0	0.0	0.0	0.0	0.0	0.0	0.2	0.4	0.6	0.7	0.9	1.1	1.3	1.4	1.6	1.8	1.9	2.1	2.2	2.4	2.5	2.7	2.8	3.0	3.1	3.3	3.4
146	0.0	0.0	0.0	0.0	0.0	0.0	0.0	0.0	0.0	0.0	0.0	0.0	0.0	0.0	0.0	0.0	0.2	0.4	0.6	0.8	1.0	1.2	1.4	1.5	1.7	1.9	2.0	2.2	2.4	2.5	2.7	2.8	3.0	3.1	3.3	3.4	3.6	3.7	3.8
144	0.0	0.0	0.0	0.0	0.0	0.0	0.0	0.0	0.0	0.0	0.0	0.0	0.0	0.0	0.2	0.4	0.6	0.8	1.0	1.2	1.4	1.6	1.8	2.0	2.1	2.3	2.5	2.6	2.8	3.0	3.1	3.3	3.4	3.6	3.7	3.8	4.0	4.1	4.3
142	0.0	0.0	0.0	0.0	0.0.	0.0	0.0	0.0	0.0	0.0	0.0	0.0	0.2	0.4	0.7	0.9	1.1	1.3	1.5	1.7	1.9	2.1	2.2	2.4	2.6	2.8	2.9	3.1	3.2	3.4	3.6	3.7	3.9	4.0	4.2	4.3	4.4	4.6	4.7
140	0.0	0.0	0.0	0.0	0.0	0.0	0.0	0.0	0.0	0.0	0.2	0.4	0.7	0.9	1.1	1.3	1.6	1.8	2.0	2.2	2.3	2.5	2.7	2.9	3.1	3.2	3.4	3.6	3.7	3.9	4.0	4.2	4.3	4.5	4.6	4.8	4.9	5.0	5.2
138	0.0	0.0	0.0	0.0	0.0	0.0	0.0	0.0	0.1	0.4	0.7	0.9	1.1	1.4	1.6	1.8	2.0	2.2	2.4	2.6	2.8	3.0	3.2	3.4	3.5	3.7	3.9	4.0	4.2	4.3	4.5	4.7	4.8	4.9	5.1	5.2	5.4	5.5	5.7
136	0.0	0.0	0.0	0.0	0.0	0.0	0.0	0.3	0.6	0.9	1.1	1.4	1.6	1.9	2.1	2.3	2.5	2.7	2.9	3.1	3.3	3.5	3.7	3.8	4.0	4.2	4.4	4.5	4.7	4.8	5.0	5.1	5.3	5.4	5.6	5.7	5.9	6.0	6.1
134	0.0	0.0	0.0	0.0	0.0	0.2	0.5	0.8	1.1	1.4	1.7	1.9	2.1	2.4	2.6	2.8	3.0	3.2	3.4	3.6	3.8	4.0	4.2	4.4	4.5	4.7	4.9	5.0	5.2	5.3	5.5	5.6	5.8	5.9	6.1	6.2	6.4	6.5	6.7
132	0.0	0.0	0.0	0.0	0.3	0.7	1.0	1.3	1.6	1.9	2.2	2.4	2.7	2.9	3.1	3.3	3.6	3.8	4.0	4.1	4.3	4.5	4.7	4.9	5.0	5.2	5.4	5.5	5.7	5.9	6.0	6.2	6.3	6.5	6.6	6.8	6.9	7.0	7.2
130	0.0	0.0	0.0	0.5	0.9	1.2	1.6	1.9	2.2	2.4	2.7	3.0	3.2	3.4	3.7	3.9	4.1	4.3	4.5	4.7	4.9	5.1	5.2	5.4	5.6	5.8	5.9	6.1	6.2	6.4	6.6	6.7	6.9	7.0	7.2	7.3	7.4	7.6	7.7
128	0.0	0.0	0.6	1.0	1.4	1.8	2.1	2.4	2.7	3.0	3.3	3.5	3.8	4.0	4.2	4.4	4.6	4.8	5.0	5.2	5.4	5.6	5.8	6.0	6.1	6.3	6.5	6.6	6.8	7.0	7.1	7.3	7.4	7.6	7.7	7.8	8.0	8.1	8.3
126	0.0	0.6	1.1	1.6	2.0	2.4	2.7	3.0	3.3	3.6	3.8	4.1	4.3	4.6	4.8	5.0	5.2	5.4	5.6	5.8	6.0	6.2	6.4	6.5	6.7	6.9	7.0	7.2	7.4	7.5	7.7	7.8	8.0	8.1	8.3	8.4	8.6	8.7	8.8
124	0.5	1.2	1.7	2.2	2.6	2.9	3.3	3.6	3.9	4.2	4.4	4.7	4.9	5.2	5.4	5.6	5.8	6.0	6.2	6.4	6.6	6.8	7.0	7.1	7.3	7.5	7.6	7.8	8.0	8.1	8.3	8.4	8.6	8.7	8.9	9.0	9.1	9.3	9.4
122	1.1	1.8	2.3	2.8	3.2	3.6	3.9	4.2	4.5	4.8	5.0	5.3	5.5	5.8	6.0	6.2	6.4	6.6	6.8	7.0	7.2	7.4	7.6	7.7	7.9	8.1	8.2	8.4	8.6	8.7	8.9	9.0	9.2	9.3	9.5	9.6	9.8	9.9	10.0
120	1.7	2.4	3.0	3.4	3.8	4.2	4.5	4.8	5.1	5.4	5.7	5.9	6.2	6.4	6.6	6.8	7.0	7.2	7.4	7.6	7.8	8.0	8.2	8.4	8.5	8.7	8.9	9.0	9.2	9.4	9.5	9.7	9.8	9.9	10.1	10.2	10.4	10.5	10.7
118	2.3	2.7	3.2	3.7	4.2	4.4	4.7	5.0	5.4	5.7	6.1	6.3	6.7	6.9	7.1	7.3	7.5	7.7	7.9	8.2	8.5	8.8	9.1	9.4	9.7	10.0	10.3	10.7	11.0	11.2	11.3	11.5	11.6	11.7	11.9	12.0	12.2	12.3	12.4
116	4.3	4.6	4.9	5.2	5.5	5.8	6.1	6.3	6.6	6.9	7.2	7.5	7.8	8.1	8.4	8.7	9.0	9.3	9.6	9.9	10.2	10.5	10.7	11.0	11.3	11.6	11.9	12.2	12.5	12.8	13.1	13.3	13.4	13.5	13.7	13.8	14.0	14.1	14.2
114	6.3	6.6	6.8	7.1	7.4	7.7	7.9	8.2	8.5	8.8	9.1	9.3	9.6	9.9	10.2	10.4	10.7	11.0	11.3	11.6	11.8	12.1	12.4	12.7	12.9	13.2	13.5	13.8	14.1	14.3	14.6	14.9	15.2	15.3	15.5	15.6	15.8	15.9	16.0
112	8.3	8.5	8.8	9.0	9.3	9.6	9.8	10.1	10.4	10.6	10.9	11.1	11.4	11.7	11.9	12.2	12.5	12.7	13.0	13.2	13.5	13.8	14.0	14.3	14.5	14.8	15.1	15.3	15.6	15.9	16.1	16.4	16.6	16.9	17.2	17.4	17.6	17.7	17.8
110	10.2	10.5	10.7	11.0	11.2	11.5	11.7	12.0	12.2	12.5	12.7	13.0	13.2	13.4	13.7	13.9	14.2	14.4	14.7	14.9	15.2	15.4	15.7	15.9	16.2	16.4	16.6	16.9	17.1	17.4	17.6	17.9	18.1	18.4	18.6	18.9	18.8	18.9	19.0
108	12.2	12.5	12.7	12.9	13.2	13.4	13.6	13.8	14.1	14.3	14.5	14.8	15.0	15.2	15.5	15.7	15.9	16.2	16.4	16.6	16.8	17.1	17.3	17.5	17.8	18.0	18.2	18.5	18.7	18.9	19.1	19.4	19.6	19.8	20.1	20.3	20.5	20.7	20.8
106	14.2	14.4	14.6	14.9	15.1	15.3	15.5	15.7	15.9	16.1	16.4	16.6	16.8	17.0	17.2	17.4	17.7	17.9	18.1	18.3	18.5	18.7	18.9	19.2	19.4	19.6	19.8	20.0	20.2	20.4	20.7	20.9	21.1	21.3	21.5	21.7	22.0	22.2	22.4
104	16.2	16.4	16.6	16.8	17.0	17.2	17.4	17.6	17.8	18.0	18.2	18.4	18.6	18.8	19.0	19.2	19.4	19.6	19.8	19.9	20.2	20.4	20.6	20.8	21.0	21.2	21.4	21.6	21.8	22.0	22.2	22.4	22.6	22.8	23.0	23.2	23.4	23.6	23.8
102	18.2	18.4	18.6	18.7	18.9	19.1	19.3	19.5	19.7	19.8	20.0	20.2	20.4	20.6	20.8	20.9	21.1	21.3	21.5	21.7	21.9	22.0	22.2	22.4	22.6	22.8	23.0	23.1	23.3	23.5	23.7	23.9	24.1	24.2	24.4	24.6	24.8	25.0	25.2
100	20.2	20.3	20.5	20.7	20.8	21.0	21.2	21.3	21.5	21.7	21.8	22.0	22.2	22.4	22.5	22.7	22.9	23.0	23.2	23.4	23.5	23.7	23.9	24.0	24.2	24.4	24.5	24.7	24.9	25.0	25.2	25.4	25.5	25.7	25.9	26.0	26.2	26.4	26.6
99	21.2	21.3	21.5	21.6	21.8	22.0	22.1	22.3	22.4	22.6	22.8	22.9	23.1	23.2	23.4	23.6	23.7	23.9	24.0	24.2	24.4	24.5	24.7	24.8	25.0	25.2	25.3	25.5	25.6	25.8	26.0	26.1	26.3	26.4	26.6	26.8	26.9	27.1	27.2
98	22.2	22.3	22.5	22.6	22.8	22.9	23.1	23.2	23.4	23.5	23.7	23.8	24.0	24.1	24.3	24.4	24.6	24.7	24.9	25.0	25.2	25.4	25.5	25.7	25.8	26.0	26.1	26.3	26.4	26.6	26.7	26.9	27.0	27.2	27.3	27.5	27.6	27.8	27.9
97	23.1	23.3	23.4	23.6	23.7	23.9	24.0	24.2	24.3	24.4	24.6	24.7	24.9	25.0	25.2	25.3	25.5	25.6	25.7	25.9	26.0	26.2	26.3	26.5	26.6	26.8	26.9	27.0	27.2	27.3	27.5	27.6	27.8	27.9	28.1	28.2	28.3	28.5	28.6
96	24.1	24.3	24.4	24.5	24.7	24.8	25.0	25.1	25.2	25.4	25.5	25.6	25.8	25.9	26.0	26.2	26.3	26.5	26.6	26.7	26.9	27.0	27.1	27.3	27.4	27.6	27.7	27.8	28.0	28.1	28.2	28.4	28.5	28.6	28.8	28.9	29.1	29.2	29.3
95	25.1	25.3	25.4	25.5	25.6	25.8	25.9	26.0	26.2	26.3	26.4	26.5	26.7	26.8	26.9	27.1	27.2	27.3	27.4	27.6	27.7	27.8	28.0	28.1	28.2	28.3	28.5	28.6	28.7	28.9	29.0	29.1	29.2	29.4	29.5	29.6	29.8	29.9	30.0
94	26.1	26.2	26.4	26.5	26.6	26.7	26.8	27.0	27.1	27.2	27.3	27.5	27.6	27.7	27.8	27.9	28.1	28.2	28.3	28.4	28.5	28.7	28.8	28.9	29.0	29.1	29.3	29.4	29.5	29.6	29.7	29.9	29.9	30.1	30.2	30.4	30.5	30.6	30.7
93	27.1	27.2	27.3	27.5	27.6	27.7	27.8	27.9	28.0	28.1	28.2	28.4	28.5	28.6	28.7	28.8	28.9	29.0	29.1	29.3	29.4	29.5	29.6	29.7	29.8	29.9	30.1	30.2	30.3	30.4	30.5	30.6	30.7	30.8	31.0	31.1	31.2	31.3	31.4
92	28.1	28.2	28.3	28.4	28.5	28.6	28.7	28.8	28.9	29.1	29.2	29.3	29.4	29.5	29.6	29.7	29.8	29.9	30.0	30.1	30.2	30.3	30.4	30.5	30.6	30.7	30.8	30.9	31.1	31.2	31.3	31.4	31.5	31.6	31.7	31.8	31.9	32.0	32.1
91	29.1	29.2	29.3	29.4	29.5	29.6	29.7	29.8	29.9	29.9	30.1	30.2	30.3	30.4	30.5	30.6	30.7	30.8	30.9	30.9	31.0	31.1	31.2	31.3	31.4	31.5	31.6	31.7	31.8	31.9	32.0	32.1	32.2	32.3	32.4	32.5	32.6	32.7	32.8
90	30.1	30.2	30.3	30.4	30.4	30.5	30.6	30.7	30.8	30.9	31.0	31.1	31.2	31.3	31.3	31.4	31.5	31.6	31.7	31.8	31.9	32.0	32.1	32.2	32.2	32.3	32.4	32.5	32.6	32.7	32.8	32.9	33.0	33.0	33.1	33.2	33.3	33.4	33.5
89	31.1	31.2	31.2	31.3	31.4	31.5	31.6	31.7	31.7	31.8	31.9	32.0	32.1	32.1	32.2	32.3	32.4	32.5	32.6	32.6	32.7	32.8	32.9	33.0	33.0	33.1	33.2	33.3	33.4	33.5	33.5	33.6	33.7	33.8	33.9	33.9	34.0	34.1	34.2
88	32.1	32.1	32.2	32.3	32.4	32.4	32.5	32.6	32.7	32.7	32.8	32.9	33.0	33.0	33.1	33.2	33.3	33.3	33.4	33.5	33.6	33.6	33.7	33.8	33.8	33.9	34.0	34.1	34.1	34.2	34.3	34.4	34.4	34.5	34.6	34.7	34.7	34.8	34.9
87	33.1	33.1	33.2	33.3	33.3	33.4	33.5	33.5	33.6	33.7	33.7	33.8	33.9	33.9	34.0	34.1	34.1	34.2	34.3	34.3	34.4	34.5	34.5	34.6	34.7	34.7	34.8	34.9	34.9	35.0	35.0	35.1	35.2	35.2	35.3	35.4	35.4	35.5	35.6
86	34.1	34.1	34.2	34.2	34.3	34.3	34.4	34.5	34.5	34.6	34.6	34.7	34.8	34.8	34.9	34.9	35.0	35.0	35.1	35.2	35.2	35.3	35.3	35.4	35.5	35.5	35.6	35.6	35.7	35.7	35.8	35.9	35.9	36.0	36.0	36.1	36.2	36.2	36.3
85	35.1	35.1	35.2	35.2	35.3	35.3	35.4	35.4	35.5	35.5	35.6	35.6	35.7	35.7	35.8	35.8	35.9	35.9	36.0	36.0	36.1	36.1	36.2	36.2	36.3	36.3	36.4	36.4	36.5	36.5	36.6	36.6	36.7	36.7	36.8	36.8	36.9	36.9	37.0
84	36.0	36.1	36.1	36.2	36.2	36.3	36.3	36.3	36.4	36.4	36.5	36.5	36.6	36.6	36.6	36.7	36.7	36.8	36.8	36.9	36.9	36.9	37.0	37.0	37.1	37.1	37.2	37.2	37.2	37.3	37.3	37.4	37.4	37.4	37.5	37.5	37.6	37.6	37.7

LISTED PUT OPTION PRICE WHEN EXERCISE PRICE IS 130

NUMBER OF WEEKS BEFORE THE OPTION EXPIRES

Common Stock Price	1	2	3	4	5	6	7	8	9	10	11	12	13	14	15	16	17	18	19	20	21	22	23	24	25	26	27	28	29	30	31	32	33	34	35	36	37	38	39
170	0.0	0.0	0.0	0.0	0.0	0.0	0.0	0.0	0.0	0.0	0.0	0.0	0.0	0.0	0.0	0.0	0.0	0.0	0.0	0.0	0.0	0.0	0.0	0.0	0.0	0.0	0.0	0.0	0.2	0.3	0.5	0.7	0.8	1.0	1.2	1.3	1.5	1.6	1.8
168	0.0	0.0	0.0	0.0	0.0	0.0	0.0	0.0	0.0	0.0	0.0	0.0	0.0	0.0	0.0	0.0	0.0	0.0	0.0	0.0	0.0	0.0	0.0	0.0	0.0	0.0	0.2	0.4	0.6	0.7	0.9	1.1	1.2	1.4	1.5	1.7	1.8	2.0	2.1
166	0.0	0.0	0.0	0.0	0.0	0.0	0.0	0.0	0.0	0.0	0.0	0.0	0.0	0.0	0.0	0.0	0.0	0.0	0.0	0.0	0.0	0.0	0.0	0.0	0.2	0.4	0.6	0.8	0.9	1.1	1.3	1.4	1.6	1.8	1.9	2.1	2.2	2.4	2.5
164	0.0	0.0	0.0	0.0	0.0	0.0	0.0	0.0	0.0	0.0	0.0	0.0	0.0	0.0	0.0	0.0	0.0	0.0	0.0	0.0	0.0	0.1	0.2	0.4	0.6	0.8	1.0	1.2	1.3	1.5	1.7	1.8	2.0	2.2	2.3	2.5	2.6	2.8	2.9
162	0.0	0.0	0.0	0.0	0.0	0.0	0.0	0.0	0.0	0.0	0.0	0.0	0.0	0.0	0.0	0.0	0.0	0.0	0.0	0.1	0.3	0.5	0.7	0.8	1.0	1.2	1.4	1.6	1.7	1.9	2.1	2.2	2.4	2.6	2.7	2.9	3.0	3.2	3.3
160	0.0	0.0	0.0	0.0	0.0	0.0	0.0	0.0	0.0	0.0	0.0	0.0	0.0	0.0	0.0	0.0	0.0	0.0	0.3	0.5	0.7	0.9	1.1	1.3	1.5	1.6	1.8	2.0	2.2	2.3	2.5	2.7	2.8	3.0	3.1	3.3	3.5	3.6	3.8
158	0.0	0.0	0.0	0.0	0.0	0.0	0.0	0.0	0.0	0.0	0.0	0.0	0.0	0.0	0.0	0.0	0.3	0.5	0.7	0.9	1.1	1.3	1.5	1.7	1.9	2.1	2.2	2.4	2.6	2.8	2.9	3.1	3.3	3.4	3.6	3.7	3.9	4.0	4.2
156	0.0	0.0	0.0	0.0	0.0	0.0	0.0	0.0	0.0	0.0	0.0	0.0	0.0	0.0	0.2	0.5	0.7	0.9	1.1	1.3	1.5	1.7	1.9	2.1	2.3	2.5	2.7	2.9	3.0	3.2	3.4	3.5	3.7	3.9	4.0	4.2	4.3	4.5	4.6
154	0.0	0.0	0.0	0.0	0.0	0.0	0.0	0.0	0.0	0.0	0.0	0.0	0.2	0.4	0.7	0.9	1.1	1.4	1.6	1.8	2.0	2.2	2.4	2.6	2.8	3.0	3.1	3.3	3.5	3.7	3.8	4.0	4.1	4.3	4.5	4.6	4.8	4.9	5.1
152	0.0	0.0	0.0	0.0	0.0	0.0	0.0	0.0	0.0	0.0	0.1	0.4	0.6	0.9	1.1	1.4	1.6	1.8	2.0	2.3	2.5	2.7	2.9	3.0	3.2	3.4	3.6	3.8	3.9	4.1	4.3	4.4	4.6	4.8	4.9	5.1	5.2	5.4	5.5
150	0.0	0.0	0.0	0.0	0.0	0.0	0.0	0.0	0.0	0.3	0.6	0.9	1.1	1.4	1.6	1.9	2.1	2.3	2.5	2.7	2.9	3.1	3.3	3.5	3.7	3.9	4.1	4.2	4.4	4.6	4.8	4.9	5.1	5.2	5.4	5.6	5.7	5.9	6.0
148	0.0	0.0	0.0	0.0	0.0	0.0	0.0	0.2	0.5	0.8	1.1	1.3	1.6	1.9	2.1	2.3	2.6	2.8	3.0	3.2	3.4	3.6	3.8	4.0	4.2	4.4	4.6	4.7	4.9	5.1	5.2	5.4	5.6	5.7	5.9	6.0	6.2	6.3	6.5
146	0.0	0.0	0.0	0.0	0.0	0.0	0.3	0.7	1.0	1.3	1.6	1.9	2.1	2.4	2.6	2.8	3.1	3.3	3.5	3.7	3.9	4.1	4.3	4.5	4.7	4.9	5.1	5.2	5.4	5.6	5.7	5.9	6.1	6.2	6.4	6.5	6.7	6.8	7.0
144	0.0	0.0	0.0	0.0	0.1	0.5	0.9	1.2	1.5	1.8	2.1	2.4	2.6	2.9	3.1	3.4	3.6	3.8	4.0	4.2	4.4	4.6	4.8	5.0	5.2	5.4	5.6	5.7	5.9	6.1	6.3	6.4	6.6	6.7	6.9	7.1	7.2	7.4	7.5
142	0.0	0.0	0.0	0.2	0.6	1.0	1.4	1.7	2.0	2.3	2.6	2.9	3.2	3.4	3.7	3.9	4.1	4.3	4.5	4.8	5.0	5.2	5.4	5.5	5.7	5.9	6.1	6.3	6.4	6.6	6.8	7.0	7.1	7.3	7.4	7.6	7.7	7.9	8.0
140	0.0	0.0	0.2	0.7	1.2	1.6	1.9	2.3	2.6	2.9	3.2	3.4	3.7	4.0	4.2	4.4	4.7	4.9	5.1	5.3	5.5	5.7	5.9	6.1	6.3	6.5	6.6	6.8	7.0	7.2	7.3	7.5	7.7	7.8	8.0	8.1	8.3	8.4	8.6
138	0.0	0.2	0.8	1.3	1.7	2.1	2.5	2.8	3.1	3.4	3.7	4.0	4.3	4.5	4.8	5.0	5.2	5.4	5.7	5.9	6.1	6.3	6.5	6.7	6.8	7.0	7.2	7.4	7.6	7.7	7.9	8.1	8.2	8.4	8.5	8.7	8.8	9.0	9.1
136	0.0	0.8	1.4	1.9	2.3	2.7	3.1	3.4	3.7	4.0	4.3	4.6	4.8	5.1	5.3	5.6	5.8	6.0	6.2	6.4	6.6	6.8	7.0	7.2	7.4	7.6	7.8	8.0	8.1	8.3	8.5	8.6	8.8	9.0	9.1	9.3	9.4	9.6	9.7
134	0.6	1.4	2.0	2.5	2.9	3.3	3.7	4.0	4.3	4.6	4.9	5.2	5.4	5.7	5.9	6.2	6.4	6.6	6.8	7.0	7.2	7.4	7.6	7.8	8.0	8.2	8.4	8.5	8.7	8.9	9.1	9.2	9.4	9.5	9.7	9.9	10.0	10.2	10.3
132	1.2	2.0	2.6	3.1	3.5	3.9	4.3	4.6	4.9	5.2	5.5	5.8	6.0	6.3	6.5	6.8	7.0	7.2	7.4	7.6	7.8	8.0	8.2	8.4	8.6	8.8	9.0	9.2	9.3	9.5	9.7	9.8	9.9	10.2	10.3	10.5	10.6	10.8	10.9
130	1.9	2.6	3.2	3.7	4.1	4.5	4.9	5.2	5.6	5.9	6.1	6.4	6.7	6.9	7.2	7.4	7.6	7.8	8.1	8.3	8.5	8.7	8.9	9.1	9.3	9.4	9.6	9.8	9.9	10.1	10.3	10.5	10.6	10.8	10.9	11.1	11.3	11.4	11.6
128	2.5	2.8	3.4	3.9	4.4	4.8	5.2	5.5	5.9	6.2	6.4	6.7	7.1	7.3	7.6	7.8	8.0	8.2	8.5	8.7	9.1	9.4	9.7	10.1	10.4	10.7	11.1	11.4	11.7	11.9	12.1	12.3	12.4	12.6	12.7	12.9	13.1	13.2	13.4
126	4.3	4.6	5.0	5.3	5.6	5.9	6.2	6.6	6.9	7.2	7.5	7.8	8.2	8.5	8.8	9.1	9.4	9.8	10.1	10.4	10.7	11.0	11.4	11.7	12.0	12.3	12.6	13.0	13.3	13.6	13.9	14.1	14.2	14.4	14.5	14.7	14.9	15.0	15.2
124	6.3	6.6	6.9	7.2	7.5	7.8	8.1	8.4	8.7	9.0	9.4	9.7	9.9	10.3	10.6	10.9	11.2	11.5	11.8	12.1	12.4	12.7	13.0	13.3	13.6	13.9	14.2	14.5	14.8	15.1	15.4	15.7	16.0	16.2	16.3	16.5	16.7	16.8	17.0
122	8.3	8.6	8.9	9.2	9.4	9.7	10.0	10.3	10.6	10.9	11.2	11.5	11.8	12.0	12.3	12.6	12.9	13.2	13.5	13.8	14.1	14.4	14.6	14.9	15.2	15.5	15.8	16.1	16.4	16.7	17.0	17.2	17.5	17.8	18.1	18.3	18.5	18.6	18.8
120	10.3	10.5	10.8	11.1	11.4	11.6	11.9	12.2	12.5	12.7	13.0	13.3	13.6	13.8	14.1	14.4	14.6	14.9	15.2	15.5	15.7	16.0	16.3	16.6	16.8	17.1	17.4	17.7	17.9	18.2	18.5	18.7	19.0	19.3	19.6	19.8	20.1	20.4	20.6
118	12.3	12.5	12.8	13.0	13.3	13.5	13.8	14.1	14.3	14.6	14.8	15.1	15.3	15.6	15.9	16.1	16.4	16.6	16.9	17.2	17.4	17.7	17.9	18.2	18.4	18.7	19.0	19.2	19.5	19.7	19.9	20.2	20.5	20.8	21.0	21.3	21.5	21.8	22.0
116	14.2	14.5	14.7	15.0	15.2	15.5	15.7	15.9	16.2	16.4	16.7	16.9	17.1	17.4	17.6	17.9	18.1	18.4	18.6	18.8	19.1	19.3	19.6	19.8	20.0	20.3	20.5	20.8	21.0	21.3	21.5	21.7	22.0	22.2	22.5	22.7	23.0	23.2	23.4
114	16.2	16.5	16.7	16.9	17.1	17.4	17.6	17.8	18.0	18.3	18.5	18.7	18.9	19.2	19.4	19.6	19.8	20.1	20.3	20.5	20.8	21.0	21.2	21.4	21.7	21.9	22.1	22.3	22.6	22.8	23.0	23.2	23.5	23.7	23.9	24.1	24.4	24.6	24.8
112	18.2	18.4	18.6	18.8	19.1	19.3	19.5	19.7	19.9	20.1	20.3	20.5	20.7	20.9	21.2	21.4	21.6	21.8	22.0	22.2	22.4	22.6	22.8	23.1	23.3	23.5	23.7	23.9	24.1	24.3	24.5	24.7	25.0	25.2	25.4	25.6	25.8	26.0	26.2
110	20.2	20.4	20.6	20.8	21.0	21.2	21.4	21.6	21.8	22.0	22.1	22.3	22.5	22.7	22.9	23.1	23.3	23.5	23.7	23.9	24.1	24.3	24.5	24.7	24.9	25.1	25.3	25.5	25.7	25.9	26.0	26.2	26.4	26.6	26.8	27.0	27.2	27.4	27.6
108	22.2	22.4	22.5	22.7	22.9	23.1	23.3	23.4	23.6	23.8	24.0	24.2	24.3	24.5	24.7	24.9	25.0	25.2	25.4	25.6	25.8	25.9	26.1	26.3	26.5	26.7	26.8	27.0	27.2	27.4	27.6	27.7	27.9	28.1	28.3	28.5	28.6	28.8	29.0
106	24.2	24.3	24.5	24.7	24.8	25.0	25.1	25.3	25.5	25.6	25.8	26.0	26.1	26.3	26.5	26.6	26.8	26.9	27.1	27.3	27.4	27.6	27.8	27.9	28.1	28.3	28.4	28.6	28.7	28.9	29.1	29.2	29.4	29.6	29.7	29.9	30.1	30.2	30.4
104	26.1	26.3	26.4	26.6	26.7	26.9	27.0	27.2	27.3	27.5	27.6	27.8	27.9	28.1	28.2	28.4	28.5	28.7	28.8	29.0	29.1	29.3	29.4	29.6	29.7	29.8	29.9	30.1	30.3	30.4	30.6	30.7	30.9	31.0	31.2	31.3	31.5	31.6	31.8
102	28.1	28.3	28.4	28.5	28.7	28.8	28.9	29.1	29.2	29.3	29.5	29.6	29.7	29.9	29.9	30.1	30.2	30.4	30.5	30.6	30.8	30.9	31.0	31.2	31.3	31.4	31.6	31.7	31.8	32.0	32.1	32.2	32.4	32.5	32.6	32.8	32.9	33.0	33.2
100	30.1	30.2	30.3	30.5	30.6	30.7	30.8	30.9	31.0	31.2	31.3	31.4	31.5	31.6	31.8	31.9	32.0	32.1	32.2	32.3	32.4	32.6	32.7	32.8	32.9	33.0	33.2	33.3	33.4	33.5	33.6	33.7	33.8	34.0	34.1	34.2	34.3	34.4	34.6
99	31.1	31.2	31.3	31.4	31.5	31.7	31.8	31.9	32.0	32.1	32.2	32.3	32.4	32.5	32.6	32.7	32.9	33.0	33.1	33.2	33.3	33.4	33.5	33.6	33.7	33.8	33.9	34.0	34.2	34.3	34.4	34.5	34.6	34.7	34.8	34.9	35.0	35.1	35.2
98	32.1	32.2	32.3	32.4	32.5	32.6	32.7	32.8	32.9	33.0	33.1	33.2	33.3	33.4	33.5	33.6	33.7	33.8	33.9	34.0	34.1	34.2	34.3	34.4	34.5	34.6	34.7	34.8	34.9	35.0	35.1	35.2	35.3	35.4	35.5	35.6	35.7	35.8	35.9
97	33.1	33.2	33.3	33.4	33.5	33.6	33.7	33.7	33.8	33.9	34.0	34.1	34.2	34.3	34.4	34.5	34.6	34.7	34.8	34.9	35.0	35.0	35.1	35.2	35.3	35.4	35.5	35.6	35.7	35.8	35.9	36.0	36.1	36.2	36.3	36.4	36.4	36.5	36.6
96	34.1	34.2	34.3	34.3	34.4	34.5	34.6	34.7	34.8	34.9	34.9	35.0	35.1	35.2	35.3	35.4	35.5	35.5	35.6	35.7	35.8	35.9	36.0	36.0	36.1	36.2	36.3	36.4	36.5	36.6	36.6	36.7	36.8	36.9	37.0	37.1	37.2	37.2	37.3
95	35.1	35.2	35.2	35.3	35.4	35.5	35.5	35.6	35.7	35.8	35.9	35.9	36.0	36.1	36.2	36.2	36.3	36.4	36.5	36.6	36.6	36.7	36.8	36.9	36.9	37.0	37.1	37.2	37.2	37.3	37.4	37.5	37.6	37.6	37.7	37.8	37.9	37.9	38.0
94	36.1	36.1	36.2	36.3	36.3	36.4	36.5	36.6	36.6	36.7	36.8	36.8	36.9	37.0	37.0	37.1	37.2	37.3	37.3	37.4	37.5	37.5	37.6	37.7	37.7	37.8	37.9	38.0	38.0	38.1	38.2	38.2	38.3	38.4	38.4	38.5	38.6	38.6	38.7
93	37.1	37.1	37.2	37.2	37.3	37.4	37.4	37.5	37.6	37.6	37.7	37.7	37.8	37.9	37.9	38.0	38.1	38.1	38.2	38.2	38.3	38.4	38.4	38.5	38.5	38.6	38.7	38.7	38.8	38.9	38.9	39.0	39.0	39.1	39.2	39.2	39.3	39.3	39.4
92	38.1	38.1	38.2	38.2	38.3	38.3	38.4	38.4	38.5	38.5	38.6	38.6	38.7	38.8	38.8	38.9	38.9	39.0	39.0	39.1	39.1	39.2	39.2	39.3	39.4	39.4	39.5	39.5	39.6	39.6	39.7	39.7	39.8	39.8	39.9	39.9	39.9	40.1	40.1
91	39.0	39.1	39.1	39.2	39.2	39.3	39.3	39.4	39.4	39.5	39.5	39.6	39.6	39.6	39.7	39.7	39.8	39.8	39.9	39.9	39.9	40.0	40.1	40.1	40.2	40.2	40.2	40.3	40.3	40.4	40.4	40.5	40.5	40.6	40.6	40.7	40.7	40.8	40.8

LISTED PUT OPTION PRICE WHEN EXERCISE PRICE IS 140

NUMBER OF WEEKS BEFORE THE OPTION EXPIRES

Common Stock Price	1	2	3	4	5	6	7	8	9	10	11	12	13	14	15	16	17	18	19	20	21	22	23	24	25	26	27	28	29	30	31	32	33	34	35	36	37	38	39
182	0.0	0.0	0.0	0.0	0.0	0.0	0.0	0.0	0.0	0.0	0.0	0.0	0.0	0.0	0.0	0.0	0.0	0.0	0.0	0.0	0.0	0.0	0.0	0.0	0.0	0.0	0.0	0.2	0.4	0.6	0.8	0.9	1.1	1.3	1.4	1.6	1.8	1.9	2.1
180	0.0	0.0	0.0	0.0	0.0	0.0	0.0	0.0	0.0	0.0	0.0	0.0	0.0	0.0	0.0	0.0	0.0	0.0	0.0	0.0	0.0	0.0	0.0	0.0	0.0	0.2	0.4	0.6	0.8	1.0	1.1	1.3	1.5	1.7	1.8	2.0	2.2	2.3	2.5
178	0.0	0.0	0.0	0.0	0.0	0.0	0.0	0.0	0.0	0.0	0.0	0.0	0.0	0.0	0.0	0.0	0.0	0.0	0.0	0.0	0.0	0.0	0.0	0.2	0.4	0.6	0.8	1.0	1.2	1.3	1.5	1.7	1.9	2.1	2.2	2.4	2.6	2.7	2.9
176	0.0	0.0	0.0	0.0	0.0	0.0	0.0	0.0	0.0	0.0	0.0	0.0	0.0	0.0	0.0	0.0	0.0	0.0	0.0	0.0	0.0	0.2	0.4	0.6	0.8	1.0	1.2	1.4	1.6	1.7	1.9	2.1	2.3	2.5	2.6	2.8	3.0	3.1	3.3
174	0.0	0.0	0.0	0.0	0.0	0.0	0.0	0.0	0.0	0.0	0.0	0.0	0.0	0.0	0.0	0.0	0.0	0.0	0.0	0.2	0.4	0.6	0.8	1.0	1.2	1.4	1.6	1.8	2.0	2.2	2.3	2.5	2.7	2.9	3.0	3.2	3.4	3.5	3.7
172	0.0	0.0	0.0	0.0	0.0	0.0	0.0	0.0	0.0	0.0	0.0	0.0	0.0	0.0	0.0	0.0	0.0	0.1	0.4	0.6	0.8	1.0	1.2	1.4	1.6	1.8	2.0	2.2	2.4	2.6	2.8	2.9	3.1	3.3	3.5	3.6	3.8	3.9	4.1
170	0.0	0.0	0.0	0.0	0.0	0.0	0.0	0.0	0.0	0.0	0.0	0.0	0.0	0.0	0.0	0.1	0.3	0.5	0.8	1.0	1.2	1.4	1.6	1.9	2.1	2.3	2.4	2.6	2.8	3.0	3.2	3.4	3.5	3.7	3.9	4.0	4.2	4.4	4.5
168	0.0	0.0	0.0	0.0	0.0	0.0	0.0	0.0	0.0	0.0	0.0	0.0	0.0	0.0	0.3	0.5	0.7	1.0	1.2	1.4	1.7	1.9	2.1	2.3	2.5	2.7	2.9	3.1	3.3	3.4	3.6	3.8	4.0	4.2	4.3	4.5	4.7	4.8	5.0
166	0.0	0.0	0.0	0.0	0.0	0.0	0.0	0.0	0.0	0.0	0.0	0.0	0.2	0.4	0.7	1.0	1.2	1.4	1.7	1.9	2.1	2.3	2.5	2.7	2.9	3.1	3.3	3.5	3.7	3.9	4.1	4.3	4.4	4.6	4.8	4.9	5.1	5.3	5.4
164	0.0	0.0	0.0	0.0	0.0	0.0	0.0	0.0	0.0	0.0	0.1	0.3	0.6	0.9	1.2	1.4	1.7	1.9	2.1	2.4	2.6	2.8	3.0	3.2	3.4	3.6	3.8	4.0	4.2	4.4	4.5	4.7	4.9	5.1	5.2	5.4	5.6	5.7	5.9
162	0.0	0.0	0.0	0.0	0.0	0.0	0.0	0.0	0.0	0.2	0.5	0.8	1.1	1.4	1.6	1.9	2.1	2.4	2.6	2.8	3.0	3.3	3.5	3.7	3.9	4.1	4.3	4.5	4.6	4.8	5.0	5.2	5.4	5.5	5.7	5.9	6.0	6.2	6.4
160	0.0	0.0	0.0	0.0	0.0	0.0	0.0	0.0	0.4	0.7	1.0	1.3	1.6	1.9	2.1	2.4	2.6	2.9	3.1	3.3	3.5	3.7	4.0	4.2	4.4	4.6	4.8	4.9	5.1	5.3	5.5	5.7	5.8	6.0	6.2	6.4	6.5	6.7	6.8
158	0.0	0.0	0.0	0.0	0.0	0.0	0.2	0.5	0.9	1.2	1.5	1.8	2.1	2.4	2.6	2.9	3.1	3.3	3.6	3.8	4.0	4.2	4.5	4.7	4.9	5.1	5.2	5.4	5.6	5.8	6.0	6.2	6.3	6.5	6.7	6.9	7.0	7.2	7.3
156	0.0	0.0	0.0	0.0	0.0	0.3	0.7	1.0	1.4	1.7	2.0	2.3	2.6	2.9	3.1	3.4	3.6	3.9	4.1	4.3	4.5	4.8	5.0	5.2	5.4	5.6	5.8	5.9	6.1	6.3	6.5	6.7	6.9	7.0	7.2	7.4	7.5	7.7	7.8
154	0.0	0.0	0.0	0.0	0.4	0.8	1.2	1.6	1.9	2.2	2.5	2.8	3.1	3.4	3.6	3.9	4.1	4.4	4.6	4.8	5.1	5.3	5.5	5.7	5.9	6.1	6.3	6.5	6.7	6.8	7.0	7.2	7.4	7.5	7.7	7.9	8.0	8.2	8.4
152	0.0	0.0	0.0	0.4	0.9	1.3	1.7	2.1	2.4	2.8	3.1	3.4	3.6	3.9	4.2	4.4	4.7	4.9	5.1	5.4	5.6	5.8	6.0	6.2	6.4	6.6	6.8	7.0	7.2	7.4	7.6	7.7	7.9	8.1	8.3	8.4	8.6	8.7	8.9
150	0.0	0.0	0.5	1.0	1.5	1.9	2.3	2.6	3.0	3.3	3.6	3.9	4.2	4.5	4.7	5.0	5.2	5.5	5.7	5.9	6.1	6.4	6.6	6.8	7.0	7.2	7.4	7.6	7.7	7.9	8.1	8.3	8.5	8.6	8.8	9.0	9.1	9.3	9.5
148	0.0	0.4	1.0	1.6	2.0	2.5	2.9	3.2	3.6	3.9	4.2	4.5	4.8	5.0	5.3	5.5	5.8	6.0	6.3	6.5	6.7	6.9	7.1	7.3	7.5	7.7	7.9	8.1	8.3	8.5	8.7	8.8	9.0	9.2	9.4	9.5	9.7	9.9	10.0
146	0.2	1.0	1.6	2.1	2.6	3.0	3.4	3.8	4.1	4.5	4.8	5.1	5.3	5.6	5.9	6.1	6.4	6.6	6.8	7.1	7.3	7.5	7.7	7.9	8.1	8.3	8.5	8.7	8.9	9.1	9.3	9.4	9.6	9.8	9.9	10.1	10.3	10.4	10.6
144	0.7	1.6	2.2	2.7	3.2	3.6	4.0	4.4	4.7	5.1	5.4	5.7	5.9	6.2	6.5	6.7	7.0	7.2	7.4	7.7	7.9	8.1	8.3	8.5	8.7	8.9	9.1	9.3	9.5	9.7	9.8	10.0	10.2	10.4	10.5	10.7	10.9	11.0	11.2
142	1.4	2.2	2.8	3.4	3.8	4.2	4.6	5.0	5.3	5.7	6.0	6.3	6.6	6.8	7.1	7.3	7.6	7.8	8.1	8.3	8.5	8.7	8.9	9.1	9.3	9.5	9.7	9.9	10.1	10.3	10.5	10.6	10.8	11.0	11.2	11.3	11.5	11.7	11.8
140	2.0	2.8	3.5	4.0	4.5	4.9	5.3	5.6	6.0	6.3	6.6	6.9	7.2	7.5	7.7	8.0	8.2	8.5	8.7	8.9	9.1	9.3	9.6	9.8	9.9	10.2	10.4	10.5	10.7	10.9	11.1	11.3	11.4	11.6	11.8	12.0	12.1	12.3	12.4
138	2.6	2.9	3.7	4.2	4.7	5.1	5.5	5.9	6.3	6.6	6.9	7.2	7.5	7.9	8.1	8.4	8.6	8.9	9.1	9.3	9.6	9.9	10.4	10.7	11.1	11.4	11.8	12.2	12.5	12.7	12.9	13.1	13.2	13.4	13.6	13.8	13.9	14.1	14.2
136	4.3	4.7	5.0	5.4	5.7	6.1	6.4	6.8	7.1	7.5	7.8	8.2	8.5	8.9	9.2	9.6	9.9	10.3	10.6	10.9	11.3	11.6	12.0	12.3	12.7	13.0	13.4	13.7	14.1	14.4	14.7	14.9	15.0	15.2	15.4	15.6	15.7	15.9	16.0
134	6.3	6.7	7.0	7.3	7.7	8.0	8.3	8.7	9.0	9.3	9.6	9.9	10.3	10.6	11.0	11.3	11.6	12.0	12.3	12.6	13.0	13.3	13.6	14.0	14.3	14.6	15.0	15.3	15.6	16.0	16.3	16.6	16.8	17.0	17.2	17.4	17.5	17.7	17.8
132	8.3	8.6	8.9	9.3	9.6	9.9	10.2	10.5	10.8	11.2	11.5	11.8	12.1	12.4	12.7	13.1	13.4	13.7	14.0	14.3	14.6	15.0	15.3	15.6	15.9	16.2	16.5	16.8	17.2	17.5	17.8	18.1	18.4	18.7	19.0	19.2	19.3	19.5	19.6
130	10.3	10.6	10.9	11.2	11.5	11.8	12.1	12.4	12.7	13.0	13.3	13.6	13.9	14.2	14.5	14.8	15.1	15.4	15.7	16.0	16.3	16.6	16.9	17.2	17.5	17.8	18.1	18.4	18.7	19.0	19.3	19.6	19.9	20.2	20.5	20.8	21.1	21.3	21.4
128	12.3	12.6	12.9	13.1	13.4	13.7	14.0	14.3	14.6	14.8	15.1	15.4	15.7	16.0	16.3	16.6	16.8	17.1	17.4	17.7	18.0	18.3	18.5	18.8	19.1	19.4	19.7	19.9	20.3	20.5	20.8	21.1	21.4	21.7	22.0	22.2	22.5	22.8	23.1
126	14.3	14.5	14.8	15.1	15.3	15.6	15.9	16.2	16.4	16.7	17.0	17.2	17.5	17.8	18.0	18.3	18.6	18.8	19.1	19.4	19.7	19.9	20.2	20.5	20.7	21.0	21.3	21.5	21.8	22.1	22.3	22.6	22.9	23.1	23.4	23.7	24.0	24.2	24.5
124	16.3	16.5	16.8	17.0	17.3	17.5	17.8	18.0	18.3	18.5	18.8	19.0	19.3	19.5	19.8	20.1	20.3	20.6	20.8	21.1	21.3	21.6	21.8	22.1	22.3	22.6	22.8	23.1	23.3	23.6	23.9	24.1	24.4	24.6	24.9	25.1	25.4	25.6	25.9
122	18.2	18.5	18.7	19.0	19.2	19.4	19.7	19.9	20.1	20.4	20.6	20.9	21.1	21.3	21.6	21.8	22.0	22.3	22.5	22.8	23.0	23.2	23.5	23.7	23.9	24.2	24.4	24.7	24.9	25.1	25.4	25.6	25.8	26.1	26.3	26.6	26.8	27.0	27.3
120	20.2	20.4	20.7	20.9	21.1	21.3	21.6	21.8	22.0	22.2	22.4	22.7	22.9	23.1	23.3	23.6	23.8	24.0	24.2	24.4	24.7	24.9	25.1	25.3	25.6	25.8	26.0	26.2	26.4	26.7	26.9	27.1	27.3	27.5	27.8	28.0	28.2	28.4	28.7
118	22.2	22.4	22.6	22.8	23.0	23.2	23.4	23.7	23.9	24.1	24.3	24.5	24.7	24.9	25.1	25.3	25.5	25.7	25.9	26.1	26.3	26.5	26.7	27.0	27.2	27.4	27.6	27.8	28.0	28.2	28.4	28.6	28.8	29.0	29.2	29.4	29.6	29.8	30.0
116	24.2	24.4	24.6	24.8	25.0	25.1	25.3	25.5	25.7	25.9	26.1	26.3	26.5	26.7	26.9	27.1	27.2	27.4	27.6	27.8	28.0	28.2	28.4	28.6	28.8	29.0	29.1	29.3	29.5	29.7	29.9	30.1	30.3	30.5	30.7	30.9	31.1	31.2	31.4
114	26.2	26.4	26.5	26.7	26.9	27.1	27.2	27.4	27.6	27.8	27.9	28.1	28.3	28.5	28.6	28.8	29.0	29.2	29.3	29.5	29.7	29.9	30.0	30.2	30.4	30.6	30.7	30.9	31.1	31.3	31.4	31.6	31.8	32.0	32.1	32.3	32.5	32.7	32.8
112	28.2	28.3	28.5	28.6	28.8	29.0	29.1	29.3	29.4	29.6	29.8	29.9	30.1	30.2	30.4	30.6	30.7	30.9	31.0	31.2	31.3	31.5	31.7	31.8	32.0	32.1	32.3	32.5	32.6	32.8	32.9	33.1	33.3	33.4	33.6	33.7	33.9	34.1	34.2
110	30.1	30.3	30.4	30.6	30.7	30.9	31.0	31.1	31.3	31.4	31.6	31.7	31.9	32.0	32.2	32.3	32.4	32.6	32.7	32.9	33.0	33.2	33.3	33.4	33.6	33.7	33.9	34.0	34.2	34.3	34.5	34.6	34.7	34.9	35.0	35.2	35.3	35.5	35.6
108	32.1	32.3	32.4	32.5	32.6	32.8	32.9	33.0	33.2	33.3	33.4	33.5	33.7	33.8	33.9	34.0	34.2	34.3	34.4	34.6	34.7	34.8	34.9	35.1	35.2	35.3	35.5	35.6	35.7	35.8	36.0	36.1	36.2	36.4	36.5	36.6	36.7	36.9	37.0
106	34.1	34.2	34.3	34.4	34.6	34.7	34.8	34.9	35.0	35.1	35.2	35.3	35.5	35.6	35.7	35.8	35.9	36.0	36.1	36.2	36.4	36.5	36.6	36.7	36.8	36.9	37.0	37.1	37.3	37.4	37.5	37.6	37.7	37.8	37.9	38.0	38.2	38.3	38.4
104	36.1	36.2	36.3	36.4	36.5	36.6	36.7	36.8	36.9	37.0	37.1	37.2	37.3	37.4	37.5	37.5	37.6	37.7	37.8	37.9	38.0	38.1	38.2	38.3	38.4	38.5	38.6	38.7	38.8	38.9	39.0	39.1	39.2	39.3	39.4	39.5	39.6	39.7	39.8
102	38.1	38.2	38.2	38.3	38.4	38.5	38.6	38.6	38.7	38.8	38.9	39.0	39.1	39.1	39.2	39.3	39.4	39.5	39.5	39.6	39.7	39.8	39.9	39.9	40.0	40.1	40.2	40.3	40.4	40.4	40.5	40.6	40.7	40.8	40.8	40.9	41.0	41.1	41.2
100	40.1	40.1	40.2	40.3	40.3	40.4	40.5	40.5	40.6	40.7	40.7	40.8	40.9	40.9	41.0	41.0	41.1	41.2	41.2	41.3	41.4	41.4	41.5	41.6	41.6	41.7	41.8	41.8	41.9	42.0	42.0	42.1	42.2	42.2	42.3	42.4	42.4	42.5	42.6
99	41.1	41.1	41.2	41.2	41.3	41.3	41.4	41.5	41.5	41.6	41.6	41.7	41.7	41.8	41.9	41.9	42.0	42.0	42.1	42.2	42.2	42.3	42.3	42.4	42.4	42.5	42.6	42.6	42.7	42.7	42.8	42.8	42.9	43.0	43.0	43.1	43.1	43.2	43.2
98	42.0	42.1	42.1	42.2	42.2	42.3	42.3	42.4	42.4	42.5	42.5	42.6	42.6	42.7	42.7	42.8	42.8	42.9	42.9	43.0	43.0	43.1	43.1	43.2	43.2	43.3	43.3	43.4	43.4	43.5	43.5	43.6	43.6	43.7	43.7	43.8	43.8	43.9	43.9

LISTED PUT OPTION PRICE WHEN EXERCISE PRICE IS 150

Common Stock Price	NUMBER OF WEEKS BEFORE THE OPTION EXPIRES																																						
	1	2	3	4	5	6	7	8	9	10	11	12	13	14	15	16	17	18	19	20	21	22	23	24	25	26	27	28	29	30	31	32	33	34	35	36	37	38	39
196	0.0	0.0	0.0	0.0	0.0	0.0	0.0	0.0	0.0	0.0	0.0	0.0	0.0	0.0	0.0	0.0	0.0	0.0	0.0	0.0	0.0	0.0	0.0	0.0	0.0	0.0	0.0	0.0	0.2	0.4	0.6	0.8	1.0	1.2	1.4	1.5	1.7	1.9	2.1
194	0.0	0.0	0.0	0.0	0.0	0.0	0.0	0.0	0.0	0.0	0.0	0.0	0.0	0.0	0.0	0.0	0.0	0.0	0.0	0.0	0.0	0.0	0.0	0.0	0.0	0.0	0.2	0.4	0.6	0.8	1.0	1.2	1.4	1.6	1.7	1.9	2.1	2.3	2.4
192	0.0	0.0	0.0	0.0	0.0	0.0	0.0	0.0	0.0	0.0	0.0	0.0	0.0	0.0	0.0	0.0	0.0	0.0	0.0	0.0	0.0	0.0	0.0	0.0	0.2	0.4	0.6	0.8	1.0	1.2	1.4	1.6	1.8	1.9	2.1	2.3	2.5	2.7	2.8
190	0.0	0.0	0.0	0.0	0.0	0.0	0.0	0.0	0.0	0.0	0.0	0.0	0.0	0.0	0.0	0.0	0.0	0.0	0.0	0.0	0.0	0.0	0.1	0.4	0.6	0.8	1.0	1.2	1.4	1.6	1.8	2.0	2.2	2.3	2.5	2.7	2.9	3.1	3.2
188	0.0	0.0	0.0	0.0	0.0	0.0	0.0	0.0	0.0	0.0	0.0	0.0	0.0	0.0	0.0	0.0	0.0	0.0	0.0	0.0	0.1	0.3	0.5	0.8	1.0	1.2	1.4	1.6	1.8	2.0	2.2	2.4	2.6	2.7	2.9	3.1	3.3	3.5	3.6
186	0.0	0.0	0.0	0.0	0.0	0.0	0.0	0.0	0.0	0.0	0.0	0.8	0.0	0.0	0.0	0.0	0.0	0.0	0.0	0.3	0.5	0.7	0.9	1.2	1.4	1.6	1.8	2.0	2.2	2.4	2.6	2.8	3.0	3.2	3.3	3.5	3.7	3.9	4.0
184	0.0	0.0	0.0	0.0	0.0	0.0	0.0	0.0	0.0	0.0	0.0	0.0	0.0	0.0	0.0	0.0	0.0	0.2	0.4	0.7	0.9	1.1	1.4	1.6	1.8	2.0	2.2	2.4	2.6	2.8	3.0	3.2	3.4	3.6	3.8	3.9	4.1	4.3	4.5
182	0.0	0.0	0.0	0.0	0.0	0.0	0.0	0.0	0.0	0.0	0.0	0.0	0.0	0.0	0.0	0.1	0.4	0.6	0.9	1.1	1.3	1.6	1.8	2.0	2.2	2.4	2.7	2.9	3.1	3.3	3.4	3.6	3.8	4.0	4.2	4.4	4.5	4.7	4.9
180	0.0	0.0	0.0	0.0	0.0	0.0	0.0	0.0	0.0	0.0	0.0	0.0	0.0	0.0	0.3	0.5	0.8	1.1	1.3	1.5	1.8	2.0	2.2	2.5	2.7	2.9	3.1	3.3	3.5	3.7	3.9	4.1	4.3	4.4	4.6	4.8	5.0	5.2	5.3
178	0.0	0.0	0.0	0.0	0.0	0.0	0.0	0.0	0.0	0.0	0.0	0.0	0.1	0.4	0.7	1.0	1.3	1.5	1.8	2.0	2.2	2.5	2.7	2.9	3.1	3.3	3.5	3.7	3.9	4.1	4.3	4.5	4.7	4.9	5.1	5.3	5.4	5.6	5.8
176	0.0	0.0	0.0	0.0	0.0	0.0	0.0	0.0	0.0	0.0	0.0	0.3	0.6	0.9	1.2	1.4	1.7	2.0	2.2	2.5	2.7	2.9	3.1	3.4	3.6	3.8	4.0	4.2	4.4	4.6	4.8	5.0	5.2	5.4	5.5	5.7	5.9	6.1	6.2
174	0.0	0.0	0.0	0.0	0.0	0.0	0.0	0.0	0.0	0.1	0.5	0.8	1.1	1.4	1.6	1.9	2.2	2.4	2.7	2.9	3.2	3.4	3.6	3.8	4.1	4.3	4.5	4.7	4.9	5.1	5.3	5.5	5.6	5.8	6.0	6.2	6.4	6.5	6.7
172	0.0	0.0	0.0	0.0	0.0	0.0	0.0	0.0	0.3	0.6	0.9	1.3	1.6	1.8	2.1	2.4	2.7	2.9	3.2	3.4	3.6	3.9	4.1	4.3	4.5	4.7	5.0	5.2	5.4	5.6	5.7	5.9	6.1	6.3	6.5	6.7	6.8	7.0	7.2
170	0.0	0.0	0.0	0.0	0.0	0.0	0.0	0.4	0.8	1.1	1.4	1.7	2.1	2.3	2.6	2.9	3.2	3.4	3.7	3.9	4.1	4.4	4.6	4.8	5.0	5.2	5.4	5.6	5.8	6.0	6.2	6.4	6.6	6.8	7.0	7.2	7.3	7.5	7.7
168	0.0	0.0	0.0	0.0	0.0	0.1	0.5	0.9	1.3	1.6	1.9	2.3	2.6	2.8	3.1	3.4	3.7	3.9	4.2	4.4	4.6	4.9	5.1	5.3	5.5	5.7	6.0	6.2	6.4	6.6	6.7	6.9	7.1	7.3	7.5	7.7	7.8	8.0	8.2
166	0.0	0.0	0.0	0.0	0.1	0.6	1.0	1.4	1.8	2.1	2.5	2.8	3.1	3.4	3.6	3.9	4.2	4.4	4.7	4.9	5.2	5.4	5.6	5.8	6.0	6.3	6.5	6.7	6.9	7.1	7.3	7.4	7.6	7.8	8.0	8.2	8.4	8.5	8.7
164	0.0	0.0	0.0	0.2	0.7	1.1	1.6	1.9	2.3	2.7	3.0	3.3	3.6	3.9	4.2	4.4	4.7	5.0	5.2	5.4	5.7	5.9	6.1	6.4	6.6	6.8	7.0	7.2	7.4	7.6	7.8	8.0	8.2	8.4	8.5	8.7	8.9	9.1	9.2
162	0.0	0,0	0.1	0.7	1.2	1.7	2.1	2.5	2.8	3.2	3.5	3.8	4.1	4.4	4.7	5.0	5.2	5.5	5.7	6.0	6.2	6.5	6.7	6.9	7.1	7.3	7.5	7.7	7.9	8.1	8.3	8.5	8.7	8.9	9.1	9.3	9.4	9.6	9.8
160	0.0	0.0	0.7	1.3	1.8	2.2	2.6	3.0	3.4	3.8	4.1	4.4	4.7	5.0	5.3	5.5	5.8	6.1	6.3	6.5	6.8	7.0	7.2	7.5	7.7	7.9	8.1	8.3	8.5	8.7	8.9	9.1	9.3	9.4	9.6	9.8	9.9	10.2	10.3
158	0.0	0.6	1.3	1.8	2.3	2.8	3.2	3.6	4.0	4.3	4.7	5.0	5.3	5.6	5.8	6.1	6.4	6.6	6.9	7.1	7.4	7.6	7.8	8.0	8.2	8.5	8.7	8.9	9.1	9.3	9.5	9.6	9.8	10.0	10.2	10.4	10.6	10.7	10.9
156	0.3	1.2	1.9	2.4	2.9	3.4	3.8	4.2	4.6	4.9	5.2	5.5	5.9	6.1	6.4	6.7	7.0	7.2	7.5	7.7	7.9	8.2	8.4	8.6	8.8	9.0	9.2	9.5	9.7	9.8	10.0	10.2	10.4	10.6	10.8	11.0	11.1	11.3	11.5
154	0.9	1.8	2.5	3.0	3.5	4.0	4.4	4.8	5.2	5.5	5.8	6.1	6.5	6.7	7.0	7.3	7.6	7.8	8.1	8.3	8.5	8.8	9.0	9.2	9.4	9.6	9.8	10.0	10.2	10.4	10.6	10.8	11.0	11.2	11.4	11.6	11.7	11.9	12.1
152	1.5	2.4	3.1	3.6	4.1	4.6	5.0	5.4	5.8	6.1	6.4	6.8	7.1	7.4	7.6	7.9	8.2	8.4	8.7	8.9	9.2	9.4	9.6	9.8	10.0	10.3	10.5	10.7	10.9	11.1	11.3	11.4	11.6	11.8	12.0	12.2	12.4	12.5	12.7
150	2.1	3.0	3.7	4.3	4.8	5.2	5.6	6.0	6.4	6.8	7.1	7.4	7.7	8.0	8.3	8.5	8.8	9.1	9.3	9.5	9.8	10.0	10.2	10.5	10.7	10.9	11.1	11.3	11.5	11.7	11.9	12.1	12.3	12.4	12.6	12.8	13.0	13.2	13.3
148	2.7	3.2	3.9	4.5	5.0	5.4	5.8	6.3	6.7	7.1	7.4	7.7	8.0	8.3	8.7	8.9	9.2	9.5	9.7	9.9	10.2	10.6	11.0	11.4	11.8	12.1	12.5	12.9	13.3	13.5	13.7	13.9	14.1	14.2	14.4	14.6	14.8	15.0	15.1
146	4.4	4.7	5.1	5.5	5.9	6.2	6.6	7.0	7.4	7.7	8.1	8.5	8.9	9.2	9.6	9.9	10.4	10.7	11.1	11.5	11.9	12.2	12.6	13.0	13.4	13.7	14.1	14.5	14.9	15.2	15.5	15.7	15.9	16.0	16.2	16.4	16.6	16.8	16.9
144	6.4	6.7	7.1	7.4	7.8	8.2	8.5	8.9	9.2	9.6	9.9	10.3	10.7	11.0	11.4	11.7	12.1	12.5	12.8	13.2	13.5	13.9	14.3	14.6	15.0	15.3	15.7	16.0	16.4	16.8	17.1	17.5	17.7	17.8	18.0	18.2	18.4	18.6	18.7
142	8.3	8.7	9.0	9.4	9.7	10.1	10.4	10.7	11.1	11.4	11.8	12.1	12.5	12.8	13.1	13.5	13.8	14.2	14.5	14.9	15.2	15.5	15.9	16.2	16.6	16.9	17.3	17.6	17.9	18.3	18.6	19.0	19.3	19.6	19.8	20.0	20.2	20.4	20.5
140	10.3	10.7	11.0	11.3	11.6	12.0	12.3	12.6	12.9	13.3	13.6	13.9	14.3	14.6	14.9	15.2	15.6	15.9	16.2	16.5	16.9	17.2	17.5	17.9	18.2	18.5	18.8	19.2	19.5	19.8	20.2	20.5	20.8	21.1	21.5	21.8	22.0	22.1	22.3
138	12.3	12.6	12.9	13.2	13.6	13.9	14.2	14.5	14.8	15.1	15.4	15.7	16.1	16.4	16.7	17.0	17.3	17.6	17.9	18.2	18.5	18.9	19.2	19.5	19.8	20.1	20.4	20.7	21.0	21.4	21.7	22.0	22.3	22.6	22.9	23.2	23.5	23.8	24.1
136	14.3	14.6	14.9	15.2	15.5	15.8	16.1	16.4	16.7	17.0	17.3	17.6	17.8	18.1	18.4	18.7	19.0	19.3	19.6	19.9	20.2	20.5	20.8	21.1	21.4	21.7	22.0	22.3	22.6	22.9	23.2	23.5	23.8	24.1	24.4	24.7	25.0	25.3	25.5
134	16.3	16.6	16.8	17.1	17.4	17.7	18.0	18.2	18.5	18.8	19.1	19.4	19.6	19.9	20.2	20.5	20.8	21.0	21.3	21.6	21.9	22.2	22.5	22.7	23.0	23.3	23.6	23.9	24.1	24.4	24.7	25.0	25.3	25.5	25.8	26.1	26.4	26.7	26.9
132	18.3	18.5	18.8	19.1	19.3	19.6	19.9	20.1	20.4	20.6	20.9	21.2	21.4	21.7	22.0	22.2	22.5	22.8	23.0	23.3	23.6	23.8	24.1	24.4	24.6	24.9	25.1	25.4	25.7	25.9	26.2	26.5	26.7	27.0	27.3	27.5	27.8	28.1	28.3
130	20.2	20.5	20.7	21.0	21.2	21.5	21.7	22.0	22.2	22.5	22.7	23.0	23.2	23.5	23.7	24.0	24.2	24.5	24.7	25.0	25.2	25.5	25.7	26.0	26.2	26.5	26.7	27.0	27.2	27.5	27.7	28.0	28.2	28.5	28.7	29.0	29.2	29.5	29.7
128	22.2	22.5	22.7	22.9	23.2	23.4	23.6	23.9	24.1	24.3	24.6	24.8	25.0	25.3	25.5	25.7	26.0	26.2	26.4	26.7	26.9	27.1	27.4	27.6	27.8	28.1	28.3	28.5	28.8	29.0	29.2	29.5	29.7	29.9	30.2	30.4	30.6	30.9	31.1
126	24.2	24.4	24.7	24.9	25.1	25.3	25.5	25.7	26.0	26.2	26.4	26.6	26.8	27.0	27.3	27.5	27.7	27.9	28.1	28.4	28.6	28.8	29.0	29.2	29.4	29.7	29.9	30.1	30.3	30.5	30.8	31.0	31.2	31.4	31.6	31.8	32.1	32.3	32.5
124	26.2	26.4	26.6	26.8	27.0	27.2	27.4	27.6	27.8	28.0	28.2	28.4	28.6	28.8	29.0	29.2	29.4	29.6	29.8	30.0	30.2	30.4	30.6	30.9	31.1	31.3	31.5	31.7	31.9	32.1	32.3	32.5	32.7	32.9	33.1	33.3	33.5	33.7	33.9
122	28.2	28.4	28.6	28.7	28.9	29.1	29.3	29.5	29.7	29.9	30.1	30.2	30.4	30.6	30.8	31.0	31.2	31.4	31.5	31.7	31.9	32.1	32.3	32.5	32.7	32.8	33.0	33.2	33.4	33.6	33.8	34.0	34.2	34.3	34.5	34.7	34.9	35.1	35.3
120	30.2	30.3	30.5	30.7	30.9	31.0	31.2	31.4	31.5	31.7	31.9	32.0	32.2	32.4	32.6	32.7	32.9	33.1	33.2	33.4	33.6	33.8	33.9	34.1	34.3	34.4	34.6	34.8	35.0	35.1	35.3	35.5	35.6	35.8	36.0	36.1	36.3	36.5	36.7
118	32.2	32.3	32.5	32.6	32.8	32.9	33.1	33.2	33.4	33.6	33.7	33.9	34.0	34.2	34.3	34.5	34.6	34.8	34.9	35.1	35.3	35.4	35.6	35.7	35.9	36.0	36.2	36.3	36.5	36.7	36.8	37.0	37.1	37.3	37.4	37.6	37.7	37.9	38.0
116	34.1	34.3	34.4	34.6	34.7	34.8	35.0	35.1	35.3	35.4	35.5	35.7	35.8	36.0	36.1	36.2	36.4	36.5	36.6	36.8	36.9	37.1	37.2	37.3	37.5	37.6	37.8	37.9	38.0	38.2	38.3	38.5	38.6	38.7	38.9	39.0	39.2	39.3	39.4
114	36.1	36.2	36.4	36.5	36.6	36.7	36.9	37.0	37.1	37.2	37.4	37.5	37.6	37.7	37.9	38.0	38.1	38.2	38.4	38.5	38.6	38.7	38.8	39.0	39.1	39.2	39.3	39.5	39.6	39.7	39.8	39.9	40.1	40.2	40.3	40.5	40.6	40.7	40.8
112	38.1	38.2	38.3	38.4	38.5	38.6	38.8	38.9	39.0	39.1	39.2	39.3	39.4	39.5	39.6	39.7	39.8	39.9	40.1	40.2	40.3	40.4	40.5	40.6	40.7	40.8	40.9	41.0	41.1	41.2	41.4	41.5	41.6	41.7	41.8	41.9	42.0	42.1	42.2
110	40.1	40.2	40.3	40.4	40.5	40.6	40.6	40.7	40.8	40.9	41.0	41.1	41.2	41.3	41.4	41.5	41.6	41.7	41.8	41.8	41.9	42.0	42.1	42.2	42.3	42.4	42.5	42.6	42.7	42.8	42.9	43.0	43.1	43.1	43.2	43.3	43.4	43.5	43.6
108	42.1	42.2	42.2	42.3	42.4	42.5	42.5	42.6	42.7	42.8	42.8	42.9	43.0	43.1	43.2	43.2	43.3	43.4	43.5	43.5	43.6	43.7	43.8	43.8	43.9	44.0	44.1	44.1	44.2	44.3	44.4	44.5	44.5	44.6	44.7	44.8	44.8	44.9	45.0
106	44.1	44.1	44.2	44.2	44.3	44.4	44.4	44.5	44.5	44.6	44.7	44.7	44.8	44.9	44.9	45.0	45.0	45.1	45.2	45.2	45.3	45.3	45.4	45.5	45.5	45.6	45.6	45.7	45.8	45.8	45.9	46.0	46.0	46.1	46.1	46.2	46.3	46.3	46.4

Index

Index

Index

Index

Purchasers of THE COMPLEAT OPTION PLAYER are eligible to receive a FREE copy of one issue of Kenneth R. Trester's Options Newsletter. To receive your FREE copy, simply fill in and mail this coupon.

NAME

MAILING ADDRESS

CITY, STATE & ZIP CODE

Return to:

Institute for Options Research, Inc.
P.O. Box 6586
Lake Tahoe, NV 89449

INSTITUTE FOR OPTIONS RESEARCH, INC.